SAINTS

THE STORY OF
THE CHURCH OF JESUS CHRIST
IN THE LATTER DAYS

Volume 2

NO UNHALLOWED
HAND
1846–1893

Published by
The Church of Jesus Christ of Latter-day Saints
Salt Lake City, Utah

© 2020 by Intellectual Reserve, Inc.

All rights reserved.

Version: 11/16

Printed in the United States of America

No part of this book may be reproduced in any form or by any means without written permission. For more information, contact permissions@ChurchofJesusChrist.org.

saints.ChurchofJesusChrist.org

Cover art by Greg Newbold

Cover design and interior layout by Patric Gerber

Library of Congress Cataloging-in-Publication Data

Names: The Church of Jesus Christ of Latter-day Saints, issuing body.

Title: Saints : the story of the Church of Jesus Christ in the latter days. Volume 2, No unhallowed hand, 1846–1893.

Other titles: Story of the Church of Jesus Christ in the latter days

Description: Salt Lake City, Utah : The Church of Jesus Christ of Latter-day Saints, 2020. | Includes bibliographical references and index. | Summary: "The second volume in a four-volume series recounting the history of The Church of Jesus Christ of Latter-day Saints"— Provided by publisher.

Identifiers: LCCN 2019043996 | ISBN 9781629726489 (paperback)

Subjects: LCSH: The Church of Jesus Christ of Latter-day Saints—History—19th century. | Mormon Church—History—19th century.

Classification: LCC BX8611 .S235 2020 | DDC 289.309/034—dc23

LC record available at https://lccn.loc.gov/2019043996

10 9 8 7 6 5 4 3 2 1

The standard of truth has been erected.
No unhallowed hand can stop the work from
progressing; persecutions may rage,
mobs may combine, armies may assemble,
calumny may defame, but the truth of God will
go forth boldly, nobly, and independent till it
has penetrated every continent, visited every clime,
swept every country, and sounded in every ear,
till the purposes of God shall be accomplished and
the great Jehovah shall say the work is done.

—*Joseph Smith, 1842*

CONTRIBUTORS

SAINTS
THE STORY OF THE CHURCH OF JESUS CHRIST
IN THE LATTER DAYS

Church Historian and Recorder
Executive Director, Church History Department
Elder LeGrand R. Curtis Jr.

Assistant Executive Director,
Church History Department
Elder Kyle S. McKay

Managing Director, Church History Department
Matthew J. Grow

Director, Publications Division
Matthew S. McBride

Managing Historian
Jed L. Woodworth

Product Manager
Ben Ellis Godfrey

Editorial Manager
Nathan N. Waite

VOLUME 2
NO UNHALLOWED HAND
1846–1893

General Editors
Matthew J. Grow
Jed L. Woodworth
Scott A. Hales
Lisa Olsen Tait

Writers
Scott A. Hales
David C. Nielsen
Angela Hallstrom
Dallin T. Morrow
James Goldberg

Editors
R. Eric Smith
Leslie Sherman Edgington
Kathryn Tanner Burnside
Nathan N. Waite
Stephanie Steed
Alison Palmer
Alison Kitchen Gainer

CONTENTS

PART 3: *The Trying Hour*
May 1869–July 1887

PART 4: *A Temple of God*
July 1887–May 1893

NO UNHALL

CARDSTON

NAUVOO

NEW YORK CITY

PHILADELPHIA

SAN
FRANCISCO

SALT
LAKE
CITY

NEW ORLEANS

MEXICO

MEXICO CITY

CAPE VERDE
ISLANDS

SANDWICH ISLANDS
(Hawaii)

JUAN
FERNÁNDEZ
ISLANDS

SOCIETY ISLANDS
(Tahiti)

The *Brooklyn*

SCAN

COPENHAGEN
LIVERPOOL

SW

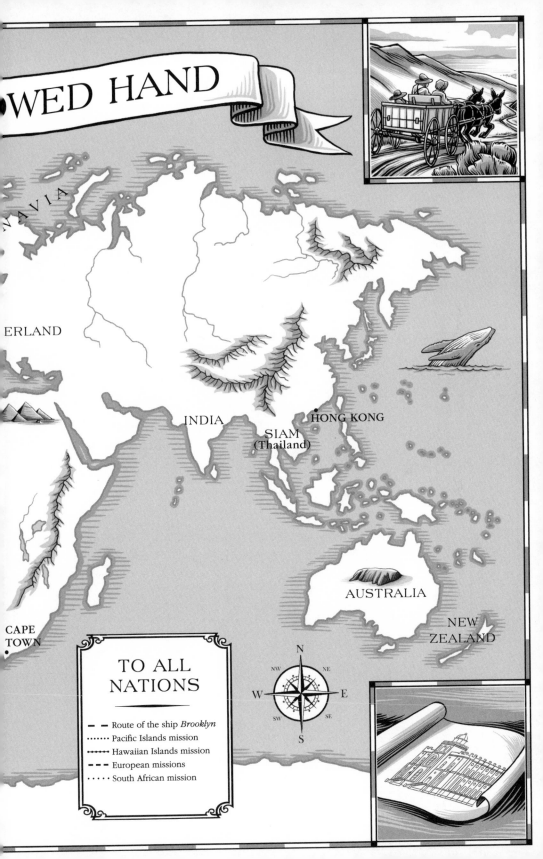

WED HAND

TO ALL NATIONS

- – – Route of the ship *Brooklyn*
- ······ Pacific Islands mission
- ••••• Hawaiian Islands mission
- – – European missions
- ····· South African mission

NAVIA

ERLAND

INDIA

SIAM
(Thailand)

HONG KONG

AUSTRALIA

NEW
ZEALAND

CAPE
TOWN

N
NW   NE
W   E
SW   SE
S

PART 1

Rise and Go

OCTOBER 1845–AUGUST 1852

Lo! a mighty host of Jacob
Tented on the western shore
Of the noble Mississippi,
Which they had been crossing o'er;
At the last day's dawn of winter,
Bound with frost and wrapt in snow:
Hark! the sound is onward, onward!
Camp of Israel! rise and go.

Eliza R. Snow, "Song for the Camp of Israel"

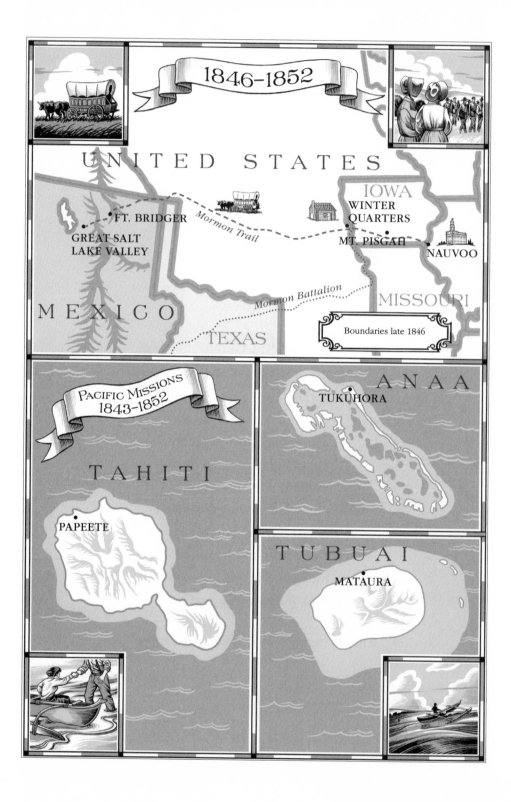

CHAPTER 1

Gather Up a Company

I want to speak about the dead."

Thousands of Latter-day Saints hushed as Lucy Mack Smith's voice echoed through the large assembly hall on the first floor of the nearly completed Nauvoo temple.

It was the morning of October 8, 1845, the third and final day of the fall conference of The Church of Jesus Christ of Latter-day Saints. Knowing she would not have many more opportunities to speak to the Saints—especially now that they planned to leave Nauvoo for a new home far to the west—Lucy spoke with a power beyond her feeble seventy-year-old body.

"It was eighteen years ago last twenty-second of September that Joseph took the plates out of the earth," she testified, "and it was eighteen years last Monday since Joseph Smith, the prophet of the Lord—"[1]

She paused, remembering Joseph, her martyred son. The Saints in the room already knew how an angel of the Lord had led him to a set of gold plates buried in a hill called Cumorah. They knew that Joseph had translated the plates by the gift and power of God and published the record as the Book of Mormon. Yet how many Saints in the assembly hall had truly known him?

Lucy could still remember when Joseph, then only twenty-one years old, had first told her that God had entrusted him with the plates. She had been anxious all morning, afraid he would return from the hill empty-handed, as he had the four previous years. But when he arrived, he had quickly calmed her nerves. "Do not be uneasy," he had said. "All is right." He had then handed her the interpreters the Lord had provided for the translation of the plates, wrapped in a handkerchief, as proof that he had succeeded in getting the record.

There had been only a handful of believers then, most of them members of the Smith family. Now more than eleven thousand Saints from North America and Europe lived in Nauvoo, Illinois, where the Church had gathered for the last six years. Some of them were new to the Church and had not had a chance to meet Joseph or his brother Hyrum before a mob shot and killed the two men in June 1844.[2] That was why Lucy wanted to speak about the dead. She wanted to testify of Joseph's prophetic call and her family's role in the Restoration of the gospel before the Saints moved away.

4

For more than a month, vigilante mobs had been torching the homes and businesses of Saints in nearby settlements. Fearing for their lives, many families had fled to the relative safety of Nauvoo. But the mobs had only grown stronger and more organized as the weeks passed, and soon armed skirmishes had broken out between them and the Saints. The state and national governments, meanwhile, did nothing to protect the Saints' rights.[3]

Believing it was only a matter of time before the mobs attacked Nauvoo, Church leaders had negotiated a fragile peace by agreeing to evacuate the Saints from the county by spring.[4]

Guided by divine revelation, Brigham Young and the other members of the Quorum of the Twelve Apostles were planning to move the Saints more than a thousand miles west, beyond the Rocky Mountains, just outside the border of the United States. As the presiding quorum of the Church, the Twelve had announced this decision to the Saints on the first day of the fall conference.

"The Lord designs to lead us to a wider field of action," apostle Parley Pratt had declared, "where we can enjoy the pure principles of liberty and equal rights."[5]

Lucy knew the Saints would help her make this journey if she chose to go. Revelations had commanded the Saints to gather together in one place, and the Twelve were determined to carry out the Lord's will. But Lucy was old and believed she would not live much longer. When she died, she wanted to be buried in Nauvoo near Joseph, Hyrum, and other family members who had passed on, including her husband, Joseph Smith Sr.

Furthermore, most of her living family members were staying in Nauvoo. Her only surviving son, William, had been a member of the Quorum of the Twelve, but he had rejected their leadership and refused to go west. Her three daughters—Sophronia, Katharine, and Lucy—were also staying behind. So too was her daughter-in-law Emma, the prophet's widow.

As Lucy spoke to the congregation, she urged her listeners not to fret about the journey ahead. "Do not be discouraged and say that you can't get wagons and things," she said. Despite poverty and persecution, her own family had fulfilled the Lord's commandment to publish the Book of Mormon. She encouraged them to listen to their leaders and treat each other well.

"As Brigham says, you must be all honest or you will not get there," she said. "If you feel cross, you will have trouble."

Lucy spoke more about her family, the terrible persecution they had suffered in Missouri and Illinois, and the trials that lay ahead for the Saints. "I pray that the Lord may bless the heads of the Church, Brother Brigham and all," she said. "When I go to another world, I want to meet you all."[6]

A LITTLE MORE THAN a month later, Wilford Woodruff, an apostle and the president of the Church's British mission, found a letter from Brigham Young waiting for him in his office in Liverpool, England. "We have had a good deal of sorrow and trouble here this fall," Brigham told his friend. "It is therefore advisable for us to remove as the only condition of peace."[7]

Wilford was alarmed but not surprised. He had read newspaper reports of mob attacks around Nauvoo. But he had not known how bad the situation was until now. "This is a strange age we live in," Wilford thought after reading the letter. The United States government claimed to protect oppressed peoples and to shelter exiles, but Wilford could not remember a time when it had helped the Saints.

"The state of Illinois and the whole United States have filled up their cup of iniquity," he wrote in his journal, "and well may the Saints go out of her midst."[8]

Fortunately, most of Wilford's family was out of harm's way. His wife, Phebe, and their youngest children, Susan and Joseph, were with him in England. Their other daughter, Phebe Amelia, was staying with relatives in the eastern United States, more than a thousand miles away from the danger.

Their oldest son, Willy, however, was still in Nauvoo in the care of close friends. In his letter, Brigham mentioned that the boy was safe, yet Wilford still felt anxious to reunite his family.[9]

As quorum president, Brigham offered Wilford instructions for what to do next. "Send no more emigrants here," he advised, "but let them wait in England till they can ship for the Pacific Ocean." As for the American missionaries in England, he wanted those who had not received their temple ordinances to return immediately to Nauvoo to receive them.[10]

In the days that followed, Wilford sent letters to the American elders preaching in England, informing them of the persecution in Nauvoo. Though he and Phebe had already received their ordinances, they decided to return home as well.

"I have a portion of my family scattered some two thousand miles apart in the States," Wilford explained in a farewell message to the British Saints. "It appears at the present time to be a duty resting upon me to return there and gather together my children that they may go out with the camp of the Saints."

Wilford appointed Reuben Hedlock, the previous mission president, to preside again in Britain. Though Wilford did not have full confidence in Reuben, who had mismanaged Church funds in the past, no one else in England had more experience in mission leadership. And Wilford had little time to find a better replacement. After reuniting with the Quorum of the Twelve, he would recommend calling another man to take Reuben's place.[11]

As WILFORD AND PHEBE prepared to return to Nauvoo, Samuel Brannan, the presiding elder of the Church in New York City, heard a rumor that the United States government would rather disarm and exterminate the

Saints than allow them to leave the country and possibly align with Mexico or Great Britain, two nations that claimed vast regions in the West. Alarmed, Sam wrote to Brigham Young immediately to report the danger.

Sam's letter reached Nauvoo amid new perils. Brigham and other apostles had been served with legal writs falsely charging them with counterfeiting, and now lawmen were seeking to arrest them.[12] After reading Sam's letter, the apostles prayed for protection, asking the Lord to lead the Saints safely out of the city.[13]

A short time later, Governor Thomas Ford of Illinois seemed to confirm Sam's report. "It is very likely that the government at Washington, DC, will interfere to prevent the Mormons from going west of the Rocky Mountains," he warned. "Many intelligent persons sincerely believe that they will join the British if they go there and be more trouble than ever."[14]

In January 1846, Brigham met often with the Quorum of the Twelve and the Council of Fifty, an organization that oversaw the temporal concerns of God's kingdom on earth, to plan the best and quickest way to evacuate Nauvoo and establish a new gathering place for the Saints. Heber Kimball, his fellow apostle, recommended that they lead a small company of Saints west as soon as possible.

"Gather up a company who can fit themselves out," he advised, "to be ready at any moment when called upon to go forth and prepare a place for their families and the poor."

"If there is an advance company to go and put in crops this spring," apostle Orson Pratt pointed out, "it will be necessary to start by the first of February." He wondered if it would be wiser to settle somewhere closer, which would allow them to plant crops sooner.

Brigham disliked that idea. The Lord had already directed the Saints to settle near the Great Salt Lake. The lake was part of the Great Basin, a massive bowl-shaped region surrounded by mountains. Much of the basin was dry desert land and a challenge to cultivate, making it undesirable for many Americans moving west.

"If we go between the mountains to the place under consideration," Brigham reasoned, "there will be no jealousies from any nation." Brigham understood that the region was already inhabited by Native peoples. Yet he was hopeful that the Saints would be able to settle peacefully among them.[15]

Over the years, the Saints had tried to share the gospel with American Indians in the United States, and they planned to do the same with the Native peoples of the West. Like most white people in the United States, many white Saints saw their culture as superior to that of the Indians and knew little about their languages and customs. But they also viewed Indians as fellow members of the house of Israel and potential allies, and they hoped to forge friendships with the Utes, Shoshones, and other western tribes.[16]

On January 13, Brigham met again with the councils to learn how many Saints were ready to leave Nauvoo with six hours' notice. He was confident that most Saints would be safe in the city until the spring deadline. To ensure speedy travel, he wanted as few families as possible to leave with the advance company.

"All those men who are in danger and who are likely to be hunted with writs," he said, "go and take their families." Everyone else was to wait to go west until the spring, after the advance company had reached the mountains and founded the new settlement.[17]

ON THE AFTERNOON OF February 4, 1846, sunlight danced across New York Harbor as a crowd huddled at the wharf to bid farewell to the *Brooklyn,* a 450-ton ship bound for San Francisco Bay on the coast of California, a sparsely settled region in northwestern Mexico. On the deck of the ship, waving to their relatives and friends below, were more than two hundred Saints, most of them too poor to travel west by wagon.[18]

Leading them was twenty-six-year-old Sam Brannan. After the October conference, the Twelve had instructed Sam to charter a ship and take a company of eastern Saints to California, where they would wait to rendezvous with the main body of the Church somewhere in the West.

"Flee out of Babylon!" apostle Orson Pratt had warned. "We do not want one Saint to be left in the United States."[19]

Sam soon chartered the *Brooklyn* at an affordable price, and workers built thirty-two small bunk rooms to accommodate the passengers. He had the Saints pack plows, shovels, hoes, pitchforks, and other tools they would need to plant crops and build homes. Unsure of what lay ahead, they stowed ample food and provisions, some livestock, three grain mills, grinding stones, lathes, nails, a printing press, and firearms. A charitable society also donated enough books to the ship to form a good library.[20]

As Sam prepared for the voyage, a politician he knew in Washington warned him that the United States was still determined to stop the Saints from leaving Nauvoo. The politician also told Sam that he and a businessman with interests in California were willing to lobby the government on the Church's behalf in exchange for half the land the Saints acquired in the West.

Sam knew the terms of the deal were not good, but he believed the men were his friends and could protect the Saints. A few days before he boarded the *Brooklyn,* Sam had a contract drawn up and sent it to Brigham, urging him to sign it. "All will go well," he promised.[21]

He also informed Brigham of his plan to establish a city at San Francisco Bay, perhaps as a new gathering place for the Saints. "I shall select the most suitable spot," he wrote. "Before you reach there, if it is the Lord's will, I shall have everything prepared for you."[22]

By the time the *Brooklyn* left its moorings, Sam was certain he had ensured safety for the Saints leaving Nauvoo and a smooth voyage for his company. The ship's course would follow ocean currents around the stormy southern tip of South America and into the heart of the Pacific. When they reached California, they would found their city and start a new life in the West.

As a steamship guided the *Brooklyn* away from the wharf, the crowd of loved ones on the pier gave three cheers to the Saints, who responded with three cheers of their own. The vessel then made its way to the narrow mouth of the harbor, spread its topsails, and caught a breeze that carried it into the Atlantic Ocean.[23]

ON THE SAME DAY the *Brooklyn* sailed for California, fifteen wagons in the Saints' advance company crossed the Mississippi River into Iowa Territory, just west of Nauvoo, and set up camp at nearby Sugar Creek.

Four days later, Brigham Young met one last time with the apostles in the Nauvoo temple.[24] Though the temple as a whole remained undedicated, they had already dedicated its attic and administered the endowment there to more than five thousand eager Saints. They had also sealed approximately thirteen hundred couples for time and eternity.[25] Some of these sealings were plural marriages, which a few faithful Saints had begun practicing privately in Nauvoo following a principle the Lord had revealed to Joseph Smith in the early 1830s.[26]

Brigham had planned to stop administering ordinances on February 3, the day before the first wagons left the city, but Saints had thronged the temple all day, anxious to receive the ordinances before their departure. At first, Brigham had dismissed them. "We shall build more temples and have further opportunities to receive the blessings of the Lord," he had insisted. "In this temple we have been abundantly rewarded, if we receive no more."

Expecting the crowd to disperse, Brigham had started to walk home. But he had not gone far before he returned and found the temple overflowing with people hungering and thirsting for the word of the Lord. That day, 295 more Saints had received their temple blessings.[27]

Now, with the ordinance work of the temple completed, the apostles knelt around the altar of the temple and prayed for a safe journey west. No one could tell what trials they might face in the weeks and months to come. Guidebooks and maps described unmarked trails for much of the way to the mountains. Rivers and streams were abundant along the way, and plenty of buffalo and game animals roamed the plains. But the terrain was still unlike anything the Saints had ever traveled before.[28]

Unwilling to leave anyone in danger, the Saints had covenanted together to help anyone who wanted to go west—especially the poor, sick, or widowed. "If you will be faithful to your covenant," Brigham had promised the Saints in the temple at the October conference, "the great God will shower down means upon this people to accomplish it to the very letter."[29]

On February 15, the burden of this covenant weighed heavily on Brigham as he crossed the Mississippi. That afternoon, he pushed and pulled wagons up a snowy, muddy hill four miles west of the river. When only a few hours of daylight remained before evening would darken the way ahead, Brigham remained determined not to rest until every Latter-day Saint wagon west of the river arrived safely at Sugar Creek.[30]

By now, the plan to send a small advance company ahead to the mountains that year was already delayed. Brigham and other Church leaders had left the city later than planned, and some Saints—ignoring counsel to stay in Nauvoo—had crossed the river and camped with the advance company at Sugar Creek. After fleeing the city so quickly, many families on the trail were disorganized, ill-equipped, and underprepared.

Brigham did not yet know what to do. These Saints would surely slow the others down. But he would not send these Saints back to the city now that they had already left. In his mind, Nauvoo had become a prison, no place for the people of God. The road west was freedom.

He and the Twelve would simply have to press forward, trusting that the Lord would help them find a solution.[31]

CHAPTER 2

Glory Enough

Cold wind blew as Brigham Young arrived at Sugar Creek on the evening of February 15, 1846. Scattered around a snowy patch of woods, not far from an icy brook, hundreds of Saints shivered in damp coats and blankets. Many families collected around fires or underneath tents fashioned from bedsheets or wagon covers. Others huddled together in carriages or wagons for warmth.[1]

Right away Brigham knew he needed to organize the camp. With the help of other Church leaders, he divided the Saints into companies and called captains to lead them. He warned against taking unnecessary trips back to Nauvoo, being idle, and borrowing without permission. Men were to protect the camp constantly and monitor cleanliness, and each family was to pray together mornings and evenings.[2]

A good spirit soon settled over the camp. Safely out of Nauvoo, the Saints worried less about mobs or government threats to stop the exodus. In the evenings, a brass band played lively music while the men and women danced. Saints who practiced plural marriage also became less guarded and began to speak openly about the principle and how it linked their families together.[3]

Brigham, meanwhile, spent hours refining plans for the move west.[4] While fasting and praying in the temple shortly before leaving Nauvoo, he had seen a vision of Joseph Smith pointing to a flag flying over a mountaintop. "Build under the point where the colors fall," Joseph had instructed him, "and you will prosper and have peace."[5] Brigham knew the Lord had a place prepared for the Church, but guiding thousands of Saints there would be a monumental task.

During this time, letters arrived in camp from Sam Brannan, who was now sailing for California on the *Brooklyn*. Among the letters was the contract promising a safe exodus for the Saints in exchange for land in the West. Brigham read the contract carefully with the apostles. If they did not sign it, Sam's letters suggested, the president of the United States could order the Saints to disarm and cease gathering together.[6]

Brigham was unconvinced. As wary as he was of the government, he had already decided to try working with it rather than against it. Shortly before leaving Nauvoo, in fact, he had instructed Jesse Little, the new presiding elder in the eastern states, to lobby for the

Church and accept any honorable offer from the federal government to assist the Saints' exodus. Brigham and the apostles quickly perceived that the contract was nothing more than an elaborate scheme designed to favor the men who had drafted it. Rather than sign the agreement, the apostles decided to trust in God and look to Him for protection.[7]

As the month rolled on, temperatures dropped below freezing, and the surface of the Mississippi River turned to ice, allowing easy passage across the river. Soon around two thousand people were camped at Sugar Creek, although some returned to Nauvoo time and again on one errand or another.

The traffic back and forth troubled Brigham, who believed these Saints were neglecting their families and focusing too much on their property in the city. With the westward trek already behind schedule, he decided it was time for the Saints to move on from Sugar Creek, even if the companies were underequipped.

On March 1, five hundred wagons started west across the Iowa prairie. Brigham still wanted to send an advance company over the Rocky Mountains that year, but first the Saints needed every resource to move the camp farther from Nauvoo.[8]

WHILE THE SAINTS WITH Brigham were leaving Sugar Creek, forty-three-year-old Louisa Pratt remained in Nauvoo, preparing to leave the city with her four young daughters. Three years earlier, the Lord had called her husband, Addison, on a mission to the Pacific Islands. Since then, unreliable mail service between Nauvoo and Tubuai, the island in French Polynesia where Addison was serving, had made it hard to stay in contact with him. Most of his letters were several months old when they arrived, and some were older than a year.

Addison's latest letter made it clear that he would not be home in time to go west with her. The Twelve had instructed him to remain in the Pacific Islands until they called him home or sent missionaries to replace him. At one point, Brigham had hoped to send more missionaries to the islands after the Saints received the endowment, but the exodus from Nauvoo had postponed that plan.[9]

Louisa was willing to make the journey without her husband, but thinking about it made her nervous. She hated to leave Nauvoo and the temple and did not relish the idea of traveling by wagon over the Rocky Mountains. She also wanted to see her aging parents in Canada—possibly for the last time—before going west.

If she sold her ox team, she could get enough money to visit her parents and book passage for her family on a ship bound for the California coast, thus avoiding overland travel altogether.

Louisa had almost made up her mind to go to Canada, but something did not feel right. She decided to write to Brigham Young about her concerns with overland travel and her desire to see her parents.

"If you say the ox team expedition is the best way for salvation, then I shall engage in it heart and hand," she wrote, "and I believe I can stand it as long without grumbling as any other woman."[10]

A short time later, a messenger arrived with Brigham's response. "Come on. The ox team salvation is the safest way," he told her. "Brother Pratt will meet us in the wilderness where we locate, and he will be sorely disappointed if his family is not with us."

Louisa considered the counsel, steeled her heart against the difficult trail ahead, and decided to follow the main body of the Saints, come life or death.[11]

THAT SPRING, THE SAINTS traveling through Iowa began calling themselves the Camp of Israel, after the ancient Hebrews the Lord had led out of captivity in Egypt. Day after day, they battled the elements as unrelenting snow and rain turned the Iowa prairie soft and muddy. Rivers and streams ran high and swift. Dirt roads dissolved into mire. The Saints had intended to cross most of the territory in a month, but in that time they had covered only a third of the distance.[12]

On April 6, the sixteenth anniversary of the organization of the Church, rain fell all day. Brigham spent hours up to his knees in mud, helping the Saints along the road to a place called Locust Creek. There he helped to arrange wagons, pitch tents, and chop wood until all the Saints were settled in the camp. One woman who saw him in the mud, pushing and pulling to free a mired wagon, thought he looked as happy as a king, despite the challenges surrounding him.

That evening, freezing rain and hail bombarded the camp, coating it in ice. In the morning, William Clayton, Brigham's clerk and captain of the brass band, found the camp in disarray. Many tents lay flat on the frozen ground. A fallen tree had crushed a wagon. Some men in the band were also out of provisions.[13]

William shared what he had with his band, although his own family had little. One of the first Saints to have practiced plural marriage, William traveled with three wives and four children. Another wife, Diantha, was still in Nauvoo, under the care of her mother. She was pregnant with her first child and in frail health, adding to William's anxiety on the trail.

While the Claytons rested at Locust Creek with the Camp of Israel, Brigham proposed a plan to establish a way station midway across Iowa where Saints could wait out the bad weather, build cabins, and plant crops for those who would come later. Some Saints would then tend the way station while others returned to Nauvoo to guide companies across Iowa. The rest of the camp would push on with him to the Missouri River.[14]

On April 14, William was out all night rounding up horses and cattle that had broken loose in camp. In the morning, he needed sleep, but someone in camp received a letter mentioning Diantha and the birth of her baby. That evening, William celebrated the birth, singing and playing music with the band long into the night.

The skies were clear the next morning, and William saw better days ahead for the Camp of Israel. Sitting down with ink and paper, he wrote a hymn of encouragement for the Saints:

> *Come, come, ye Saints, no toil nor labor fear;*
> *But with joy wend your way.*
> *Though hard to you this journey may appear,*
> *Grace shall be as your day.*
> *'Tis better far for us to strive*
> *Our useless cares from us to drive;*
> *Do this, and joy your hearts will swell—*
> *All is well! All is well!*[15]

ONE HUNDRED MILES TO the east, Wilford Woodruff stood on the deck of a riverboat on the Mississippi River, gazing at the Nauvoo temple through a spyglass. When he had last seen the temple, its walls were still unfinished. Now it had a roof, gleaming windows, and a majestic tower topped with a weather vane shaped like an angel.[16] Portions of the temple had already been dedicated for ordinance work, and soon the building would be finished and ready to be fully dedicated to the Lord.

Wilford's voyage home from Britain had been treacherous. Hard winds and waves had battered the ship to and fro. Wilford had held on, seasick and miserable. "Any man that would sell a farm and go to sea for a living," he had groaned at the time, "has a different taste from mine."[17]

Phebe had set sail from England first, taking their children Susan and Joseph on board a ship filled with Saints who were emigrating to the United States. Wilford had remained in Liverpool a little longer to settle some financial matters, transfer the leadership of the Church to the new mission president, and solicit donations to finish construction on the temple.[18]

"The building of the temple of God is of equal interest to every truehearted Saint, wherever his lot may be cast," he had reminded Church members.[19] Although the temple would have to be abandoned soon after its completion, Saints on both sides of the Atlantic Ocean were determined to finish it in obedience to the Lord's commandment to the Church in 1841.

"I grant unto you a sufficient time to build a house unto me," the Lord had declared through Joseph Smith, "and if you do not these things at the end of the appointment ye shall be rejected as a church, with your dead, saith the Lord your God."[20]

Even though many British Saints were impoverished, Wilford had encouraged them to donate what they could to help pay for the temple, promising blessings for their sacrifice. They had given generously, and Wilford was grateful for their consecration.[21]

Upon arriving in the United States, Wilford picked up his daughter Phebe Amelia in Maine and traveled south to visit his parents, whom he persuaded to go west with him.[22]

After disembarking at Nauvoo, Wilford reunited with his wife and met with Orson Hyde, the presiding apostle in the city, who had little good news to report. Among the Saints still in Nauvoo were some who felt restless and abandoned. A few were even questioning the Twelve's claim to leadership in the Church. Among them were Wilford's sister and brother-in-law, Eunice and Dwight Webster.[23]

The news grieved Wilford for days. He had taught and baptized Eunice and Dwight a decade earlier. Recently, they had been drawn to a man named James Strang, who claimed that Joseph Smith had secretly appointed him to be his successor. Strang's claim was false, but his charisma had won over some Saints in Nauvoo, including former apostles John Page and William Smith, the prophet Joseph's younger brother.[24]

On April 18, Wilford became incensed when he learned that Dwight and Eunice were trying to convince his parents to follow Strang rather than go west. Wilford called his family together and denounced the false prophet. He then left to load his wagons.

"I have much to do," he wrote in his journal, "and little time to do it."[25]

THAT SPRING, WORKERS RACED to finish the temple before its public dedication on May 1. They installed a brick floor around the baptismal font, fitted decorative woodwork into place, and painted the walls. The work proceeded all day and often into the night. Since the Church had little money to pay the laborers, many of them sacrificed part of their wages to ensure the temple was ready to dedicate to the Lord.[26]

Two days before the dedication, workers finished painting the first-floor assembly hall. The next day, they swept the dust and debris out of the large room and prepared for the service. The workers were not able to put finishing touches on every room, but they knew that would not keep the Lord from accepting the temple. Confident they had fulfilled God's command, they painted the words "The Lord has beheld our sacrifice" above the pulpits along the east wall of the assembly hall.[27]

Conscious of the debt they owed the workers, Church leaders announced that the first session of the dedication would be a charitable event. Those who attended were asked to contribute a dollar to help pay the impoverished laborers.

On the morning of May 1, fourteen-year-old Elvira Stevens left her camp west of the Mississippi and crossed the river to attend the dedication. An orphan whose parents had died soon after the family moved to Nauvoo, Elvira now lived with her married sister. Since no one else in her camp could join her for the dedication, she went alone.

Knowing that it might be years before another temple was built in the West, the apostles had administered the endowment to some young single people, including Elvira. Now, three months later, she climbed the steps to the temple doors once more, contributed her dollar, and found a seat in the assembly hall.[28]

The session opened with singing from a choir. Orson Hyde then offered the dedicatory prayer. "Grant that Thy Spirit shall dwell here," he pleaded, "and may all feel a sacred influence on their hearts that His hand has helped this work."[29]

Elvira felt heavenly power in the room. After the session, she returned to her camp, but she came back for the next session two days later, hoping to feel the same power again. Orson Hyde and Wilford Woodruff gave sermons on temple work, priesthood, and the resurrection. Before closing the meeting, Wilford praised the Saints for finishing the temple even though they would have to abandon it.

"Thousands of the Saints have received their endowment in it, and the light will not go out," he said. "This is glory enough for building the temple."

After the session, Elvira returned to her camp, crossing the river one last time.[30] Saints in Nauvoo, meanwhile, spent the rest of the day and night packing up and removing chairs, tables, and other furnishings until the temple was empty and left in the hands of the Lord.[31]

A FEW WEEKS AFTER the temple dedication, Louisa Pratt and her daughters started west with a company of Saints. Ellen was now fourteen, Frances was twelve, Lois was nine, and Ann was five. They had two yoke of oxen, two cows, and a wagon loaded with new clothes and provisions.

Before crossing the river into Iowa, Louisa called at the post office and found a long letter from Addison dated January 6, 1846—five months earlier. Addison reported that he was now in Tahiti with some Tubuaian friends, the married couple Nabota and Telii, on their way to help his fellow missionary Benjamin Grouard with missionary work on the nearby Anaa atoll. He had sent Louisa sixty dollars and loving words for her and the children.

Addison expected to serve among the island Saints for many years to come, but not without his family. "If you can get any books," he wrote, "and have any leisure time, I think you and the children had better attend to the studying of the Tahitian language, for in my opinion you may have use for it within a few years."[32]

The letter pleased Louisa, and she found her journey west surprisingly joyful. The spring rains had ended, and she liked riding horseback beneath clear skies while a hired man drove her wagons. She rose early every morning, gathered up stray cattle, and helped to drive them during the day. Occasionally she worried about how far she was traveling from her parents and other relatives, but her belief in Zion comforted her. The revelations spoke of Zion as a place of refuge, a land of peace. That was what she wanted in her life.

"Sometimes I feel cheerful," she wrote in her journal on June 10. "The Lord has called us, and appointed us a place where we can live in peace and be free from the dread of our cruel persecutors!"[33]

Five days later, Louisa and her company arrived at Mount Pisgah, one of two large way stations the Saints had established along the Iowa trail. The encampment hugged the base of some low, sloping hills crowned with a grove of oak trees. As Brigham had envisioned, the Saints there lived in tents or log cabins and cultivated crops to supply food for companies who would arrive later. Other areas of the camp provided pastureland for the livestock.

Louisa selected a site in the shade of some oak trees for her family. The place was beautiful, but overhead the sun beat down on the encamped Saints, many of whom were exhausted from the rain and mud they had battled that spring.

"May the Lord reward them for all their sacrifices," Louisa thought.[34]

FARTHER AHEAD ON THE trail, Brigham and the Camp of Israel stopped at a place called Mosquito Creek, not far from the Missouri River. They were hungry, two months behind schedule, and desperately poor.[35] Yet Brigham still insisted on sending an advance company over the Rocky Mountains. He believed that a group of Saints needed to finish the journey that season, for as long as the Church wandered without a home, its enemies would try to scatter it or block its way.[36]

Brigham knew, however, that outfitting such a group would strain the Saints' resources. Few had money or provisions to spare, and Iowa provided limited opportunities for paid labor. To survive on the prairie, many Saints had sold prized possessions along the trail or worked odd jobs to earn money for food and supplies. As the camp moved west and settlements thinned, these opportunities would only become harder to find.[37]

Other matters also weighed on Brigham. The Saints who did not belong to the advance company needed a place to spend the winter. The Omahas and other Native peoples who inhabited the land west of the Missouri River were willing to let the Saints camp there over the winter, but government agents were reluctant to allow them to settle on protected Indian lands for a long period of time.[38]

Brigham also knew the sick and impoverished Saints in Nauvoo were depending on the Church to take them west. For a time, he had hoped to assist them by selling valuable property in Nauvoo, including the temple. But so far this effort had been unsuccessful.[39]

On June 29, Brigham learned that three officers from the United States Army were coming to Mosquito Creek. The United States had declared war on Mexico, and President James Polk had authorized the men to recruit a battalion of five hundred Saints for a military campaign to the California coast.

The next day, Brigham discussed the news with Heber Kimball and Willard Richards. Brigham had no quarrel with Mexico, and the idea of helping the United States galled him. But the West could become American territory if the United States won the war, and assisting the army could improve the Saints' relationship with the nation. More important, the enlisted men's pay could help the Church fund its westward migration.[40]

Brigham spoke with the officers as soon as they arrived. He learned that their orders had come after Thomas Kane, a well-connected young man on the East Coast, had heard about the Saints' plight and introduced Jesse Little to important officials in Washington, DC. After some lobbying, Jesse had met with President Polk and persuaded him to help the Saints move west by enlisting some of them in military service.

Seeing the benefits of the arrangement, Brigham endorsed the orders wholeheartedly. "This is the first offer we have ever had from the government to benefit us," he declared. "I propose that the five hundred volunteers be mustered, and I will do my best to see all their families brought forward, as far as my influence can be extended, and feed them when I have anything to eat myself."[41]

DRUSILLA HENDRICKS WAS FURIOUS with Brigham's decision to cooperate with the United States. Her husband, James, had been shot in the neck during a skirmish with

Missourians in 1838, leaving him partially paralyzed. Like others in camp, she still resented the government for not helping the Saints at that time. Even though her son William was old enough to volunteer for the battalion, she did not want to let him join. With her husband's paralysis, she depended on her son for help.[42]

Recruiters visited the camp daily, often with Brigham or other apostles. "If we want the privilege of going where we can worship God according to the dictates of our conscience," Brigham testified, "we must raise the battalion."[43] Many Saints swallowed their resentment and supported the endeavor, but Drusilla could not bear parting with her son.

Sometimes the Spirit whispered to her, "Are you afraid to trust the God of Israel? Has He not been with you in all your trials? Has He not provided for your wants?" She would acknowledge God's goodness, but then she would remember the government's cruelty, and her anger would return.

On the day of the battalion's departure, William rose early to bring in the cows. Drusilla watched him as he walked through the tall, wet grass, and she worried that her lack of faith would do him more harm than good. He could get hurt traveling on the trail with his family just as easily as he could marching with the battalion. And if that happened, she would regret having made him stay.

Drusilla started breakfast, unsure what to do about William. Climbing onto the wagon to get flour, she again felt the Spirit's whisper: Didn't she want the greatest blessings of the Lord?

"Yes," she said aloud.

"Then how can you get it without making the greatest sacrifice?" the Spirit asked. "Let your son go in the battalion."

"It is too late," she said. "They are to be marched off this morning."

William returned, and the family gathered for breakfast. As James blessed the food, Drusilla was startled when a man interrupted the camp. "Turn out, men!" he shouted. "We lack some men yet in the battalion."

Drusilla opened her eyes and saw William staring at her. She studied his face, memorizing each feature. She knew then that he would join the battalion. "If I never see you again until the morning of the resurrection," she thought, "I shall know you are my child."

After breakfast, Drusilla prayed alone. "Spare his life," she pleaded, "and let him be restored to me and to the bosom of the Church."

"It shall be done unto you," the Spirit whispered, "as it was unto Abraham when he offered Isaac on the altar."

Drusilla searched for William and found him sitting in the wagon, his head buried in his hands. "Do you want to go with the battalion?" she asked. "If you do, I have had a testimony that it is right for you to go."

"President Young said it is for the salvation of this people," William said, "and I might as well have a hand in it as anyone."

"I have held you back," Drusilla said, "but if you want to go, I shall hold you no longer."[44]

CHAPTER 3

Word and Will
of the Lord

Wilford and Phebe Woodruff arrived at the Missouri River with their children in early July 1846. Unable to persuade his sister and brother-in-law to follow the apostles instead of James Strang, Wilford had left Nauvoo soon after the temple dedication with his parents and other Saints.

Their arrival in camp coincided with the departure of William Hendricks and the other army recruits. Named the Mormon Battalion, they numbered more than five hundred men. The battalion employed twenty women as laundresses. Other women also accompanied their husbands on the march, and some brought along their children. In total, more than thirty women traveled with the battalion.[1]

Wilford was at first suspicious of the government's effort to recruit Latter-day Saint men. But he soon changed his mind, especially after Thomas Kane visited the camp. Though Thomas was only mildly curious about the restored gospel, he had been instrumental in persuading the government to assist the Church. He cared deeply about fighting injustice, and he was genuinely eager to help the Saints in their dire circumstances.

Thomas impressed the apostles immediately. "From the information we received from him," Wilford noted in his journal, "we were convinced that God had begun to move upon the heart of the president and others in this nation."[2]

Three days before the battalion marched off, Brigham Young spoke to its officers. He counseled them to keep their bodies clean, to be chaste, and to wear their temple garments if they had received the endowment. He told them to behave honorably toward the Mexicans and not to dispute with them. "Treat prisoners with the greatest civility," he said, "and never take life, if it can be avoided."

Brigham assured the men that they would have no fighting to do, however. He urged them to perform their duties without murmuring, pray daily, and take their scriptures.[3]

After the battalion departed, Brigham turned again to the next stage of the Saints' journey. Cooperating with the United States had allowed him to secure permission to establish a winter camp on Indian lands west of the Missouri River. He now planned to winter the Saints at a place called Grand Island, two hundred miles west, and from there send the advance company over the Rocky Mountains.[4]

As the apostles counseled together, Wilford spoke of other important Church matters that needed their immediate attention. Reuben Hedlock, the man he had appointed to preside over the British mission, had alienated many British Saints by squandering funds they had consecrated for emigration. Wilford foresaw problems within the mission, including the loss of many new converts, until Reuben was released and replaced by more responsible leadership.[5]

The quorum also knew that impoverished Saints were still in Nauvoo at the mercy of mobs and false prophets. If the apostles did not do more to help these Saints, as they had promised to do in the temple at the October conference, then the quorum would be breaking a solemn covenant with the Saints and the Lord.[6]

Acting decisively, the quorum resolved to send three of the apostles in camp—Parley Pratt, Orson Hyde, and John Taylor—to England to lead the British mission. They then sent wagons, teams, and supplies back to Nauvoo to evacuate the poor.[7]

As the quorum sent men and provisions east, Brigham realized his plan to push farther west that year was no longer possible, especially since the battalion had reduced the number of able-bodied men in camp. Thomas Kane recommended building their winter camp at the Missouri River, and Brigham ultimately agreed.[8]

On August 9, 1846, the apostles announced that the Saints would spend the winter in a temporary settlement just west of the river. Brigham wanted to go over the Rocky Mountains and build a temple as soon as possible. But before then, he would gather the Saints together and look after the poor.[9]

AROUND THIS TIME, FOG enveloped the *Brooklyn* as it sailed into San Francisco Bay, six weary months after leaving New York Harbor. Standing on the ship's deck, Sam Brannan peered through the haze and glimpsed a rugged shoreline. Just inside the bay, he saw a crumbling Mexican fort. Flapping in the breeze above it was the American flag.[10]

Sam had feared something like this would happen. The flag was a sure sign the United States had seized San Francisco from Mexico. He had learned about the war with Mexico when the *Brooklyn* anchored at the Hawaiian Islands. There the commander of an American warship said the Saints would be expected to assist the U.S. military in capturing California from the Mexicans. The news angered the Saints, who had not traveled west to fight for a nation that had rejected them.[11]

As they sailed farther into the bay, Sam could see trees along the sandy shoreline and a few wandering animals. In the distance, tucked between some hills, lay Yerba Buena, an old Spanish town.

The *Brooklyn* docked in the harbor, and the Saints disembarked later that afternoon. They pitched tents in the hills outside of Yerba Buena or found shelter in abandoned homes and an old military barracks nearby. Using materials they had brought from New York, the Saints set up mills and a printing shop. A few of them also found work among the town's settlers.[12]

Although disappointed that the California coast now belonged to the United States, Sam was determined to establish the kingdom of God there. He sent a group of men to a valley several days' journey east of the bay to found a settlement called New Hope. There they built a sawmill and a cabin, then cleared the land and sowed acres of wheat and other crops.

Sam wanted to take some men east to find Brigham and lead the rest of the Saints to California as soon as the snow melted off the mountains the following year. Enamored by the healthy climate, fertile soil, and good harbor, he believed the Lord's people could not ask for a better gathering place.[13]

THAT SUMMER, LOUISA PRATT and her daughters camped at the Mount Pisgah way station on the Iowa trail. The place was beautiful, but the water was tepid and foul tasting. Sickness soon overran the settlement, and many Saints died. Louisa's family escaped in early August in good health, but they felt awful about leaving so many sick friends behind.

Louisa's company camped a short time later beside a mosquito-infested creek, and soon she and others were running fevers. The company stopped to rest and then pushed on to the Missouri River, where a long line of wagons waited to be ferried across. When it was finally Louisa's turn, something frightened the cattle, causing great confusion on the ferry and aggravating Louisa's illness.

On the other side of the river, Louisa's fever soared, robbing her of sleep. Around midnight, her groans awoke the ferryman's wife, who found her in terrible condition. The woman quickly directed Louisa's daughters to make a separate bed for themselves so their mother could get some rest. She then gave Louisa warm coffee and some food to revive her.[14]

The next day, the company rolled into the Saints' new settlement, Winter Quarters, the largest of several settlements of Saints along the Missouri River. About twenty-five hundred people lived in Winter Quarters on land shared by the Omahas and other local Indian tribes.[15] Most of the Saints occupied cabins made from logs or sod, but some lived in tents, wagons, or cave-like dwellings called dugouts.[16]

The women of Winter Quarters immediately surrounded Louisa, anxious to help her. They gave her brandy and sugar as medicine, which at first made her feel better. But soon her fever worsened, and she began to shake violently. Afraid she was dying, she cried to the Lord for mercy.[17]

Some of the women who attended to Louisa anointed her with oil, laid their hands on her, and blessed her by the power of their faith. In Nauvoo, Joseph Smith had taught the Relief Society that healing was a gift of the Spirit, a sign that followed all believers in Christ.[18] The blessing comforted Louisa, giving her strength to endure her sickness, and she soon hired a nurse to care for her until her fever broke.

She also paid a man five dollars to build her a cabin of sod and willow brush. The cabin had only a blanket for a door, but it was well lit and large enough for her to sit in a rocking chair beside her fireplace while she recovered her strength.[19]

AT WINTER QUARTERS, THE Saints plowed and planted fields, built mills beside a nearby stream, and established stores and shops. The settlement was laid out in city blocks similar to the Lord's pattern for the city of Zion, as revealed to Joseph Smith in 1833. North of town, Brigham, Heber Kimball, and Willard Richards built homes close to a small council house where the Quorum of the Twelve and the newly called Winter Quarters high council met. Near the center of town was a public square for preaching and other community meetings.[20]

The trek through Iowa had worn down many Saints, and keeping their families fed, clothed, and sheltered continued to sap their strength.[21] Also, flies and mosquitoes from the muddy riverbank often swarmed the new settlement, and malarial aches and chills harassed Saints for days and weeks at a time.[22]

During these trials, most Saints obeyed the commandments. But some stole, cheated, criticized the apostles' leadership, and refused to pay tithing. Brigham had little patience for this behavior. "Men get led away by degrees," he declared, "until the devil gets possession of their tabernacle and they are led captive at the will of the devil."[23]

To encourage righteousness, Brigham admonished the Saints to work together, keep covenants, and avoid sin. "We cannot be sanctified all at once," he said, "but have to be tried and placed in all kinds of shapes and proven to the utmost to see whether we will serve the Lord unto the end."[24]

He also organized them into small wards, appointed bishops, and instructed the high council to uphold a firm code of conduct. Some Saints also gathered into special adoptive families. At this time, Saints were not sealed to their deceased parents if their parents had not joined the Church in this life. Before leaving Nauvoo, Brigham had therefore encouraged around two hundred Saints to be sealed, or spiritually adopted, as sons and daughters into the families of Church leaders who were friends or mentors in the gospel.

These adoption sealings were performed through an ordinance in the temple. Adoptive parents often offered temporal and emotional support, while adoptive sons and daughters, some of whom had no other family in the Church, often responded with faithfulness and devotion.[25]

Some of the challenges at Winter Quarters and other temporary settlements were impossible to avoid. By the time cold weather set in, over nine thousand Saints lived in the area, including thirty-five hundred who lived in Winter Quarters. Accidents, sickness, and death plagued every settlement. Malaria, tuberculosis, scurvy, and other illnesses claimed about one person in ten. About half of the deceased were infants and children.[26]

Wilford Woodruff's family suffered along with the others. In October, while Wilford cut timber, a falling tree struck him and broke some of his ribs. Soon after, his little son Joseph caught a severe cold. Wilford and Phebe attended to the boy constantly, but nothing they did helped, and soon they buried his body in the settlement's newly plotted cemetery.

Some weeks after Joseph's death, Phebe delivered a baby prematurely, and the child died two days later. One evening, Wilford came home and found Phebe distraught, looking at a portrait of herself holding Joseph. Losing the children pained them both, and Wilford longed for when the Saints would find a home, live in peace, and enjoy the blessings and safety of Zion.

"I pray my Heavenly Father to lengthen out my days," he wrote in his journal, "to behold the house of God stand upon the tops of the mountains and to see the standard of liberty reared up as an ensign to the nations."[27]

AMID THE SUFFERING IN Winter Quarters, Brigham received word that a mob of about a thousand men had attacked the small community of Saints still in Nauvoo. About two hundred Saints fought back, but they were defeated in battle after a few days. City leaders negotiated for a peaceful evacuation of the Saints, many of whom were poor and sick. But as the Saints left the city, the mob harassed them and ransacked their homes and wagons. A mob seized the temple, desecrated its interior, and mocked the Saints as they fled to camps on the other side of the river.[28]

When Brigham learned about the desperation of the refugees, he dispatched a letter to Church leaders, reminding them of the covenant they had made in Nauvoo to help the poor and assist every Saint who wanted to come west.

"The poor brethren and sisters, widows and orphans, sick and destitute, are now lying on the west bank of the Mississippi," he declared. "Now is the time for labor. Let the fire of the covenant, which you made in the house of the Lord, burn in your hearts, like flame unquenchable."[29]

Though they had sent twenty relief wagons to Nauvoo two weeks earlier and had little food and few supplies to spare, the Saints at Winter Quarters and neighboring settlements sent additional wagons, ox teams, food, and other supplies back to Nauvoo. Newel Whitney, the presiding bishop of the Church, also purchased flour for the impoverished Saints.[30]

When relief parties found the refugees, many of the Saints there were feverish, ill-equipped for cold weather, and desperately hungry. On October 9, as they prepared to make the journey to the Missouri River, the Saints watched as a flock of quail filled the sky and landed on and around their wagons. Men and boys scrambled after the birds, catching them with their hands. Many recalled how God had also sent Moses and the children of Israel quail in their time of need.

"This morning we had a direct manifestation of the mercy and goodness of God," wrote Thomas Bullock, a Church clerk, in his journal. "The brethren and sisters praised God and glorified His name that what was showered down upon the children of Israel in the wilderness is manifested unto us in our persecution."

"Every man, woman, and child had quails to eat for their dinner," Thomas wrote.[31]

MEANWHILE, THOUSANDS OF MILES away on the Anaa atoll in the Pacific Ocean, an Aaronic Priesthood holder named Tamanehune addressed a conference of more than eight hundred Latter-day Saints. "A letter should be sent to the Church in America," he proposed, "requesting them to send out here immediately from five to one hundred elders." Ariipaea, a member of the Church and a local village leader, seconded the proposal, and the South Pacific Saints raised their hands in assent.[32]

Presiding at the conference, Addison Pratt agreed wholeheartedly with Tamanehune. Over the last three years, Addison and Benjamin Grouard had baptized more than a thousand people. But in that time they had received only one letter from any of the Twelve, and it had given no instructions for returning home.[33]

In the six months since that letter had arrived, the two missionaries had heard nothing else from family, friends, or Church leaders. Whenever a newspaper came to the island, they scoured its pages for news about the Saints. One paper they read claimed that half the Saints in Nauvoo had been slaughtered while the rest had been forced to flee to California.[34]

Anxious to learn the fate of Louisa and his daughters, Addison decided to return to the United States. "To know the truth, even if it is bad," he told himself, "is better than to remain in doubt and anxiety."[35]

Addison's friends Nabota and Telii, the husband and wife who had served with him on Anaa, decided to return to Tubuai, where Telii was beloved as a spiritual teacher among her fellow women of the Church. Benjamin planned to remain on the islands to lead the mission.[36]

When the Pacific Saints learned of Addison's coming departure, they urged him to return quickly and bring more missionaries with him. Since Addison already planned to return to the islands with Louisa and his daughters, provided they were still alive, he readily agreed.[37]

A ship arrived at the island a month later, and Addison sailed with Nabota and Telii for Papeete, Tahiti, where he hoped to catch a ship to Hawaii and then California. When they arrived in Tahiti, he learned to his dismay that a package of letters from Louisa, Brigham Young, and the *Brooklyn* Saints had just been forwarded from the island to Anaa.

"I thought that I had got case-hardened to disappointments," he lamented in his journal, "but this made impressions on my mind that I had heretofore been a stranger to."[38]

AS COLDER WEATHER SETTLED over Winter Quarters, Brigham prayed often to know how to prepare the Church for the journey beyond the Rocky Mountains. After almost a year on the trail, he had learned that organizing and equipping the Saints for the road ahead was vital to their success. Yet setback after setback had also shown him how important it was to rely on the Lord and follow His direction. As in the days of Joseph, only the Lord could direct His Church.

Soon after the start of a new year, Brigham felt the Lord open his mind to new light and knowledge. In a meeting with the high council and the Twelve on January 14, 1847, he began recording a revelation from the Lord to the Saints. Before Brigham went to bed, the Lord gave him further instructions for the coming journey. Taking out the unfinished revelation,

Brigham continued recording the Lord's directions for the Saints.[39]

The next day, Brigham presented the revelation to the Twelve. Called the "Word and Will of the Lord," it emphasized the need to organize the Saints into companies under the leadership of the apostles. In the revelation, the Lord commanded the Saints to provide for their own needs as well as work together on their journey, looking after widows, orphans, and the families of Mormon Battalion members.

"Let every man use all his influence and property to remove this people to the place where the Lord shall locate a stake of Zion," the revelation directed. "If ye do this with a pure heart, in all faithfulness, ye shall be blessed."[40]

The Lord also commanded His people to repent and humble themselves, treat each other kindly, and cease drunkenness and evil-speaking. His words were presented as a covenant, directing the Saints to "walk in all the ordinances," keeping the promises made in the Nauvoo temple.[41]

"I am the Lord your God, even the God of your fathers, the God of Abraham and of Isaac and of Jacob," He declared. "I am he who led the children of Israel out of the land of Egypt; and my arm is stretched out in the last days."

Like the ancient Israelites, the Saints were to praise the Lord and call on His name in times of distress. They were to sing and dance with a prayer of thanksgiving in their hearts. They were not to fear the future but to trust in Him and bear their afflictions.

"My people must be tried in all things," the Lord declared, "that they may be prepared to receive the glory that I have for them, even the glory of Zion."[42]

THE APOSTLES PRESENTED THE new revelation to the Saints at Winter Quarters a few days later, and many rejoiced when they heard it. "The Lord has once more remembered His servants and favored them with a revelation of His will," one woman wrote to her husband in England. "Peace and unity reign in our midst," she exclaimed, "and the Spirit of God is prevalent amongst us."[43]

But some problems persisted in Winter Quarters. Since leaving Nauvoo, the apostles had continued to perform spiritual adoptions among the Saints. Brigham observed that a few Saints were urging friends to be adopted into their families, believing their eternal glory depended on the number of people sealed to them. Jealousy and competition rose as they argued over who would have the biggest family in heaven. The contention left Brigham wondering if any of them would make it there at all.[44]

In February, while speaking on the practice of spiritual adoption, Brigham admitted that he still did not know much about it. He deeply loved the dozens of Saints who had been adopted through the ordinance into his family. He nevertheless felt unschooled in this practice and wondered about what it meant.[45]

"I will attain to more knowledge on the subject," he promised the Saints, "and consequently will be enabled to teach and practice more."[46]

The next day, he felt sick and lay down to rest. As he slept, he dreamed that he saw Joseph Smith sitting in a chair in front of a large window. Taking Joseph's right hand, Brigham asked his friend why he could not be with the Saints.

"It is all right," Joseph said, rising from his chair.

"The brethren have great anxiety to understand the law of adoption or sealing principles," Brigham said. "If you have a word of counsel for me, I should be glad to receive it."

"Tell the people to be humble and faithful and sure to keep the Spirit of the Lord," Joseph said. "If they will, they will find themselves just as they were organized by our Father in Heaven before they came into the world."

Brigham awoke with Joseph's words echoing in his mind: "Tell the people to be sure to keep the Spirit of the Lord and follow it, and it would lead them just right."[47] The counsel did not answer his questions about adoption sealings, but it reminded him to obey the Spirit so that he and the Saints could be guided to greater understanding.

FOR THE REST OF the winter, the apostles continued to seek revelation as they prepared to send wagon companies over the Rocky Mountains. Under their leadership, a small advance company would leave Winter Quarters in the spring, cross the mountains, and establish the new gathering place for the Saints. To obey the Lord's command and fulfill prophecy, they would raise an ensign to the nations and begin work on a temple. Larger companies, made up mainly of families, would soon follow them, obeying the Word and Will of the Lord on their journey.[48]

Before leaving Nauvoo, the Quorum of the Twelve and the Council of Fifty had contemplated settling in the Salt Lake Valley or the Bear River Valley to the north. Both valleys were on the far side of the Rocky Mountains, and descriptions of them were promising.[49] Brigham had seen in a vision the spot where the Saints would settle, but he had only a general sense of where to find it. Still, he prayed that God would direct him and the advance company to the right gathering place for the Church.[50]

The advance company was composed of 143 men selected by the apostles. Harriet Young, the wife of Brigham's brother Lorenzo, asked if she and her two young sons could accompany Lorenzo on the journey. Brigham then asked his wife Clara, who was Harriet's daughter from her first marriage, to join the company as well. Heber Kimball's plural wife Ellen, an immigrant from Norway, also joined the company.[51]

Just as the advance company was preparing to leave, Parley Pratt and John Taylor returned to Winter

Quarters from their mission to England. Along with Orson Hyde, who was still overseeing the Church in Britain, they had appointed new mission leaders and restored order among the Saints. Now, believing they had been away from their families for too long, Parley and John declined Brigham's entreaties to join the rest of the quorum on the trek west. Brigham therefore left them in charge of Winter Quarters.[52]

On the afternoon of April 16, 1847, the advance company began their journey under cold and gloomy skies. "We mean to open up the way for the salvation of the honest in heart from all nations, or sacrifice everything in our stewardship," the apostles declared in a farewell letter to the Saints at Winter Quarters. "In the name of Israel's God, we mean to conquer or die trying."[53]

CHAPTER 4

An Ensign to the Nations

In April 1847, Sam Brannan and three other men left San Francisco Bay in search of Brigham Young and the main body of the Saints. They did not know exactly where to find them, but most emigrants followed the same trail west. If Sam and his small company headed east along the trail, they would eventually cross paths with the Saints.

After stopping briefly to pick up supplies at New Hope, the men trekked northeast to the foothills of the Sierra Nevada mountains. People who knew the Sierras well had warned Sam not to cross them so early in the year. The mountain pass was still choked with snow, they said, which meant the journey could be a two-month ordeal.

Yet Sam was sure he could cross the mountains quickly. Urging their pack animals forward, he and his men hiked for hours up the mountains. The snow was deep but tightly packed, making it easier to find footing along the trail. The mountain streams ran high, however, forcing the men to risk dangerous swims or hazardous alternative routes.

On the far side of the mountain range, the trail led them along hulking granite crags to a view of a beautiful pine-wooded valley with a lake as blue as the sky. Descending to the valley, they found a few abandoned cabins at a campsite littered with human remains. Months earlier, a wagon train bound for California had become stranded in the snow. The emigrants had built the cabins to wait out a bad winter storm, but low on food and unprepared for the cold, many of them slowly starved or froze to death, while some resorted to cannibalism.[1]

Their story was a grim reminder of the dangers of overland travel, but Sam refused to let their tragedy frighten him. He was captivated by the wilderness. "A man cannot know himself," he exulted, "until he has traveled in these wild mountains."[2]

BY MID-MAY, BRIGHAM YOUNG and the advance company had covered more than three hundred miles. Each morning, the bugle awoke the camp at five o'clock, and travel began at seven. Sometimes delays slowed the company's progress, but most days they managed to travel between fifteen and twenty miles. In the evening they circled their wagons, gathered for evening prayers, and extinguished campfires.[3]

The dull routine was sometimes broken by buffalo sightings. The large, shaggy animals traveled in massive herds, rumbling across hills and bottomlands so fluidly that the prairie itself seemed to be moving. The men were eager to hunt the animal, but Brigham counseled them to do so only when necessary and to never waste the meat.[4]

The company traveled along an existing trail that other westbound settlers had blazed a few years earlier. With each passing mile, the grassy prairie slowly gave way to desert meadows and rolling hills. From the top of a bluff, the landscape looked as rough as a stormy sea. The trail followed the Platte River and crossed several creeks that provided water for drinking and cleaning. Yet the ground itself was sandy. Sometimes the company spotted a tree or a patch of green grass along the trail, but much of the land was stark and forbidding as far as the eye could see.[5]

Sometimes, a member of the company would ask Brigham where they were going. "I will show you when we come to it," he would say. "I have seen it, I have seen it in vision, and when my natural eyes behold it, I shall know it."[6]

Every day, William Clayton estimated the company's mileage and corrected the sometimes imprecise maps that guided them. Not far into the journey, he and Orson Pratt worked with Appleton Harmon, a skilled craftsman, to build a "roadometer," a wooden device that accurately measured distances through a system of cogs attached to a wagon wheel.[7]

Despite the company's progress, Brigham was often frustrated when he saw the actions of some members of the company. Most of them had been in the Church for years, served missions, and received the ordinances of the temple. Yet many ignored his counsel on hunting or idled away their free time with gambling, wrestling, and dancing late into the night. Sometimes Brigham woke in the morning to the sound of men arguing over something that had happened during the night. He worried that their quarrels would soon lead to fistfights or worse.

"Do we suppose," he asked the men on the morning of May 29, "that we are going to look out a home for the Saints, a resting place, a place of peace, where they can build up the kingdom and bid the nations welcome, with a low, mean, dirty, trifling, covetous, wicked spirit?"[8] Each of them, he declared, ought to be men of faith and sober minds, given to prayer and meditation.

"Here is an opportunity," he said, "for every man to prove himself, to know whether he will pray and remember his God, without being asked to do it every day." He urged them to serve the Lord, remember their temple covenants, and repent of their sins.

Afterward, the men grouped themselves together in priesthood quorums and covenanted, by uplifted hand, to do right and walk humbly before God.[9] The next day, when the men partook of the sacrament, a new spirit prevailed.

"I have never seen the brethren so still and sober on a Sunday," Heber Kimball noted in his journal, "since we started on the journey."[10]

WHILE THE ADVANCE COMPANY traveled west, roughly half the Saints in Winter Quarters were outfitting wagons and packing provisions for their journey. In the evenings, after finishing their preparations, they often gathered together to sing and dance to fiddle music, and on Sundays they met to hear sermons and talk about their coming trek.[11]

Not everyone was eager to go west, however. James Strang and other dissenters continued to lure Saints away with promises of food, shelter, and peace. Strang and his followers had started a community in Wisconsin, a sparsely settled territory some three hundred miles northeast of Nauvoo, where some dissatisfied Saints were gathering. Already several families in Winter Quarters had packed up their wagons and left to join them.[12]

As the presiding apostle in Winter Quarters, Parley Pratt begged the Saints to ignore apostates and follow the Lord's authorized apostles. "The Lord has called us to gather," he reminded them, "and not scatter all the time." He told them he and John Taylor wanted to send companies west at the end of spring.[13]

Parley had to delay the departure, though. Before the advance company left, the Twelve had organized several companies according to revelation. These companies were composed mostly of families that had been sealed by adoption to Brigham Young and Heber Kimball. The apostles instructed them to pack enough provisions for the coming year and to bring with them poor Saints and the families of the men in the Mormon Battalion. If people would not keep the covenant to provide for these needy families, their wagons could be confiscated and given to those who would.[14]

But Parley saw problems in carrying out the quorum's plan. Many Saints in these companies, including some company captains, were not ready to leave. Some of them lacked the resources to make the journey, and without sufficient supplies they would be a heavy burden on others in the companies who barely had enough provisions for their own families. At the same time, there were other Saints who had not been organized into companies but who were ready and eager to go, fearing they would lose more loved ones to sickness and death if they stayed another year in Winter Quarters.[15]

Parley and John decided to reorganize the companies, adapting the original plan to suit the roughly fifteen hundred Saints who were ready to go west. When some Saints objected to the changes, questioning Parley's authority to modify the Twelve's plan, the two apostles tried to reason with them.

In Brigham's absence, John explained, the apostle with the most seniority had authority to direct Church members. Since Brigham was not in Winter Quarters, John felt it was Parley's responsibility—and right—to make decisions for the settlement.

Parley agreed. "I think it is best to act according to our circumstances," he said.[16]

AS WILFORD WOODRUFF TRAVELED west with the advance company, he often reflected on its sacred mission. "It should be understood," he wrote in his journal, "that we are piloting a road for the house of Israel to travel in for many years to come."[17]

One night, he dreamed that the company arrived at the new gathering place. As he gazed upon the land, a glorious temple appeared before him. It appeared to be built of white and blue stone. Turning to some men standing near him in the dream, he asked if they could see it. They said they did not, but that did not diminish the joy Wilford felt in beholding it.[18]

By June, the weather turned hot. The short grasses that fed their cattle turned brown in the dry air, and timber was harder to find. Often, the only fuel for fires was dried buffalo dung.[19] The company, however, remained diligent in keeping the commandments as Brigham instructed, and Wilford saw evidence of God's blessings in preserving their food supplies, animals, and wagons.

"We have had peace and union in our midst," he wrote in his journal. "Great good will grow out of this mission if we are faithful in keeping the commandments of God."[20]

On June 27, the advance company encountered a well-known explorer named Moses Harris on the trail. Harris told the Saints that neither the Bear River Valley nor the Salt Lake Valley was good for settlement. He recommended that they settle in a place called Cache Valley, northeast of the Great Salt Lake.

The following day, the company encountered another explorer, Jim Bridger. Unlike Harris, Bridger spoke highly of the Bear River and Salt Lake Valleys, although he warned them that cold nights in the Bear River Valley would likely prevent them from cultivating corn. He said the Salt Lake Valley had good soil, several freshwater streams, and year-round rain. He also praised Utah Valley, south of the Great Salt Lake, yet he cautioned them about disturbing the Ute Indians who lived in that region.[21]

Bridger's words about the Salt Lake Valley were encouraging. Though Brigham was unwilling to identify a stopping place until he saw it, he and other members of the company were most interested in exploring the Salt Lake Valley. And if it was not where the Lord wanted them to settle, they could at least stop there, plant crops, and create a temporary settlement until they found their permanent home in the basin.[22]

Two days later, as the men in the advance company were building rafts to cross a fast-moving river, Sam Brannan and his companions walked into the camp just before sunset, surprising everyone. The company listened raptly as Sam entertained them with stories of the *Brooklyn,* the founding of New Hope, and his own perilous journey across mountains and plains to find them. He told them the Saints in California had planted acres of wheat and potatoes to prepare for their arrival.

Sam's enthusiasm for the climate and soil of California was infectious. He urged the company to claim the San Francisco Bay area before other settlers arrived. The land was ideal for settlement, and important men in California were friendly to the Saints' cause and ready to welcome them.

Brigham listened to Sam, quietly skeptical of the proposal. The allure of the California coast was beyond question, but Brigham knew the Lord wanted the Saints to establish the new gathering place closer to the Rocky Mountains. "Our destination is the Great Basin," he declared.[23]

Just over a week later, the company turned off the well-beaten trail they had been following to take another, fainter trail south to the Salt Lake Valley.[24]

THAT SUMMER, LOUISA PRATT moved her family into a cabin she had purchased for five dollars. It was her third home in Winter Quarters. After the chimney failed on her sod home, she had moved the family into a damp dugout, which was little more than a five-foot hole in the ground with a leaky roof.

In the new house, Louisa paid some men to install a floor of split logs. She then had a bowery built in front of her house that could seat twenty-five people, and she and her daughter Ellen opened a school for children. Her daughter Frances, meanwhile, planted and tended a garden and chopped wood for heating the home and cooking.

Louisa's health was still poor. After recovering from her fever and shakes, she took a bad fall on the snow and ice and hurt her knee. While living in the dugout, she developed scurvy and lost her front teeth. But she and her daughters had suffered less than many of the Saints. Everyone had neighbors and friends who had died from the sicknesses that raged through camp.[25]

After purchasing the home and making repairs, she had little money left. When her supply of food was almost gone, she visited her neighbors and asked if they would be interested in purchasing her feather bed, but they did not have any money either. While speaking with them, Louisa mentioned that she had nothing in her house to eat.

"You do not seem troubled," one of them said. "What do you expect to do?"

"Oh, no, I do not feel troubled," Louisa said. "I know deliverance will come in some unexpected way."

As she made her way home, she visited another neighbor. During the conversation, the neighbor mentioned Louisa's old-fashioned iron crane, which was used for holding pots in a fireplace. "If you will sell it," the neighbor said, "I will give you two bushels of cornmeal." Louisa agreed to the bargain, recognizing the Lord was blessing her once again.

That spring, Louisa felt healthier and ventured out to worship with the Saints. The women in the settlement had begun to meet together to strengthen each other by exercising their spiritual gifts. During one meeting, the women spoke in tongues while Elizabeth Ann Whitney, who had been a spiritual leader among the Saints for many years, interpreted. Elizabeth Ann said that Louisa would have health, cross the Rocky Mountains, and there have a joyful reunion with her husband.

Louisa was startled. She had assumed that she would reunite with Addison in Winter Quarters and then make the journey west with him. Without his help, she could see no way, physically or financially, to make the journey.[26]

AS THE MEMBERS OF the advance company headed into the heart of the Rocky Mountains, the trail grew steeper and the men and women tired more easily. Ahead of them, clearly visible above the rolling plains, were snow-capped peaks much taller than any mountain they had seen in the eastern United States.

One night in early July, Brigham's wife Clara awoke with a fever, a headache, and intense pain in her hips and back. Others soon complained of the same symptoms, and they struggled to keep pace with the rest of the company. Every step they took on the stony ground was agonizing for their feeble limbs.[27]

Clara felt better as the days passed. The strange sickness seemed to attack quickly, then subside a short time later. On July 12, however, Brigham came down with a fever. He became delirious through the night. The next day, he felt somewhat better, but he and the apostles decided to rest most of the company while Orson Pratt pressed on with a band of forty-two men.[28]

About a week later, Brigham instructed Willard Richards, George A. Smith, Erastus Snow, and others to continue on and catch up with Orson's advance company. "Halt at the first suitable spot after reaching the Salt Lake Valley," he instructed, "and put in our seed potatoes, buckwheat, and turnips, regardless of our final location."[29] Remembering Jim Bridger's report on the region, he cautioned the company against going south into Utah Valley until they had become better acquainted with the Ute people who inhabited it.[30]

Clara, her two young half brothers, and her mother stayed behind with Brigham and the other sick pioneers. Once the company felt strong enough to continue, they followed a crude trail across uneven terrain choked with underbrush. In some places, the canyon walls were so high that heavy dust became trapped in the air, making it difficult to see what lay ahead.

On July 23, Clara and the sick company climbed a long, steep trail to the summit of a hill. From there they descended through a thick grove of trees, winding their way down a path riddled with stumps left by those who cut the trail. A mile down the hill, the wagon carrying Clara's brothers overturned in a ravine and smashed against a rock. Men quickly cut a hole in the wagon cover and pulled the boys to safety.

While the company rested at the bottom of the hill, two riders from Orson's company arrived in camp with reports that they were near the Salt Lake Valley. Exhausted, Clara and her mother pushed ahead with the rest of the company until the early evening. Above them, the sky looked ready for a storm.[31]

THE NEXT MORNING, JULY 24, 1847, Wilford drove his carriage for several miles down a deep ravine. Brigham lay behind him in the carriage, too feverish and weak to walk. Soon they traveled along a creek through another canyon until they arrived at a level bench of land that opened to a view of the Salt Lake Valley.

Wilford gazed with wonder at the vast country below. Fertile fields of thick green prairie grass, watered by clear mountain streams, stretched for miles before them. The streams emptied into a long narrow river that ran lengthwise down the valley floor. A rim of tall mountains, their jagged peaks high in the clouds, surrounded the valley like a fortress. To the west, glistening like a mirror in the sunlight, was the Great Salt Lake.

After a journey of more than a thousand miles through prairie, desert, and canyons, the sight was breathtaking. Wilford could imagine the Saints settling there and establishing another stake of Zion. They could build homes, cultivate orchards and fields, and gather God's people from around the world. And before long, the Lord's house would be established in the mountains and exalted above the hills, just as Isaiah had prophesied.[32]

Brigham could not see the valley clearly, so Wilford turned the carriage to give his friend a better view. Looking out across the valley, Brigham studied it for several minutes.[33]

"It is enough. This is the right place," he told Wilford. "Drive on."[34]

BRIGHAM HAD RECOGNIZED THE spot as soon as he saw it. At the north end of the valley was the mountain peak from his vision. Brigham had prayed to be led directly to that place, and the Lord had answered his prayers. He saw no need to look elsewhere.[35]

Below, the valley floor was already alive with activity. Even before Brigham, Wilford, and Heber Kimball descended the mountain, Orson Pratt, Erastus Snow, and other men had established a base camp and begun plowing fields, planting crops, and irrigating the land. Wilford joined them as soon as he reached the camp, planting half a bushel of potatoes before eating his evening meal and settling in for the night.

The following day was the Sabbath, and the Saints gave thanks to the Lord. The company met to hear sermons and partake of the sacrament. Though feeble, Brigham spoke briefly to encourage the Saints to keep the Sabbath, take care of the land, and respect each other's property.

On the morning of Monday, July 26, Brigham was still convalescing in Wilford's carriage when he turned to Wilford and said, "Brother Woodruff, I want to take a walk."

"All right," Wilford said.[36]

They set out that morning with eight other men, traveling toward the mountains to the north. Brigham rode in Wilford's carriage part of the way, his hands clutching a green cloak around his shoulders. Before they reached the foothills, the ground leveled off into a plain, and Brigham stepped out of the carriage and walked slowly over the light, rich soil.

As the men followed Brigham, admiring the land, he stopped suddenly and thrust his cane into the ground. "Here shall stand the temple of our God," he said.[37] He could already see a vision of it in front of him, its six spires rising up from the valley floor.[38]

Brigham's words struck Wilford like lightning. The men were about to walk on, but Wilford asked them to wait. He broke off a branch from a nearby sagebrush and drove it into the ground to mark the spot.

The men then continued on, envisioning the city the Saints would build in the valley.[39]

LATER THAT DAY, BRIGHAM pointed at the mountain peak north of the valley. "I want to go up on that peak," he said, "for I feel fully satisfied that that was the point shown me in the vision." The round, rocky peak was easy to climb and clearly visible from all parts of the valley. It was an ideal place to raise an ensign to the nations, signaling to the world that the kingdom of God was again on the earth.

Brigham set out immediately for the summit with Wilford, Heber Kimball, Willard Richards, and others. Wilford was the first to reach the top. From the peak, he could see the valley spread out before him.[40] With its high mountains and spacious plain, this valley could keep the Saints safe from their enemies as they tried to live the laws of God, gather Israel, build another temple, and establish Zion. In his meetings with the Twelve and the Council of Fifty, Joseph Smith had often expressed his desire to find such a place for the Saints.[41]

Wilford's friends soon joined him. They called the place Ensign Peak, evoking Isaiah's prophecy that the outcasts of Israel and the dispersed of Judah would assemble from the four corners of the earth under a common banner.[42]

Someday they wanted to fly a massive flag over the peak. But for now, they did their best to mark the occasion. What happened is uncertain, but one man recalled that Heber Kimball took out a yellow bandana, tied it to the end of Willard Richards's cane, and waved it back and forth in the warm mountain air.[43]

CHAPTER 5

Bowed Down to the Grave

In the summer of 1847, Jane Manning James traveled west with her husband, Isaac, and two sons, Sylvester and Silas, in a large caravan of about 1,500 Saints. Apostles Parley Pratt and John Taylor led the caravan with the help of several captains who oversaw companies of about 150 to 200 Saints. Parley and John had organized the caravan in late spring after deciding to modify the Quorum of the Twelve's original migration plan.

The caravan had left Winter Quarters in mid-June, about two months after the advance company's departure.[1] Though only in her twenties, Jane was used to long overland journeys. After being denied passage on a canal boat in 1843, likely because of the color of their skin, she and a small group of black Latter-day Saints had walked almost eight hundred miles from western New York to Nauvoo. Later, Jane and Isaac had walked across the muddy prairies of Iowa with the Camp of Israel. For most of that time, Jane had been pregnant with her son Silas, who was born along the trail.[2]

Overland travel was rarely exciting. Days were long and tiring. The landscape of the plains was generally dull, unless an unusual rock formation or a buffalo herd came into view. Once, while traveling along the bank of the North Platte River, Jane's company was startled when a herd of buffalo charged at them. The company drew their wagons and cattle together while some men shouted and cracked whips at the stampede. Just before trampling the company, the herd divided down the middle, with some buffalo moving to the right while others moved to the left. In the end no one was harmed.[3]

Jane, Isaac, and their children were the only black Saints in their company of almost 190 people. Yet there were some other black Saints living in wards and branches throughout the Church. Elijah Able, a seventy who had served a mission to New York and Canada, attended a midwestern branch with his wife, Mary Ann. Another man, Walker Lewis, whom Brigham Young had described as "one of the best elders" in the Church, attended a branch on the East Coast with his family.[4]

Many Church members opposed slavery, and Joseph Smith had run for United States president on a platform that included a plan to end the institution. The

Church's missionary efforts, however, had led to the baptisms of some slaveholders and some slaves. Among the enslaved Saints were three members of the advance company—Green Flake, Hark Lay, and Oscar Crosby.[5]

In 1833, the Lord had declared that it was "not right that any man should be in bondage one to another." But after the Saints were driven from Jackson County, Missouri, partly because some of them opposed slavery and showed sympathy for free blacks, Church leaders had cautioned missionaries against stirring up tension between enslaved people and slaveholders. Slavery was one of the most intensely debated issues in the United States at the time, and for many years it had divided churches as well as the country.[6]

Having lived all her life in the northern United States, where slavery was illegal, Jane had never been enslaved. She had worked in the homes of Joseph Smith and Brigham Young and knew that white Saints generally accepted black people into the fold.[7] Like other groups of Christians at this time, however, many white Saints wrongly viewed black people as inferior, believing that black skin was the result of God's curse on the biblical figures Cain and Ham.[8] Some had even begun to teach the false idea that black skin was evidence of a person's unrighteous actions in the premortal life.[9]

Brigham Young shared some of these views, but before leaving Winter Quarters, he had also told a mixed-race Saint that all people were alike unto God. "Of one blood has God made all flesh," he had said. "We don't care about the color."[10]

Establishing Zion beyond the Rocky Mountains granted the Saints an opportunity to create a new society where Jane, her family, and others like them could be welcomed as fellow citizens as well as Saints.[11] But prejudices ran deep, and change seemed unlikely in the near future.

ON AUGUST 26, WILFORD WOODRUFF rode his horse through rows of corn and potatoes to the foothills overlooking the Salt Lake Valley. From there he could see the beginning of a great settlement. In a month's time, he and the advance company had begun building a sturdy fort, planted acres of crops, and drawn up plans for the new gathering place. At the center of the settlement, on the spot where Brigham had thrust his cane into the earth, was a square patch of ground they now called the "temple block."[12]

Wilford's first days in the valley had been full of wonder. A herd of antelope grazed on the west side of the valley. Flocks of mountain goats played in the hills. Wilford and the other pioneers had discovered sulfurous hot springs near Ensign Peak. At the Great Salt Lake, the men had floated and rolled like logs on the warm, briny water, trying in vain to sink beneath its surface.[13]

Four days after arriving in the valley, Wilford had been riding alone several miles from camp when he saw twenty American Indians on a ridge ahead of him. In coming west, the Saints knew they would encounter Native peoples along the trail and in the Great Basin. Yet they had expected to find the Salt Lake Valley largely unoccupied. In reality, the Shoshones, the Utes, and a few other tribes often came to the valley to hunt and gather food.

Cautiously turning his horse around, Wilford started back to camp at a slow trot. One of the Indians galloped after him, and when only a hundred yards separated them, Wilford halted his horse, turned to face the rider, and tried to communicate with improvised sign language. The man was friendly, and Wilford learned that he was a Ute who wanted peace and commerce with the Saints. Since then, the Saints had made additional contact with Indians, including the Shoshones from the north.[14]

Now, with cold weather only weeks away, Wilford, Brigham, Heber Kimball, and some other members of the advance company planned to return to their families in Winter Quarters and bring them west in the spring. "I wish to God we had not got to return," Heber had said. "This is a paradise to me. It's one of the most lovely places I ever beheld."[15]

Not everyone agreed with him about the valley. Despite its streams and grassy fields, the new settlement was drier and more desolate than any place the Saints had ever gathered. From the moment he arrived, Sam Brannan had pleaded with Brigham to continue on to the green fields and fertile soil of the California coast.[16]

"I am going to stop right here," Brigham had told Sam. "I am going to build a city here. I am going to build a temple here." He knew the Lord wanted the Saints to settle in the Salt Lake Valley, far from other western U.S. settlements, where he was sure other emigrants would soon take up residence. Brigham appointed Sam to serve as president over the Church in California, however, and sent him back to San Francisco Bay with a letter for the Saints.[17]

"If you choose to tarry where you are, you are at liberty to do so," Brigham noted in his letter. Yet he invited them to join the Saints in the mountains. "We wish to make this a stronghold, a rallying point, a more immediate gathering place than any other," he told them. California, on the other hand, was to be a way station for Saints headed to the valley.[18]

For his part, Wilford had never seen a better site for a city than the Salt Lake Valley, and he was eager for more Saints to arrive. He and the Twelve had spent all winter planning an orderly migration—one that provided a way for all Saints, regardless of position or wealth, to make it to the valley. The time had now come for the plan to unfold for the benefit of Zion.[19]

WHEN ADDISON PRATT LEFT Tahiti in March 1847, he had hoped to find his family in California with the rest of the Saints. Yet having received no word from them—or anyone in the Church—in the last year, he did not know if they would actually be there. "To reflect that I am now on my way to them is a pleasant thought," he wrote in his journal. "But the next thought that arises is: Where are they? Or where am I to find them?"[20]

Addison arrived at San Francisco Bay in June. There he found the *Brooklyn* Saints awaiting the return of Sam Brannan and the arrival of the main body of the Church. Believing Louisa and their children were on their way to the coast, Addison volunteered to go to the Saints' settlement, New Hope, with four other men to harvest the Church's wheat.

The group left a short time later in a boat. New Hope lay more than a hundred miles inland on a tributary of the San Joaquin River. For days, the men sailed along low marshy country with tall bulrushes by the riverbanks. Nearer the settlement, the ground hardened, and they traveled the rest of the way on foot over grassy prairies.

The site for New Hope was beautiful, but a nearby river had flooded a short time before, washing out some of the Saints' wheat and leaving behind pools of stagnant water. At night, as Addison lay down to sleep, swarms of mosquitoes besieged the settlement. Addison and the others tried to beat them away or smoke them out, but with no success. And to make matters worse, coyotes and owls howled and hooted until daybreak, robbing the tired settlers of peace and quiet.[21]

The wheat harvest started the next morning. But Addison's sleepless night caught up with him by noon, and he napped beneath the shade of a tree. This became an everyday routine as mosquitoes and the din of wild animals kept him awake night after night. When the harvest was over, Addison was happy to go.

"Had it not have been for the mosquitoes," he wrote in his journal, "I should have enjoyed myself well there."[22]

Back at San Francisco Bay, Addison began preparing a home for his family. By then, some members of the Mormon Battalion had arrived in California and received an honorable release. Sam Brannan also returned to the bay, still convinced that Brigham was foolish to settle in the Salt Lake Valley. "When he has fairly tried it," he told some battalion veterans, "he will find that I was right and he was wrong."

Sam delivered Brigham's letter to the Saints in California, however, and many of those who had sailed on the *Brooklyn* or marched with the Mormon Battalion decided to emigrate to the Salt Lake Valley in the spring. Sam also had a letter for Addison from Louisa. She was still in Winter Quarters, but she too planned to come to the valley in the spring and settle with the body of the Saints.

Addison's plans changed immediately. Come spring, he would head east with the departing Saints and meet up with his family.[23]

BRIGHAM YOUNG WAS STILL feeling sick in late August when he and the return company left the Salt Lake Valley for their trip back to Winter Quarters. Over the next three days, the small company traveled rapidly through dusty canyons and over steep Rocky Mountain passes.[24] When they arrived on the other side, Brigham was glad to learn that Parley Pratt and John Taylor's large caravan of Saints was only a few hundred miles away.

Brigham's joy vanished a short time later, however, when he learned that the caravan was four hundred wagons larger than he had anticipated. The Twelve had spent all winter organizing Saints into companies according to the revealed will of the Lord. Now it appeared that Parley and John had disregarded that revelation and acted of their own accord.[25]

A few days later, Brigham and the return company met up with the caravan. Parley was in one of the lead companies, so Brigham quickly called a council with Church leaders to ask him why he and John had disobeyed the quorum's instructions.[26]

"If I've done anything wrong, I am willing to right it," Parley told the council. But he insisted that he and John had acted within their authority as apostles. Hundreds of Saints had died that year in Winter Quarters and other settlements along the Missouri River. And many families had been desperate to leave the area before another deadly season set in. Since some Saints in the companies the Twelve had organized were not yet prepared to leave, he and John had chosen to form new companies to accommodate those who were ready.[27]

"Our companies were perfectly organized," Brigham countered, "and if they could not get through, we were responsible to them." The Word and Will of the Lord had clearly directed each company to "bear an equal proportion" of the poor and the families of the men serving in the Mormon Battalion. Yet Parley and John had left many of these people behind.[28]

Brigham also disagreed that two apostles could overturn the decision of the quorum. "If the Quorum of the Twelve do a thing, it is not in the power of two of them to rip it up," he said. "When we got the machine moving, it was not your business to stick your hands among the cogs to stop the wheel."[29]

"I've done the best I could," Parley said. "You say I could have done better, and if I am to take blame in it, and say I've done wrong—I've done wrong. I am guilty of an error and am sorry for it."

"I forgive you," Brigham replied. "And if I don't do right," he added, "I want every man so to live in the sunshine of glory to correct me when I'm wrong. I feel bowed down to the grave with the burden of this great people."[30]

Brigham's weariness was evident in his face and gaunt frame. "I look upon myself as a weak, poor little man. I was called by the providence of God to preside," he said. "I want you to go right into the celestial kingdom with me."

"I want to know if the brethren are satisfied with me," Parley said.

"God bless you forever and ever," Brigham said. "Don't think any more about it."[31]

DRUSILLA HENDRICKS AND HER family were camped farther down the wagon train when Brigham and his group arrived. While most of the families of Mormon Battalion members were still in Winter Quarters, the Hendrickses and some others had gathered enough resources to join those going west. More than a year had passed since Drusilla watched her son William march away with the battalion, and she was anxious to reunite with him in the valley—or sooner.[32]

Already Drusilla's company had encountered returning battalion soldiers along the trail. The faces of many Saints, anxious to see their loved ones, brightened hopefully when they saw the troops. Sadly, William was not among them.

They saw more battalion soldiers a month later. These men captivated the Saints with descriptions of the Great Basin and let them taste salt they had brought with them from the Great Salt Lake. But William was not with this group either.[33]

Over the next several weeks, Drusilla and her family labored over mountain trails, crossed rivers and streams, climbed steep hills, and navigated canyons. Their hands, hair, and faces became caked with dust and grime. Their clothes, already threadbare and tattered from the long journey, offered little protection from the sun, rain, and dirt. When they reached the valley in early October, some in their company were too ill or exhausted to celebrate.[34]

More than a week passed after Drusilla and her family arrived in the valley, and still they had no news about William. After the battalion arrived at the California coast, some veterans had stayed behind to work and earn money while others headed east to the Salt Lake Valley or Winter Quarters. For all Drusilla knew, William could be anywhere between the Pacific Ocean and the Missouri River.[35]

With winter approaching, Drusilla and her family had almost no warm clothing, little food, and no way to build a house. Their situation looked bleak, but she trusted in God that all would work out. One night, Drusilla dreamed of the temple the Saints would build in the valley, as Wilford Woodruff had a few months earlier. Joseph Smith stood on top of it, looking exactly as he had in life. Drusilla called her husband and children to her and said, "There is Joseph." The prophet spoke with them, and two doves flew down to the family.

Waking from the dream, Drusilla believed the doves represented the Spirit of the Lord, a sign of divine approval of the decisions she and her family had made. She believed that their sacrifices had not gone unnoticed.

Later that day, a group of footsore battalion veterans arrived in the valley. This time, William was among them.[36]

WHILE THE HENDRICKS FAMILY was reuniting in the Salt Lake Valley, the men of Brigham's return company were still venturing east on the trail. They had been traveling rapidly and were now exhausted and running low on food. Their horses were growing weaker and starting to give out. In the mornings, some animals needed help getting to their feet.[37]

Amid these difficulties, Brigham remained unsettled about his meeting with Parley.[38] Although he had forgiven his fellow apostle and told him to forget the matter, their disagreement revealed a need for clarification—and possibly changes—in how the Church was currently led and organized.

In Joseph's day, a First Presidency had presided over the Church. After the prophet's death, however, the First Presidency had been dissolved, leaving the Twelve to preside in its place. According to revelation, the Twelve Apostles formed a quorum equal in authority to the First Presidency. Yet they also had a sacred duty to serve as a traveling council and take the gospel to the world.[39] As a quorum, could they adequately fulfill this mandate while still shouldering the duties of the First Presidency?

Brigham had occasionally considered reorganizing the First Presidency, yet he had never thought the time was right. Since leaving the Salt Lake Valley, questions about the future of Church leadership had loomed over him.[40] He pondered the matter quietly on the road to Winter Quarters, and more and more he felt the Spirit urging him to act.

One day, while resting beside a river, he turned to Wilford Woodruff and asked if the Church should call members of the Twelve to form a new First Presidency.

Wilford thought it over. Altering the Quorum of the Twelve—a quorum established by revelation—was a serious matter.

"It would require a revelation to change the order of that quorum," Wilford observed. "Whatever the Lord inspires you to do in this matter, I am with you."[41]

CHAPTER 6

Seven Thunders Rolling

In the fall of 1847, Oliver Cowdery was living with his wife, Elizabeth Ann, and their daughter Maria Louise in a small town in Wisconsin Territory, nearly five hundred miles from Winter Quarters. He was forty-one years old and practicing law with his older brother. Almost two decades had passed since Oliver had served as Joseph Smith's scribe for the translation of the Book of Mormon. He still believed in the restored gospel, yet for the last nine years he had been living apart from the Saints.[1]

Phineas Young, Brigham Young's older brother, was married to Oliver's younger sister Lucy, and the two men were close friends and often exchanged letters. Phineas frequently let Oliver know he still had a place in the Church.[2]

Other old friends reached out to Oliver as well. Sam Brannan, Oliver's former apprentice in the Kirtland printing office, had invited him to sail with the Saints on the *Brooklyn*. William Phelps, who had once briefly left the Church himself after falling out with Joseph Smith, likewise invited Oliver to go west. "If you believe that we are Israel," William wrote, "come on and go with us, and we will do you good."[3]

But Oliver's resentment ran deep. He believed that Thomas Marsh, Sidney Rigdon, and other Church leaders had turned Joseph and the high council against him in Missouri. And he feared that his disaffection from the Church had hurt his reputation among the Saints. He wanted them to remember the good things he had done, especially his part in the translation of the Book of Mormon and the restoration of the priesthood.[4]

"I have been sensitive on this subject," he once wrote to Phineas. "You would be, under the circumstances, had you stood in the presence of John with our departed brother Joseph, to receive the lesser priesthood, and in the presence of Peter, to receive the greater."[5]

Oliver also was unsure if the Quorum of the Twelve had authority to preside over the Church. He respected Brigham Young and the other apostles he knew, but he did not have a witness that they were called of God to lead the Saints. For now, he believed the Church was in a dormant state, awaiting a leader.

In July, around the time the advance company entered the Salt Lake Valley, former apostle William

McLellin had visited Oliver. William wanted to start a new church in Missouri based on the restored gospel, and he hoped that Oliver would join him. The visit prompted Oliver to write his wife's brother David Whitmer, a fellow witness of the Book of Mormon. Oliver knew William was planning to visit David as well, and he wanted to know what David thought about William and his work.[6]

David wrote back six weeks later, noting that William had indeed visited him. "We have established, or commenced to establish, the church of Christ again," David announced, "and it is the will of God that you be one of my counselors in the presidency of the church."[7]

Oliver considered the offer. Forming a new church presidency with David and William in Missouri would give him another chance to preach the restored gospel. But was it the same gospel he had embraced in 1829? And did David and William have authority from God to establish a new church?[8]

EARLY IN THE MORNING on October 19, 1847, apostles Wilford Woodruff and Amasa Lyman spotted seven men emerging from a distant scattering of trees. Normally, strangers on the trail posed no threat. But the sudden appearance of these men set Wilford on edge.

For the last two days, he and Amasa had been hunting buffalo with several other men to feed Brigham Young's struggling return company. Winter Quarters, their destination, was still more than a week's journey away. Without the buffalo meat piled into the hunters' three wagons, the company would be hard-pressed to finish their journey. Many of them were already sick.[9]

The apostles watched the strangers carefully, wondering at first if they were Indians. But as the figures drew nearer, the apostles could see that they were white men—possibly soldiers—on horseback. And they were charging full speed at the hunting party.

Wilford and the hunters drew their weapons in defense. But when the strangers rode up, Wilford was surprised and delighted to see the face of Hosea Stout, the police chief in Winter Quarters. The Saints in Winter Quarters had learned about the return company's desperate straits, and Hosea and his men had been dispatched to supply provisions for the travelers and their animals.[10]

The assistance bolstered the return company, and they pressed forward. On October 31, when they were about a mile from the settlement, Brigham signaled his company to stop and assemble. The hard day of travel was almost over, and the men were anxious to see their families, but he wanted to say a few words before they disbanded.

"Thanks for your kindness and willingness to obey orders," he said. In a little over six months, they had traveled more than two thousand miles with no major accidents and no deaths. "We have accomplished more than we expected," Brigham declared. "The blessings of the Lord have been with us."[11]

He dismissed the men, and they returned to their wagons. The company then drove the remaining mile to Winter Quarters. As the wagons rolled into the settlement shortly before sunset, Saints emerged from their cabins and hovels to welcome the men back. Crowds formed along the streets to shake hands with them and rejoice in all they had accomplished under the guiding hand of the Lord.[12]

WILFORD WAS OVERJOYED TO see his wife and children again. Three days earlier, Phebe had given birth to a healthy baby girl. Now the Woodruffs had four living children: Willy, Phebe Amelia, Susan, and newborn Shuah. Wilford also had one son, James, with his plural wife, Mary Ann Jackson, whom he had married shortly after returning from England. Mary Ann and James had gone to the Salt Lake Valley earlier that year with Wilford's father.

"All was cheerful and happy," Wilford wrote of his homecoming, "and we felt it a blessing to again meet."[13]

That winter, the nine apostles in Winter Quarters and the surrounding settlements counseled together often. During these meetings, the future of the quorum weighed heavily on Brigham's mind. On the journey back from the Salt Lake Valley, the Spirit had revealed to Brigham that the Lord wanted the Twelve to reorganize the First Presidency so that the apostles could be free to proclaim the gospel of Jesus Christ throughout the world.[14]

Brigham had long been reluctant to speak to the quorum about the subject. He understood that his responsibilities as president of the Twelve set him apart from the other apostles, giving him authority to receive revelation for the quorum and everyone within its stewardship.

But he also understood that he could not act alone. The Lord had revealed in 1835 that the Twelve were to make decisions unanimously or not at all. By divine direction, the apostles were supposed to act "in all righteousness, in holiness, and lowliness of heart" when making decisions. If they were going to do anything as a quorum, they would need to come together in unity and harmony.[15]

On November 30, Brigham finally spoke to the quorum about reorganizing the First Presidency, certain that it was the Lord's will to move forward. Orson Pratt immediately questioned the need for change. "I would like to see the Twelve hold together perfectly and unitedly," he said.

Orson believed that the Twelve could lead the Church in the absence of a First Presidency because a revelation had declared the two quorums to be equal in authority. The prophet Joseph Smith had also taught that a majority of the Twelve could make authoritative decisions when a full quorum was not present. For Orson, this meant that seven apostles could stay at Church headquarters to govern the Saints while the remaining five took the gospel to the nations.[16]

Brigham listened to Orson, but he disagreed with his conclusion. "Which is better," Brigham asked, "to untie the feet of the Twelve and let them go to the nations, or always keep seven at home?"

"It is my feeling," said Orson, "there should not be a three-member First Presidency, but the Twelve be the First Presidency."[17]

As Orson and Brigham spoke, Wilford turned the matter over in his mind. He was willing to sustain a new First Presidency if it was the Lord's revealed will. But he also worried about the consequences of a change. If three of the Twelve formed a First Presidency, would three new apostles be called to take their place in the quorum? And how would the reorganization of the presidency affect the role of the Twelve in the Church?

For now, he wanted the Twelve to continue as they were. Splitting up the quorum would feel like severing a body in two.[18]

THE MOUNTAINS SURROUNDING THE Salt Lake Valley seemed to catch fire in the fall of 1847 as their foliage changed to brilliant hues of red, yellow, and brown. From where her family camped amid other Saints on the temple block, Jane Manning James could see most of the mountains and much of the Saints' new settlement, which they had begun calling Great Salt Lake City, or simply Salt Lake City. About a mile southwest of her tent lay a square-shaped fort where some Saints were building cabins for their families. Since the valley had few trees, they constructed these buildings with timber from the nearby canyons or from hard adobe bricks.[19]

When Jane arrived in the valley, the Saints who had come with the advance company were already running low on food. Newcomers like Jane had few provisions to spare. The milk of most cows in the valley had dried up, and the cattle were fatigued and scrawny. John Smith, the newly appointed president of the Salt Lake Stake, led the high council and bishops in providing for everyone in the valley until crops were ready to harvest, but few went to bed with full stomachs.[20]

Yet even with a lack of food, the settlement developed rapidly. Women and men worked together to build homes and make their surroundings comfortable. Men ventured up the canyons to cut timber and haul it down to the valley. With no sawmill, each log had to be cut into planks by hand. Roofs were made from poles and dried grass. Windows were often made from greased paper instead of glass.[21]

At this time, the women of the Church continued to meet together informally. Elizabeth Ann Whitney and Eliza Snow, former leaders of the Nauvoo Relief Society, often led meetings for mothers as well as for young women and little girls. As they had done in Winter Quarters, the women exercised spiritual gifts and strengthened one another.[22]

Like other Saints, Jane and her husband, Isaac, worked together to make a home in the valley. Jane's son Sylvester was old enough to help with chores.[23] And there was always something to do. Children could help their mothers gather wild parsnips, thistles, and sego lily roots to boost their dwindling provisions. The Saints could hardly afford to waste food. When a cow was slaughtered, they ate everything they could, head to hoof.[24]

Snow began to fall in early November, blanketing the tops of the mountains with white powder. Temperatures dropped in the valley, and the Saints readied themselves for their first winter.[25]

ON AN OVERCAST DAY in late November, the apostles at Winter Quarters met to discuss Oliver Cowdery. Most of them had known him in Kirtland and had heard his powerful testimony of the Book of Mormon. Along with David Whitmer and Martin Harris, he had helped the prophet Joseph Smith call some of them to the Quorum of the Twelve and had taught them their responsibilities. Phineas Young had also assured them that Oliver was committed to Zion and had softened his heart toward the Church.[26]

With Willard Richards acting as clerk, the apostles composed a letter to Oliver. "Come," they wrote, "and return to our Father's house, from whence thou hast wandered." Describing Oliver as a beloved prodigal son, they invited him to be rebaptized and ordained again to the priesthood.

"If you desire to serve God with all your heart and become partaker of the blessings of the celestial kingdom, do these things," they declared. "Thy soul will be filled with rejoicing."

They gave Phineas the letter and asked him to deliver it in person.[27]

A SHORT TIME LATER, Brigham met with eight other apostles at the home of Orson Hyde, who had returned from his mission in England. "I want to have a decision," he said. "From the time I had been in Great Salt Lake City till now, the tappings of the Spirit to me is, the Church ought to be now organized." He testified that the quorum needed to sustain a First Presidency to govern the Church so the apostles could lead missionary efforts abroad.

"I want every man to go with the conviction of the Lord. Just learn which way that the Lord goes and go with that," he counseled. "An elder who resists the current of the Spirit will spit in his own face."

Heber Kimball and Orson Hyde agreed that it was time to reorganize the First Presidency. But Orson Pratt once again expressed concern. He worried that the First Presidency would not seek advice from the Quorum of the Twelve and that the Twelve might also defer too quickly to the presidency's authority, accepting its decisions before thinking through matters themselves. The Church had functioned well enough under the Twelve, he reasoned. Why change now?[28]

Brigham asked to hear the thoughts of each of the quorum members present. When his turn came, Wilford Woodruff shared his hesitations about creating a First Presidency, but he expressed his willingness to align his will with God's. "Our president seems to be moved upon by the Spirit," he said. "He stands between us and God, and I for one don't want to tie his hands."[29]

"I don't want to see this quorum divided," George A. Smith said next. He wished to delay his decision until he was certain of the mind of God, but he was open to change. "If it's the will of the Lord that this course should be taken," he declared, "I'll twist myself to it."

"My feelings are precisely like yours," said Brigham. "I would not be divided in our feelings or separated no more than you would." Still, he knew the Lord's will. "It is in me like seven thunders rolling," he declared. "God has brought us where we are, and we have got to do it."[30]

Amasa Lyman and Ezra Benson, the two newest apostles, agreed with him. "I want to help with the Quorum of the Twelve," Ezra said, "and I mean to stick to Brother Brigham." He compared himself to a machine in a mill, ever ready to serve its function. He said he was perfectly willing to have the First Presidency lead him as the Lord saw fit.

"Amen!" said several apostles.

Orson Pratt stood. "I don't consider we should act as machines," he said. "If we are to be governed in all cases in that way, we have no room in the least degree to look at a thing in this light."[31]

"It's of importance now to organize the Church," Brigham told Orson. "What we have done is a mere patching to what we have to do. If you tie us up, we can't do anything."[32]

Brigham's words hung over the room, and the Holy Ghost was poured out upon the apostles. Orson knew what Brigham had said was true.[33] The apostles brought the question of reorganization to a vote, and each member of the quorum raised his hand to sustain Brigham Young as the president of The Church of Jesus Christ of Latter-day Saints.

"I suggest that Brother Young appoint his two counselors tonight," said Orson.[34]

THREE WEEKS LATER, ON December 27, 1847, about a thousand Saints from settlements along the Missouri River gathered for a special conference. They had built a log tabernacle for the occasion on the east side of the river at a place later called Kanesville. The building was larger than any cabin in the area, but it could not hold everyone who wanted to attend.

Inside, the Saints sat shoulder to shoulder on hard log benches. Though the winter had been intensely cold so far, when the Saints arrived at the log tabernacle the weather was unseasonably pleasant. The day before, Heber Kimball had promised them that if they attended the meeting, they would have one of their best days ever and a fire would be lit that would never go out.[35]

On a platform at the front of the room, the apostles sat with the Winter Quarters high council. The meeting opened with singing and prayer, followed by sermons from some of the apostles and other Church leaders. Orson Pratt spoke about the importance of the First Presidency.

"The time has come when the Twelve must have their hands liberated to go to the ends of the earth," Orson said, certain now of the Lord's will. "If there is no First Presidency, it confines the Twelve too much to one place." Reorganizing the presidency, he testified, allowed the Church to turn its eyes to the distant parts of the earth, where thousands of people could be waiting for the gospel.[36]

After the sermons, it was proposed that Brigham Young be sustained as president of the Church. The Saints then raised their hands in unison to sustain him. Taking the stand, Brigham proposed that Heber Kimball and Willard Richards be sustained as his counselors.

"This is one of the happiest days of my life," he told the Saints. The road ahead would not be easy, but as the Saints' leader, he would dedicate himself completely to fulfilling the Lord's will.

"I will do right," he promised. "As He dictates, so I will perform."[37]

CHAPTER 7

Keep Up Good Courage

The spring of 1848 brought warmer days and a few hard rains to the Salt Lake Valley. Roofs leaked and the ground turned soft and muddy. Snakes slithered through cabins, catching adults off guard and terrifying children. Tiny mice, with teeth as sharp as needles, scampered across cabin floors and chewed their way into food sacks, trunks, and coat sleeves. Sometimes at night, Saints would awake with a start as rodents scurried across them.[1]

One of the oldest men in the valley was sixty-six-year-old John Smith. He was the uncle of the prophet Joseph Smith and the father of apostle George A. Smith. After being baptized in 1832, John had served on the Kirtland high council and presided over stakes in Missouri and Illinois. He now served as president of the Salt Lake Stake, making him responsible for the well-being of the settlement.[2]

Suffering from poor health, John shouldered his new duties with the help of his younger counselors, Charles Rich and John Young, and a newly formed high council.[3] As stake president, John oversaw city planning, land distribution, and public building projects.[4] Illness sometimes kept him out of council meetings, yet he was mindful of everything happening in the valley and responded quickly to problems.[5]

In letters to Brigham, John wrote hopefully about the Saints in Salt Lake City. "Considering all the circumstances, great union and harmony prevail in our midst," he noted. Throughout the settlement, people were farming or making tables, chairs, beds, washtubs, butter churns, and other household items. Many families now had cabins in or around the fort. In fields along creeks and irrigation ditches, winter wheat had come up and acres of new crops had been planted for the summer.[6]

Yet John also wrote openly about the challenges in the city. Several Saints had already become discontented with life in the valley and left for California. That winter a group of Indians who had long hunted for food in Utah Valley drove off and killed some of the Saints' cattle. Violence nearly broke out, but the Saints and the Indians negotiated peace.[7]

Of greatest concern, however, was the lack of food. In November, John had authorized a company of men to travel to the California coast to purchase livestock, grain, and other supplies. But the company had not returned yet, and food supplies were running out. There were nearly seventeen hundred Saints to feed, and thousands more were on the way. A failed harvest could carry the settlement to the brink of starvation.[8]

John had faith in the Lord's plan for the valley, trusting that He would ultimately provide for His people.[9] But life in Salt Lake City remained fragile. If something happened to upend its tenuous peace and stability, the Saints could be in serious trouble.

"GOLD!" SHOUTED SAM BRANNAN as he ran through the streets of San Francisco. "Gold from the American River!" He waved his hat wildly in the air and held up a small bottle, its sandy contents glinting in the sun. "Gold!" he cried. "Gold!"[10]

For weeks, Sam and the California Saints had heard rumors that gold had been found at a place called Sutter's Mill along the American River, about 140 miles northeast of San Francisco. But he did not know if the rumors were true until he spoke with a group of Mormon Battalion veterans who had been present when the gold was discovered. He soon visited the place himself and found men squatting in the shallow water, dipping baskets and pans into the silty riverbed. In a matter of five minutes, he watched someone pull eight dollars' worth of gold out of the river.[11]

San Francisco went into a frenzy over the gold dust in Sam's bottle. Men quit their jobs, sold their land, and hurried to the river. Sam, meanwhile, plotted how to make a fortune of his own. California had gold for the taking, but he did not need to take up the hard and often fruitless work of gold digging to get rich. All he needed to do was sell shovels, pans, and other supplies to gold seekers. The demand for these materials would always be high as long as there was a gold rush.[12]

Like many other California Saints, Addison Pratt prospected for gold at a place called Mormon Island while he waited for snow to melt from the trail over the Sierra Nevada mountains. To make more money, Sam had convinced the veterans to give him 30 percent of all the gold discovered in the area, supposedly to purchase cattle for the Saints in the Salt Lake Valley.

Addison doubted any money from Mormon Island would ever go toward helping the Church. In the months he had lived in San Francisco, Addison had observed that Sam, for all his professions of faith and devotion, was becoming more and more interested in self-promotion and getting rich than in the kingdom of God.

Fortunately, Addison did not have to wait long— four days later he learned that the mountain passes were clear. He secured a wagon and a team to pull it and soon started off for the valley in company with around fifty Saints from the *Brooklyn* and the Mormon Battalion.[13]

WHEN HARRIET YOUNG HAD arrived in the Salt Lake Valley with the advance company, she had looked over the new gathering place with dismay. It appeared parched and barren and lonely. "Weak and weary as I am," she had said, "I would rather go a thousand miles farther than remain in such a forsaken place as this."[14] Her husband, Lorenzo, felt the same. "My feelings were such as I cannot describe," he noted in his journal. "Everything looked gloomy, and I felt heartsick."[15]

Harriet and Lorenzo built a home near the temple block during the mild winter and moved out of the cramped fort. As soon as March arrived, they planted spring wheat, oats, corn, potatoes, beans, and peas to feed their family. A few weeks later, a severe frost struck the valley, damaging crops and threatening the success of the harvest. The frost lingered well into May, but by working together, the Youngs managed to salvage most of their crop.[16]

"We still keep up good courage, hoping for the best," Lorenzo wrote in his journal. As was the case with everyone else in the valley, their provisions were running low and they needed a successful harvest to replenish their food supply.[17]

On May 27, 1848, however, swarms of wingless crickets descended on the valley from the mountains and swept across the Youngs' yard at an alarming speed. The crickets were large and black, with armor-like shells and long antennae. They consumed the Youngs' bean patch and peas in a matter of minutes. Harriet and Lorenzo tried to beat the crickets back with handfuls of brush, but there were too many.[18]

The insects soon spread far and wide, feeding ravenously on the Saints' crops, leaving dry stalks where corn or wheat used to be. The Saints did everything they could think of to stop the crickets. They smashed them. They burned them. They tried hitting pots and pans together, hoping the noise would drive them away. They dug deep trenches and tried to drown them or block their paths. They prayed for help. Nothing seemed to work.[19]

As the destruction continued, President John Smith assessed the damage. The frost and crickets had wiped out whole fields of crops, and now more Saints were thinking seriously about leaving the valley. One of his counselors urged him to write to Brigham immediately. "Tell him not to bring the people here," the counselor said, "for if he does, they will all starve to death."

John was silent for a few moments, deep in thought. "The Lord led us here," he said at last, "and He has not led us here to starve."[20]

MEANWHILE, IN WINTER QUARTERS, Louisa Pratt did not think she could afford to make the journey to the Salt Lake Valley that spring, but Brigham Young told her that she had to go. The women in Winter Quarters had promised her that the Lord would reunite her with her husband in the valley. And the previous fall, Addison had written to her and Brigham about his plan to leave for Salt Lake City in the spring. He would be disappointed if his family was not there.[21]

"I hope I shall see my dear family," Addison had written. "This has been a long and grievous separation to me, but the Lord has thus far brought me through it, and I still live in hope of seeing them."[22]

Brigham asked Louisa to provide all she could to support her family, and he promised to help her with the rest. She began selling items she no longer needed, praying all the while for strength and courage to make the journey. After five years apart, Louisa was anxious to see Addison again. Five years was an unusually long time for a mission in the Church. Most elders left for no more than a year or two at a time. She wondered if he would recognize his family. Ellen, Frances, Lois, and Ann had grown so much in his absence. Only Ellen, the oldest, had strong memories of her father. Ann, the youngest, could not remember him at all.

Surely the girls would not know him from any other man on the street. And would Louisa herself recognize him?[23]

Louisa succeeded in selling her belongings at a fair price. Mindful of her poverty and aware of the great sacrifices she and Addison had made, Brigham had her wagon outfitted and supplied with one thousand pounds of flour and another yoke of oxen. He also hired a man to drive her team and gave her fifty dollars' worth of goods from the store, including new clothes for her and her daughters.[24]

Brigham was ready to lead the company west in the first week of June. Most of his wives and children were emigrating with him. At the same time, Heber Kimball was leaving Winter Quarters with a company of around seven hundred people, including his family. Willard Richards would follow a month later with a company of almost six hundred.[25]

Though well supplied for her journey, Louisa still dreaded the long road ahead. She put on a cheerful face, however, gave her cabin to a neighbor, and set out for the West. Her company traveled three wagons abreast in a line stretching almost as far as the eye could see. At first, Louisa found little joy in traveling. But soon she took pleasure in seeing the green prairie grass, the colorful wildflowers, and the dappled patches of ground along the riverbanks.

"The gloom on my mind wore gradually away," she recorded, "and there was not a more mirthful woman in the whole company."[26]

In early June, crickets were still devouring crops in the Salt Lake Valley. Many Saints fasted and prayed for deliverance, but others were beginning to wonder if they should quit their work, load up their wagons, and abandon the settlement. "I have stopped building my mill," one man informed John Smith. "There will be no grain to grind."

"We are not going to be broken up," John said firmly. "Go ahead with your mill, and if you do so, you shall be blessed, and it shall be an endless source of joy and profit to you."[27]

Yet Saints continued to talk about moving to California. San Francisco Bay took two months to reach by wagon, and for some, setting out on another long journey sounded better than slowly starving to death.[28]

John's counselor Charles Rich sympathized with those who wanted to leave. If the crickets continued to feed on their crops, the Saints would have little left to eat. As it was, some Saints were barely surviving on roots, thistle stalks, and soups made from boiling old oxhides.

One Sabbath day, Charles called the Saints together for a meeting. The skies overhead were clear and blue, yet a solemn mood hung over the crowd. In nearby fields, the crickets clung tenaciously to stalks of wheat and corn, eating away the crops. Charles climbed atop an open wagon and raised his voice. "We do not want you to part with your wagons and teams," he said, "for we might need them."

As Charles spoke, the crowd heard a shrill noise coming from the sky. Looking up, they saw a small flock of seagulls from the Great Salt Lake flying over the valley. A few minutes later, a larger flock swooped down and lighted on the Saints' fields and gardens. At first, the birds appeared to be consuming the rest of the crops, finishing the devastation begun by the frost and crickets. But as the Saints looked more closely, they saw that the gulls were feasting on the crickets, disgorging what they could not digest, and then returning to eat some more.[29]

"The seagulls have come in large flocks from the lake and sweep the crickets as they go," John Smith reported to Brigham on June 9. "It seems the hand of the Lord is in our favor."[30] There were more crickets than the seagulls could eat, but the birds kept the insects under control. The Saints saw the seagulls as angels sent from God, and they thanked the Lord for answering their prayers in time to save their damaged fields and replant their crops.[31]

"The crickets are still quite numerous and busy eating," John observed two weeks later, "but between the gulls, our efforts, and the growth of our crops, we shall raise much grain in spite of them." The harvest would not be as large as they had hoped, but no one in the valley would starve. And the company John had sent to California in November had returned with almost two hundred head of cattle, various fruits, and some seed grains.

"We are gaining a fund of knowledge," John was pleased to report, "and, as a large majority, feel encouraged and well satisfied."[32]

Two months into their journey, Louisa and her daughters stopped at Independence Rock, a hulking granite monolith that stood like a massive turtle shell beside the Sweetwater River. Climbing with effort to the top of the rock, they saw the names of travelers etched and painted on the stone. Along the trail, with none but themselves for company, Louisa had often thought of the Saints as being alone in the great wilderness. But the names, so many and so unfamiliar, reminded her that they were not the first people to pass this way—nor likely the last.

She felt less like an outcast then, even though her family had been driven from Nauvoo. Blessings had come in their exile. If the Saints had not fled into the wilderness, she realized, they would not have seen how much beauty there was in nature.

From where she stood, Louisa could see the surrounding country clearly. Brigham's company was camped along the base of the rock, wagons circled in the usual fashion. Beyond them, the Sweetwater River wound like a serpent across the plains, its surface a silvery blue as it disappeared behind Devil's Gate, an imposing pair of cliffs five miles to the west.

God, she remembered, had made a beautiful world for His children to enjoy. "All things which come of the earth," one of the revelations read, "are made for the benefit and the use of man, both to please the eye and to gladden the heart."

Louisa and other members of her company carved their names into Independence Rock, then followed a crevice through a narrow passage that brought them to a natural spring of fresh, cold water. They drank and drank, grateful it was not the murky river water they had relied on since leaving Winter Quarters. Satisfied, they left the spring and found their way back to camp.

In the coming weeks, Louisa and her daughters traveled through high canyons, deep mud, and willow brush. Her daughters were keeping pace, and each day they grew more independent, burdening no one. One morning, thirteen-year-old Frances woke up and made a fire before anyone else in camp. People soon came to their campsite to compliment her and borrow a flame to start their own fire.

"Slowly we move along, gaining a little every day," Louisa wrote in her journal. "I feel now as if I could go another thousand miles."[33]

CHAPTER 8

This Time of Scarcity

Louisa Pratt and her daughters arrived in the Salt Lake Valley with Brigham Young's wagon company on the afternoon of September 20, 1848. They had thought all morning about eating fresh vegetables in the promised land, and finally, after old friends greeted them and shook their hands, they sat down to feast on corn harvested from the valley.

Since Addison's company had not yet arrived from California, Mary Rogers, the wife of a man who had helped Louisa in Winter Quarters, invited the family to stay with her. Louisa did not know Mary well, but she gladly accepted the invitation. Mary was nearly ready to give birth, and staying with her while they waited for Addison gave Louisa and her daughters a chance to help her and repay the kindnesses shown to their family.

Days passed with no sign of Addison. Mary had her baby, and Louisa took care of her and the child night and day. Then, on September 27, some veterans of the Mormon Battalion rode into the city with news that Addison was a day's journey away. The girls were elated. "They tell me I have a father, but I do not know him," eight-year-old Ann told her friends. "Is it not strange to have a father and not know him?"

The next morning dawned bright and clear, and Louisa went to her wagon to dress for the reunion.[1] As sixteen-year-old Ellen scrubbed the Rogerses' floor on her hands and knees, a family friend stepped into the cabin. "Ellen," he said, "here is your father."

Ellen sprang to her feet as a rough, sunburned man entered the room. "Why, Pa," Ellen said, taking his hands into hers, "have you come?" After more than five years, she almost did not recognize him.

Frances and Lois soon burst into the room, and Addison's unkempt appearance surprised them. They called for Ann, who was playing outside. She entered the cabin, eyeing Addison warily and keeping her hands behind her back. "That is Pa," one of her sisters said. They tried to get Ann to shake his hand, but she ran out of the room.

"It is not," she cried.[2]

Louisa soon came in and saw Addison's travel-worn face. He looked almost like a stranger, and she hardly knew what to say. Sadness swept over her as she realized how much her family had changed in his absence.

Nothing short of building the kingdom of God, she thought, could justify such a long separation.[3]

Emotion overtook Addison as well. His daughters were no longer the little girls he remembered—especially Ann, who had been three years old when he left. Louisa's voice had changed as a result of losing teeth to scurvy at Winter Quarters. Addison felt like an outsider, and he longed to get to know his family again.

The next morning, Ann had still not spoken to Addison, so he brought her out to his wagon, opened a trunk, and placed several seashells and other curiosities in a pile beside her. As he set each item down, he told her where it came from and said that he had picked it out just for her. He then poured sugarplums, raisins, and cinnamon candy over the pile.

"You believe now that I am your father?" he asked.

Ann gazed at the gifts and then back at him. "Yes!" she cheered.[4]

THE FOLLOWING MONTH, OLIVER Cowdery stepped onto a platform to address the Saints at a conference near Kanesville, on the east side of the Missouri River. He did not recognize many of the people in front of him. The Church had grown rapidly since he left it a decade earlier. His brother-in-law Phineas Young was one of the few people he knew at the conference.

It was partly Phineas's determination that had led Oliver to meet with the Saints at the Missouri River settlements.[5] But Oliver had also concluded that David Whitmer's new church did not have proper authority. The priesthood was with The Church of Jesus Christ of Latter-day Saints.

Sitting near Oliver on the platform was Orson Hyde, the presiding apostle at Kanesville. Almost fourteen years earlier, Oliver had ordained Orson as one of the first apostles in the latter days. Like Oliver, Orson had left the Church in Missouri, but he had found his way back soon after and reconciled with Joseph Smith face-to-face.[6]

After collecting his thoughts, Oliver addressed the Saints. "My name is Cowdery, Oliver Cowdery," he said. "I wrote with my own pen the entire Book of Mormon, save a few pages, as it fell from the lips of the prophet as he translated it by the gift and power of God." He testified that the Book of Mormon was true and that it contained the principles of salvation. "If you will walk by its light and obey its precepts," he declared, "you will be saved in the everlasting kingdom of God."

He then spoke of the restoration of the priesthood and the prophetic call of Joseph Smith. "This holy priesthood we conferred upon many," he testified, "and is just as good and valid as if God had conferred it in person."[7]

As he spoke to the Saints, Oliver longed to have the blessings of the priesthood in his life again. He understood that he would not occupy the same position of authority he once held in the Church, but that did not matter. He wanted to be rebaptized and welcomed back as a humble member of the Church of Jesus Christ.

Two weeks after the conference, Oliver met with Church leaders in the log tabernacle at Kanesville. "For a number of years I have been separated from you," he acknowledged. "I now desire to come back." He knew baptism was the doorway to the kingdom of God, and he wanted to enter it. "I feel that I can honorably return," he said.

A few people, however, questioned Oliver's sincerity. To them, Oliver replied, "My coming back and humbly asking to become a member through the door covers the whole ground. I acknowledge this authority."

Orson Hyde put the decision to a vote. "It is moved," he said, "that Brother Oliver be received by baptism and that all old things be forgotten."

The men voted unanimously in Oliver's favor. One week later, Orson baptized him, welcoming him back to the gospel fold.[8]

MEANWHILE, IN CITIES AND towns across the globe, rumors about gold in California spread like wildfire, luring people away from homes, jobs, and families with the prospect of easy wealth. In the fall of 1848, thousands of people—many of them young men—swarmed to the California coast, hoping to strike it rich.[9]

Knowing the gold would tempt the impoverished Saints, Brigham Young addressed the matter soon after he arrived back in Salt Lake City. "If we were to go to San Francisco and dig up chunks of gold," he told the Saints, "it would ruin us." He urged them to stay on the land the Lord had given them. "To talk of going away from this valley for anything," he said, "is like vinegar to my eyes."[10]

Resolved to stay in the valley, come what may, Brigham began putting the Church and city in order. At the October 1848 conference, the Saints once more sustained him, Heber Kimball, and Willard Richards as the First Presidency of the Church.[11] A short time later, he reconvened the Council of Fifty to manage the city while the Saints petitioned the United States Congress to establish a territorial government in the area.

As part of the treaty ending the recent war with Mexico, the United States had acquired Mexico's northern territories. Soon, settlers and politicians were eagerly planning to form new territories and states from the land, with little regard for the situation of Native peoples or former Mexican citizens in the area.

Wanting the Saints to have the freedom to govern themselves, Brigham and other Church leaders hoped to organize a territory in the Great Basin. Establishing a territory came with risk, however. Unlike states, which granted citizens the right to elect their own leaders, territories relied on the president of the United States to choose some of the most important government officials. If the president appointed officials who were hostile to the Church, the Saints could face more persecution.[12]

The Council of Fifty met regularly that winter to discuss the needs of the Saints and to draft their petition to Congress. The territory they proposed covered much of the Great Basin and a portion of the southern California coast—a vast area that provided ample space for new settlements and an ocean port to aid the gathering. The Saints called the proposed territory "Deseret," after the Book of Mormon word for honeybee, a symbol of hard work, industry, and cooperation.[13]

The council completed the petition to Congress in January while the Salt Lake Valley shivered under severe winter weather.[14] In some places, the Saints endured three feet of snow and sharp, bone-chilling winds. Deeper snow in the mountains made collecting firewood difficult. Grain supplies were again running low, and cattle were succumbing to hunger and cold. Some Saints seemed to be surviving on faith alone. Others talked again about going to the warmer climate of the California goldfields—with or without the First Presidency's blessing.[15]

On February 25, 1849, Brigham prophesied that the Saints who stayed would prosper and build thriving settlements. "God has shown me that this is the spot to locate His people," he testified. "He will temper the elements for the good of His Saints. He will rebuke the frost and the sterility of the soil, and the land shall become fruitful."

Now was not the time to dig for gold, Brigham told the Saints. "It is our duty to preach the gospel, gather Israel, pay our tithing, and build temples," he said. Wealth would come later.

"The worst fear that I have about this people," he said, "is that they will get rich in this country, forget God and His people, wax fat, and kick themselves out of the Church and go to hell."[16]

"I am not troubled about your poverty," Heber Kimball agreed in a sermon to the Saints a short time later. He prophesied that goods would soon be cheaper in the valley than in the large cities of the eastern United States. "If you are faithful," he promised, "you shall have every desire of your hearts."[17]

THAT WINTER, TWENTY-EIGHT-YEAR-OLD ELIZA Partridge Lyman lived in a small log room in the fort with her infant son; her widowed mother, Lydia; her sisters Emily, Caroline, and Lydia; her brother Edward Partridge Jr.; and sometimes her husband, apostle Amasa Lyman, who divided his time among her and his other wives. Nine-year-old Francis Lyman, Amasa's oldest son from his first wife, Louisa Tanner, also lived in the room so he could attend school in the fort.[18]

Around four thousand Saints had settled in the valley, and many of them still lived in wagons and tents.[19] Eliza's room provided some shelter from the bitter winds, even when the roof leaked during rain or snow. But it offered no safeguards against sickness and hunger. That season, Eliza's son and her brother came down with whooping cough, and every day the family's food supplies got smaller.[20]

Scarcity was a problem everywhere, and the Saints had to eat sparingly if they wanted to survive the winter. The Timpanogos, their Ute neighbors in nearby Utah Valley, were hungry as well. The Saints' arrival had strained the area's natural resources, especially the fishing waters the Timpanogos relied on for food. Though the Saints and the Timpanogos had tried to maintain good interactions, a few Timpanogos soon began raiding the Saints' cattle to relieve their own hunger.[21] Eager to maintain peace, Brigham urged the Saints not to seek vengeance and to instead preach the gospel to the Indians.[22]

Eliza's stepbrother Oliver Huntington sometimes worked as a translator and scout among the Utes. As the raids persisted, Little Chief, a leader of the Timpanogos, asked Oliver and Brigham to punish the raiders before their actions turned the Saints against his people. Brigham responded by sending Oliver and an armed company to Utah Valley to stop the raids.

With help from Little Chief, the company tracked down the band of raiders, surrounded them, and ordered their surrender. The band refused to give up and instead attacked the company. A skirmish broke out, and the company killed four raiders.[23]

The raids ended with the skirmish, but hunger and scarcity remained. "We baked the last of our flour today and have no prospect of getting any more until after harvest," Eliza wrote in her journal on April 8. Around this time, the First Presidency called her husband on a mission to San Francisco to oversee the California branches and collect tithing. He would then lead a company of California Saints to the valley in the fall.[24]

Amasa left five days later, too poor to buy more flour for his family. On April 19, Eliza and some of her family moved out of the fort and set up house in tents and wagons on a city lot. She spun candlewicks and sold them for corn and meal, which she divided among the large Lyman family.[25]

Others helped her as well. Her sister Emily, who was a wife of Brigham Young, brought the family fifteen pounds of flour after Brigham heard that they were out of bread. On April 25, Jane Manning James, who had known Eliza and Emily when the sisters lived in the Nauvoo Mansion as plural wives of Joseph Smith, gave Eliza two pounds of flour—half of what Jane had herself.[26]

Eliza spun more candlewicks, planned a garden, and had fruit trees planted on her lot. Wind and snowstorms continued to plague the valley well into May, and Eliza's tent burned down one day while she was visiting her mother. But by the end of the month, she found reason for hope in the Saints' ripening fields.

"Saw a head of wheat," she wrote in her journal, "which looks encouraging in this time of scarcity."[27]

THROUGH THE HARSH WINTER of 1848–49, Louisa Pratt watched her husband struggle to adjust to life after his mission. Much had changed in the Church while he was away. The Saints had received the temple endowment, embraced the doctrine of eternal marriage and exaltation, and created new covenant relationships with God and each other. Plural marriage, practiced privately among the Saints, was also new to Addison.[28]

Sometimes Addison disagreed with Louisa about the newly revealed principles. What was familiar to her seemed peculiar to him. He was also bothered that Saints in the valley did not strictly heed the Word of Wisdom's warnings against hot drinks and tobacco. Still, Louisa was happy to have him home. He attended Sabbath meetings with the family and served as a president of his seventies quorum.[29]

The Pratts passed the winter in the fort. Louisa's sister and brother-in-law Caroline and Jonathan Crosby lived with them until they had a home of their own. Addison worked to support his family and taught Tahitian language classes to prospective missionaries.[30]

When spring arrived, the First Presidency and Quorum of the Twelve called Addison and his family to the Pacific Islands with eleven other missionaries, including six families. The Pratts were excited to go, and they prepared to leave after the fall harvest. On July 21, Addison received the endowment on the top of Ensign Peak, which Church leaders had consecrated for that purpose in the absence of a temple. The family then began to dispose of goods and property they did not need.[31]

Thousands of gold seekers from the eastern states, meanwhile, scrambled over the Rocky Mountains on their way to California. Soon Salt Lake City became a favorite spot for them to rest and resupply before continuing on to the goldfields. Most gold seekers were young farmers, laborers, or merchants. Many of them had never ventured far from their hometowns, let alone crossed an entire continent.[32]

Their arrival fulfilled Heber Kimball's prophecy much sooner than anyone expected.[33] The gold seekers had flour, sugar, groceries of every kind, shoes, clothing, fabric, and tools. Desperate for fresh vegetables, lighter wagons, and pack animals, many of the gold seekers stopped at the fort to barter. Often they sold hard-to-find goods to the Saints at bargain prices. Sometimes they simply discarded or gave away items they were tired of carrying.[34]

The gold seekers boosted the economy in Salt Lake City, but they also exhausted grazing lands between Salt Lake and California when they left, making overland travel almost impossible late in the season. And stories circulated that dangerous men preyed on the travelers, making the road unsafe for families.[35] The stories did not scare Louisa, but Brigham worried about the safety of the departing families, and soon Church leaders decided to send Addison without Louisa and the children.

The family was heartbroken. "Pa will not be so safe," Frances insisted. "The robbers would be more likely to plunder a lone man, and take his team from him, than they would if he had his family."

"Poor child," Louisa said, "you know but little about robbers."

Louisa understood that the gospel required sacrifices, and if anyone asked her, she said she was perfectly willing to let Addison go. But she thought her family was in no condition to be separated only a year after their reunion.[36]

Brigham planned to postpone the mission until the spring, when the grazing would be better and fewer gold seekers would be on the road. That fall, however, a wagon train passing through Salt Lake City hired Captain Jefferson Hunt, a veteran of the Mormon Battalion, to conduct it safely to California by way of a less-traveled route to the Southwest. When Brigham learned of the company, he asked Addison and two missionaries to go with them to assist Captain Hunt and then sail for the islands once they reached California.[37]

Louisa felt like heaven and earth had turned against her. She and Addison hardly spoke to each other. When alone, she prayed, freely venting her grief and pain to God. "Will my sufferings never come to an end?" she groaned.[38]

The day Addison left the valley, Louisa and Ellen rode with him to his campsite and stayed the night. In the morning, he blessed them and they said goodbye. Although she had been dreading the farewell for weeks, Louisa felt comforted as she rode back to the fort, her heart much lighter than it had been for some time.[39]

CHAPTER 9

As the Spirit Dictates

On October 6, 1849, the first day of the Church's fall conference, the First Presidency and Quorum of the Twelve announced the Church's most ambitious missionary effort since the death of Joseph Smith. "The time is come," Heber Kimball declared in his opening address. "We want this people to take an interest with us in bearing off the kingdom to all nations of the earth."[1]

Since coming to the valley, the Saints had spent their strength on settlement and survival. But the harvest that year had yielded a large crop, producing enough food for the winter. After the Saints began moving out of the fort and building homes in the city, Church leaders organized them into twenty-three wards, each presided over by a bishop. New settlements also began to dot the Salt Lake Valley and the valleys to the north and south, and many Saints started constructing shops, mills, and factories. The gathering place was beginning to blossom as the Saints readied it to welcome the people of God.[2]

The Twelve would lead the new missionary effort. Earlier that year, Brigham had called Charles Rich, Lorenzo Snow, Erastus Snow, and Franklin Richards to fill vacancies in the quorum. Now the First Presidency sent Charles to California to assist Amasa Lyman; Lorenzo to Italy with Joseph Toronto, an Italian Saint; Erastus to Denmark with Peter Hansen, a Danish Saint; Franklin to Great Britain; and veteran apostle John Taylor to France.[3]

At the conference, Heber also spoke about the Perpetual Emigrating Fund, a new program designed to help the Saints keep the covenant they had made in the Nauvoo temple to help the poor. "We are here and are healthy and have plenty to eat, drink, and to do," Heber said. Yet many impoverished Saints remained stranded in the Missouri River settlements, the Iowa way stations, Nauvoo, and Great Britain. Sometimes, these Saints became discouraged and left the Church.

"Shall we fulfill that covenant," he asked, "or shall we not?"[4]

Under the new program, Saints donated money to help the poor gather to Zion. Emigrants then received loans to cover travel costs, which they were to pay back once they got settled in Zion. For the program to work, however, it needed cash contributions—something few Saints could provide in a barter economy. The First Presidency called on Saints to donate their surplus to the fund, but they also discussed the possibility of sending missionaries to dig for gold in California.[5]

Brigham remained wary of that option. He believed the hunger for gold corrupted and distracted good people from the cause of Zion. Yet gold could serve a sacred purpose if it helped to finance the Church and emigration.[6] If he called missionaries to the goldfields of California, they could possibly gather much-needed funds for God's work.

But such missionaries would have to be good, righteous men who cared no more for gold than they did the dust beneath their feet.[7]

AT FIRST GLANCE, GEORGE Q. Cannon appeared no different from the gold seekers who were tramping through the Salt Lake Valley on their way to California. He was twenty-two years old, unmarried, and full of youthful ambition. But he had no desire to leave home. He loved the grand mountains and peaceful spirit of the valley. And he was not one to waste time digging for gold. Every minute mattered to him. He wanted to read books, build an adobe house on his city lot, and someday marry a young woman named Elizabeth Hoagland.[8]

George and Elizabeth had traveled west in the same company two years earlier. An orphan since his teens, George had come with his aunt and uncle Leonora and John Taylor to prepare a home for the rest of his family. His younger brothers and sisters were due to arrive in the valley any day. They were traveling with his old-est sister and brother-in-law, Mary Alice and Charles Lambert, who had taken them in when their parents died. George was eager to reunite with them.[9]

Before George's family arrived, however, Church leaders called him on a mission to dig for gold in California.[10] The assignment came as a shock, and Elizabeth was not happy. "I am only called for a year," George told her, trying to be consoling. "Would you prefer that I went for perhaps three years to France?"

"I would rather you went to save souls than to find gold, even though the time be longer," Elizabeth said.[11]

George could not disagree. As a boy in England, he had looked up to missionaries like his uncle John and Wilford Woodruff, anticipating the day when he would serve a mission as well.[12] But a call to dig for gold was hardly what he had imagined.

After the first day of the October conference, George met with newly called missionaries and others. Brigham spoke to them at length about honoring the things of God. "A man must always live with the love of the priesthood in his heart," he taught, "and not the love of the things of this world."[13]

In the days that followed, George was busy prepar-ing for his mission. On October 8, John Taylor, Erastus Snow, and Franklin Richards blessed him to prosper on his mission and be a good example to the other mis-sionaries. They promised him that angels would watch over him and that he would return home safely.[14]

Three days later, sorrow and dread weighed on George as he left home with the other gold missionaries. He had moved several times in his life, but he had never been far from a family member for more than a day or two. He did not know what to expect.

The gold missionaries planned to meet up with Addison Pratt and Jefferson Hunt and follow them to California. On their way out of the valley, the missionaries stopped at a party for the elders headed to Europe. Around a hundred Saints had gathered to see them off. Some were feasting at tables spread with all kinds of foods while others were dancing beneath a large tent made from wagon covers. As George rode up to the party, he saw Brigham Young's carriage coming toward him.

The carriage stopped, and George dismounted to shake Brigham's hand. Brigham said he would remember George and pray for him while he was away. Grateful for the prophet's kind words, George enjoyed the good humor and camaraderie of his fellow Saints for one more night. In the morning, he and the gold missionaries mounted their horses and headed south for California.[15]

IN MARCH 1850, BRIGHAM'S wife Mary Ann visited Louisa Pratt to see if she needed any help from the Church. Louisa did not know how to respond. Friends like Mary Ann often offered help or invitations to dinner, but life without Addison was as lonely as ever, and nothing seemed to change that.

"Have you a desire to go to your husband?" Mary Ann asked.[16]

Louisa told her that a friend had already volunteered to take her family to California if the Church ever decided to send them to the Pacific Islands. In confiding this to Mary Ann, Louisa worried that she sounded too eager to go. Staying in Salt Lake City would likely keep her and Addison apart another five years. But joining him on the islands came with risks as well. Ellen and Frances would soon be old enough to marry. Was now the best time to take them away from the valley?

She prayed often to learn the Lord's will. But part of her simply wanted Addison to write her a letter asking her to come. Knowing what he wanted would make her decision easier. But another part of her wondered if he even wanted her to join him at all. Had he accepted this latest mission call simply because he wanted to go away again?

"Were I an elder," Louisa told Willard Richards one day, "I would never consent to stay so long from my family." She said she would fulfill her mission as quickly as possible and then return home. Willard smiled and said nothing, but Louisa thought he agreed with her.[17]

Louisa attended conference on the morning of April 7. George A. Smith spoke for nearly two hours. When he finished, Heber Kimball took the stand. "Here are a few appointments of elders to the nations," he said. Heber called two men to the Pacific Islands, but he said nothing about Louisa and her daughters. He then said, "Thomas Tompkins is proposed to go to the islands where Brother Addison Pratt has been laboring and take Brother Pratt's family to him."[18]

An indescribable sensation shot through Louisa, and she heard little else of the meeting. After the session, she sought out Mary Ann in the crowd and urged her to ask Brigham to consider calling her sister and brother-in-law Caroline and Jonathan Crosby to the mission as well. Mary Ann agreed, and the Crosbys received the call the following day.

Shortly before they left, Louisa and her daughters visited Brigham. He told Louisa that she was called and set apart to go to the islands and assist Addison in teaching the people. He then blessed her that all her wants would be supplied and that she would have power over the adversary, do a good work, and return from her mission in peace.[19]

As the Pratts and Crosbys set out for the islands, the newly called missionaries to Europe disembarked in England and the apostles took a short tour of the British mission, which included branches in Wales and Scotland. Thirty-one-year-old Danish missionary Peter Hansen, meanwhile, was eager to continue on to Denmark, despite instructions from Erastus Snow not to go there until he and the other Scandinavian mission-aries could join him.

Peter respected his mission president, but it had been seven years since he had been in his homeland, and he greatly desired to be the first missionary to preach the gospel there. A steamship bound for Copenhagen was in a nearby harbor, and Peter decided that he could not wait a moment longer.

He arrived in the Danish capital on May 11, 1850. Walking along its streets, he felt glad to be back in his native country. Yet he was troubled that no one there enjoyed the light of the restored gospel. When Peter left Denmark seven years earlier, the nation had no laws protecting religious liberty and forbade the preaching of all doctrines but those of the state-supported church.[20]

Growing up, Peter had bristled under these restric-tions, so when he learned that his brother in the United States had embraced a new faith, he had made every effort to join him. The decision angered his father, a stern man with rigid beliefs. On the day of Peter's departure, his father smashed his suitcase and burned its contents.

Peter left anyway and did not look back. He moved to the United States and joined the Church. He then began translating the Book of Mormon into Danish and traveled in the advance company to the Salt Lake Valley. In Denmark, meanwhile, lawmakers had granted all churches the right to circulate their beliefs.[21]

Hoping his labors would benefit from this new climate of religious freedom, Peter sought out members of churches that shared some beliefs with the Saints. In speaking with a Baptist pastor, he learned that the state church still persecuted people for their religious convictions, despite the new law. Peter sympathized with them, having experienced persecution for his beliefs in the United States. He soon started sharing the restored gospel with the pastor and his congregation.

Out of a sense of duty, Peter also searched for his father, who had learned of his arrival as a missionary. One day, Peter spotted him on the street and greeted him. The old man looked at him blankly. Peter revealed who he was, and his father raised his hand to brush him away.

"I have no children," he said. "And you, you have come to disturb the public peace in this land."

Peter returned to his labors, unsurprised and unfazed by his father's anger. He sent letters to Erastus in England, informing him of his activities in the mission, and continued to work on his translation of the Book of Mormon. He also wrote and published a Danish pamphlet and translated several hymns into his native language.

Erastus was not happy with Peter's decision to disobey his instructions, but when he arrived in Copenhagen on June 14, Erastus was pleased that Peter had laid a foundation for the Lord's work to move forward.[22]

ON SEPTEMBER 24, 1850, APOSTLE Charles Rich rode into a central California mining camp in search of the gold missionaries. It was evening, the time when gold seekers returned to their tents and shanties, lighted lanterns and stoves, and changed their wet clothing. Along the riverbank where they worked, the land looked torn apart by a thousand shovels and pickaxes.[23]

Almost one year had passed since the gold missionaries left Salt Lake City. So far no one had struck it rich. Some missionaries had found enough gold to send small quantities of it back to Salt Lake City, some of which was melted down and minted into currency. But they had used most of what they found to cover the high cost of food and supplies.[24] Some local Saints who had grown wealthy during the gold rush, meanwhile, offered little assistance. Sam Brannan was quickly becoming one of the richest men in California, yet he had stopped paying tithing and disavowed any connection to the Church.

Charles found the gold missionaries in their camp. When he had last visited the mining camp, several months earlier, the missionaries and other gold seekers had been damming the river, hoping to expose the gold in its silty bottom. Most of them still spent their days working on the dam or searching for gold. George Q. Cannon ran the camp store.[25]

In the morning, Charles spoke to the men about the future of the mission. Prime mining season was almost over, and the mission's lack of success had confirmed Brigham's reservations about gold seeking. Rather than stay the winter in California, where the cost of living was high, Charles proposed that some of the missionaries finish their missions on the Hawaiian Islands. The missionaries could live cheaply there while preaching to the many English-speaking colonists.[26]

George told Charles he was ready to do whatever Church leaders thought best. If they wanted him to go to Hawaii, he would go. Besides, the goldfields were a rough place for a young Latter-day Saint. It was not uncommon to hear about theft and even murders taking place in the camps. George himself had once been assaulted by some miners who forced whiskey down his throat.[27]

Before leaving camp, Charles set the missionaries apart for their new mission. "When you arrive at the islands," he told them, "act as the Spirit dictates in regard to your duties." He said the Spirit would know better than he did what course they should take when they got to the islands.[28]

The missionaries soon returned to the river to finish the dam and pan for more gold. A few weeks later, they found enough gold for each to receive more than $700. After that, they did not find any more.[29]

They left the mining camp soon after and headed for the coast. One night they held a meeting for California Saints and others interested in the gospel. George was anxious. Missionaries were expected to speak at such gatherings, but he had never preached to nonbelievers. He knew he would have to speak eventually, but he did not want to go first.

After the meeting started, however, the elder conducting asked him to preach. George stood reluctantly. "I am in the harness," he told himself, "and it will not do for me to balk." He opened his mouth, and words came easily enough. "How professedly anxious the world is to get hold of truth," he said. "How thankful we ought to be that we are in possession of it, and of the principle whereby we might progress from one truth to another."

He spoke for five more minutes, but then his thoughts became jumbled, his mind went blank, and he stammered through the rest of his sermon. Embarrassed, he took his seat, sure his first experience as a preaching missionary could not have gone worse.

Yet he was not completely discouraged. He was on a mission, and he was not going to back down or fail in his charge.[30]

AROUND THIS TIME, FIFTEEN-YEAR-OLD Frances Pratt sighted the island of Tubuai from the deck of a ship carrying more than twenty American Saints to the South Pacific mission. Frances, who had been unhappy and withdrawn for most of the voyage, brightened instantly. She explored the island through a spyglass, hoping to catch a glimpse of her father on shore. Her older sister, Ellen, was sure he would board the ship as soon as it landed.

Louisa longed to reunite with Addison as well, but she had been seasick the entire voyage, and she could think of little else but solid ground, some decent food, and a soft bed. Her sister Caroline suffered by her side, nauseated and barely able to walk.[31]

After two days of battling contrary winds and dangerous reefs, the ship dropped anchor near the island, and two Tubuaian men paddled out to greet them. When they climbed aboard the ship, Louisa asked if Addison was on the island. No, replied one of the men. He was being held on the island of Tahiti as a prisoner of the French governor, who was suspicious of any foreign missionaries who did not belong to the Catholic Church.

Louisa had steeled herself against bad news, but her daughters had not. Ellen sat down and folded her hands in her lap, her face like stone. The other girls paced the deck.

Soon another boat arrived, and two American men climbed on deck. One of them was Benjamin Grouard. When Louisa last saw him in Nauvoo, he had been a lively young man. Now, after seven years as a missionary in the Pacific, he looked solemn and dignified. With eyes wide with joy and surprise, he greeted the newcomers warmly and invited them ashore.[32]

On the beach, Tubuaian Saints welcomed Louisa and the other passengers. Louisa asked if she could meet Nabota and Telii, Addison's friends from his first mission. A man took her by the hand. "'O vau te arataʻi ia ʻoe," he said. *I will lead you.*[33]

He set off into the island and Louisa followed, trying her best to communicate with him. The rest of the crowd trailed close behind, laughing as they went. Louisa marveled at the tall palm trees towering overhead and the lush vegetation that covered the island. Here and there she saw long, low dwellings plastered over with white lime made from coral.

Telii was overjoyed when she met the new missionaries. Though recovering from sickness, she rose from her bed and began preparing a feast. She roasted pork in a pit, fried fish, prepared bread from flour made from an island root, and set out an array of fresh fruit. By the time she finished cooking, Saints from all over the island had gathered to meet the new arrivals.

The company feasted as a full moon rose high in the sky. Afterward, the Tubuaian Saints crowded into the house and sat on grass mats while the American Saints sang hymns in English. The island Saints then sang hymns in their own language, their voices loud and clear in perfect harmony.

As she enjoyed the music, Louisa glanced outside the house and admired the stunning scenery. Tall shade trees with brilliant yellow flowers surrounded the house. Moonlight filtered through the branches in a thousand different shapes. Louisa thought of the distances her family had crossed, and the suffering they had experienced to come to such a beautiful place, and she knew God's hand was in it.[34]

TWO MONTHS AFTER LOUISA arrived in Tubuai, the gold missionaries climbed up a mountainside overlooking Honolulu on the island of Oahu and dedicated the

Hawaiian Islands for missionary work. The next evening, the mission president assigned George Q. Cannon to work on the island of Maui, southeast of Oahu, with James Keeler and Henry Bigler.[35]

Maui was a slightly larger island than Oahu. Lahaina, its principal town, lay along a flat stretch of beach and had no harbor. From the ocean, most of the town was obscured by palm trees and heavy foliage. A tall mountain range loomed in the distance behind it.[36]

The missionaries went to work, but they soon discovered that there were fewer white settlers than expected on the island. George grew discouraged. The gold missionaries had come to Hawaii expecting to teach English-speaking settlers, yet none of them seemed interested in the restored gospel. If they preached only to the white population, they realized, their mission would be short and unfruitful.

One day, they discussed their options. "Shall we confine our labors to the white people?" they asked themselves. They had never been instructed to preach to the Hawaiians, but neither had they been told not to. In California, Charles Rich had simply counseled them to rely on the Spirit to direct their mission.

George believed their call and duty was to share the gospel with all people. If he and the other missionaries made an effort to learn the language of the land, as Addison Pratt had done on Tubuai, they could magnify their calling and touch the hearts and minds of more people. Henry and James felt the same way.[37]

The Hawaiian language, the missionaries quickly discovered, was difficult for them to understand. Each word seemed to run into the next.[38] Yet many Hawaiians were eager to help them learn. Since there were not many textbooks on Maui, the missionaries ordered some from Honolulu. George's desire to speak was very strong, and he never missed an opportunity to practice the language. Sometimes he and others spent all day at home, reading and studying it.

Gradually, George began to use the language more confidently. One evening, as he and his companions sat at home talking in Hawaiian with their neighbors, George realized all at once that he understood most of what they said. Leaping to his feet, he placed his hands on the sides of his head and exclaimed that he had received the interpretation of tongues.

He could not distinguish every word they said, but he caught their general meaning. Gratitude filled him, and he knew he had been blessed by the Lord.[39]

CHAPTER 10

Truth and Righteousness

George Q. Cannon gripped his travel bag as he stepped into a stream winding through Maui's verdant 'Iao Valley. It was March 8, 1851, near the end of Hawaii's wet season. Four days earlier, he had left his home in Lahaina and started walking north along the shoreline. "I must push out among the Natives and commence preaching to them," he had told his fellow missionaries. He was anxious to improve his Hawaiian and bear testimony. The Lord had revealed to him that there were people on Maui prepared to receive the truth. George did not know who they were, but he expected to recognize them as soon as he found them.

He had now traveled nearly forty miles without success. Glowering storm clouds and torrential downpours had left him wondering if he had picked the wrong time of the year to take his journey.

As George waded farther out into the stream, he slipped and tumbled into the water. Picking himself up, he clambered out of the water and climbed a nearby hill to Wailuku, a small town with a few houses, a women's school, and a tall church made from lava rocks.[1]

Several Protestant missionaries lived in the town, and George wanted to bear testimony to them. But he was tired and embarrassed by his wet, filthy clothes. Maybe it was better to return to Lahaina, he told himself, than to try to share the gospel when the weather was so poor.

George found the road out of town and started for home. Just outside of Wailuku, while he paused to change his shirt and shave, he suddenly felt impressed to return to the town. He quickly retraced his steps, and as he passed the churchyard, two women emerged from a nearby house. "E ka haole!" they called back into the house. *Oh, the white man!*[2]

Three men appeared at the door behind them and approached the gate just as George was passing. One of the men asked where he was going. George explained that he was thinking about returning to Lahaina because of the weather. The man said it would be better to wait a few days and invited George to stay at his house.

The man's name was Jonathan Napela. He was a respected judge in the area and one of the *aliʻi,* or island nobility. He and the two other men, William Uaua and

H. K. Kaleohano, had been educated at the best school on the island. As George spoke with them, he knew at once that he had found the people God had prepared.[3]

The next day, George taught Napela about the Book of Mormon and the prophet Joseph Smith. "We do not take the Book of Mormon for the Bible," he explained, "but prove one by the other." Napela was interested in George's message, but he said he wanted to know for himself if it was true.[4]

Soon George had to return to Lahaina. He promised to come back to Wailuku, however, to teach Napela and his friends. He testified that he had told them the truth and invited them to study the restored gospel further.

"Prove all things," George said, quoting the Bible, "and hold fast to that which is good."[5]

WHILE GEORGE WAS RETURNING to Lahaina, Brigham Young was bracing himself for changes in the Salt Lake Valley. After the Saints petitioned Congress for a territorial government, Thomas Kane, who had earlier befriended the Saints and helped them raise the Mormon Battalion, advised Brigham in a letter to petition for statehood instead. Unlike territories, which relied on the president of the United States to appoint some of their top officers, states allowed voters to elect their own leaders, giving the people more control in the government.[6]

The legislature quickly drew up a statehood petition. To ensure the petition reached Congress in time, the legislature created a record for a constitutional convention that never occurred and sent it with other documents to their delegates in Washington, DC.[7] The First Presidency had hoped to send Oliver Cowdery to Washington to help lobby for statehood, but Oliver had become sick while staying with his wife's family in Missouri and had died in March 1850. Phineas Young had been at his side when he passed away.

"His last testimony will never be forgotten," Phineas had written Brigham soon after. "He said to his friend there was no salvation but in the valley and through the priesthood there."[8]

When the statehood petition arrived in Washington, Congress was enmeshed in a long and contentious debate over slavery and its expansion into the western lands acquired after the war with Mexico. The debate overshadowed the statehood petition, and ultimately Congress organized a territory in the Great Basin as part of a broader compromise to pacify the warring factions within the government.

Congress rejected the name *Deseret* and called the new territory *Utah,* after the Ute Indians. Utah was much smaller than what the Saints had proposed, and it lacked an ocean harbor, but the territory still encompassed vast tracts of land. To the Saints' satisfaction, the president appointed Church members to more than half of the top government positions, including Brigham Young as governor. The remaining appointments went to officers from outside the territory who were not members of the Church.[9] These officers included two of the three members of the newly created territorial supreme court, limiting the Saints' power to enforce their own laws.

Brigham and the Saints cautiously welcomed the officers to Utah in the summer of 1851. They were ambitious eastern men who were nevertheless reluctant to move to the faraway territory. Their first meetings with the Saints were strained and awkward. Past persecution had made the Saints suspicious of outsiders, and the officers felt ignored and disrespected when they arrived. They also knew little about the Saints and their beliefs aside from rumors they had heard about plural marriage in the Church.[10]

At the time, the Saints had not yet publicly proclaimed their belief in plural marriage. When the Lord commanded Joseph Smith to practice the principle, an angel had charged him to keep it private and teach it only to Saints with unwavering integrity. Early Church members had honored monogamy as the only legitimate form of marriage, and any alternative to it would be shocking. But the Lord had promised to exalt these Saints for their obedience and sacrifice.

By the time of his death, Joseph had married some plural wives for time and eternity. He had been sealed to others for eternity alone, which meant their marriage relationship would begin in the next life. He had also taught plural marriage to his closest associates, and they had continued to keep the practice private after his death. For Joseph and the early Saints, plural marriage was a solemn religious principle, not a way to gratify lust.[11]

When the federal officers arrived in the territory in the summer of 1851, plural marriages had become more common in the Church, making it harder for the Saints to shield the practice from visitors. In fact, at parties and other social gatherings, the officers met the wives of Brigham Young and Heber Kimball, who made no effort to conceal their relationship to their husbands.[12]

On July 24, 1851, the officers joined the Saints in commemorating the fourth anniversary of the pioneers' arrival in the valley. The celebration began with cannon fire, patriotic music, and a parade. General Daniel Wells, a prominent Church member and commander of the territorial militia, then spoke about the Saints' past trials and predicted a day when the United States would be scourged for its unwillingness to help the Church.[13] The Saints loved the speech, but it offended the officers.

Several weeks later, another officer, Judge Perry Brocchus, arrived from the eastern states. Brocchus had accepted his appointment to Utah hoping that the Saints would elect him to represent them in the U.S. Congress. When he came to the territory, though, he was disappointed to learn that a Church member named John Bernhisel had already been elected to the office. He was also alarmed and disgusted by what the other officers reported about Daniel Wells's July 24th speech.

In September, Brocchus requested permission to speak at a special conference of the Church. He claimed that he wanted to solicit funds for a monument to George Washington, the first president of the United States. Brigham was wary of the request, but he agreed to let the judge speak.[14]

Brocchus began by praising the Saints' generosity. He quoted from the Book of Mormon and spoke of his desire to serve and befriend them. But he was slow to arrive at his point. And when he finally invited the Saints to donate to the monument, he insinuated that plural wives ought to forsake their marriages before contributing to the fund.[15] "You must become virtuous and teach your daughters to become virtuous," he said.[16]

Insulted, the congregation demanded that Brocchus sit down. Yet the judge continued to speak. He condemned Daniel Wells's July 24th speech and accused the Saints of being disloyal. "The government of the United States has not injured you," he said. "Missouri is the place for redress, and Illinois also."[17]

His words struck a nerve with the Saints. What did he know about their past suffering? Angry hissing and shouting erupted from the congregation as the Saints called on Brigham to respond to the insults.

Once Brocchus finished his speech, Brigham stood and paced back and forth across the stand.[18] "Judge Brocchus is either profoundly ignorant or corruptly wicked," he roared. "We love the government and the Constitution, but we do not love the damned rascals that administer the government."[19]

FAR FROM THE TURMOIL in Utah Territory, the Church continued to grow in the South Pacific. After being detained for weeks, Addison Pratt and his companion, James Brown, finally received permission from the French governor of Tahiti to stay on the islands as long as they obeyed certain restrictions limiting how they shared the gospel and conducted the Church.

Under the new restrictions, Latter-day Saint missionaries could not preach against the nation's established religion or interfere with political or civil matters. The restrictions also limited how the missionaries could support themselves, correct wayward Church members, acquire land for the Church, and hold meetings. If they failed to comply with these regulations, the missionaries could be expelled from the country.[20]

Addison assigned James to work with a nearby branch while he returned to Tubuai to reunite with his family and lead the mission. The voyage to Tubuai lasted seven days. As the island came in sight of his boat, he took out a spyglass and saw his daughters on the beach looking eagerly back at him with a spyglass of their own. Ribbons of smoke soon appeared on the island as the Tubuaian Saints began preparing a feast for his arrival.

When the boat drew closer to the island, a canoe came out to take Addison to shore. Anxious to reunite with his family, Addison was ready to jump into the canoe, but the ship's chaplain stopped him. "Let no one leave the vessel till we have tendered thanks to the Lord," he said.

Addison knelt down with the other passengers, and the chaplain offered a prayer. As soon as he heard "Amen," Addison leapt into the canoe and was soon brought to the arms of his family and friends. Once again Addison was surprised by how much his daughters had grown. Everyone appeared well and ready to celebrate his safe arrival. And Louisa was relieved to have him back.

"I was brought down to the verge of seasickness on the passage from California," she told him matter-of-factly, "but am now in good health and spirits."

Addison moved into his family's home, which had a fence and a small garden. Benjamin Grouard and the other elders were building a ship, the *Ravaai,* in a nearby town so they could visit the far-flung islands of the mission. Addison soon started making sails for the ship.[21]

Louisa, meanwhile, taught school with her sister Caroline in the Saints' meetinghouse, a breezy room with six large windows on each wall. Classes started early in the morning, and Louisa drilled fidgeting boys and girls in the English language, teaching them their numbers, the days of the week, and the months of the year. The Tubuaian Saints, in turn, spent their evenings tutoring Louisa and the other missionaries in the Tahitian language.[22]

The faith of the Tubuaian Saints impressed Louisa. They took pleasure in prayer and reading their Bibles. They often rose before dawn, calling their families together for morning devotions. A bell would clang every Sabbath morning at seven o'clock, and around one hundred Saints would assemble at the meetinghouse with Bibles tucked beneath their arms. For the sacrament, they sometimes used fruit and coconut water.[23]

Many Tubuaian Saints were anxious to gather with the Saints in the United States, but no one could afford the costly voyage. When one missionary family, the Tompkinses, decided to return home after eight months on the island, Addison asked them to raise funds to gather the island Saints to southern California.[24]

When the Saints completed the *Ravaai,* the missionaries spread throughout the islands. Ellen joined Addison on his voyage while Louisa stayed behind to continue the school. Addison and Ellen returned six weeks later, and Louisa often joined her husband in ministering on the island, giving her opportunities to practice the language and reflect on the Lord's work.

Sometimes she wondered if she was making a difference. "I hope much good will arise from my coming here, though it may not be realized at present," Louisa wrote. "I have endeavored to sow good seed; the fruit may be gathered up after many days."[25]

BACK IN THE EASTERN United States, news of Brigham Young's thundering rebuke of Judge Brocchus caused an uproar. Newspapers accused the Church of being in open rebellion against the nation. One editor recommended sending the military to occupy Utah and maintain peace.[26]

The source of the news was Brocchus himself. Although Brigham had tried to make peace with him after the conference, Brocchus refused to apologize to the Saints and penned a scathing account of Brigham's reaction to his speech. "The ferment created by his remarks was truly fearful," Brocchus wrote. "It seemed as if the people (I mean a large portion of them) were ready to spring upon me like hyenas and destroy me."[27]

The *Deseret News,* the Church's new newspaper, dismissed the charges as baseless. Realizing the harm Brocchus's account could do to the Church, however, the First Presidency asked Thomas Kane for help, hoping his talents as a lobbyist and writer could prevent a scandal.[28] Brocchus and two other officers, meanwhile, left Utah and immediately began sharing their stories, turning public opinion against the Saints.[29]

Thomas Kane agreed to help, and he worked closely with John Bernhisel, Utah's representative in Congress, to share the Saints' side of the story with the president of the United States and other government officials. Brigham also sent Jedediah Grant, the outspoken mayor of Salt Lake City and a trusted Latter-day Saint, to help Thomas in Washington, DC.[30]

Jedediah arrived ready to defend the Church. With the public decidedly against the Saints, many people were calling on the president to remove Brigham from the governor's office. Brocchus and the other officers, moreover, had written a detailed report of their tenure in Utah to the president. The report claimed that Brigham and the

Church dominated the region, controlled the minds and property of Church members, and practiced polygamy.[31]

After the report was published, Jedediah took a copy to Thomas and they reviewed it together. Thomas read the claims about polygamy and dismissed them outright. They were nothing but absurd rumors, he believed.

Jedediah grew uncomfortable. The rumors were not all false, he told Thomas. In fact, the Saints had been practicing plural marriage for as long as Thomas had known them.[32]

Thomas was stunned. For five years, he had loved and defended the Saints, often putting his reputation on the line for them. Why had they never told him that they practiced plural marriage? He felt betrayed and humiliated.[33]

Thomas agonized for days over the knowledge, unsure if he could continue to help the Saints. He assumed that polygamy disadvantaged women and threatened family unity. He worried that defending the Saints might forever associate his name with the practice.[34]

Yet he also admired the Saints and valued their friendship. He wanted to aid oppressed and misunderstood people in their times of trouble, and he could not abandon the Saints now.[35]

On December 29, Thomas wrote to John Bernhisel with a plan for counteracting the officers' report. "As I still recognize the relations of personal respect and friendship toward you," he stated, "I will be ready to assist you if you desire me to."

But he urged the Saints to do two things: stop concealing plural marriage and explain the practice to the public.[36]

AFTER A YEAR ON Tubuai, Louisa Pratt and Caroline Crosby felt comfortable enough with the Tahitian language to hold regular prayer meetings with the women of the Church. At these meetings, the women sang hymns together and discussed the gospel. Louisa and Caroline grew fond of the women of the Church, especially Queen Pitomai, the wife of King Tamatoa of Tubuai.

Since Ellen Pratt had quickly mastered the language, her mother and aunt often depended on her to translate for them at the prayer meetings. At the October 30 meeting, however, Caroline sang the opening hymn in Tahitian with two Tubuaian women, and Louisa gave a sermon in the language.

Louisa's subject was the Book of Mormon. Before the meeting, she had written out her talk and Benjamin Grouard had translated it into Tahitian. As Louisa read the talk, the women in the room appeared to understand her, and afterward they asked her to tell them more about the ancient Nephites.

As her confidence with Tahitian increased, Louisa grew more eager to share the gospel. One day, shortly after her forty-ninth birthday, she taught a group of women about baptisms for the dead, surprising herself at how well she did. "Little do we know what we can do till we make a thorough trial," she reflected. "Past the meridian of life, I learned a new language."[37]

Several weeks later, on November 29, the *Ravaai* stopped at Tubuai on its way to visit other islands. One of the missionaries on board was James Brown, who was again a prisoner of Tahiti's French government. He had been arrested on the Anaa atoll after French priests overheard him encouraging the Saints there to gather to the United States. Deeming his words political, French officials arrested him for sedition and banished him from the country.

James thought he had to stay on the *Ravaai,* subsisting on bread and water, until the crew dropped him off on an island outside French jurisdiction. But Queen Pitomai boarded the ship and invited him on shore. "This is my island," she said. "I will be responsible for all the trouble that may arise."

James remained on Tubuai for ten days, then left to serve on an island just outside of French jurisdiction. His banishment was evidence that the French government was growing stricter, making it almost impossible for foreign missionaries from many faiths to do their work. Discouragement and frustration, coupled with homesickness, soon beset the Saints from the United States, and they decided it was time to return home.[38]

Louisa knew many of the faithful Tubuaian Saints wanted to go with them to the United States. Telii, the Pratts' closest friend, planned to make the journey, but family responsibilities on the island prevented her from going. Louisa also wanted to bring some of her students to Salt Lake City, but their parents would not let them go. Others who wished to go lacked money to pay their way.

"We shall intercede to have you removed to the Church when we get home," Louisa told the women at their March 11 prayer meeting. "In the meantime, you must pray for yourselves and for us."[39]

Three weeks later, the Tubuaian women gathered for their final prayer meeting with Louisa and Caroline. Knowing this was their last meeting together affected Caroline deeply. She could see that some of the women were sad to see them go. Yet the Spirit filled the meeting, and the women spoke and prayed together until late in the evening. Louisa said goodbye to her students and left Telii in charge of them. Caroline gave a quilt she had made to Queen Pitomai, who gave her a beautiful dress in return.[40]

On April 6, 1852, the missionaries on Tubuai boarded the *Ravaai*. The island Saints came to the beach to bid them farewell, bringing food for the voyage. "Be comforted," Louisa told them. "I will pray that at some future time you might come to the Church of Christ in America, even to Zion in the valley of the Rocky Mountains." Everyone wept, and they shook hands for the last time.

The *Ravaai* set sail at about four o'clock in the afternoon. The Tubuaian Saints waded into the ocean alongside the boat for as long as possible, blessing the missionaries. As the ship moved quietly across the still

waters, and the island receded from view, the missionaries could hear the faint farewell of the Saints on shore.

"'Ia ora na 'outou." *Peace be with you.*[41]

A FEW MONTHS LATER, Brigham met with his closest advisers in Salt Lake City. Thanks to Thomas Kane,
John Bernhisel, and Jedediah Grant, the controversy
with the territorial officers was over for now. Brigham
remained the governor, and new federal officers were
sent to replace Brocchus and others who had left Utah.
Yet Church leaders had still made no official statement
about plural marriage, as Thomas had urged them to do.

Brigham contemplated the best way to announce
the practice. With its headquarters in Utah securely
established, the Church had never been stronger. Also,
plural marriage now had a central role in the lives of
many Saints, greatly affecting how they understood
their covenant relationship to God and their families.
Keeping the practice private for much longer seemed
both impossible and unnecessary. The time was right
to make plural marriage public, and they decided to
explain the practice more fully to the Saints and the
wider world at an upcoming two-day conference on
missionary work.[42]

The conference began on August 28, 1852. On that
day, the First Presidency called 107 men to missions
in India, Siam, China, South Africa, Australia, Jamaica,
Barbados, and other places across the globe. "The

missions we will call for during this conference are, generally, not to be very long ones," George A. Smith quipped. "Probably from three to seven years will be as long as any man will be absent from his family."[43]

As missionaries, they were expected to carry the gospel of Jesus Christ to the peoples of the world. "Let truth and righteousness be your motto," Heber Kimball counseled, "and don't go into the world for anything else but to preach the gospel, build up the kingdom of God, and gather the sheep into the fold."[44]

The next day, Orson Pratt stood to deliver the sermon on plural marriage to the Saints. His words would be published in the *Deseret News,* and other newspapers across the world would quickly reprint its report. Orson designed the sermon to teach missionaries the doctrinal foundations of plural marriage so they could teach and defend the practice while serving in the mission field.[45]

"The Latter-day Saints have embraced the doctrine of plurality of wives as part of their religious faith," Orson declared from the stand. "We shall endeavor to set forth before this enlightened assembly some of the causes and whys and wherefores."[46]

He spoke for the next two hours, drawing on his own understanding of the practice. The scriptures offered few doctrinal statements on plural marriage. The Bible told of righteous men and women, such as Abraham and Sarah, who followed the principle but revealed little about why they did so. The Book of Mormon, however, explained that God sometimes commanded people to practice plural marriage to raise up children unto Him.[47]

Orson taught the congregation that plural marriage was not about sexual indulgence, as many people outside the Church assumed, but rather about helping to carry out God's eternal work on earth. At times, Orson suggested, the Lord asked His people to practice plural marriage to multiply and replenish the earth, share the promises and blessings of the Abrahamic covenant, and bring more of Heavenly Father's spirit children into the world. In these families, such children could learn the gospel from righteous parents and grow up to help establish the kingdom of God.[48]

Orson also noted that the Lord governed the practice with strict laws. Only the prophet held the keys to the marriage covenant, and no one could perform a plural marriage without his consent. Those who practiced plural marriage, moreover, were expected to keep their covenants and live righteous lives.[49]

"We can only just touch here and there upon this great subject," Orson stated as he concluded his remarks. Faithful Saints were heirs to all that God possessed, he declared. By making and keeping eternal marriage covenants, they could nurture families as numerous as the sands upon the seashore.

"I feel to say hallelujah to His great and holy name," Orson said, "for He reigns in the heavens, and He will exalt His people to sit with Him upon thrones of power, to reign forever and ever."[50]

LATER THAT DAY, BRIGHAM spoke to the Saints about revelation. He noted that some of the Lord's revelations were difficult to accept when they were first revealed. He recounted his own struggle, twenty years earlier, to accept Joseph Smith's vision of the afterlife and the three kingdoms of glory.[51]

"When that first came to me, it was so directly contrary and opposed to my education and traditions," he admitted. "I didn't reject it, but I could not understand it." His faith in the revelation grew as he sought clarity from the Lord. "I would think and pray, read and think, pray and reflect," he told the Saints, "until I knew and fully understood it for myself, by the visions of the Holy Spirit."[52]

Brigham then bore witness of the Lord's revelation to Joseph Smith on eternal marriage, testifying that God still revealed His words to the Church. "If it was necessary to write them, we would write all the time," he said. "We would rather the people, however, would live so as to have revelations for themselves, and then do the work we are called to do. That is enough for us."[53]

Afterward, Brigham's clerk, Thomas Bullock, read the Lord's revelation on plural marriage to an overflowing congregation. Most of the Saints, including those who practiced plural marriage, had never read the revelation before. Some rejoiced knowing that they could finally proclaim the principle freely to the world.[54]

Immediately following the conference, the newly called missionaries met to receive instruction before they set out to preach on every inhabited continent. Excitement filled the room as the men thought about the work of the Lord rolling forth with new momentum. With the summer almost over, they had little time to waste.

"I want you to go as quick as possible," Brigham told the missionaries, "and get over the plains before snow falls."[55]

PART 2

—◆—

By Sea and by Land

SEPTEMBER 1852–MAY 1869

The time is far spent—there is little remaining,
To publish glad tidings, by sea and by land,
Then hasten, ye heralds! go forward proclaiming,
Repent for the Kingdom of Heaven's at hand.

Eliza R. Snow, "The Time Is Far Spent"

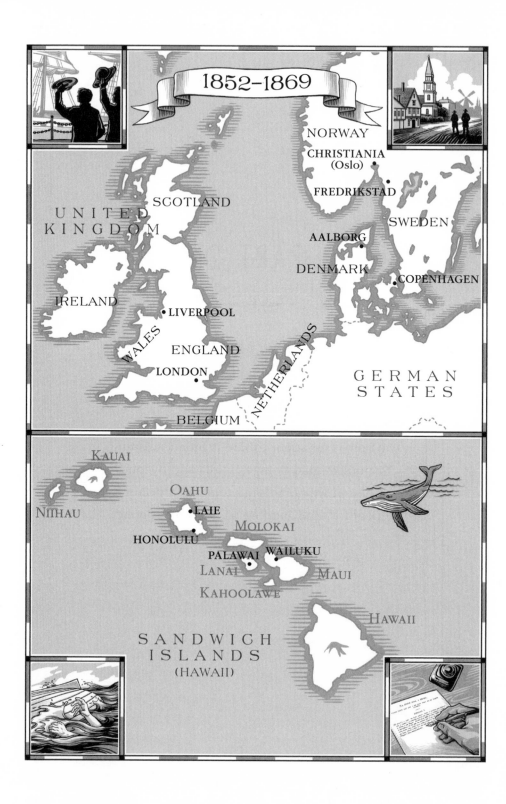

1852–1869

NORWAY

CHRISTIANIA
(Oslo)

FREDRIKSTAD

SWEDEN

UNITED
KINGDOM

SCOTLAND

AALBORG

DENMARK

COPENHAGEN

IRELAND

LIVERPOOL

WALES

ENGLAND

NETHERLANDS

GERMAN
STATES

LONDON

BELGIUM

KAUAI

OAHU

LAIE

MOLOKAI

NIIHAU

HONOLULU

PALAWAI

WAILUKU

LANAI

MAUI

KAHOOLAWE

HAWAII

SANDWICH
ISLANDS
(HAWAII)

CHAPTER 11

A Glorious Privilege

Most mornings, Ann Eliza Secrist heard her two-year-old son, Moroni, calling for his father. She was days away from giving birth, and until recently her husband, Jacob, could simply attend to the boy himself. But on September 15, 1852, she and her three small children had stood in the doorway of their unfinished home in Salt Lake City and watched as Jacob drove his team up a hill east of the city. At the top of the hill he had waved his hat back at them, gazed once more at the city, and then disappeared behind the rise.[1]

Jacob was among the scores of missionaries called into service at the August 1852 conference. With instructions to leave as soon as possible, he joined a company of eighty elders bound mainly for Great Britain and other European nations. He was one of four missionaries sent to Germany, where he was assigned to labor for three years.[2]

So far, Ann Eliza was coping with her husband's absence as well as she could. She and Jacob had grown up together in a small town in the eastern United States. During their courtship, Jacob had worked in another state, and while he was away they exchanged long, loving letters. They married in 1842, joined the Church soon after, and then followed the Saints west. Both of them had strong testimonies of the restored gospel, and Ann Eliza did not want to murmur about Jacob's mission call. But time seemed to pass slowly while he was away, and she felt weighed down with grief.[3]

Thirteen days after her husband's departure, Ann Eliza delivered a black-haired baby boy. She wrote Jacob the next day. "We had the babe weighed, and it weighed ten pounds and a half," she reported. "He is not yet named. If you have got a name for it, write its name in your letter."[4]

Ann Eliza could only guess how long it would take for Jacob to receive the news. Mail came sporadically to the valley most months of the year, and it stopped altogether when winter snows on the plains made mail routes virtually impassable. She had little reason to expect a reply from her husband before spring.

Not long after the baby's birth, however, Ann Eliza received a letter from Jacob, sent while he was still on the trail east. She could tell from its contents that he had not yet received her letter. He told her that he had seen their family in a dream. The three children had been playing together on the floor while Ann Eliza lay in bed with a newborn baby boy.

If she gave birth to a son, Jacob wrote, he wanted her to name him Nephi.

Ann Eliza had her answer. She named the baby Heber Nephi Secrist.[5]

IN THE SUMMER OF 1852, twenty-year-old Johan Dorius arrived in the Vendsyssel district of northern Denmark.[6] A shoemaker's apprentice from Copenhagen, Johan had set aside his tools to serve a mission in his homeland. He had joined the Church with his father, Nicolai, and younger sister Augusta shortly after the first Latter-day Saint missionaries arrived in Denmark. His older brother Carl had joined the Church a little over a year later.[7]

The Church had grown rapidly in Denmark since Peter Hansen and Erastus Snow opened the mission. Within two years of their arrival, they had published the Book of Mormon in Danish—the first non-English edition of the book—and started a monthly newspaper called the *Skandinaviens Stjerne*. Now Denmark was home to more than five hundred members organized into twelve branches.[8]

Johan's mother, Ane Sophie, despised the new and unpopular church, however, and she used her husband's membership in it as grounds for divorce. Around the time that Ane Sophie and Nicolai separated, Johan had been called with other new converts to serve local missions and Augusta left Denmark with the first group of Scandinavian Saints to gather to Zion.[9]

In Vendsyssel, Johan traveled south to meet with Saints in a rural village called Bastholm.[10] They met in the home of a local Church member. Johan felt joyful and inspired as he spoke to the congregation. Having already preached in the area, he knew most everyone in the room.

Around noon, just before the meeting ended, a mob of farmhands with tools and clubs entered the house and lurked around the doorway. Earlier that year, Danish Saints had petitioned the nation's legislature for protection against mobs, but nothing was done. New converts in nearby Sweden had faced similar opposition, prompting some believers to be baptized in a tanner's vat rather than risk being seen in a river.[11]

After the meeting ended, Johan approached the door to leave. The mob drew closer together, and Johan felt something prick his leg. He ignored the pain and stepped outside, but almost instantly the farmhands grabbed him from behind and clubbed him across the back. Searing pain shot through his body as the men jabbed him with sticks and sharp tools until his flesh was raw and bleeding.

Somehow Johan escaped and fled to the nearby home of a Church member named Peter Jensen. There his friends removed his torn clothes, cleaned his wounds, and put him to bed. A man anointed and blessed him, and an elderly woman stood watch in his room. After an hour and a half, however, drunken men pounded on the door. The old woman dropped to her knees and prayed for help. "They will have to hit me before they can hit you," she told Johan.

A moment later, the drunken men burst into the room. The woman tried to stop them, but they shoved her against the wall. They surrounded the bed and started thrashing Johan's bruised and lacerated body. Desperate to keep conscious and composed, Johan thought about God. But then the mob seized his arms and dragged him out of bed and into the night.[12]

SOREN THURA WAS PASSING near the Jensen home when he saw the mob carrying Johan to a nearby river. Some of the men were yelling and swearing wildly. Others were bellowing songs. Soren strode up to them and elbowed his way between their shoulders. Their breath reeked of brandy. Soren glanced at Johan. The young man looked small and frail in his nightshirt.

The men recognized Soren immediately. He was a veteran of the Danish cavalry and had a reputation in Bastholm for being a powerful athlete. Assuming he would want to join them, the men told him that they had caught a "Mormon preacher" and were going to throw him into the river. "We will show this Mormon priest how to baptize," they said.

"Let him go," Soren said. "I will take care of this boy, and I dare any of you cowards to prevent me." Soren was easily taller and stronger than anyone in the mob, so they dropped the missionary, hit him a few more times, and scurried away.[13]

Soren took Johan back to the Jensen home and returned the following day to check on him. Johan believed that God had sent Soren to rescue him. "This is no more than what befell God's people in earlier times," Johan testified, "and such chastisements are intended to humble us before the Lord."

Johan's message moved Soren, and he returned day after day to talk with the young man about his mission and the restored gospel.[14]

WHILE JOHAN RECOVERED FROM his beating, his fourteen-year-old sister, Augusta, was crossing the Rocky Mountains in a wagon train of around one hundred emigrating Saints. The road they traveled was sandy and well-worn after five years of heavy migration to the Salt Lake Valley. Yet even with a clear path, they were anxious about the trail ahead. Fall weather had arrived on the plains, throwing icy winds across the flatlands as temperatures dropped to an almost unbearable cold.

To make matters worse, the oxen were getting tired, and the Saints had used up the last of their flour, forcing them to send a rider ahead for more provisions. With no way of knowing how long it would take for relief to arrive, the Saints plodded on with empty stomachs.

They were more than 150 miles from Salt Lake City, and the steepest part of their journey still lay ahead.[15]

Augusta and her friends often walked far in front of the wagon train and then waited for it to catch up. Along the way, they thought about the homes they had left behind. The twenty-eight Danes in the company had sailed to the United States with Erastus Snow, who had already gone ahead to Salt Lake City while Augusta and the rest of the company followed in another wagon train. Most of the Scandinavian emigrants, Augusta included, knew hardly a word of English. But every morning and night they joined the English-speaking Saints to pray and sing hymns.[16]

So far, the journey to Salt Lake City was proving much harder and longer than Augusta had expected. As she listened to Americans speaking their incomprehensible language, she realized how little she knew about her new home. She also felt homesick. In addition to her brothers Carl and Johan, she had three younger sisters named Caroline, Rebekke, and Nicolena. She wanted everyone in her family to join her in Zion someday. But she did not know if that would ever happen, especially after her parents' divorce.[17]

On the trail west, Augusta survived on meager rations as the wagon train climbed ridges, descended steep ravines, and crossed narrow mountain creeks. At the mouth of Echo Canyon, about forty miles from Salt Lake City, women in the company spotted the man who had been sent ahead for provisions. Soon a wagon came loaded with bread, flour, and crackers, which the company captains distributed to the relieved Saints.[18]

The wagon train rolled into the Salt Lake Valley a few days later. Erastus Snow greeted the Danish Saints as they came to the city and invited them to his home for a dinner of raisin bread and rice. After months of eating little more than bland bread and buffalo meat, Augusta thought she had never tasted anything more wonderful.[19]

ON NOVEMBER 8, 1852, GEORGE Q. Cannon opened his small brown journal and wrote, "Busily engaged in writing." All day he had been hunched over a table in the home of Jonathan and Kitty Napela, translating the Book of Mormon into Hawaiian. Now, as he reflected on his day's work, he asked the Lord to help him finish the project.

"I consider it a glorious privilege," George mused in his journal. "I feel to rejoice while engaged in it, and my heart burns and swells while contemplating the glorious principles contained therein."[20]

When George met Jonathan Napela in March 1851, he could not have known how important Napela would become to the Lord's work in Hawaii. Yet it took until January 1852—almost a year after their first meeting—for Napela to accept baptism.[21] Napela knew the restored gospel was true, but opposition from members of the community and the local Protestant church kept him from joining the Church right away. George, meanwhile, had succeeded in baptizing many people and organizing four branches on Maui.[22]

With Napela's help and encouragement, George had begun translating the Book of Mormon soon after Napela's baptism. Hour after hour, George studied passages from the book and tried his best to write out a Hawaiian translation on a sheet of paper. He then read what he had written to Napela, who helped him refine the translation. A well-educated lawyer, Napela was excellently suited to guide George through the complexities of his native tongue. He had also studied the principles of the gospel carefully and quickly grasped truth.

This process had gone slowly at first, but their desire to share the message of the Book of Mormon with Hawaiians spurred them forward. Soon they felt the Spirit rest over them, and they found themselves working quickly through the book, even when they came upon passages expressing complex doctrine and ideas. George's fluency in Hawaiian also improved daily as Napela introduced him to new words and expressions.[23]

On November 11, fellow missionaries laboring on another island brought George three letters and seven issues of the *Deseret News* from Utah. Hungry for information from home, George read the letters and papers as soon as he had the chance. In one letter, he learned that apostle Orson Pratt had read the revelation on plural marriage to the Saints and preached on it publicly. The news did not surprise him.

"This is what I have been expecting," he noted in his journal. "I believe it to be the proper time."[24]

Another letter reported that Church leaders had learned about the translation of the Book of Mormon and approved of the project. The third letter informed him that apostle John Taylor, his uncle, had recently returned from his mission to France and wanted George to come home as well. Elizabeth Hoagland, the young woman George had been courting before his mission, was also anticipating his return. Willard Richards of the First Presidency, however, wanted George to consider finishing the translation before coming home.

George knew that he had served a faithful mission. He had grown from a homesick, tongue-tied young man to a powerful preacher and missionary. If he chose to go home now, no one could say that he had not magnified the calling the Lord had given him.

Still, he believed that the ancestors of the Hawaiian people had prayed for the chance for their descendants to hear and enjoy the blessings of the gospel. And he longed to rejoice with his Hawaiian sisters and brothers in the celestial kingdom. How could he leave Hawaii before finishing his translation?[25] He would stay to complete his work.

A few days later, after spending the morning with Saints on Maui, George reflected on the goodness of God, and his heart filled with joy and unspeakable happiness.

"My tongue and language are far too feeble to express the feelings I experience when pondering upon the work of the Lord," he exclaimed in his journal. "Oh, that my tongue, and my time and talents, and all I have or possess may be employed to His honor and glory, in glorifying His name, and in spreading a knowledge of His attributes wherever my lot may be cast."[26]

THAT FALL, JOHAN DORIUS and other Danish missionaries were sent to preach the gospel in Norway. Like Denmark, Norway granted some religious freedom to Christians who did not belong to the state church. But books and newspapers had been warning Norwegians about the dangers of the Latter-day Saints for more than a decade, turning public opinion against the Church.[27]

One day, Johan and his companion held a meeting in a small house near the city of Fredrikstad. After the congregation sang "The Spirit of God like a Fire Is Burning," Johan spoke of the origins of the Church and declared that God had again revealed Himself to humankind. When he finished, a young woman demanded that he prove the truth of his words with the Bible. He did so, and she was impressed by what he said.[28]

Two days later, Johan and his companion stopped for the night at an inn outside Fredrikstad. The innkeeper asked who they were, and the young men introduced themselves as Latter-day Saint missionaries.

The innkeeper grew wary. County officials had strictly forbidden her to shelter Latter-day Saints.

As the missionaries spoke to the innkeeper, a police officer stepped out of a nearby room and demanded to see Johan's passport. "It is in Fredrikstad," Johan explained.

"You are under arrest," said the officer, who then turned to Johan's companion and demanded his passport. When the missionary could not produce it, the officer arrested him too and led both men to a room to await interrogation. To their surprise, Johan and his companion found the room full of Norwegian Saints—women and men—who had also been arrested. Among them were several Danish missionaries, including one who had been in custody for two weeks.[29]

Lately, government officials in the area had begun to round up and interrogate missionaries and other Church members. Many Norwegians were deeply suspicious of the Saints and believed their faith in the Book of Mormon disqualified them from the protections granted under the nation's religious freedom laws.

News that Church members in the United States practiced plural marriage had also led some Norwegians to see the Saints as troublemakers who wanted to corrupt the traditional faith and values of the Norwegian people. By interrogating and imprisoning Latter-day Saints, officials hoped to expose them as non-Christian and stop the spread of the new religion.[30]

Johan was soon transported to Fredrikstad and placed in jail with four other missionaries, including Christian Larsen, a Church leader in Norway. The jailer and his family treated the missionaries civilly, allowing them to pray, read and write, sing, and talk about the gospel. But no one was free to leave.[31]

After several weeks, the county judge and other officials questioned some of the missionaries. The judge treated the men like criminals, hardly listened to what they said, and refused to let them speak when they tried to explain that their message was in harmony with Christianity and the Bible.

"For what purpose have you come to this country?" the officials asked Christian.

"To teach the people the true gospel of Jesus Christ," Christian said.

"Would you return to Denmark, if you were liberated from prison?"

"Not till God shall release me through His servants who sent me here."

"Will you refrain from preaching and baptizing?"

"If you or any of your priests can convince me that our doctrine and faith is not in accordance with the doctrines of Christ," said Christian, "for I desire to obtain salvation and to do the will of God."

"We consider it beneath the dignity of our priests to argue with you," said the chief interrogator. "I now forbid you to mislead any more souls by your false doctrines."[32]

While Johan and the missionaries waited for their day in court, they shared a cell with Johan Andreas Jensen. A sea captain, Jensen was a deeply religious man who had given his earthly goods to the poor and started preaching and crying repentance in the streets. In his enthusiasm to proclaim God's word, he had tried to share his religious views with King Oscar I of Sweden and Norway, but he had been rejected every time he sought an audience. Frustrated, Jensen had called the king an "exalted sinner" and had been promptly arrested and imprisoned.

Soon the missionaries shared the restored gospel with Jensen. At first, the captain was not interested in the message, but he prayed for them, and they prayed for him. One day, as the missionaries bore testimony to Jensen, everyone in the cell was suddenly filled with joy. Jensen wept intensely and his face shone. He declared that he knew the restored gospel was true.

The missionaries petitioned the court to release Jensen long enough to be baptized, but their request was rejected. Jensen, however, assured the missionaries that he would be baptized as soon as he was released from prison.[33]

"This brought us all to humble thanksgiving to God, and truly it was a glorious day for us," Johan recorded in his journal. "We sang and praised God for His goodness."[34]

CHAPTER 12

Their Faces Are Zionward

On the morning of April 6, 1853, Brigham Young stood with his counselors, Heber Kimball and Willard Richards, at the partially excavated foundation for the new temple in Salt Lake City. He had been looking forward to this day for months—if not years—and he could not have asked for a clearer blue sky. It was the Church's twenty-third anniversary and the first day of its spring general conference. Thousands of Saints had come to the temple block, as they did twice a year, to hear the words of their leaders. But today was different. Today they had also come to witness the laying of the temple's cornerstones.[1]

Brigham felt like rejoicing. He had broken ground for the temple and Heber had dedicated its site two and a half months earlier. Since then, workers had not had enough time to fully excavate the massive foundation, but they had dug deep trenches along its walls large enough to fit the enormous sandstone cornerstones. Finishing the excavation would take another two months of labor.[2]

With the Saints assembled, Brigham and his counselors laid the cornerstone in the southeast corner of the foundation.[3] Each cornerstone weighed more than five thousand pounds.[4] The temple would have six spires and would be much taller than the temples in Kirtland and Nauvoo, requiring a solid foundation to support its weight. In a meeting with architect Truman Angell, Brigham had sketched the temple on a slate and explained that its three eastern spires would represent the Melchizedek Priesthood while its three western spires would represent the Aaronic Priesthood.[5]

After the cornerstones were laid, Thomas Bullock, a Church clerk, read a sermon prepared by Brigham Young about the purpose of temples. Though many Saints had received the endowment in the Nauvoo temple or in the Council House, a building in Salt Lake City that Brigham had temporarily authorized for some temple work, most of them had experienced the ordinance only once and may not have fully grasped its beauty and significance. Other Saints, including many newly arrived Europeans, had not had a chance to receive the endowment. To help them understand the sacred ordinance and its importance, Brigham provided a description.[6]

"Your endowment," the sermon explained, "is to receive all those ordinances in the house of the Lord, which are necessary for you, after you have departed this life, to enable you to walk back to the presence of the Father, passing the angels who stand as sentinels, enabled to give them the key words, the signs, and tokens pertaining to the holy priesthood, and gain your eternal exaltation in spite of earth and hell."[7]

Even before coming to the valley, Brigham had planned to build another temple as soon as the Church found a new gathering place. And once he arrived in the valley, he saw the temple in a vision. "Five years ago last July, I saw here the temple cornerstone not ten feet from where we lay the stone," he testified to the Saints at the conference. "I never look at that ground but what the vision of it is before me."[8]

As the Saints dedicated themselves to the project and paid their tithing, Brigham promised, the temple would rise in beauty and grandeur, surpassing anything they had seen or imagined.[9]

NOT LONG AFTER THE cornerstone ceremony, Ann Eliza Secrist received four letters in one day from her husband, Jacob. Each letter recounted a different stage in his journey to the mission field. The most recent letter, dated January 28, 1853, indicated that he had finally arrived in Hamburg, a city in the German Confederation.[10]

Eight months after Jacob's departure, Ann Eliza was more at peace with his absence. The *Deseret News* often printed letters from elders throughout the world, giving the Saints reports of missionary work in such far-flung places as Australia, Sweden, Italy, and India. Sometimes these reports described fierce opposition to the missionaries. Two days before Jacob's letters arrived, in fact, Ann Eliza had read in the *Deseret News* about government efforts to expel a missionary from Hamburg.

Rather than fear for Jacob, Ann Eliza wrote him an encouraging letter. "It is of no use to try to stop this work," she testified, "for it will roll on in spite of all the devils on earth and in hell, and nothing can stay its progress."[11]

Whenever Ann Eliza wrote her husband, she mentioned their children's health. That winter they had come down with scarlet fever, but each of them recovered from the disease by the spring. Then they contracted chicken pox, which vexed them for a month. During this time, the children often talked about their father, especially when they sat down to a meal that they knew he would have enjoyed.

She also wrote about the family farm, located about twenty miles north of Salt Lake City. Jacob and Ann Eliza had hired men to keep it running while the family lived in the city, and recently one farmworker had demanded glass, nails, and lumber from Ann Eliza to finish a house on the property. She supplied materials from her house in the city, even though it was unfinished as well. The same man later demanded payment for work he had originally agreed to do for free. Without any cash or wheat on hand, Ann Eliza had sold a cow to pay him.[12]

In her next letter to Jacob, however, Ann Eliza was pleased to report that the farm was prospering with a fine crop. She also noted that she felt strongly that she and the children should return to the farm, build a small house on the property, and live there. But she did not want to make such an important decision without first seeking Jacob's advice. "I want to know your mind on the subject," she stated, "and I want you to write me as soon as possible concerning it."

She sent the request with more love and reassurance. "Although we are separated far, far from each other by large oceans, vast prairies, and snowcapped mountains, yet I continually think of you and your welfare," she wrote. "Do not let anything trouble you concerning me, for I believe that God, whose service you are in, will protect me."[13]

THAT SPRING, ON THE island of Maui, newspaper reports about Orson Pratt's August 1852 sermon on plural marriage were causing an uproar. Hawaiians had once practiced polygamy, but the government had outlawed the practice and now prosecuted those who violated the law. Protestant missionaries had quickly seized on the teachings in Orson's sermon and twisted them to ridicule the Saints and cast doubt on the Church.[14]

Convinced that truth and openness were the best way to respond to lies and misconceptions about the Church, George Q. Cannon set aside the translation of the Book of Mormon, translated the revelation on plural marriage, and preached about the practice to a crowd of a thousand people. George's sermon dispelled confusion over plural marriage and clarified that individuals were not expected to practice it unless the Lord commanded them to do so.[15]

Before his sermon, George had shown his translation of the revelation to Jonathan Napela. Napela was pleased with it. Before his baptism in 1852, Napela had felt pressure from his Protestant friends to abandon the Church. Working closely with George in the Church had strengthened his faith. Though translating the Book of Mormon was hard work, now and then he and George would stop to discuss the book. Napela could feel changes happening in his life. It was like the passage in the book of Alma: a seed had been planted, and now it was growing. The restored gospel of Jesus Christ felt right and good, and he wanted to share it with others.[16]

Napela began accompanying missionaries on their visits, and he preached the gospel with power and eloquence. One day he even wrote to Brigham Young to share the story of his conversion. "It is very plain to us that this is the church of God," Napela testified, "and my thoughts are buoyant to go to your place, when the proper time arrives."[17]

When new missionaries arrived on the islands, their clumsiness with the language was almost comical. Napela offered to give them language lessons—a proposal they readily accepted. He provided them with

Hawaiian Bibles and dictionaries, a place to study, and something to eat. Every morning and evening, the elders recited passages from the Bible in Hawaiian and Napela drilled them in the basics of his language. By the end of each day, his students were exhausted.

"I have always been a hardworking man," one missionary said, "but this is the hardest work I have ever done."[18]

After a few days of instruction from Napela, the elders could pronounce some words—even if they understood nothing they read. Within a month, elders were taking their books to quiet places in the woods to practice the language by translating Bible chapters from English into simple Hawaiian.[19]

When Napela concluded his instruction, the elders fanned out across the islands, better equipped to fulfill their missions. Soon Napela was ordained an elder, becoming one of the first Hawaiians to hold the Melchizedek Priesthood. The gospel had taken root in him, and thanks in part to his own efforts, it was starting to take root in Hawaii.[20]

WILLIAM WALKER GLIMPSED CAPE Town, South Africa, for the first time on April 18, 1853.[21] The city lay on the southwest end of a bay at the base of a high, flat-topped mountain. Another peak, almost as high as the other, rose above the west side of the city. From where William stood, on the deck of a ship about one mile from the coast, the peak looked like a massive lion stretched out on its belly.[22]

Eight months earlier, William and his companions, Jesse Haven and Leonard Smith, had been among the 108 men called into missionary service at the special August 1852 conference. William himself had been in the mountains southeast of Salt Lake City, cutting timber to build a sawmill, when his call was announced. He went to the city a few days later to hire men to help with the mill, and on his way there he learned about his new assignment.[23]

A veteran of the Mormon Battalion who was deeply committed to the cause of Zion, William had started preparing immediately for his mission. At thirty-two, he was leaving behind two wives, two small children, and a two-story adobe house in the city. He sold his share in the sawmill, purchased enough provisions to support his family for a year, and left Salt Lake City fifteen days later.[24]

After their ship dropped anchor at Cape Town, William and his companions disembarked and found themselves a world apart from Utah.[25] Cape Town was an old Dutch settlement that had since come under British rule. White British colonists and Afrikaners—the descendants of the early Dutch colonists—made up a portion of the city's thirty thousand inhabitants, while nearly half of its population were mixed race or black, including many Muslims and formerly enslaved people.[26]

On the evening of April 25, the missionaries held their first meeting in the town hall. Jesse opened his New Testament and preached from Galatians to an approving congregation. Leonard followed with a sermon about Joseph Smith, the Book of Mormon, and revelation. Some people in the audience began to make noise and heckle the missionaries. A riot broke out, and the meeting ended in chaos. When the missionaries returned to the hall the next day to hold another meeting, the doors were locked.[27]

The missionaries fasted and prayed that the Lord would open the hearts of the people to receive the truth and to show them some hospitality. Most nights the elders went to bed hungry. "Our friends seem to be very scarce," William noted in his journal. "The devil is determined to starve us out."[28]

Another factor complicating their work was race. A year earlier, the Utah legislature had debated the status of black slavery in Utah. Neither Brigham Young nor the legislators wanted slavery to become widespread in the region, but several Saints from the southern United States had already brought enslaved people into the territory. Brigham believed in the humanity of all people, and he opposed slavery as it existed in the American South, where enslaved men and women were considered property and lacked basic rights. But like most people from the northern United States, he believed black people were suited for servitude.[29]

During the debates, Brigham declared publicly for the first time that people of black African descent could no longer be ordained to the priesthood. Before this time, a few black men had been ordained, and no restriction existed then or afterward for other races or ethnicities. As he explained the restriction, Brigham echoed a widespread but mistaken idea that God had cursed people of black African descent. Yet he also stated that at some future time, black Saints would "have all the privileges and more" enjoyed by other Church members.[30]

Apostle Orson Pratt, who served in the legislature, opposed allowing slavery in the territory and warned lawmakers against inflicting slavery upon a people without the authority of God. "Shall we take then the innocent African that has committed no sin," he asked, "and damn him to slavery and bondage without receiving any authority from heaven to do so?"[31]

Likewise, Orson Spencer, a former mission president who served in the legislature, had questioned how this restriction would impact missionary work. "How can the gospel be carried to Africa?" he had asked. "We can't give them the priesthood. How are they going to have it?"[32]

Such questions about the priesthood restriction went unresolved, however, and the legislature ultimately voted to create a system of black "servitude" in the territory.[33]

If Brigham's speech directly influenced the actions of William and his fellow missionaries in South Africa, their writings made no mention of it. The speech did not prohibit black men and women from joining the Church. But while other churches sought to make converts among black populations, William, Jesse, and Leonard focused their efforts primarily on the city's white inhabitants.[34]

One day, after a month of unsuccessful preaching, William went several miles outside the city in search of new places to preach. Rain fell in sheets, and William's trousers and shoes were soon drenched. After a while he stopped at an inn and introduced himself as a Latter-day Saint missionary.

The innkeeper stared at him blankly. "I don't care who in the devil you are," the innkeeper said, "just so you pay your way."

"We travel and preach the gospel without purse or scrip," William started to explain, but the innkeeper promptly turned him away.

William plodded wearily into the rainy night, his feet aching and blistered. Soon the wind picked up, and he begged for shelter at every home he passed. By the time he reached the town of Mowbray, four miles from Cape Town, he had been rejected sixteen times.

In Mowbray he called at a house and two men appeared at the door. William asked the younger of the two men if he had a room or a bed to spare. The young man wanted to help him, but he did not have a place to put him up for the night.

Disappointed, William stepped back out into the rain. But soon the older man caught up with William and offered him a place to sleep at his home. As they walked, he introduced himself as Nicholas Paul, the business partner of the other man at the door, Charles Rawlinson. They were building contractors from England who had moved to South Africa for work.

William and Nicholas arrived at Nicholas's house a little after nine. William's clothes were soaking wet, so Nicholas's wife, Harriet, quickly made a fire. She then served a warm meal, and William sang a hymn and prayed. They then spoke for two hours before sleepiness overtook them and they retired for the night.[35]

A FEW DAYS AFTER meeting Nicholas and Harriet Paul, William arranged to preach to some convicts at a prison near the Pauls' home. Nicholas attended the sermon with Charles Rawlinson, and both men were impressed by William's message. Harriet told the missionary that he was welcome to stay with them anytime. Soon the Pauls offered to host a Church meeting in their home.

Nicholas employed forty to fifty people in Mowbray and had a good reputation. Yet when some people in town heard about the upcoming meeting, they threatened to smash in his windows and doors and break up the gathering. Nicholas said all were welcome to attend, but he threatened to shoot anybody who tried to insult William or anyone else in the house. When the day of the meeting arrived, William preached without interruption to a full house.[36]

With Nicholas's help, the Church in Cape Town began to grow. One night, not long after the first meeting in the Pauls' home, William told Nicholas not to postpone baptism if he was convinced of the truth. Nicholas said he was ready to be baptized, but it was dark and rainy outside, and he did not think William would go out in such a night.

"Yes, I would," William said. "I never stop for rain or dark."

William baptized Nicholas immediately, and in the coming days he also baptized Harriet as well as Charles and his wife, Hannah.[37] Meanwhile, Jesse Haven wrote several pamphlets about the doctrine of the Church and the principle of plural marriage, and the missionaries distributed them throughout the city.[38]

By the first days of September, the Latter-day Saint missionaries had baptized more than forty people and organized two branches southeast of Cape Town.[39] Among the new members were two black women, Sarah Hariss and Raichel Hanable, and an Afrikaner woman named Johanna Provis.[40]

With two branches organized, the missionaries called the South African Saints together on September 13 and assigned five men and three women to serve missions in the Cape Town area or distribute pamphlets in their neighborhoods.[41] But Jesse Haven felt the area needed even more missionaries.

"If we had half a dozen more elders here, there would be plenty of work for them to do," he wrote the First Presidency. "Those that have been baptized are well united—are determined to do right. They rejoice they have lived to see this day, and their faces are Zionward."[42]

AROUND THIS TIME, GEORGE Q. Cannon and Jonathan Napela finished their translation of the Book of Mormon into Hawaiian. George could hardly contain his joy. Nothing on his mission had brought him more pleasure and spiritual growth. After starting the project, he had felt more of the Spirit when preaching, more power when testifying, and more faith when administering the ordinances of the priesthood. His heart overflowed with gratitude.[43]

Several days later, at a conference of twenty missionaries at Wailuku, George and the other elders discussed the best way to publish the book. George had worked as a printer's apprentice in the *Times and Seasons* office in Nauvoo, so he had a sense of what it would take to accomplish the project. They could either hire a printer on the islands, or they could purchase a printing press and supplies and publish the book themselves.

"For my own part," George said, "I do not consider that my mission is fully filled until I see the Book of Mormon in press."[44]

The missionaries agreed and decided to print the book themselves. They appointed George and two other men to travel throughout the islands to raise money for the publication by collecting donations from the Saints and selling advance copies of the book.

Next, the men discussed the gathering of the Saints. More than three thousand Hawaiians had joined the Church in the three years since missionaries had come to the islands, but their poverty and Hawaii's strict emigration laws prohibited them from permanently leaving the kingdom. When apprised of the problem, Brigham Young counseled the Hawaiian Saints to find "a fitting island, or portion of an island" where they could gather in peace until the way opened up for them to come to Utah.[45]

Francis Hammond, one of the missionaries assigned to find the temporary gathering place, recommended the Palawai Basin on Lanai, an island just west of Maui. "I have never seen a place better calculated for the colonizing of the Saints on these islands than this," he had observed when he first saw the area. Its only fault, he believed, was a lack of rainfall during part of the year. But if the Saints built reservoirs, as they did in Salt Lake City, they would have plenty of water during the drought season.

The following day, the Hawaiian Saints voted to sustain the decisions to publish the Book of Mormon and find a gathering place in the islands.[46] Two weeks later, George, Napela, and several missionaries traveled to Lanai to explore the Palawai Basin. They set out after breakfast on October 20 and climbed up the steep, rocky slope of a mountain until the land leveled off for a short distance and they could overlook the basin. The basin was about two miles wide, beautifully formed, and secluded from the view of the sea.

"It was a splendid piece of land and seemed to be well adapted for a gathering place," George wrote in his journal. "It reminded me of Deseret."[47]

CHAPTER 13

By Every Possible Means

By the fall of 1853, Augusta Dorius had been living in Salt Lake City for about a year. The city was nowhere near as large as Copenhagen. Most of the buildings were log cabins or adobe structures with one or two stories. Aside from the large Council House, where many government and Church meetings were held, the Saints had built an office and stockyard for collecting tithing and a social hall for dances, plays, and other community events. Nearby, on the temple block, were various workshops for temple construction and a new adobe tabernacle that seated close to three thousand people.[1]

Like other young immigrant women in the valley, Augusta worked as a hired girl for a family. Living and working with them helped her learn English quickly. Still, she missed Denmark and her family.[2] Her brother

Johan had been released from prison in Norway, and now he and Carl were preaching the gospel in Denmark and Norway, sometimes as companions. Her father also preached throughout Denmark when he was not caring for Augusta's three younger sisters. Augusta's mother lived in Copenhagen, still uninterested in the Church.[3]

Late in September, Augusta rejoiced when a company with more than two hundred Danish Saints arrived in Salt Lake City. Although her family was not among them, the arrival of fellow Danes helped Augusta feel more at home in Utah. But almost as soon as the company arrived, Brigham Young called the newly arrived Danes to help settle another part of the territory.[4]

Since coming to the Rocky Mountains, the Saints had established settlements beyond the Salt Lake Valley, including Ogden to the north and Provo to the south. Other towns had grown up in between and beyond these settlements. Brigham had also sent families to build an ironworks in southern Utah to manufacture iron products and make the territory more self-sufficient.[5]

Brigham sent the Danes to strengthen settlements in Sanpete Valley, about a hundred miles southeast of Salt Lake City.[6] Settlers had first come to Sanpete in the fall of 1849 at the invitation of Walkara, a powerful Ute leader who received baptism the following spring.[7] Around this time, however, problems had arisen when three settlers in nearby Utah Valley killed a Ute named Old Bishop in an argument over a shirt.

When the Utes retaliated, Brigham had first urged the settlers not to fight back. His general policy was to teach the Saints to live in peace with their Indian neighbors. But after counseling with the leader of the Provo settlement, who concealed the murder of Old Bishop from him, Brigham had ultimately ordered the militia to wage a campaign against the Ute attackers. In early 1850, the militia struck a camp of about seventy Utes along the Provo River. After two days of fighting, the camp scattered, and the militia pursued most of the band to the south end of Utah Lake, where the militia surrounded and killed the remaining Ute men.

The swift and bloody campaign had put an end to fighting around Provo.[8] But the tension it created spread quickly to Sanpete Valley, where settlers had claimed choice land, blocking the Indians' access to fishing and hunting grounds. Out of hunger and desperation, some Indians began raiding cattle or demanding food from the settlers.[9]

Territorial leaders had also angered Walkara and his people by regulating trade in the area, including some Indians' longstanding practice of taking captives from other tribes to sell as slaves. Though Utah's laws prohibited Indians from selling their captives to Spanish and Mexican slave-traders, Walkara and other Indians could still sell them to Saints as indentured servants. Many of these captives were women and children, and the Saints often purchased them, believing they were rescuing them from torture, neglect, or death. Some

Saints employed the former captives as laborers, while others treated them as family members.

The loss of the Spanish and Mexican market was a severe blow to the Utes' livelihood, especially since they had come to depend more on the slave trade after losing their land to new settlements.[10]

Tensions had reached a breaking point in July 1853 when a man in Utah Valley killed a Ute in a fight and Walkara retaliated.[11] Militia leaders in Salt Lake City ordered militia units to respond defensively and refrain from killing Utes, but some settlers acted against orders, and both sides attacked each other brutally.[12]

Although moving to Sanpete Valley would place her in the middle of this conflict, Augusta chose to join the Danish Saints. Traveling south, they saw that wary settlers had abandoned smaller farms and towns and had built forts.[13]

In Sanpete Valley, the company settled in a place called Spring Town. The town's fifteen families had arranged their cabins in a tight circle. Since there were no spare cabins, Augusta and the other new settlers lived in their wagons. Every morning and evening a drumbeat ordered the settlement's inhabitants to roll call, where Bishop Reuben Allred appointed guards and assigned other duties. Because Augusta had learned English while working for the family in the Salt Lake Valley, the bishop hired her to be his interpreter for the Danish Saints.[14]

In time, the settlement ran low on food, and the bishop sent swift riders to the nearby town of Manti for help. When the party returned, they came with word that Walkara had moved south and was no longer a threat.[15] In other parts of the territory, it appeared the war was coming to an end.[16]

But heavy snows and freezing temperatures that winter made both the settlers and the Utes more desperate than ever as provisions grew scarce. Fearing that an attack on their town was imminent, Spring Town leaders decided that everyone needed to move to Manti for safety. In December, Augusta and the other settlers abandoned the town as a hard snowstorm swirled around them.[17]

WHILE AUGUSTA WAS GETTING settled in Manti and the conflict with Walkara's people remained unresolved, thirty-five-year-old Matilda Dudley met with several of her friends in Salt Lake City to discuss what they could do to help Indian women and children.[18]

Since the start of the conflict with Walkara, Brigham Young and other Church leaders had urged the Saints to stop hostility toward the Utes and other Native peoples. "Seek by every possible means to reach the Indians with a peaceful message," he pleaded.

At the October 1853 general conference, Brigham had observed that missionaries were traveling the globe to gather Israel while Indians—remnants of the house of Israel—already lived in their midst. He then called more than twenty missionaries to spend the winter learning the Indians' languages so that they could serve among them in the spring.

Brigham likewise counseled the Saints not to seek revenge if Indians took horses, cattle, or other property from them. "Shame on you if you feel like killing them," he said. "Instead of murdering them, preach the gospel to them."[19] Parley Pratt also urged the Saints to feed and clothe Indian women and children.[20]

Such words had inspired Matilda, a single mother with one son. When she was a baby in the eastern United States, Indians had killed her father and then kidnapped her and her mother. But an elderly Indian man had shown compassion by intervening to save their lives. She had since come to cherish the values of union, humility, and love. And she believed that it was important for her and her friends to organize a society of women to make clothes for the Indians.[21]

One of her friends, Amanda Smith, agreed to help. Amanda was a survivor of the Hawn's Mill massacre and a former member of the Female Relief Society of Nauvoo. Though Brigham Young had suspended Relief Society meetings nine months after the death of Joseph Smith, Amanda and other women in the Church had continued serving their communities and knew the good that Relief Societies could do.[22]

On February 9, 1854, Matilda convened the first official meeting of her new relief organization. Women from different parts of the city met at her house and elected officers for the group. Matilda became their president and treasurer and asked that every member pay twenty-five cents to join the society. She also proposed that together they make a rag carpet and sell it to raise money for material to make clothes for the Indian women and children.[23]

The women began to meet weekly through the rest of winter and spring, sewing rags for the carpet and enjoying each other's company. "The Spirit of the Lord was with us," Amanda Smith recorded, "and union prevailed."[24]

WHEN SPRING ARRIVED IN the Salt Lake Valley, the men called to the Indian mission headed south, accompanied by a group of twenty missionaries assigned to the Hawaiian Islands. Around the same time, Brigham Young and several Church leaders also left Salt Lake City to visit the southern settlements and meet with Walkara. The Ute leader had recently promised to end the conflict in exchange for gifts and a pledge to end the territory's opposition to the slave trade.[25]

Knowing conflict would continue until the settlers and the Utes honored the territorial laws and respected each other's rights, Brigham arranged to meet Walkara at a place called Chicken Creek, not far from the settlement of Salt Creek, where settlers had killed nine Utes the previous fall.[26]

Brigham's party arrived at Chicken Creek on May 11. About a dozen people in the Ute camp, including

Walkara's daughter, were ill. Several warriors guarded Walkara's tent. With the Utes' permission, Brigham and other Church leaders entered the tent and found Walkara wrapped in a blanket and lying on the dirt floor. Other Ute leaders from neighboring valleys sat nearby.

Walkara looked sick and ill-tempered. "I do not want to talk. I want to hear President Young talk," he said. "I have neither heart nor spirit and am afraid."

"I have brought some beef cattle for you," Brigham said. "I want one killed so you can have a feast while we are here." He helped Walkara sit up and then sat down beside him.[27]

"Brother Brigham, lay your hands upon me," Walkara said, "for my spirit has gone away from me, and I want it to come back again." Brigham gave him a blessing, and though Walkara soon appeared to improve, he still refused to speak.[28]

"Let Walkara have some sleep and rest awhile, and then he may talk perhaps," Brigham said to the other men in the tent.[29] He gave the Utes gifts of cattle, tobacco, and flour, and that night the entire camp feasted.[30]

The next morning, Brigham blessed Walkara's daughter, and the company's doctor administered medicine to her and the other sick people in camp. Brigham then promised to continue his friendship with the Utes and offered to supply them with food and clothes if they promised not to fight. Yet he did not agree to lift the prohibition on the slave trade.[31]

Walkara agreed to no longer attack the settlers. "We now understand each other," he said. "All can now go on the road in peace and not be afraid." The two men shook hands and smoked a peace pipe.[32]

As Brigham continued south with his party of Church leaders and missionaries, he spoke to settlement after settlement about the Indians.[33] "The Lord has told me it is the duty of this people to save the remnants of the house of Israel, who are our brethren," Brigham told one congregation.

He reminded them that many Saints, before coming west, had prophesied or seen visions of sharing the gospel with Indians and teaching them skills like sewing and farming. But now these same people wanted nothing to do with the Indians. "The time has come," he declared, "that you will have to carry out that which you have seen years and years ago."[34]

After visiting Cedar City, the Saints' southernmost settlement in the territory, Brigham parted ways with the men headed to the Indian and Hawaiian missions. Returning north, he used his first Sunday home to talk to the women of Salt Lake City about each ward organizing relief societies like Matilda Dudley's to help clothe Indian women and children.[35]

Wards in the Salt Lake Valley soon organized more than twenty Indian Relief Societies. The women visited individual homes and asked for donations of cloth or carpet, sewing supplies, and items they could sell for cash.[36]

AMONG THE MISSIONARIES WHO traveled south with
Brigham Young was fifteen-year-old Joseph F. Smith, the
youngest son of Hyrum Smith, the martyred patriarch.
On the night of May 20, 1854, after Brigham had started
for home, Joseph spread a blanket down in Cedar City
and stretched out to sleep on the hard ground. He had
been on the road all afternoon, traveling through the
territory on his way to the California coast. Yet he could
not sleep. He looked up at the sky, saw the countless
stars of the Milky Way, and felt homesick.

Joseph was the youngest of twenty missionaries
going to Hawaii. Although two of his father's cousins had
been called alongside him, he felt cut off from everyone
he loved and revered.[37] Young men his age were not
usually called on missions. Joseph was a special case.

His temper had been "white hot" for almost ten
years—ever since his father and uncle had been murdered. And it had only grown hotter as he got older and
came to feel that people had not shown proper respect
to his mother, Mary Fielding Smith. Joseph believed
that she had often been overlooked after her husband's
death, especially during the journey west.[38]

He remembered how their company captain had
complained that Mary and her family would slow down
his wagon train. Mary had vowed that she and her family would beat him to the valley, however, and Joseph
had wanted to help her keep her vow. Though only
nine years old at the time, he drove a wagon, tended
cattle, and did whatever his mother asked him to do.

In the end, her strong will and faith had brought the family to the valley ahead of the captain, just as she said they would.[39]

The family settled south of Salt Lake City, and Mary died of a lung infection in the fall of 1852. Joseph had fainted when he learned about her death.[40] For a time, he and his younger sister, Martha Ann, lived on a farm with a kind woman, but she died too. Their aunt Mercy Thompson then took care of Martha Ann while apostle George A. Smith, their father's cousin, took Joseph under his wing.

Joseph also relied on the support of his older siblings. Although his oldest sister, Lovina, had remained in Illinois with her husband and children, his older brother John and his older sisters Jerusha and Sarah lived nearby.

Like many young men his age, Joseph worked as a herdboy, watching over his family's cattle and sheep.[41] But even with this work to occupy him, he soon grew wild and volatile. When he received his mission call, he could have rejected it, as some men did, and followed his anger down another path. But the example of his parents meant too much to him. In a matter of weeks, he was ordained to the Melchizedek Priesthood, endowed, and set apart to preach the gospel of Jesus Christ.[42]

As he lay beneath the stars in Cedar City, he did not know much about where he was going or what to expect when he got there. He was only fifteen, after all. Sometimes he felt strong and important, but other times he sensed his own weakness and insignificance.

What did he know about the world or preaching the gospel?[43]

A CAUTIOUS PEACE SETTLED over Sanpete Valley in the summer of 1854. By then, Augusta Dorius had joined Bishop Reuben Allred and a company of fifteen families in building a fort seven miles north of Manti. Most people in the company were Danes from Spring Town, but a Canadian Saint named Henry Stevens, his wife, Mary Ann, and their four children had gone with them. Henry and Mary Ann had been members of the Church for many years and were among the more recent pioneers to Sanpete Valley.[44]

Bishop Allred settled the company along a creek near a low mountain ridge. The site appeared ideal for settlement, though fear of attacks by Indians who lived off the land had kept most people away from the area.

The Saints began building their fort immediately. Quarrying limestone from the nearby mountains, they built walls nine feet high with portholes every twenty feet for defense. At the front of the structure, which they named Fort Ephraim, they built a tower and a massive gate where guards could keep a lookout for danger. Inside, the fort was large enough to corral the settlers' horses, cattle, and sheep during the night. Around the inner walls were houses made of mud and logs for the settlers.

Augusta lived with Bishop Allred and his wife, Lucy Ann. The Allreds had seven children living with them, including Rachel, a young Indian girl they had adopted. Though the Ephraim settlers were poorly equipped, they were hopeful about the future of their new settlement. During the day, the children played in the fort while the women and men worked.[45]

More than two years had passed since Augusta left Denmark. Many families had taken her in and cared for her, but she wanted a family of her own. At sixteen, she had reached an age at which some women on the frontier married. She had even received a few marriage proposals, but she had felt too young to marry.

Then Henry Stevens proposed to her, and she gave the proposal serious consideration. Some women thrived in plural marriages, but others found the practice difficult and sometimes lonely. Often, those who chose to live the principle did so more out of faith than romantic love. From the pulpit, and in private, Church leaders often counseled those who practiced plural marriage to cultivate selflessness and the pure love of Christ within their homes.[46]

In Sanpete Valley, about a quarter of the settlers belonged to families who practiced plural marriage.[47] As Augusta reflected on the principle, she felt that it was right. Though she barely knew Henry and Mary Ann, who was frail and often sick, she believed they were good people who wanted to care and provide for her. Still, joining their family would be an act of faith.

Augusta ultimately decided to accept Henry's proposal, and they soon traveled to Salt Lake City to be sealed together in the Council House. When they returned to Fort Ephraim, Augusta took her place among the family. Like most married women, she milked cows; made candles, butter, and cheese; spun wool and wove cloth; and made clothing for the family, sometimes adorning the women's clothing with fine crochet work.

The family had no stove, so Augusta and Mary Ann did their cooking in the fireplace that also heated and lit their simple home. In the evening, they sometimes attended dances and other activities with their neighbors.[48]

ON SEPTEMBER 26, RAINFALL OBSCURED the Hawaiian Islands from Joseph F. Smith and the other missionaries bound for the port of Honolulu. In the late afternoon, the rains lifted and the sun cut through the mist, revealing a beautiful view of the nearest island. From the deck of the ship, the missionaries could see runoff from the shower cascading down a narrow canyon to the Pacific Ocean.[49]

The missionaries arrived in Honolulu the following day, and Joseph was sent to the home of Francis and Mary Jane Hammond on the island of Maui. Most of the original missionaries to Hawaii, including George Q. Cannon, had already returned to the United States. Under Francis's leadership, missionary work continued to thrive on the island, although many Saints were preparing to move to the new gathering place on Lanai, where the Saints had established a settlement in the Palawai Valley.[50]

Almost as soon as Joseph arrived at the Hammonds' home, he came down with what the missionaries called "Lahaina fever." Mary Jane, who operated a school for the Hawaiians while her husband preached, began to nurse Joseph back to health and introduced him to local Church members.[51]

On October 8, 1854, Joseph's first Sunday on Maui, she took him to a Sabbath meeting with six Hawaiian Saints. Having heard that Joseph was the nephew of the prophet Joseph Smith, the Saints were anxious to hear him preach. They seemed to have an immediate love for him, even though he could not speak a single sentence to them in their own language.

In the days that followed, Joseph's health took a turn for the worse. After teaching school, Mary Jane gave Joseph some herbal tea and soaked his feet to try to help his fever break. He sweat through the night, and in the morning he felt better.

Soon Francis gave him a tour of Lanai. It was home to only about a hundred Saints, but the missionaries expected more than a thousand to gather there in the coming months. To prepare for their arrival, some missionaries had begun plowing fields, sowing crops, and plotting a city.[52]

After his visit to Lanai, Joseph went back to Maui, where Jonathan and Kitty Napela lived. Joseph wanted to be a good missionary, so he dedicated himself to the work, studying the language and meeting often with Hawaiian Saints.

"I am happy to say that I am ready to go through thick and thin for this cause in which I am engaged," he wrote George A. Smith, "and truly hope and pray that I may prove faithful to the end."[53]

CHAPTER 14

Hard to Be Separated

By the end of March 1855, Ann Eliza Secrist had not heard from her husband, Jacob, in nine months. Some mail had been destroyed during the recent conflict with Walkara. And the winter closure of the mail routes certainly accounted for part of the silence. She wanted to write to him, but she did not know where to send her letters. The last she had heard, Jacob was preaching the gospel in Switzerland. But a recent letter from Daniel Tyler, a mission leader in that country, indicated that he did not know where Jacob was serving.[1]

More than a year earlier, Jacob had written that he would soon be returning to Utah. The third anniversary of his mission call was six months away, and Ann Eliza expected him home around that time. Other missionaries who had left the territory with him had already returned, and the children were beginning to ask why their father had not come home as well.[2]

Much had happened in the family recently. When fighting broke out between the settlers and the Utes, Ann Eliza had decided not to move back to the farm but instead to stay in Salt Lake City, where it was safer. For a time she had rented part of their house in the city to a newly arrived family of Scottish immigrants. She had also raised two fat hogs that provided much of the family's food for the winter. The children were attending school, improving as readers, and learning the gospel. Throughout Jacob's absence she had been careful with the family's resources and had tried to stay out of debt.[3]

On March 25, 1855, three Swiss Saints visited Ann Eliza and the children. One of the Saints was Serge Louis Ballif, an early convert to the Church in Switzerland. He had been a leader in the Swiss mission when Jacob arrived. Before Serge and his family emigrated to Zion, Jacob had given him a written history of his mission and gifts to give to Ann Eliza and the children.

At the end of his mission history, Jacob wrote down some reflections on his missionary service. "I have done but little as yet, and how much good I shall do while in Switzerland, time will only prove," he wrote. "I have seen some few rejoice much under my instructions and trust I shall see the time yet in this country that Saints will rejoice in my teachings, which are simple."[4]

To Louisa and Mary Elizabeth, Jacob had sent pairs of scissors, which he instructed the girls to keep shiny.

To Moroni he sent a small box full of toy soldiers and some marbles to share with his two-year-old brother, Nephi. He also promised to bring the boys swords from Europe.[5]

After reading about Jacob's experiences, Ann Eliza wrote him in care of the mission office in Liverpool, England. She kept her letter brief, unsure if it would find its way to Jacob before he returned home. As always, she shared news of the children and the farm.

"I have done all along the very best I knew how since you went away," she wrote. "Praying God to bless and preserve you continually is the sincere wish of your affectionate wife."[6]

ON MAY 5, 1855, GEORGE Q. Cannon awoke to a frosty spring morning in the Salt Lake Valley. He had been home from Hawaii since late November.[7] Twelve days after his return, he had borrowed an ill-fitting suit and married Elizabeth Hoagland in her parents' home—a moment he and Elizabeth had been anticipating since before George left on his first mission.[8]

Now, five months after their wedding, the couple had been invited to attend the dedication of the Endowment House, a new building on the temple block in which the Saints could receive sacred ordinances while the temple was under construction.

Following the dedication, Elizabeth would receive her endowment, and she and George would be sealed together. The couple would then leave for San Francisco, where George had been called on a mission to publish the translation of the Book of Mormon in Hawaiian.

George and Elizabeth arrived at the Endowment House just before eight o'clock. It was a simple, un-adorned building with solid adobe walls, four chimneys, and a sandstone foundation. Inside, the house was divided into several rooms for the endowment and sealing ordinances.

Brigham Young convened the dedicatory service on the top floor, and Heber Kimball offered a dedicatory prayer. When the prayer was finished, Brigham pronounced the structure clean and declared it to be the house of the Lord.[9] Heber, Eliza Snow, and others then administered the endowment to five men and three women, including Elizabeth. Afterward, Heber sealed George and Elizabeth together for time and eternity.

As planned, the couple said goodbye to their families later that day. George expected their parting to be hard on Elizabeth, a schoolteacher who had never left her family, but she remained composed. Abraham Hoagland, her father and a Salt Lake City bishop, blessed the couple and encouraged them to do right. "Take care of Elizabeth and treat her kindly," he told George.[10]

The couple traveled south along the same route George had taken to California in 1849. On May 19, they arrived in Cedar City at the same time as the First Presidency, who had come to inspect the town's fledgling iron industry. George was impressed with the Saints' progress there. Aside from establishing the ironworks, they had built comfortable homes, a meetinghouse, and a protective wall around the city.[11]

The following day, Brigham organized a stake and called a man named Isaac Haight to preside over it.[12]

Later, at the Haight home, George and Elizabeth visited with Brigham Young and Jedediah Grant, who had been called to the First Presidency after the death of Willard Richards in 1854. Brigham and Jedediah blessed George to write and publish with wisdom and inspiration and to speak without fear. They also blessed Elizabeth to accomplish a good work alongside George and to one day be reunited with her loved ones in the valley.

Afterward, Brigham encouraged George to develop his writing talents as much as possible. "Roar!" Jedediah added. "Let them know you are a Cannon."[13]

AROUND THE TIME THE Cannons left for California, thirteen-year-old Martha Ann Smith received a letter from her older brother Joseph F. Smith in Hawaii. "I am well and hearty," he wrote cheerfully, "and have grown considerably since you saw me last."

Whether he meant that his growth was physical or spiritual, Joseph did not say. He seemed far more interested in dispensing brotherly advice to his younger sister than in describing his new life as a missionary in the Pacific.

"I could give you much counsel, Marty, that would be beneficial to you as long as you live upon this earth," he declared grandly. He encouraged her to listen to her older siblings and not fight with her sisters. "Be sober and prayerful," he advised her, "and you will grow up in the footsteps of your mother."[14]

Martha Ann appreciated her brother's advice. She had been just eleven years old when her mother died, but her memories remained vivid. Growing up, Martha Ann had rarely seen her widowed mother smile. In fact, if Martha Ann or her siblings ever made their mother laugh, they considered it quite an accomplishment. Yet Mary had been a loving mother, and Martha Ann's world now seemed empty without her.

Martha Ann had fewer memories of her father, Hyrum Smith. She had been only three when he died, but she still recalled a time when her mother had made him a pair of trousers. After he put them on, he had walked proudly back and forth with his hands in his pockets. She remembered him being loving, kind, and affectionate with his children.[15]

Soon after the Smith family arrived in the Salt Lake Valley, they had settled along a creek not far from a canyon southeast of the city, and they worked together to establish a farm. A few years later, they and their neighbors were organized into the Sugar House Ward under the leadership of Bishop Abraham Smoot, one of Wilford Woodruff's earliest converts. The ward took its name from the Church-owned factory in the area, which Bishop Smoot operated to produce molasses from beets.[16]

Martha Ann and her siblings supported each other as new trials came their way. The mild winter of 1854–55 had created drought conditions across Utah Territory, which depended on runoff from heavy mountain snowfall to replenish its streams and rivers. The drought strained Martha Ann's family as it did everyone else. As weeks passed and little rain fell, the land in the valley grew drier, killing crops the Saints had planted earlier that year. Irrigation ditches started to dry out and crack.[17]

To make matters worse, hordes of grasshoppers infested the settlements, devouring the meager crops and ruining the prospects for a good harvest. The Saints in Sugar House and other settlements tried to plant more seeds, but the drought made cultivation difficult, and the grasshoppers kept coming.[18]

Trial after trial seemed to follow the Smiths, and it was anyone's guess how the drought and infestation would affect the Saints. As the youngest in her family, Martha Ann did not have the same kinds of responsibilities her older siblings had.[19] But every Saint was expected to work together to overcome hardship and help establish Zion. What could she do?

Joseph offered more advice in his next letter. "Have patience and long-suffering," he wrote. "Be a Mormon, out and out, and you will be blessed."[20]

ON THE PRAIRIE A thousand miles to the east, at a small emigrant settlement called Mormon Grove, Danish convert Nicolai Dorius and a wagon train of nearly four hundred Saints from Denmark, Norway, Nova Scotia, and England started for the Salt Lake Valley.[21] Company leaders expected the journey to take four months, which meant that Nicolai could expect to reunite with his daughter Augusta, now seventeen years old, as early as September.[22]

Six months earlier, Nicolai had left Copenhagen with his three youngest daughters, Caroline, Rebekke, and Nicolena. His sons Johan and Carl were still serving missions in Norway, so he was unable to say goodbye to them personally.[23]

Emigrants like Nicolai were eager to come to Zion not only because of their faith in the restored gospel of Jesus Christ but also because they wanted to escape the wickedness of the world and find a better life for themselves and their families in the promised land. Inspired by the American missionaries' enthusiastic descriptions of Utah, many of them pictured the Salt Lake Valley as a Garden of Eden and made every sacrifice to get there.[24]

It had taken about six weeks to cross the ocean. Peter Hansen, the first missionary to Denmark, took charge of the company on board the ship. He and his two counselors organized the Saints into seven districts and called elders to maintain order and cleanliness in each unit. When the ship docked at New Orleans, its captain praised their good behavior.

"In the future," he said, "if I have my choice, I will bring none but Latter-day Saints."[25]

At New Orleans, Nicolai and his daughters had boarded a steamboat and traveled up the icy Mississippi River with their company. Tragedy struck when six-year-old Nicolena took sick and died not long after leaving New Orleans. More people died in the days that followed. By the time Nicolai arrived in Mormon Grove, fourteen-year-old Caroline had died as well, leaving only him and eleven-year-old Rebekke to reunite with Augusta when they arrived in Utah.[26]

At Mormon Grove, the emigrating Saints found temporary work to earn money to purchase oxen, wagons, and supplies for the journey west.[27] They were also organized into companies. Nicolai, Rebekke, and other Saints from Denmark and Norway were placed in a company led by Jacob Secrist.[28] After being away from his wife and four children for nearly three years, Jacob was anxious to reunite with them in Utah. Since he did not speak Danish, the most common language spoken in the company, he relied on Peter Hansen to translate for him.[29]

The company left Mormon Grove on June 13, 1855. Moving west, Jacob was often impatient with the Scandinavian emigrants. Most of them had never driven oxen before, and sometimes it took four men to keep two oxen moving in a straight line.[30] More concerning was the health of the company. Emigrating Saints usually had few, if any, deaths in their companies.[31] But on the first day out, a man in the Secrist company died of cholera. Eight more deaths followed over the next two weeks.[32]

The elders in the camp fasted and gave blessings of healing and comfort to the sick, but cholera continued to claim more lives. Near the end of June, Jacob himself became too sick to keep up with the wagons. Other company leaders sent a carriage back for him, and when he rejoined the camp, the elders blessed him. His health continued to worsen, however, and he died on the afternoon of July 2. The emigrants wanted to transport his remains to his wife and children in the valley, but with no way to preserve the body, they buried him along the trail.[33]

Nicolai, Rebekke, and the rest of the company pressed on through August and the early weeks of September. There were no more outbreaks of cholera among them. On September 6, they climbed the last mountain pass and camped beside a stream a short distance from their destination.

The next morning, the emigrants washed themselves and put on clean clothes in preparation for their arrival in the Salt Lake Valley. Peter Hansen said they ought to clean up after they got to the city, since they had a dusty road ahead of them, but the emigrants decided to risk the dust.

They traveled the last few miles full of hope, eager to see the place they had heard so much about. But as they entered the valley, they did not see a Garden of

Eden. They found a drought-stricken basin covered in sagebrush, bone-white salt beds, and grasshoppers as far as the eye could see.[34]

NEWS OF JACOB SECRIST'S death appeared in the *Deseret News* on August 8, about a month before his company arrived in the valley. His death was reported along with those of two other missionaries, Albert Gregory and Andrew Lamoreaux, who had also died on their way home to Utah. "These our brethren were prosecuting their way homeward with heart beating joyously," the news article stated. "But the decrees of an all-wise Providence went forth, and like good soldiers they meekly bowed with their armor on and now rest from their labors, and their works will follow them."[35]

Around this time, Ann Eliza received her final letter from Jacob. The letter was dated May 21 from St. Louis. "I am in good health and about ready to start up the Missouri River," it read in part. "May the God of Israel bless you with the blessings of His Spirit, and health, faith, and long life."[36]

After his company arrived in early September, two men delivered Jacob's personal belongings and a horse to Ann Eliza. As promised, Jacob had brought back a sword for each of the boys as well as material for nice suits. For the girls he had brought back dresses and fabric. His wagon also contained his letters and other papers and a year's supply of goods for the family.[37]

As she had planned to do a few years earlier, Ann Eliza moved with her children back to the farm north of Salt Lake City. The letters she and Jacob had exchanged were stowed and preserved. In one of them, which Ann Eliza had sent during the first year of Jacob's mission, she reflected on the sacrifice they had been called to make.

"It looks hard to be separated from those that we love most dear on earth," she had written, "but when I contemplate what they are sent for, even to assist in rolling forth the kingdom of God, I have no cause to complain or murmur."

"Nor need I do," she wrote, "knowing that my exaltation will be greater in that world, where there is no sorrowing nor weeping, but all tears shall be wiped from our eyes."[38]

BY THE OCTOBER 1855 general conference, Brigham Young knew the Saints in Utah Territory were in trouble. Grasshoppers had ravaged many of their gardens and fields, and the drought had destroyed what the grasshoppers had not. Dust clouds blew across the valleys, and wildfires burned through the dry canyons, destroying fodder for cattle. With no way to feed the ox teams hauling stone to the temple site, work on the house of the Lord ceased.

Brigham and his counselors believed the drought and infestation were a "gentle chastening" from the Lord. "Give heed unto the whisperings of the Spirit and tempt not the Lord to bring upon us a heavier rod of discipline," they instructed the Saints that fall, "that we may more fully escape those judgments of high heaven's King."[39]

More concerning to Brigham was the effect of the devastation on the gathering. While the missions to India, China, and Siam had resulted in few conversions, the missions in Europe and South Africa had produced branches of Saints who now wanted to gather to Zion. Emigration was expensive, however, and most of the new converts were poor and needed loans from the Perpetual Emigrating Fund.[40]

Unfortunately, the drought had wrecked the economy in Utah, which depended almost entirely on successful harvests. Robbed of their livelihood, many Saints could not pay tithing or repay their loans to the fund. And soon the Church accrued a steep debt by borrowing money to help finance the large wagon trains coming west that year.[41]

In an October 1855 epistle to the Saints, the First Presidency reminded Church members that donating to the emigrating fund helped to bring their fellow Saints to a place where they could enjoy industry and honest labor. "This is true charity," the presidency declared, "not only to feed the hungry and clothe the naked, but to place them in a situation where they can produce by their own labor their subsistence."[42]

Brigham and his counselors urged the Saints to donate what they could to the Perpetual Emigrating Fund.

Aware that most Saints could not contribute much, they also proposed a more affordable way to gather. Rather than coming to Zion with expensive oxen and wagons, future emigrants could come by handcarts instead.

Pulling handcarts over the plains, the First Presidency explained, would be faster and cheaper than traveling by wagon. Each handcart would consist of a wooden box sitting on an axle and two wagon wheels. Since handcarts were smaller than wagons, the emigrants would not be able to carry as many supplies and provisions with them. But wagons from the valley could meet the handcarts partway to provide assistance as needed.

"Let all the Saints, who can, gather up for Zion and come while the way is open before them," the First Presidency declared. "Let them come on foot, with hand-carts or wheelbarrows; let them gird up their loins and walk through, and nothing shall hinder or stay them."[43]

Brigham immediately shared the plan with apostle Franklin Richards, the European mission president. "I want to see it fairly tried," he wrote. "If it is once tried, you will find that it will become the favorite mode of crossing the plains."[44]

CHAPTER 15

In Storms and in Calms

On January 26, 1856, apostle Franklin Richards published the First Presidency's epistle in the *Latter-day Saints' Millennial Star,* the Church's newspaper in England. As editor of the paper, Franklin gave his enthusiastic support to the handcart plan. "The faithful poor in foreign lands have the consolation of knowing that they are not forgotten," he rejoiced.[1]

Since the earliest days of the Church, the Lord had commanded the Saints to gather together to prepare themselves for the tribulations preceding the Second Coming of Jesus Christ.[2] Franklin believed that these hardships were coming soon and that the European Saints needed to act quickly to avoid them.

Knowing that some Saints worried about the difficulty of gathering by handcart, he presented the proposal as a test of faith. He also reminded emigrants that the ordinances of exaltation awaited them in the Endowment House. "Come, all ye faithful, who have stood firm in storms and in calms," he declared. "We are ready to welcome you home and bestow upon you those blessings for which you have long hungered."[3]

With his time as mission president almost over, Franklin planned to return home to Utah as well. Writing to other returning missionaries, he advised them to assist the handcart emigrants until everyone had arrived safely in the valley.

"On your journey home," he directed, "you should constantly seek how you can aid them by your experience, direct and comfort them by your counsels, cheer them by your presence, strengthen their faith, and keep the spirit of union and peace in their midst."

"The Saints look to you, and have a right to, as the angels of their deliverance," he wrote. "Discharge the responsibility like men of God, for it is upon you."[4]

THAT WINTER, JESSE HAVEN traveled to London after serving for almost three years as president of the South African mission. His companions, William Walker and Leonard Smith, had already come to England a few months earlier with fifteen South African Saints bound for Zion.[5] In a matter of days, both William and Leonard would be sailing out of Liverpool with nearly five hundred emigrating Church members.[6]

Eager to reunite with his family, Jesse looked forward to his own voyage home. Still, he already missed the South African Saints. Finding people to teach had been a constant challenge in such a large and diverse region, yet he and his companions had achieved great success and left behind many friends.[7] More than 170 people had been baptized in South Africa, and most of them were still faithful.

While Jesse would have liked to accomplish more on his mission, he believed the Church in South Africa would grow larger with time and that many more of its members would come to Zion.

"It is not so easy a matter as one might suppose, at first thought, to establish the gospel in a country," Jesse wrote in his official report to the First Presidency, "where the people speak three or four different languages, and where they are of all kinds, grades, conditions, castes, and complexions, and where only two or three hundred thousand inhabitants are scattered over a territory twice as big as England."[8]

On a sunny day in March, soon after Jesse's arrival in Britain, another group of about five hundred Saints left Liverpool for Zion. These Saints were from the United Kingdom, Switzerland, Denmark, East India, and South Africa. Before they departed, Jesse bid farewell to the South African emigrants, sad that he could not join them on the voyage. He would be leaving England two months later with an even larger group of emigrants.[9]

Many of these emigrants expected to travel by handcart once they reached the Great Plains. Since arriving in England, Jesse had heard much about handcarts, but he felt unsure about using them. "I don't know but what they will do well, yet I have not much faith in them," he confided in his journal. "I am inclined to think that the plan will prove a failure, yet as it is recommended by President Brigham Young, I shall back it up and recommend it too."[10]

On May 25, Jesse left England on a ship with more than 850 Church members, most of whom were longtime British Saints who had received financial assistance from the Perpetual Emigrating Fund. They were the largest company of Saints to cross the Atlantic Ocean so far. Before they departed, apostle Franklin Richards called Edward Martin to lead them and appointed Jesse as one of his counselors. A capable leader, Edward was one of the first British converts, a veteran of the Mormon Battalion, and one of the many missionaries sent throughout the world in 1852.[11]

Franklin and other mission leaders saw the Saints off at the docks in Liverpool. Before the ship set sail, they gave the emigrating Saints three cheers. The Saints responded with three cheers of their own, and Franklin and the other leaders said goodbye, giving one more cheer as a parting blessing for the Saints.[12]

THE SHIP ARRIVED IN Boston just over a month later. Like others on board, Elizabeth and Aaron Jackson had been members of the Church for years. Elizabeth's parents had joined the Church in 1840, not long after the first missionaries came to England, and Elizabeth had been baptized a year later at the age of fifteen. She had married Aaron, an elder in the Church, in 1848. Both had worked in the British silk mills.[13]

Traveling with the Jacksons were their three children—seven-year-old Martha, four-year-old Mary, and two-year-old Aaron Jr.—and Elizabeth's nineteen-year-old sister, Mary Horrocks.

In Boston, the family boarded a train with most of their company and traveled to Iowa City, a point of departure for westbound Saints. When they arrived, Elizabeth and Aaron expected to find handcarts ready for them, but the number of Saints going west that season was higher than expected. Three handcart companies had already left Iowa City that summer, and a fourth company, led by returning missionary James Willie, would soon be leaving. There were not enough handcarts ready for everyone.[14]

Knowing they needed to leave soon to get to the Salt Lake Valley before winter, the newly arrived emigrants helped to assemble handcarts. The emigrants split into two handcart companies, one led by Edward Martin and the other by Jesse Haven. Other emigrants joined two wagon companies also led by returning missionaries.[15]

The four companies left Iowa City in late July and early August. About five people were assigned to each handcart, and they were allowed to bring seventeen pounds of personal items apiece. A handcart weighed around two hundred pounds when fully loaded. Each handcart company also traveled with mule teams and wagons laden with tents and provisions.[16]

Toward the end of August, the companies stopped in a town called Florence, not far from the old Winter Quarters site. Franklin Richards, who was traveling with a smaller and faster-moving company of returning missionaries, was already there, preparing to continue on to Utah for the upcoming general conference. In a meeting, Franklin discussed with company leaders whether the emigrants should spend the winter in Florence or continue to Zion, despite the risk of meeting bad weather on the trail ahead.[17]

In their epistles to the Saints throughout the world, the First Presidency had warned emigrants repeatedly about the dangers of starting for the valley late in the season. Wagon companies needed to leave Florence no later than spring or early summer to arrive in Salt Lake City by August or September. While Church leaders believed that handcart companies could travel faster than wagon companies, no one was sure they would, since the first handcart companies were still on the trail. If the Martin company left Florence in late August, they would still be on the trail in late October or early November, when it sometimes began to snow.[18]

Knowing this, some men urged Franklin to recommend wintering the company in Florence. Others counseled him to send the emigrants on to Zion, regardless of the danger. Two weeks earlier, the Willie handcart company had faced the same dilemma, and most members had decided to move ahead on the advice of Captain Willie and other leaders, who promised that God would protect them from harm. Franklin also had faith that God would open a way for the emigrants to arrive safely in the valley, but he wanted them to decide for themselves if they should stay or go.[19]

Gathering the companies together, Franklin warned them about the dangers of traveling so late in the emigration season. Some infants and elderly Saints would likely perish, he said. Other members of the company would suffer disease and exhaustion. If the emigrants wanted, they could spend the winter in Florence living off the provisions already purchased for their journey. Franklin even offered to buy additional provisions for their stay.[20]

Several returning missionaries spoke after Franklin. Most encouraged the Saints to continue to the valley. Brigham Young's son Joseph urged them not to press forward that season. "Such would cause untold agonies, sickness, and much loss of life," he said. "I do not wish such upon my conscience but wish all to stay here for the winter and then go on in the spring."

When the missionaries finished, Franklin arose again and asked the emigrants to vote on the matter. "If you knew that you should be swallowed up in storms," he asked, "would you stop or turn back?"[21]

With cheers, most emigrants removed their hats, raised their hands, and voted to continue to Zion.[22]

Franklin merged the two handcart companies under the leadership of Edward Martin and assigned Jesse Haven to help lead a wagon company with Captain William Hodgetts. The companies left Florence a few days later with a large herd of cattle.

Though Elizabeth and Aaron Jackson were young and healthy, the daily grind of pulling their heavy handcart over rocky trails, patches of deep sand, and streams soon took a toll on their bodies. Some emigrants also struggled to keep up with the company when poorly made handcarts broke down. At the end of every day, the Saints arrived in camp with hungry stomachs and a sure knowledge that the backbreaking work would begin again in the morning.[23]

IN SEPTEMBER 1856, AS the handcart and wagon companies traveled west, the First Presidency and Quorum of the Twelve began preaching repentance and moral reform throughout Utah Territory. Although many Saints lived righteous lives, Church leaders were concerned that too many Saints were not actively striving to become a Zion people or to prepare for the Second Coming. They worried as well about the influence of those in the territory who did not belong to the Church, the weak faith and commitment among some emigrants, and those who had left the Church and now fought against it.

Jedediah Grant, second counselor in the First Presidency, led reform efforts under Brigham Young's direction. Beginning in early September, Jedediah urged the Saints to forsake evil and be rebaptized to renew their covenants and remit their sins. Soon other Church leaders joined him, spreading the message far and wide until a spirit of reformation filled the air.[24]

Their sermons were often fiery. "I am speaking to you in the name of Israel's God," Jedediah proclaimed in Salt Lake City on September 21. "You need to be baptized and washed clean from your sins, from your backslidings, from your apostasies, from your filthiness, from your lying, from your swearing, from your lusts, and from everything that is evil before the God of Israel."[25]

In the Sugar House Ward, Martha Ann Smith was already interested in improving herself, thanks in part to the constant advice she received from her brother Joseph in Hawaii. At first, she believed that going to school would help. Since the territory had no public school system, she attended a school run by her ward. But now that the school term had ended, she was looking for other ways to better herself.

In the spring, Martha Ann had begun living with her older brother John and his family, and her new home provided opportunities for personal improvement. As much as Martha Ann liked John, she did not care for his wife, Hellen, or his in-laws. "They will tell lies behind my back and make fun of your sisters and call them liars," she confided in a letter to Joseph. Knowing Joseph might scold her for speaking ill of family, she added, "If you should know them as well as I do, you would not blame me."[26]

That summer, however, a letter from the East drew Martha Ann's attention away from family squabbles. Lovina, her oldest sister, wrote that she was finally moving to the valley with her husband and four children. Almost immediately, John headed east to bring them supplies and help them on the trail.

Martha Ann and her sisters expected John to come with Lovina and her family in one of the handcart or wagon companies arriving that fall. But when the first companies arrived that season, John and Lovina were not among them. In fact, news of their whereabouts did not come until the third handcart company arrived in early October.

"The handcart company has come into the valley," Martha Ann informed Joseph, "and they said that the company that John is in is three weeks behind."

They had no news about Lovina and her family.[27]

JOHN SMITH WAS NOT three weeks behind. He arrived in the valley two days later with Franklin Richards and the small company of returning missionaries. While heading east, John had crossed paths with them at Independence Rock, about 350 miles from Salt Lake City. They informed him that Lovina's family had reached Florence late in the season and had decided not to go any farther that year.[28]

Disappointed, John thought about continuing east. The weather on the plains was still warm and clear.

He could travel the remaining seven hundred miles to Florence, spend the winter with Lovina and her family, and help them come west in the spring. But if he did that, he would have to leave Hellen and their children to fend for themselves in Utah. John asked Franklin what he should do, and the apostle advised him to return to the valley with him and his company.[29]

On October 4, the evening they arrived in Salt Lake City, Franklin told the First Presidency that the Willie and Martin companies and two wagon companies were five hundred, maybe six hundred, miles away. Altogether, more than a thousand Saints were still east of the Rocky Mountains, and Franklin did not think the Martin company would be able to arrive before the end of November.[30]

Franklin's report alarmed the presidency. Knowing some companies had left England late in the season, they had assumed that Franklin and the emigration agents would instruct them to wait until spring to come west. The Church had sent no provisions east to resupply the remaining companies, which meant that the emigrants would not have enough food to sustain them through their journey. If the companies did not perish in ice and snow, they would succumb to starvation—unless the Saints in the valley came to their rescue.[31]

In Church services the next day, Brigham spoke urgently about the imperiled emigrants. "They must be brought here; we must send assistance to them," he declared. "That is my religion. That is the dictation of the Holy Ghost that I possess. It is to save the people."[32]

Brigham called on the bishops to assemble mule teams and supplies immediately. He asked for men to be ready to leave as soon as possible and called on women to begin organizing donations of blankets, clothes, and shoes.

"Your faith, religion, and profession of religion will never save one soul of you in the celestial kingdom of our God," he said, "unless you carry out just such principles as I am now teaching you. Go and bring in those people now on the plains."[33]

Before they left the meeting, some women removed their warm stockings, petticoats, and anything else they could spare and piled them into wagons.[34] Other women and men immediately began collecting food and supplies and preparing to care for the emigrants once they arrived.

Two days later, more than fifty men and twenty relief wagons left the valley and began crossing the mountains. More followed over the coming weeks. Among the first rescuers were five of the missionaries who had returned home in Franklin Richards's company just three days earlier.[35]

CHAPTER 16

Not Doubting nor Despairing

As the first rescue teams hurried east, Edward Martin's company camped near Jesse Haven and the Hodgetts wagon train at Fort Laramie, a military outpost halfway between Florence and Salt Lake City. The emigrants' food supply was dwindling, and there were no relief teams from the valley in sight.

The man in charge of the fort opened his stores to the Saints, who sold their watches and other goods to purchase a little more flour, bacon, and rice. But even then their provisions would not be enough to satisfy their needs for the remaining five hundred miles of the journey.[1]

Jesse Haven feared for the handcart Saints. A pound of flour per day was not enough to sustain a person pulling a handcart over sandy trails and rocky bluffs, and that allotment would soon have to be reduced. The strain was especially hard on the elderly Saints, who had begun to die in alarming numbers.

"They are truly a poor and afflicted people," Jesse reported in a letter to Brigham Young. "My heart bleeds for them."[2]

The emigrants struggled on. Jesse's wagon company traveled close to the Martin company, lending help where they could. The handcart emigrants were moving more slowly. Not long after leaving the fort, Aaron Jackson, the British silk worker, came down with a fever. The sickness sapped his strength, and he seemed to lose the will to go forward.

Aaron wanted to eat more than his ration, but there was no food to spare. After surveying the company's food stores, Captain Martin had reduced the daily ration in his company to three-fourths of a pound of flour per person. Aaron's family and friends tried to keep him moving, but the exertion wore him down even more.[3]

On the morning of October 19, Aaron sat down to rest beside the trail while the others in the company pressed on to the North Platte River. By noon, he still felt too weak to move. The temperature had dropped drastically over the last few days, and snow was beginning to fall. If he did not get up and rejoin his company soon, he would freeze to death.

Sometime later, two men from the company found Aaron, put him in a wagon with other sick Saints, and brought him to the North Platte. He found his family at the edge of the river, preparing to pull their handcart across. Since the wagon's oxen were too weak to pull their load safely through the current, Aaron had to climb out to cross the river on foot.

He stepped feebly into the icy water as his wife, Elizabeth, and sister-in-law Mary stayed with the children and the handcart. He managed to walk a short distance, but then he stepped onto a sandbar and collapsed from exhaustion. Mary quickly waded out to him and pulled him to his feet while a man on horseback rode over, picked him up, and carried him to the other side of the river.[4]

A north wind blew through the company, and hail began to fall. Mary returned to the handcart, and she and Elizabeth pulled it across the river. As other emigrants struggled to cross, women and men stepped back into the river to rescue friends. Some carried the Saints who were too old, too young, or too sick to cross on their own. Nineteen-year-old Sarah Ann Haigh waded into the freezing water again and again, helping several people across.

Unable to walk any farther, Aaron Jackson was placed on a handcart and carried to the evening's campsite, his feet dangling over the back of the cart. Elizabeth and Mary followed soon after, ready to attend to him once they reached camp. Behind them, Saints staggered on into the fading afternoon, their tattered clothes freezing stiff against their bodies.[5]

THAT NIGHT, ELIZABETH HELPED her husband to bed and fell asleep beside him. When she awoke a few hours later, she listened for Aaron's breathing and heard nothing. Alarmed, she placed her hand on him and found his body cold and stiff.

Elizabeth cried out for help, but there was nothing anyone could do. She thought about lighting a fire so she could look at Aaron, but she had no way to kindle it.

Lying down beside her husband's lifeless body, Elizabeth could not sleep. She waited and prayed, grieving as she watched for the first signs of daylight. The hours passed slowly. She knew she still had her children to take care of—and she still had her sister Mary to help her. But even Mary was getting sick. The only person Elizabeth could truly rely on was the Lord. That night she asked Him for help, trusting that He would comfort her and aid her children.

When morning came, the emigrants were discouraged to find several inches of snow on the ground. A group of men carried Aaron away with thirteen other people who had died overnight. Since the ground was too hard to break, they wrapped the dead in blankets and covered them with snow.[6]

Captain Martin instructed the company to move on, despite the weather. The emigrants pushed and pulled their handcarts through a few miles of deepening snowdrift and bitter winds. The wet snow stuck to the wheels, making the handcarts heavier and harder to pull.[7]

The following day, the company trudged on through still deeper snow.[8] Many did not have adequate shoes or boots to protect against the cold. Their feet turned raw and bloody from frostbite. The Saints tried to keep their spirits up by singing hymns.[9] But four days after crossing the North Platte, they had made little progress.

Feeble and emaciated, the emigrants struggled to keep moving. The flour was now almost gone. Cattle were dying off but were too lean to provide much nourishment. Some people did not have enough strength to set up their tents, so they slept in the snow.[10]

On October 23, Captain Martin decided to rest the company at a place called Red Buttes. As the days passed, the situation in camp only got worse. The temperature continued to drop, and deaths in the company soon totaled more than fifty. At night, wolves crept into camp, dug through the graves, and fed on the bodies.[11]

Every day, Captain Martin called the Saints together to pray for deliverance and ask a blessing on the sick and suffering in camp. He looked tired and sorrowful, but he assured the Saints that help was coming.[12]

On the evening of October 27, Elizabeth sat down on a rock and held her children close. Thousands of miles from England, destitute and snowbound in a rocky mountain country, she was growing despondent. She was now a widow. Her children were fatherless. They had nothing to protect them from the winter storms but threadbare clothes and some blankets.

Sometime in the night, she fell asleep and dreamed that Aaron was standing beside her. "Cheer up, Elizabeth," he said, "deliverance is at hand."[13]

The next day, after eating their meager breakfast, the emigrants spotted three figures coming down a nearby hill on horses. As the figures got closer, the Saints recognized Joseph Young, the twenty-two-year-old son of Brigham Young who had served as a missionary in England for three years. With him were Daniel Jones and Abel Garr, two men from the Salt Lake Valley. They rode into camp, called everyone together, and distributed the food and supplies they carried on their animals.

"There are plenty of provisions and clothing coming for you on the road," Joseph announced, "but tomorrow morning you must make a move from here." Other rescuers were forty-five miles away in wagons stocked with food, clothes, and blankets. If the emigrants pressed on, they would meet up with them in a few days.[14]

The emigrants cheered, threw their arms around the men, and kissed their cheeks. Families laughed and embraced each other as tears poured from their eyes. "Amen!" they shouted.

The company sang a hymn and retired to their tents when night came. They would start west in the morning.[15]

THREE DAYS LATER, ON October 31, the Martin company met the other rescuers on the trail. George D.

Grant, the leader of the small team, was stunned by what he saw. Five or six hundred Saints tugged and pulled their handcarts in a ragged line some three or four miles long. He could see they were worn down after pulling their handcarts all day through the snow and mud. Some people lay in the carts, too sick or exhausted to move. Children were crying, some as they struggled alongside their parents in the snow. Everyone looked cold, and some people's limbs were stiff and bleeding from exposure to the snow.[16]

Over the next few days, the rescuers helped the Martin company move west. Hoping to protect the emigrants against the weather, the rescue team wanted to move them to a cove not far from two high cliffs called Devil's Gate. But to get there, the emigrants had to cross the icy Sweetwater River. With the horror of their last river crossing still fresh in their minds, many emigrants were terrified to cross. Some of them were able to cross the river in wagons. Others went over on foot. Several rescuers and a few of the emigrants carried people over the icy current. Five young rescuers—David P. Kimball, George W. Grant, Allen Huntington, Stephen Taylor, and Ira Nebeker—spent hours in the frigid water, heroically helping the company make the crossing.

Once the emigrants were settled in the cove, which they later named Martin's Cove, it began to snow again. The camp became unbearably cold, and more people died. One emigrant described the cove as "an overcrowded tomb."[17]

By November 9, Jesse Haven and the other Saints in the remaining two wagon companies were with the Martin company at the cove. The weather had cleared, and the rescuers decided to keep moving the company west, despite not having enough supplies and provisions to sustain every emigrant for the remaining 325 miles to Salt Lake City. The emigrants discarded most of their handcarts and nearly all their possessions, keeping only what they had to fight off the cold. Only about a third of the Saints in the Martin company could walk. The rescuers placed others in wagons.[18]

George D. Grant understood that the emigrants needed more help than his men could offer. "We go on doing all we can, not doubting nor despairing," George reported in a letter to Brigham. "I have never seen such energy and faith among the 'boys,' nor so good a spirit as is among those who came out with me."

"We have prayed without ceasing," he testified, "and the blessing of God has been with us."[19]

Ephraim Hanks, Arza Hinckley, and other rescuers found the company west of Martin's Cove and supplied additional food and support for the emigrants. Ten more rescue wagons reached the emigrants at a place called Rocky Ridge, still about 250 miles from Salt Lake City. By then, more than 350 men from the valley had ventured into the deepening snow to help. They set up camps along the trail, cleared away snow, lit fires, and provided more wagons so no one had to walk. Rescuers also cooked meals for the emigrants and danced and sang to distract them from their suffering.[20]

The weather remained harsh, but the Saints felt God supporting them. "Almost every day angry storms arise very threatening, and judging from their appearance one would think that we should be unable to withstand the tempest," wrote Joseph Simmons, one of the rescuers, to a friend in the valley. "Without the help of high heaven, we should have been snowbound in the mountains long ago."[21]

As Brigham learned more about the Saints still on the trail, he struggled to focus on anything but their suffering. "My mind is yonder in the snow," he told a congregation on November 12. "I cannot go out or come in but what in every minute or two minutes my mind reverts to them."[22]

On November 30, as he presided over a Sabbath meeting in Salt Lake City, Brigham learned that relief wagons carrying the members of the Martin company would arrive later that day. He quickly canceled the rest of the day's meetings. "When those persons arrive," he said, "I want to have them distributed in the city among the families that have good and comfortable houses."[23]

The emigrants came into the city at noon. By then, they were utterly destitute. Over one hundred people in the company had died. Many of the survivors had frostbitten hands and feet, some needing amputation.

Had the rescuers not come when they did, many more people would have perished.

The Saints in the territory welcomed the new emigrants into their homes. Elizabeth Jackson and her children moved into her brother Samuel's home in Ogden, north of Salt Lake City, where they rested and recuperated from their brutal journey.[24]

Jesse Haven, who arrived in Salt Lake City two weeks after the Martin company, wept when he saw the valley for the first time in four years. He went straight home to see his wives, Martha and Abigail, and his son, Jesse, who had been born while he was in South Africa. He then visited Brigham Young, grateful that the prophet had sent the rescue parties out to save the Saints.

"The fall of 1856 will long be remembered by me," he wrote in his journal soon after arriving in the valley. "I have been in this Church nineteen years. I saw more suffering last fall than I ever saw before among the Saints."[25]

Patience Loader, a member of the Martin company, later recalled how the Lord had blessed her with strength to endure the journey. "I can say we put our trust in God," she testified. "He heard and answered our prayers and brought us through to the valleys."[26]

CHAPTER 17

The Folks Are Reforming

While the winter of 1856–57 brought snow and ice to the Salt Lake Valley, Joseph F. Smith was laboring on the Big Island of Hawaii. Like George Q. Cannon, he had learned the Hawaiian language quickly and had become a leader in the mission. Now, almost three years after receiving his call, he was eighteen years old and eager to continue serving the Lord.[1]

"I do not feel as though I have done my mission as yet," he wrote his sister Martha Ann, "and I do not want to go home till then."[2]

A short time later, Joseph received a letter from his brother John in Utah. "Christmas passed, and the New Year's Day soon followed it," John reported. "There was no excitement." Although the Saints normally enjoyed large dances and parties during the holidays, Church leaders had discouraged such festivities this year. The moral reformation Jedediah Grant had started the previous fall was still underway, and such celebrations were deemed inappropriate.

"We have forgotten ourselves and gone to sleep, laid aside our religion, and gone to amuse ourselves with temporal things," John explained further. Recently called as the presiding patriarch of the Church, an office his father and grandfather had held, twenty-four-year-old John fully supported the reformation, although his intense shyness kept him from joining other leaders in public preaching.[3]

Other letters from home described the reformation for Joseph. Since September, Church leaders had been rebaptizing penitent Saints in any nearby pool of water—even if they had to break ice to do it.[4] The First Presidency, moreover, had instructed bishops to stop administering the sacrament in their wards until more Saints were rebaptized and proved their willingness to keep their covenants.[5]

Joseph's aunt Mercy Thompson believed the reformation was having a positive effect on her and the Saints. "I feel astonished at the dealings of the Lord with me," she wrote to Joseph. "I do feel that the Lord has more than fulfilled His promises to me."[6]

To encourage righteousness, Church leaders admonished the Saints to confess their sins publicly at ward meetings. In a letter to Joseph, Mercy wrote about Allen Huntington, one of the young men who had helped carry handcart emigrants across the Sweetwater River. Allen had always been a wild young man, but shortly after the handcart rescue, he stood up in the Sugar House Ward, acknowledged his past sins, and spoke about how the rescue had changed his heart.

"He had seen so much of the power of God that he did rejoice while traveling to meet the companies on the road and bringing them in," Mercy reported. "He exhorted his young comrades to turn away from their follies and seek to build up the kingdom of God. His mother wept with joy. His father rose and declared it was the happiest time he ever saw."[7]

Some men were also called as "home missionaries" to visit with families in the Church. During these visits, the missionaries asked a set of formal questions to learn how well family members kept the Ten Commandments, loved one another and their neighbors, and worshipped with their ward members.[8]

As they encouraged greater righteousness, Church leaders called on more men and women to practice plural marriage. Soon after the reformation began, Brigham Young urged John Smith to marry a second wife. The thought of John marrying another woman troubled his wife, Hellen, deeply. But if the Lord wanted her and John to obey the principle, then Hellen preferred to get the marriage ceremony over with as soon as possible. Perhaps living the principle would be easier afterward.

John married a woman named Melissa Lemmon. "It was a trial to me, but thank the Lord it is over with now," Hellen wrote to Joseph in Hawaii. "The Lord is going to try His people in all things, and I think that is the greatest trial. But I pray to my Heavenly Father to give me wisdom and strength of mind to stand every trial as they come along."[9]

Joseph also learned more about the reformation in letters from his sister Martha Ann. "I have been baptized and am commencing to live my religion," she wrote in February. "I am just beginning to see my faults and mend my ways." After months of feuding with Hellen, Martha Ann had finally made peace with her sister-in-law.[10]

"The folks are reforming, and they treat me well now," Martha Ann told Joseph. "We are all good friends."[11]

With many young people in her ward getting married, Martha Ann wondered if it was time for her to marry as well. She was secretly in love with William Harris, the stepson of Bishop Abraham Smoot. "My hand trembles when I say love, but it is so, very so," she confided to Joseph. "He is a good young man and has gained my affections."

She pleaded with her brother to keep the secret. "Do not say anything about it in any of your letters except mine," she wrote, "and tell me what you think about it."

William would soon be leaving on a mission to Europe, however, which Martha Ann considered a sore trial. "I am getting over it now; that is, I am striving to overcome it," she lamented in her letter. "I suppose it is all good."[12]

BY THE SPRING OF 1857, Brigham Young and other Church leaders were pleased with the Saints' reformation and reinstituted the sacrament throughout the Church. Brigham said time and again that the Saints were a "God-blessed people."[13]

Yet some problems had arisen during the reformation. Leaders had spoken harshly of apostates and locals who were not members of the Church. Feeling intimidated, some people left the territory. Bishops, home missionaries, and Church members also clashed sometimes when frequent home visits and public confessions proved embarrassing, disruptive, or intimidating. With time, Church leaders began encouraging that interviews and confessions be done in private.[14]

Church leaders typically used moderate and uplifting language in their sermons to encourage the Saints to do better. The Book of Mormon provided clear examples of how forceful preaching could inspire people to reform, however, and Church leaders had often used extreme language that winter to call the Saints to repentance. At times, Brigham and others had even drawn on Old Testament scriptures to teach that certain grievous sins could be forgiven only through the shedding of the sinner's blood.[15]

Such teachings harked back to the hellfire and brimstone language of Protestant revival preachers who tried to frighten sinners into reform.[16] Brigham understood that he sometimes let his fiery sermons go too far, and he did not intend for people to be put to death for their sins.[17]

One day Brigham received a letter from Isaac Haight, the stake president in Cedar City, about a man who had confessed to a sexual sin with his fiancée after he had received his endowment. The man had since married the woman and said he would do anything to make restitution for his sin, even if that meant having his blood shed.

"Will you tell me what to say to him?" Isaac asked.

"Tell the young man to go and sin no more, repent of all his sins, and be baptized for the same," Brigham replied.[18] Amid the reformation's hard admonitions, he often counseled leaders to help sinners repent and seek mercy. Both Brigham's forceful preaching and his counsel for mercy were intended to help Saints repent and draw closer to the Lord.[19]

As their season of reformation wound down, the Saints once again grew frustrated with the federally appointed officials in the territorial government. Early in 1857, Utah's legislature petitioned James Buchanan, the newly elected president of the United States, to grant them greater freedom to appoint their own government leaders.

"We will resist any attempt of government officials to set at naught our territorial laws," they warned, "or to impose upon us those which are inapplicable and of right not in force in this territory."[20]

The local government officials, meanwhile, were equally frustrated with the Saints' disdain toward outsiders, intimidation of federally appointed leaders, and lack of separation of church and state in the territorial government. In March, some officials resigned their appointments and returned east with stories of the Saints' plural marriages and seemingly undemocratic government, much as Perry Brocchus and others had done a few years earlier.

Early that summer, after the snowy plains thawed and mail routes reopened, the Saints learned that their strongly worded petition and reports of their treatment of former territorial officers had deeply alarmed and angered President Buchanan and his advisers. The president viewed the Saints' actions as rebellious, and he appointed new men to the vacant offices in Utah.[21] Eastern newspapers and politicians, meanwhile, demanded that he use military action to oust Brigham as governor, quell the Saints' rumored rebelliousness, and see that the new federal officials were seated and protected.

To its critics, the plan sounded excessive and expensive, but rumors soon spread that the president intended to carry it out. Buchanan saw it as his duty to establish federal authority in Utah. At the time, the United States was experiencing significant tensions over the matter of slavery, and many people feared that slaveholders in the southern states might someday form their own country. Sending an army to Utah might dissuade other regions from challenging the federal government.[22]

With his term as governor up, Brigham now expected the president to try to appoint an outsider to replace him. The change would not affect his standing with the Saints, but it would lessen his ability to help them politically. If the president removed him from office and sent an army to enforce the change, the Saints would have little hope for self-rule. They would again be subject to the whims of men who scorned the kingdom of God.[23]

About a month after Brigham heard the rumors of Buchanan's intentions, he learned that apostle Parley Pratt had been murdered. His murderer, Hector McLean, was the estranged husband of Eleanor McLean, one of Parley's plural wives. Eleanor had joined the Church in California after years of suffering from Hector's abuse and alcoholism. Hector had blamed Parley when Eleanor left him, and he sent their children to live with relatives in the southern United States. Eleanor attempted to reunite with her children, and Parley followed soon after to assist her. In May 1857, however, Hector hunted Parley down and brutally killed him.[24]

Parley's murder shocked Brigham and the Saints. For more than twenty-five years, Parley had been a leading Latter-day Saint writer and missionary. His tract *A Voice of Warning* had helped to bring countless people into the Church. The loss of his tireless service and incomparable voice pained the Saints deeply.

Yet newspaper editors throughout the nation celebrated Parley's murder. To them, Hector McLean had justly slain the man who had wrecked his home. One newspaper even recommended that President Buchanan appoint Hector as the new governor of Utah.[25]

Like those who had persecuted the Saints in Missouri and Illinois, Parley's murderer was never brought to justice.[26]

AS TENSIONS INCREASED BETWEEN the Saints and the United States government, Martha Ann Smith prepared to say goodbye to William Harris, who would soon be leaving for the European mission. Martha Ann expected to marry William when he returned home. On the day he met with the First Presidency to be set apart for his mission, she helped his mother, Emily Smoot, prepare his belongings for the journey.

As they worked, William burst into the room. "Get your sunbonnet, Martha, and come on," he said. While setting William apart, Brigham Young had suggested that William bring Martha Ann to the city and marry her before leaving for Europe.

Startled, Martha Ann turned to Emily. "What shall I do? What shall I do?" she asked.

"Honey," said Emily, "put on the calico dress and go on."

Martha Ann quickly changed into her calico dress and climbed into the wagon beside William. They were married in the Endowment House, and Martha Ann moved in with William and the Smoot family.

Two days later, William loaded his belongings into a handcart and left the valley in a company of seventy other missionaries.[27]

When the missionaries arrived in New York City several weeks later, William was astonished by the hostility many people felt toward the Saints. "We hear all kinds of abuse about the Mormons and the authorities of the Church," he wrote Joseph F. Smith, his new brother-in-law. "The topic of conversation is Utah, Utah in every newspaper that you see. They say that they are going to send out a governor for Utah and troops, and he will enforce the law of the United States, set the women at liberty, and if old Young resists, hang him up by the neck."[28]

ON JULY 24, 1857, THE tenth anniversary of the Saints' arrival in the valley, the Smoot family joined Brigham Young and two thousand other Saints for a picnic at a mountain lake east of Salt Lake City. Brass bands from various settlements played as the Saints spent the morning fishing, dancing, and visiting with each other. American flags flew from the tops of two tall trees. Throughout the morning, Saints fired cannons, watched the territorial militia drill, and heard speeches.

Around noon, however, Abraham Smoot and Porter Rockwell rode into camp, interrupting the festivities. Abraham had just returned from a Church business trip to the eastern United States. On the way, he had seen freight wagons traveling west to supply an army of fifteen hundred troops the president was now officially sending to Utah with a new governor. The government had also stopped mail service to Utah Territory, effectively cutting off communication between the Saints and the East.[29]

The next day, Brigham and the Saints traveled back to the city to prepare for invasion. On August 1, Daniel Wells, the commander of the territorial militia, ordered his officers to get every community ready for war. The Saints needed to stockpile provisions, letting nothing go to waste. He forbade them from selling grain and other goods to wagon trains going to California. If the army laid siege to the valleys, the Saints would need every ounce of their supplies to survive.[30]

Brigham also requested that mission presidents and Church leaders in outlying branches and settlements send missionaries and other Saints home to Utah.

"Release those of the elders who have been laboring there for any great length of time," he instructed George Q. Cannon, who now presided over the Pacific mission in San Francisco. "Induce as many of our young men to return as possible, as their parents are exceedingly anxious to see them."[31]

Brigham had heard rumors that General William Harney, a man known for his brutality, was leading the army to Utah. Though Harney claimed to feel no hostility toward most Saints, he was apparently determined to punish Brigham and other Church leaders.[32]

"Whether I am to be hung with or without trial," Brigham speculated, "is yet to be decided."[33]

WHILE THE SAINTS IN and around Salt Lake City prepared for invasion, George A. Smith visited the territory's southern settlements to warn them about the coming army. On August 8, he arrived in Parowan, a town he had helped to establish six years earlier. The Saints there loved and trusted him.[34]

News about the army had already reached the town, and everyone was on edge. They feared that additional troops from California would invade southern Utah first, attacking the weaker settlements there before working their way north. Impoverished settlements like Parowan, existing on the edge of survival, would be no match for the army.[35]

George worried about the safety of his family and friends in the area. The army intended to wage a war of extermination against the Church, he told them. To ensure their survival, he urged the Parowan Saints to give excess grain to their bishop to store for the uncertain times ahead. They should also use all their wool to make clothes.[36]

The next day, George spoke more forcibly. The Church was hated back east, he claimed. If the Saints did not trust in God, the army would divide them in two and conquer them easily.

"Take care of your provisions, for we will need them," he instructed. He knew the Saints would be tempted to help and feed the soldiers when they came—whether out of kindness or a desire to profit off them.

"Will you sell them grain or forage?" George asked. "I say curse the man who pours oil and water on their heads."[37]

CHAPTER 18

Too Late, Too Late

During the summer of 1857, Johan and Carl Dorius
made their way to Zion in a handcart company of
around three hundred Scandinavian Saints.[1] Most of
the company had arrived in the eastern United States in
May. Having stayed to preach the gospel in Norway and
Denmark long after his father and sisters had emigrated
to Zion, Johan felt his heart beat for joy when he finally
saw the United States.[2] On shore, however, he and his
company soon learned about the murder of Parley Pratt
and the army of fifteen hundred troops marching to
subdue the Saints in Utah.[3]

They also learned about the handcart emigrants who
perished on the trail the year before. As Brigham had
anticipated, handcart travel under normal circumstances
had proved to be faster and cheaper than traditional

wagon trains. Of the five handcart companies that had come to the valley, the first three had arrived without major incident. And the tragic outcomes of the other two could have been avoided with better planning and counsel from some of the emigration leaders. To avoid additional catastrophes, emigration agents now made sure to send off all handcart companies with enough time to reach the valley safely.[4]

In late August, Johan, Carl, and their company traveled for a time near the well-armed, well-supplied army marching to Utah. Though many people believed that the army wanted to overpower and oppress the Saints, the emigrants received no harassment or abuse while traveling alongside them.[5]

One day, about two hundred miles from the Salt Lake Valley, the emigrants found one of the army's oxen on the trail with an injured foot. "You people can have that ox," the leader of the army's provision wagons said. "I suppose you might need a little meat."

The Saints gladly accepted the animal. Relief wagons from the valley were supposed to be on the way, but they had not yet arrived. Short on other sources for food, the Saints saw the beef as a blessing from God.

The handcarts eventually outpaced the army. As they neared Utah, Johan was eager to begin the important work ahead of him. While crossing the Atlantic, he had married a Norwegian Saint named Karen Frantzen. His brother Carl had married Elen Rolfsen, another Norwegian Saint, at the same time. In Utah, the former missionaries planned to settle down for the first time in years—probably near the rest of the Dorius family—and enjoy their new lives in Zion.[6]

Yet some uncertainty lay on the horizon. The soldiers had treated the Saints kindly on the trail. Would they do the same when they marched into the territory?

ON AUGUST 25, 1857, JACOB Hamblin, the president of the Indian mission in southern Utah, accompanied George A. Smith back to Salt Lake City. They traveled north with a group of leaders from the Paiute Indian tribe. Knowing Paiutes could ally with the Saints if violence broke out with the army, Brigham had invited the leaders to the city for a council.[7] Jacob would act as a translator during the meetings.[8]

About midway to Salt Lake City, the small company camped across the creek from a wagon train of emigrants mainly from Arkansas, a state in the southern United States. After sunset, a few men from the Arkansas company approached camp and introduced themselves.[9]

The company had around 140 people, most of them young and eager to start a new life in California. Several were married and traveling with small children. Their leaders were Alexander Fancher and John Baker. Captain Fancher, who had traveled to California before, was a natural leader who was known for his integrity and courage. He and his wife, Eliza, were the parents of nine children, each of whom was in the company.

Captain Baker traveled with three of his grown children and an infant grandson.

The company had mules, horses, and oxen to pull their wagons and carriages. They also traveled with hundreds of longhorn cattle, which they could sell for a profit when they arrived in California, provided they kept the cattle fed and healthy on the trail.[10]

Around the time Captain Fancher had first traveled to California, the southern route through Utah had plenty of open grazing land and watering spots. Since then, new settlements along the road had claimed this ground, making it difficult for large wagon trains to care for their livestock without the Saints' cooperation. Now, with the army approaching, many Saints were treating outsiders with suspicion and hostility. Many also obeyed the counsel not to sell provisions to outsiders.[11]

The Saints' indifference worried the Arkansas company. The road ahead passed through some of the hottest and driest country in the United States. The journey would be difficult without a place to resupply, feed and water their animals, and rest.[12]

Jacob Hamblin told the company about good campsites along the road. The best was a lush valley, just south of his ranch, with plenty of water and grass for the cattle. It was a peaceful spot called Mountain Meadows.[13]

SEVERAL DAYS LATER, THE Arkansas company stopped at Cedar City, two hundred and fifty miles south of Salt

Lake City, to purchase supplies before moving on to Mountain Meadows. Cedar City was the last major settlement in southern Utah and home to the Saints' iron industry, which was now struggling. Its residents were poor and relatively isolated.[14]

The company found a man outside of town willing to sell them fifty bushels of unmilled wheat. Some members of the company took the wheat and some corn they had purchased from Indians to a mill operated by Philip Klingensmith, the local bishop, who charged an exceptionally high price to grind the grain.[15]

Other members of the company, meanwhile, tried to make purchases at a store in town. What happened next remains unclear. Years later, Cedar City settlers recalled that the store clerk did not have the items the emigrants needed—or that he simply refused to sell them.[16] Some people remembered a few members of the company growing angry and threatening to help the soldiers exterminate the Saints once the army arrived. Other settlers said that one man in the company claimed to have the gun that killed the prophet Joseph Smith.[17]

Captain Fancher tried to rein in the angry men.[18] But some of them apparently found the home of the mayor, Isaac Haight, who also served as the stake president and a major in the territorial militia, and shouted threats at him.[19] Isaac slipped out his back door, found John Higbee, the town marshal, and urged him to arrest the men.

Higbee confronted the men and told them that disturbing the peace and using foul language were against the local laws. The men dared him to arrest them. Then they left town.[20]

LATER IN THE DAY, Isaac Haight and other Cedar City leaders sent a message to William Dame, the commander of the district militia and the stake president in nearby Parowan, seeking advice on what to do about the emigrants. Though the vast majority of the company had caused no trouble, and no one had physically harmed any of the residents, people in town were seething when the emigrants left. Some of them had even begun plotting revenge.

William shared Isaac's message with a council of Church and town leaders, and they determined that the Arkansas company was probably harmless. "Do not notice their threats," William counseled Isaac in a letter. "Words are but wind—they injure no one."[21]

Dissatisfied, Isaac sent for John D. Lee, a Latter-day Saint in a neighboring town. John taught farming to local Paiutes and had a good relationship with them. He was a hard worker and was eager to prove himself in the southern settlements.[22]

While he waited for John to arrive, Isaac met with other leaders in Cedar City to lay out his plan for revenge. South of Mountain Meadows, along the road to California, was a narrow canyon where Paiutes could attack the wagon train, kill some or all of the men, and take their cattle. The Paiutes were generally peaceful, and some of them had joined the Church. But Isaac believed that John could convince them to attack the company.[23]

Once John arrived, Isaac told him about the emigrants, repeating the rumor that one of them had bragged about having the gun that killed the prophet Joseph.[24] "Unless something is done to prevent it," Isaac said, "the emigrants will carry out their threats and rob every one of the outlying settlements in the south."[25]

He asked John to convince the Paiutes to attack the company. "If they kill part or all of them," he said, "so much the better." But no one could know that white settlers had ordered the attack.

Blame had to fall on the Paiutes.[26]

ON THE AFTERNOON OF Sunday, September 6, Cedar City leaders met again to discuss the Arkansas company, now camped at Mountain Meadows. Convinced that a member of the company was connected to the deaths of Joseph and Hyrum Smith or that some people in the company wanted to help the army kill the Saints, a few councilmen supported the plan to provoke the Paiutes into attacking the company.[27]

Others in the council urged caution, and soon more men expressed reservations about the plan.[28] Frustrated, Isaac leapt out of his seat and stormed out of the room. The council, meanwhile, proposed sending an express rider to seek advice from Brigham Young.[29] But by noon on Monday, no rider had been sent.

That same day, September 7, Isaac received a message from John D. Lee. That morning, John and a group of Paiutes had attacked the emigrants at Mountain Meadows. Though the Paiutes had at first been reluctant to participate, John and other local leaders had promised to reward them with plunder if they joined in the strike.[30]

Isaac reeled at the news. According to the plan, the attack should have happened after the Arkansas company left the meadows, not before. John now reported that seven emigrants had been killed and another sixteen wounded. The emigrants had circled their wagons, fought back, and killed at least one Paiute.[31]

With a siege underway at Mountain Meadows, Isaac wrote to Brigham Young for advice. He reported that the Paiutes had attacked a wagon train. He noted that the emigrants had threatened the Saints in Cedar City, but he omitted the settlers' role in plotting and carrying out the attack.[32]

Isaac handed the letter to James Haslam, a young member of the militia, and ordered him to ride a horse to Salt Lake City as quickly as possible.[33] He then wrote to John. "You will use your best endeavors to keep the Indians off the emigrants," he wrote, "and protect them from harm until further orders."[34]

That evening, Isaac learned that after John and the Paiutes attacked the company, armed Latter-day Saints had searched the area for two of the company's members who had left Mountain Meadows earlier that week to round up stray cattle. The men had found the emigrants and shot one of them. The other emigrant had escaped and returned to the company's camp, aware that two white men had attacked him.

If the emigrants had not previously known that Latter-day Saints were involved in the attack on their camp, they knew now.[35]

TWO DAYS LATER, ON September 9, Isaac met with marshal John Higbee, who had just returned from the siege.[36] Since the initial killings, John D. Lee had led smaller attacks on the company.[37] Higbee knew the emigrants would eventually run out of water and supplies. But more wagon trains would be passing through the area, perhaps within the next few days, and could discover the Saints' role in the attack.[38]

To hide the settlers' involvement, Isaac and Higbee decided that the local militia had to end the siege. Everyone in the company who could implicate the attackers had to be killed.[39]

After the meeting, Isaac went to Parowan to get permission from William Dame to order the militia to attack the emigrants. Still believing the emigrants were victims of an Indian attack, William and his council wanted to send the militia to Mountain Meadows to protect the company and help them continue on their way.[40]

In a private meeting with William, however, Isaac admitted that Latter-day Saints had been involved in the attacks and that the emigrants knew it. He said their only option now was to kill any survivor old enough to testify against the settlers.[41]

Weighing these words, William put aside his council's decision and authorized an attack.[42]

THE NEXT DAY, SEPTEMBER 10, Brigham Young met with Jacob Hamblin in Salt Lake City to learn how Paiutes stored food. If the Saints had to flee to the mountains when the army arrived, Brigham wanted to know how to survive in rugged terrain.[43]

But already the army seemed like less of a threat than the Saints had first imagined. An army representative had recently come to the city and stated that the soldiers did not intend to harm the Saints. It also seemed unlikely that most of the army would arrive in the area before winter.[44]

As Brigham and Jacob spoke, the messenger from Cedar City, James Haslam, interrupted the meeting with his message about the siege at Mountain Meadows.[45] Brigham read the note and then looked at the messenger. James had ridden 250 miles in three days—with practically no sleep. Realizing there was little time to waste, Brigham asked him if he could carry his response back to Cedar City. He said he could.[46]

Brigham told him to get some sleep and return for his reply.[47] James left, and Brigham wrote his response. "In regard to emigration trains passing through our settlements, we must not interfere with them until they are first notified to keep away," he instructed. "You must not meddle with them. The Indians we expect will do as they please, but you should try and preserve good feelings with them."

"Let them go in peace," Brigham insisted.[48]

An hour later, Brigham handed the letter to James and walked with him to the hitching post outside his office. "Brother Haslam," he said, "I want you to ride for dear life."[49]

ALTHOUGH THE SAINTS IN Salt Lake City no longer expected soldiers to invade their streets that season, the Saints in southern Utah remained unaware of the army's professions of peace and of Brigham's instructions not to interfere with emigration trains. The Cedar City Saints still believed the army intended to destroy them.

For more than a week, the women in town had watched the men in their families grow more agitated over the Arkansas emigrants. The men stayed out late, held councils, and plotted ways to handle the situation. Now the militia was marching off to Mountain Meadows.[50]

On the afternoon of September 10, the women met for their monthly Relief Society meeting. Some of the women had felt threatened when the emigrants passed through Cedar City. A few of them, including Annabella Haight and Hannah Klingensmith, were wives of the leaders who had participated in the events of the past week.[51]

"These are squally times," Annabella told the women, "and we ought to attend to secret prayer in behalf of our husbands, sons, fathers, and brothers."

"Attend strictly to secret prayer in behalf of the brethren that are out acting in our defense," agreed Lydia Hopkins, the president of the Relief Society. She and her counselors then instructed the women and appointed several members to visit other women throughout the city.

Before closing the meeting, they sang a hymn.

Repent and be washed clean from sin,
And then a crown of life you'll win;
For the day we seek is nigh, is nigh at hand.[52]

AT MOUNTAIN MEADOWS, MEANWHILE, between sixty and seventy militiamen from Cedar City and other neighboring settlements joined John D. Lee at the ranch of Jacob Hamblin, who had not yet returned from Salt Lake City.[53] A few militiamen were teenagers, but most were in their twenties and thirties.[54] A few of them arrived thinking they had come to bury the dead.[55]

In the evening, John Higbee, John D. Lee, Philip Klingensmith, and other leaders reviewed the plan of attack with the militiamen. One by one, the men agreed to the plan, convinced that if they let the Arkansas company go free, the enemies of the Church would learn the truth about the siege.[56]

The next morning, September 11, twenty-three-year-old Nephi Johnson was on a hilltop overlooking Mountain Meadows. Since he was fluent in the Paiute language, he was ordered to lead the Indians in the attack. Nephi wanted to wait until after hearing back from Brigham Young, but the militia insisted on striking now. Nephi believed he had no choice but to cooperate.[57]

He watched as a sergeant in the militia, carrying a white flag of truce, met one of the emigrants outside the company's barricade and offered to help the survivors. After the emigrants accepted the offer, John D. Lee approached the barricade to negotiate the rescue. He instructed the company to hide their guns in wagons and leave their cattle and goods as gifts for the Paiutes.[58]

John ordered the emigrants to follow him. Two wagons with the sick, the wounded, and small children led the way, followed by a line of women and older children. The older boys and men walked some distance behind, each one with an armed militiaman at his side. Some of the men and women carried young children in their arms.[59]

Nephi knew what would happen next. The emigrants would proceed toward the Hamblin ranch. At some point, Higbee would signal each militiaman to turn and shoot the emigrant next to him. Nephi would then order the Paiutes to attack.[60]

Soon John D. Lee and the emigrants passed beneath where Nephi hid with the Paiutes. Nephi waited for Higbee's signal, but it did not come. Confused, the Paiutes struggled to stay hidden as they hurried to keep up with the procession.[61] Finally, Higbee turned his horse to face the militia.

"Halt!" he yelled.[62]

WHEN THE MILITIAMEN HEARD Higbee's signal, most of them turned their guns on the men and boys and killed them instantly. One loud shot seemed to echo across the meadow as gun smoke shrouded the emigrants.[63] Nephi signaled the Paiutes to attack, and they sprang from their positions and fired on the closest emigrants.[64]

The emigrants who survived the first volley of fire fled for their lives. Higbee and other men on horseback cut them off while attackers on the ground chased and slaughtered them, sparing only some of the youngest children.[65] At the wagons with the sick and wounded, John D. Lee saw to it that no one survived who could tell the tale.[66]

Afterward, the stench of blood and gunpowder hung over Mountain Meadows. More than 120 emigrants had been killed since the first attack four days earlier. As some attackers looted bodies, Philip Klingensmith rounded up seventeen small children and carted them to the Hamblin ranch. When Jacob Hamblin's wife Rachel saw the children, most of them crying and covered in blood, her heart broke. One of the youngest children, a one-year-old girl, had been shot in the arm.[67]

John D. Lee wanted to separate the wounded girl from her two sisters, but Rachel persuaded him to keep them together.[68] That night, while Rachel cared for the anguished children, John bedded down outside the house and went to sleep.[69]

EARLY THE NEXT MORNING, Isaac Haight and William Dame arrived at the Hamblin ranch. It was the first time either of them had visited Mountain Meadows since the siege began.[70] When he learned how many people had been killed, William was shocked. "I must report this matter to the authorities," he said.

"And implicate yourself with the rest?" said Isaac. "Nothing has been done except by your orders."[71]

Later, John D. Lee led both men to the massacre site. Signs of the carnage were everywhere, and some men were burying the bodies in shallow graves.[72]

"I did not think that there were so many women and children," William said, his face pale.[73]

"Colonel Dame counseled and ordered me to do this thing, and now he wants to back out and go back on me," Isaac said to John, his voice filling with rage. "He has got to stand up to what he did, like a little man."

"Isaac," William said, "I did not know there were so many of them."

"That makes no difference," Isaac said.[74]

LATER, AFTER THE DEAD were buried, Philip Klingensmith and Isaac told the militiamen to keep their role in the massacre a secret.[75] James Haslam, the messenger sent to Salt Lake City, returned soon after with Brigham Young's instructions to let the wagon company go in peace.

Isaac began to weep.[76] "Too late," he said. "Too late."[77]

CHAPTER 19

The Chambers of the Lord

On September 13, 1857, Johan and Carl Dorius pulled their handcarts into Salt Lake City side by side with their wives, Karen and Elen. Having discarded extra baggage along the trail to lighten their loads, they and their company entered the city in the same threadbare rags they had been wearing for weeks. Some of the women had replaced their worn-out shoes with rough burlap cloth wrapped around their feet. Still, after months on the trail, the emigrants were grateful to be in Zion and proudly flew the Danish flag from their lead handcart.[1]

As the emigrants made their way through the city, Saints brought out cakes and milk to welcome them. The Dorius brothers soon spotted their father in the crowd. Nicolai greeted them joyfully and introduced his new wife, Hannah Rasmusen, who was also from Denmark.

The brothers and their families then rolled their hand-carts to a campground in the city, unloaded their few belongings, and followed Nicolai and Hannah back to a small, comfortable home at the south end of town.[2]

Nicolai and Hannah had traveled west in the same wagon company as one another two years earlier. Hannah had been married then, but her husband abandoned her and their teenage son, Lewis, along the trail. Knowing the pain of a failed marriage, Nicolai could sympathize with her. They were sealed in the Endowment House on August 7, 1857, and Lewis soon adopted the Dorius name as his own.[3]

While Johan, Carl, and their wives rested from their journey, Saints throughout the territory were preparing for the coming army. Taking no chances, Brigham Young declared martial law on September 15 and issued a proclamation forbidding the army from entering the territory. Although messengers from the army insisted that the troops were coming simply to install a new territorial governor, the Saints' spies had visited the army's camps and heard soldiers boasting about what they would do to the Saints once they reached Utah.[4]

Harrowed by the memory of militias and mobs plundering homes, burning settlements, and killing Saints in Missouri and Illinois, Brigham was prepared to evacuate the valley and destroy Salt Lake City if the army invaded. "Before I will suffer what I have in times gone by," he declared in mid-September, "there shall not be one building, nor one foot of lumber, nor a stick, nor a tree, nor a particle of grass and hay that will burn left in reach of our enemies."[5]

He continued to speak about the matter in the days leading up to the October conference. "Let us walk in the precepts of our Savior," he told the Saints. "I know that all will be made right, and an all-wise, overruling Providence will bring us off victorious."[6]

Although they did not speak English, Johan and Carl Dorius attended a general conference for the first time on October 7. At the close of the meeting, Brigham offered the benediction. "Bless Thy Saints in the valleys of the mountains," he prayed. "Hide us in the chambers of the Lord, where Thou hast gathered Thy people, where we have rested in peace for many years."[7]

One week later, Nicolai and Hannah moved to Fort Ephraim in Sanpete Valley, where Nicolai's daughters Augusta and Rebekke lived. Johan and Karen, meanwhile, stayed in the city with Carl and Elen. Like most Saints who migrated to the valley, they were rebaptized to renew their covenants. They also began preparing to receive the temple ordinances in the Endowment House.

Johan and Carl were also on hand to defend the city.[8]

AROUND THIS TIME, JOHN D. Lee met with Brigham Young and Wilford Woodruff in Salt Lake City to report on the massacre that had taken place at Mountain Meadows. Much of what John told them about the Arkansas company was misleading. "Many of them belonged to the mob in Missouri and Illinois," he lied. "As they traveled along south, they went damning Brigham Young, Heber C. Kimball, and the heads of the Church."[9]

John also repeated a false rumor about the emigrants poisoning cattle and provoking the Paiutes. "The Indians fought them five days until they killed all their men," he claimed, saying nothing about the Saints' own participation. "They then rushed into their corral and cut the throats of their women and children, except some eight or ten children which they brought and sold to the whites."

Concealing his own role in the attack, John claimed that he had gone to the meadows only after the massacre to help bury the bodies. "It was a horrid, awful job," he reported. "The whole air was filled with an awful stench."

"It is heartrending," Brigham said, believing the report.[10] John wrote out his account of the massacre two months later and sent it to Salt Lake City. Brigham then included long extracts from the letter in his official report of the massacre to the commissioner of Indian affairs in Washington, DC.[11]

MEANWHILE, RUMORS OF THE massacre spread to California. Within a month of the massacre, the first detailed account of the killings appeared in a Los Angeles newspaper.[12] Other papers soon picked up the story.[13]

Most of these reports speculated that Saints had been involved in the attack. "Who can be so blind as not to see that the hands of Mormons are stained with this blood?" one editorial asked.[14]

Ignorant of the Cedar City Saints' leading role in the massacre, George Q. Cannon treated these reports with contempt. Writing as editor of the *Western Standard,* the Church's San Francisco newspaper, he accused reporters of stirring up hatred against the Saints. "This continual abuse and piling on of false charges," he wrote, "we are tired of hearing. We know that the Mormons in Deseret are an industrious, peaceable, God-fearing people, and that they have been most foully abused and vilified."[15]

Around this time, missionaries throughout the world began returning home, responding to Brigham Young's call to help their families and protect Zion against the army. On October 22, eighteen-year-old Joseph F. Smith and other elders from the Hawaiian mission arrived penniless at the *Western Standard* office. George gave Joseph an overcoat and warm blanket and sent him and his companions on their way.[16]

A little over a month later, on December 1, apostles Orson Pratt and Ezra Benson arrived at San Francisco with elders from the British mission. Knowing the president of the United States had declared the Saints to be in open rebellion against the government, the apostles had traveled under assumed names to avoid detection on their way to Utah. In the city, they called on George and urged him to return with them to Zion.

With so much hostility directed at the Saints in California, George needed no prodding. He had already finished printing the Book of Mormon in Hawaiian, one of his mission's main objectives. "I leave San Francisco without a sigh of regret," he wrote in his journal.[17]

Meanwhile, many Saints, hearing that bands of men were attacking Church members to avenge the Mountain Meadows massacre, fled California in small companies.[18] Joseph F. Smith found work driving a team of cattle to Utah. One day, he was gathering firewood when some men rode into camp and threatened to kill any "Mormon" they found.

Some men in camp hid in the brush beside a nearby creek. Joseph almost fled into the woods as well, but then he stopped himself.[19] He had once encouraged his sister Martha Ann to "be a Mormon, out and out."[20] Shouldn't he do the same?

Joseph walked into camp with firewood still in his arms. One of the riders trotted up to him with a pistol in his hand. "Are you a Mormon?" he demanded.

Joseph looked him in the eye, fully expecting the man to shoot him. "Yes, sirree," he said. "Dyed in the wool. True blue, through and through."

The man gazed back at Joseph, bewildered. He lowered his pistol and seemed for a moment to be paralyzed. "Shake, young fellow," he then said, reaching out his hand. "I am glad to see a man that stands up for his convictions."

He and the other riders then turned and rode out of camp, and Joseph and the company thanked the Lord for delivering them safely from harm.[21]

WHILE MANY CALIFORNIA SAINTS left for Utah immediately, others were not prepared to leave. Several families had also built homes and profitable businesses in San Bernardino, the largest settlement of California Saints. They took pride in their beautiful farms and orchards. No one was eager to see years of hard work go to waste.[22]

Among them were Addison and Louisa Pratt, who had lived in the town since returning from the Pacific Islands in 1852. Louisa was willing to move again, no matter how much she prized her home and orchard in California. But Addison was more hesitant to leave. The crisis in Utah bore down on him like a weight, and he had grown sullen.

Addison had faced several disappointments during the last five years. He had tried to serve another mission in the South Pacific, but the French protectorate government at Tahiti all but banned him from preaching. His former companion Benjamin Grouard, moreover, had drifted away from the Church.[23]

Addison also preferred California's warm climate to Utah's often unpredictable weather. And he was fiercely loyal to the United States. If American soldiers invaded Utah, he did not think he could fight them in good conscience.

His unwillingness to move bothered Louisa. Their three oldest daughters were now married. Two of them, Ellen and Lois, were planning to move to Utah with their husbands. Ann, the youngest daughter, also wanted to go. Only Frances and her husband were staying in California.[24]

At night, while all of San Bernardino slept, Louisa often went outside to water the trees in her orchard, which were just beginning to bear fruit. "Must I go and leave them?" she wondered. To the north, a canyon road wound up the dark mountain to the top of a high pass. On the other side of the mountain lay hundreds of miles of sterile desert. Choosing to make the arduous journey to Utah would be easier, she felt, if Addison were more eager to go.[25]

As she reflected on the choice before her, Louisa felt her heart beat with love for the Church. At baptism, she had promised to unite herself with the Saints. And she knew if Church members chose to go their own way, they would soon become a community of strangers. Her decision became clear. She would go back to Utah.

Louisa and Ann left California in early January with Ellen, Lois, and their families. Nothing Louisa said could convince Addison to go with them. He simply said that he would join her in the valley the next year, perhaps bringing Frances and her husband with him. He then traveled with his family over the mountain and made sure they had a place in a wagon company.

For days afterward, Louisa and her daughters wept for the loved ones they had left behind.[26]

BY LATE MARCH 1858, United States troops, now under the command of General Albert Sidney Johnston, were camped on the outskirts of Utah Territory. Trying to slow the troops' advance, the Saints' militia had spent part of the fall raiding the army's supplies and burning wagons and forts. The raids had frustrated and humiliated the soldiers, who spent the winter hunkered down in the snow beside the charred ruins of their wagons, surviving on poor rations and cursing the Saints.

That winter, Thomas Kane, the Saints' trusted eastern ally, had also come to Salt Lake City, taking a risky sea voyage to California via the Isthmus of Panama and then coming overland to Utah. With the unofficial support of President James Buchanan, he met with Brigham and other Church leaders before going to the army camps to try to negotiate peace. The leaders of the army, however, scoffed at Thomas's talk of peace.[27]

"Our enemies are determined to blot us out of existence if they can," Brigham told the Saints at a special conference in Salt Lake City.[28] To save lives and perhaps win sympathy from potential allies in the eastern states, he announced a plan to move the Saints living in Salt Lake City and surrounding areas to Provo and other settlements farther south.[29] The bold move would upend the lives of many Church members, and Brigham was not entirely certain that it was the right choice to make.

"'Can a prophet or an apostle be mistaken?' Do not ask me any such question, for I will acknowledge that all the time," he declared. "But I do not acknowledge that I designedly lead this people astray one hair's breadth from the truth, and I do not knowingly do a wrong, though I may commit many wrongs."[30]

Brigham believed it was best to act decisively rather than risk having the Saints endure the same horrors they had experienced in Missouri and Illinois. Within days, he called five hundred families to move south immediately and plant crops for the thousands of Saints who would follow. He also sent men to scout out a new place to settle and instructed the Saints in southern towns to prepare to receive the exiles.[31] Soon the Saints in the Salt Lake Valley were loading wagons and preparing to move.[32]

A few weeks later, Alfred Cumming, the newly appointed governor of Utah Territory, arrived in Salt Lake City at the invitation of Thomas Kane. As a gesture of peace, he came without an army escort.[33] Alfred was fifty-five years old and had served the United States government in various capacities during his career. He also seemed to lack the usual prejudices toward the Saints.

Upon entering Salt Lake City, he saw people loading furniture and goods into wagons, gathering together livestock, and heading south. "Don't move! You shall not be hurt!" Alfred cried out to them. "I will not be governor if you don't want me!"[34] His words did nothing to change their minds.

While in Salt Lake City, Alfred and Thomas investigated some of the charges of rebellion made against the Saints and met with Brigham and other Church leaders. After a few days, Alfred was satisfied that the charges had been exaggerated.[35]

More than a week after his arrival, he spoke to a congregation in Salt Lake City. "If I err in my administration," he told the Saints, "I desire, friends, that you will come and counsel me." He acknowledged that the Saints had been grossly misrepresented outside of Utah and promised to perform his responsibilities in good faith.[36]

When he finished, the Saints were still wary, but Brigham stood up and voiced his support. It was a lukewarm welcome, but Alfred had reason to hope the Saints would accept him as their new governor.[37]

DESPITE THE GOVERNOR'S REASSURING words, the road south to Provo was choked with wagons, carriages, and livestock for forty miles or more.[38] Brigham's family occupied several buildings in Provo. Other Saints had little idea where they would live once they reached the southern settlements. There were not enough homes for everyone, and some families had nowhere to live but in wagons or tents. And with the army still on the way, many people wondered how soon they would see smoke rising from the Salt Lake Valley.[39]

On May 7, Martha Ann Smith Harris moved with her mother-in-law and the rest of the Smoot family to a place called Pond Town, about fifteen miles south of Provo.[40] Before leaving Salt Lake City, Bishop Smoot placed five kegs of gunpowder in the foundation of his house to make it easier to destroy if the army seized the city. Other members of the Sugar House Ward followed the Smoots to Pond Town, and Bishop Smoot and his counselors soon recommended organizing a new ward there.[41]

The move interrupted Martha Ann's usual routine of spinning and weaving, milking cows, making butter, teaching school, and helping her mother-in-law learn to read and write. But it also gave her and everyone else in the family new work to do.[42] The Saints in Pond Town and other settlements gathered near fresh water, built shelters, planted crops and gardens, and set up shops and mills.[43]

The spring winds blew cold at first, and the crude shelters did little to keep out the elements.[44] Poor water and supply shortages plagued the temporary settlements, but most Saints were content to be away from the army. In time they adjusted to their new homes.[45]

Most of Martha Ann's family on the Smith side moved south, but her brother Joseph, newly returned from Hawaii, remained in Salt Lake City to serve in the militia with other young men, including Johan and Carl Dorius. "I am doing little or nothing here now," Joseph reported in a letter. "The city, houses, and country look deserted and lonely."[46]

Martha Ann heard little from her husband, William, who was still on a mission in England. He had last written her in late November 1857, soon after Brigham Young had called the missionaries home. "Martha dear, my mind is full of reflection, and I hardly know where to commence," William had written. "From present prospects, I will cross the raging main shortly to my home in the West."

"So goodbye, love," he had added, "till we meet."

In his letter, William had indicated that he would be home in the spring. But spring was nearly over, and Martha Ann had seen no sign of him.[47]

BEFORE THE MOVE SOUTH, around eight thousand people had lived in Salt Lake City. Midway through June, only around fifteen hundred people remained. Most of the houses and shops had been abandoned and their doors and windows boarded up. The Saints' gardens were green and flourishing nicely despite the lack of care. Sometimes the only sound in the city was the faint trickling of the irrigation ditches lining the streets.[48]

A government peace commission arrived around this time and offered Brigham Young and the Saints full pardons from the president for their crimes, whatever they might be, in exchange for obedience to the government. The Saints did not believe they had committed crimes, but they accepted the pardons nonetheless.

In the eastern United States, people continued to mistrust and misunderstand the Saints. But now that government officials had visited Utah and Brigham had peacefully yielded his governorship to Alfred Cumming, many easterners no longer believed the Saints were in rebellion.[49] Newspaper editors who had been critical of Brigham Young were now critical of President James Buchanan.

"The Mormon war has been unquestionably a mass of blunders from beginning to end," wrote one reporter. "Whichever way we look at it, it is a great mass of stupid blunders."[50]

On June 26, 1858, the army marched into Salt Lake City. The place looked like a ghost town. There was grass growing in the streets and in the dooryards of houses. Before leaving, the Saints had buried the temple's foundation to protect it from plundering soldiers. When the troops passed by the temple lot, they saw what looked like a plowed field.[51]

AT THE END OF the Utah War, as the crisis came to be known, Brigham Young encouraged everyone to return to their homes. Many Saints started back northward in early July. At a narrow point where the mountains divided the Utah and Salt Lake Valleys, they watched the army marching toward them. The troops were headed for Camp Floyd, a new outpost in a remote area called Cedar Valley, forty miles southwest of Salt Lake City.[52]

As the army passed near the Saints, some soldiers harassed the young women or the men who traveled in carriages with their plural wives. Eventually the road became too congested, so returning Saints waited three hours for the army to pass. When the roads finally cleared, the Saints continued home.[53]

The move south had scattered the Church like crumbs across the southern valleys, and it would take time and means to gather them back north. As the Saints returned home, they found their houses, farms, and public works in disarray. Many wards had stopped functioning. Most Relief Societies and Sunday Schools had disbanded altogether.[54]

When the Smoot family left Pond Town in mid-July, Martha Ann drove a team of horses for her in-laws. On July 12, as she rounded the mountain and drove into the Salt Lake Valley, she saw a figure in the distance riding toward her on a white mule. They drew closer together, and to Martha Ann's surprise, the rider was her husband, William, home from his mission.[55]

CHAPTER 20

Handwriting on
the Wall

In the summer of 1858, around the time the army passed through Salt Lake City, a schoolteacher named Karl Maeser received a flattering offer from the family of John Tyler, a former president of the United States. For months Karl had been teaching music lessons to the children of John and Julia Tyler at a spacious plantation in the southern United States. A German immigrant, Karl had impressed the Tylers with his good education, gentlemanly manners, and subtle humor. Now they wanted to pay him a salary to live near them and continue teaching their children.[1]

The offer was almost too generous to refuse. A financial crisis had crippled the economy shortly after Karl and his wife, Anna, arrived from Germany. Tens of thousands of people lost their jobs in cities across the United

States, Canada, and Europe. For a time, Karl and Anna had struggled to find work and put food on the table. Teaching the Tyler children gave the Maesers and their three-year-old son, Reinhard, some financial stability.[2]

But Karl did not intend to accept the Tylers' offer. He had once told Julia Tyler that all he needed to be happy was a little house and a garden for his family. What he had not told her was that he and Anna were Latter-day Saints who had come to the United States to gather to Zion. One reason Karl had sought work in the South, aside from providing for his family, was to make enough money to migrate west.[3]

Karl had first learned about the Church while living in Germany. After reading a book hostile to the Church and its message, he contacted the leaders of the European mission. Apostle Franklin Richards and a missionary named William Budge soon came to Germany and taught his family the gospel. Karl and Anna accepted it quickly.

Since joining the Church was illegal in Germany, Franklin had baptized the schoolteacher at night. When Karl came out of the water, he had lifted his hands to the sky and prayed, "Father, if what I have done just now is pleasing unto Thee, give me a testimony, and whatever Thou shouldst require of my hands I shall do."[4]

Karl did not know English at the time, so he and Franklin had talked through an interpreter. But as they walked back to the city, Karl and Franklin suddenly began to understand each other, as if both were speaking the same language. This manifestation of the gift of tongues was the witness Karl had sought, and he intended to remain true to his word, regardless of the cost.[5]

Now, three years later, he was still striving to keep the promise he had made at his baptism. Determined to go to Zion, Karl turned down the Tylers' offer and moved his family to Philadelphia, a large city in the northeastern states, where he was soon called to preside over a small branch of the Church.[6]

Before the recent crisis in Utah, such branches had played a vital role in supporting missionary work and emigration, defending the Church against critics, and lobbying the government on the Church's behalf. But after Brigham Young summoned missionaries home and urged eastern Saints to come west, many of the eastern branches lacked enough members or funds to carry on these activities.[7]

Being a Latter-day Saint could be challenging in the East. The Church's reputation in the region had plummeted over the last decade. Many people continued to believe the Saints were rebellious and unpatriotic. A Church leader received a death threat in New York City, and some Saints were tarred and feathered for their beliefs. Others kept their membership in the Church quiet to avoid further persecution.[8]

In Philadelphia, Anna earned money as a seamstress and housekeeper while Karl ministered to branch members, attended regional Church conferences, and helped plan the next emigration season. They did what they could to strengthen their small branch.[9] But for the Church to prosper there and throughout the world, the Saints needed to oppose the false ideas and misunderstandings about them that abounded.

And they needed more missionaries to return to the field and continue the work of salvation.

IN EARLY SEPTEMBER 1858, George Q. Cannon was publishing the *Deseret News* in a central Utah town called Fillmore. The newspaper was normally headquartered in Salt Lake City, but when the Saints moved south earlier that year, George and his family had packed up the heavy printing equipment and hauled it about 150 miles to Fillmore.[10]

Now that it was safe to return to Salt Lake City, George decided to bring the printing operation back north. On September 9, he and his younger brother David loaded the printing equipment into wagons and headed back to the city with George's growing family. George and Elizabeth now had a one-year-old son, John, and another baby on the way. George had also married a second wife, Sarah Jane Jenne, and she too was expecting.

Four days after leaving Fillmore, the Cannons stopped to rest in a town about seventy miles from Salt Lake City. While George was unhitching his teams, a man in a mule-drawn carriage rode up beside him. He was a messenger from Brigham Young and had been searching for George since the night before. He said that Brigham had expected George to be in the city already. The Church was sending missionaries out again, and a company of elders was waiting to leave with George on his mission to the eastern United States.

George was confused. What mission to the East? Within half an hour, he and Elizabeth packed a small suitcase and rushed off to Salt Lake City with John while David followed soon after with Sarah Jane and the printing equipment. George arrived in the city the next morning at five o'clock and went to Brigham's office immediately after breakfast. Brigham greeted him and asked, "Are you ready?"

"I am," George said.

Brigham turned to one of the men beside him. "I told you it would be so," he said. A clerk then handed George instructions for his mission.[11]

Once again, the Utah territorial legislature was petitioning the United States Congress for statehood and the right to elect or appoint all local government officials. Knowing another statehood petition would fail if public opinion about the Church remained low, Brigham wanted George to go on a special mission to preside over the eastern Saints, publish positive newspaper articles about the Church, and improve its reputation throughout the country.[12]

George felt the weight of the mission immediately. He had to leave the following day, hardly giving him time to settle his family in the valley. Yet he believed the

Lord would provide a way to carry out His will. George's experiences in Hawaii and California had prepared him for a mission of this size and responsibility. And he knew his siblings and other relatives, including his aunt and uncle Leonora and John Taylor, would be able to help his wives and children.

Brigham blessed George and set him apart as a missionary. George then blessed Elizabeth and John and committed them and Sarah Jane, who was still traveling north, to the care of the Lord. The next afternoon he and a small group of missionaries headed east across the Rocky Mountains.[13]

MEANWHILE, IN SANPETE VALLEY'S Fort Ephraim, Augusta Dorius Stevens finally had most of her family near her. Her sisters-in-law Elen and Karen had followed her father, Nicolai, to Fort Ephraim when the Saints moved south. Augusta's older brothers Carl and Johan had come a short time later, after being released from guard duty in Salt Lake City. Her younger sister Rebekke also lived in town. Only their mother, Ane Sophie, was still in Denmark and not a member of the Church.[14]

Since marrying Henry Stevens four years earlier, Augusta had run the household and taken care of Henry's ailing first wife, Mary Ann, whom she loved dearly.[15] At age nineteen, Augusta also became the first president of the Fort Ephraim Female Relief Society. Along with attending to the sick and suffering, she and her Relief

Society sisters wove cloth, made quilts, provided food and shelter for the needy, and cared for orphans. When someone in town passed away, they washed and dressed the dead, made burial clothes, comforted mourners, and preserved the body before the funeral with ice from the San Pitch River.[16]

Shortly before the Dorius family was reunited, Augusta gave birth to a boy named Jason, who died during an epidemic before he was a year old. Despite her grief, Augusta had found a home and certainly comfort within the large community of Scandinavian Saints in Sanpete Valley, who drew on shared customs, traditions, and languages to endure the trials of their new home. While on their missions, her brothers had taught and baptized many of these Saints, which no doubt strengthened her bonds with them.

When Carl and Johan arrived at Fort Ephraim in 1858, they tried their hand at farming, but grasshoppers destroyed their crops. More experienced settlers like Augusta and Henry had suffered similar challenges while farming in Sanpete Valley. The first Saints who came to the area had faced several years of devastating frosts and insect infestations. To survive, they lived together in two forts, worked a common field, and shared irrigation water. When a good crop finally came in, they filled their granaries and stored other food.[17]

In the summer of 1859, Augusta's life changed when Brigham Young called several Sanpete families to settle near the old Spring Town settlement, where

Augusta had lived briefly when she first came to the valley. Augusta and Henry moved there a short time later. Men surveyed a townsite and 640 acres for farming. The farmland was then surveyed into 5- and 10-acre lots and divided among the families. Soon houses, cabins, and a log meetinghouse graced the new settlement. With so many Danes living in the area, residents nicknamed it Little Denmark.[18]

After settling in Spring Town, Henry began building a gristmill. While cutting and hauling timber in the mountains that winter, he caught a terrible cold and soon developed a nagging cough. The cough turned into asthma, making it hard for Henry to work. There were no doctors in town, so Augusta tried every remedy she could find to ease Henry's breathing. Nothing helped.[19]

About a year after Augusta and Henry moved to Spring Town, the First Presidency called Augusta's brothers Johan and Carl back to Scandinavia on missions. Since neither brother had means for travel, the Saints in Fort Ephraim and Spring Town provided them with a wagon, a horse, and a mule.[20]

IN THE SUMMER OF 1860, a few months after the Dorius brothers started on their missions, George Q. Cannon was called home from his mission to the East.[21] Over the past two years, he and the Saints' longtime ally Thomas Kane had published several positive articles about the Church in newspapers and lobbied on behalf of the Church.

Working closely with Karl Maeser and other Church leaders, George had also strengthened the Saints in New York, Boston, Philadelphia, and other eastern branches.[22]

But public opinion remained staunchly against the Church. A new political party, the Republicans, had recently formed to put an end to slavery and polygamy, denouncing these practices as the "twin relics of barbarism."[23] Republicans linked the two practices because they wrongly assumed that women were coerced into plural marriage with no way to escape. Of the two issues, however, slavery was causing a greater rift in the nation, leading many people, including George, to predict a national calamity.

"No man who loves liberty and free and liberal institutions can witness these things without feeling that the glory of our nation is rapidly fading away," George wrote in a letter to Brigham Young. "The destruction of the government of the United States is inevitable. It will be merely a question of time."[24]

During his mission, George also received a letter from Brigham about a recent decision of the First Presidency and Quorum of the Twelve. In a meeting in October 1859, Brigham had proposed calling a new apostle to replace Parley Pratt. He asked the Twelve for recommendations. "Any man who will be faithful will have intelligence enough to magnify his calling," Brigham told the Twelve.

"I would like to know on what principle men are to be selected," said Orson Pratt, Parley's younger brother.

"If a man was suggested to me of good natural judgment, possessing no higher qualifications than faithfulness and humility enough to seek the Lord for all his knowledge and who would trust in Him for his strength," Brigham replied, "I would prefer him to the learned and talented."

"If the Lord should designate a boy twelve years old, he is the person we would all be willing to sustain," Orson said. "But if left to my own judgment to choose, I would select a man of experience who was tried in many places, faithful, and diligent, and a man of talent who could defend the Church in any position in which he might be placed."

Brigham listened as the apostles recommended several men for the position. "I nominate George Q. Cannon for one of the Twelve," he then said. "He is modest, but I don't think he will let modesty smother his obligations to do his duty."[25]

George's call was announced at the spring general conference, while George was preparing to return home. He received the appointment with a sense of his own weakness and unworthiness. "I trembled with fear and dread," the thirty-three-year-old wrote Brigham soon after learning of the call, "and joy to think of the goodness and favor of the Lord and the love and confidence of my brethren."[26]

As he traveled home a few months later, George hurried ahead of several wagon companies and two handcart companies, which he had organized with Saints from the eastern branches, Europe, and South Africa.[27]

Mindful of the handcart tragedy of 1856, George wisely sent the last handcart company ahead of several wagon trains. "I have endeavored to take all possible steps to avoid any mishap," he informed Brigham, "and sincerely trust that with the blessing of the Lord they will all reach their destinations in safety."[28]

AMONG THE SAINTS TRAVELING west with George that season was Church patriarch John Smith. John had come east in late 1859 to try once more to help his sister Lovina and her family gather to Utah. While they waited for the emigration season to begin, he and Lovina visited their Smith relatives in Nauvoo, including their aunt Emma and her children.[29]

Emma led a quiet life in Nauvoo. She still lived in the Nauvoo Mansion and owned former Church property, which Joseph had given her before his death in 1844. He had deeded the land to her in good faith, but some of his creditors later demanded this property be sold to pay them back, believing he had cheated them. They failed to prove their accusations. The matter was settled in 1852 when a federal judge decreed that all the land Joseph had held as trustee for the Church in excess of ten acres could be sold to pay his debts. As Joseph's widow, Emma was awarded one-sixth of the proceeds of the sale, which she used to buy back some of the land to support her family.[30]

John and Lovina found their relatives well but divided in matters of religion. Their cousin Julia had married a Catholic and converted to her husband's religion. Joseph and Emma's four sons, however, still considered themselves Latter-day Saints, although they rejected some of the principles their father had taught in Nauvoo, particularly plural marriage.[31]

This was no surprise to John. Although Emma knew that her husband had privately taught and practiced plural marriage, her son Joseph Smith III believed that Brigham Young had introduced the principle to the Saints after the prophet Joseph's death. When John's family had evacuated Nauvoo in 1848, John had tried to convince Joseph III to come west with him and continue the work of their fathers. Joseph III had flatly refused.

"If you mean by this that I must support spiritual wifery and the other institutions which have been instituted since their deaths," Joseph III had responded, "I most assuredly shall be your most inveterate adversary."[32]

For many years, Joseph III had shown little interest in leading a church. But on April 6, 1860, after John and Lovina's visit, Joseph III and Emma had attended a conference of a "New Organization" of Saints who had rejected the leadership of Brigham Young and remained in the Midwest. During that meeting, Joseph III had accepted leadership over the New Organization and distanced himself from the Saints in Utah by condemning plural marriage.[33]

A few months later, John started west with Lovina and her family. Traveling in their company were Karl and Anna Maeser. Unaccustomed to life on the rugged trail, the young schoolteacher did his best to drive an ox team, but he eventually hired a driver to do the work for him. Whooping cough plagued the children in the company for part of the journey, but the trail was uneventful much of the time.[34]

On August 17, about 160 miles from Salt Lake City, Lovina's fourteen-year-old son, Hyrum Walker, accidentally shot himself in the arm. Hoping to save his nephew's life, if not his arm, John quickly put another man in charge of the company, placed Hyrum in a mule cart, and rushed him and Lovina ahead to the valley.

The mule cart arrived in Salt Lake City nine days later, and a doctor was able to mend Hyrum's arm. With his nephew safe, John returned to his company and led them into the city on September 1.[35]

ON NOVEMBER 4, 1860, WILFORD Woodruff welcomed a man named Walter Gibson back to Salt Lake City. Walter was a world traveler and adventurer. As a young man, he had traveled to Mexico and South America, sailed the oceans, and escaped a Dutch prison on the island of Java.[36]

According to Walter, he had heard a voice in prison prompting him to establish a powerful kingdom in the

Pacific. For years he had searched for a people to help him in this mission, but he could never find the right group until he heard about the Latter-day Saints. In May 1859, he had written to Brigham Young and proposed a plan to gather the Church to the Pacific Islands. He traveled to Salt Lake City with his three children a short time later and joined the Church in January 1860.[37]

Wilford had befriended Walter that winter, often attending lectures he gave on his travels or meeting him at social gatherings.[38] Brigham had no interest in Walter's proposal for a new gathering place, but he had recognized potential in the new convert.[39] Walter seemed knowledgeable, well-spoken, and eager to serve in the Church. In April 1860, the First Presidency had called him on a short mission to the East, which Walter had enthusiastically accepted.[40]

Now, six months later, Walter had returned to Utah with exciting news. While in New York City, he had told an official at the Japanese embassy about the Saints and received an invitation to come to Japan. Believing he could forge a good relationship with the Japanese, Walter wanted to accept the invitation and prepare the way for missionary work in that land. From there, he believed, the restored gospel could spread to Siam and other nations in the region.

"I shall be governed, as I have been instructed, entirely by the Spirit of God," he told the Saints at a meeting on November 18. "I feel I shall be at home with all the nations of the children of the human family."[41]

The prospect of sending Walter to Asia excited Wilford. "The Lord opened the door before him in a marvelous manner," he noted in his journal.[42]

Brigham agreed. "Brother Gibson is going to leave us now to go on a mission," he told the Saints at the meeting. "As far as I can learn, he came here because the Lord led him here."[43]

The following day, Heber Kimball and Brigham placed their hands on Walter's head. "Inasmuch as thou will let thine eye be single to the glory of God, and call upon His name, and seek His wisdom, and seek to be humble and meek before the Lord, and let thine eye be for the good and welfare of the children of man," Heber declared, "thou shall be blessed mightily, and thou shall gather up the house of Israel and bring many to repentance and baptize and confirm upon them the Holy Ghost."[44]

Walter and his daughter, Talula, started for the Pacific two days later.[45]

ONE MONTH AFTER WALTER'S departure, South Carolina, a state in the southern United States, withdrew from the nation, fearing the recent election of Abraham Lincoln to the U.S. presidency would alter the economic and political balance of power in the country and lead to the end of slavery. Wilford Woodruff immediately recognized the alarming event as a fulfillment of a revelation Joseph Smith had received twenty-eight years earlier. On

Christmas Day 1832, the Lord had warned the prophet that a rebellion would soon begin in South Carolina and end in the death and misery of many people.[46]

"With the sword and by bloodshed the inhabitants of the earth shall mourn," the Lord had declared, "and with famine, and plague, and earthquake, and the thunder of heaven, and the fierce and vivid lightning also, shall the inhabitants of the earth be made to feel the wrath, and indignation, and chastening hand of an Almighty God, until the consumption decreed hath made a full end of all nations."[47]

"We may prepare ourselves for an awful time in the United States," Wilford wrote in his journal on January 1, 1861. "The handwriting has been seen upon the wall, and our nation is doomed to destruction."[48]

CHAPTER 21

The Same Great Work

War excitement is driving the people mad," apostles Orson Pratt and Erastus Snow wrote to Brigham Young in the spring of 1861. "Armies are enlisting, drilling, marching, and concentrating for the terrible conflict. And the time may soon come when no man will be permitted to remain in the North or in the South who will not fight."[1]

South Carolina's dramatic exit from the United States had sparked widespread rebellion throughout the South. In the months that followed, ten more southern states left the nation, and the U.S. government scrambled to fortify its military bases. Southern forces quickly seized all but the strongest forts, however, and President Abraham Lincoln recruited seventy-five thousand soldiers to put down the rebellion. The force soon proved too small to handle the crisis.[2]

Orson had been watching the conflict build since he and Erastus had traveled east in the fall to oversee the eastern mission. As a young missionary in the 1830s, Orson had carried in his pocket a copy of Joseph Smith's prophecy on war, which he would sometimes read to congregations. Most people thought it was nonsense back then, but it was having a different effect now.[3] Orson read the revelation in public and arranged to have it published in the *New York Times*.[4] Other newspapers also published the prophecy.

"Have we not had a prophet among us?" asked one Philadelphia newspaper that printed the revelation. "In view of our present troubles, this prediction seems to be in progress of fulfillment, whether Joe Smith was a humbug or not."[5]

As the armies of the North and South mobilized for civil war, the missionaries under Orson and Erastus rallied the eastern Saints to gather to Zion. Church leaders scoured the cities and countryside for Saints who had wandered from the fold and urged them to return.[6]

The response was overwhelming. Around a thousand Saints from Philadelphia, New York, and Boston boarded a train for Florence in June. "The train was so lengthy and heavy," Orson reported to Brigham, "that two engines were required to drag it along." Five hundred Church members from the midwestern states also started west on foot and by wagon.[7]

But the massive migration was not limited to Americans. Saints came west across the Atlantic Ocean in droves in the spring of 1861. The year before, the First Presidency had called George Q. Cannon to join Amasa Lyman and Charles Rich in presiding over the British mission and directing emigration.[8] That season, they sent two thousand Saints from Europe and South Africa to Zion.

Rather than supply handcarts for the many emigrants who could not pay their way to Utah, the Church sent two hundred wagons and seventeen hundred oxen—many of them donated by Utah wards—to the Missouri River. The needy Saints were then divided into four "down and back" wagon companies that carried them to Utah at the relatively low price of fourteen dollars for adults and seven dollars for children.[9]

Meanwhile, people throughout the country wondered if Utah would stay with the Union, join the Southern rebels, or form an independent nation. Many Saints still blamed the United States government for failing to redress the losses they had suffered in Missouri and Illinois. They also resented the government-appointed officials, the army's presence in Utah, and Congress's refusal to grant Utah statehood.[10]

Yet Brigham Young believed the right course for Utah was to stay in the nation, regardless of its policies against the Saints. "Utah has not seceded," he assured lawmakers in the East, "but is firm for the Constitution and laws of our once happy country."[11]

AFTER CIVIL WAR BROKE out in the East, regular reports of bloody battles came west with the mail. The grim accounts told of hundreds, sometimes thousands, of deaths.[12] Some people in the Church believed that God was punishing the United States for its treatment of the Saints.[13]

A handful of Saints went east to take part in the war, but most Church members were content to stay in Utah and build up Zion. That summer, Brigham Young proposed to uncover the temple foundation, which had lain buried since the move south, and begin the temple walls. He also announced a plan, already underway, to build a large theater a few blocks from the temple site.[14]

Though the city's Social Hall already functioned as a small playhouse, Brigham wanted a theater that would inspire the minds and imaginations of the Saints. Drama had a way of teaching and edifying people in ways sermons could not. Having a magnificent theater in Salt Lake City would also show visitors that the Saints were a cultured and refined people, countering the negative images of Saints in many newspapers.[15]

The idea to build a theater had come to Brigham earlier that year. He and Heber Kimball had attended a play in the home of the Bowring family, who had equipped the ground floor of their house with a small stage. Henry and Marian Bowring were members of the Mechanics' Dramatic Association, an acting company composed mainly of British Saints, including some handcart pioneers. Marian herself had come west with her daughter, Emily, in the Martin handcart company.

Brigham and Heber enjoyed the performance at the Bowrings' theater, and they returned the following evening to attend another play with their families.[16] Soon Brigham proposed combining the Mechanics' Dramatic Association with another acting company, the Deseret Dramatic Association, and building a larger theater so more Saints could enjoy the best entertainment in the territory.

Though Brigham believed in the value of work, he also encouraged the Saints to rest and enjoy life. "The people must have amusements," he declared. He believed that recreation and physical exercise were important to both body and soul.[17]

To pay for the theater, Brigham diverted funds from a stalled construction project, the Seventies Hall of Science.[18] The theater project received additional funding that summer when the U.S. Army troops stationed in Cedar Valley were summoned back east to fight in the Civil War. Before the soldiers departed, Brigham sent Hiram Clawson, his son-in-law and manager of the new theater, to purchase some of the army's iron, livestock, dry goods, and other materials at a bargain. Brigham then sold these items at a higher price to fund the construction of the theater.[19]

On August 5, the First Presidency and their clerks visited the construction site for the theater. Stepping down from the carriage, Brigham inspected the stone foundation with Heber. "The rocks look of a very en-during character," Heber said.

Brigham agreed. "I always like to see some kind of a building going on."[20]

In the weeks and months that followed, the theater sprang up quickly.[21] Unaware of the careful planning happening behind the scenes on the larger and more complex temple, some people lamented that construc-tion on the house of the Lord seemed to be moving much slower than on the theater. Workers had only recently begun digging up the buried foundation of the temple and cutting large granite blocks in a new quarry twenty miles to the south. Why were the Saints spending so much time and money on a theater while the house of the Lord was still unbuilt?[22]

Their objections did not trouble Brigham. He did not want work on the temple to be hurried, and he was not concerned about the cost of construction—as long as it was done properly. Before the temple foun-dation was buried in 1858, workers had not installed the stones properly, making portions of the sandstone foundation susceptible to cracking under the temple's massive weight.[23] Once the foundation was excavated, he had the workers repair the damaged sandstone and replace any stone that was beyond repair with granite from the quarry.

"Do a good work on this temple," he told the temple foremen. He wanted the workers to take the time to do it right. "I want to see the temple built in a manner that it will endure through the Millennium," he declared. "This is not the only temple we shall build. There will be hundreds of them built and dedicated to the Lord."[24]

The Salt Lake Theatre opened on March 6, 1862, for a special dedicatory service with a prayer and speeches from Church leaders. Afterward, the theater company performed a comedy called *The Pride of the Market*. Two nights later, the theater opened its doors to the public. Hundreds of people, eager to get a seat, crowded outside the theater two hours before the performance. When the curtain rose, there was not an empty seat in the house.

The Saints' enthusiasm for the theater pleased Brigham. "Hell is a great distance from us, and we can never arrive there, unless we change our path," he declared during the festivities, "for the way we are now pursuing leads to heaven and happiness."[25]

ON MAY 5, GEORGE Q. CANNON received a puzzling telegram from Salt Lake City. He was in the Liverpool office of the British and European mission, where he had served as president for the last year and a half.

"Join Senator Hooper Washington," the telegram read. "May twenty-fifth."

A tremor shot through George's body, and he grabbed a nearby desk to steady himself. He could hardly breathe. Once again, an assignment from Salt Lake City had taken him by surprise. And the vagueness of this assignment only made it more shocking. Why was he needed in Washington, DC?[26]

George knew that Utah's territorial legislature had recently drafted another statehood petition for the United States Congress. That meant two senators would be elected to go to Congress to represent the proposed state and lobby for the petition. The telegram seemed to suggest that William Hooper, Utah's former delegate to Congress, was one of the senators.[27] Had George been elected as the other?

George had a taste for politics. As a boy, he had received a blessing promising him that he would some-day occupy a responsible position in government. But as much as he wanted to represent Utah in Congress, he cast the desire aside, just in case Church leaders needed him in Washington for a different reason.[28]

Recently, Justin Morrill, a member of the United States House of Representatives, had introduced a law in Congress that would outlaw bigamy, or marriage to more than one spouse at the same time, in all U.S. territories.[29] Perhaps the Saints needed George to lobby for their right to practice plural marriage. If passed, the Morrill law would make criminals of George and other Saints who practiced the principle. It would also limit the Church's influence in Utah by restricting the amount of property it could own.[30]

On the day of his departure, George blessed his wife Elizabeth and daughter, Georgiana, who had been born while the couple was in England. Neither Elizabeth nor the baby was healthy enough to go with him, so George entrusted them to the care of their new friends in England while he was away.

When he arrived in the United States two weeks later, he learned that he had indeed been elected to serve alongside William Hooper in the Senate if the statehood petition was approved. The appointment granted them no official authority, but they could try to persuade lawmakers to vote against the Morrill antibigamy bill and in favor of Utah's bid to become a state.[31]

On June 13, George and William visited President Abraham Lincoln, hoping to win his support for their petition. George expected the president to look tired and careworn after more than a year of civil war, but Lincoln chatted and joked with them in a friendly manner. He was a tall, plain man with a bearded face and awkward limbs. He listened politely as George and William made their case for statehood, but he made no promise to support their petition.[32]

George and William left the White House disappointed. The meeting had been like other discussions they'd had with other politicians in Washington. Most lawmakers seemed open-minded about statehood for Utah, but they were unwilling to promise their votes. Believing they could not support Utah statehood after having voted for the antibigamy law, a few lawmakers refused to consider granting statehood to Utah until its constitution outlawed plural marriage.[33]

Outrage over the Mountain Meadows massacre also kept some people from supporting the Saints and their bid for statehood.[34] About a year after John D. Lee gave his report of the massacre, Church investigators had discovered that John and other Church members were involved in the attack. A short time later, government officials had conducted their own investigations. They tried to bring John D. Lee, Isaac Haight, John Higbee, and others to justice, but no witnesses came forward to testify against them. Investigators located the eleven girls and six boys who survived the attack, however, and returned them to relatives or friends in the summer of 1859.[35]

George and William hoped that their diligence to win support for the petition was making a good impression on lawmakers in Washington. Still, neither man knew if their efforts were enough to win statehood for the people of Utah.[36]

WHILE THE STATEHOOD PETITION was under review in Washington, missionary work in Denmark, Norway, and Sweden was thriving. More than two years had passed since Johan and Carl Dorius had left Sanpete Valley to serve their second mission to Scandinavia. For most of that time, Carl had presided over the Saints in Norway with Johan as his first counselor.[37]

When the brothers had arrived in Scandinavia, Johan had gone immediately to Norway. Carl, however, had visited their estranged mother, Ane Sophie, in Copenhagen. At first, Ane Sophie did not recognize her son. But once Carl told her who he was, she kissed him again and again on the forehead, overjoyed that he was back from America. Like Nicolai, her former husband and Carl's father, she had remarried. She and her husband, Hans Birch, had adopted a girl named Julia, now eight years old.[38]

As Carl and Ane Sophie spoke for the first time in three years, he marveled at the changes that had come over her. Before he and Johan had left for Zion, she had been embarrassed to walk beside them in public. But the Church's reputation in Denmark had since improved, and the day after Carl arrived, Ane Sophie agreed not only to go out in public with him but also to attend a Church meeting.

When mother and son entered the hall where the Saints met, they found the room full. Carl recognized many faces in the congregation from his first mission, and after he addressed the group, several people came up to shake his hand and welcome him back to the country.

Ane Sophie rarely left her son's side in the days that followed. After Carl visited the Church's headquarters in Denmark, he was a little embarrassed that he was still wearing the same shabby suit he had worn during his last mission. His mother took him out to get a new suit and then joined him as he visited old friends in the city. As they talked together, Carl could tell that his mother was more interested in the Church than ever before.

After visiting Ane Sophie, Carl joined Johan in Norway. The brothers discovered that many Norwegian branches had shrunk because of emigration, but around 600 Saints still resided in Norway, with around 250 in the capital city of Christiania. The Norwegian government had yet to legalize religious freedom, so the missionaries were cautious when they preached or baptized publicly.[39]

In early 1862, as Carl was preaching in southern Norway, police apprehended him and ten other missionaries, questioned them in front of a mocking crowd, and threatened them with fines and imprisonment. Such harassment did little to stop the work. By the spring of that year, 1,556 Scandinavian Saints were preparing to emigrate to Zion—the largest emigration yet.

Around this time, Carl returned to Copenhagen to visit his mother again. Ane Sophie had a good spirit about her. She seemed more serious and still interested in the Church. Once again, she attended Church meetings with Carl, sometimes bringing Julia along.

In June 1862, Carl took his mother and Julia to Christiania for a short trip. The prejudice and bitterness Ane Sophie had once felt toward the Saints were gone, and she and Julia agreed to have Carl baptize and confirm them into the Church. After the ordinances were performed, the Saints in Norway showered Ane Sophie with attention, happy to finally meet the mother of their mission leader.[40]

312

ON JULY 20, ELIZABETH CANNON received a letter from George. His work in Washington was done, and he was eager to return to Liverpool on one of the next two departing steamships. The letter did not give Elizabeth much hope that George would catch the earlier ship. But she would be glad to see him, whenever he arrived.

The next day, she rode out to a grassy hill overlooking Liverpool with Georgiana and watched her play in the grass. Having left her little sons John and Abraham in the care of family in Utah, Elizabeth was grateful to have Georgiana with her. "She is a great comfort to me in the absence of my dear husband," she noted in her journal the following day. "I could not content myself were it not for her."[41]

She could not have known, when George left on his first mission to California and Hawaii, how hard their absences from each other would be. Helping to gather God's people was a vital part of the latter-day work, but it often took an immense emotional and physical toll on the women who stayed behind to care for family and look after home and property while their husbands were away. Elizabeth had been fortunate enough to go with George on some of his missions,[42] which is more than most wives of missionaries could say. But that did not make the long separations easier when they happened.

A few days after receiving George's letter, Elizabeth was tidying up the house while Georgiana played with

Rosina Mathews, a little English girl the Cannons had taken into their home. As the girls played, Rosina glanced out a window overlooking the street. "Here comes Pa," she sang out.

"You must be mistaken," Elizabeth said.

"He is in a cab," Rosina insisted, "at the door."

Just then Elizabeth heard the familiar sound of George's footsteps on the stairs. When she saw him, her heart leapt with joy, and she could scarcely speak. Georgiana ran up to him, and he took her in his arms. He looked well after his long journey and was pleased to see Elizabeth stronger and healthier than when he had left.

That afternoon, the family took a walk. "We all enjoyed ourselves very much together, after so long a separation," Elizabeth wrote in her journal. "Our home was happy again."[43]

Despite George's best efforts, his lobbying in Washington had been unsuccessful. President Lincoln signed the antibigamy bill into law on July 8. A short time later, lawmakers informed George and William that Congress had more important matters to decide than statehood for Utah—especially since the American Civil War was only getting worse.[44]

Now that George was back in Europe, he wanted to tour the mission with Elizabeth. They left Liverpool in September in company with John Smith, the Church patriarch, who was passing through England on his way to a mission in Scandinavia. Along the way they picked up John's brother Joseph F. Smith and his cousin Samuel Smith, who had been serving missions in London since 1860. Another Smith cousin, Jesse Smith, was president of the Scandinavian mission, and he had invited his cousins to visit with him once John arrived in Europe.

The party left England on September 3 and passed through Hamburg, Germany, on their way to Denmark. Joseph and Samuel looked tired and thin from overwork, but they seemed to improve with each passing day. In Denmark, Elizabeth felt somewhat awkward traveling through a country where she did not know the language. When she attended a conference in the city of Aalborg, though, she enjoyed mingling with the Saints.[45]

George and the other missionaries addressed the congregation with help from interpreters, and afterward they gathered on a hill overlooking the city to talk and sing together. Most of the songs were in English and Danish, but George and Joseph entertained the Saints by singing in Hawaiian as well. The joy they felt as fellow Saints, despite differences in language and nationality, stood in stark contrast to the discord then afflicting the United States.[46]

"Enjoyed myself very much indeed; was highly pleased with the people," Elizabeth wrote that day in her journal. "I could not make myself understood, yet we were in the same great work and partook of the same spirit."[47]

CHAPTER 22

Like Coals of Living Fire

Evening was settling over Washington, DC, on June 5, 1863, when T. B. H. Stenhouse met with President Abraham Lincoln. A thirty-nine-year-old editor from Scotland, Stenhouse was a highly respected Latter-day Saint on both sides of the Atlantic.

As a young man, he had served missions in England, Italy, and Switzerland. Later, he led missionaries in the eastern United States and wrote articles for the widely read *New York Herald* and the *Deseret News*. He and his wife, Fanny, were well loved among the Saints in Salt Lake City and were often introduced when distinguished visitors came to the valley.[1]

In meeting Lincoln, Stenhouse wanted to gauge the president's openness to letting the Saints govern themselves. Few people in Utah expected Lincoln to enforce the new antibigamy law. To convict a Church member of bigamy, prosecutors would have to prove that a plural marriage had taken place—an almost impossible task when marriages occurred privately in the Endowment House and public officials had no access to its records. Furthermore, prosecutors in Utah were unlikely to convict someone of bigamy as long as Church members sat on juries.[2]

Yet many Saints were angry about the men Lincoln had appointed to govern them in Utah. Alfred Cumming, the person who replaced Brigham Young as governor in 1858, had resigned in 1861 as a friend to the Saints. The governor Lincoln selected to replace him, John Dawson, quickly fell out of favor with the Saints when he tried to crush the 1862 statehood petition.[3] Lincoln's next appointment, Stephen Harding, was a native of Palmyra, New York, who had been acquainted with Joseph Smith in his youth. Despite this connection, Harding quickly offended the Saints when he tried to strengthen the antibigamy law by proposing laws to keep Church members off of juries.[4]

The president listened to Stenhouse. He joked about not remembering Governor Harding's name and expressed hope that the officials he sent to Utah would behave themselves better.

Still, the American Civil War had entered its third bloody year, leaving Lincoln's face creased and careworn. Trying to turn the tide of the war, he had recently issued a proclamation freeing slaves in all Southern states and allowing blacks to join the United States Army. But the Southern army had just defeated federal forces in a large, costly battle sixty miles southwest of Washington, leaving him with bigger issues to deal with than disputes between the Saints and government officials.[5]

"In my younger days," Lincoln told Stenhouse, "I was plowing a piece of newly cleared land, and by and by I came to a big log. I could not plow over it, for it was too high, and it was so heavy I could not move it out of the way, and so wet I could not burn it. I stood and looked at it and studied it and finally concluded to plow around it."[6]

"You go back," the president continued, "and tell Brigham Young that if he will let me alone, I will let him alone."[7]

Not long after, Lincoln fired Governor Harding and appointed a more moderate politician to take his place.[8]

THE FOLLOWING JANUARY, THIRTY-THREE-YEAR-OLD Alma Smith received a letter from the island of Lanai. The brief, urgent letter was signed by six Hawaiian Church members. Among them was Solomona, an elder who had been set apart as a leader of the Church on Lanai when Alma and all other Utah missionaries left Hawaii in 1858.[9]

Alma read the letter, carefully translating the Hawaiian words into English. "The matter that we wish to write to you about," it read, "is concerning our prophet living here, Walter M. Gibson. Is it true that he is our leader?"[10]

It was no surprise that Walter Gibson was on Lanai. But the word "prophet" was alarming. The First Presidency had sent the well-known adventurer on an ambitious mission to Japan and other nations in Asia and the Pacific Ocean in 1861. A short time later, he had notified them that he and his daughter, Talula, had settled with the Saints on Lanai.[11]

Since then, Walter had kept Brigham Young informed on the promising growth of the mission and the Lanai settlement. One Hawaiian newspaper report from 1862, reprinted in the *Deseret News,* had nothing but praise for Walter's work among the Saints in Hawaii.[12] Still, why were the Saints there calling him their prophet? Walter was a missionary, nothing more.

Alma kept reading. The letter told of Walter rejecting Brigham Young's authority and establishing his own form of priesthood on the island. "He has ordained a quorum of twelve apostles, also a quorum of seventies, a number of bishops and high priests," Solomona and the other Saints wrote. "The certificates of ordinations could only be obtained by the payment of money, and if the money was not paid, the candidate was not ordained."[13]

Walter's management of Church lands was also troubling. Using donations from the Hawaiian Saints, he had purchased land in his name and now claimed it for himself. "Gibson says this land is not for the Church, nor

319

have the brethren any right or title to it," the Hawaiian Saints reported. "It belongs to him alone."

The Saints urged Alma to show their letter to Brigham Young. "We are greatly surprised at this foreigner," they wrote. "We greatly distrust him."[14]

Alma took the letter to Brigham, who read it to the Quorum of the Twelve on January 17, 1864. The apostles agreed that they had to take immediate action. Walter had set himself up as a prophet, swindled land from the Church, and oppressed the Hawaiian Saints.

"I want two of the Twelve to take several of the young brethren who have been over there before," Brigham said, "and go to the islands and set the churches in order."[15]

He selected apostles Ezra Benson and Lorenzo Snow to lead the mission. He then asked Alma Smith and two other former missionaries to Hawaii, Joseph F. Smith and William Cluff, to go and assist them.[16]

"Do what is necessary," he instructed.[17]

ON THE MORNING OF March 31, 1864, a schooner carrying the two apostles and three missionaries dropped anchor in the outer harbor of Lahaina, Maui, in the Hawaiian Islands. While Joseph F. Smith remained on deck with the group's luggage, a small boat was lowered into the water, and Ezra Benson, Lorenzo Snow, William Cluff, Alma Smith, and the ship's captain climbed aboard and began making their way to shore.

In the distance, closer to the beach, tall waves swelled dangerously high over the reef. Having traveled in and out of the harbor many times as a missionary, William Cluff worried that the water was too rough for the boat. But the captain assured him that there was nothing to fear if they stayed their course.

Moments later, a massive wave struck the boat, lifting its back end out of the water. The boat sped rapidly toward the reef, where it caught another wave that raised its back end so high that the oars no longer touched the water. When the wave broke, the boat swung around and capsized, plunging the men into the churning swells.[18]

For a moment, there was no sign of the passengers. Then William, Ezra, and Alma surfaced, gasping for air, and swam to the overturned boat. The men looked around for Lorenzo and the captain, but they were nowhere in sight.

Some Hawaiians saw the accident from the shore and immediately came to the rescue. As some rescuers fished William, Ezra, and Alma out of the water, others dove in to search for the two missing men. The divers quickly found the captain lying on the ocean floor, but there was still no sign of Lorenzo.

Suddenly, William spotted a Hawaiian man swimming toward their boat, dragging Lorenzo's body behind him. They swung the boat around, and William and Alma pulled the apostle out of the water and placed him facedown across their knees. His body was cold and stiff. He was not breathing.

When they reached shore, William and Alma carried Lorenzo up the beach, stretched him across the side of a barrel, and rolled him back and forth until water poured from his mouth. They then rubbed his arms and chest with a strong-smelling oil and rolled him across the barrel once more to make sure all the water was out of him. Lorenzo still showed no sign of life.

"We have done all that can be done," said a man from shore who assisted them. "It is impossible to save your friend."

Neither William nor Alma was willing to believe that God had brought Lorenzo all the way to Hawaii just to let him die. As a little boy, Alma himself had almost died when a mob attacked his family at Hawn's Mill, Missouri. The mob had killed his father and brother and shot him in the hip, obliterating the joint. He nearly bled to death in the smoke-filled blacksmith shop where he was wounded, but his mother had called on God for help, and the Spirit showed her how to heal his wound.[19]

Acting on faith, William and Alma tried once more to revive Lorenzo. A thought crossed William's mind to place his mouth over Lorenzo's and blow as hard as he could into the apostle's lungs. He blew in and out, again and again, until he heard a faint rattle in Lorenzo's throat. The noise encouraged him, and he blew again until the rattle turned into a groan.

"What is the matter?" Lorenzo whispered at last.

"You have been drowned," William said. He asked the apostle if he recognized him.

"Yes, Brother William, I knew you would not forsake me," he said. "Are you brethren all safe?"

"Brother Snow," said William, "we are all safe."[20]

THE FOLLOWING SUNDAY, JOSEPH F. Smith joined his companions as they traveled to the Church settlement on Lanai. When they arrived, some Hawaiian Saints recognized the former missionaries and welcomed them back with expressions of love.[21]

Walter met the apostles and missionaries at the gate of his large thatched house. He was not expecting them, and his gaze was anxious and inquiring. He shook hands with them coldly and introduced them to his daughter, Talula, who was in her twenties. He then ushered them into his house and served a large breakfast of sweet potatoes, boiled goat, and other foods. The whole time his manner was distant and formal.[22]

After breakfast, Walter took the men to his Sabbath meeting with the Hawaiian Saints. An elaborately dressed "supreme bishop" rang a bell to assemble the congregation together. As the Saints filed in, fifteen or twenty young men wearing wreaths of flowers and green leaves sat down on a bench at the head of the meetinghouse. Seventeen boys and seventeen girls, each dressed in a uniform, then took seats near a table where the bishop sat with men Walter had set apart as apostles.

When Walter entered the room, the congregation stood and bowed reverently as he passed them and sat down at the head of the table. After the opening prayer, he rose and acknowledged the five visitors from Utah. "I do not know what they have come for," he said, "but they will perhaps tell us."

"This I will say," he added. "I have come here among you, bought you land, and here I will remain immovably, and in this I will not yield!"[23]

Over the next two days, the apostles met privately with Walter. His misdeeds, they learned, went well beyond selling priesthood ordinations.[24] It was almost too strange to believe.

When Walter came to Lanai, he saw an opportunity to begin the vast Pacific empire he had long dreamed of establishing.[25] He persuaded the Hawaiian Saints to donate their livestock and personal property to him so that he could purchase land on the island.[26] Inspiring the Saints with his dream of empire, he organized a militia on the island and trained its members to invade other islands. He also sent missionaries to Samoa and other Polynesian islands to prepare those lands for his rule.

The people soon began treating him like a king. No one entered his house to speak with him except on hands and knees. To inspire awe, he designated a hollowed-out boulder near his house to be the cornerstone of a temple. He placed a Book of Mormon and other documents in the rock, covered it with brush, and warned the Saints that they would be smitten if they went near it.

When the apostles and missionaries finished their investigation, Ezra Benson and Lorenzo Snow called all the Saints together to address Walter's future as a leader. With Joseph acting as translator, Ezra condemned Walter's seizure of Church lands and abuses of priesthood authority.

"It is our duty to disfellowship him," Ezra declared, "and if he does not veer his boat into the channel and repent, we shall have to cut him off from the Church."[27]

Walter whispered something to Talula, and she quickly fetched a stack of papers ornately decorated with seals and ribbons. "Gentlemen, here is my authority," he said, pointing to three signatures at the bottom of one page. "You will not fail to recognize the names of Brigham Young and his two counselors here."

Lorenzo read the document. It was a simple missionary license to preach the gospel to the islands of the sea. "This document does not appoint you to preside over the Hawaiian mission," Lorenzo said. "You have assumed that authority."[28]

"I have seen President Young," Walter said. "He laid his hands on me and blessed me. And God Almighty poured out mightily His Spirit upon me, before I saw him, when I lay in that prison, and revealed to me that I had a great and mighty work to do."

Walter spoke quickly, fervently pleading with the Hawaiians in the room. "I am your patriarch," he said. "These men have come to take your land and send your earnings away. Is this love? Who loves you? Is it not I?

Then who are my children and my friends? Let them stand up!"

Joseph F. Smith watched the congregation. Walter's words had moved them, and almost everyone stood up. Sadness filled Joseph's heart and cast a dark shadow over his hopes for the settlement.[29]

WALTER WAS ODDLY KIND to the five men after the meeting. When they decided to leave the island the following evening, he offered them horses to ride to the beach and the use of his personal boat and a crew to take them back to Maui. He also presented Ezra Benson with a nice walking stick and $9.75—all the money in his pocket. He adamantly refused to surrender his preaching license, however, or the land that he had swindled from the Saints.[30]

After leaving Lanai, Ezra Benson and Lorenzo Snow returned to Utah, leaving Joseph F. Smith to preside over the Hawaiian mission. Since the missionaries could not legally recover the land Walter had taken from the Saints on Lanai, they decided to rekindle faith on the other islands. Joseph assigned Alma Smith to labor on Maui and the Big Island of Hawaii while he labored on Oahu and William Cluff on Kauai.[31]

Some Saints regretted their earlier support of Walter. Jonathan Napela, who had helped George Q. Cannon translate the Book of Mormon, had served as the president of Walter's twelve apostles for the last two years.

But he felt deceived when he realized that Walter had never had the authority to ordain him to that office.[32]

Napela began meeting with Saints on Maui. Most of them were disillusioned with Walter. He had sold off most of their meetinghouses and forbidden them from worshipping together, preaching the gospel, reading the scriptures, and praying as families. As a result, they were spiritually weak and discouraged over everything Walter had taken from them.[33]

Alma too spent much of his time crisscrossing Maui's rocky, mountainous terrain to visit the scattered Saints. By the start of summer, he could tell that Walter's influence was waning. More Saints were leaving Lanai, often coming to Maui with little else but the clothes on their backs. Yet their time with Walter had tried their faith, and few Church members were keeping their baptismal covenants when they returned.

"We cannot even see that the gospel has benefited them one iota, because not one of them has lived it!" Joseph complained in a report to Brigham Young. "With our examples constantly before them, and our teachings ringing in their ears, we should expect a few to do better, but it is not so."[34]

Brigham counseled Joseph and the other American missionaries to come home if the Spirit prompted them. He believed the Hawaiian Saints were ultimately responsible for their own spiritual growth. "It seems to me that you will be able to leave the affairs of the mission in the hands of the Native brethren," he wrote Joseph and the other missionaries. The Hawaiian Saints had received the gospel and priesthood many years earlier and had all the resources necessary to run the Church on their own.[35]

By the time Brigham's counsel arrived in Hawaii, Joseph's attitude toward the Hawaiian Saints had softened. "We do not feel like deserting the mission," he wrote to Brigham. But he did want to decrease the number of American missionaries on the islands and call several Hawaiian elders to preside over the various islands in the mission.

Joseph announced the change in October and called Hawaiians to leadership positions at a mission-wide conference in Honolulu. After he spoke, Kaloa, a Hawaiian elder, testified of his determination to serve in the Church. "I was a boy when these brethren first came to the islands," he said. "I am now a man. Let us no longer be children, but men in faith and good works."

Napela then arose and urged the Saints to righteousness. "We were deceived and led away by Gibson's cunning words and thereby have broken the sacred covenants we had made," he said. "But we are now undeceived; therefore, let us renew our covenants and be faithful."

Kanahunahupu, another Hawaiian elder, also testified. "The words that have been spoken today," he said, "are like coals of living fire."[36]

AT THE END OF the conference, Joseph F. Smith and William Cluff announced that they would soon be returning to Utah. Brigham notified Joseph a few weeks later that he intended to call Francis Hammond, Joseph's former mission leader in Hawaii, to replace him.[37]

Since losing the Lanai settlement, Joseph and the other missionaries had been looking for a new place to gather the Saints. In the summer, they had found a place on the Big Island of Hawaii that seemed promising, but the cost was more than the Hawaiian Saints could afford.

After the failure of the Lanai settlement, moreover, many Saints had become reluctant to risk more money on another gathering place. Families wanted the new settlement on their island and near their home.[38]

After the fall conference, however, Brigham Young authorized mission leaders to purchase land with money from the Church.[39] Undecided about the tract of land on the Big Island, Joseph and William continued to look for potential gathering places to recommend to Francis as they toured the branches on Kauai and Oahu one last time.

One day on Oahu, while Joseph and William were visiting a small branch near a plantation called Laie, William went for a walk alone. The plantation was situated on six thousand acres at the base of tall, wooded mountains along the northeast shore of the island. Unlike the settlement in Lanai, Laie had good access to water.

Feeling depressed and somewhat lonely, William knelt down in a nearby thicket to pray. When he arose, still listless, he found a path that wound through grassy plots and dense brush. He followed it some distance when, to his surprise, he saw a vision of Brigham Young walking up the path.

William greeted him as if he were really there, and they sat down in the grass. Brigham commented on the beauty of the plantation, the rich soil, the green mountains, and the waves gently crashing on the beach. "This is a most delightful place," he said at last. "Brother William, this is the place we want to secure as headquarters for this mission."

William then found himself alone, full of wonder and amazement, confident that he had found the right gathering place for the Hawaiian Saints.[40]

CHAPTER 23

One Harmonious Whole

Susie Young had always been a sickly child. By the time she turned nine years old, in the spring of 1865, she had survived pneumonia, whooping cough, and other serious illnesses. She would wheeze when she ran too fast or played too hard. Sometimes her father, Brigham Young, would gently take her in his arms, hold her close, and softly say, "Wait a minute, daughter. Don't get in such a hurry. Take time to breathe."[1]

Susie rarely wanted to wait a minute. Something was always happening in the house she shared with many of her father's wives and most of his younger children. The long two-story home was called the Lion House, and it stood next door to her father's office, a block east of the temple site in Salt Lake City. The upper floor of the Lion House had many bedrooms and sitting rooms for family

331

members. On the ground floor were more bedrooms and a large parlor for entertaining guests and holding family prayers. In the basement were storage rooms and cellars, a laundry room and kitchen, and a dining room large enough to seat the entire family.

On the front balcony of the home, keeping vigil over the street, crouched the regal statue of a lion.[2]

Nearly thirty of Susie's fifty-five brothers and sisters lived there at one time. Sometimes the family also took in orphans, including Ina Maybert, a girl from India. A neighborhood boy named Heber Grant often played at the house with Susie's brothers and joined the Youngs for family prayers. He was the only child of Rachel Ivins and Brigham Young's former counselor Jedediah Grant. In the wintertime, Heber liked to grab hold of Brigham's sleigh and let it pull him across the ice.[3]

The Young family tried to keep an orderly household, with a strict schedule for meals, schooling, and prayers. But that did not stop Susie and her siblings from sliding down banisters, running up the stairs, and playing hide-and-seek.[4] As a small girl, Susie thought it was perfectly normal to have such a large family and for her father to live with more than a dozen wives. In fact, her family was not typical even among plural families, which were usually far smaller by comparison. Unlike her father, most men in the Church who practiced plural marriage had only two wives.[5]

Her own mother, Lucy Bigelow Young, was a devoted parent who showered her with care and love. Zina

332

Huntington Young and Emily Partridge Young, two of her father's wives who lived for a time in the Lion House, were like second mothers to her. So too was her father's wife Clara Decker Young, who often stayed up late to chat and give advice to Susie and her sisters.[6]

Another wife, Eliza Snow, was a poet who studied books in her spare time and encouraged Susie's budding creativity. Eliza was intelligent, eloquent, and extremely self-disciplined. Her bedroom, sitting room, and writing table were tidy and carefully arranged. Some people thought Eliza was cold and aloof, but Susie knew her to be kind and tender—especially when nursing the sick.[7]

The Lion House was not always free of conflict, but the family tried to make their living arrangement a success. Brigham did not like comparing plural marriage to the customs of the world. "It is from heaven," he told the Saints. "The Lord has instituted it for an express purpose of raising up a royal nation, a holy priesthood, a nation peculiar to Himself, one that He can own and bless."[8]

"If I ever had a trial on the earth of my faith, it was when Joseph Smith revealed this doctrine to me," he testified further. "I had to pray unceasingly and I had to exercise faith, and the Lord revealed to me the truth of it, and that satisfied me."[9]

The joy he felt in bringing his many children up in the gospel of Christ was a fruit of that faith.[10] In the evening, he would ring a bell, calling everyone together for family prayers. "We thank Thee for our homes in these peaceful vales, and for these mountain fastnesses which

Thou has preserved as a gathering place for Thy people," he would often pray, speaking gently to the Lord with real love in his voice. "Bless the poor, the needy, the sick and afflicted. Comfort the hearts of those that mourn. Be a stay and a staff to the aged and a guide to the youth."[11]

Brigham often pondered on the Saints' welfare. Times were changing, and construction was now underway for a railroad that would span North America.[12] He had invested money in the venture, certain the railroad would make travel to and from Utah faster, cheaper, and less tiring for missionaries and emigrants. Yet he knew it would bring more temptations to the territory, and he wanted to prepare the Saints spiritually and economically for its arrival.[13]

He also wanted to fortify his own family, so that spring, Susie and her siblings learned that he had hired Karl Maeser to be their private schoolteacher. Some of Susie's brothers bristled under Professor Maeser's instruction and dropped out of school. But Susie was captivated by his lessons.

Books, especially the scriptures, came alive in the classroom. Professor Maeser encouraged the Young children to ask questions and puzzle out solutions to problems. Though she was ever eager to learn something new, Susie sometimes became frustrated when she made mistakes in her schoolwork.[14]

Professor Maeser was patient. "Only those who have the courage to make mistakes," he told her, "ever learn worthwhile lessons and truths."[15]

JOHAN DORIUS WAS WORKING that spring as a shoe-maker in Fort Ephraim. He and his brother Carl had been home from their Scandinavian missions for two years. Before leaving Denmark, they had hoped to bring their mother back with them. But since Ane Sophie's new husband was not willing to leave Copenhagen, she had decided to stay. Disappointed, the brothers had sailed from Denmark a few days later with a company of three hundred Saints.

Since returning to Utah, Johan had been trying to earn money. During his absence, his wife, Karen, had built a two-room house on their empty lot in Spring Town, cultivated crops, and kept a yard full of livestock. Karen had looked forward to joyful days with her husband and children in the new home, but soon after Johan's return, he had received permission to marry a second wife, a Norwegian convert named Gunild Torgersen. Karen was sorely tried by the new arrangement, but she was sustained by her faith in the Lord. Since their house now proved too small, the family moved to a large city lot in Ephraim within the year.[16]

Around that time, tensions between the Saints and the Ute Indians in Sanpete Valley increased. With more emigrants gathering to Utah, towns grew rapidly and new settlements often cut the Utes off from traditional sources of food and water. Some settlers also kept large herds of cattle on acres of grasslands in central Utah, further pushing the Utes out of the area.[17]

Aware of these problems, Brigham Young urged the Saints to feed the Indians and treat them kindly. "We are settled upon their lands, which materially interrupts their success in hunting, fishing, etc.," he wrote one Church leader. "For these reasons, it behooves us to exercise toward them all possible kindness, liberty, patience, and forbearance."[18]

Although Brigham hoped to inspire greater compassion for the Indians, food was already scarce in some settlements, and few Saints were eager to share their provisions. When settlers refused to share their food, the Utes often resorted to raiding cattle for sustenance.[19]

Violence finally erupted in the spring of 1865 after peace talks between the Saints and Utes in Sanpete Valley ended badly. Within weeks, a band of Utes led by a man named Black Hawk began raiding cattle and killing settlers.[20] The conflict grew worse as spring turned to summer. In June, Brigham and the United States government tried to persuade Ute leaders to move the tribe to a reservation—land set aside by the government for Indians to live on—but attacks on settlements continued. Brigham then ordered the militia to stop the raiders while doing no harm to women, children, or peaceful Ute men. Yet both sides attacked each other more viciously.[21]

On the afternoon of October 17, Johan Dorius watched in horror as Black Hawk and his men attacked a young Danish couple, their infant son, and a young Swedish woman in the fields outside of Ephraim. After

Black Hawk's men rode off to raid the settlement's cattle, Johan and several Saints rushed out to the fields. The couple was dead, and the Swedish woman was dying, but somehow the infant boy was unharmed. Johan picked him up and carried him back into town.[22]

With the militia in pursuit of Black Hawk's band, Church leaders ordered the Saints in Sanpete Valley and the surrounding areas to act cautiously and defensively. But overwhelmed by fear and mistrust, some Saints in the thick of the conflict disregarded their words.[23]

Six months after the attack on Fort Ephraim, Church members in a small, poorly fortified community called Circleville captured around twenty peaceful Paiutes, whom they suspected to be spies for Black Hawk. The settlers bound the men and held them under guard in the local meetinghouse. The women and children, meanwhile, were placed in an empty cellar. When some of the Paiute men tried to escape, the settlers shot them and executed the remaining captives, one by one, including the women and older children.[24]

Brigham strongly condemned the violence. "When a man shoots down an innocent Indian, he is guilty of murder," he said.[25] Brigham blamed the Saints, not the Utes, for the conflict. "If the elders of Israel had always treated the Lamanites as they should," he declared, "I don't believe we should have ever had any difficulty with them."[26]

Widespread violence continued to rage between the Saints and Indians in central Utah for another year.

Saints in smaller communities moved to larger towns, and settlers posted guards to protect their cattle. After the Saints stopped a major Indian raid in July 1867, Black Hawk and two chiefs surrendered to government agents. Some Utes continued to raid the Saints' cattle, but the conflict was virtually over.[27]

LATER THAT YEAR, ON October 6, the Saints held their general conference for the first time in a spacious new tabernacle just west of the temple site. The First Presidency had announced plans to construct a larger meeting place on the temple block in 1863. The oval building was topped with a large dome shaped like a turtle shell. Forty-four sandstone piers supported the dome, which veteran bridge builder Henry Grow fashioned from an arching latticework of wooden trusses, bound tightly together with wooden pegs and strips of rawhide. Since the innovative design used no interior columns to support the massive ceiling, the Saints at conference had an unobstructed view of the speakers at the pulpit.[28]

That fall, Brigham Young continued to follow the progress of the railroad. The American Civil War had ended with a Northern victory in the spring of 1865, giving the railroad project fresh momentum as the nation looked westward for new opportunities. Brigham served on the board of directors of one of the railroad companies, but his support for the venture did not remove his anxiety about the changes it would bring to the territory—and its economy.[29]

In the Doctrine and Covenants, the Lord instructed His people to "be one," share economic burdens, and "stand independent above all other creatures beneath the celestial world."[30] Over the years, Brigham and other leaders had employed various efforts to unify the Saints and keep them tethered to one another. One effort was the Deseret alphabet, a phonetic system designed to fix perceived problems with English spelling, teach young Saints to read, and help immigrants learn English rapidly and feel at home in Utah.[31]

Also, to achieve economic independence for Zion, Brigham began promoting a cooperative movement among the Saints. In his sermons, he frequently encouraged Church members to grow their own food, make homespun clothes, and build mills, factories, and foundries. He also criticized merchants in and out of the Church who came to the territory to sell hard-to-find eastern goods at a profit, thus enriching themselves instead of the cause of Zion.[32]

Knowing the railroad would bring even more merchants and goods to compete with the Saints' home industries, Brigham pleaded with Church members to support local businesses and seek financial independence from outside markets.[33] For him, the Saints' economic salvation was as important as their spiritual salvation. An attack on Zion's economy was an attack on Zion itself.

Brigham also began seeking ways to strengthen the Saints through institutions within the Church. In 1849, Scottish Saint Richard Ballantyne had organized the valley's first Sunday School. Since then, many wards had operated Sunday Schools independently of each other, often using different textbooks and lesson material. Recently, however, George Q. Cannon had founded the *Juvenile Instructor,* an illustrated magazine with gospel lessons that could be used in Sunday Schools at low cost to teachers and students. In November 1867, Brigham and other Church leaders selected George as president of a Sunday School Union to encourage wards and branches throughout the Church to organize Sunday Schools of their own.[34]

The basic, foundational classes of the Sunday Schools catered mostly to the young boys and girls of the Church. For the grown men in the Church, Brigham decided to organize a School of the Prophets in each of the larger towns of the territory. Nearly thirty-five years earlier, the Lord had commanded Joseph Smith to organize such schools in Kirtland and Missouri to foster unity and faith among priesthood holders in the young Church and to prepare men to proclaim the gospel.[35]

Brigham wanted the new School of the Prophets to nurture greater spiritual unity and devotion among the men of the Church. He believed it could help them understand the importance of economic cooperation, covenant keeping, and Zion building before the coming of the railroad.

A School of the Prophets opened in Salt Lake City on December 2, 1867. In the weeks that followed, Brigham urged its members to run their businesses in ways that would benefit the Saints instead of outsider merchants. "We are to be one and to understand each other," he taught. And he condemned Church members who purchased goods when and where they pleased, regardless of the needs of Zion.

"They have no business in this kingdom," he declared.[36]

Six days after organizing the School of the Prophets in Salt Lake City, Brigham spoke to bishops about reorganizing ward Relief Societies, which had largely disbanded during the threatened conflict with the United States Army ten years earlier. Brigham hoped that ward Relief Societies would promote greater unity among the Saints by helping the neediest members.[37]

Since the bishops knew little about the purpose of Relief Societies, he asked Eliza Snow to assist them in organizing societies in their wards. Eliza was honored to help. Few people understood the purpose of the Relief Society as well as she did. As the secretary of the Female Relief Society of Nauvoo, Eliza had written careful minutes of the meetings, recorded Joseph Smith's teachings to the women, and preserved them in a record book.

Eliza enjoyed working with the bishops, and they appreciated her help.[38] When Brigham told her the following spring that he had another mission for her, she did not ask what it was. She simply said, "I shall endeavor to fulfill it."

"I want you to instruct the sisters," Brigham told her. He believed the women of the Church needed Eliza to help them understand the Relief Society's role in building Zion.

Eliza felt her heart beat faster. Teaching the women of the Church was an enormous assignment. Women in the Church did not usually speak in public meetings outside of testimony meetings. Now Eliza would be expected to visit every settlement in the territory, meet individually with each ward and branch Relief Society, and speak publicly.[39]

Shortly after her meeting with Brigham, Eliza published an article in the *Deseret News*. "What is the object of the Female Relief Society?" she asked her readers. "I would reply—*to do good*—to bring into requisition every capacity we possess for doing good, not only in relieving the poor but in saving souls."

Drawing on the records of the Nauvoo Relief Society, she urged the women to step forward and embrace their duties. "If any of the daughters and mothers in Israel are feeling in the least circumscribed in their present spheres," she wrote, "they will now find ample scope for every power and capability for doing good."[40]

On the afternoon of April 30, 1868, Eliza visited the Female Relief Society of the Salt Lake City Thirteenth Ward. About twenty-five women were present, including

Zina Huntington Young, Emily Partridge Young, and Bathsheba Smith, all of whom had belonged to the Relief Society in Nauvoo. The ward's newly called Relief Society president, Rachel Grant, conducted the meeting with her two counselors, twin sisters Annie Godbe and Margaret Mitchell.[41]

Now forty-seven years old, Rachel Grant had lived in Nauvoo in the early 1840s, but she had not belonged to the original Relief Society. Learning about plural marriage had tried her faith severely, and she returned to live with her family in the eastern states after the death of Joseph Smith. She had remained in contact with missionaries and other Church members, however, and had decided to come to Utah in 1853 after much prayer and soul-searching. Two years later, she married Jedediah Grant as a plural wife and bore her only child, Heber, nine days before her husband's untimely death. Since then, she had cared for Heber with the meager income she earned working as a seamstress.[42]

After opening the Relief Society meeting, Rachel called upon Eliza to instruct the women. "The prophet Joseph Smith anticipated great results from the formation of Female Relief Societies," Eliza told the women, "that much good might be done by the sisters in visiting the sick and afflicted." She encouraged them to conduct orderly meetings, do good works, and care for one another.

"The society should be like a mother with her child," she explained. "She does not hold it at a distance but draws it near and folds it in her bosom, showing the necessity of union and love."

When Eliza finished speaking, Rachel said that she was proud of the women and that she hoped they would gain strength by meeting together. Eliza then encouraged the women to open their mouths. She testified that they could find strength in speaking to one another.

"The enemy is always pleased when we do not overcome our feelings of timidity and keep our tongues from speaking words of encouragement and determination," she said. "When that diffidence is once broken through, we soon gain confidence."

"The time will come," she promised, "when we will have to be in large places and act in responsible situations."[43]

As words and branches organized Relief Societies, Eliza met with Sarah Kimball, another founding member of the Nauvoo society, to outline the duties of Relief Society officers.[44] She then began visiting Relief Societies throughout the territory, often drawing on the minutes of the original Relief Society to instruct the women in their duties. "This organization belongs to the organization of the Church of Christ, in all dispensations when it is in perfection," Eliza taught the women of the Church. When she could not visit Relief Societies personally, she wrote them letters.[45]

344

Brigham, meanwhile, organized more branches of the School of the Prophets and counseled their members to study all types of knowledge and become one in heart and mind.[46] In April 1868, he went to Provo to establish a school under Abraham Smoot, whom he had sent with John Taylor, Wilford Woodruff, Joseph F. Smith, and others to reform the rowdy, unruly town. While there, Brigham and Abraham urged the members of the Provo school to do business primarily with each other, thus keeping their resources and profits with the Saints.

"Every member has an influence," Abraham said, "and we should use it in the proper direction."[47]

A few weeks later, Brigham's counselor Heber Kimball was in a buggy accident in Provo. He was thrown violently from the cab and struck his head on the ground. He lay there for some time, exposed to the chilly air, until a friend found him. Brigham hoped that Heber, one of his oldest friends, would recover from the accident. Heber had a stroke in early June, however, and died later that month, surrounded by family.

His death occurred eight months to the day after his wife Vilate's death. "I shall not be long after her," Heber had prophesied at her passing. At Heber's funeral, Brigham chose to pay a simple tribute to his friend and counselor's righteousness.

"He was a man of as much integrity," he declared, "as any man who ever lived on the earth."[48]

AT THE TIME OF Heber's death, railroad workers—
among them many Chinese immigrants, former slaves,
and Civil War veterans—were rushing to complete the
transcontinental line. In August, Brigham encouraged
the men in the Church to assist in the construction.
Once the two railroad lines merged north of the Great
Salt Lake, he hoped to build a connecting line through
Salt Lake City and other points south to speed up
travel between the settlements and to haul stone for
the temple.[49]

One night after family prayers, however, Brigham
shared his anxiety about the railroad with some of his
wives, friends, and older children. "We left the world, but
the world is coming to us," he said. The Sunday School,
School of the Prophets, and Relief Society were in place
to support and strengthen the Saints. But had he and
his generation done enough to prepare the youth for
what was coming?

"They will not have the same kind of trials their
fathers and mothers have passed through," he said. "They
will be tried with the pride and follies and pleasures of a
sinful world." If his generation did not help young people
develop faith in Jesus Christ, worldly temptations could
lead them astray.[50]

Ultimately, Brigham trusted that the gospel of Jesus
Christ would continue to unite and protect the people
of God, including the youth.

The restored gospel, he reflected at the start of
1869, "has sent forth its teachers to the ends of the earth,

has gathered people of almost every tongue and creed under heaven, of the most varied educations and the most opposite traditions, and welded them into one harmonious whole."

"A creed that can take the heterogeneous masses of mankind and make them a happy, contented, and united people," he stated, "has a power within it that the nations know little of. That power is the power of God."[51]

IN MARCH 1869, THE townspeople of Ogden crowded onto high bluffs to get a view of the tracklayers for the railroad. The track had finally come to the heart of the territory, one railroad tie and stretch of steel at a time. Soon the trains would arrive, belching black smoke and gray steam into the sky.[52]

Brigham visited the Saints in the southern settlements later that year. There were now Sunday Schools, Schools of the Prophets, and Relief Societies in many of the towns he visited. At his request, the Saints were also opening new stores, called "cooperatives" or "co-ops," to promote economic cooperation rather than competition among the Saints. Brigham wanted every town to have a co-op store to provide the Saints with their basic needs at a fair price.[53]

In early May, he counseled the Saints of central Utah to live by every word of God. "It is not proven that people are the saints of God because they live in these valleys," he said. "If we want to prove to God or men that we are saints, then we must live for God and none else."[54]

The eastern and western railroad lines finally met the following day, May 10, 1869, in a valley west of Ogden. The railroad companies rigged telegraph wires to the hammers that drove the last spikes home on the line. Each blow of the hammers sent an electric pulse down the telegraph wire to Salt Lake City and other cities across the nation, proclaiming that a railroad now connected the Atlantic and Pacific shores of the United States of America.[55]

The Saints in Salt Lake City celebrated the event in the new tabernacle on the temple block. That evening, all the public offices and buildings kept their lights aglow long after hours to illuminate the city. On a hill north of town the Saints lit a massive bonfire that could be seen for miles.[56]

PART 3

$$\longrightarrow \bowtie \longleftarrow$$

The Trying Hour

MAY 1869–JULY 1887

God grant us wisdom, grace and power,
To bravely stand the trying hour,
Till Zion, pure, redeem'd, and free,
Moves on in peaceful majesty.

Eliza R. Snow, "A Brother's and a Sister's Love"

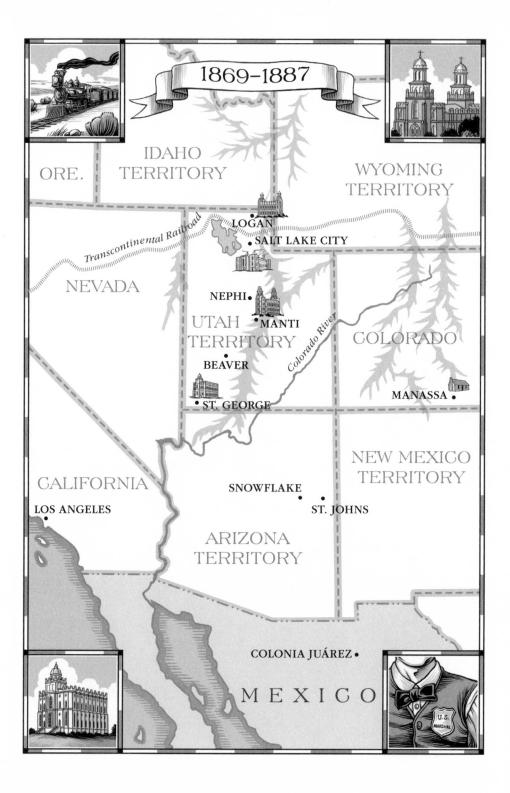

CHAPTER 24

An Immense Labor

Cooperative stores have sprung into existence in almost every place throughout the territory where a store is needed," wrote George Q. Cannon in a May 19, 1869, editorial in the *Deseret Evening News*. "Let every female in the territory have an interest in these stores, and the trade will flow as naturally to them as water downhill."[1]

The editorial's views on women and their importance in the cooperative movement impressed Sarah Kimball, the president of the Salt Lake City Fifteenth Ward Relief Society. Cooperation was crucial for the Saints to become a self-sustaining people. Women made many of the goods sold at co-ops and frequently purchased stock in the institutions.

Brigham Young taught that all efforts to establish Zion, no matter how mundane, were part of the sacred work of the Lord. Recently, he had urged the Saints to shop only at cooperatives and other businesses where the words "Holiness to the Lord" appeared somewhere on the establishment. By supporting these stores, the women worked for the good of the Saints, not outsider merchants.[2]

Sarah and her Relief Society were already working to promote the ideals of cooperation. The year before, they had begun building a Relief Society hall in their ward. Patterned after Joseph Smith's store in Nauvoo, where the original Relief Society was organized, the new hall had two floors. On the upper floor, the women would have a workroom dedicated to worship, art, and science. On the ground floor, they would run a cooperative store that sold and traded wool cloth, spools of cotton, carpet rags, dried fruit, moccasins, and other goods made by Relief Society members.[3] Like other small cooperative stores, it could also act as a retail distributor for the largest co-op in the city, Zion's Cooperative Mercantile Institution (Z.C.M.I.).

When completed, the Relief Society hall would be the first of its kind in the Church. Relief Societies usually met in homes or in ward buildings. But Sarah, who had been a founding member of the original Relief Society in Nauvoo, had wanted a place where the women of the Fifteenth Ward could develop and strengthen their God-given powers and abilities.[4]

Sarah had been a driving force behind the hall's construction over the last year. Though a man had offered to donate a city lot to the project, she and the other women in the society had insisted on paying one hundred dollars for it.[5] Later, after the ward had broken ground on the new building, Sarah used a mallet and silver trowel to help a mason lay the cornerstone.

"The object of the building," she had declared, standing atop the stone, "is to enable the society to more perfectly combine their labors, their means, their tastes, and their talents, for improvement—physically, socially, morally, intellectually, spiritually, and financially—and for more extended usefulness."[6]

In the six months since then, the women had hired builders and supervised the construction work, which was now nearing completion. In the spirit of cooperation, they had raised money and pooled their resources to furnish the hall with window blinds and carpets. When some people asked how the Fifteenth Ward Relief Society had been so successful, considering they were hardly the wealthiest ward in the Church, Sarah had simply replied, "It is because we have acted in unison and have kept in motion that which we received."[7]

The day after the editorial appeared in the *Deseret Evening News,* Sarah shared it with her Relief Society. "With woman to aid in the great cause of reform, what wonderful changes can be effected!" it read. "Give her responsibility, and she will prove that she is capable of great things."

Sarah believed a new day was dawning for women. "There never was a time," she told her Relief Society, "when woman, and her abilities and duties, were as much spoken of both in public and private as the present."[8]

AS THE FIFTEENTH WARD Relief Society built their meeting hall, powerful steam engines sped passengers and freight across the country. Though wary of worldly influences coming to the territory, the First Presidency believed the new transcontinental railroad would make it easier and more affordable to send elders to the mission field and gather people to Zion. So, one week after workers completed the transcontinental line, Brigham Young broke ground for a Church-owned railroad connecting Salt Lake City to Ogden.[9]

Joseph F. Smith, meanwhile, worked as a clerk in the Church Historian's Office in Salt Lake City. He was thirty years old and had more responsibilities in the Church than ever. Three years earlier, not long after returning from Hawaii, he had been called to the apostleship and set apart as a counselor in the First Presidency.[10]

Now, as the spring of 1869 was turning into summer, Joseph F. was preparing for a new challenge. His cousins Alexander and David Smith were coming to the territory. Sons of the prophet Joseph Smith, they lived in Illinois and belonged to the Reorganized Church of Jesus Christ of Latter Day Saints. Alexander and David sustained their older brother Joseph Smith III as a prophet and the rightful successor of their father's work.

Like Joseph III, Alexander and David believed that their father had never taught or practiced plural marriage. They claimed instead that Brigham Young had introduced the principle after their father's death.[11]

Though Joseph F. sometimes exchanged letters with his cousins, they were not close. He had last seen Alexander three years earlier, in 1866, when Alexander had stopped to preach in Salt Lake City on his way to a mission in California. Knowing the Saints would dispute his claims about his father and plural marriage, Alexander had come prepared with statements that his father and Hyrum Smith had published in the *Times and Seasons,* the Church's newspaper in Nauvoo, which appeared to condemn plural marriage and to deny the Saints' involvement in that practice.[12]

In 1866, Joseph F. had wanted to counter his cousin's claims, but he was at a loss. To his surprise, he could find little documented evidence connecting the prophet Joseph to plural marriage. He knew that Joseph Smith had taught the principle to several faithful Saints, including Brigham Young and others now living in Utah Territory. But he found that they had documented almost nothing about the experience.

There was also the Lord's revelation on marriage, which had been recorded by Joseph Smith in 1843 and published for the first time in 1852. The revelation described how a man and woman could be sealed together for eternity by priesthood authority. It also explained that God sometimes commanded plural marriage to raise up children in righteous families and help fulfill His covenant to bless Abraham with a numberless posterity.[13]

The revelation was strong evidence that Joseph Smith had taught and practiced plural marriage. Alexander had refused to accept its authenticity, however, and Joseph F. had been unable to find additional written evidence of the prophet's plural marriages.[14] "So far as the books are concerned," he had acknowledged to his cousin, "you have them on your side."[15]

After learning that Alexander would be returning to Utah with David, Joseph F. began again to look for evidence of Joseph Smith's plural marriages.[16] Plural marriage had become a fundamental part of Joseph F.'s life, and he was determined to defend it. A few years earlier, his first wife, Levira, had divorced him, partly because his marriage to a second wife, Julina Lambson, had aggravated existing tensions in the relationship. Since then, Joseph F. had married a third wife, Sarah Ellen Richards.[17] For him, an attack on the practice threatened the covenant relationships that formed the foundation of his family.

Over the last three years, Joseph F. had also understood more about how his uncle and father responded to the grave dangers they faced in Nauvoo. To defend themselves and the Church against critics, they had sometimes deflected rumors of plural marriage in Nauvoo by publishing statements that carefully denounced false practices without condemning the authorized practice itself. Their caution helped explain why almost no written evidence existed to connect the prophet and Hyrum to the practice.[18]

To remedy this gap in the historical record, Joseph F. began collecting signed statements from people who had been involved in early plural marriages. Some of the women he spoke to had been sealed to Joseph Smith for this life and the next. Others had been sealed to the prophet for eternity alone. Joseph F. also gathered information about what his aunt Emma knew about the practice. His oldest sister, Lovina, had lived with Emma for a time after most of the Saints had traveled west. She testified that Emma had once told her that she consented to and witnessed her husband's sealings to some of his plural wives.

Through the early weeks of summer, Joseph F. continued to collect statements, every day waiting for his cousins to arrive.[19]

ON JULY 22, 1869, SARAH Kimball called to order the first meeting in the Fifteenth Ward's newly completed Relief Society hall. "The house has been built for the good of all," she announced to the women in the room.[20]

Two weeks later, on August 5, the First Presidency dedicated the building. At the ceremony, a choir sang a new hymn that Eliza Snow had written about the Relief Society hall's role in protecting Zion:

May union in this Hall abide
With God-like strength and skill:

And Father, let Thy wisdom guide,
And each department fill.
We dedicate this House to Thee,
As love and labor's bower:
May Zion's welfare ever be
Its ruling motive power.[21]

The First Presidency was pleased that the building embraced the ideals of economic cooperation and local manufacturing. In his remarks to the society, Brigham emphasized the importance of women and men working together for Zion. "The earth has to be revolutionized," he said. "There is an immense labor to be performed, and all the means, talent, and assistance that can be procured will be required."

"The assistance of the ladies is as requisite as that of the men," he continued. "Our Relief Societies are for the benefit of the poor and for the benefit of the rich. They are for the benefit of every condition and for the benefit of the whole of the community of the Latter-day Saints."[22]

Sarah added her testimony of the value of cooperation at a meeting later that month. She taught that cooperation was a part of the Lord's pattern for Zion. In her mind, local manufacturing was crucial to the Saints' well-being.

"The subject must not be lost sight of," she insisted, "even for a single meeting."[23]

ALEXANDER AND DAVID SMITH arrived in Salt Lake City that summer and stayed their first night with Joseph F.'s older brother John, the presiding patriarch of the Church, and his wife Hellen. Two days later, Alexander and David called at Brigham Young's office, hoping to get permission to preach in the tabernacle, which was sometimes made available for other religious groups to hold meetings. Brigham considered the brothers' request, but he and other Church leaders were wary of their motives and did not grant permission.[24]

In the Historian's Office, Joseph F. Smith continued to collect evidence that Joseph Smith had taught and practiced plural marriage, greatly expanding what he and the Church knew about plural marriage in Nauvoo. Aside from gathering more statements, he combed through the journals of William Clayton, who had been the prophet Joseph's clerk, friend, and confidant. William's journal was one of the few records from Nauvoo that detailed early plural marriages, and it provided evidence of the prophet's participation.[25]

When Joseph F. was not in the Historian's Office or with his family, he was officiating in the Endowment House. In early August, he and George Q. Cannon administered the endowment to their friend Jonathan Napela, who had come to Salt Lake City from Hawaii in late July to receive the ordinance, visit Church headquarters, and meet Brigham Young and other Saints.[26]

Alexander and David Smith, meanwhile, were still in the city, attracting crowds whenever they spoke. Hoping to weaken Brigham Young's authority, wealthy merchants who opposed the Church's cooperative movement rented a large Protestant church where the brothers could give lectures criticizing Brigham's leadership and the Church. As Alexander had done three years earlier, they also relied heavily on quotations from the *Times and Seasons* to deny their father's involvement in plural marriage.

At the same time, Joseph F. Smith and other Church leaders gave sermons on Nauvoo plural marriage in ward buildings throughout the city.[27] On August 8, Joseph F. spoke to a congregation in Salt Lake City. He presented some of the evidence he had collected about early plural marriages and addressed his father's and uncle's statements about the practice in the *Times and Seasons.*

"I only know these facts," he told the congregation. "Everybody knows the people then were not prepared for these things, and it was necessary to be cautious," he said. "They were in the midst of enemies and in a state where this doctrine would have sent them to the penitentiary."

Joseph F. believed his father and uncle had done what they did to preserve their lives and protect other men and women who were also practicing plural marriage. "The brethren were not free as they are here," he continued. "The devil was raging about Nauvoo, and there were the traitors on every hand."[28]

IN SEPTEMBER, A LATTER-DAY Saint editor named Elias Harrison mocked Alexander and David Smith's mission in a column of the *Utah Magazine,* a periodical he published with the financial backing of his friend William Godbe, one of the wealthiest merchants in the Church. With an unsparing pen, Elias belittled the Reorganized Church and accused the Smith brothers of being "singularly ignorant" of their father's ministry.

"Their especial zeal is spent in trying to prove that their father did not practice polygamy, basing their arguments on certain assertions in the Book of Mormon, Doctrine and Covenants, and in the *Times and Seasons,*" wrote Elias. "But what does this amount to? David and Alexander can prove Joseph Smith denied polygamy, and we can prove he practiced it."[29]

Though Elias often defended the Church in his writing, he did so to conceal his real motives for publishing the *Utah Magazine.* Since the beginning of the cooperative movement, he and William Godbe had quietly resisted the First Presidency's counsel to support fellow Saints and avoid merchants who did not use their profits to strengthen the local economy.[30] For William, opposing the First Presidency required great subtlety. Aside from being a successful businessman, he was a Salt Lake City councilman and a member of the Thirteenth Ward bishopric. And he was a son-in-law and close friend of Brigham Young.[31]

Like Elias, William believed the prophet was old-fashioned and exerted too much influence over the lives of the Saints. Before the cooperative movement began, merchants like William had enjoyed more control over the local market, allowing them to charge high prices and get rich. Under the new system, however, the Church sought to keep prices low to benefit poor Saints and the local cooperative stores.

With his grasp on the market weakening, William had become irritated with Brigham's emphasis on the sacredness of cooperation. More and more, he and Elias had begun using the *Utah Magazine* to prepare other like-minded people to stage a revolt within the Church.[32]

Their desire to revolt had taken shape one year earlier on a business trip to New York. At that time, both men had begun trying to communicate with the dead through Spiritualist séances. Spiritualism had become popular in the aftermath of the American Civil War as people yearned to communicate with loved ones who had perished in the conflict. Church leaders had long condemned such practices, however, as counterfeit revelations from the adversary.

Ignoring these warnings, William and Elias immersed themselves in séances and came to believe that they had spoken with the spirits of Joseph Smith, Heber Kimball, the apostles Peter, James, and John, and even the Savior. Convinced these communications were real, William and Elias felt called on a special mission to rid the Church of everything they considered to be false. When they returned to Utah, they began to publish subtle criticisms of Church leaders and policies alongside more positive columns in the *Utah Magazine*.[33]

Soon after publishing his column on the Smith brothers, Elias grew more aggressive in his attacks on

Brigham Young and Church policies. He argued that the cooperation movement robbed the Saints of the competitive drive necessary to stimulate Utah's economy, which he thought was too weak to sustain itself on local manufacturing. He also reasoned that the Saints were too selfish to sacrifice their own interests for the good of the community.[34]

Then, on October 16, Elias published an editorial urging the Saints to develop Utah's mining industry. Over the years, Brigham Young had approved of some Church-supported mining, but he worried that the discovery of valuable minerals would bring greater social problems and class divisions to the territory. This concern had led him to preach aggressively against independent mining ventures in the territory.[35]

It soon became clear that Elias and William were carefully conspiring against the Church. On October 18, Orson Pratt, Wilford Woodruff, and George Q. Cannon met with the two men and some of their friends. Elias was full of bitterness, and neither man was willing to sustain the First Presidency. Five days later, at a meeting of the Salt Lake City School of the Prophets, William stated that he had followed Brigham's economic counsel against his better judgment and did not believe the prophet had a right to guide the Saints in commercial matters. Elias spoke even more defiantly against Brigham's leadership. "It is false! It is false!" he shouted.[36]

A few days later, the Salt Lake City high council met with Elias and William at the city hall. Elias accused

Church leaders of acting as if they and their words were infallible. In rejecting counsel, William claimed that he and Elias were only following a higher spiritual authority, an allusion to their Spiritualist séances.

"We do not ignore the priesthood by any means," he insisted, "but we do admit the existence of a power behind the veil from which influences and instructions do come and have always come by which the will may be guided in its onward path."

After the two men spoke, Brigham addressed the high council. "I have never sought but one thing in this kingdom," he said, "and that has been to get men and women to obey the Lord Jesus Christ in everything."

He affirmed that all people had a right to think for themselves, just as Church leaders had a right to counsel them according to revelation. "We work in harmony with our Savior," he declared. "He works in harmony with His Father, and we cooperate with the Son for the salvation of ourselves and the human family."

Brigham also rejected the idea that Church leaders could not make mistakes. "Man having the priesthood may be fallible," he declared. "I do not pretend to be infallible." But his fallibility did not mean God could not work through him for the good of the Saints.

If William and Elias wanted to continue criticizing the Church in the *Utah Magazine,* Brigham believed they were free to do so. He would continue to preach and practice cooperation, regardless of what they or outsider merchants did or said. "I will leave it to the people to do as they have a mind to," he said. "I have the right to counsel them, and they have the right to take my counsel or let it alone."

When the hearing ended, the stake president proposed excommunicating William and Elias from the Church for apostasy. The high council sustained the motion, and all but six people in the room—each an associate of Elias and William—sustained the decision.[37]

CHAPTER 25

The Dignity of Our Calling

On October 30, 1869, five days after meeting with the high council, Elias Harrison and William Godbe published statements in the *Utah Magazine* denying the apostasy charges against them. They accused Church leaders of tyranny and complained that the Saints were not free to think or act for themselves. Convinced that spirits had spoken to them in séances, both men believed they had been called to reform the Church. And they were determined to keep publishing their magazine and to rally the Saints to their cause.

"From out of our mountain valleys shall yet be borne a banner emblazoned with a wider creed, a nobler Christianity, a purer faith than earth has ever seen," Elias promised.[1]

Though he cautioned the Saints against reading the *Utah Magazine,* Brigham Young made no effort to shut it down.[2] During his nearly four decades in the Church, he had seen opposition movements come and go without lasting success. While Elias and William railed against him, he left Salt Lake City to tour settlements in Utah and Sanpete Valleys.

As he journeyed south, Brigham saw thriving towns where small forts and adobe shacks had once been. Some Saints operated workshops and factories to manufacture goods. Though no town was entirely self-sufficient, a few had cooperative stores up and running.[3]

Whenever Brigham visited a settlement, the Saints brought out their best for him, sometimes providing lavish feasts. He received these meals graciously, but he preferred simpler food that demanded less work from those who prepared it. Years earlier, while dining with Saints on his mission to England, Brigham had eaten with nothing more than a simple cup and a pocketknife, using a slice of bread for a plate. It had taken all of five minutes to clean up after the meal, giving the Saints more time to visit together.

As he traveled south through Utah, though, Brigham noticed that many women were missing Church meetings because they were busy preparing or cleaning up after elaborate meals.[4] He also lamented that many well-to-do men and women in the Church had developed extravagant lifestyles, sometimes at the expense of their spiritual well-being. Brigham wanted all Saints, himself included, to retrench, or simplify their lifestyles.

"The idle habits, the wasteful extravagance of men, are ridiculous in our community," he declared.

In the School of the Prophets, Brigham had counseled men not to follow the fashions of the world but to develop their own styles cut from fabric made in the territory. At other times, he encouraged women to refrain from making ornate dresses with expensive materials from the eastern states and to instead use cloth made in the territory. For him, extravagance often sparked competitiveness among the Saints and took time away from their spiritual development. He felt that it was a sign of worldliness, incompatible with the cooperative spirit of Zion.[5]

This concern was still on Brigham's mind when his party arrived in Gunnison, a town at the south end of Sanpete Valley. There he spoke with Mary Isabella Horne, a Salt Lake City resident who was visiting her son in the town. Mary Isabella was known for being a determined and faithful leader of Latter-day Saint women. Like Brigham, she had been a member of the Church since the 1830s and had endured her share of privation for the gospel's sake. Now she was the president of the Salt Lake City Fourteenth Ward Relief Society.[6]

"Sister Horne, I am going to give you a mission, to begin when you return to your home—the mission of teaching retrenchment among the wives and daughters of Israel," Brigham said. "It is not right that they should spend so much time in the preparation of their food and the adornment of their bodies, and neglect their spiritual education."

Mary Isabella was reluctant to take on the responsibility. Teaching retrenchment meant encouraging women to simplify their work and standard of living. Yet women often found purpose, satisfaction, and worth in preparing fine meals and making beautiful clothing for themselves and their families. By challenging them to simplify their work, Mary Isabella would be asking them to change how they saw themselves and their contributions to the community.[7]

Brigham urged her to accept the mission, however, believing it would give women more opportunities to grow spiritually. "Call the sisters of the Relief Society together and ask them to begin a reform in eating and housekeeping," he said. "I wish to get up a society whose members would agree to have a light, nice breakfast in the morning, for themselves and their children, without cooking forty different kinds of food."

Though still unsure how to undertake such a mission, Mary Isabella accepted the call.[8]

AROUND THIS TIME, JAMES Crockett traveled to Kirtland, Ohio, with his cousin William Homer. James was not a Latter-day Saint, but William had just finished a mission to Europe and planned to visit the Saints' former gathering place before returning home to Utah. Kirtland was less than one hundred miles from James's house, and the cousins decided to make the journey together.

In Kirtland, William wanted to visit Martin Harris, one of the Three Witnesses of the Book of Mormon, who now worked as the self-appointed caretaker of the Kirtland temple. Martin's son had married William's sister, and William hoped to persuade the old man to reunite with his family in Utah Territory.

Martin's relationship to the Church was fraught, however. After the collapse of the Kirtland Safety Society more than thirty years earlier, Martin had turned against Joseph Smith and drifted from one group of former Latter-day Saints to another. When his wife, Caroline, had emigrated with their children to Utah in the 1850s, he had refused to go with them.

After arriving in Kirtland, James and William called on Martin at his cottage. He was a small, poorly dressed man with a thin, leathery face and a discontented look in his eyes. William introduced himself as a missionary from Utah and the brother-in-law of Martin's son.

"One of those Brighamite 'Mormons,' are you?" Martin groused.[9]

William tried to give Martin news about his family in Utah, but the old man did not seem to hear him. Instead, he said, "You want to see the temple, do you?"

"If we may," said William.

Martin retrieved a key and led James and William to the temple. The outside of the building was in fair condition. The plaster on the outside walls was still intact, and the building had a new roof and some new windows. Inside, however, James saw that plaster was falling off the ceiling and walls, and some of the woodwork was stained and marred.

Walking from room to room, Martin testified of the sacred events that had occurred in the temple. But he grew tired after a while, and they stopped to rest.

"Do you still believe that the Book of Mormon is true and that Joseph Smith was a prophet?" William asked Martin.

The old man seemed to spring to life. "I saw the plates. I saw the angel. I heard the voice of God," he declared, his voice throbbing with sincerity and conviction. "I might as well doubt my own existence as to doubt the divine authenticity of the Book of Mormon or the divine calling of Joseph Smith."

The testimony electrified the room. Though he came to Kirtland an unbeliever, James was thrilled by what he heard. In an instant, Martin seemed to change from a bitter old man to a man of noble convictions, inspired of God and endowed with knowledge.

William asked Martin how he could bear such a powerful testimony after leaving the Church.

"I never did leave the Church," Martin said. "The Church left me."

"Wouldn't you like to see your family again?" William asked. "President Young would be only too glad to furnish means to convey you to Utah."

Martin scoffed. "He would not do anything that was right."

"Send him a message by me," William said.

Martin considered the offer. "You call on Brigham Young," he said. "Tell him I should like to visit Utah, my family, my children. I would be glad to accept help from the Church, but I want no personal favor."

William agreed to deliver the message, and Martin said goodbye to his visitors. As the cousins stepped outside, James placed his hands on William's shoulders and looked him squarely in the eye.

"There is something within me that tells me that the old man told the truth," he said. "I know the Book of Mormon is true."[10]

WHILE WILLIAM HOMER RETURNED to Utah Territory with Martin's message, legislators in Washington, DC, were proposing new laws to strengthen the 1862 Morrill Anti-Bigamy Act. In December 1869, Senator Aaron Cragin proposed a bill that, among other things, would deny the Saints their right to a trial by jury in polygamy cases. Later that month, Representative Shelby Cullom introduced another bill that would fine, imprison, and deny citizenship to Latter-day Saints who practiced plural marriage.[11]

On January 6, 1870, three days after a copy of the Cullom Bill arrived in Utah Territory, Sarah Kimball and the women of the Salt Lake City Fifteenth Ward Relief

Society met on the second floor of their Relief Society hall to plan a protest against the proposed legislation. They believed antipolygamy laws violated religious freedom, infringed on their consciences, and sought to demean the Saints.

"We would be unworthy of the names we bear and of the blood in our veins," she said, "should we longer remain silent while such an infamous bill was before the House."[12]

The women drafted resolutions to use their moral influence to stop the bills. They expressed their indignation against the men who introduced the legislation to Congress and resolved to petition the governor of Utah for the right of women to vote in the territory. They also resolved to send two female representatives to Washington, DC, to lobby on the Saints' behalf.

An hour into the meeting, Eliza Snow arrived at the hall to lend her support. She believed Relief Society members owed it to themselves and their families to defend the Church and their way of life. Too often, critics of the Church used popular newspapers, political cartoons, novels, and speeches to portray the women of the Church as poor, oppressed victims of plural marriage. "We should rise up in the dignity of our calling and speak for ourselves," she told the women.[13]

The weather was cold and snowy the following week, but more than three thousand women braved the elements on January 13 to gather in the old adobe tabernacle in Salt Lake City for a "Great Indignation

Meeting" to protest the Cragin and Cullom Bills. Sarah Kimball presided at the meeting. Aside from a handful of reporters, no men were present.

After the meeting opened, Sarah approached the pulpit. Though women throughout the nation had often spoken publicly on political issues, especially women's suffrage and the abolition of slavery, it could still be a controversial thing to do. Yet Sarah was determined to give Latter-day Saint women a public voice. "Have we transgressed any law of the United States?" she called out to the assembly.

"No!" the women shouted back.

"Then why are we here today?" asked Sarah. "We have been driven from place to place, and why? Simply for believing in and practicing the counsels of God as contained in the gospel of heaven."[14]

A committee of several Relief Society presidents— including Mary Isabella Horne, Rachel Grant, and Margaret Smoot—presented a formal statement of protest against the antipolygamy bills. "We unitedly exercise every moral power and every right which we inherit as the daughters of American citizens," they declared, "to prevent the passage of such bills, knowing that they would inevitably cast a stigma on our republican government by jeopardizing the liberty and lives of its most loyal and peaceable citizens."[15]

Other women spoke forcefully at the meeting. Amanda Smith described how her husband and son had been killed and another son wounded at the Hawn's

Mill massacre three decades earlier. "Let us stand by the truth if we die for it!" she cried as the tabernacle erupted in applause.

Phebe Woodruff condemned the United States for denying religious freedom to the Saints. "If the rulers of our nation will so far depart from the spirit and the letter of our glorious Constitution as to deprive our prophets, apostles, and elders of citizenship and imprison them for obeying this law," she declared, "let them grant us this our last request, to make their prisons large enough to hold their wives, for where they go we will go also."

Eliza Snow spoke last. "My desire is that we may as mothers and sisters in Israel defend truth and righteousness and sustain those who preach it," she said. "Let us be more energetic to improve our minds and develop that strength of moral character which cannot be surpassed on the face of the earth."[16]

IN THE DAYS THAT followed, newspapers across the nation published full reports of the Great Indignation Meeting.[17] Soon after, the *Deseret News* reported speeches made at other indignation meetings in settlements throughout the territory. Since the Cragin and Cullom Bills characterized plural marriage as a kind of slavery, many women who spoke at these meetings emphasized their right to marry the man of their choice.[18]

In meetings of the territorial legislature, meanwhile, Joseph F. Smith and other members of Utah's House of

Representatives were considering the question of women's voting rights in the territory.[19] The United States was in the process of bestowing the vote on all male citizens, including formerly enslaved men. But in the entire country, only Wyoming Territory allowed women to vote, despite a growing national movement to give the vote to all citizens over the age of twenty-one.[20]

Several months earlier, some U.S. lawmakers had proposed granting voting rights to Utah's women, certain they would vote to outlaw plural marriage. Many Saints in the territory, male and female, supported women's suffrage, however, precisely because they trusted it would strengthen the Saints' ability to make laws that preserved religious freedom in their own community.[21]

On January 29, 1870, Joseph attended a meeting of the Salt Lake City School of the Prophets at which Orson Pratt, his fellow apostle and a top leader in the territorial legislature, voiced his support for women's suffrage. The legislature voted unanimously to pass the bill several days later. Joseph then sent an official copy of the bill to the acting governor, who signed it into law.[22]

While a new law granting voting rights to women was cause for celebration, it did little to ease the Saints' anxieties about the antipolygamy bills under review in Washington, which Congress could pass whether Utah's voters supported them or not.[23]

Adding to this anxiety was growing opposition to the Church from within the territory. Joseph's cousins Alexander and David had left Utah a few months earlier, their mission less successful than they had hoped.[24] But William Godbe and Elias Harrison had recently organized their followers into the "Church of Zion" and proclaimed themselves the forerunners of a "New Movement" to reform the Church and the priesthood.[25] They also began a newspaper, the *Mormon Tribune,* and aligned with merchants in the city to form the "Liberal Party" to combat the Saints' political dominance in the territory.[26]

Amid this resistance, Joseph and other apostles continued to sustain Brigham Young's leadership. "If God has any revelation to give to man," Wilford Woodruff testified to the School of the Prophets, "he will not give it to me, nor Billy Godbe, but it will come through President Young. He will speak through His mouthpiece."[27]

A few men did resign their membership in the school to join the New Movement. And others, including the once-stalwart missionary T. B. H. Stenhouse, were beginning to waver.[28]

On March 23, the United States House of Representatives passed the Cullom Bill and sent it to the Senate for approval. Three days later, after the alarming news reached Salt Lake City, some men in the School of the Prophets feared that conflict with the United States was imminent.

George Q. Cannon urged them to be cautious. "The spirit of fighting seems to be easily brought out when circumstances call it forth," he said. "Let us keep our tongues still and not implicate ourselves by unwise talking."

Daniel Wells, a counselor in the First Presidency, believed that it was wise to prepare quietly for a fight. But he wondered aloud if the Saints had not brought this opposition upon themselves by failing to live the principles of cooperation. "How many of even this school are this day trading with and sustaining our open enemies in this city, instead of sustaining the servants of God in their counsels?" he asked. "Let us repent and do better."[29]

Joseph F. Smith echoed these words in a letter to his sister Martha Ann. "I would have no trouble in my mind were it not for the fact that I do not believe as a people we have lived as near to God as we should have done," he wrote. "It may be the Lord has a scourge prepared for us on this account."[30]

WHEN MARY ISABELLA HORNE returned to Salt Lake City, she recruited Eliza Snow and Margaret Smoot to help with her new retrenchment mission. She invited about a dozen Relief Society presidents to her home and asked Eliza and Margaret to work with Sarah Kimball to draft guiding principles for the Ladies' Cooperative Retrenchment Society. As instructed, they would create a society to help the women in the Church simplify meals and fashions, which in turn would allow more time to focus on spiritual and intellectual growth.

Mary Isabella believed that retrenchment should place all women on equal social standing throughout the Church. Some women hesitated to make friends with their wealthier neighbors, feeling embarrassed that they did not serve elaborate dishes and food. Mary Isabella wanted the women to feel free to socialize with and learn from each other. She believed that any table spread neatly with wholesome food was respectable, no matter how plain and simple it appeared.[31]

As retrenchment took root among the women of the Church, Brigham Young's fourteen-year-old daughter Susie Young noticed that her father's wives were dressing more simply and preparing less elaborate meals. But she and her sisters loved to wear dresses trimmed with fancy store-bought ribbons, buttons, bows, and lace.[32]

One evening in May 1870, after family prayers, her father spoke to some of his daughters in the Lion House about starting a retrenchment association. "I should like you to get up your own fashions," Brigham said. "Retrench in everything that is bad and worthless, and improve in everything that is good and beautiful. Not to be unhappy, but to live so that you may be truly happy in this life and in the life to come."[33]

In the days that followed, Eliza instructed the young women in retrenchment principles and asked them to remove unnecessary ornaments from their clothes. The result was anything but stylish. Where ribbons and bows had once been were now spots of unfaded cloth. If retrenchment was supposed to make them appear different from the rest of the world, it was succeeding.[34]

Still, Susie and her sisters understood that retrenchment, like cooperation, was supposed to give the Saints a new pattern for living, untangling them from distracting fads and fashions so they were free to live the commandments with all their hearts.[35]

A few days after meeting with their father, some of Susie's sisters organized the First Young Ladies' Department of the Ladies' Cooperative Retrenchment Association. Welcoming young married women and single women alike, they resolved to dress modestly, support and sustain each other in good works, and be good examples to the world. Ella Empey, one of Susie's married sisters, was selected as president, and Susie was presented the following day as the general reporter for the society.[36]

"Inasmuch as the Church of Jesus Christ is likened to a city set on a hill to be a beacon of light to all nations," they resolved, "it is our duty to set examples for others, instead of seeking to pattern after them."[37]

CHAPTER 26

For the Best Good
of Zion

During the spring and summer of 1870, retrenchment spread from Salt Lake City to Relief Societies throughout the territory—even in rural communities where Saints already lived simple lives. Eager to keep pace with their sisters in the city, President Elizabeth Stickney and the women of the Santaquin Relief Society held a picnic in their schoolhouse. They prepared a simple meal of brown bread and bean soup, enjoyed each other's company, and spun twenty skeins of yarn for homemade cloth.[1]

The need to retrench became even more essential after another grasshopper infestation ravaged the Saints' crops in many settlements. In a May meeting with the Salt Lake City School of the Prophets, George A. Smith lamented that few people had listened to the First Presidency's repeated counsel to store grain. He then compared the grasshoppers to critics of the Church in the local and national government.

"There are many who expect to fatten themselves on our overthrow and pick the bones of the Mormons," he said. "They may determine to send armies here to destroy us, and scatter us, and lay waste to our habitations, but it will not prove our religion to be false."

With the Cullom Bill under review in the Senate, the eyes of the nation's lawmakers were on the Saints. George believed that critics in Salt Lake City were trying to turn public opinion against the Church, so he counseled the men of the school to be patient and wise and not to give offense. He also warned them not to look to wicked men to lead the Saints.[2]

Though George did not mention William Godbe and Elias Harrison by name, they were likely among the men he had in mind. After organizing their Church of Zion, William and Elias had spoken of a "Coming Man" who would lead their New Movement. William had reached out to Joseph Smith III, perhaps to recruit his leadership, but Joseph had not joined their cause.[3]

That spring, however, Amasa Lyman announced his decision to join the Church of Zion, immediately sparking rumors that he would lead it. Amasa had been released from the Quorum of the Twelve in 1867 for apostasy, and few people were surprised when he embraced the New Movement. Yet his oldest son, Francis Lyman, was speechless when he learned of his father's decision. He tried to reason with Amasa but soon was too heartsick to argue. He fled the room and wept for hours.[4]

Brigham encouraged members of the School of the Prophets to leave such dissenters alone and refrain from criticizing them. In the meantime, he vowed to continue building up God's kingdom. "I intend to use my influence to strengthen Israel until Jesus reigns whose right it is to reign," he declared.

In July, he asked the men in the School of the Prophets to share their views on the Atonement of Jesus Christ. After listening to their testimonies, he bore witness of the Savior's sacrifice and acknowledged the dangers facing the Saints, including the disaffection of former stalwarts. "We have got the gospel," he said, "but if we expect to receive the benefits of it, we have got to live according to its precepts."

He urged the men to follow the counsel of the Lord's servants, promising that God would bless them if they did.[5]

THAT SUMMER, MARTIN HARRIS came to Utah on the transcontinental railroad. After learning of Martin's desire to come west, Brigham Young had been eager to assist one who had given so much time and money to the Church in the past. He asked Edward Stevenson, a seasoned missionary, to collect donations for Martin and then help the old man make the long journey from

Kirtland. "Send for him," Brigham had instructed, "even if it were to take the last dollar of my own."[6]

Martin's arrival caused a stir in Salt Lake City, though he was not the first former Church member to come to the territory. Thomas Marsh, the original president of the Quorum of the Twelve, had been re-baptized and come west thirteen years earlier, his heart full of regret for leaving the Church in 1838. Martin's status as a Book of Mormon witness set him apart, however. At eighty-seven years old, he was one of the last living participants in some of the earliest miracles of the new dispensation.[7]

Soon after arriving in the city, Martin visited Brigham Young, and the prophet invited him to speak at the tabernacle on September 4. When that day arrived, Martin stood at the pulpit for thirty minutes and quietly spoke about his search for truth during the religious revivals of the late 1810s.[8]

"The Spirit told me to join none of the churches, for none had authority from the Lord," he testified. "The Spirit told me that I might just as well plunge myself into the water as to have any one of the sects baptize me, so I remained until the Church was organized by Joseph Smith the prophet."[9]

In the weeks that followed, Martin reunited with his wife, children, and other family members in the territory. His older brother, Emer, had died the previous year in northern Utah's Cache Valley. But their widowed sister, Naomi Bent, lived in Utah Valley. On September 17, she went with Martin to the Endowment House, where Edward Stevenson rebaptized him, after which Orson Pratt, John Taylor, Wilford Woodruff, and Joseph F. Smith reconfirmed him a member of the Church. Martin and Naomi were then baptized and confirmed for several of their ancestors.[10]

The following month, Martin bore witness of the truth and divine origin of the Book of Mormon at the Church's October general conference. Afterward, George A. Smith approached the pulpit. "It is remarkable to have the testimony of Martin Harris," he said. "The Book of Mormon, however, carries evidence with it. The promise has been fulfilled that those who do the will of God should know of the doctrine that it is true."

"Thus," he said, "the Book of Mormon has thousands of witnesses."[11]

IN LATE NOVEMBER 1870, Susie Young sang and strummed a guitar as she traveled south in a carriage bound for St. George, a settlement of Saints in southern Utah. Riding with her were her mother, Lucy, and younger sister Mabel. After years of living in the bustling Lion House, they were moving to a home of their own in St. George. Susie's father, Brigham Young, was coming to southern Utah as well, though not permanently. Now nearly seventy years old, he suffered from arthritis and preferred to spend the winter season in St. George's warmer climate.[12]

Susie sang partly to lighten the mood in the carriage. On October 3, a few days before the Church's fall conference, she and her eighteen-year-old sister, Dora, had quietly slipped away from their mother's birthday party to meet up with Dora's fiancé, Morley Dunford. The three of them had then gone to a Protestant minister—one of several now living in the valley—who married Dora and Morley while Susie stood watch.

For Susie, the elopement had been like something out of a thrilling novel or stage play. But it had devastated her parents. Dora had been engaged to Morley for two years. He was handsome and came from a family of faithful Latter-day Saint merchants. He had a drinking problem, however, and Brigham and Lucy did not think he was a good match for their daughter. In fact, one reason they had wanted to move their daughters to St. George was to put three hundred miles between Dora and Morley.[13]

But Dora's marriage meant that she would not be moving south with the rest of the family. Susie could now see how sad that made their mother feel. Even as Lucy sang and joked with the others in the carriage, her eyes betrayed her grief. Susie tried her best to cheer her mother up, but nothing really seemed to help.[14]

With no railroad between Salt Lake City and St. George, the journey south took fourteen days over rough roads.[15] St. George sat in a large river valley rimmed by rocky, red cliffs. On a tour of the area about a decade earlier, Brigham had looked over the valley and prophesied that a city would spring up from it, with homes and spires and steeples. A short time later, he sent apostle Erastus Snow and more than three hundred families on a mission to the area to grow cotton, a crop that had been raised with some success in other southern Utah settlements.

Since then, the Saints in St. George had worked hard to fulfill Brigham's prophecy. The region was extremely hot for much of the year, and snowfall was rare. Two nearby rivers, after they were dammed, provided just enough water to grow crops and fruit trees amid the desert scrub. When rain fell, it sometimes came in torrents, washing out the settlers' dams. Timber was also scarce, so the Saints built instead with stone and adobe. Many who came to settle the valley left soon after they arrived. Those who stayed clung to their faith, trusting the Lord would help them establish a home.[16]

The settlers had since built wide streets, several nice homes, a courthouse, and a nearby cotton mill. In the center of town, they were also constructing a stately sandstone tabernacle where they could meet and worship together.[17]

When Susie and her family arrived in St. George, they settled into a comfortable home in the city and met their new neighbors. Her father, meanwhile, spent time considering the needs of the settlement and of Saints everywhere. The temple in Salt Lake City was years away from completion, and the Endowment House, which administered only some of the ordinances of the temple, was a temporary solution for a long-term need. The Saints needed an operating temple, where they could make covenants with Heavenly Father and perform all necessary ordinances for the living and the dead.[18]

In January 1871, just before Brigham planned to travel back to Salt Lake City, he attended a council of local Church leaders in the home of Erastus Snow, who presided over the Church in the region. As the meeting was drawing to a close, Brigham asked the men what they thought about building a temple in St. George.

Excitement filled the room. "Glory! Hallelujah!" Erastus exclaimed.[19]

AFTER BRIGHAM RETURNED TO Salt Lake City, he wrote Erastus about his plans for the new temple. It would be smaller and less ornate than the temple in Salt Lake City. It would be crafted from stone and plastered inside and out. Like the temple in Nauvoo, it would have a single tower rising from one end of the roof and a baptismal font in the basement.

"We wish the Saints in the south to unite their efforts with one heart and one mind for the prosecution of this work," he wrote.

Brigham looked forward to returning to St. George in the fall to begin construction on the temple,[20] but the Church in other parts of the territory needed his attention in the meantime. Over the last year, Amasa Lyman had been preaching for the Church of Zion and attending séances at which Spiritualist mediums claimed to speak for Joseph and Hyrum Smith, Chief Walkara, and other Saints who had died. People reported hearing rapping noises or seeing a table levitate during the meetings.[21]

While these séances drew some Saints to the New Movement, most were wary of them, and the Church of Zion soon floundered. By the time Brigham returned to Salt Lake City in February 1871, the New Movement was less a religious organization than it was a group of people with a shared goal of ending the Church's influence in the area.

In April, the leaders of the New Movement changed the name of their newspaper from the *Mormon Tribune* to the *Salt Lake Tribune.* Then, in July, they dedicated the Liberal Institute, a spacious meetinghouse in which they could deliver sermons, hold séances, and stage lectures and Liberal Party political meetings. The New Movement had also succeeded in drawing away Brigham's former friends T. B. H. and Fanny Stenhouse, who had been on the cusp of leaving the Church for several months.[22]

The New Movement, however, posed less of a threat to the Church than did James McKean, the newly appointed chief justice of the Utah Supreme Court. Judge McKean was determined to stamp out what he considered to be theocracy in Utah. Around the time of his appointment, the Cullom antipolygamy bill had failed to pass in the Senate and United States president Ulysses

Grant had sent McKean to Utah specifically to enforce the existing antipolygamy law.[23]

"In this country a man may adopt any religion that he pleases," Judge McKean declared soon after his arrival, "but no man must violate our laws and plead religion as an excuse."[24]

In the fall of 1871, about a month before he planned to return to St. George, Brigham learned that Robert Baskin, the United States attorney for Utah and one of the authors of the Cullom Bill, intended to charge him and other Church leaders with various crimes. A former Church member named Bill Hickman even agreed to try to implicate Brigham and other Church leaders in a murder Bill had committed during the Utah War fourteen years earlier.[25]

Bill Hickman was now under arrest for another murder, and he had cut a deal with the court to be lenient with him in exchange for his testimony. He was a lawless man whose word would never hold up in an impartial court of law, especially since several reputable people knew the facts of the crime and denied Brigham's involvement. Still, John Taylor, who had been with Joseph Smith at the Carthage jail, urged Brigham not to place his life in the hands of the court. Doubtful he would share Joseph's fate, Brigham said, "Things are entirely different to what they were then."[26]

The first charges came on October 2, when a United States marshal arrested Brigham for living with more than one woman as his wife. Daniel Wells and George Q. Cannon were arrested on similar charges.

The arrests ignited a firestorm of rumors. Outside the territory, newspapers predicted that civil war would break out in Salt Lake City and reported that the Saints had stockpiled guns and positioned a cannon on the foothills of the mountains.[27] In reality, the streets of Salt Lake City were quiet. Church leaders cooperated with the lawmen, and lawyers began preparing for Brigham to answer the charges in court the following week.[28]

When that day came, the courtroom was crowded. Thousands stood in the street outside the city building. Brigham arrived fifteen minutes before the judge and sat patiently, his coolness disarming his critics.[29]

After Judge McKean arrived, Brigham's lawyers tried to stop the hearing, claiming that officials had not followed proper procedure when they assembled a grand jury with no Church members. When McKean denied this request, the lawyers tried to find fault with the charges themselves, hoping to have them dropped altogether. Once again the judge denied their request.[30]

During the hearing, McKean revealed that he saw the case not as a trial of Brigham's innocence or guilt but as a crucial battle in a war between the Saints' revelations and federal law. "While the case at bar is called *The People versus Brigham Young*," he stated, "its other and real title is *Federal Authority versus Polygamic Theocracy*." He was not interested in being an impartial judge. In his eyes, the prophet was already guilty.[31]

Assuming the trial would not be scheduled until March, during the next term of the court, Brigham left for St. George nearly two weeks later. A few days after that, arrest warrants were issued for him and other Church leaders—this time for the trumped-up murder charge.[32]

ON NOVEMBER 9, 1871, AFTER days of chilly weather and some rain, the sky over St. George was clear and pleasant. Just south of town, Susie Young stood in a large crowd on a newly surveyed city block where the Saints had gathered to break ground on the temple.[33]

Brigham had made few public appearances since coming to St. George that fall. With illness and a court hearing hanging over his head, he had to be cautious. Some people feared that marshals would try to capture him and drag him back to Salt Lake City. At night, he stayed at Erastus Snow's house, where armed men stood guard to protect him.[34]

At the temple block, Susie gripped a pencil and notebook, ready to take notes on the ceremony. Before moving to St. George, she had been the star pupil of one of her father's stenographers, and she took pride in being a reporter. From her place in the crowd, she would be able to record everything that happened. She could easily see her father and mother standing close together and her sister Mabel clinging to her mother's hand.[35]

After the choir sang an opening hymn, George A. Smith knelt and offered the dedicatory prayer, asking the Lord to preserve the prophet from his enemies and lengthen his days. Susie then watched her father and other Church leaders break ground at the southeast corner of the block.

The Saints sang "The Spirit of God like a Fire Is Burning," and Brigham climbed onto a chair so that everyone could hear him give instructions for the "Hosanna Shout," a solemn cheer given at dedication ceremonies and public events since the Kirtland temple.

Following his lead, the Saints raised their right hands and shouted three times, "Hosanna, hosanna, hosanna to God and the Lamb!"[36]

A FEW WEEKS LATER, Brigham received notice that Judge McKean had scheduled his court date for December 4 even though he knew the prophet was far from Salt Lake City. Brigham was reluctant to leave St. George, however, and the judge pushed the court date to early January. Meanwhile, Brigham consulted with his lawyers and advisers about the course he should take. He knew that he would be arrested once he returned to Salt Lake City, and he was now more concerned about his safety than before. He wanted assurances that he would not be killed while in custody.[37]

For a time, he considered going into hiding, as Joseph Smith had done in Nauvoo. Murder was a capital offense, and if a biased jury found him guilty, he could be executed. But in mid-December his lawyers urged him to return to the city, confident that he would be safe. Members of the Quorum of the Twelve and other friends were divided on the matter, yet they agreed that he should act as he saw best.[38]

One night, Brigham dreamed that two men were trying to take control of a large meeting of Saints. After he awoke, he knew what he needed to do. "I feel like going home and running the meeting, with the help of God and my brethren!" he told his friends.[39]

On his way back to Salt Lake City, Brigham stopped in a small settlement for the night. The Saints there were distraught over his choice to go to trial, knowing that Judge McKean had all but pronounced him guilty. One man even sobbed when he learned what Brigham intended to do. The prophet understood his fear, but he knew the right course to take.

"God will overrule all for the best good of Zion," he said.[40]

CHAPTER 27

Fire in the Dry Grass

Rumors about Brigham Young's return to Salt Lake City abounded in the weeks leading up to his January 1872 court date. Territorial prosecutors were sure Brigham would rather become a fugitive from justice than appear before a judge.[1]

In late December, however, Daniel Wells received an urgent letter from the prophet. "We shall be on hand at the time appointed to make our appearance in the court," Brigham informed him.[2] On the day after Christmas, he traveled seventy miles through snowstorms to meet Daniel in Draper, a town twenty miles south of Salt Lake City. From there, they boarded a northbound train, and Brigham arrived home shortly before midnight.

A United States marshal arrested the prophet one week later and escorted him to Judge McKean's courtroom. Brigham remained calm and confident throughout the proceedings. Noting his old age and ill health, the prophet's lawyers asked the judge to release him on bail. McKean denied the request and placed Brigham under house arrest.[3]

The trial was scheduled to begin a short time later, and the *Salt Lake Tribune* predicted that every newspaper in the United States and Great Britain would publish its proceedings. The "Great Trial" was postponed, however, and days soon stretched into weeks. Brigham stayed at home most of the time, usually under the watch of marshals. But sometimes he attended social events, as when he and a deputy marshal went to a surprise birthday party for Eliza Snow in the Fourteenth Ward building.[4]

From Washington, DC, George Q. Cannon sent Brigham regular reports about a case the Saints had brought before the United States Supreme Court, the highest court in the country. The case argued that Judge McKean's practice of deliberately excluding Saints from grand juries in Utah Territory was illegal. If the Supreme Court ruled against the judge's practice, every charge issued by an improperly formed grand jury in Utah—including charges against the prophet—would be thrown out immediately.[5]

The Supreme Court decided the case in April. Both Judge McKean and George were in the courtroom to hear the ruling. Though some of his associates were confident that the court would rule in their favor,

McKean looked anxious as the presiding judge read the court's decision.[6]

"Upon the whole," the presiding judge declared, "we are of the opinion that the jury in this case was not selected and summoned in conformity with law."[7]

Judge McKean left the room cursing the ruling and insisting that he had done nothing wrong. Soon telegraph wires carried the news to Utah. All criminal charges issued by illegally formed grand juries in the territory had been erased. Brigham Young was free.[8]

"The Supreme Court has risen above religious prejudices and political influences," George rejoiced in a letter to Brigham later that day. Yet George worried about the court's decision, certain it would only embitter the Saints' enemies more.

"I shall be surprised," George wrote, "if there will not be a strong effort made to secure adverse legislation against us."[9]

THAT APRIL, SAINTS FROM all around Hawaii came to Oahu for a conference in Laie, their gathering place for the last seven years. About four hundred Saints lived in the settlement year-round. It had a small chapel, a school, and a large farm where local Saints and missionaries from Utah raised sugarcane.

At the conference, thirteen local missionaries testified of their recent experiences. Under the direction of Jonathan Napela, who had been called to oversee proselytizing on the islands, the missionaries had baptized more than six hundred people. The number of Saints in Hawaii was now well over two thousand.[10]

Each elder bore witness of the miracles he had seen in the mission field. Recently, the Lord had healed a paralyzed man after missionaries exercised faith and prayed in his behalf.[11] Another man, who broke his arm after falling off his mule, was fully healed after two missionaries blessed him. Other elders had administered repeatedly to a little girl who could not walk. After each blessing she improved little by little until she was able to run and play again.[12]

After the conference, the missionaries continued to preach the gospel and heal the sick. Among those who sought their help was Keʻelikōlani, the governor of the Big Island of Hawaii. She asked the Saints to pray for her half brother, King Kamehameha V, who was close to death. Napela knew the king well, so he and another longtime elder in the Church, H. K. Kaleohano, went to the palace and offered to pray for him.

"We have heard of your great affliction," they said, "and we sincerely desire your restoration of health." The king accepted their offer, and the missionaries bowed respectfully. Kaleohano then offered a fervent prayer.

When the missionary finished, Kamehameha appeared much better. He told the elders that some people in the government had been pressuring him to stop the Saints from preaching on the islands, but he had refused to listen to them. The constitution of Hawaii granted religious liberty to the people, and he insisted on upholding it.

The king spoke pleasantly with Napela and Kaleohano for a long time. As the elders were about to leave, some men arrived with fish for the king's household. When Kamehameha saw them, he pointed to Napela and Kaleohano. "Don't you forget these kings," he said.

He gave the elders each a basket of fish and bid them goodbye.[13]

AROUND THE TIME OF the April conference in Laie, newspapers across the United States were raving about a newly published exposé of plural marriage by Fanny Stenhouse, who had become the most prominent woman in the New Movement. In the book, Fanny portrayed Latter-day Saint women as oppressed and discontented.[14]

The women of the Church were appalled at this characterization. Believing it was better for Latter-day Saint women to represent themselves than be misrepresented by others, twenty-three-year-old Lula Greene began publishing a newspaper for women in Utah. She called her newspaper the *Woman's Exponent*.[15]

Lula was a gifted writer who served as president of a small branch of the Young Ladies' Retrenchment Association. After publishing Lula's poetry, the editor of the *Salt Lake Daily Herald* had wanted her to write for his newspaper. But after his staff had balked at hiring her, the editor had suggested that she start a paper of her own.

The idea had intrigued Lula. The recent indignation meetings had shown the powerful influence Latter-day Saint women could have when they spoke up on issues that mattered to them. But women in and out of the Church rarely had opportunities to express their opinions so publicly. Many of the good things said and done by Relief Societies and the Retrenchment Association, moreover, went unmentioned and unnoticed, especially by people outside the territory.

Lula had first shared the plans for the newspaper with Eliza Snow, who then consulted with Brigham Young, Lula's great-uncle. Both gave their support to the endeavor. At Lula's request, Brigham appointed Lula on a special mission to serve as the paper's editor.[16]

The first issue of the *Woman's Exponent* was published in June 1872. The paper featured local, national, and world news as well as editorials, poetry, and reports from Relief Society and retrenchment meetings.[17] Lula also printed letters to the editor, giving Latter-day Saint women a place to share their stories and express their views.

In July, Lula published a letter from an Englishwoman named Mary, who contrasted her hard life as a hired girl in London and New York with her life in Utah. "We 'Mormon women' ought to write and tell the world—whether it is pleased to believe us or not—that we are not the poor, oppressed beings we are represented to be," Mary stated. "I have not been oppressed here but have been free to come, free to go, free to work or let it alone."

"I like the *Exponent* so far very much," she added. "It tells of sound sense."[18]

MEANWHILE, IN NORTHERN UTAH, the Northwestern bands of the Shoshone Nation were on the brink of starvation. Nearly ten thousand white settlers, most of them Latter-day Saints, were living on indigenous Shoshone lands in Cache Valley and the surrounding area, straining the region's natural food sources.[19]

When the Saints first came to Cache Valley in the mid-1850s, a Shoshone leader named Sagwitch had cultivated a good relationship with local Church officials, particularly Bishop Peter Maughan, who sometimes provided aid to the Shoshones from the tithing office. Tensions between the two peoples had increased in the late 1850s, however, as more Saints settled in the valley and game grew scarcer.

To provide food for themselves and their families, some Shoshones started raiding the Saints' cattle, treating this as compensation for their lost lands and depleted resources. Perhaps hoping to stop the raids, the Saints grudgingly tried to feed the Shoshones with gifts of flour and beef. But these gifts did not make up for the privation the settlers had created by moving into Cache Valley.[20]

During this time, the Shoshones had also clashed repeatedly with the United States government. Colonel Patrick Connor, the commander of the U.S. Army troops stationed at Salt Lake City, used the conflict as grounds for attacking the Shoshones. One morning in January 1863, as Sagwitch and his people camped near the Bear River, they awoke to find soldiers advancing on them. The Shoshones retreated to their defenses and tried to fight off the soldiers. The army quickly surrounded them, however, and fired mercilessly on their position.

Approximately four hundred Shoshone men, women, and children died in the assault on the camp. Sagwitch survived the attack, as did his infant daughter and three sons. But his wife, Dadabaychee, and two stepsons were among the women and children slain.[21]

Following the massacre, Saints from nearby settlements came to assist the wounded Shoshones. The attack had left Sagwitch deeply suspicious of the Saints, however. Porter Rockwell, a Latter-day Saint who sometimes worked as an army scout, had led the soldiers to the Shoshones' camp. Some Cache Valley Saints had also watched the massacre unfold from a nearby hilltop, and others had sheltered and fed the army after the attack. Even Peter Maughan, who described the soldiers' actions as "inhuman," believed the Shoshones had provoked the violence. Some Saints went so far as to call the assault an act of divine intervention.[22]

Now, a decade after the massacre, Sagwitch and his people remained resentful of white settlers. Although the

Saints' willingness to use Church resources to provide food and supplies to the Shoshones had earned back some trust, the loss of innocent lives, land, and resources had left the Shoshones in desperate straits.[23]

In the spring of 1873, a respected Shoshone leader named Ech-up-wy had a vision in which three Indians entered his lodge. The largest of them—a handsome, broad-shouldered man—told him that the Saints' God was the same God that the Shoshones worshipped. With the Saints' help, they would build houses, cultivate the earth, and receive baptism.

In the vision, Ech-up-wy also saw Shoshones working small farms with a few white men alongside them. One was George Hill, a Latter-day Saint who had served a mission among the Shoshones fifteen years earlier. He was a man who spoke their language and sometimes distributed food and other provisions among them.

After hearing about Ech-up-wy's vision, a group of Shoshones set out for George's home in Ogden.[24]

A SHORT TIME LATER, George Hill awoke to learn that a group of Shoshones was outside his house, waiting to speak to him. When George greeted his visitors, one of their leading men explained to him that they had learned through inspiration that the Saints were the Lord's people. "We want you to come to our camp and preach to us and baptize us," he said.

George did not feel he could baptize them without permission from Brigham Young. Disappointed, the Shoshones departed for home, but they returned later and again asked for baptism. Once more, George told them that he had to wait for the prophet's direction.[25]

Not long afterward, George met with Brigham in Salt Lake City. "There has been a load resting on my shoulders for some time," Brigham said. "I have tried to shake it off. Now I am going to give it to you. It is going to be your load from now on. I want you to take charge of the mission to the Indians in all this northern country."

He counseled George to establish a gathering place for the Shoshones and teach them to farm the land. "I don't know just how you should go about this," he said, "but you will find a way."[26]

On May 5, 1873, George traveled by train to a town about thirty miles north of Ogden. From there he started on foot for Sagwitch's camp, twelve miles away. Before he had walked a mile, an old Shoshone man named Tig-we-tick-er approached him, laughing. That morning, he said, Sagwitch had prophesied that George would be visiting their camp.

Tig-we-tick-er gave George directions to the camp and promised to return soon to hear him preach. George walked on and encountered two more Shoshones who repeated Sagwitch's words. Amazed, George wondered how Sagwitch knew the exact day and time of his coming. To him it was a sign that the Lord's work was truly beginning among the Shoshones.

Soon, George saw Sagwitch approaching on horse-back, leading another horse behind him. "I thought you would be tired," Sagwitch said, "so I brought you a horse to ride."

They rode into camp together. Scores of people were waiting to be taught. George preached for an hour or two and found many who wanted to join the Church. That afternoon, he baptized 101 Shoshones, including Sagwitch, and confirmed them at the water's edge. He then left camp with just enough time to catch the last train to Ogden.[27]

The following day, George sent a letter to Brigham Young. "I never felt better in my life nor ever spent a happier day," he wrote. The Shoshones likewise seemed happy, he noted, and they planned to hold prayer meetings each night. Mentioning their dire need for provisions, he requested sacks of flour for the people.[28]

George then wrote about the baptisms in a letter to his friend Dimick Huntington, who also knew the Shoshones' language. "My only desire is that I have the Spirit of God to assist me," George stated, "that I may be able to accomplish the work that is required at my hands."

"Dimick, help me all you can," he pleaded. "The work is extending like fire in the dry grass."[29]

AROUND THE TIME THE Northwestern Shoshones embraced the restored gospel, Jonathan Napela learned that his wife, Kitty, had been ordered to go to the island of Molokai after contracting Hansen's disease, or leprosy. Hoping to stop the spread of the disease in Hawaii, King Kamehameha V had established a colony on Molokai's Kalaupapa peninsula to quarantine people who showed signs of infection. Since leprosy was thought to be incurable, banishment to the colony was usually a life sentence.

Anxious not to part with Kitty, Napela secured work on Kalaupapa as the colony's assistant supervisor. His new duties included distributing rations and reporting regularly to the board of health. The job placed him in close contact with infected people, increasing his chances of contracting the disease.

When he and Kitty arrived at the colony in the spring of 1873, Napela began preaching the gospel and holding meetings every Sunday with Saints afflicted with leprosy. He also befriended Father Damien, a Catholic priest serving Kalaupapa, and Peter Kaeo, a member of the Hawaiian royal family who had contracted the disease and arrived not long after Kitty and Napela.[30]

In the colony, Peter lived in relative comfort in a cottage overlooking the peninsula. He employed servants, received gifts from his wealthy family, and had little contact with the island's suffering. When he learned that a man had died in the settlement, Peter was apparently shocked and told Kitty about it.

"It is nothing new," she responded. "They die almost every day."[31]

On August 30, 1873, Peter joined Napela as he assessed the needs of the people in the colony. The morning sky was overcast as they went across the peninsula to the huts and sheds where some of the residents lived. Napela stopped first at a cave and spoke to three men, three women, and a small boy about their rations. Peter was horrified. The disease had completely disfigured the faces of some of them. Others were missing fingers.

Later, Napela and Peter met a woman with a severely swollen leg. She had been on Molokai for three years and had worn out her dresses and underclothing. Napela told her that if she came to the colony store on Monday, she would receive new clothes.

In October, the board of health learned that Napela was giving away food to needy people in the colony who were not authorized to receive it. They dismissed him from his post and ordered him to leave Kalaupapa. Napela immediately told Kitty the news. When Peter found the couple a short time later, they were weeping. Kitty had been unwell lately, and Napela did not want to leave her.[32]

Napela petitioned the board of health to let him stay as Kitty's caretaker. "I vowed before God to care for my wife in health and sickness, and until death do us part," he wrote. "I am sixty years old and do not have much longer to live. During the brief time remaining, I want to be with my wife."

The board approved his request.[33]

IN DECEMBER 1873, AFTER years of lobbying for the Church and Utah in Washington, DC, George Q. Cannon was sworn in as the territory's delegate to the United States House of Representatives.[34] George had spiritually prepared himself for this moment. He had felt weak and alone the night before, but after praying for help, he felt blessed with joy, comfort, and strength.

"I am here without a man who is in sympathy with me," he reflected in his journal, "but I have a Friend more powerful than they all. In this I rejoice."[35]

In the early 1870s, public opinion of the Church was as low as ever in the United States. President Ulysses Grant was determined to end plural marriage in Utah, having already promised to stop efforts to bestow Utah statehood until that happened. In the spring of 1874, Senator Luke Poland presented another bill designed to strengthen the Morrill Anti-Bigamy Act by seizing greater control over Utah's courts.[36]

Fanny and T. B. H. Stenhouse, meanwhile, continued to write critically about the Church and speak against plural marriage to audiences across the country.[37] Likewise, Ann Eliza Young, an estranged plural wife of Brigham Young who had sued him for divorce, had begun giving public speeches denouncing the Church. After a show in Washington, DC, during which Ann Eliza condemned George Q. Cannon's election to Congress, President Grant spoke with her and heartily agreed with her views.[38]

Fasting and praying for guidance, George tried to use his influence to stop the Poland Bill. He also sought help from allies. Recently, Thomas Kane and his wife, Elizabeth, had spent the winter with Brigham Young in Utah. Influenced by hostile books and newspaper reports, Elizabeth had come to the territory expecting to find women who were oppressed and hopeless. Instead, she met kind, sincere women who were devoted to their religion. Soon after the trip, Elizabeth's impressions of the Saints were published in a book. In it, she portrayed the Saints fairly, though she continued to oppose plural marriage.

Thanks in part to Elizabeth's book, George persuaded his fellow lawmakers to soften some aspects of the Poland Bill. But none of his efforts stopped President Grant from signing it into law in mid-June.[39]

That summer and fall, William Carey, the United States attorney in Utah, took steps to begin prosecuting well-known Saints who practiced plural marriage. George returned to Utah during this time, and in October he was arrested on charges associated with his plural marriages. Facing the prospect of more arrests among the Saints, Church leaders decided to set up a test court case to challenge the legality of the Morrill antipolygamy law.

Striking a deal with Carey, they agreed to let him convict one man for polygamy so that Church lawyers could appeal the case before a higher court. In exchange, the federal attorney promised that he would not prosecute anyone else until the appeal process on the test case concluded. In making this deal, Church leaders hoped the higher court would decide that the antipolygamy law violated the Saints' religious rights and would overturn the conviction.

George Q. Cannon was released on bail shortly after his arrest. That evening, he encountered George and Amelia Reynolds strolling along the south wall of the temple block. George Reynolds was a young British Saint who served as secretary to Brigham Young. That summer he had married Amelia, his first plural wife. Knowing Reynolds well, George Cannon recommended him as the ideal candidate for contesting the antipolygamy law.

Reynolds agreed. Since the test case could go forward only if he was convicted, Reynolds soon provided a list of people who could stand as witnesses against him in court. He was arrested for bigamy a short time later. The judge then released him on bail and set a date for his trial.[40]

CHAPTER 28

Until the Coming of the Son of Man

On June 19, 1875, Brigham Young left Salt Lake City to visit settlements in central Utah.[1] He had just turned seventy-four years old, and travel was becoming more difficult. Every time he moved, his joints ached with arthritis. Yet visiting the settlements brought him closer to the Saints—and put welcome distance between him and the Church's recent legal difficulties.

After George Reynolds was indicted for bigamy, United States attorney William Carey had broken his promise with Church leaders and charged George Q. Cannon with bigamy as well. George Cannon's case was later dismissed, but Reynolds was tried, convicted, fined $300, and sentenced to a year in prison. The territorial supreme court overturned Reynolds's conviction, however, after his lawyers successfully argued that he had been charged by an illegally formed grand jury. Now that Reynolds was free, prosecutors vowed to bring him to trial again.[2]

Brigham's estranged plural wife Ann Eliza Young, moreover, had lately joined forces with critics of the Church to sue the prophet for divorce. When she demanded more than $200,000 in alimony and other claims, Brigham's lawyers rejected her suit, believing it extravagant. They also argued that Ann Eliza could not divorce Brigham in court because the United States did not recognize plural marriage as legal. Judge James McKean ruled in Ann Eliza's favor, however, and sent Brigham to jail for one night when he, on the advice of his lawyers, refused to pay until after they had appealed the ruling in a higher court.

Newspapers throughout the country recognized the judge's actions as a stunt to embarrass Brigham, and they condemned and ridiculed McKean for it. A few days later, the president of the United States replaced him with another judge, and Brigham went on to pay Ann Eliza's $3,000 legal fees.[3]

Two days after leaving Salt Lake City, Brigham and his company met with the Relief Society in Moroni, a small town in Sanpete Valley. Eliza Snow and Mary Isabella Horne, who were traveling in the company, encouraged the women to continue to cooperate and to be self-sustaining in economic matters. Mary Isabella urged them to put the kingdom of God first in their lives. "What we expect to receive," she said, "we must work for."

Eliza then spoke about religious education. Some families in Sanpete Valley were sending their children to a newly opened school run by a missionary of another faith, and Church leaders worried that his lessons would contradict what the children were learning from their parents and the Church.

"Zion should be the place to educate the children of Zion," Eliza told the women. "Let the children understand that your religion is uppermost in your mind."[4]

In other Sanpete settlements, Brigham encouraged the Saints to embrace a more cooperative economic system. Two years earlier, a nationwide depression had hurt Utah's economy. Several cooperative stores and industries in the territory had weathered the financial crisis, however, strengthening Brigham's belief in cooperation.

Since then, he had called on Saints to live like the ancient people of Enoch, who were united in heart and mind and had no poor among them.[5] The system, known as the United Order of Enoch, called to mind the Lord's revelation on the law of consecration. Members of the order were to provide for one another like a family, freely contributing labor and personal property to promote home-grown industries and improve the local economy.

Many Saints had already organized united orders in their communities. Though the orders differed from one another in structure, they shared the values of economic cooperation, self-sufficiency, and simplicity.[6]

While meeting with the Sanpete Saints, apostle Erastus Snow spoke of how the United Order had blessed Saints in southern Utah. "There is a tendency with us to labor in that selfish way that tends to exalt the few at the expense of the many poor," he noted. "This is in itself an evil."

"The United Order is to learn what to do with the property we have," Brigham added later that day, "and to use ourselves to the accomplishment of God's designs."[7]

Before finishing his Sanpete tour, Brigham spoke with local Church leaders. "We can build temples here cheaper than the one at Salt Lake," he told them. "Do you feel like taking hold and building a temple here yourselves?"

Each man in the room raised his hand to show his support, and they agreed that the prophet should select the site. Brigham had visited several possible locations, and he announced his decision the next day.

"I would say my spirit rests entirely upon the spur of the mountain pointing into Manti," he said.[8]

WHEN BRIGHAM RETURNED FROM central Utah, a man named Meliton Trejo was in Salt Lake City translating the Book of Mormon into Spanish. A veteran soldier from Spain, Meliton had come to the city from the Philippines in the late summer of 1874. He arrived in Utah dressed in a military uniform, and his appearance had quickly attracted the gaze of passersby.

Meliton had come to the territory knowing little about the Church. He had heard of the Saints in the Rocky Mountains and wanted to visit them someday. One night in the Philippines, after praying for direction, he had been prompted in a dream to make the journey. He resigned from the army, sewed all the money he had inside his vest, and sailed for San Francisco.

Once in Salt Lake City, Meliton met a Spanish-speaking man who introduced him to Brigham Young and other Church leaders.[9] Brigham had recently asked two men, Daniel Jones and Henry Brizzee, to prepare for a mission to Mexico. Brigham believed that some of the descendants of Book of Mormon peoples lived there, and he longed to send the gospel to them. But he also knew that Parley Pratt had tried to take the gospel to Latin America in 1851 and that the effort had been unsuccessful partly because the Book of Mormon was not available in Spanish.[10]

As part of Daniel and Henry's preparation, Brigham had asked them to study the language and eventually translate the Book of Mormon. Both men knew some Spanish, but the thought of translating a book of scripture was daunting. Neither felt he had enough experience with the language. They needed a native speaker who could assist them.

Daniel and Henry considered Meliton's arrival a godsend. They taught him the gospel, and Meliton wholeheartedly accepted baptism.[11] Daniel then invited Meliton to stay with him for the winter to work on the translation.

Meliton spent several months translating the sacred text. When money ran out, Daniel received permission from Brigham Young to ask the Saints for donations. More than four hundred donors gave money to support Meliton and to pay for the printing.

After revising the translation, Daniel arranged for one hundred pages of excerpts from the translation to be printed as *Trozos selectos del Libro de Mormon*.[12] Brigham wanted Daniel to make sure the translation was accurate, however, so Daniel arranged to reread the translation with Meliton. As they read, Daniel asked God to help him find any errors in their work. Whenever he sensed a rough spot in the text, he would ask Meliton for help. Meliton would then study the translation closely and find the needed correction. Daniel felt the Lord was guiding their work.

Shortly after *Trozos selectos* was printed, Daniel and other missionaries were called to Mexico. Meliton was not assigned to go with them, but he hoped the missionaries' efforts would bear fruit.[13]

The missionaries departed in the fall of 1875. Before leaving, Daniel and the others carefully loaded fifteen hundred copies of *Trozos selectos* on the backs of pack mules. Then they started down the dirt road, eager to introduce the Book of Mormon to the people of Mexico.[14]

AROUND THIS TIME, SALT Lake City buzzed with news of an upcoming visit from President Ulysses Grant. No

United States president had ever visited the territory, and a delegation of territorial officials, city dignitaries, and private citizens quickly formed to welcome him. Brigham Young was invited to join the delegation, as were John Taylor and Joseph F. Smith.[15]

Grant arrived in the territory in October, and Brigham met him and his wife, Julia, on a train in Ogden. Brigham was able to greet the party briefly before the president excused himself to visit the train's observation car.

"I am anxious to see the country," Grant explained.

After the president left, Julia said, "I am at a loss to know how to address you, Mr. Young."

"I am sometimes called governor," Brigham replied, "sometimes president, and, again, General Young." He had received the last title years earlier as an officer in the Nauvoo Legion.

"As I am accustomed to the military title, I will call you the last," Julia said. Her husband, a hero of the American Civil War, had been an army officer for much of his life.

"Well, madam," said Brigham, "you will now have the opportunity of seeing this poor, despised, and hated people."

"Oh, no, General Young," Julia responded. "To the contrary, your people can only be respected and admired for their endurance, perseverance, and faith." She then added, "There is but one objection to your people—to you, General."

Julia did not need to state her objection; her husband was a staunch opponent of plural marriage. "Well," Brigham said, "without that we would not have the population we have."

"That is prohibited by the laws of the country," Julia said, "and would have been wiped out long ago by the strong arm of the government except through charity for the young and innocent that would necessarily suffer."

Before Brigham could reply, a staff officer invited him to join the president in the observation car, and Brigham took leave of the First Lady.

Later, after arriving in Salt Lake City, Brigham parted with the Grants, expressing hope that they would enjoy their visit. From the train depot, the Grants then left for a tour of the city with George Emery, the territorial governor. As they drove near the temple block, they saw rows of children, dressed in white, lining the streets with their Sunday School teachers. As the Grants' carriage passed, the children strewed flowers in the street and sang to the visitors.

Impressed, President Grant asked, "Whose children are these?"

"Mormon children," said the governor.

The president was silent for several seconds. Everything he had heard about the Saints had led him to believe they were a degenerate people. But the appearance and behavior of these children suggested otherwise.

"I have been deceived," he murmured.[16]

THAT WINTER, SAMUEL CHAMBERS stood up to testify in a meeting of the Salt Lake Stake deacons quorum. Like the men seated around him, he was middle-aged. "I came here for my religion," Samuel told the men. "I disposed of all I had and have come here to help to build up the kingdom of God."

Samuel had been a member of the Church for over thirty years. Born into slavery in the southern United States, he had been baptized at age thirteen after a missionary taught him the gospel. Because he was enslaved, Samuel could not join the rest of the Saints in Nauvoo. He had little contact with the Church in the years that followed, but he kept his faith through the influence of the Holy Spirit.

When the Civil War ended and enslaved people in the United States were freed, he and his wife, Amanda, had no money to move to Utah. They worked for five years, saving every penny they could, before they could make the trip. They came to Utah in April 1870 with Samuel's son, Peter. Amanda's brother and sister-in-law, Edward and Susan Leggroan, moved with their three children to Utah as well.[17]

The Chambers and Leggroan families settled next door to one another in the Salt Lake City First Ward. Richard and Johanna Provis, a mixed-race couple from South Africa, also lived in the ward. The Leggroans joined the Church in 1873 and soon thereafter moved with the Chamberses to the Eighth Ward, where Jane Manning James, her husband, Frank Perkins, and a few other black Saints also lived.[18]

In these wards, black Saints and white Saints worshipped side by side. Although the Church did not extend priesthood ordination to black Saints at this time, Samuel served as an unordained assistant to the deacons quorum and bore his testimony each month at quorum meetings. Amanda participated with Jane in the Relief Society. They paid their tithes and offerings and attended their Church meetings regularly. When calls came to donate to the St. George temple, Samuel donated five dollars and Jane and Frank donated fifty cents each.

Samuel and Amanda, along with several other black Saints, had also recently participated in baptisms for the dead in the Endowment House. Samuel and Amanda were baptized for more than two dozen friends and relatives. Edward Leggroan was baptized for his wife's first husband. Jane Manning James was baptized for a childhood friend.[19]

Samuel cherished his membership in the Church and the opportunity to bear testimony to the deacons quorum. "If I don't bear my testimony," he said, "how do you know how I feel, or how you feel? But if I rise and speak, I know I have a friend, and if I hear you speak as I speak, I know we are one."[20]

LATE IN THE AFTERNOON on April 5, 1876, a thundering blast shattered the spring air over Salt Lake City. A giant fireball rose up from the hill to the north where stone bunkers housed black powder. Something had ignited the explosives, destroying the arsenal.

In the Twentieth Ward's schoolhouse, where Karl Maeser taught classes, the blast sent part of the plaster ceiling crashing to the floor. Since he was scheduled to give a lecture in the schoolhouse that night, Karl knew at once that he had to speak to his bishop about the damage.[21]

Karl found his bishop meeting with Brigham Young at the prophet's office. Karl reported the extensive damage to the schoolhouse and told them that classes could not continue until it was repaired.

"That is exactly right, Brother Maeser," Brigham said. "I have another mission for you."[22]

Karl's heart sank. Only a few years had passed since he had returned from a mission to Germany and Switzerland. His steady employment in the Twentieth Ward school had been a blessing for his family. They were comfortably settled in Salt Lake City and felt at home.[23]

But Brigham did not want him to go far. Like Eliza Snow, Brigham and other Church leaders were worried about educating the rising generation of young people, whose faith had not been tried by the early persecution of the Church or solidified through experiences of conversion and immigration.[24]

Brigham was not opposed to secular knowledge or universities; some of his sons had even attended colleges in the eastern United States. Yet he worried that young Saints in Utah were being taught by people who were deeply critical of the restored gospel. The University of Deseret, first established in 1850, enrolled students from other churches and did not teach Latter-day Saint beliefs as part of the curriculum. Brigham wanted the youth of the Church to have educational opportunities that strengthened their faith and helped create a Zion society.[25]

To achieve these ends, in fact, he had recently founded a school in Provo called Brigham Young Academy. Its first term had just ended, and now he invited Karl to take charge of it.

Karl did not respond to Brigham's invitation right away. But two weeks later, after he had accepted the appointment, Karl visited the prophet. "I am about to leave for Provo, Brother Young, to start my work in the academy," he said. "Have you any instructions?"

"Brother Maeser," said Brigham, "I want you to remember that you ought not to teach even the alphabet or the multiplication table without the Spirit of God."[26]

LATER THAT YEAR, EVERY ward in Salt Lake City held a party to raise money to finish the St. George temple. Knowing twenty-year-old Heber Grant was a reliable young man with many friends, Bishop Edwin Woolley of the Thirteenth Ward asked him to organize his ward's party. "I want you to make a success of it," he told Heber.

The previous year, Heber had been called as a counselor in the presidency of his ward's Young Men's

Mutual Improvement Association (Y.M.M.I.A.), a new organization formed in 1875 after Brigham Young asked wards to organize their young men just as they had organized their young women. As a leader in the Y.M.M.I.A., Heber was responsible for helping young men develop their talents and strengthen their testimonies of the gospel.[27]

Heber had misgivings about Bishop Woolley's request. "I will do my level best," he said, "but you must guarantee, if it doesn't pay, to put up the difference."

He explained that young people wanted to attend dances where they could waltz. The popular dance involved partners holding each other close while spinning around the dance floor in a large circle. Although some people considered the waltz to be less proper than more traditional quadrille dances, Brigham Young was known to allow three waltzes per party. Bishop Woolley disapproved of the dance, however, and had prohibited it at Thirteenth Ward parties.[28]

"Well," Bishop Woolley said, "you can have your three waltzes."

"There's another thing," Heber continued. Without a good band for the dance, he would have a hard time selling tickets. "You won't allow Olsen's Quadrille Band to play in your ward because the flute player once got drunk," he told the bishop. "There is only one first-class string band, and that is Olsen's."

Reluctantly, the bishop agreed to let Heber hire the band as well. "I have let that young man have everything he wanted," he said as he walked away. "I'll roast him in public if he doesn't make a success of it."

Heber recruited the bishop's son Eddie to help sell tickets and prepare the ward building for the party. They cleared away desks from a large room, placed borrowed rugs on the floor, and hung pictures of Brigham Young and other Church leaders on the walls. They then recruited several young men to promote the dance at their workplaces.

On the day of the dance, Heber sat at the door with an alphabetical list of everyone who had purchased tickets. No one was allowed inside who had not paid a dollar and a half for a ticket. Then Brigham Young showed up—without a ticket.

"I understand this is for the benefit of the St. George temple," Brigham said. He threw down ten dollars. "Is that enough for my ticket?"

"Plenty," Heber said, unsure if he should give the prophet change.

That evening, Heber counted the money while Brigham counted the waltzes. The ward brought in more than eighty dollars, which was more than any other ward had collected for the temple. And the young people danced their three waltzes.

Before the party ended, however, Heber whispered to the band leader to play a waltz quadrille, a waltz that contained elements of the classic square dance.

As the band began playing, Heber took a seat beside Brigham to hear what he would say when he saw the fourth waltz. Sure enough, as soon as the young people began the dance, Brigham said, "They are waltzing."

"No," Heber explained, "when they waltz, they waltz all around the room. This is a quadrille."

Brigham looked at Heber and laughed. "Oh, you boys, you boys," he said.[29]

SOON AFTER THE THIRTEENTH Ward dance, Brigham headed south with Wilford Woodruff to dedicate portions of the St. George temple. Although the temple would not be finished until spring, some ordinance rooms were ready for use.[30] In the Nauvoo temple and the Endowment House, the Saints had performed endowments only for the living. Once the St. George temple was dedicated, they would perform endowments for the dead for the first time.[31]

As Brigham neared the settlement, he could easily spot the temple. From a distance, it looked like the Nauvoo temple, but up close its exterior was simpler. It had rows of tall windows and unadorned buttresses to support its high white walls. A domed tower rose above fortresslike battlements that lined the roof.[32]

On New Year's Day 1877, over twelve hundred people squeezed inside the temple basement for the dedication of the baptistry.[33] After climbing to the top step of the baptismal font, Wilford Woodruff called the Saints to attention. "I realize that this assembly cannot bow the knee in their crowded condition," he said, "but you can bow your heads and your hearts unto God."

After Wilford offered the dedicatory prayer, the congregation moved upstairs to an assembly hall. Brigham's arthritis had lately made walking nearly impossible, so three men carried him into the room. Erastus Snow then dedicated the hall, and the three men carried Brigham up more stairs to dedicate a sealing room.

When Brigham returned to the assembly hall, he struggled to stand at the pulpit. Steadying himself with a hickory cane, he said, "I cannot consent in my feelings to retire from this house without exercising my strength—the strength of my lungs, stomach, and speaking organs."

Brigham wanted the Saints to dedicate themselves to redeeming the dead. "When I think upon this subject, I want the tongues of seven thunders to wake up the people," he declared. "Can the fathers be saved without us? No. Can we be saved without them? No. And if we do not wake up and cease to long after the things of this earth, we will find that we as individuals will go down to hell."

Brigham lamented that many Saints were pursuing worldly things. "Supposing we were awake to this thing, namely the salvation of the human family," he said, "this house would be crowded, as we hope it will be, from Monday morning until Saturday night."

At the close of his sermon, Brigham raised his cane in the air. "I do not know whether the people are satisfied with the services of the dedication of the temple or not," he stated. "I am not half-satisfied, and I never expect to be satisfied until the devil is whipped and driven from off the face of the earth."

As he spoke, Brigham struck the pulpit forcefully with his cane, leaving dents in the wood.

"If I mar the pulpit," he said, "some of these good workmen can fix it up again."[34]

ON JANUARY 9, WILFORD WOODRUFF waded into the temple's baptismal font with Brigham's daughter Susie, now eighteen years old and married to a young man named Alma Dunford. Using a crutch and walking stick, Brigham stood as witness as Wilford baptized Susie for one of her deceased friends, the first baptism for the dead in the St. George temple. Afterward, Wilford and Brigham laid their hands on Susie's head and confirmed her on the deceased's behalf.

Two days later, Wilford and Brigham supervised the first endowments for the dead performed in any temple. Wilford then spent nearly every day afterward doing temple work. He began wearing a white suit, the first time someone had worn white clothes rather than normal dress clothes as part of the temple ceremonies. Susie's mother, Lucy, who likewise dedicated herself to temple work, wore a white dress as an example for women.[35]

As Wilford worked in the temple, Brigham asked him and other Church leaders to write out the endowment ceremony and the other temple ordinances. Since the time of Joseph Smith, the words of the ordinances had been preserved only through word of mouth. Now that the ordinances would be performed at a distance from Church headquarters, Brigham wanted the ceremonies written down to ensure that they would occur the same way in each temple.[36]

In standardizing the ordinances, Brigham was fulfilling a charge Joseph Smith had given him after the first endowments in Nauvoo. "This is not arranged right, but we have done the best we could under the circumstances," Joseph had told him then. "I wish you to take this matter in hand and organize and systematize all these ceremonies."[37]

Wilford and others worked for weeks on the assignment. After writing down the ceremonies, they read them to Brigham, who accepted or revised them as the Spirit directed. When they finished, Brigham said to Wilford, "Now you have before you an example to carry on the endowments in all the temples until the coming of the Son of Man."[38]

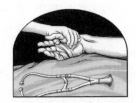

CHAPTER 29

To Die in the Harness

Brigham Young left the red cliffs of southern Utah in mid-April 1877. Heading home to Salt Lake City, he knew his days were numbered. "I feel many times that I could not live an hour longer," he told the St. George Saints before he left. "I know not how soon the messenger will call for me, but I calculate to die in the harness."[1]

A few days later, he stopped in Cedar City to speak to a reporter about John D. Lee and the Mountain Meadows massacre.[2] The federal government had spent more than a decade investigating those who had carried out the killings. John and other men, including Parowan stake president William Dame, had been arrested several years earlier to stand trial for their part in the massacre, generating renewed national interest in the nearly twenty-year-old crime.[3] The charges against William and others had since been dropped, but John had gone to trial twice before being convicted and executed by firing squad for his leading role in the attack.

During the trials, prosecutors and reporters had hoped that John would implicate the prophet in the massacre. But even though he was angry with Brigham for not shielding him from punishment, John had refused to blame him for the murders.[4]

John's execution had ignited a national furor among people who falsely assumed that Brigham had ordered the massacre.[5] In some places, anger toward the Church was making it hard for missionaries to find people to teach, and some elders were choosing to return home. Brigham generally did not respond to such attacks on him or the Church, but he wanted to go on the record about the massacre and agreed to answer the reporter's questions.[6]

The reporter asked Brigham if John had received orders from Church headquarters to kill the emigrants. "None that I have any knowledge of," Brigham replied, "and certainly none from me." He said if he had known about the plan to kill the emigrants, he would have tried to stop it.

"I would have gone to that camp and fought the Indians and white men who took part in the perpetration of the massacre to the death, rather than such a deed should have been committed," he said.[7]

Several days later, Brigham stopped in Sanpete Valley to dedicate the temple site in Manti. While there, the Spirit whispered to him that he needed to reorganize the Church's priesthood structure.[8]

Brigham had already begun making some changes to Church organization. Two years earlier, he had restructured the Quorum of the Twelve to give seniority to apostles who had remained faithful to their testimonies since the time of their call. This move had granted John Taylor and Wilford Woodruff greater seniority than Orson Hyde and Orson Pratt, who had both left the quorum briefly during Joseph Smith's lifetime. The change made John Taylor the senior member of the Twelve and Brigham's likely successor as president of the Church.[9]

But on the road and in meetings with local Church leaders, Brigham could see other changes that needed to be made. Some of the Church's thirteen stakes were overseen by stake presidents, while members of the Twelve presided over others—sometimes without counselors or high councils. Some wards had bishops and others had presiding bishops, and hardly anyone knew how the two callings differed. A few wards had no bishop at all.[10]

Aaronic Priesthood quorums were also disorganized. Aaronic Priesthood holders took care of ward buildings, visited families, and taught the gospel. Yet many wards lacked enough Aaronic Priesthood holders to form quorums, often because grown men were usually the only ones given the Aaronic Priesthood, and they were normally ordained to the Melchizedek Priesthood soon thereafter.

In the spring and summer of 1877, Brigham, his counselors, and the Quorum of the Twelve worked together to reorganize wards and stakes and strengthen Aaronic and Melchizedek Priesthood quorums. They directed that all Church members should belong to a ward where a bishop could look after them with the help of two counselors. They designated one man, Edward Hunter, to serve as the only presiding bishop in the Church.

The First Presidency and the Twelve also asked local priesthood leaders to ordain young men to offices in the Aaronic Priesthood. They specifically asked adult teachers and priests to bring young men with them on visits to the Saints, thus training the boys in their priesthood duties. Each settlement was asked to organize a Mutual Improvement Association (M.I.A.) for the young women and young men.

Traveling throughout the territory week after week, the First Presidency and the Twelve released apostles from stake presidencies and called new stake presidents to take their place. They made sure each stake president had two counselors and each stake had a high council. They also asked each stake to hold a quarterly conference.[11]

The strain of traveling and preaching soon wearied Brigham. He looked pale and tired. "In my anxiety to see the house of God set in order," he admitted, "I have somewhat overtaxed my strength."[12]

ON JUNE 20, FRANCIS LYMAN received a telegram from George Q. Cannon, who was now serving as a counselor in the First Presidency. "President asks are you willing to act as president of Tooele Stake?" it read. "If so can you be here to accompany the Twelve Saturday morning?"[13]

Francis lived in Fillmore, Utah. The Tooele Stake was over one hundred miles to the north. He had never lived there and knew few people in the stake. In Fillmore, where he had lived for more than a decade, he held high positions in local government. If he agreed to serve in Tooele, he would have to uproot his family and move with them to a new place.

And Saturday morning was just three days away.

At thirty-seven, Francis was a committed Latter-day Saint who had served a mission to the British Isles and had taken an active part in his priesthood quorum. He had also gathered his family genealogy, looking forward to the day when ordinance work could be done in the house of the Lord.

"The height of my ambition," he had once noted in his journal, "is to live the life of a Latter-day Saint and to lead my family to do likewise."[14]

But he was still coming to terms with the decision of his father, Amasa Lyman, to join William Godbe's New Movement. He had always hoped that his father would come back into the Church. They had worked together on the family genealogy and had recently enjoyed some happy interactions. Yet Amasa had died in February, still separated from the Church.

Near the end, Francis had visited his father on his sickbed. "Don't go away," Amasa had said. "I want you to be near me."

"How long?" Francis asked.

"Forever," he whispered.[15]

After Amasa's death, Francis was anxious to have his father's membership and priesthood restored, which would allow the family to feel whole again. In April, Francis had asked Brigham Young what could be done. Nothing for the present, Brigham had said. The matter was in the hands of the Lord.

Francis had accepted Brigham's decision, and he willingly undertook the prophet's new assignment for him in Tooele. "I will be with the Twelve on Saturday morning," he telegrammed George Q. Cannon.[16]

The Tooele Stake was created on June 24, 1877, and Francis was set apart as its president on the same day.[17] Prior to that time, the six principal settlements in the Tooele area had branches of the Church supervised by a presiding bishop named John Rowberry. Upon the creation of the new stake, each of the branches became a ward ranging in size from twenty-seven families to two hundred.[18]

Realizing that some Tooele Saints might grumble that their new president was a young man from another stake, Francis soon bought a house in the center of town and called two local men as his counselors. He then invited Bishop Rowberry to join him on visits to the various wards, where they organized new priesthood quorums and presidencies and spoke to the Saints, encouraging them in their devotions to the Lord.[19]

"Our temporal and spiritual interests of the kingdom are inseparably connected," Francis taught the members of his new stake. "Be humble before the Lord and possess the light of His Holy Spirit for our constant guide."[20]

IN MID-JULY 1877, JANE Richards sat on the stand beside Brigham Young in the Weber Stake tabernacle in Ogden. The occasion was a conference for the city's Relief Societies and Young Ladies' Associations. Jane, the president of the Ogden Ward Relief Society, had organized the event and invited Brigham to speak.[21]

Leading such a large group of women had not always come easily for Jane. She had first joined the Relief Society as a young woman in Nauvoo.[22] But when she was called to lead the Ogden Ward Relief Society in 1872, she had hesitated. Her health had always been poor, despite the strength she found in priesthood blessings, and it was particularly bad when she received her call.

One day, her friend Eliza Snow had visited her. Eliza urged her to live, certain that Jane still had something more to do in her life. While ministering to Jane, Eliza promised her that if she accepted the calling to lead the Relief Society in Ogden, she would have health and blessings from the Lord.

Jane was healed a short time later by the power of God, but she still spent weeks pondering whether she should accept the call. Finally, her bishop and Relief Society sisters implored her to do so. "The Lord has raised you from a bed of sickness to do us good," they said, "and we want you to accept the office." Jane then realized that her service contributed to a greater good, no matter how tired and fearful she felt.[23]

Now, five years later, the Weber Stake tabernacle was crowded with women and men anxious to hear the prophet. After Brigham addressed the Saints, other Church leaders spoke. Among them was Jane's husband, apostle Franklin Richards, who had recently been released as the Weber Stake president as part of the priesthood reorganization.

During one talk, Brigham turned to Jane and quietly asked her thoughts on organizing stake Relief Societies and having them hold quarterly conferences. He had recently been considering doing so as part of his efforts to better organize the Church, and he had already consulted several people on the matter, including Bathsheba Smith, another woman active in Relief Society leadership.[24]

The question surprised Jane, but not because the idea of a stake Relief Society was hard to imagine. Though Relief Societies currently functioned only at the ward level, she and her counselors in the Ogden Ward already acted like an informal stake Relief Society presidency when they advised smaller Relief Societies in the area. What truly surprised her was the notion of Relief Societies holding regular conferences.

Jane had little time to get used to the idea. Before the conference ended, Brigham called her to serve as the Weber Stake Relief Society president and asked her to collect reports from ward Relief Society presidents about the spiritual and financial conditions of the women in their congregations. If his health permitted, he intended to meet with them again at their next conference to hear their reports.

Following the conference, Brigham asked Jane to travel with his company to neighboring settlements. On the way, he taught her about the duties of her new calling and the importance of keeping careful records of what she and the Relief Society accomplished. Leading a stake Relief Society would be a major undertaking. Before the recent Church reorganization, Jane had advised three Relief Societies in Ogden. The newly formed Weber Stake, in contrast, had sixteen wards.[25]

When Jane returned to Ogden, she met with her ward Relief Society. "I would like to hear from all the sisters and know how they feel about what President Young told us," she said.

For the rest of the meeting, Jane listened as the women bore testimony and shared their experiences at the conference. Many of them expressed their love for the gospel. "We have the light and knowledge of the Holy Spirit," Jane told the sisters, "and when we lose that, great is the darkness."

At the next meeting a few days later, Jane added to her testimony. "I wish to live my religion," she declared, "and do all the good I can."[26]

THAT SUMMER, WHILE THE Church underwent major reorganization, Susie Young Dunford wondered if it was time to make changes in her own life. Her husband, Alma, had just left on a mission to Britain. But rather than missing him, she was grateful he was gone.

Her marriage had been unhappy almost from the start. Like his cousin Morley, who had married Susie's sister Dora, Alma drank alcohol regularly. After the Word of Wisdom was revealed in 1833, many Saints had not followed its counsel closely. But in 1867, Susie's father, Brigham Young, had begun urging the Saints to obey it more exactly by abstaining from coffee, tea, tobacco, and hard liquor.

Not everyone accepted the counsel, and Alma was often defensive about his drinking. Sometimes he even became abusive. One night, after he had been drinking, he had thrown Susie and their six-month-old daughter, Leah, out of the house, yelling at them to never come back.

Susie had come back, hopeful that things would change. She and Alma had a son now as well, Bailey, and she wanted to make her marriage successful. But nothing changed. When Alma received his mission call, she was relieved. Sometimes young men like Alma were sent on missions to help them grow up and reform their behavior.

Susie enjoyed the newfound peace and quiet in her home. The more time she spent away from Alma, the less she wanted to see him again.[27]

Alma's family lived beside Bear Lake, near Utah's northern border, and Susie planned to visit them that summer. Before heading north, however, she went to see her father about another matter weighing on her mind.[28]

Recently, Saints had published a book in New York City called *The Women of Mormondom* to counter the depictions of Latter-day Saint women found in the books and lectures of Fanny Stenhouse, Ann Eliza Young, and other critics of the Church. *The Women of Mormondom* contained the testimonies of several prominent women in the Church and presented their experiences in a positive light.

To help promote the book, Susie wanted to go on a national speaking tour with two of her father's wives, Eliza Snow and Zina Young, and her sister Zina Presendia Williams. Susie had always longed to be a great speaker and writer, and she was eager to travel the country and give lectures.[29]

Brigham spoke favorably to Susie about the tour, but he wanted her to undertake it for the right reasons. He knew she was ambitious, and he had always tried to support her developing talents by sending her to school with some of the best teachers in the territory.

But he did not want her to seek worldly acclaim at the expense of her family.

"If you were to become the greatest woman in the world," he told her, "and you should neglect your duty as wife and mother, you would wake up on the morning of the First Resurrection and find you had failed in everything."

As usual, her father was not mincing words. But Susie did not feel rebuked. His manner was gentle and understanding, and he seemed to see into her soul. "All that you can do after you have satisfied the righteous claims of your home and family," he reassured her, "will redound to your credit and to the honor and glory of God."

"I wish I knew the gospel was true," Susie admitted as they continued to talk. She wanted to know it was true deep within her soul, the way her parents knew it.[30]

"There is only one way, daughter, that you can get the testimony of the truth," Brigham said simply, "and this is the way I attained my testimony and the way your mother got hers. On your knees before the Lord, go in prayer and He will hear and answer."

A thrill swept through Susie, and she knew what her father said was true. "If it had not been for Mormonism," he then told her, "I would be today a carpenter in a country village."

Brigham had set aside his trade long before Susie was born, but he was still the same man of faith who had left his home in New York to shake the hand of a prophet of God in Kirtland. Before he passed away, Susie wanted him to know what he meant to her.

"How proud and grateful I am," she said, "that I have been permitted to come upon the earth as your daughter."[31]

ON THE EVENING OF August 23, 1877, Brigham sat with Eliza Snow in the room where his family normally prayed together. They spoke about the plan to send Eliza, Zina, Zina Presendia, and Susie east to promote *The Women of Mormondom* and give people a better understanding of the Church.

"It is an experiment, but one that I should like to see tried," Brigham said.

He stood and picked up his candle. Earlier that evening, he had spoken with bishops in Salt Lake City, instructing them to make sure priests and teachers were meeting monthly with each member of their ward. He had then appointed a committee to oversee the construction of an assembly hall next to the Salt Lake temple. Now he was tired.

"I think now I shall go and take my rest," he told Eliza.

During the night, sharp pains seized Brigham's abdomen. In the morning, his son Brigham Young Jr. rushed to his side and took him by the hand. "How do you feel?" he asked. "Do you think you will pull through?"

"I don't know," Brigham said. "Ask the Lord."

For two days he lay in bed, enduring the agony with little sleep. Despite the pain, he made jokes, trying to ease the worry of the family and friends who gathered around him. Whenever anyone asked him if he suffered, he said, "No, I don't know that I do."

Apostles and other Church leaders gave him blessings, rallying his spirits. But after four days, he began to slip in and out of consciousness. His symptoms became worse, and the doctor operated on his abdomen to no avail.

On August 29 the doctor gave him medicine for the pain and moved his bed closer to the window for fresh air. Outside, a crowd of Saints stood in reverent silence in the yard of the Lion House. Brigham's family, meanwhile, knelt in prayer around his bed.

Lying beside the window, Brigham revived for a moment. He opened his eyes and gazed up at the ceiling. "Joseph," he said. "Joseph, Joseph, Joseph."

His breathing then grew shorter and shorter until it ceased.[32]

CHAPTER 30

A Steady, Onward
Movement

When Wilford Woodruff arrived in Salt Lake City three days after Brigham Young's death, thousands of mourners were filing through the tabernacle, where Brigham's body lay in state. The prophet's casket was simple and had a glass panel on its lid, allowing the Saints to view his face one more time.

Saints in Utah believed that Brigham's leadership had helped fulfill Isaiah's prophecy of the desert blossoming as a rose. Under Brigham's direction, the Saints had irrigated the valleys of the mountains, watering the farms, gardens, orchards, and pastures that sustained several hundred settlements of Latter-day Saints. Most of these settlements had taken root, fostering communities of Saints who strove to live the principles of unity and cooperation. A few settlements, like Salt Lake City, were rapidly become urban centers of manufacturing and commerce.

But Brigham's success as a planner and pioneer did not surpass his service as a prophet of God. Many of the people honoring Brigham that morning had heard him speak or seen him out among the Saints in the territory. Some had known him as a missionary in the eastern United States or England. Others remembered how he guided the Church safely through the uncertainty following Joseph Smith's death. Others still had crossed the Great Plains and Rocky Mountains at his side. Many people, including the tens of thousands of Saints who had gathered to Utah from Europe and other parts of the world, had never known the Church without him.

As Wilford stood over the casket, he thought his old friend looked natural. The Lion of the Lord was at rest.[1]

On September 2, 1877, the day after the viewing, Saints filled the tabernacle for Brigham's funeral while thousands more stood outside. Rows of looping garlands hung from the tabernacle's arched ceiling, and black fabric draped the organ. The Saints did not dress in black, as was customary at funerals in the United States. Brigham had asked them not to.[2]

The Church had not yet sustained a new First Presidency after Brigham's death, so John Taylor officiated at the meeting as president of the Quorum of the Twelve.[3] Several apostles paid tribute to the deceased prophet. Wilford spoke of Brigham's great desire to build temples and redeem the dead. "He felt the weight of this dispensation resting upon him," Wilford said. "I rejoice that he lived long enough to enter into one temple and attend to its dedication, and to commence the work of others."[4]

John testified that God would continue to lead the Church through the turmoil of the latter days. Already, the *Salt Lake Tribune* had predicted that Brigham's death would lead to squabbling among Church leaders and disaffection among the Saints.[5] Other critics hoped the courts would bring the Church's ruin. George Reynolds, who had been retried and convicted for bigamy, was now appealing his case before the United States Supreme Court. If the court upheld his conviction, the Saints would be virtually powerless to defend their way of life.[6]

But John did not fear the future. "The work we are engaged in is not the work of man. Joseph Smith did not originate it; neither did Brigham Young," he declared. "It emanated from God. He is its author."

"And it is for us, as Latter-day Saints, now to magnify our calling," he said, "that as the changing scenes we are anticipating shall come upon all nations—revolutions succeeding revolutions—we may have a steady, onward movement, guided by the Lord."[7]

AFTER THE DEATH OF her father, Susie Young Dunford struggled to know what to do about her failing marriage. When her husband, Alma, left on a mission, she had hoped the experience would change him. But he continued to be angry and defensive in his letters to her.[8]

Not wanting to act rashly, Susie considered her options, praying continually about her dilemma. Shortly before his death, her father had reminded her that the roles of wife and mother were central to her success in life. Susie wanted to fulfill those roles righteously. But did that mean she had to stay in an abusive marriage?[9]

One night, Susie dreamed that she and Alma were visiting her father in the Lion House. Brigham had an assignment for them, but rather than give it to Alma, as he usually did when he was alive, he gave it to Susie. As she left to fulfill the assignment, Susie encountered Eliza Snow in the hall. Why had her father given her the assignment, Susie asked, when he had always asked Alma in the past?

"He did not understand then," Eliza said in the dream. "But he does now."

Eliza's words lingered with Susie after she awoke. It was a comfort to realize that her father might have a different perspective in the spirit world than he had in life.

Susie filed for divorce soon after, and Alma returned from England and began consulting lawyers. Church leaders often tried to reconcile couples who wanted to divorce. But leaders also believed that any woman who wanted a divorce from an unhappy marriage should receive one.[10] This was no less true for women who struggled to adapt to the challenges of plural marriage. Since the local court system did not recognize these marriages, local Church leaders handled divorce cases involving plural wives.[11]

Because Susie was Alma's only wife, her case was different. As a woman in an abusive marriage, she could expect to receive a divorce, but she and Alma had to go before a civil court. Courts throughout the United States and Europe usually sided with men in divorce cases at this time. Although Church leaders counseled husbands to provide amply for former wives and their children, Alma insisted on getting custody of the children and nearly all the family's property.

Susie's and Alma's divorce hearing lasted two days. In the end, Alma received full custody of their four-year-old daughter, Leah. Since their son, Bailey, was only two, the court placed him under Susie's care while designating Alma his legal guardian.[12]

Losing her children tore at Susie's heart, and she left the courtroom distraught over the ruling. But because the divorce had left her with no property and no means of financial support, she had little time to dwell on her pain. She badly needed a plan for what to do next.[13]

A short time after the divorce, Susie spoke to President John Taylor about her future. She had left school at age fourteen, but now she wanted to return. President Taylor was supportive and offered to help her get started at the local secondary school. As Susie left his office, however, she encountered apostle Erastus Snow.

"If you want to go to school, I'll tell you the place to go," he said. "A place where you can fill your soul with the rich light of inspiration as well as crowd your mind with the learning of the ancients and moderns. This place is the Brigham Young Academy at Provo."

The next day, Susie took a train south to see the academy. Even though her father had founded the school, she knew little about it or its purpose. When she arrived, she met with the principal, her old schoolteacher Karl Maeser. He greeted her warmly and added her name to the rolls of the academy.[14]

MEANWHILE, ON THE KALAUPAPA Peninsula on the island of Molokai, Jonathan Napela's health had taken a turn for the worse. When Napela had begun living among the people with leprosy on the peninsula, he was not afflicted with the disease ravaging so many other Hawaiians, including his wife, Kitty. Now, almost five years later, the disease had taken hold of him too. His face was swollen almost beyond recognition, and many of his teeth had fallen out. His hands, which had blessed countless people for more than twenty years, were riddled with sores.[15]

On January 26, 1878, Napela and Kitty welcomed into their home two missionaries, Henry Richards and Keau Kalawaia, as well as Nehemia Kahuelaau, the presiding Church authority on Molokai. Keau and Nehemia were longtime Hawaiian Saints, and both had served several missions. Henry was the youngest brother of apostle Franklin Richards and had served his first mission to the islands in the 1850s, a few years after Napela's baptism. Henry had last seen Napela in Salt Lake City in 1869, but now, less than a decade later, he was surprised by how much Napela's appearance had changed.[16]

The next day was the Sabbath, and Napela planned to take his guests to visit the branches on the peninsula. Despite his illness, Napela continued to lead the Church in Kalaupapa, overseeing seventy-eight Saints in two branches. But before Henry could travel throughout the settlements, he needed to present a visitor's permit to Father Damien, the Catholic priest who served as the colony's superintendent. Because the Hawaiian board of health advised visitors against spending the night with people who had leprosy, Henry would stay at Father Damien's house until morning.

Father Damien had in fact already contracted leprosy, but the disease was still in its earliest stages and no one knew about his condition. Like Napela, he had devoted his life to caring for the spiritual and physical well-being of the exiles on Kalaupapa. Though he and Napela disagreed on some religious matters, they had become close friends.[17]

In the morning, Napela and Henry attended a branch meeting in the home of Lepo, the branch president of the Saints on the eastern shore of the peninsula. Between forty and fifty people, many of whom were not members of the Church, attended the meeting. Some of them appeared healthy. Others were covered from head to foot in sores. The sight of their suffering moved

Henry to tears. He and Keau spoke for forty-five minutes each. When they finished, Nehemia and Napela gave brief remarks.

After the morning meeting, Napela took Henry and Keau to visit the other branch on the peninsula. Henry then spent the rest of the evening and the following morning visiting the sickest people in the settlement with Father Damien.

Napela, Nehemia, and Keau were waiting for Henry when he returned. Before his visitors left, Napela asked them for a blessing. It would not be long before he and Kitty were bedridden, and they would probably never see Henry again.

Henry placed his hands on Napela's head and spoke the words of the blessing. With heavy hearts, the old friends then said goodbye, and Henry, Keau, and Nehemia started back up the steep mountain trail.[18]

LATER THAT SUMMER, IN rural Farmington, Utah, Aurelia Rogers had dinner with two prominent Relief Society leaders from Salt Lake City, Eliza Snow and Emmeline Wells. The women had come to Farmington for a Relief Society conference, and Aurelia, a local Relief Society secretary, had an idea she urgently wanted to share with them.[19]

Aurelia was keenly aware of the needs of children. When she was twelve, her mother had died, leaving her and her older sister in charge of four younger siblings while their father served a mission. Now in her forties, she had seven living children, the youngest a boy just three years old. Lately, she had worried about the young boys in her community. They were rowdy and often stayed out late at night.

"What will our girls do for good husbands?" Aurelia asked during dinner. "Could there not be an organization for little boys, and have them trained to make better men?"

Eliza was intrigued. She agreed that young boys needed more spiritual and moral guidance than they received in Sunday School or their regular day schools.

Eliza took the idea to John Taylor, who gave his approval. She sought the support of Aurelia's bishop, John Hess, as well. Eliza wrote him about the proposed organization, and Bishop Hess soon called Aurelia as president of the ward's new Primary Mutual Improvement Association.

As Aurelia planned how to reach out to the boys in her ward, she realized their meetings would be incomplete without the girls. She wrote Eliza, asking if she should also invite the girls to take part in Primary.

"We must have the girls as well as the boys," Eliza wrote back. "They must be trained together."[20]

On a Sunday in August 1878, Aurelia and Bishop Hess met with parents in Farmington to organize the Primary. The bishop spoke first. "I hope parents will feel the importance of this movement," he said. "If anything in this life should engross the attention of parents, it should be the care of their children." He set apart Aurelia and her counselors, and Aurelia spoke strongly about the need for an organization to support parents in teaching children.

"I feel that this move will be of much benefit," she said. She then compared the children in Farmington to an orchard of young trees. "The roots of the trees should be looked to," she said, "for if the root is sound, the tree will be sound, and there will be but little trouble with the branches."[21]

More than two hundred children gathered two Sundays later for the first meeting of the Primary. Aurelia did her best to maintain order. She organized the children into classes by age and assigned the oldest child in each class to act as a monitor. At the next meeting, she invited the children to raise their hands to sustain her and the other leaders.

Aurelia's teachings to the children were simple and sincere: No child is better than another. Avoid contention with others. Always return good for evil.[22]

IN SEPTEMBER 1878, ABOUT a month after the organization of the Primary, President Taylor sent apostles Orson Pratt and Joseph F. Smith on a mission to gather more information about early Church history. Orson was the Church historian, and Joseph had long worked in the Historian's Office.

Traveling east, Orson and Joseph stopped in Missouri to visit David Whitmer, one of the Three Witnesses of the Book of Mormon. The apostles wanted to interview him and see if he would sell them the manuscript that had been used by the printer to typeset the first edition of the Book of Mormon. Martin Harris had passed away in Utah in 1875, and David was the only one of the Three Witnesses still alive.

David agreed to speak to the apostles in their hotel room. He had not returned to the Church after his 1838 excommunication, though recently he had helped found a church that used the Book of Mormon as scripture. Now over seventy years old, David expressed surprise when Orson introduced himself. In 1835, David had assisted Joseph Smith, Oliver Cowdery, and Martin Harris in calling Orson as one of the first apostles of the dispensation. At the time, Orson had been a shy, slender young man. Now he had a broad waist, a receding hairline, and a long white beard.[23]

Soon after the interview began, Orson asked David if he remembered when he saw the gold plates Joseph Smith used to translate the Book of Mormon.

"It was in June 1829," David said. "It was just as though Joseph, Oliver, and I were sitting just here on a log, when we were overshadowed by a light." David related that an angel had then appeared with the ancient records, the Urim and Thummim, and other Nephite artifacts.

453

"I saw them just as plain as I see this bed," he said, striking the bed beside him with his hand. "I heard the voice of the Lord as distinctly as I ever heard anything in my life, declaring that the records of the plates of the Book of Mormon were translated by the gift and power of God."

Orson and Joseph asked more questions about the Church's past, and David answered them with as much detail as he could. They inquired about the printer's manuscript of the Book of Mormon, which Oliver Cowdery had given to David. "Would you not part with it to a purchaser?" Orson asked.

"No. Oliver charged me to keep it," David said. "I consider these things sacred and would not part with nor barter them for money."[24]

The next day, David showed the manuscript to the apostles. As he did so, he noted that the Lord had wanted His servants to take the Book of Mormon to all the world.

"Yes," Joseph replied, "and we have sent that book to the Danes, the Swedes, the Spanish, the Italians, the French, the Germans, the Welsh, and to the islands of the sea."

"So, Father Whitmer," Joseph continued, "the Church has not been idle."[25]

LATER THAT FALL, IN Utah, sixty-seven-year-old Ane Sophie Dorius traveled to the St. George temple with her oldest son, Carl. Nearly thirty years had passed since Ane Sophie had divorced Carl's father, Nicolai, after he joined the Latter-day Saints. She had since cast aside her bitterness toward the Church, embraced the everlasting gospel, and left her native Denmark to gather to Zion. Now she was about to participate in sacred ordinances that would begin to mend her fractured family.[26]

Ane Sophie had emigrated to Utah in 1874, two years after Nicolai passed away. Before he died, Nicolai had expressed hope that he and Ane Sophie would one day be sealed together for eternity.[27]

When Ane Sophie arrived in Utah, she settled in Sanpete Valley near the families of her three surviving children with Nicolai—Carl, Johan, and Augusta. Over the years, Ane Sophie had seen her sons during their several missions to Scandinavia. But when she reunited with Augusta, who was thirty-six years old and the mother of seven children, it was the first time they had seen each other in over two decades.[28]

Settling in Ephraim, Ane Sophie embraced her new life as a mother and grandmother. When Brigham Young and other Church leaders reorganized the wards and stakes in 1877, they split the Ephraim Ward in half and called Carl to serve as the bishop of the Ephraim South Ward. Afterward, whenever Ane Sophie attended a play or musical performance in town, she would enter without a ticket and simply proclaim with a smile, "I am Bishop Dorius's mother."

Ane Sophie had been a successful baker in Denmark, and her family in Utah benefited from her talents after her arrival. She enjoyed dressing nicely for get-togethers where Danish pastries were served. On her birthday, she would wear a red geranium on her dress, bake a large cake, and invite all her family and friends to celebrate with her.[29]

Ane Sophie and Carl entered the St. George temple on November 5, and Ane Sophie was baptized for her mother and for her sister who had passed away when she was young. Carl received the ordinance for Ane Sophie's father. Ane Sophie received her endowment the following day and later performed the ordinance for her mother and sister while Carl performed it on behalf of his grandfather. Ane Sophie's parents were also sealed together, with her and Carl acting as proxies.

On the day she received her endowment, Ane Sophie was sealed to Nicolai, with Carl acting as proxy, healing the bond that had been broken in mortality. Carl was then sealed to his parents, with apostle Erastus Snow, one of the first missionaries to Denmark, acting as proxy for his father.[30]

IN EARLY JANUARY 1879, Emmeline Wells and Zina Presendia Williams, one of Brigham Young's daughters, left Utah to attend a national convention of women's rights leaders in Washington, DC.[31] Since the indignation meetings of 1870, Latter-day Saint women had continued to champion women's rights publicly in Utah and the rest of the country. Their work had even attracted the attention of some of the nation's leading activists for women's rights, including Susan B. Anthony and Elizabeth Cady Stanton, who together came to Salt Lake City and spoke to Latter-day Saint women in the summer of 1871.[32]

While attending the convention in Washington, Emmeline and Zina Presendia intended to lobby Congress on behalf of the Church and Utah's women. Recently, in ongoing efforts to weaken the Saints politically, some legislators had proposed taking the right to vote away from Utah women. Emmeline and Zina Presendia wanted to defend their right to vote, speak out against the government's efforts to interfere with the Church, and seek political support at a time when George Reynolds's bigamy conviction was being reviewed by the United States Supreme Court.[33]

This was not the first time Emmeline had undertaken an enormous challenge for the Church. In 1876, at the height of a grasshopper infestation, Brigham Young, Eliza Snow, and leaders of the retrenchment movement had called her to lead efforts to store grain in the territory. By the end of 1877, she had led the Relief Societies and Young Ladies' Associations in collecting more than ten thousand bushels of grain and building two granaries in Salt Lake City. Following her instructions, many Relief Societies in the territory had also stored grain in bins in their Relief Society halls or ward buildings.[34]

Emmeline, a plural wife of Daniel Wells, was also known as a staunch defender of plural marriage and the rights of Latter-day Saint women. In 1877, she became the editor of the *Woman's Exponent,* and she used its columns to express her opinions on a variety of matters, both political and spiritual. Though swamped with work since taking the lead on the newspaper, she believed that publishing it was vital to the cause of the Latter-day Saints.[35]

"Our paper is improving and benefiting society," Emmeline noted in her journal soon after taking over the *Woman's Exponent*. "I desire to do all in my power to help elevate the condition of my own people, especially women."[36]

When Emmeline and Zina Presendia arrived in Washington, George Q. Cannon, Susan B. Anthony, and Elizabeth Cady Stanton welcomed them to the city. They also learned that two days earlier, the Supreme Court had unanimously upheld George Reynolds's conviction, ruling that the United States Constitution protected religious beliefs but not necessarily religious action. The court's decision, which could not be appealed, meant that the federal government was free to pass and enforce laws prohibiting plural marriage.[37]

In the days that followed, Emmeline and Zina Presendia attended the women's convention, defending plural marriage and their right to vote. "The women of Utah have never broken any law of that territory," Emmeline declared, "and it would be unjust as well as impolitic to deprive them of this right."

"The women of Utah do not propose to relinquish their rights," Zina Presendia added, "but to aid their sisters throughout the land."[38]

On January 13, Emmeline, Zina Presendia, and two other women from the convention went to the White House to meet President Rutherford Hayes. The president invited the group into his library and listened politely as the women read the resolutions of the convention, including some that rebuked him for not doing more to support women's rights.

Emmeline and Zina Presendia also cautioned the president against enforcing the Morrill antipolygamy law of 1862. "Many thousand women would be made outcasts," they said, "and their children made illegitimate before the world."

President Hayes expressed sympathy, but he made no promises to help. His wife, Lucy, soon entered the room, listened graciously to Emmeline and Zina Presendia's appeal, and gave the visitors a tour of the White House.[39]

In the following weeks, Emmeline and Zina Presendia testified before a congressional committee and spoke to leading politicians on behalf of the Saints. They also presented a memorial to Congress asking for the repeal of the Morrill law. In the memorial, they asked Congress to pass laws that would recognize the legal status of the wives and children in existing plural marriages.[40] Some people were impressed by their courageous defense of the Saints' beliefs. Others treated them like curiosities or complained about plural wives being allowed to speak at the national women's rights convention.[41]

Before leaving Washington, Emmeline and Zina Presendia attended two parties hosted by Lucy Hayes. Despite their efforts, Emmeline and Zina Presendia had been unable to change the president's view of the Saints, and he remained determined to destroy the Church's "temporal power" in Utah. Still, Emmeline appreciated Lucy's kindness and admired her simple tastes, charming manner, and firm refusal to serve alcohol in the White House.

At a reception on January 18, Emmeline presented Lucy with a copy of *The Women of Mormondom* and a personal letter. Inside the book she had written a short message:

"Please accept this token of the esteem of a Mormon wife."[42]

CHAPTER 31

The Shattered Threads of Life

On a cold day in January 1879, Ovando Hollister took a seat in John Taylor's office. Ovando was a tax collector in Utah Territory who sometimes wrote articles for a newspaper in the eastern states. After the United States Supreme Court's ruling on the George Reynolds case, the newspaper wanted Ovando to learn what John, the Church's senior apostle, thought about the decision.

John did not usually grant interviews to reporters, but since it was a government representative asking, he felt obligated to make known his views on religious freedom and the Supreme Court ruling. "A religious faith amounts to nothing unless we are permitted to carry it into effect," he told Ovando. The court's decision was unjust, he explained, because it restricted the Saints' right to practice their beliefs. "I do not believe that the

Supreme Court of the United States nor the Congress of the United States has any right to interfere with my religious views," he said.

Was it worth continuing the practice of plural marriage, Ovando asked, if it meant constant opposition from the government?

"I would respectfully say we are not the parties who produce this antagonism," John said. He believed the United States Constitution protected the Saints' right to practice plural marriage. By passing an unconstitutional law, John reasoned, Congress had created whatever tension existed between the Church and the nation. "It now becomes a question whether we should obey God or man," he said.

"Could you not consistently surrender polygamy," asked Ovando, "on the ground that there is no prospect of changing the opinion and law of the country against it?" He did not think the Church could survive much longer if it continued to resist the antipolygamy law.

"We leave that with God," said John. "It is His business to take care of His Saints."[1]

THAT SPRING, AT BRIGHAM Young Academy, Susie Young started each school day at eight thirty in the morning. Students met in a two-story brick building on Center Street in Provo. They ranged from young children to women and men in their twenties. Most were not used to school being held daily and starting on time. But Principal Karl Maeser insisted on punctuality.[2]

Susie loved being at the academy. One of her classmates, James Talmage, was a recent immigrant from England with a passion for science. Another, Joseph Tanner, worked at Provo's wool mill and had persuaded Principal Maeser to start evening classes for factory workers.[3] The mill's president, Abraham Smoot, led the academy's board of directors. His daughter Anna Christina taught the younger students part of the day while pursuing her own studies. Her younger brother Reed also attended, preparing for a career in business.[4]

Principal Maeser nurtured his students' love for the gospel and for learning. Brigham Young had asked him to make the Bible, the Book of Mormon, and the Doctrine and Covenants standard textbooks at the school. Students took courses in gospel principles alongside the usual academic subjects. Each Wednesday afternoon, Principal Maeser called the students together for a devotional. After a prayer, they would bear testimony and share what they were learning in class.[5]

As he had done years earlier when teaching in the Young home in Salt Lake City, Principal Maeser urged Susie to develop her potential. He encouraged her to write and reminded her to aim for a high standard in her work. He also entrusted her to help take the official minutes of the devotionals.

Since Utah had few trained educators, Principal Maeser often recruited teachers from among his older students. One day, while walking home after school with Susie and her mother, Lucy, he had stopped abruptly in the middle of the road.

"Does Miss Susie understand music well enough to give lessons?" he asked.

"Of course she does," Lucy replied. "She has given lessons ever since she was fourteen."

"I must think of that," the principal said.

Within a few days, Susie had started organizing the academy's music department under Principal Maeser's direction. Since the academy had no piano, she bought one that she and her students could use. Once she had a classroom, James Talmage helped her schedule teaching hours, rehearsal times for concerts, and individual lessons for her students. She now spent most of her time as a music teacher.[6]

As much as Susie enjoyed the academy, she still struggled to come to terms with her divorce. Her son, Bailey, was with her in Provo, but her ex-husband had sent her daughter, Leah, to live with his family at Bear Lake, more than 150 miles to the north. Susie worried that she had made a mess of her life, and she wondered if she had ruined her chances for happiness.

Lately, though, she had begun exchanging letters with Jacob Gates, a friend from St. George who was serving a mission in Hawaii. At first their letters were no more than friendly, but she and Jacob had begun to confide more in one another. Susie shared her regrets about her first marriage, her joy in the academy, and her longing to do more with her life than teach music classes.

"No, Jake, I ain't going to make a schoolma'am," she told him in one letter. "Hope to be a writer sometime. When I learn enough."

After the term ended, Susie planned to go to Hawaii with Zina Young, one of her father's widows whom she called her "other mother," to visit Relief Societies. She hoped to see Jacob while she was there. Though she feared that life had passed her by, she still had faith that Heaven was mindful of her.

"God is good," Susie wrote to Jacob, "and He will help me to pick up the shattered threads of life and mend them into something useful."[7]

AFTER A FOUR-DAY TRAIN ride, George Reynolds arrived at the Nebraska state prison, about nine hundred miles east of Salt Lake City, to serve his two-year sentence for bigamy. Inside, the guards confiscated his possessions, including his clothes and temple garments. After he bathed, they cut his hair short and shaved off his beard.

He was assigned a cell and given a coarse shirt, a pair of shoes, a cap, and a blue-and-white-striped prison uniform. Three times a day, Reynolds was marched with the other prisoners in silence to the food table, where he would retrieve his meal and then return to his cell to eat alone. After a few days, prison officials gave back his garments, and he felt grateful that his religious beliefs were respected at least in this regard.

For ten hours a day, six days a week, Reynolds worked as bookkeeper in the prison's knitting shop. On Sundays, he attended a short religious service held for the prisoners. Once every two weeks, prison regulations allowed him to write his wives, Mary Ann and Amelia. He asked them to write as often as they could but to keep in mind that their letters would be opened and read before they were delivered to him.[8]

After a month, Reynolds was moved to the territorial prison in Utah, a transfer George Q. Cannon had lobbied for in Washington, DC.[9]

In Ogden, Reynolds's family embraced him as he switched lines and boarded the train for Salt Lake City. His younger children did not recognize him without his beard.

"Be assured there are many worse places in the world than in prison for conscience's sake," Reynolds later wrote to his family. "It cannot take away the peace which reigns in my heart."[10]

THAT SUMMER, IN THE southern United States, twenty-two-year-old Rudger Clawson and his mission companion, Joseph Standing, were preaching in a rural area in the state of Georgia. Rudger, a former clerk in Brigham Young's office, was a relatively new missionary. Twenty-four-year-old Joseph, on the other hand, had already served one mission and now presided over the branches of the Church in the area.[11]

The region where they worked had been devastated by the American Civil War, and many people there were suspicious of outsiders. Since the decision in the George Reynolds case, the region had become more hostile toward Latter-day Saints. Preachers and newspapers were spreading rumors about the elders, and mobs were forcing their way into the homes of people they suspected of harboring "Mormon" missionaries.

Joseph was terrified of being caught by a mob, knowing they sometimes tied their victims to a log and whipped them. He told Rudger that he would rather die than be whipped.[12]

On the morning of July 21, 1879, Rudger and Joseph saw a dozen men ahead of them on the road. Three of the men were on horseback, with the rest on foot. Each man carried a gun or club. The elders paused as the men regarded them silently. Then, in one swift motion, the men threw off their hats and charged at the missionaries. "You are our prisoners," one man shouted.

"If you have a warrant of arrest, we would like to see it," Joseph said. His voice was loud and clear, but he looked pale.

"The United States of America is against you," one man said. "There is no law in Georgia for the Mormons."

With guns drawn, the mob led the missionaries deep into the surrounding woods. Joseph tried to talk to their leaders. "It is not our intention to remain in this part of the state," he said. "We preach what we understand to be the truth and leave people to embrace it or not."

His words had no effect. The mob soon split up, and some of the men took Rudger and Joseph to a place beside a spring of clear water.

"I want you men to understand that I am the captain of this party," said an older man. "If we ever again find you in this part of the country, we will hang you by the neck like dogs."

For about twenty minutes, the missionaries listened as the men accused them of coming to Georgia to carry their wives and daughters off to Utah. Many of the rumors in the South about the missionaries were based on highly inaccurate ideas about plural marriage, and some men felt honor bound to protect the women in their families by any means necessary.

The talk ended when the three riders arrived at the spring. "Follow us," said a man with a rifle.

Joseph sprang to his feet. Were they going to whip him? One of the mobbers had left a pistol on a stump, and Joseph snatched it up.

"Surrender!" he shouted at the mob.

A man to the left of Joseph stood up and shot him in the face. Joseph stood still for a moment, reeled around, and collapsed to the forest floor. Smoke and dust billowed up around him.

The leader of the men thrust a finger at Rudger. "Shoot that man!" he cried. Rudger looked around him. Every man with a gun had it aimed at his head.

"Shoot," Rudger said, folding his arms. His eyes were open, but the world seemed to go dark.

"Don't shoot," the leader of the mob called out, changing his mind. The other men lowered their weapons, and Rudger stooped down beside his companion. Joseph had rolled onto his back. He had a large gunshot wound in his forehead.

"Isn't this terrible that he should have shot himself?" said someone in the mob.

What had happened was murder, not suicide, Rudger knew. But he dared not disagree with the man. "Yes, it is terrible," he replied. "We must send for help." No one in the mob moved, and Rudger grew anxious. "You must go, or you must send me," he insisted.

"You go and get help," a man told him.[13]

ON SUNDAY, AUGUST 3, JOHN Taylor gazed at ten thousand solemn faces from the pulpit of the tabernacle in Salt Lake City. Behind him the stands were draped in black cloth and adorned with floral arrangements. Men ordained to the priesthood sat together as quorums while other Saints filled the remaining seats on the floor and in the gallery. Near the stands, in full view of the congregation, was Joseph Standing's casket, decorated with flowers.[14]

After the mob released him, Rudger Clawson had found help from a friend living nearby and sent a telegram to Salt Lake City reporting Joseph's murder. He had then returned to the murder scene with a coroner to retrieve his companion's body, which had been disfigured by more bullets in his absence. A week and a half later, Rudger brought the body back to Utah by train in a heavy metal box. News of the murder had spread quickly to all parts of the territory.[15]

John shared the Saints' outrage and sadness. But he believed they should feel proud as well as sorrowful. Joseph had died righteously in the cause of Zion. His murder would not stop the work of God from moving forward.[16] The Saints would continue to build temples, send missionaries throughout the world, and expand Zion's borders.

Under Brigham Young's leadership, the Saints had established hundreds of settlements in the western United States, spreading outward from Utah to neighboring Nevada, Wyoming, New Mexico, and Idaho. During the last year of his life, Brigham sent two hundred colonists to settle along the Little Colorado River in northeastern Arizona.

More recently, at John Taylor's call, seventy converts from the southern United States had joined Scandinavian Saints in settling a town called Manassa in the neighboring state of Colorado. In southeastern Utah, a large company of Saints was crossing the land's deep canyons to make a home along the San Juan River.[17]

John knew the principles of truth would continue to fill the world, despite the unhallowed hands that tried to strike them down. "Men may clamor for our property; they may clamor for our blood just as much as men have at any other time," he declared, "but in the name of Israel's God, Zion will go on and prosper."[18]

WIND BLEW ACROSS TARO fields as Zina and Susie Young rode a carriage over the high mountains dividing the island of Oahu. Zina and Susie were on their way from Honolulu to Laie, the gathering place for Hawaiian Saints. The road down the far side of the slopes was so steep that an iron rod had been installed along one side to keep travelers from falling. And it took the help of two men pulling on a strong rope to steady the carriage as it descended into the green valley below.[19]

The Church was now well established on the Hawaiian Islands, with roughly one in every twelve Hawaiians a Latter-day Saint.[20] When Zina and Susie arrived in Laie, Saints greeted them with a banner, music, and dancing. They sat their visitors down for a welcome meal and performed a song they had written especially for the occasion.

As she settled in for a two-month stay, Zina met Saints who were, like her, gray-haired pioneers. Among them was Relief Society president Mary Kapo, the sister-in-law of Jonathan Napela, the steadfast Hawaiian missionary and Church leader. Earlier that summer, Napela had passed away on Molokai, firm in his testimony, just two weeks before his wife, Kitty.[21]

Zina loved her time with the Hawaiian Saints. She and Susie met often with the Relief Society and young women. At their first meeting, the Hawaiian sisters brought a melon, a small bag of sweet potatoes, a cucumber, some eggs, a fish, and a cabbage. "I thought the donation was for the poor," Zina wrote in her journal, "but they were tokens of friendship for us."[22]

One evening, some Saints gathered at a home to hear Jacob Gates, Susie's missionary friend, play "O My Father" on an organ Zina had bought for the Saints in Laie. As she listened to the Hawaiians sing, Zina thought of her friend Eliza Snow, who had written the hymn in Nauvoo so many years ago. The hymn taught about Heavenly Parents and other truths Zina had first learned from the prophet Joseph Smith. Now the hymn was being sung in an altogether different part of the world.[23]

Three days later, Susie and Jacob took a trip up the canyon together. Susie had written Jacob a short love letter two weeks earlier while he spent the day away from Laie, attending to missionary work.

"I am thinking of you now, away up in the hills," she wrote. "Are you wishing, like me, that work had not to be done today, that we might talk over the future and express in a thousand ways that in our minds?"[24]

While Susie and Jacob courted, Zina planned to commemorate the second anniversary of Brigham Young's death with the Hawaiian Saints. On August 29, Church members throughout Laie marked the occasion with her and Susie. Young boys and girls decorated the meetinghouse while Relief Society sisters purchased beef for a feast and other Saints dug a pit to cook the meat.

Zina appreciated their efforts. They were honoring not only her late husband, she felt, but also the principles he had worked to establish among the Saints.

The following Sunday, Zina helped to organize a new Relief Society with thirty members. She and Susie departed the next day. As they traveled farther and farther from the island, Zina asked Susie if she was glad to be heading toward home. Susie felt torn. She was eager to see her children again, but she also longed to be with the man she now hoped to marry.

"I wish I could do myself up in an envelope and be sent to you," she wrote Jacob during the voyage. "I cannot see you now, and all I can do is to sit and dream and dream of the happy past and the blessed future."[25]

MELITON TREJO WAS LIVING in southern Arizona when he received a call from President Taylor to serve a mission in Mexico City. It had been over three years since Meliton had bidden farewell to the first missionaries heading to Mexico. While on their journey, the missionaries distributed hundreds of copies of Meliton's translation of Book of Mormon passages. Church leaders soon began to receive letters from readers of *Trozos selectos* asking for more missionaries.

Meliton had proven himself through his work on the translation, and now he prepared himself to accompany James Stewart and newly called apostle Moses Thatcher on the journey to Mexico's capital.

The three missionaries met in November in New Orleans, where they boarded a steamship to Veracruz. From there, they traveled to Mexico City by train.[26] The day after they arrived, they were met at their hotel by Plotino Rhodakanaty, a leader of a group of around twenty believers in Mexico City. Plotino, a native of Greece, welcomed them warmly. His letters to President Taylor had been instrumental in persuading the apostles to send missionaries to the city.[27] While Plotino waited for them, he and other unbaptized converts had started a newspaper about the restored gospel called *La voz del desierto* (The voice of the desert).[28]

Later that week, the missionaries went to a quiet olive orchard just outside the city, and Moses baptized Plotino and his friend Silviano Arteaga in a warm, spring-fed pool. "All nature was smiling around us, and I believe angels were rejoicing above," Moses wrote in his journal.[29]

Within a few days, Meliton had baptized six more people. The missionaries organized a branch and began to hold meetings in Plotino's home. They taught each other the gospel and administered to the sick. Moses called Plotino to serve as branch president, with Silviano and another recent convert, José Ybarola, as counselors.

After careful planning and prayer, the missionaries decided to translate Parley Pratt's *Voice of Warning* and other Church tracts. Joining the Church sometimes carried a cost, as Plotino learned when he lost his job as a schoolteacher for refusing to deny his new faith. But the small branch was growing, and missionaries and converts alike felt that they were taking part in something momentous.

Meliton, James, and Plotino finished the translation of *Voice of Warning* on January 8, 1880. A few days later, Moses wrote to President Taylor, reporting the progress of the mission.

"We shall avail ourselves of every opportunity to secure useful knowledge and at the same time do all we can to extend the knowledge of the truths of the gospel," he assured John. "And we believe the Lord has and will continue to help us."[30]

CHAPTER 32

Stand Up and Take the Pelting

George Q. Cannon and his wife Elizabeth were in Washington, DC, at the start of 1880. A new session of Congress was beginning, and George was still serving as Utah's territorial representative. This year, he and Elizabeth had brought their two young daughters with them. They hoped to give the nation's politicians and newspaper editors a positive view of Latter-day Saint families.[1]

Many people knew, of course, that George and Elizabeth practiced plural marriage. In fact, George had four wives and twenty living children. Yet, as one reporter observed, the Cannons did not match popular caricatures of the Saints. "If the virtues of an institution are to be rated by their refining and intelligent results," one reporter wrote, "there should be no prejudices against polygamy."[2]

But prejudice against the Saints had only worsened since the United States Supreme Court's decision a year earlier in the George Reynolds case. In his annual address to the nation, issued in December 1879, President Rutherford Hayes had condemned polygamy and urged law enforcement officials to uphold the Morrill antipolygamy act.[3]

The president's message emboldened some congressmen to oppose plural marriage more aggressively. One legislator introduced a bill proposing a constitutional amendment outlawing polygamy. Another declared his intention to expel George Q. Cannon from Congress. Citizens from all over the country, meanwhile, began pressuring their representatives to do more to eradicate plural marriage.

"The clouds seem to be gathering thick and portentous around us," George wrote to John Taylor on January 13. "If the Lord does not furnish lightning rods to draw off the electricity in some other direction, which I feel satisfied He will, I see no other way for us to do than to stand up and take the pelting."[4]

ONE NIGHT, AROUND THIS time, Desideria Quintanar de Yáñez had a dream in which she saw a book called *Voz de amonestación* being printed in Mexico City. When she woke up, she knew she had to find the book.[5]

Desideria, a descendant of the Aztec ruler Cuauhtémoc, was well respected in Nopala, the town where she and her son José lived. Though most people in Mexico were Catholic, Desideria and José belonged to a local Protestant congregation.[6]

Desideria felt she needed to go to Mexico City to search for the mysterious book, but the city was about seventy-five miles away. A railroad line could carry her part of the way, but most of her traveling would be on foot along unpaved roads. Desideria was in her sixties and in no condition to make the arduous journey.[7]

Determined to find the book, she told her son about the dream. José believed her and soon left for Mexico City in search of the unknown book.[8]

When José returned, he shared his astonishing experience with Desideria. He found Mexico City teeming with hundreds of thousands of people, and his search for the book seemed hopeless. But one day, while walking through the city's busy streets, he met Plotino Rhodakanaty, who told him about a book called *Voz de amonestación*.

Plotino sent José to a hotel to meet with missionary James Stewart. There José learned that *Voz de amonestación* was the Spanish translation of a book called *Voice of Warning,* which Latter-day Saint missionaries had been using for decades to introduce English-speaking people to their faith. It testified of the Restoration of the gospel of Christ and the coming forth of the Book of Mormon, a sacred record of ancient inhabitants of the Americas.[9]

Voz de amonestación was not yet off the printing press, but James gave José religious tracts to take home with him. José brought the tracts to his mother, and she studied them carefully. Desideria then asked for missionaries to come to Nopala and baptize her.

Meliton Trejo came to town in April and, at their request, baptized Desideria, José, and José's daughter Carmen. A few days later, José returned to Mexico City and received the Melchizedek Priesthood. When he came home, his arms were laden with tracts and books, including ten copies of the newly printed *Voz de amonestación*.[10]

IDA HUNT'S EARLIEST MEMORY was of her grandfather Addison Pratt bouncing her on his knee. At the time, Ida's family lived on a farm near San Bernardino, California. Her parents, John and Lois Pratt Hunt, had settled there when Ida was about a year old. But a few years later, at the prodding of Ida's grandmother Louisa Pratt, her family had moved to Beaver, a small town in southern Utah, where Louisa had been living since 1858.

Addison died in California in 1872. Though he and Louisa could never resolve their differences and lived apart for most of the last fifteen years of their marriage, they remained affectionate toward their daughters and grandchildren. Ida loved both of them dearly.[11]

Ida lived one block away from Louisa's house, and she spent countless afternoons at her grandmother's side, learning one lesson or another. In 1875, when Ida was seventeen, she and her family moved away from Beaver. Three years later, Church leaders called the family to move again, this time to the town of Snowflake in Arizona Territory. But rather than go with her family, Ida decided to return to Beaver to live with her grandmother for a while.

Back in Beaver, Ida was indispensable to her grandmother and two aunts, Ellen and Ann, who lived nearby. She assisted with chores and helped care for sick family members. Not all of Ida's time was spent at home, however. Her evenings were often filled with dinners, parties, and concerts. She soon began keeping company with a young man named Johnny.

In the spring of 1880, Ida's family and friends in Snowflake pleaded for her to come home, and Ida made the difficult decision to leave Beaver. Louisa could hardly speak as she said goodbye to her granddaughter and wished her a safe journey. Her only consolation was the thought that Ida's relationship with Johnny might bring her back to Beaver.[12]

Ida traveled to Snowflake with the family of Jesse Smith, president of the Eastern Arizona Stake. Two of his wives, Emma and Augusta, had a sacred, unselfish quality about their relationship with one another that Ida admired. Her own parents did not practice plural marriage, so she had little experience observing how plural families worked. But the more time she spent with the Smiths, the more she considered practicing plural marriage herself.[13]

Doing so would set Ida apart from other Saints her age. Though most Saints accepted and defended plural marriage, the number of plural families in the Church was in decline. The practice was largely limited to Saints in the American West, and plural marriages between Church members were not performed in Europe, Hawaii, or other places throughout the world.

At the height of the practice in the late 1850s, about half of the people in Utah could expect to be part of a plural family during their lives. That number had since dropped to around twenty or thirty percent, and it continued to shrink.[14] Since plural marriage was not required of Church members, Saints could remain in good standing with God and the Church if they chose not to practice it.[15]

Several months after Ida arrived in Snowflake, she received news that her grandmother had died. Overcome by grief, Ida regretted leaving Louisa. If she had stayed in Beaver, she told herself, she could have comforted her grandmother during the last months of her life.

Around this time, Ida also received a letter from Johnny. He wanted to come to Arizona and marry her. But by then she hoped to marry a man who was willing to practice plural marriage. Johnny lacked faith in the gospel, and Ida knew he was not the right person for her.[16]

IN 1880, THE CHURCH celebrated its fiftieth anniversary. Recalling that ancient Israel held a Jubilee celebration every fifty years to forgive debts and free people from bondage, President John Taylor canceled the debts of thousands of poor Saints who had gathered to Zion with money borrowed from the Perpetual Emigrating Fund. He asked Saints who owned banks and businesses to cancel some of the debts owed them, and he urged Church members to donate livestock to the needy.

He also asked Emmeline Wells, the president of the Relief Society's grain committee, to loan bishops as much wheat from Relief Society granaries as they needed to feed the poor in their wards.[17]

In June, President Taylor attended a conference of the Salt Lake Stake Relief Society. The meeting included representatives from the Primary Association and Young Ladies' Mutual Improvement Association (Y.L.M.I.A.), which were seen as auxiliaries to the Relief Society. During the proceedings, Eliza Snow nominated Louie Felt, a ward Primary president, to supervise the Primary for the entire Church. The congregation sustained Louie and also approved two women to serve as her counselors.

Later at the same meeting, President Taylor asked a secretary to read an account of the organization of the Nauvoo Relief Society in 1842. President Taylor had attended that first meeting at which Emma Smith had been elected president of the society. He had also given Emma's counselors, Sarah Cleveland and Elizabeth Ann Whitney, authority to act in their calling.

After the secretary finished reading the account, President Taylor spoke on the powers and duties the Relief Society gave to women. Mary Isabella Horne then proposed that he appoint Eliza Snow as president of all Relief Societies in the Church. Eliza had served as secretary of the original Relief Society, and she had been advising all ward Relief Societies for more than a decade. But there had been no general president of the Relief Society since Emma Smith led the organization in the 1840s.

President Taylor nominated Eliza to be the Relief Society general president, and the congregation sustained her. Eliza then chose Zina Young and Elizabeth Ann Whitney as her counselors, Sarah Kimball as the secretary, and Mary Isabella Horne as the treasurer. Like Eliza, they had all been members of the Relief Society in Nauvoo and had served in the organization since its reestablishment in Utah.

Later that afternoon, at the final meeting of the conference, Eliza nominated Elmina Taylor, one of Mary Isabella Horne's counselors in a stake Relief Society presidency, to serve as general president of the Young Ladies' Mutual Improvement Association. Elmina was sustained along with counselors, a secretary, and a treasurer.[18]

Women throughout the territory rejoiced in these new general presidencies.

"I am greatly pleased to see my sisters moving in such order," Phebe Woodruff declared at a Relief

Society meeting one month later. Belinda Pratt, a stake Relief Society president, wrote in her journal: "What an age we are living in! How great the responsibilities of the sisters of the Church. What a work they are accomplishing!"[19]

Other inspired changes occurred in the Church that year. Since the death of Brigham Young three years earlier, the Quorum of the Twelve had led the Church without a First Presidency. After discussing and praying about the matter, the quorum unitedly sustained John Taylor as president of the Church and George Q. Cannon and Joseph F. Smith as his counselors. Later, in a crowded session of the October general conference, the Saints raised their hands to support the new presidency.[20]

Following the sustaining, George Q. Cannon arose and proposed that the Pearl of Great Price, a collection of some of Joseph Smith's writings and inspired translations, be made a new standard work of the Church. Although missionaries had been using editions of the Pearl of Great Price since its publication in 1851, this was the first time Church members had been asked to accept it as a volume of scripture.

"It is gratifying to see the oneness of feeling and united sentiment which has been manifested in our votes," President Taylor said afterward. "Now continue to be united in other things, as you have been in this, and God will stand by you henceforth."[21]

SIX MONTHS LATER, IN the bustling waterfront town of Trondheim, Norway, Anna Widtsoe stepped out of an icy fjord as a newly baptized member of The Church of Jesus Christ of Latter-day Saints. Though her body was cold, she had the fire of the gospel burning inside her, and she was filled with love for the Saints who surrounded her.

Anna's path to baptism had not been easy. Her husband had died unexpectedly three years earlier, leaving her and her two young sons, John and Osborne, alone. They now lived off a small pension and her income from sewing dresses. After her husband's death, Anna had turned to God, and she wondered why He had taken her husband from her.

She had read the Bible since her childhood and knew its stories. Now she studied it for answers. As she did, she felt herself growing closer to God. But something in the doctrines of the church she attended felt incomplete and unsatisfying.

One day a cobbler named Olaus Johnsen returned a pair of shoes she had asked him to repair. Inside each shoe was a religious tract. She read the tract and was curious to learn more, so she brought another pair of shoes to the cobbler on a warm spring day a short time later. At the shop, though, she was reluctant to ask the shoemaker too many questions. Just as she was opening the door to leave, he called to her.

"I can give you something of more value than soles for your child's shoes," he said.

"What can you, a shoemaker, give me?" she asked.

"I can teach you how to find happiness in this life and to prepare for eternal joy in the life to come," he said.

"Who are you?" Anna asked.

"I am a member of the Church of Christ," Olaus said. "We are called Mormons. We have the truth of God."

At that, Anna fled the shop. Latter-day Saints had a reputation in Norway for being fanatics. But the tract intrigued her, and soon she attended a meeting with the Trondheim Saints at the home of Olaus and his wife, Karen. Rigid class distinctions marked Norwegian society, and Anna was distracted by the Johnsens' humble home and the impoverished people who worshipped there. When her husband was alive, she had belonged to a wealthier class, and she tended to look down on poor people.

Over the next two years, Anna met regularly with the missionaries, despite her reservations. One day at home, she felt the Spirit powerfully. Class distinctions meant nothing to the Lord, but her prejudice was strong as she thought about the unpopular Church, its members, and their poverty. "Must I step down to that?" she asked herself.

She then answered her own question: "Yes, if it is the truth, I must do so."[22]

MEANWHILE, IN THE UNITED States, James Garfield succeeded Rutherford Hayes as the nation's president.

Like Hayes, he condemned the Church and charged Congress with putting an end to plural marriage once and for all. When a disgruntled man shot Garfield a few months into his term, there was some speculation that the gunman was a Latter-day Saint.[23] But the accusation was false. John Taylor quickly condemned the attack, expressed sympathy for the ailing president, and refused to blame him for the political stance he had taken against the Church.

"He, like the rest of us, is a fallible being," John told the Saints. "We are all fallible, and it is not every man who can resist the pressure which is brought to bear upon him."[24]

President Garfield died of his wound a few months later. His successor, Chester Arthur, was no less determined to stop plural marriage.[25] As Utah's delegate to Congress, George Q. Cannon felt the pressure immediately. In December 1881, Senator George Edmunds introduced a bill in Congress that would make it easier to prosecute Saints for practicing plural marriage.

If the Edmunds Act passed, Saints could be imprisoned for "unlawful cohabitation," which meant that courts no longer had to prove that a plural marriage had taken place. Any Church member who appeared to be practicing plural marriage could be prosecuted under the law. Plural couples who lived in the same house or were seen together in public would be at risk of arrest.

The law would also take away voting rights from men and women in plural marriages, subject them to fines and prison terms, and bar them from serving on juries and holding political office.[26]

Adding to George's pressure was the fact that his wife Elizabeth was back in Utah, sick with pneumonia. He wanted to be with her. On January 24, 1882, however, George received a telegram with a message from Elizabeth. "Stand to your post," she urged him. "God can raise me up in answer to your prayers there as well as here."

Two days later, George received another telegram. It reported that Elizabeth had passed away. "The thought that we are separated for the remainder of this life and that I shall never behold her face again nor have the pleasure of her affectionate attentions and sweet society in the flesh almost stuns me," George wrote in his journal.[27]

The Edmunds Act passed a short time later, disqualifying George from serving in Congress. On April 19, he addressed the House of Representatives for the last time. He felt calmer than usual, but he was outraged by his colleagues' decision to pass the Edmunds Act. The Saints practiced plural marriage because God had commanded them to do so, he said. They had no desire to force their belief on anyone but merely wished to be granted the right to obey God as they saw fit.

"So far as the condemnation of the world is concerned, we are willing to be placed on the same plane with Abraham," George added.

Afterward, a few congressmen complimented George on his speech. Other representatives confessed that they had felt pressure to oppose him. Most just seemed content that he was leaving.[28]

THE EDMUNDS ACT DID not change Ida Hunt's mind about plural marriage. In the fall of 1881, she had lived with Ella and David Udall in the town of St. Johns, Arizona, about forty-five miles from Snowflake. During that time, she had worked in the local cooperative store with David, who was the bishop in St. Johns, and had grown as close to Ella as a sister.[29]

Soon after David became a bishop, he and Ella had concluded that it was time for them to practice plural marriage. A short time later, David proposed marriage to Ida with Ella's consent. Ida wanted to accept his proposal, but she could tell that Ella was still struggling with the idea of sharing her husband. So, instead of responding to David's offer, Ida returned to Snowflake, her heart in turmoil.[30]

Later, Ida wrote a letter to learn Ella's true feelings about the marriage proposal. "I cannot allow the matter to go farther without first having received some assurance of your willingness to such a step being taken," she told her friend. "It is not only your right but your imperative duty to state plainly any objections you may have."

"I promise you," she assured Ella, "I shall not be offended."[31]

Ella sent a short reply six weeks later. "The subject in question is one which has caused me a great amount of pain and sorrow, more perhaps than you would imagine," she wrote, "yet I feel as I have done from the beginning, that if it is the will of the Lord I am perfectly willing to try to endure it and trust that it will be overruled for the best good of all."[32]

On May 6, 1882, Ida left Snowflake on an eighteen-day journey to the St. George temple with David, Ella, and their little daughter, Pearl. As they rolled slowly across the desert, Ida could see that Ella was still unhappy about the marriage. Ida was careful with her words and actions, concerned that she might say or do something to cause Ella more pain. Together they read books aloud and played with Pearl to stave off uncomfortable silences.

One night, Ida spoke privately with David, worried about Ella's unhappiness and afraid that she had made the wrong choice in accepting David's proposal. His loving, encouraging words brought hope to her heart. She went to bed that night reassured that God would support them through their trials as they tried to be obedient.

Ida and David were sealed in the St. George temple on May 25. In the face of an uncertain future, Ida felt she could trust David to care for her, and she prayed that her love for him would only increase. Ella also seemed to find comfort in the words and counsel of the man who performed the ceremony.

That night, the family stayed at the home of one of Ella's sisters. After everyone else went to bed, Ella slipped into Ida's room, unable to sleep. For the first time, the two women talked face-to-face about their new relationship to each other—and their hopes and desires for the future.

Both women believed that Ida's marriage to David was God's will. But now that the Edmunds Act was in force, the events of the day had placed their family even more at odds with the government.

"Marriage under ordinary circumstances is a grave and important step," Ida wrote that night in her journal, "but entering into plural marriage, in these perilous times, is doubly so."[33]

CHAPTER 33

Until the Storm
Blows Past

On the day before Christmas 1882, Māori chief Hare Teimana stood on the edge of a cliff beside his village near Cambridge, New Zealand. Below, he could see a man climbing resolutely up the cliff. But why was this stranger climbing to the village when he could more easily take a road? Why was he in such a hurry to reach the summit? Did he have something important to say?

As Hare watched the stranger climb, he realized that he knew him. One night a few months earlier, the apostle Peter, dressed in white, had appeared in Hare's room. He told Hare that a man was coming to the Māori people with the same gospel Jesus Christ had preached while He was on the earth. Peter said Hare would know this man when he saw him.[1]

Protestant and Catholic missionaries had converted most Māori to Christianity by the 1850s, so Hare was familiar with Peter's mission in Christ's ancient Church. He also believed in the reality of visions and revelations. Māori looked to their *matakite,* or seers, to receive direct guidance from God. Even after converting to Christianity, some *matakite,* tribal chiefs, and family patriarchs had continued to see visions and receive divine directions for their people.[2]

The year before, in fact, Māori leaders had asked Pāora Te Pōtangaroa, a revered *matakite,* which church Māori should join. After fasting and praying for three days, Pāora had said the church they should join had not yet arrived. But he said it would come sometime in 1882 or 1883.[3]

Recognizing the man on the cliff as the person Peter spoke of in his vision, Hare was eager to hear what he had to say. The climber was exhausted when he reached the village, though, and Hare had to wait for him to catch his breath. When the man finally spoke, it was in Māori. He said his name was William McDonnel, and he was a missionary from The Church of Jesus Christ of Latter-day Saints. He gave Hare some religious tracts and testified that they contained the same gospel Christ had taught during His ministry. He also spoke of Christ commissioning Peter to proclaim the gospel after His Ascension.[4]

Hare's interest was piqued, but William was anxious to rejoin his two mission companions, who had taken the road to the village. When William started to leave,

Hare grabbed him by the collar of his coat. "You stop here and tell me all about the gospel," he demanded.

William began sharing all he knew, and Hare continued to grip his collar tightly. Fifteen minutes passed, and William spotted his companions, mission president William Bromley and Thomas Cox, who had arrived at the village from the main road. He waved his hat high in the air to get their attention, and Hare finally let go of his collar. Then, with William acting as translator, the men spoke to Hare, expressing their desire to meet with Māori in that area.

Hare invited them to return later that day. "You can have a meeting in my house," he said.[5]

THAT EVENING, WILLIAM McDONNEL sat down with President Bromley and Thomas Cox in Hare Teimana's house. Irish by birth, William had moved to New Zealand after a ship's captain told him it was a good country. He later settled among Māori for several years and learned their language. He then moved to the city of Auckland, New Zealand, where he was married in 1874 and joined the Church a few years later.[6]

Though missionaries had been called to preach in New Zealand and neighboring Australia since the early 1850s, the Church in New Zealand was small. Over the past three decades, at least 130 members had gathered to the Salt Lake Valley, thinning out the branches in New Zealand much as in other countries.

Most of the members were European immigrants like William. But soon after William's baptism, President Bromley came to New Zealand with a charge from Joseph F. Smith, the new second counselor in the First Presidency, to take the gospel to Māori people.[7] President Bromley prayed to find the right people to send, and he felt that William was one of the men to do it. William baptized the first Māori to receive the ordinance in New Zealand, a man named Ngataki, six months later.[8]

Now, sitting among Māori women and men in Hare's house, the missionaries carried out Joseph F. Smith's mandate. President Bromley would read a passage from the Bible in English, and William would turn to the same section in the Māori Bible and hand it to someone to read. The group listened attentively to the message, and William told the group that he would come back the following evening.

Before the missionaries left, Hare took William to see his daughter Mary. She had been ill for weeks, and the doctors said it was only a matter of time before she died. William had just taught that elders with the priesthood of God could perform healing blessings, and Hare wondered if they would bless his daughter.

The girl looked as if she might die at any moment. William, President Bromley, and Thomas knelt beside her and placed their hands on her head. A good spirit enveloped the room, and Thomas blessed her with life.

That night, William was unable to sleep. He had faith that Mary could be healed. But what if it was not

God's will? How would it affect the faith of Hare and other Māori if she died?

Just after sunrise, William started for Hare's house. In the distance, he saw a woman from the village coming toward him. When she reached him, she lifted him off the ground in an embrace. She then took him by the hand and pulled him to Hare's house.

"How is the girl?" William asked.

"Plenty good!" the woman said.

When William entered the house, he found Mary sitting up in bed and looking around the room. He shook hands with her and asked her mother to get her some strawberries to eat.[9]

That evening, Hare and his wife, Pare, accepted baptism, as did one other person in the village. The group made their way to the Waikato River, where William waded into the current, raised his right arm to the square, and immersed each of them in the water. Afterward, he returned home to Auckland while Thomas Cox and his wife, Hannah, continued ministering to Māori in Cambridge.

Two months later, on February 25, 1883, the first Māori branch of the Church was organized.[10]

AFTER HER BAPTISM, ANNA Widtsoe was anxious to heed the Lord's call to gather to Zion. Anthon Skanchy, one of the missionaries who had taught her the gospel, wrote often to encourage her and her young sons to join him and other Scandinavian Saints in Utah. Having already immigrated to Logan, Utah, where the Saints were finishing a temple similar in size and appearance to the temple in Manti, he understood her desire to leave Norway.

"Everything will work together for your good," he assured her in a letter. "You and your little ones will not be forgotten."[11]

As eager as Anna was to move to Utah, she knew she would miss her homeland. Her late husband was buried there, and she cared deeply about the other Church members in her town. Often, when European Saints left their branches to come to Zion, they left vacancies in local Church leadership, making it difficult for the tiny congregations to thrive. Anna was a counselor in her branch Relief Society, and if she decided to move to Utah, the small group of women would certainly feel her loss.

She also had her two sons to consider. Eleven-year-old John and five-year-old Osborne were smart, well-behaved boys. In Utah, they would have to learn a new language and adapt to a new culture, which would put them behind other children their age. And how would she support them? Since her baptism, Anna's dressmaking business had flourished. If she left Norway, she would lose her husband's pension and would have to reestablish her business in a new place.[12]

Anna had also become reacquainted with Hans, a former suitor, who seemed interested in rekindling their romance. He was not a member of the Church, but he seemed supportive of her faith. Anna did not have much hope that he would join the Saints, though, since he seemed more interested in worldly pursuits than in seeking the kingdom of God.[13]

As Anna turned these matters over in her mind, she realized that staying in Norway would only hold her and her sons back. The Norwegian government did not recognize the Church nor consider it Christian. Mobs hounded missionaries, and ministers frequently criticized the Church in sermons and pamphlets. Aside from her younger sister Petroline, who had taken an interest in the Church, Anna's own family had also rejected her once she joined the Saints.

In the fall of 1883, Anna decided to leave Norway. "I am traveling home to Utah as soon as I can," she wrote Petroline in September. "If we cannot leave everything, even our life if required, we are no disciples."[14]

Money was an obstacle, however. Her family would never help her make the move, and Anna did not know how she would pay the cost of emigrating. Then two returned missionaries and a Norwegian Saint donated some money to her. Hans also gave her some money for the journey, and the Church permitted her to use some of her tithing to help pay for her family's passage.

At her final meeting with her Relief Society, Anna expressed how happy she was that God's kingdom was again on the earth—and that she had the opportunity to help build it. As she listened to the testimonies of her Relief Society sisters, she wished that she and they might always live so that the Spirit of God would be with and enlighten them.

In October 1883, Anna, John, and Osborne boarded a ship in Oslo and headed for England. On shore, their fellow Norwegian Saints waved farewell with handkerchiefs. Norway's majestic coastline had never looked so beautiful to Anna. For all she knew, she would never see it again.[15]

DURING THE EARLY SUMMER of 1884, Ida Hunt Udall was serving as the president of the Young Ladies' Mutual Improvement Association of the Eastern Arizona Stake, a position that required her to watch over and teach the young women in Snowflake, St. Johns, and other settlements in the area. Though she was not able to visit every association in the stake very often, she found joy when they met together for quarterly conferences.[16]

Since her marriage to David Udall, Ida had moved back to St. Johns, where the Saints were facing strong opposition. The town was run by powerful citizens who did not want Saints settling in the county. Known as the Ring, the group harassed Church members and tried to prevent them from voting. They also published a newspaper that encouraged readers to terrorize the Saints.

"How did Missouri and Illinois get rid of the Mormons?" one article asked. "By the use of the shotgun and rope."[17]

At home with David and Ella, though, Ida had found peace. For a while, Ella had struggled to get used to Ida's new status in the home, but the two women had grown closer as they helped each other through sicknesses and other day-to-day challenges. Since joining the family, Ida had assisted Ella during the births of two daughters, Erma and Mary. Ida herself was still childless.

On July 10, 1884, five days after Mary was born, Ida was cleaning up dinner when David's brother-in-law Ammon Tenney appeared at the door. He had been indicted for polygamy, and his wife Eliza, David's sister, had been subpoenaed to testify against him. Rather than submit to the law and be a key witness at her husband's trial, Eliza had decided to hide from the marshals.[18]

"The next call might be for you," Ammon warned Ida. As the bishop of St. Johns—and a known polygamist—her husband would be a prime target for prosecution. If a marshal with a subpoena caught Ida, she could be forced to testify against David in court. Under the Edmunds Act, he could be fined $300 and sentenced to six months in prison for unlawful cohabitation. And the punishment for polygamy was even harsher. If convicted, David could be fined $500 and sentenced to five years in prison.[19]

Ida's first thought was of Ella, who was recovering from the birth of her daughter. Ella still needed her help, and Ida did not want to leave her. But staying in the house only put the family in more danger.

Ida hastily threw a shawl over her head and silently slipped outside. Eliza and other women were hiding from the marshals in a neighbor's house, and Ida joined them. Most of the women had left children behind, with no choice but to trust their little ones to the care of others.

Day after day they kept a watchful eye on the road, ducking beneath a bed or behind curtains whenever a stranger came near the house.

After Ida had been at the neighbor's house for six days, a friend offered to secretly transport her and the other women to Snowflake. Before leaving town, Ida returned home and quickly packed a few items for her journey. As she kissed Ella and the children goodbye, she had the impression that many long days would pass before she saw them again.[20]

Ida spoke to the young women organization in the Snowflake Ward soon after her arrival, her ordeal in St. Johns still fresh in her mind. "Those who suffer persecution for the gospel's sake have a peace and contentment which they could scarcely expect," she testified. "We cannot expect to glide along in this Church without trials. Our lives will no doubt be placed in jeopardy."[21]

BY THE END OF summer, several Saints in Utah Territory had been arrested under the Edmunds Act, but no one had been prosecuted and imprisoned. Among the Saints arrested was Rudger Clawson, who had witnessed the murder of his mission companion, Joseph Standing, five years earlier. Rudger was married to two women,

Florence Dinwoody and Lydia Spencer. After his arrest, Lydia went into hiding, leaving the prosecution without a key witness.[22]

Rudger's trial began in October. At the hearing, Latter-day Saint witnesses, including President John Taylor, tried to be as unhelpful to the court as possible. When prosecutors asked the prophet where the Church's marriage records could be located, his answers were vague.

"If you wanted to see it," one lawyer asked him, "is there any means of ascertaining where it is?"

"I could find out by inquiry," President Taylor said.

"Will you be good enough to do so?" asked the lawyer.

"Well," said the prophet wryly, "I am not good enough to do so." The courtroom then erupted in laughter.[23]

After a week of hearing similar testimonies, the twelve-man jury failed to come to a decision on the case, and the judge adjourned the court. But that same night, a deputy marshal tracked down Lydia Clawson and subpoenaed her to testify against Rudger in court.

A new trial soon began. After hearing the testimonies of several witnesses who had appeared at the previous trial, the prosecuting attorney called Lydia to the witness stand. She looked pale but determined. When the clerk tried to swear her in, she refused to take the oath.[24]

"Don't you know it is wrong for you not to be sworn?" the judge asked Lydia.

"It may be," she replied.

"You may have to be imprisoned," the judge warned.

"That depends on you," said Lydia.

"You take a fearful responsibility in undertaking to defy the government," the judge said. He then committed her into the custody of the marshal and adjourned the court.

That night, after being transported to the state penitentiary, Lydia received a message from Rudger. He begged her to testify against him. She was pregnant, and if she refused to cooperate with the court, she might end up delivering her baby in a federal prison, hundreds of miles from home and family.[25]

The next morning the marshal accompanied Lydia to the packed courthouse, where prosecutors once again called her to the witness stand. This time, she did not resist when the clerk administered the oath. Then the prosecuting attorney asked her if she was married.

Almost whispering, Lydia said that she was.

"To whom?" he pressed.

"Rudger Clawson," she said.

Members of the jury took less than twenty minutes to deliver a guilty verdict—the first under the Edmunds Act.[26] Nine days later, Rudger appeared before the judge for sentencing. Before giving his ruling, the judge asked Rudger if he had anything to say.

"I very much regret that the laws of my country should come in contact with the laws of God," Rudger said, "but whenever they do, I shall invariably choose the latter."

The judge sat back in his chair. He had been prepared to be lenient with Rudger, but the young man's
defiance had changed his mind. With a solemn look, he
sentenced Rudger to four years in prison and fined him
$500 for polygamy and $300 for unlawful cohabitation.

The courtroom was silent. A marshal ushered
Rudger out of the room, allowed him to say goodbye
to friends and relatives, and then took him to the penitentiary. Rudger spent his first night in prison confined
with about fifty of the territory's hardened inmates.[27]

THAT WINTER, IN SETTLEMENTS across Utah Territory,
marshals continued to harass Saints at their homes, hoping to catch plural families off guard. Day and night,
fathers and mothers watched in horror as lawmen ransacked their homes and turned children out of their
beds. Some marshals sneaked through windows or
threatened to break down doors. If they found a plural
wife, they might arrest her if she refused to testify against
her husband.

As much as John Taylor wanted to encourage the
Saints to continue living their religion, he could see
that families were being torn apart, and he felt respon-
sible for their welfare.[28] Soon he began counseling with
Church leaders about moving Saints outside the United
States to avoid arrest and seek greater freedom.[29]

In January 1885, he and Joseph F. Smith left Salt
Lake City with a few apostles and trusted friends to visit

the Saints in Arizona Territory, just north of Mexico. Many Saints were living in fear there, and some had already fled to Mexico to escape the marshals.[30]

Anxious to see for themselves whether more Saints could find refuge in that country, John, Joseph, and their companions crossed the border into Mexico. There they located a few promising sites near enough water to support settlement.[31] When the company returned to Arizona a few days later, John and his companions counseled about what to do next.

In the end, they decided to buy land and establish settlements in the Mexican state of Chihuahua. John asked a few men to begin raising money. He and the others then proceeded by train to San Francisco.[32] Once there, John received an urgent telegram from George Q. Cannon. Enemies at home were active, George warned, and a plan had been laid to arrest the First Presidency.

Several men pressed John to stay in California until the danger passed. Unsure of what to do, the prophet prayed for guidance. He then announced he was returning to Salt Lake City and sending Joseph F. Smith to Hawaii on another mission. A few men protested, certain that John and others would be arrested if they returned home. But John's mind was clear—his place was in Utah.

John arrived home a few days later and called a special council with Church leaders. He told them his plan to buy land in Mexico, and he stated his intention to avoid capture by going into hiding. He had advised the

Saints to do everything in their power, short of violence, to avoid prosecution. Now he would do the same.[33]

That Sunday, John spoke publicly to the Saints in the tabernacle, despite the threat of arrest. He reminded the congregation that they had faced oppression before. "Pull up the collar of your coat and button yourself up and keep the cold out until the storm blows past," he counseled them. "This storm will blow past as others have done."[34]

Having encouraged the Saints the best he could, John left the tabernacle, climbed into a carriage, and rode out into the night.[35]

CHAPTER 34

Nothing to Fear from the Wicked

On March 8, 1885, Ida Udall awoke on her twenty-seventh birthday to glorious sunshine. But as much as she welcomed a warm day at the end of winter, Ida knew she had to be careful when stepping outside. Most days she had to stay indoors until the sun went down— or risk being recognized by a United States marshal.[1]

Eight months had passed since Ida had fled her home in St. Johns, Arizona, to go "underground," a term the Saints were beginning to use to describe life in hiding from the law. In that time, her husband, David, had been indicted for polygamy and gone to trial with five other Saints. Nearly forty men had testified at the trials, and several of them had sworn falsely against the Saints. "There seems to be no law or justice for Mormons in Arizona," David had written to Ida at the time.[2]

When the trial concluded, five of the six men were convicted of polygamy. Three men were sentenced to serve three and a half years at a penitentiary in Detroit, Michigan, two thousand miles away. David alone had avoided conviction, but only because his case had been delayed for six months while the prosecution searched for more witnesses against him—including Ida.[3]

After leaving Arizona, Ida had moved in with David's father and stepmother in Nephi, a town about eighty miles south of Salt Lake City. Only Ida's closest family members and friends knew where she was.

Ida had never spent time with her in-laws before, so at first she felt like she was living with strangers. But she had since grown to love them and had made friends with her new neighbors, including other plural wives who were hiding to protect their families. Attending Church meetings and socializing with friends now helped to brighten her long, lonely days.[4]

On Ida's birthday, her friends and family in Nephi threw her a party. But those who were dearest to her heart—her parents, David, and David's first wife, Ella— were hundreds of miles away. She had not seen David for almost six months. And his absence felt particularly hard to bear since she was expecting their first child in a few weeks.[5]

A short time after the birthday party, Ida received a copy of a newspaper from Arizona. When she opened the paper, she was stunned to see a headline announcing the death of her mother, Lois Pratt Hunt. Lois had been only forty-eight years old, and Ida was not prepared to lose her.

Ida's friends gently took the newspaper from her hands and sat with her until dusk. A few hours later, she went into labor and gave birth to a healthy, blue-eyed girl she named Pauline.

The weeks that followed were a blur of sorrow and joy, but Ida was grateful to have Pauline with her. "I was blessed with a dear little daughter of my very own," she wrote in her journal. "I thanked God that I now had something to live and labor for."[6]

THAT SPRING, IN NORTHERN Utah, Sagwitch, his wife Moyogah, and sixteen other Shoshones ascended the hill leading to the Logan temple.[7] The temple had been finished and dedicated a year earlier, a testament to the faith and hard work of Saints in northern Utah and southern Idaho. Among those who had labored tirelessly to build the temple were Sagwitch and other Shoshone Saints.[8]

The Shoshones had traveled a long road to reach the temple. Twelve years had passed since Sagwitch and over two hundred other Shoshones had joined the Church. They worshipped in their own ward and in their own language.[9] Sagwitch and Moyogah had been sealed in the Endowment House,[10] and Sagwitch's son Frank Timbimboo Warner had been called as a missionary among the Shoshones.[11]

But the U.S. Army's attack on the Shoshone camp along the Bear River still haunted the survivors, and other hardships continued to plague them. After joining the Church, Sagwitch and his people received land in northern Utah to settle on and farm. But a few months after the Shoshones arrived, people in a nearby town who were not members of the Church began to fear that white Saints were inciting Indians to attack them. The townspeople threatened the Shoshones and forced them to abandon their land just as they were beginning their harvest. The Shoshones returned the next year, but grasshoppers and stray stock invaded their fields and ate their crops.[12]

Acting under President John Taylor's direction, Church leaders soon found land for the Shoshones along Utah's northern border.[13] Now their small town, Washakie, had several homes, corrals, a blacksmith shop, a cooperative store, and a schoolhouse.[14]

Building a new life was demanding, but it had not kept Sagwitch and his people from helping to construct the temple. With the little time they had to spare, men from the community would travel by team and train to Logan, where they helped haul the stone. At other times they prepared the mortar that held the temple walls together or mixed plaster to cover the interior walls. By the time the temple was dedicated, the Shoshones had donated thousands of hours of labor to build the sacred structure.[15]

Sagwitch had taken his turn too, though he was getting old and his hand was scarred from the Bear River massacre. The slaughter was never far from his people's minds. Many survivors now reckoned their age by how many years had passed since the horrifying event.[16] They could not forget the parents, siblings, husbands, wives, children, and grandchildren they had lost.

On the day of the massacre, Sagwitch had not been able to stop the soldiers from killing his people. But in the spring of 1885, he and other Shoshones spent four days in the temple, performing ordinances on behalf of their deceased relatives, including many who had been killed at Bear River.[17]

IN JUNE 1885, JOSEPH Smith III and his brother Alexander came to Utah Territory on another mission for the Reorganized Church of Jesus Christ of Latter Day Saints. As previous missionaries from their church had tried to do, the brothers wanted to convince the Saints in Utah and elsewhere that the prophet Joseph Smith had never practiced plural marriage.[18]

Among the Saints who noted their arrival was Helen Whitney, the fifty-six-year-old daughter of Heber and Vilate Kimball. Helen was familiar with the brothers' message. In fact, she had once published a pamphlet, *Plural Marriage as Taught by the Prophet Joseph,* in response to Joseph III's claims about his father. As a plural wife of Joseph Smith herself, Helen knew for certain that the prophet had practiced plural marriage.[19]

Helen was fourteen when her father taught her the principle and asked her if she would be sealed to

Joseph. Her feelings had revolted at first, and she responded indignantly to his words. But over the course of the day, as she thought about what to do, she knew that her father loved her too much to teach her anything that was contrary to God's will. She agreed to the sealing, believing the union would help exalt her and her family and connect them to Joseph Smith in the eternities.

The arrangement had been unconventional in almost every way. Helen was young for marriage, although some women her age did marry in the United States at that time. Like some of Joseph's other wives, she was sealed to the prophet for eternity only. She and Joseph rarely interacted socially, and she never indicated that they had an intimate physical relationship. She continued to live in her parents' home and, like other plural wives in Nauvoo, kept her sealing private. But she had been the age when some young women began courting, making it hard for her to explain to her friends why she stopped attending some social gatherings.[20]

After the prophet's death, Helen had married Horace Whitney, a son of Newel and Elizabeth Ann Whitney. Helen was seventeen and Horace was twenty-two at the time, and they were deeply in love. On the day of the marriage, they promised to cling to one another for the rest of their lives and, if possible, in the eternities. But at the altar of the Nauvoo temple, they were married for this life only, since Helen had already been sealed to Joseph Smith for eternity.[21]

Later, after settling in Utah, Helen had consented to Horace's marriages to Lucy Bloxham and Mary Cravath. Lucy died a short time later, but Mary and Helen lived next door to each other and enjoyed a good relationship. Helen and Horace were happily married for thirty-eight years, and she gave birth to eleven children.[22] Horace died on November 22, 1884, and Helen now spent some of her time writing for the *Deseret News* and *Woman's Exponent.*[23]

Plural marriage had never been easy for Helen, but she defended it vigorously. "Had it not been for a powerful testimony from the Lord," she wrote, "I do not believe that I could have submitted to it for a moment."

A few years after writing *Plural Marriage as Taught by the Prophet Joseph,* Helen had published a second pamphlet, *Why We Practice Plural Marriage,* which addressed common criticisms of the practice. "There can be no evil," she told her readers, "in a thing that inspires prayer, drives selfishness from the heart, and lengthens the cords of human feelings, leading one to do greater deeds of kindness outside of his or her own little circle."[24]

Though writing sometimes exhausted Helen, the income paid for her newspaper subscription and other expenses.[25] Her editorials chastised the Church's persecutors for championing freedom and religious liberty on the one hand and pursuing a ruthless campaign against the Church on the other. Her words also provided encouragement to her fellow Saints.

"If this people will do their part, the powers of the Almighty will be made manifest in their behalf," she reassured her readers in August 1885. "We have nothing to fear from the wicked."[26]

Helen viewed Joseph III's efforts to distance his father from plural marriage as an assault on truth.[27] One day, while traveling by train through central Utah, she noticed a man who boarded her car and took a seat in front of her. He did not look like a member of the Church, and Helen wondered if he was a government official there to enforce the antipolygamy laws. After the stranger exited the train, Helen learned to her shock that he was Joseph Smith III.

"If I had known him," she wrote in her journal, "I would have been more bold to criticize and tempted to make myself known."[28]

Though Helen spent most of her life married to Horace, she knew she had been sealed to the prophet Joseph Smith. How her relationships would work themselves out in the hereafter was not always clear to her. But she intended to claim all the eternal blessings God had promised her family. God had always brought her through the furnace of affliction, and she continued to trust that He would make things right in the end.

"I have long since learned to leave all with Him, who knoweth better than ourselves what will make us happy," she wrote.[29]

A FEW MONTHS AFTER the birth of her daughter, Ida Udall was on the move again. Traveling under an assumed name, she stayed for a few weeks at a time with different friends and relatives in Utah.[30] David would be going to trial in August 1885. Since prosecutors were unable to assemble a convincing case against him for polygamy, they had turned instead to a trumped-up perjury charge his enemies in St. Johns had leveled against him some time earlier.[31]

Ida and David had last seen each other in May 1885, two months after Pauline was born. Since then, Ida had received a letter from David expressing regret over all she had to endure because of him.

"Better, it has been my feelings sometimes, that I had suffered imprisonment than to have you going by another name and running here and there for fear of being known," he wrote.[32]

But Ida was hopeful that her sacrifice would be worth the struggle, especially since many people believed that David would be acquitted. As she awaited news of the trial in Arizona, she took comfort in caring for Pauline. Attending to the baby's needs was sometimes the only thing distracting her from the wearying suspense.[33]

On August 17, news arrived that David had been convicted on the perjury charge and sentenced to three years in prison. Ida was dismayed, but she hoped she would at least be able to return to her family in Arizona. Apostle George Teasdale recommended against coming out of hiding, however. If David was pardoned in the flimsy perjury case, his enemies would again try to convict him of polygamy.

Ida followed the apostle's advice and did not return to Arizona.[34] But with every passing day, she grew more and more anxious to hear from David in prison. He could only write one letter a month to his family, so she depended on Ella to send her copies of his letters. Ella was facing her own challenges, though, especially after her youngest child, Mary, passed away in October 1885.

For three months, Ida received no letters from David. When a bundle of his letters finally arrived, she found that he had begun using a code name for her. Wary of incriminating himself, David now referred to her by her mother's name, Lois Pratt.[35]

THAT FALL, WHILE HIDING from marshals south of Salt Lake City, President Taylor called Jacob Gates on another mission to Hawaii. It had been six years since Jacob had returned from his first mission to the islands. In that time, he had married Susie Young, who now went by Susa. They were living in Provo, raising their three children together and expecting another. Bailey, Susa's son from her first marriage, also lived with them. Her daughter Leah, however, still lived with her father's family in northern Utah.

Jacob's unexpected mission call left Susa anxious and full of questions. The letter asked Jacob to leave for Hawaii in just three weeks, giving him little time to settle up his business affairs. It also did not indicate if he could take his family with him, as missionaries were sometimes permitted to do.

Susa wanted to go with him and take the children, but she was not hopeful. "From the tone of Jacob's notification, he doesn't think I will be wanted to go," she wrote to her mother the next day. "So you can imagine my prospects for the next three years."[36]

Jacob accepted the mission call promptly, but he asked President Taylor if Susa and the children could join him. "I would rather have them go with me," he wrote. He reminded the prophet that Susa had been to Hawaii before and knew the area well.[37]

No immediate response came, and Susa prepared to send Jacob off on his own. She learned that three other missionaries had already received permission to take their families to Laie, where housing was limited, so she did not expect the same blessing. Then, just a week before he needed to leave Utah, Jacob received a letter granting him permission to take his family.[38]

Susa and Jacob hurried to prepare. Among other things, they wrote to Alma Dunford, Susa's ex-husband, to ask if ten-year-old Bailey could go to Hawaii with them. Rather than write back, Alma waited until the family was leaving for Hawaii. He then confronted them at the train station in Salt Lake City with a deputy and a court order invoking his right to keep Bailey with him in Utah.

Though Bailey had always lived with Susa, the court order left her powerless to stop Alma from taking him.

As Susa parted with her son, heartbroken, the boy cried out and tried to go back to her.[39]

Susa and Jacob sailed for Hawaii a short time later with their other children. During the voyage, Susa was grief-stricken and sick. When the ship docked in Honolulu, Joseph F. Smith, who was living in exile on the island to avoid arrest, greeted them. The next morning they went to Laie, where a large crowd of Saints greeted them with dinner and a concert.[40]

Susa and Jacob soon settled into life in Laie. Susa admired the lovely scenery around her, but she struggled to adjust to the missionary quarters, which were infested with vermin. "If I feel at all lonely," she wrote in a humorous article for the *Woman's Exponent,* "I have plenty of company in mice, rats, scorpions, centipedes, cockroaches, fleas, mosquitos, lizards, and millions of ants."[41]

Mostly, she was homesick for Utah.[42] But a few months after arriving, she received a letter from Bailey. "I wish you were staying here," he wrote. "I think of you in my prayers."[43]

In those prayers, at least, Susa could take comfort.

WHEN JOHN TAYLOR WENT into hiding in early 1885, he had joined George Q. Cannon, who had entered the underground a few weeks earlier. So far, they had found refuge in the homes of a few faithful Saints in and around Salt Lake City, moving whenever neighbors began acting suspicious or John felt uneasy. Since marshals were always hunting them, they could never let their guard down.[44]

Unable to meet with the Saints in person, the First Presidency tried to handle Church business by letter. When certain matters could not be resolved that way, they would meet secretly with other Church leaders in Salt Lake City. Every trip to the city was dangerous. No Church leader who practiced plural marriage was safe.[45]

In November, federal marshals arrested apostle Lorenzo Snow, who was seventy-one years old and in fragile health.[46] Before his arrest, Lorenzo had decided to live with only one of his families to avoid the charge of unlawful cohabitation. But one of the judges involved in the case said that he needed to stop being a husband to his wives entirely. "I would prefer to die a thousand deaths," Lorenzo had stated, "than renounce my wives and violate these sacred obligations."[47]

In January 1886, the judge sentenced Lorenzo to eighteen months in jail for three counts of unlawful cohabitation. The following month, marshal Elwin Ireland and several deputies raided George Q. Cannon's farm and served subpoenas to family members living there. Ireland then issued a $500 reward for George's arrest.[48]

When George learned about the reward, he knew a pack of "human bloodhounds" would be hunting for him. Unwilling to put the prophet in danger, he decided to part ways with John for a time. John agreed and advised him to go to Mexico. A few days later, George shaved his beard and boarded a train, hoping to slip out of Utah undetected.[49]

Word had somehow gotten out that George had left town, however, and a sheriff boarded the train and arrested him. Marshal Ireland then came to escort George back to Salt Lake City.

As the train rattled along, a Church member approached George and whispered that a group of Saints was planning to rescue him before the train reached the city. George stood up and headed for a platform outside one of the train's cars. He did not want anyone to be arrested—or killed—because of him.

Looking out over the winter landscape, George thought about jumping from the train. The western desert was a desolate place, though. If he jumped at the wrong time, he might end up miles away from the nearest town. Traveling this barren land on foot could be deadly, especially for someone nearly sixty years old.

Suddenly the train lurched, pitching George overboard. His head and left side slammed onto the ground as the train chugged on, disappearing into the cold, gray distance.

Lying half-conscious on the frozen earth, George felt pain course through his head and body. The ridge of his nose had been pushed to one side, broken. A gash through one of his eyebrows cut straight to his skull, coating his face and clothes with blood.

Picking himself up, George began walking slowly along the track. Soon he saw a deputy heading toward him. Marshal Ireland had noticed him missing and had ordered the train to stop. George limped to the deputy, who escorted him to a nearby town.

There George sent a telegram with a request that no Saint interfere with his arrest. He was in the Lord's hands now.[50]

CHAPTER 35

A Day of Trial

A large crowd was waiting at the train platform when George Q. Cannon and his captors rolled into Salt Lake City on February 17, 1886. Marshal Ireland escorted George off the train and to an office in the city, where another crowd had gathered to show sympathy to the battered and bruised prisoner. Inside, the marshal gave George a mattress and let him rest while they waited for his lawyer and other visitors to arrive.[1]

George's trial was scheduled for March 17, and a judge released him on a $45,000 bond. A grand jury, meanwhile, began interrogating George's wives and children to gather evidence that he had violated the Edmunds Act.

"Those men are dead to every human sympathy," George declared when he learned of their aggressive questioning. "They are as pitiless as the most abandoned and wicked pirates."[2]

After his release, George met secretly with President Taylor. George had all but decided to go to prison, but he had prayed that the prophet would know the Lord's will on the matter. At their meeting, George explained his predicament, and President Taylor agreed that he should submit to the law. If George did not stand trial, he would forfeit the $45,000 bond, which his friends had generously agreed to pay in his behalf.

That night, however, the Lord revealed to President Taylor that his first counselor should go back into hiding. The revelation was like a flash of lightning, and after it came, the prophet immediately knelt beside his bed in grateful prayer. A few years earlier, the Lord had inspired him to invest non-tithing Church money into a mining company in order to create a special reserve fund for the Church. President Taylor believed the reserve should be used to reimburse the men who had put up George's bond.[3]

George felt that the revelation was an answer to his prayers. He and President Taylor submitted it to the four apostles in the city, and they approved the plan to carry it out.

George worried about the propriety of going back into hiding, though, especially when other men had gone to jail for their convictions. He did not want anyone in or out of the Church thinking he was a coward. Yet he now knew the Lord's will for him, and he chose to trust in it.

"If God directs a course for me to take," he wrote in his journal, "I desire to take it and leave the result with Him."[4]

AROUND THE TIME GEORGE Q. Cannon went back into hiding, Emmeline Wells was again traveling to Washington, DC, on Church business. Seven years had passed since her meeting with President Rutherford Hayes and his wife, Lucy. Opposition to the Church had only increased since then, especially now that Congress was trying to amend the Edmunds Act with an even harsher piece of legislation, which would come to be known as the Edmunds-Tucker Act.[5]

The proposed act sought, among other things, to rob Utah's women of their right to vote, and Emmeline felt duty bound to speak out against it.[6] She was hopeful that she could persuade reasonable people—especially her allies in the fight for women's rights—to see the injustice of the act.

In Washington, Emmeline spoke to lawmakers and activists who were sympathetic to her cause. Some were indignant that women in Utah might lose their right to vote. Others disagreed with a part of the act allowing the government to confiscate the Saints' private property. But opposition to plural marriage muted the enthusiasm of even those Emmeline called friends.[7]

After several weeks in Washington, she boarded a westbound train, believing she had done all she could for the Saints. On her journey, she learned that two thousand women had recently crowded into the Salt Lake Theatre to protest the government's treatment of plural families. At the meeting, Mary Isabella Horne had called on the women to speak out against the injustice. "Must we, women of The Church of Jesus Christ of Latter-day Saints, still submit to insults and injury without raising our voices against it?" she asked.[8]

Emmeline was thrilled by the strength of her sisters in the gospel, and she looked forward to reuniting with them. But on her way home, she received a telegram from President Taylor asking her to return to Washington. A committee of Latter-day Saint women had written resolutions calling for the nation's leaders to end their crusade against the Saints. The resolutions also pleaded with wives and mothers throughout the United States to come to the aid of Utah's women. The prophet wanted Emmeline to present the resolutions to Grover Cleveland, the president of the United States. Ellen Ferguson, a Latter-day Saint physician and surgeon in Salt Lake City, would join her.[9]

Within days, Emmeline was back in Washington. She and Ellen called on President Cleveland in the White House library. He was not as intimidating as they expected, but they knew it would be difficult to persuade him to support their cause. A year earlier, he had met with a delegation of Latter-day Saints from Utah and told them, "I wish you out there could be like the rest of us."[10]

The president listened attentively to Emmeline and Ellen and promised to give their resolutions serious consideration. But while he seemed sympathetic to their cause, he was not sympathetic enough to risk offending antipolygamy legislators.

"All that can be done here in presenting facts and seeking to remove prejudice seems only a drop in the ocean of public sentiment," Emmeline wrote in the *Woman's Exponent* a short time later. "But one must not be weary in well-doing, even though the opportunities may be few and the prejudice bitter."[11]

MEANWHILE, IN UTAH'S SANPETE Valley, marshals had begun rounding up polygamous Saints in Ephraim, Manti, and neighboring towns.[12] As president of the Ephraim South Ward Primary, Augusta Dorius Stevens instructed children how to act if the marshals tried to question them.[13] Unsuspecting children were often easy sources of information, so they needed to learn how to recognize the marshals and create confusion to muddle investigations.[14]

More than thirty years had passed since Augusta left her family in Copenhagen, Denmark, to come to Utah. She was only fourteen at that time. Her mother had hated the Church then and had just divorced her father. If somebody had told Augusta that her family would one day be together again in Zion, with her parents sealed by proxy in the temple, she probably would not have believed them.[15]

But that was exactly what happened, and now the Dorius family was a sizable presence in Sanpete Valley.

Augusta's father and most of her siblings were long since dead, but her mother, Ane Sophie, was now in her seventies and taking great pride in the children whose Church membership used to embarrass her. Augusta's brothers Carl and Johan had large plural families that grew year after year with more children and grandchildren. Her stepbrother, Lewis, the son of her father's second wife, Hannah, also had a large plural family. Augusta's stepsister, Julia, whom her mother had adopted in Denmark, was likewise married and raising a family in the valley.[16]

While the Dorius brothers' plural marriages put them at risk of arrest, Augusta's husband, Henry, was safe. His first wife had died in 1864, so he and Augusta were no longer practicing plural marriage. They had eight children together, five of whom were still living.[17] None of their married children practiced plural marriage either.[18]

Because she worked as a midwife and nurse, however, Augusta could still be a person of interest to the marshals. Seeing a need for better medical care among the Saints, Brigham Young and Eliza Snow had begun in the 1870s to urge Latter-day Saint women to gain medical education. Augusta became a midwife in 1876 after receiving her training in Utah. With encouragement from the Relief Society and Church leaders, other women attended medical schools in the eastern United States. Some of them also helped the Relief Society establish the Deseret Hospital in Salt Lake City in 1882.[19]

In the eyes of marshals, children were evidence of unlawful cohabitation, if not plural marriage, and midwives like Augusta could serve as witnesses in court. Augusta continued to deliver babies and visit patients, however, going door-to-door with a black satchel and a cheerful countenance.[20]

In Primary, she often told the children how blessed they were to grow up in Zion, despite its present dangers. Primary meetings provided a secure place for children to learn the gospel. Augusta taught them to be kind to the elderly and those with disabilities. She encouraged them to be polite and do all they could to share in the blessings of the temple.[21]

Like other Church leaders, she also emphasized the importance of taking the sacrament worthily each week, which the children did in Sunday School. "We must not take the sacrament if we have bad feelings in our heart toward our playmates or anyone else," she taught them. "We must be prayerful and have the Spirit of God that we may love one another. If we hate our playmate or our brother or sister, we cannot love God."[22]

And she reminded the Primary children not to forget those being harassed by the marshals. "It is a day of trial," she said, "and we must remember to offer up our humble prayers for our brethren in prison—and all Saints."[23]

THAT WINTER, WHILE LIVING on the underground in Utah, Ida Udall received a telegram from her husband, David. President Cleveland had pardoned him for perjury, and he was coming home.

Ida was overjoyed for David but sad that she could not reunite with him in St. Johns, Arizona. "How lonely and homesick it makes me to think I can join in none of the rejoicings over the return of my own husband," she lamented in her journal.[24]

Ida continued to live in Nephi, often battling feelings of loneliness and frustration at her exile.[25] In September 1886, after David had to delay a long-awaited visit to see her, she wrote him an angry letter and mailed it before she had time to change her mind.

"I told him he need not worry about coming at all on my account," she fumed later in her journal. "I thought I had fooled around long enough for someone who did not care a snap for me."

Not long after, Ida lay awake crying, regretting that she had sent the letter. Then, in a message from her sister-in-law, she learned that David prayed for her and Pauline's well-being. The thought of David praying for her and their daughter touched Ida's heart, and she wrote to him again, this time apologizing for her angry letter.[26]

She soon received a letter from David assuring her that he was her "affectionate and devoted husband," followed by another, longer letter full of hope and loving, contrite words. "Forgive me too for every unkind act, word, thought, and apparent neglect," David pleaded. "I have a testimony that the day of deliverance is near at hand and that we will have joy in the earth."[27]

In December, a polygamy indictment hanging over David was dismissed, making it possible for Ida to return to Arizona.[28] David came to Nephi in March 1887 to bring her and Pauline back, just in time for the little girl's second birthday. Pauline did not know her father, and she reacted strongly whenever he tried to hold Ida. "Keep his hands off!" she warned her mother.

The family's journey to Arizona lasted three weeks. It was the most time Ida had spent alone with her husband in the five years they had been married.[29]

A YEAR AFTER ACCOMPANYING her husband into the mission field, Susa Gates had grown used to her home in Hawaii. Jacob worked as a sugar boiler, turning the settlement's sugarcane crop into a product that could be sold.[30] Susa did her best to meet the demands of domestic life. She was pregnant again, and aside from doing laundry and cooking meals, she kept busy making shirts for Jacob, gingham dresses for their six-year-old daughter, Lucy, shirts and pants for four-year-old Jay and three-year old Karl, and new aprons for infant Joseph. She often felt tired at the end of the day, but she still found time to write and submit articles to newspapers in Utah and California.[31]

One morning in February 1887, little Jay came down with a fever and a cough. At first, Susa and Jacob assumed it was a cold, but the symptoms got worse over the next week. They cared for Jay as best they could and called in Joseph F. Smith and others to bless him. Susa marveled at the faith exercised in behalf of her son. But Jay did not get any better.

On the night of February 22, Susa stayed up with Jay, rubbing his belly with oil to try to relieve his pain. His breaths came hard and short. "Don't leave me tonight, Mama," he told her. "Stay tonight."

Susa promised she would, but after midnight, Jacob urged her to get some rest while he watched their son. Jay seemed to be sleeping soundly, so she went to bed, unwilling to believe her little boy would die. He was on a mission with his family, she told herself, and people did not die on missions.

Jay awoke later and whispered "Mama" over and over throughout the night. In the morning, he looked worse, and the family called for Joseph F. and Julina Smith. The Smiths stayed with the Gates family for the rest of the day. Jay did not improve, and that afternoon, he fell peacefully asleep and then passed away just before two o'clock.[32]

Susa's grief was inexpressible, but she had barely begun mourning when Karl came down with the same sickness. As he grew worse, the Saints from around Laie fasted and prayed, but nothing helped. The family was placed under quarantine to prevent the spread of the disease, and Karl died soon after.[33]

Though many families came to Susa and Jacob's aid, Joseph F. and Julina Smith were constantly by their side. They had lost their oldest daughter, Josephine, when she was about the age of the boys, and they understood their friends' anguish. When the boys died, Joseph was there at their bedside. Julina washed their bodies, made their burial clothes, and dressed them for the last time.[34]

In the days that followed, Jacob wept for their sons, but Susa was too stunned to cry. She worried their other children might catch the disease. After Karl's passing, she had also felt no movement from the baby in her womb. Though Jay had seen the child in a dream just before his death, Susa wondered if the baby was still alive.

Then one day she felt a slight flutter—a small sign of life. "A very faint motion comforts me with hope that life still beats under my saddened heart," she wrote her mother. She did not understand why her sons had died, but she found strength knowing that God was watching over her.

"With all this, we know that God rules in the heavens," she wrote her mother. "God has blessed me and helped me to bear my burdens. Praise His holy name forever."[35]

EARLY IN 1887, CONGRESS passed the Edmunds-Tucker Act. The new law gave Utah courts even greater power to prosecute and punish plural families. Women in the territory lost their right to vote, and children born of plural marriage were stripped of inheritance rights. Prospective voters, jurors, and local government officials were required to take an antipolygamy oath. The Church and the Perpetual Emigrating Fund ceased to exist as legal entities, and the government was given authority to confiscate certain Church properties valued at over $50,000.[36]

John Taylor, George Q. Cannon, and other Church leaders worked to keep one step ahead of the marshals. More and more Saints were finding refuge in small Church settlements in Chihuahua, Mexico, including Colonia Díaz and Colonia Juárez.[37] Other Saints had founded a settlement in Canada called Cardston.[38] These women and men were willing to move hundreds of miles to remote locales outside the United States to protect their families, follow God's commandments, and keep their sacred temple covenants.

That spring, John Taylor's health declined sharply, and George grew anxious for the prophet's well-being. Though still in hiding, the two men had lived the past six months with a family at an isolated home in Kaysville, about twenty miles north of Salt Lake City. Lately John had suffered from heart pains, shortness of breath, and sleeplessness. His memory was starting to fail, and he found it difficult to concentrate. George pressed him to see a doctor, but aside from a few herbal teas, John would take no remedy.[39]

On May 24, John did not feel well enough to attend to Church business, and he asked George to handle it himself. More business matters arose, and John asked George to resolve them too. When a message came requesting advice on an important political question, John asked George to travel to Salt Lake City to handle it.[40]

George's thoughts turned often to Joseph F. Smith, who was still in exile in Hawaii. The previous fall, he had written to Joseph about the challenges he and John were facing. "I cannot say to you how many times I have wished that you were here," he had expressed. "I have felt about the First Presidency like I would about a bird that had one wing lacking."

More recently, George had informed Joseph about John's poor health. "His will, as you know, is indomitable," he had noted in a letter. But the prophet was not a young man, and his body was slowing down. If John took a turn for the worse, George had promised to send for Joseph immediately.

That time had now come. Though George knew calling Joseph home would place him in danger, he sent word urging him to return to Utah.

"I have taken this step without communicating it to anyone, for fear that it might create alarm, or it might endanger your safety," he wrote. "I have nothing to say except that you cannot be too cautious."[41]

GEORGE BEGAN THE MORNING of July 18 signing temple recommends, a task normally reserved for the president of the Church. By now, John Taylor rarely left his bedroom and scarcely had the strength to speak. The entire burden of the First Presidency's responsibilities had fallen on George's shoulders.[42]

Later that afternoon, a covered wagon approached the house in Kaysville. When it stopped, a familiar figure emerged, and a flood of relief and joy rushed over

George as he recognized Joseph F. Smith. He brought Joseph inside to see the prophet, and they found John sitting in a chair in his bedroom, barely conscious. Joseph took John's hand and spoke to him. John appeared to recognize his counselor.

"This is the first time the First Presidency have been together for two years and eight months," George said to John. "How do you feel?"

"I feel to thank the Lord," John whispered.[43]

Over the next week, John's condition worsened. One evening, George and Joseph were handling Church business when they were suddenly called into John's bedroom. John was lying motionless in bed, his breath short and faint. After a few minutes, his breathing stopped completely. It happened so peacefully that George thought of a baby falling asleep.

For George, losing John was like losing his best friend. John had been like a father to him. They had not always seen eye to eye, but George considered him one of the noblest men he had ever known. He thought about the First Presidency's reunion just one week earlier. Now they were separated again.

George and Joseph quickly began making plans to notify the apostles. George had already written about the prophet's failing health to Wilford Woodruff, the president of the Quorum of the Twelve, and Wilford was slowly making his way to Salt Lake City from St. George, taking care to avoid the marshals. Most of the other apostles were still in hiding.

In their absence, George knew he was in a delicate position. Since the Church president had died, he and Joseph could no longer act as members of the First Presidency. Yet the Church still faced grave dangers and needed leadership. If he continued to manage Church affairs, independent of the Twelve, he might displease the other apostles. But what choice did he have? The quorum was scattered, and some matters simply could not be put off or ignored.

George also knew that he and Joseph had to act quickly. If John's death became public too soon, the marshals might learn of their whereabouts and come after them. He and Joseph were no longer safe.

"We must break camp," George announced, "and get away from here as soon as possible."[44]

PART 4

A Temple of God

JULY 1887–MAY 1893

Glad tidings of joy to the spirits in prison,
To the Saints of all countries and Isles of the sea,
For a Temple of God in the midst
of the mountains;
And joy in the courts of the highest will be.

Eliza R. Snow, "The Temple"

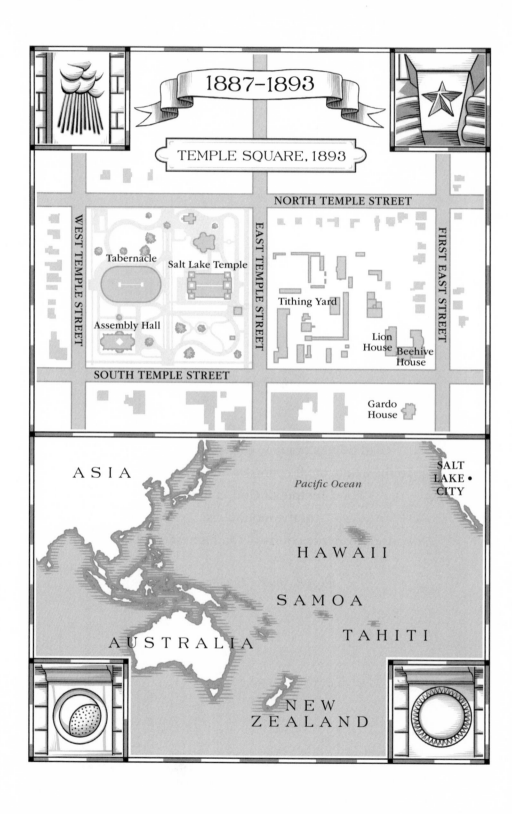

1887–1893

TEMPLE SQUARE, 1893

NORTH TEMPLE STREET

WEST TEMPLE STREET

EAST TEMPLE STREET

FIRST EAST STREET

Tabernacle

Salt Lake Temple

Tithing Yard

Assembly Hall

Lion House

Beehive House

SOUTH TEMPLE STREET

Gardo House

ASIA

Pacific Ocean

SALT LAKE • CITY

HAWAII

SAMOA

TAHITI

AUSTRALIA

NEW ZEALAND

CHAPTER 36

The Weak Thing
of This World

On July 29, 1887, Wilford Woodruff stood with George Q. Cannon and Joseph F. Smith at the window of the Church president's office in Salt Lake City. Together, they watched John Taylor's funeral procession slowly make its way through the city. Throngs of people lined the streets as more than a hundred carriages, buggies, and wagons rolled past. Emmeline Wells expressed what many Saints felt when she wrote that President Taylor "was a man the people might always be sure of as a leader and of whom they might also be justly proud."[1]

Only the threat of arrest kept Wilford and the other two apostles from stepping outside to pay their respects to their friend and prophet. Like most of his quorum, Wilford rarely appeared in public to avoid being arrested for polygamy or unlawful cohabitation. When his wife

Phebe passed away in 1885, Wilford had been at her bedside. But he did not attend her funeral three days later, fearing he would be captured. Now, as president of the Quorum of the Twelve and the senior leader of the Church, Wilford had become even more of a target for the marshals.

Wilford had never aspired to lead the Church. When he received the news of John's death, the burden of responsibility weighed heavy on his shoulders. "Marvelous are Thy ways, O Lord God Almighty," he had prayed, "for Thou has certainly chosen the weak thing of this world to perform Thy work on the earth."[2]

Wilford assembled the Twelve a few days after the funeral to discuss the future of the Church. As had been the case after the deaths of Joseph Smith and Brigham Young, the quorum did not immediately organize a new First Presidency. Rather, in a public statement, Wilford reaffirmed that in the absence of a First Presidency, the Twelve Apostles had the authority to lead the Church.[3]

Over the next several months, the apostles accomplished much under Wilford's leadership. Although the Manti temple was nearly ready to dedicate, the larger and more ambitious Salt Lake temple was still far from complete. The original plans for the temple had called for two large assembly halls to occupy the building's upper and lower floors. While on the underground, however, John Taylor had considered a new floor plan that would eliminate the lower assembly hall, providing much more space for endowment rooms. Now, Wilford and the Twelve consulted with builders on the best way to carry out these plans. They also approved a proposal to finish the temple's six towers in granite rather than in wood, as originally intended.[4]

Wilford and other Church leaders quietly prepared to make another attempt at Utah statehood as well. Since efforts to arrest Church leaders had prevented the Saints from holding general conference in Salt Lake City for the past three years, the Twelve also negotiated with local marshals to allow Wilford and apostles who had not been charged with polygamy or unlawful cohabitation to come out of hiding and hold conference in the city.[5]

As the apostles met together, Wilford noticed discord beginning to arise in their meetings. Several new apostles had been called to the quorum since Brigham Young's death a decade earlier, including Moses Thatcher, Francis Lyman, Heber Grant, and John W. Taylor. Now each of them seemed to have serious misgivings about George Q. Cannon. They believed he had made many poor decisions as a businessman, politician, and Church leader.

Among their concerns was George's recent handling of a Church discipline case involving his son, a prominent Church leader who had committed adultery. They also did not like that George had made decisions on his own for the Church during John Taylor's final illness. Nor did they like that George was advising Wilford on Church business, even though the First Presidency had been dissolved and George had returned to his place among the Twelve. In the minds of the junior apostles, George was acting out of self-interest and excluding them from the decision-making process.[6]

George believed he had been misjudged, however. He admitted to making small mistakes from time to time, but the accusations against him were false or based on incomplete information. Wilford understood the immense pressures George had faced over the last few years, and he continued to express trust in him and depend on his wisdom and experience.[7]

On October 5, the day before the general conference, Wilford gathered the apostles together to seek reconciliation. "Of all men under heaven," he said, "we should be united." He then listened for hours as the younger apostles again aired their grievances. When they finished, Wilford spoke about Joseph Smith, Brigham Young, and John Taylor, each of whom he had known and worked with closely. As great as these men were, he had seen imperfection in them. But they would not have to answer to him, Wilford said. They would answer to God, who was their judge.

"We should treat Brother Cannon with consideration," Wilford said. "He has his failings. If he did not, he would not be with us."

"If I have hurt any of your feelings," George added, "I humbly ask your pardon."

The meeting ended after midnight, with the opening prayer of general conference only hours away. Despite George's plea for forgiveness, Moses Thatcher and Heber Grant still believed that he had not adequately answered for his mistakes, and they told the brethren they did not yet feel reconciled.

In his journal, Wilford described the evening in three short words: "It was painful."[8]

AROUND THIS TIME, SAMUELA Manoa guided his canoe over the teal-blue water of Pago Pago Harbor. Behind him, the craggy mountain peaks of Tutuila, a Samoan island, rose into the sky. Just ahead, a large sailing vessel sat at the harbor's entrance, waiting for a local sailor to help pilot the ship safely through the reefs.

A resident of the neighboring island of Aunu'u, Samuela knew the harbor well. When his canoe finally reached the waiting ship, Samuela called to the captain and offered his help. The captain threw a rope ladder over the side of the ship and welcomed Samuela aboard.

Samuela followed the captain to his office in the lower deck. It was early in the morning, and the captain wondered if Samuela might like to cook some ham and eggs for himself before navigating the harbor. Samuela thanked him and was given old newspapers to light a cooking fire.

Samuela could read a little English and saw that one of the newspapers came from California. As he placed the paper in the fire, a headline stood out amid the flickering light. It was an announcement of a conference for members of The Church of Jesus Christ of Latter-day

Saints. Samuela's heart leaped, and he snatched up the paper and put out the flames.[9]

The date of the conference had long since passed, but Samuela was more interested in the name of the church than the event itself. This church was *his* church, and now, for the first time in years, he knew it was still thriving in the United States.

As a young man in the 1850s, Samuela had been baptized by Latter-day Saint missionaries in Hawaii. In 1861, however, Walter Gibson had seized control of the Saints' settlement on Lanai and told Samuela and others that the Church in Utah had been destroyed by the United States Army. Unaware of Walter's fraud, Samuela had believed him and supported his leadership. When Walter sent him and another Hawaiian Saint, Kimo Belio, on a mission to Samoa in 1862, he had accepted the call.[10]

Samuela and Kimo were the first Latter-day Saint missionaries to Samoa, and they had baptized around fifty Samoans during their first few years there. But mail service was unreliable, and the missionaries struggled to stay in contact with the Saints in Hawaii.[11] Since Church leaders in Utah had not issued the call to open a mission in Samoa, no new missionaries were sent to assist Samuela and Kimo, and the congregation of Samoan Saints dwindled.[12]

Kimo had since died, but Samuela had remained in Samoa and made it his home. He married and started a business. His neighbors continued to know him as the

Latter-day Saint missionary from Hawaii, but some of them had begun doubting the existence of the church he claimed to represent.[13]

Samuela had long wondered if Walter had lied to him about the destruction of the Church in the United States.[14] Now, twenty-five years after coming to Samoa, he finally had a reason to hope that if he wrote to Church headquarters, someone might respond.[15]

Clutching the newspaper, Samuela hurried to find the ship's captain to ask for help writing a letter to Church leaders in Utah. In the letter, he requested that missionaries be sent to Samoa as soon as possible. He had been waiting for several years, he wrote, and was eager to see the gospel preached once again among the Samoans.[16]

BY THE FALL OF 1887, Anna Widtsoe and her two sons, John and Osborne, had lived in the northern Utah town of Logan for nearly four years. Anna's sister Petroline had also joined the Church in Norway and come to Utah, settling in Salt Lake City, eighty miles to the south.[17]

Anna now worked as a seamstress, putting in long hours to make enough money to support her boys. She wanted her sons to be schoolteachers, as their late father had been, and she made education a priority in their lives. Since fifteen-year-old John worked at the local cooperative store to help earn money for the family, he could not attend school during the day. He instead taught himself algebra in his spare time and took private lessons in English and Latin from a British Saint. Nine-year-old Osborne, meanwhile, attended the local grade school and excelled in his studies.[18]

A few years before the Widtsoes arrived, Brigham Young had donated land for a school in the area similar to the one he had established in Provo. Brigham Young College opened in Logan in 1878, and Anna was determined to send her sons there as soon as they were ready, even if it meant that John could no longer work at the store. Some people thought she was wrong to emphasize education over manual labor, but she believed that developing the mind was as important as developing the body.[19]

Anna also ensured that the boys participated in Church programs and meetings. On Sundays they attended sacrament meeting and Sunday School. Osborne attended the ward Primary during the week, and John attended Aaronic Priesthood meetings on Monday evenings. As a deacon, he had chopped firewood for widows and helped take care of the stake tabernacle, where the ward held its meetings. Now, as a priest, he met with the bishopric and other priests and visited a few families every month as a "ward teacher." John also belonged to the Young Men's Mutual Improvement Association.

Anna attended Relief Society meetings on Thursdays. The Saints in Logan were from all over the United States and Europe, but their faith in the restored gospel bound them together. It was common in local Relief Society meetings to hear women speak or bear testimony in their native language while others interpreted for them. Anna learned English after a year of living in Logan, but with so many Scandinavian Saints in the area, she had many opportunities to speak Norwegian.[20]

At her Church meetings, Anna came to learn and understand more about the restored gospel. She had not been taught the Word of Wisdom in Norway, and she continued to drink coffee and tea in Utah, especially when she had to work late at night. She struggled for two months without success to give up these drinks. But one day she walked briskly to her cupboards, pulled out her coffee and tea packages, and threw them into the fire.

"Never again," she said.[21]

Anna and her sons also participated in temple work. She and John had witnessed President Taylor dedicate the Logan temple in 1884. A few years later, John was baptized and confirmed for his father, John Widtsoe Sr., in the temple. On the same day, he and Osborne were also baptized and confirmed for other deceased relatives, including their grandfathers and great-grandfathers. Anna and her sister Petroline then went to the temple and received their endowment. Anna returned to be baptized and confirmed for her mother and other kindred dead.

The Logan temple had become precious to her. The heavens had seemed to open on the day it was dedicated, rewarding her for all the sacrifices she had made to come to Zion.[22]

FOR MUCH OF 1887, Eliza Snow's health was fading. Now eighty-three years old, the beloved poet and Relief Society general president had already outlived many of the Saints of her generation, and she knew her death was coming. "I have no choice as to whether I shall die or live," she reminded her friends. "I am perfectly willing to go or stay, as our Heavenly Father shall order. I am in His hands."

Eliza's condition worsened as the year wore on. Zina Young and other close friends watched over her constantly. At ten o'clock on December 4, 1887, Patriarch John Smith visited her bedside in the Lion House in Salt Lake City. He asked her if she recognized him, and she smiled. "Of course I do," she said. John gave her a blessing, and she thanked him. Early the next morning, Eliza passed away peacefully with her brother Lorenzo at her side.[23]

As a leader of Latter-day Saint women, Eliza had organized and ministered to Relief Societies, Young Ladies' Mutual Improvement Associations, and Primaries in nearly every settlement in the territory. She had also presided over women's temple work in the Endowment House for more than thirty years. In each of these settings, Eliza had inspired women to employ their talents in helping God save the human family.

"It is the duty of each of us to be a holy woman," she had once taught them. "We shall feel that we are called to perform important duties. No one is exempt from them. There is no sister so isolated, and her sphere so narrow, but what she can do a great deal toward establishing the kingdom of God upon the earth."[24]

In the December 15 issue of the *Woman's Exponent,* Emmeline Wells honored her as an "Elect Lady" and "Zion's Poetess." "Sister Eliza has ever been brave, strong, and unflinching in the positions she has held," Emmeline wrote. "The daughters of Zion should emulate her wise example and follow in her footsteps."[25]

THE FOLLOWING APRIL, THE Saints sustained Eliza's friend Zina Young as the new general president of the Relief Society. Like Eliza, Zina had been a plural wife of both Joseph Smith and Brigham Young.[26] When Eliza became general president of the Relief Society in 1880, she had chosen Zina as her counselor. Over the years, the two women had worked, traveled, and grown old together.[27]

Zina was known for her loving, personal ministering and powerful spiritual gifts. For years she had presided over the Deseret Silk Association, one of the Relief Society's cooperative programs. She was also an experienced midwife who served as the vice president of the Deseret Hospital, a hospital the Relief Society operated in Salt Lake City. Though she accepted her new calling with some trepidation, she was determined to help the Relief Society thrive as it had under Eliza.[28]

Shortly after receiving her call, Zina traveled north to Canada to visit her only daughter, Zina Presendia Card. Before his death, John Taylor had asked Zina Presendia's husband, Charles, to establish a settlement in Canada for polygamous Saints in exile.[29] Until now, illness and the winter season had prevented Zina from visiting her daughter. But Zina Presendia was expecting a baby, and Zina wanted to be by her side.[30]

Zina arrived in Cardston, the new Canadian settlement, just as the wildflowers were beginning to bloom. Surrounded by fields of swaying grass, the town seemed perfectly situated to flourish.[31]

Zina could see that her daughter was flourishing as well, despite years of hardship. Widowed at age twenty-four, Zina Presendia had raised two young sons on her own for several years before the younger boy, Tommy, died of diphtheria at the age of seven. Three years later, she married Charles as a plural wife.[32]

Although Zina Presendia was unaccustomed to frontier living, she had made a comfortable home in a small log cabin. She had covered the cabin's rough-hewn interior with a soft flannel fabric she had made herself, each room a different color. Once spring arrived, she also tried to keep a fresh bouquet of flowers on the dining room table.[33]

Zina Young spent about three months in Cardston. During her stay, she met regularly with the Relief Society. On June 11, she taught the women that Cardston had been held in reserve for the Saints of God. There was a spirit of union among the people, she said, and the Lord had great blessings in store for them.[34]

The day after the meeting, Zina Presendia went into labor. Zina was by her side, both as a midwife and as a mother. After only three hours of labor, Zina Presendia gave birth to a plump, healthy girl—her first daughter.

The baby's mother, grandmother, and great-grand-mother had all been named Zina. It seemed fitting to name her Zina as well.[35]

EVEN BEFORE SAMUELA MANOA'S letter arrived in Salt Lake City, the Spirit had been working on Church leaders to expand missionary efforts in Samoa. Early in 1887, apostle Franklin Richards had called thirty-one-year-old Joseph Dean and his wife Florence to serve a mission to Hawaii. When he set them apart, he had instructed them to take the gospel to other islands in the Pacific as well, including Samoa.[36]

Joseph had been sent to the Pacific partly to protect him and his family from the marshals. He had fulfilled a mission to Hawaii with his first wife, Sally, ten years earlier. After returning to the mainland, he had married Florence as a plural wife and later served time in prison for unlawful cohabitation. Prosecutors continued to hound Joseph until he and Florence left for Hawaii. Sally, meanwhile, remained in Salt Lake City with her and Joseph's five children.[37]

Joseph wrote to Samuela several months after arriving in Hawaii, and Samuela soon replied, eager to assist in the work.[38] In May 1888, a few months after Florence gave birth to a boy they named Jasper, Joseph sent a letter to Samuela, notifying him that he and his family would be coming to Samoa the following month. A short time later, Susa and Jacob Gates threw a going-away party for the Deans, and Joseph, Florence, and their infant son set out for Samoa soon after.[39]

The first leg of their 2,000-mile trip was uneventful, but their steamship's captain had no plans to travel to the island of Aunu'u, where Samuela lived. Instead, he stopped the ship near Tutuila, about twenty miles west of Aunu'u.

Joseph knew no one on Tutuila, but he searched anxiously for a leader among the people who had come to meet the boat. Spotting a man who appeared to be in charge, Joseph thrust out his hand and said one of the few Samoan words he knew: "Talofa!"

Surprised, the man returned Joseph's greeting. Joseph then tried to tell him where he and his family were headed, speaking in Hawaiian and emphasizing the words "Aunu'u" and "Manoa."

Suddenly the man's eyes lit up. "You Manoa's friend?" he asked in English.

"Yes," Joseph said, relieved.

The man's name was Tanihiili. Samuela had sent him to find Joseph and his family and transport them safely to Aunu'u. He led them to a small open boat with a crew of twelve other Samoan men. After the Deans climbed aboard, ten of the men began rowing them out to sea while two others bailed water and Tanihiili steered. Struggling against stiff winds, the oarsmen maneuvered the boat up and over threatening waves until they brought it safely into the harbor at Aunu'u.

Samuela Manoa and his wife, Fasopo, greeted Joseph, Florence, and Jasper on the shore. Samuela was a thin man, much older than Joseph and rather frail. Tears stained his weather-worn face as he welcomed them in Hawaiian. "I feel greatly blessed that God has brought us together and that I can meet His good servant here in Samoa," he said.

Fasopo took Florence by the hand and led her to the three-room house they would all share. The following Sunday, Joseph preached his first sermon in Samoa to a house full of curious neighbors. He spoke Hawaiian, and Samuela translated. The next day, Joseph rebaptized and reconfirmed Samuela, as the Saints sometimes did at this time to renew their covenants.

A woman named Malaea was among those gathered to watch the ordinance. Moved by the Spirit, she asked Joseph to baptize her. He had already changed out of his wet baptismal clothes for the confirmation, but he put them back on and entered the water.

In the weeks that followed, fourteen more Samoans were baptized. Filled with hopeful enthusiasm, Joseph wrote to Wilford Woodruff on July 7 to share his family's experience. "I felt to prophesy in the name of the Lord that thousands of the people would embrace the truth," he reported. "That is my testimony today, and I believe I shall live to see it fulfilled."[40]

CHAPTER 37

To the Throne of Grace

Wilford Woodruff and George Q. Cannon arrived at the Manti temple in the middle of the night on May 15, 1888. They had left Salt Lake City a few days earlier, traveling after sundown to avoid marshals. The last leg of their trip was a forty-mile carriage ride through treacherous canyon terrain. Navigating in darkness, the driver had twice run the carriage off the road, nearly sending the apostles crashing down the mountain.[1]

Wilford had come to Sanpete Valley to dedicate the third temple in Utah. Since appearing at public events would endanger George and other Church leaders, Wilford had decided to dedicate the temple in a small, private ceremony. Later, the Saints would hold a public dedication without him for those who had a special recommend from their bishop or stake president.[2]

The beauty of the new temple was breathtaking. Constructed with cream-colored limestone from the nearby mountains, it rose atop a hill overlooking a sea of wheat fields. Delicately carved trimmings and colorful murals adorned the temple's interior, and two magnificent spiral staircases stood as if suspended in air, without a single pillar for support.[3]

Completing the temple was a bright spot in an otherwise difficult time for Wilford. Disunity within the Quorum of the Twelve continued to threaten their ability to lead the Church effectively. Eight months had passed since John Taylor's death, and some junior apostles were still finding fault with George. Wilford was ready to organize the First Presidency, but he could not do so as long as the quorum was out of harmony.

The apostles had made some progress in healing the rift in their quorum. In March, Wilford had brought them together several times to try to reconcile their differences. During one meeting, he reminded the quorum that they must be guided by humility and love. He meekly confessed his own wrongdoing in speaking too sharply at times, prompting each apostle to confess his sins and ask the others for forgiveness. Afterward, though, a few members of the quorum still remained unwilling to support the formation of a new First Presidency.[4]

The Edmunds-Tucker Act continued to threaten the Church as well. With power to confiscate Church property valued over $50,000, federal officials had taken control of the Church's tithing office, president's office, and temple block, which included the unfinished Salt Lake temple. The government had then offered to rent back the temple block for a courtesy fee of one dollar per month. Wilford had found the offer insulting, but he agreed to it to allow construction on the temple to continue.[5]

The new law had also put oversight of Utah's public schools into the hands of a federal commission, and the apostles worried that Latter-day Saint educators would be passed over when they sought teaching positions. Earlier that year, George had suggested establishing more Church-owned academies to employ these instructors and teach gospel principles to students. Wilford and the apostles had unanimously supported the plan, and on April 8 they announced the organization of a board of education to govern the new system.[6]

With these matters looming over the Church, Wilford dedicated the Manti temple on May 17, 1888. In the celestial room, he knelt at an altar and offered a prayer, thanking God for the wondrous blessing of another temple in Zion.

"Thou hast seen the labors of Thy Saints in the building of this house. Their motives and their exertions are all known to Thee," he prayed. "We this day present it to Thee, O Lord our God, as the fruit of the tithings and freewill offerings of Thy people."

That day, following the dedication, Wilford received a report that federal marshal Frank Dyer was demanding that the Church turn over all its property in Logan, including the tithing house, tabernacle, and temple. Wilford recorded a simple prayer in his journal, asking God to protect the temples from those who wished to defile them.[7]

The following week, apostle Lorenzo Snow presided at the Manti temple's public dedication. Before the first session began, many Saints in the temple's assembly hall heard angelic voices singing throughout the room. At other times, Saints saw halos or bright manifestations of light around speakers. Some people reported seeing Joseph Smith, Brigham Young, John Taylor, and other personages. While Lorenzo read the dedicatory prayer, someone in the congregation heard a voice say, "Hallelujah, hallelujah, the Lord be praised."

For the Saints, these spiritual manifestations were signs of God's watchful care. "They comfort the people," wrote one witness to the outpourings, "being an evidence that in the most cloudy times, the Lord is with them."[8]

WHILE STILL ON THEIR mission to Hawaii, Susa and Jacob Gates were beginning to think about what they would do when they returned to Utah. One day early in 1888, Jacob said, "Su, I wish you could get a position on the *Exponent* as associate editor." Susa had already published articles in the *Woman's Exponent* under the pen name "Homespun," and Jacob had great confidence in her writing talent.

Susa wanted to use her writing to help the Church. Eliza Snow had once encouraged her to "never write a line or a word that is not calculated to help and benefit this kingdom," and Susa tried to live by that counsel. Lately, she had begun thinking about writing articles in defense of the Church for magazines in the eastern United States. But she had never considered working as an editor before.[9]

The truth was, she struggled to find time to write. She was up by six o'clock most mornings, attending to three children and the never-ending tasks of running a household.[10] Barely a year had passed since the deaths of her small sons, Jay and Karl, and she still struggled with their loss, at times wishing she could leave Laie just to keep her thoughts from returning to the two graves on the hillside above her home. A cough from any of her children still made her anxious.[11] Was now the right time to take on more responsibilities?

But once the idea of working for the *Exponent* was planted in Susa's mind, it quickly took root. She wrote to Zina Young and described her desire to change the *Woman's Exponent* into a monthly magazine printed on fine paper, similar to popular women's magazines of the time.

"My whole soul is for the building up of this kingdom. I would labor so hard to help my sisters," she wrote. "The work would be a labor of love, for you know I love writing."[12]

At the same time, she sent a letter to Emmeline Wells, the newspaper's editor, and others she respected, asking for advice. Romania Pratt, one of the territory's few female physicians and a regular writer for the *Woman's Exponent,* was the first to respond.

"My dear young and gifted friend," she wrote, "I do not feel that you will be in your best situation as a member or partner in the *Exponent.*" Emmeline liked to manage the paper her own way, Romania explained, and would not welcome Susa's involvement. Instead, Romania suggested that Susa start a new magazine for the Church's young women.[13]

Susa loved the idea, and she wrote to her friend Joseph F. Smith about it. He responded a short time later, full of support. He envisioned a magazine written and produced entirely by Latter-day Saint women, and he encouraged Susa to seek "good and wise counselors" to help her.

"Not one who is capable should be denied the privilege to do their best," he wrote. "Our community is different from any other. Our prosperity lies in our own union, cooperation, and mutual effort. There is no one independent."[14]

At Joseph's recommendation, Susa wrote to Wilford Woodruff and the presidency of the Young Ladies' Mutual Improvement Association, seeking their support for the magazine. Wilford wrote back with his approval a few months later. The Y.L.M.I.A. presidency also gave her their support.

"Well, it is in the hands of the Lord," Susa wrote in her journal. As soon as she returned to the United States, she would try to make her magazine a reality.[15]

IN THE FALL OF 1888, George Q. Cannon decided that it was in his and the Church's best interest for him to go to prison. In the months before John Taylor's death, the Lord had revealed that George needed to go back into hiding with the prophet to help manage the Church. Now that John had passed away and the leadership of the Church was in the hands of the Twelve, George no longer had a duty to stay hidden.[16]

Wilford Woodruff also believed that the Saints needed to mend their relationship with the United States government in order to win statehood for Utah. Under a state government, the Saints could use their majority vote to elect leaders who would protect their religious freedoms. Since the Edmunds-Tucker Act applied only to territories, it would no longer have power to harm the Church if Utah became a state.[17] But the United States Congress was unlikely to grant statehood to Utah while a prominent apostle was a fugitive from justice.

When he learned that the United States attorney was willing to recommend a lenient sentence, George began to consider how turning himself in might benefit the Saints. His surrender could serve as an olive branch to Washington's lawmakers. He also hoped his actions might strengthen the resolve of other men to face up to similar charges.[18]

On September 17, he pleaded guilty to two counts of unlawful cohabitation, aware that he might have to spend nearly a year in jail. The chief justice, who was rumored to be more moderate in his dealings with the Saints than previous judges, gave him the relatively short sentence of 175 days behind bars.[19]

George wanted to begin his jail term as soon as possible, so on the same day as his sentencing, he was transported to the Utah territorial penitentiary. The weather-beaten prison sat on a hill in Salt Lake City.[20] Normally, when new prisoners entered the yard, inmates liked to heckle them by shouting, "Fresh fish!" But when George came in, no one yelled. Instead, the men circled around him, surprised and curious to see an apostle in prison.

Inside, George found three levels of small cells. The warden gave him a cell on the top level and told him he could stay inside without locking the heavy iron doors. George was not seeking favors, however. He wore the same black-and-white prison uniform and abided by the same rules as the rest of the inmates.[21]

After a short time in prison, George organized a Bible class. Over sixty men attended the first Sunday meeting, including several who were not Latter-day Saints. The prisoners read and discussed the first five chapters of Matthew. "A most delightful spirit prevailed," George wrote in his journal.[22]

Week followed week, and George found his time in prison to be happier than he had expected. During visiting days, he conducted Church business and met with other apostles, including Heber Grant, whose heart was beginning to soften toward him. He also received visits from friends and family, and he spent much time counseling fellow inmates.

"My cell has seemed a heavenly place," George wrote in his journal. "I feel that angels have been there."[23]

WHILE GEORGE Q. CANNON SERVED his prison sentence, Joseph F. Smith traveled to Washington, DC, to help the Church's attorney, Franklin S. Richards, lobby for Utah statehood.[24] Still a fugitive, Joseph sometimes wondered if he should follow George's example and turn himself in to the authorities. But Wilford Woodruff had assigned Joseph to oversee the Church's political activity in Washington, and Joseph believed either statehood or an act of divine intervention was the only path to lasting religious liberty for the Saints.[25]

In Washington, Joseph was free to move around town, though he was careful to avoid the halls of Congress, where someone might recognize him. He spent several days helping Franklin prepare a speech to the committee that would ultimately recommend whether Congress should vote for or against Utah statehood. Then, a few hours before the speech, he blessed Franklin that a good spirit would be with him.[26]

During the speech, Franklin represented plural marriage as a dying practice. Often, he said, the polygamy cases the government prosecuted were against elderly men who had entered into plural marriage years before. Franklin also argued that Utah's residents, a large majority of whom did not practice plural marriage, should have the liberty to elect their own officials under a state government.[27]

After days of deliberations, the committee decided to make no recommendation to Congress. Joseph was disappointed, but he thought so much of Franklin's speech that he sent copies of it to more than three thousand lawmakers and prominent persons across the country.

Not long after, however, he received a telegram informing him that George Peters, the United States attorney for Utah, was planning to summon members of Joseph's family to testify against him before a grand jury.[28]

Joseph considered it an act of betrayal. A few months earlier, Peters had extorted $5,000 from the Church with a promise that he would be lenient in future prosecutions of Latter-day Saints. Although political favors were often bought and sold at this time in the United States, Joseph's whole being had revolted at the thought of paying Peters. But after discussing the matter with Wilford, Joseph had decided that submitting to the blackmail might help protect the Saints.[29]

Joseph replied to the telegram immediately, giving instructions on where his wives and children could hide. But he felt anxious for the rest of the day. "I pray God to protect my family from the merciless grasp of the pitiless, bigoted foe," he wrote in his journal.[30]

THROUGHOUT THE WINTER OF 1888–89, the Quorum of the Twelve still could not come to an agreement over the formation of a new First Presidency. Federal marshals, meanwhile, continued to apprehend Church leaders. In December, apostle Francis Lyman surrendered to authorities, joining George Q. Cannon in prison. As president of the Twelve, Wilford Woodruff was forced to lead the Church with fewer and fewer apostles by his side.[31]

Wilford spent some of his time working on his farm, writing letters, and signing recommends for Saints wanting to attend the temples in Logan, Manti, or St. George.[32] In February 1889, George Q. Cannon was released after serving five months in prison. Wilford invited him and several friends to his office the following day to celebrate. Members of the Tabernacle Choir hauled in an organ, and the choir sang hymns. Then some Hawaiian Saints who had immigrated to Utah sang three songs, including two composed for the occasion. One of the men, Kanaka, was over ninety years old. George had baptized him while on his mission to Hawaii in the early 1850s.

That night, Wilford joined the Cannon family for a turkey dinner. "Your father has got the biggest brain and the best mind of any man in the kingdom," he told one of George's sons. Now that George was released from prison, Wilford hoped all the apostles could recognize his goodness and move forward together to lead the Church.[33]

AFTER ZINA YOUNG RETURNED to Salt Lake City from Cardston, she felt the full weight of her new responsibility as the general president of the Relief Society. She now stood at the head of more than twenty-two thousand women in hundreds of wards and branches across the world. In addition to serving as a spiritual leader, she oversaw several institutions, such as the Deseret Hospital, and multiple assets, including over thirty-two thousand bushels of grain in storage.

Zina had selected two experienced Relief Society leaders, Jane Richards and Bathsheba Smith, to support her as counselors, but the demands of the calling still felt overwhelming. Her daughter, Zina Presendia, reminded her of another person who could help. "See dear Aunt Em," she wrote. "She is a natural-made general."[34]

Zina Presendia was referring to Emmeline Wells, who served as a secretary to the Relief Society, a role that put her in charge of communications, business transactions, and arranging visits to Relief Societies throughout the territory. Emmeline's duties as editor of the *Woman's Exponent* already kept her extremely busy.[35] Even so, she willingly agreed to help Zina with her new responsibilities.

"Evidently my work will be more extensive in the future than it has been," Emmeline wrote in her journal. "Responsibilities come thick and fast upon the women of Zion."[36]

Both Zina and Emmeline felt strongly about women having the right to vote—a right the Edmunds-Tucker Act had taken from them. In the winter of 1889, Zina and Emmeline met with Wilford Woodruff and other Church leaders to discuss forming a women's suffrage association for Utah. Wilford and other members of the Quorum of the Twelve gave their full support.[37]

Soon, women's suffrage meetings began to follow regular Relief Society meetings in wards all around Utah and Idaho. Emmeline often published reports of these meetings in the *Woman's Exponent*. Zina, meanwhile, called on the United States government to return the "God-given right of suffrage" to Utah's women. "By and with it we will be enabled to do vast good to the world," she said. She also declared her commitment to working with women outside the Church. "We expect to reach out our hands to the women of America," she said, "and say we are one with you in this grand struggle."[38]

As the Relief Society grew, Zina worried that individual stakes were becoming disconnected from general Relief Society leaders and from one another. Her solution was to invite Relief Societies from outlying stakes to

Salt Lake City for a conference. The Young Men's Mutual Improvement Association had held similar conferences with success.[39]

The first general Relief Society conference was scheduled for April 6, 1889, to coincide with general conference. On that night, Zina stood in the Assembly Hall on Temple Square in front of women who had gathered to Zion from many nations. Over the past forty years, more than eighty thousand Latter-day Saints had emigrated to America from across the seas. Most came from the United Kingdom, but many others came from Scandinavia and the German-speaking areas of Europe. Still others had come from New Zealand, Australia, and other islands of the Pacific.

Zina encouraged the diverse congregation to visit each other's meetings and become acquainted with one another. "It will tend to union and harmony, promote confidence, and strengthen the cords that bind us together," she promised, "for there is more difference in our manner of speech than in the motives of our hearts."

"Sisters, let us be as one grand phalanx and stand for the right," she said. "Do not doubt the goodness of God or the truth of the work in which we are engaged."[40]

ON THE FIRST FRIDAY in April 1889, Wilford Woodruff called the apostles together. Nearly two years had passed since John Taylor's death, and Wilford had waited patiently for the quorum to find unity. He had led, as the revelations instructed, gently and meekly, with long-suffering and love unfeigned. Now, the day before the April general conference was to begin, he felt the time had come to reorganize the First Presidency.

Over the preceding months, a growing consensus had developed among the apostles that forming a First Presidency was in the best interest of the Church and that Wilford was the Lord's choice to lead them, no matter whom he chose as his counselors. Wilford had even written to Francis Lyman in prison and received his support.[41]

The apostles now unanimously agreed to form a new First Presidency. Wilford then nominated George Q. Cannon as his first counselor and Joseph F. Smith as his second.

"I can only accept this nomination by knowing that it is the will of the Lord," George said, "and that it is with the hearty and full approval of my brethren."

"I have prayed over this matter," Wilford assured him, "and I know that it is the mind and will of the Lord."

Despite lingering questions about George, Moses Thatcher voted in favor. "When I vote for him, I shall do so freely and will try and sustain him with all my might," he said. Heber Grant also voiced his support for President Woodruff's choice with only minor reservations.

The rest of the apostles sustained the new presidency wholeheartedly, and Wilford was pleased that the quorum was finally becoming united. "I have never seen a time when the Church needs the services of the Twelve more than today," he said.[42]

On Sunday, thousands of Saints filed into the tabernacle for the afternoon session of general conference. At this solemn assembly, Church members had the opportunity to sustain their new First Presidency. When the names of Wilford and his counselors were read, a sea of hands went up in support.[43]

"I have a great desire that, as a people, we may be united in heart, that we may have faith in the revelations of God and look to those things which have been promised unto us," Wilford told the Saints later in the meeting. He then bore testimony of Jesus Christ.

"In meekness and lowliness of heart He labored faithfully while He dwelt in the flesh to carry out the will of His Father," he said. "Trace the history of Jesus Christ, the Savior of the world, from the manger to the cross, onward through sufferings, mingled with blood, to the throne of grace, and there is an example for the elders of Israel, an example for all those who follow the Lord Jesus Christ."[44]

CHAPTER 38

Mine Own Due Time
and Way

Early in 1889, Joseph Dean was struggling to find people to teach in Samoa. Shortly after he and his wife Florence arrived on the island of Aunu'u the previous summer, the work had progressed quickly, and the island soon had enough Saints to form a branch with a Sunday School and Relief Society. New missionaries had also been sent from Salt Lake City to assist the Deans and the Samoan Saints.

But Samoa was in the middle of a civil war, and dangerous battles were erupting across the islands as factions fought for control. To make matters worse, the king was opposed to the Church. Rumors spread that he had made it illegal to be baptized a Latter-day Saint and that anyone who was baptized would be thrown in jail. Now fewer and fewer people were requesting baptism.[1]

Despite these challenges, the Samoan Saints built a meetinghouse, thatching the roof with coconut leaves and covering the floor with white pebbles and seashells. Florence Dean and Louisa Lee, another woman serving in the mission with her husband, held Relief Society meetings every Friday. The elders, meanwhile, bought a small sailboat so they could preach the gospel on other Samoan islands. They christened the new boat *Faaʻaliga*, the Samoan word for "revelation."[2]

In late 1888, Joseph, Florence, their young son, and several missionaries had moved from Aunuʻu to a larger neighboring island, Tutuila. But the island had a small population, and most of its men were away fighting in the war. Few people were interested in the gospel, and Joseph soon felt that he and the other missionaries were no longer making progress. He decided to go to the island of Upolu and visit Apia, a city at the center of Samoan government and trade.[3]

On Upolu, Joseph planned to contact the American consul and discuss the king's rumored threats against the Saints. He also wanted to find a man named Ifopo, who had been baptized by the Hawaiian missionary Kimo Belio some twenty-five years earlier. Ifopo had already sent Joseph two letters, and he was eager to meet missionaries who could help establish the Church on his island.[4]

On the night of March 11, Joseph and his two companions, Edward Wood and Adelbert Beesley, set sail for Upolu, a seventy-mile journey. They understood the danger of three inexperienced sailors traveling in a small boat over potentially rough waters. Yet Joseph felt the Lord wanted them to make the journey.

After a night of rough sailing, the missionaries approached Upolu. But as they neared the shore, a strong gust of wind took them by surprise. The boat tipped and immediately filled with water. The men tried to hold on to the oars, boxes, and trunks now bobbing alongside them in the waves. When they spotted another boat about a quarter mile away, they yelled and whistled until it finally turned around.

The Samoans who came to the missionaries' rescue spent over an hour righting their boat, diving under the waves to retrieve its sails and anchor, and helping the missionaries gather their possessions. Joseph was sorry that he had no money to give the men for their service, but they kindly accepted his handshake, and he asked the Lord to bless them.

By the time Joseph and his companions reached the city of Apia, they were exhausted. They offered a prayer of gratitude to God for protecting them during their journey. In the days that followed, they set out to find the American consul and search for Ifopo.[5]

BACK IN UTAH, TWENTY-NINE-YEAR-OLD Lorena Larsen was pregnant with her fourth child. Her husband, Bent, had recently finished serving a six-month prison sentence for unlawful cohabitation. Since

Lorena was a plural wife, her pregnancy could be used as evidence that Bent had violated the law again. To keep her family safe, she decided to go on the underground.[6]

Lorena first found refuge serving in the Manti temple. The temple was sixty miles from her hometown of Monroe, Utah, and her ward had been asked to provide temple workers. Lorena moved to Manti and served in the temple for a time, but it was difficult to be separated from her children, who had been left in the care of Bent and other family members. After almost suffering a miscarriage, Lorena was honorably released by the temple president, Daniel Wells.[7]

Lorena and Bent next decided to rent a home for her and her children in the town of Redmond, halfway between Monroe and Manti. Since informers were everywhere, Lorena had to keep her identity secret. Her name was now Hannah Thompson, she told her children, and if their father came to visit, they were to call him "Uncle Thompson." Again and again, Lorena stressed the importance of not revealing their true names.[8]

When the family arrived in Redmond, Lorena avoided public places and spent most of her time at home. One afternoon, however, she joined a group of friendly Relief Society sisters, and they told Lorena that when they asked her two-year-old daughter her name, she had responded, "Uncle Thompson."

Kind Saints in Redmond were quick to serve Lorena's family. On Easter Sunday, she found a bucket of fresh eggs and a pound of butter on her doorstep. Still, she missed her home in Monroe. Pregnant and alone, she struggled every day to take care of three children in a strange town.[9]

Then one night, Lorena had a dream. She saw her lawn in Monroe covered in wild bushes and vines. It hurt to see her home in ruins, so she immediately went to work digging out weeds in the yard. As she began pulling at deep roots, Lorena suddenly found herself beside a beautiful tree, heavy with the finest fruit she had ever seen. She heard a voice say, "The underground tree brings forth very choice fruit too."

In the dream, Lorena was soon surrounded by her loved ones. Her children, now fully grown, came to her, bearing dishes, bowls, and small baskets. Together, they filled the bowls with the delicious fruit and passed them among the crowd, some of whom Lorena perceived to be her descendants.

Lorena's heart rejoiced, and she awoke full of gratitude.[10]

SHORTLY AFTER ARRIVING IN Apia, Joseph Dean and his companions met with the American vice-consul in Samoa, William Blacklock, and asked if the rumors about Samoan Latter-day Saints being imprisoned were true. "It is nothing but a bluff," the vice-consul assured them. A treaty between the warring factions on the islands allowed people to worship as they pleased.[11]

Still, the threat of war loomed over the islands. Seven warships were anchored in Apia harbor—three from Germany, three from the United States, and one from Great Britain. Each nation was determined to defend its interests in the Pacific.[12]

Eager to find Ifopo, the missionaries next planned to travel by boat to his village, Salea'aumua, on the east end of the island.[13] But a storm soon descended on Apia. Howling winds and crashing waves sent Joseph and his companions scurrying for shelter. After they took cover in a loft above a local shop owner's barn, the missionaries felt the ramshackle building clatter against the gathering tempest, and they feared the structure would collapse.

The storm intensified, and the missionaries stood at a window watching in horror as the cyclone battered the huge warships in the harbor. Massive waves crashed upon the deck of one ship, sweeping men out to sea. Some sailors on another ship scrambled up the masts and rigging, clinging to the ropes like spiders, while others jumped into the roiling ocean to try swimming to safety. The ships were only one hundred yards from shore, but nothing could be done to help the men. All Joseph could do was pray for mercy. [14]

After the storm, debris and wreckage from the warships lined the beach, and about two hundred people had perished.[15] The missionaries were wary about venturing out to sea again. During cyclone season, another storm could descend without warning.[16] Setting their fears aside, however, the missionaries sailed for Salea'aumua to find Ifopo.

When they arrived, a group of Samoans rowed out to greet them, and one of the men introduced himself as Ifopo. For two decades he had stayed faithful to his testimony of the restored gospel, all the while unsure if new missionaries would ever come to his island. Now Joseph and his companions had arrived, and it was time to celebrate. They met Ifopo's wife, Matalita, and enjoyed a feast of roast pig and fruit.[17]

In the days that followed, the missionaries became acquainted with Ifopo's friends and neighbors. During one meeting, a hundred people gathered to hear Joseph speak, and the Spirit was powerful. The people were genuine in their questioning, eager to know more about the gospel.

One afternoon, Ifopo and the missionaries walked to a nearby stream. Although Ifopo had already been baptized, many years had passed, and he asked to be baptized again. Joseph waded into the water with his new friend and immersed him. Ifopo then knelt by the water's edge, and the missionaries confirmed him a member of the Church.

A few days later the wind changed, allowing Joseph and his companions to begin the journey back to Tutuila. Ifopo accompanied them beyond the reef to show them the way. When the time came to say goodbye, he pressed his nose against each of the missionaries' noses in turn, sending them off with a Samoan kiss.[18]

IN THE SPRING OF 1889, Lorena Larsen's husband, Bent, decided to evade federal marshals by fleeing to the relative safety of Colorado, a neighboring state where the Edmunds-Tucker Act did not apply. His first wife, Julia, could remain in Monroe with the rest of her family. But he wanted Lorena and her children to stay in Utah with her brother until he was sufficiently settled in Colorado to send for them.[19]

Lorena did not like the plan. Her brother was poor, she reminded Bent, and her sister-in-law had recently battled typhoid fever. They were in no position to help Lorena and her children. Lorena was also approaching the final months of her pregnancy and wanted her husband by her side.

Bent agreed, and Lorena and their children soon started for Colorado with him. The journey was over five hundred miles, through deserts and over mountains. It was wild country, and the men they encountered along the way often appeared dangerous. At one point on the trail, the only available water was pooled in holes in the rocky mountainside. Bent hunted for water while Lorena slowly drove the wagon through the canyon, periodically calling his name to ensure she had not lost him in the darkness.

Lorena was grateful when her family finally reached Sanford, Colorado, and joined the small community of Saints there. When the time came for Lorena to give birth, she was still weak from traveling. Her labor was so difficult some feared she might die. Lorena's son

Enoch was finally born on August 22, and the midwife declared he was the biggest baby she had delivered in twenty-six years.[20]

Meanwhile, laws and practices designed to injure the Church continued to bear down on families like the Larsens. Even Saints who did not practice plural marriage were affected.

In Idaho, the territorial legislature had passed a law requiring prospective voters to swear that they did not belong to a church that taught or encouraged polygamy. It did not matter whether the voters participated in the practice themselves. This effectively barred all Saints in Idaho, or almost one-fourth of the population, from voting or holding office. Latter-day Saint immigrants to the United States were likewise singled out by government officers and judges who refused to allow them to become citizens.

Cases challenging the lawfulness of these measures moved through the U.S. court system, but public sentiment against the Church ran high, and rulings in favor of the Church were few. The Church's lawyers had contested the legality of the Edmunds-Tucker Act soon after Congress passed it, however, and the Saints were hopeful that the Supreme Court would strike it down. The court had recently begun hearing the case, but it had not yet issued its ruling, leaving the Saints in suspense.[21]

Even in a remote town like Sanford, Lorena knew that her family and the Church would remain fractured and fearful as long as the government continued to deny the Saints their religious rights.[22]

AS THE LARSENS AND other Church members went underground to preserve their families and practice their faith, the First Presidency searched for new ways to protect the Saints' religious freedom. Determined to win allies in Washington, DC, and ultimately achieve statehood for Utah, Wilford Woodruff had begun encouraging Latter-day Saint newspaper editors to stop attacking the government in their publications. He urged Church leaders to stop speaking publicly about plural marriage lest they provoke the Church's critics in the government. And he had asked the president of the Logan temple to stop performing plural marriages in the house of the Lord.[23]

Under these new policies, fewer and fewer Saints entered new plural marriages. Yet some Saints still hoped to follow the principle as it had been previously taught. They were usually encouraged to go to Mexico or Canada, where Church leaders quietly performed the marriages beyond the reach of the United States government. Occasionally, though, plural marriages were still performed in Utah Territory.[24]

In September 1889, while visiting Saints north of Salt Lake City, Wilford Woodruff and George Q. Cannon met with a stake president who asked if he should issue temple recommends to Saints who wanted to enter plural marriage.

Wilford did not immediately answer the stake president's question. Instead, he reminded him that the Saints had once been commanded to build a temple in Jackson County, Missouri, but they had been forced to abandon their plans when opposition became too great. The Lord had accepted the Saints' offering nonetheless, and the consequences of not building a temple fell on the people who had prevented it.

"So it is now with this nation," said Wilford, "and the consequences of this will have to fall upon those who take this course to prevent our obeying this commandment."

He then answered the stake president's question directly. "I feel that it is not proper for any marriages of this kind to be performed in this territory at the present time," he said. Then, gesturing toward George, he added, "Here is President Cannon. He can say what he thinks about this matter."

George was dumbfounded. He had never heard Wilford speak so plainly on the subject before—and he did not know if he agreed with him. Should the Church cease performing plural marriages in Utah Territory? He personally was not as ready as Wilford to answer that question, so he made no reply, letting the conversation move to other matters.

But later, as George recorded the conversation in his journal, he continued to struggle with what Wilford had said. "To me, it is an exceedingly grave question," he wrote, "and it is the first time that anything of this kind has ever been uttered, to my knowledge, by one holding the keys."[25]

AMID GROWING QUESTIONS ABOUT the future course of the Church, Susa Gates published the first issue of the *Young Woman's Journal* in October 1889.

Susa had begun promoting the magazine after she and Jacob returned to Utah earlier that year. In June, her sister Maria Dougall, a counselor in the general Young Ladies' Mutual Improvement Association presidency, had encouraged the young women of the Salt Lake Stake to support and contribute to the new magazine. A few months later, several newspapers printed announcements of its imminent publication.[26]

Susa had also invited several Latter-day Saint writers to send their poetry and prose to the journal. For years, Saints with literary talents had honed their writing skills in such Church-supported newspapers and journals as the *Woman's Exponent,* the *Juvenile Instructor,* and the *Contributor.* In Europe, Saints had also provided writing for the British mission's *Millennial Star,* the Scandinavian mission's *Skandinaviens Stjerne* and *Nordstjarnan,* and the Swiss-German mission's *Der Stern.*[27]

The Saints sometimes called this writing "home literature," a term that brought to mind Brigham Young's notion of "home industries," or locally made products, like sugar, iron, and silk. In an 1888 sermon, Bishop Orson Whitney had encouraged the youth of the Church to create more home literature to showcase the Saints' greatest literary talents and testify of the restored gospel of Jesus Christ.

"Write for the papers, write for the magazines—especially our home publications," he had urged them. "Make books yourselves, which shall not only be a credit to you and to the land and people that produced you but likewise a boon and benefaction to mankind."[28]

In the first issue of the *Young Woman's Journal,* Susa published works of home literature by some of the best-known writers in the Church, including Josephine Spencer, Ruby Lamont, Lula Greene Richards, M. A. Y. Greenhalgh, and sisters Lu Dalton and Ellen Jakeman. She also included some of her own writing, a letter from the general Y.L.M.I.A. presidency, and a health and hygiene column by Romania Pratt.[29]

In her first editorial for the journal, Susa expressed hope that the magazine would soon feature writing from the young women throughout the Church. "Remember, girls, this is your magazine," she wrote. "Let its field of usefulness be extended from Canada to Mexico, from London to the Sandwich Islands."[30]

LATER THAT FALL, A federal judge in Utah denied U.S. citizenship to several European immigrants because they were Latter-day Saints and thus, in the judge's mind, disloyal to the United States. During the hearings, disaffected Church members claimed that the Saints made hostile, anti-government oaths in their temples. District attorneys also quoted sermons from times when Church leaders had spoken forcefully against corrupt government officials and people who had left the Church. These sermons, as well as other Church teachings about the last days and the kingdom of God, were construed as evidence that the Saints disregarded the government's authority.[31]

Wilford and other Church leaders knew they needed to respond to these claims. But responding to statements related to the temple, which the Saints had made solemn promises not to discuss, would be difficult.[32]

In late November, Wilford met with lawyers who advised Church leaders to supply the court with more information about the temple. They also recommended that he make an official announcement that no more plural marriages would be solemnized by the Church. Wilford was unsure how to respond to the lawyers' requests. Were such actions truly necessary, just to pacify the enemies of the Church? He needed time to seek God's will.[33]

Night had fallen by the time the lawyers left Wilford alone. For hours, he pondered and prayed for guidance on what to do.[34] He and the Saints had come to the Salt Lake Valley in 1847 seeking another chance to establish Zion and gather God's children to the peace and safety of its borders. Now, more than forty years later, opponents of the Church were tearing families apart, stripping women and men of their voting rights, creating obstacles for immigration and the gathering, and denying the rights of citizenship to people for simply belonging to the Church.

Before long, the Saints could lose even more—including the temples. What would happen then to the salvation and exaltation of God's children on both sides of the veil?

As Wilford prayed, the Lord answered him. "I, Jesus Christ, the Savior of the world, am in your midst," He said. "All that I have revealed and promised and decreed concerning the generation in which you live shall come to pass, and no power shall stay My hand."

The Savior did not tell Wilford exactly what to do, but He promised that all would be well if the Saints followed the Spirit.

"Have faith in God," the Savior said. "He will not forsake you. I, the Lord, will deliver my Saints from the dominion of the wicked in mine own due time and way."[35]

CHAPTER 39

In the Hands of God

On December 14, 1889, newly called apostle Anthon Lund received a telegram from the First Presidency at his home in Ephraim, Utah. Troubled by the recent cases of foreign-born Saints being denied United States citizenship, the presidency wanted to issue a response to the charge that it was impossible for Saints to be loyal citizens. Church leaders had drafted a statement denying this and other false claims and wanted to attach Anthon's name to it as a member of the Quorum of the Twelve.[1]

Anthon had defended the Church against misrepresentation ever since he was a child. After joining the Church as a boy in his native Denmark, he had been beaten by classmates for his beliefs. But rather than responding with anger, Anthon had shown them patience and kindness, eventually winning their friendship and respect. Anthon left Denmark at age eighteen to join the Saints in Utah, and in the decades since, he and his wife, Sanie, and their six children had sacrificed much to help build up the kingdom of God.[2]

Anthon replied to the First Presidency's telegram immediately, lending his name to their declaration. Although he had held many positions of responsibility in the Church, including serving in the Manti temple presidency, this was the first time his name was going out to all the world as an apostle of Jesus Christ.

Unlike the other members of the Quorum of the Twelve, Anthon had never practiced plural marriage. He was also the first modern-day apostle whose native language was not English. Wilford Woodruff was confident these differences could be assets to the quorum, and he knew that Anthon's call was God's will. Anthon's gentle manner and skill with several languages could help lead the Church into the next century.[3]

When Anthon was called into the Twelve, Wilford asked George Q. Cannon to give him an apostolic charge to prepare him for his new responsibilities. "It will require your life's labor to fill this calling properly," George had told Anthon. "You will feel, as you probably never have felt, the necessity of living near to God and invoking His power and having His guardian care, through His angels round about you."

From this charge, Anthon learned that it was his privilege as an apostle to learn God's mind and will. He was to stay true to the revelations he would receive—even when it seemed contrary to his natural judgment. "You cannot be too humble," George had reminded him. Anthon needed to express his views freely while also listening meekly to the Lord's prophet. "We should be willing to sit and watch the operations of the Spirit of God on this man whom God has chosen," George had said.[4]

The day Anthon replied to the telegram, the First Presidency and Quorum of the Twelve published their statement in the *Deseret News*. In clear language, they proclaimed that the Church abhorred violence and intended to exist in peace with the United States government, despite the hardships they had suffered under the nation's antipolygamy laws.

"We claim no religious liberty that we are unwilling to accord to others," the statement affirmed. "We desire to be in harmony with the government and people of the United States as an integral part of the nation."[5]

THAT WINTER, WHILE CHURCH leaders sought to clarify their beliefs to the nation, Jane Manning James wrote to Joseph F. Smith seeking clarity of her own. Jane was more than sixty years old now, and she worried about what the next life had in store for her. Most Saints in Utah had received temple ordinances that sealed them to loved ones in this life and the next. But Jane understood that she, as a black Latter-day Saint, was not permitted to participate in these higher ordinances.

Even so, Jane knew that God had promised to bless all nations of the earth through Abraham. Surely, she thought, that promise applied to her as well.[6]

Adding to Jane's anxiety about the next life was the present state of her family. She and her husband, Isaac, had divorced in the spring of 1870. Around 1874, she had married Frank Perkins, another black Latter-day Saint, but their marriage did not last. During these years, she had lost three children and several grandchildren to illnesses. Though four of her children were still alive, none of them were as devoted to the Church as she was.[7]

Would they be with her in the next life? If not, was there a place and a family for her there?

As a young woman, Jane had lived and worked in the home of Joseph and Emma Smith in Nauvoo. During that time, Emma had invited her to be adopted as a daughter to her and Joseph, but Jane had never given her a direct answer before Joseph's death. Now, however, Jane understood that Saints could be adopted into families through a special sealing in the temple. She believed that Emma had been inviting her to join their family in this way.[8]

In early 1883, Jane had visited President John Taylor to seek permission to receive her endowment. President Taylor discussed the matter with her, but he did not think the time had yet arrived for black Saints to receive the higher ordinances of the temple. He had reviewed the issue several years earlier when another black Saint, Elijah Able, asked to receive his temple ordinances. Though his investigation confirmed that Elijah had received the Melchizedek Priesthood in the 1830s, President Taylor and other Church leaders nevertheless decided to refuse Elijah's request on the basis of his race.[9]

Nearly two years after speaking with President Taylor, Jane had entreated him again. "I realize my race and color and can't expect my endowments," she stated at that time. Yet she noted that God had promised to bless all of Abraham's seed. "As this is the fullness of all dispensations," she asked, "is there no blessing for me?"

"You know my history," she continued. "According to the best of my ability I have lived to all the requirements of the gospel." She then recounted Emma's invitation to her and expressed her own desire to be adopted into Joseph Smith's family. "If I could be adopted to him as a child," she noted, "my soul would be satisfied."[10]

Soon after Jane sent her letter, President Taylor had left Salt Lake City to visit the southern settlements and Mexico, and he did not respond to her before his death. Four years later, Jane's stake president issued her a recommend to perform baptisms for the dead in the temple. "You must be content with this privilege, awaiting further instructions from the Lord to His servants," he wrote. A short time later, Jane traveled to the Logan temple and received baptism for her mother, grandmother, daughter, and other kindred dead.[11]

Now, in her letter to Joseph F. Smith, Jane again requested a chance to receive temple ordinances, including an adoption into the Smith family. "Can that be accomplished and when?" she asked.[12]

Jane received no reply to her letter, so she wrote again in April. Again she received no reply. Jane continued to have faith in the restored gospel and the prophets, praying that she might receive salvation in the Lord's kingdom. "I know that this is the work of God," she had once told her Relief Society. "I have never seen a time when I felt like backing out."

She also trusted in the promises she had recently received in a patriarchal blessing from John Smith, Joseph F. Smith's older brother.

"Hold sacred thy covenants, for the Lord has heard thy petitions," the blessing assured her. "His hand has been over thee for good, and thou shalt verily receive thy reward."

"Thou shalt complete thy mission and receive thine inheritance among the Saints," it promised, "and thy name shall be handed down to posterity in honorable remembrance."[13]

ON A MUDDY AFTERNOON in late April 1890, Emily Grant called at the home of her friend Josephine Smith. Both women lived in Manassa, a small Colorado town several miles south of Lorena and Bent Larsen's home in Sanford. Far from the larger settlements of Saints in Utah, Manassa had become a haven for "polygamy widows," or plural wives on the underground. Emily was lonely there, but she was striving to make a home in the windswept town for herself and her daughters, four-year-old Dessie and infant Grace.

During the short carriage ride to Josephine's home, Dessie had fussed and cried, sad that her beloved "Uncle Eli" could not join them. Emily was sad too. "Uncle Eli" was Emily's code name for apostle Heber Grant, her husband and Dessie and Grace's father. As Heber's third wife, Emily used the name in letters and around the children to protect Heber's identity.

Earlier that day, Heber had left for his home in Salt Lake City after spending two days with Emily and the girls. Emily hoped that visiting Josephine would cheer her up. But almost as soon as she and the girls arrived, Emily burst into tears. Josephine understood her friend's feelings. She herself was a plural wife of apostle John Henry Smith, who had just come to town for a short visit of his own.[14]

Emily never felt like Heber's visits were long enough. The two of them had grown up together in the Salt Lake City Thirteenth Ward, and they had married in the spring of 1884 after a lengthy courtship. As a plural wife, Emily could not make her marriage public, and she had moved often over the next six years, spending time in southern Idaho, England, and a hidden apartment in her mother's house in Salt Lake City.[15]

Now Emily was in Manassa, hoping that her long separation from Heber might someday end. Accustomed to city living, she was still adjusting to life in the small town, and she sometimes felt hundreds of miles away from civilization. Heber had tried to help by providing her with a furnished home, a team of horses, some cows and chickens, a hired hand, and a subscription to the *Salt Lake Herald*. Her mother-in-law, Rachel Grant, had also come to stay with her in the isolated town.[16]

"I have got everything in it now that I want," Emily once told Heber in a letter from Manassa. "Except you."[17]

Almost two weeks after Heber's visit, Emily wrote to him about a meeting in Manassa at which two Church leaders had said that the town's "widows" might never be able to return to Utah. "They said the next move in Congress would be to confiscate the property of the leaders of the Church," she reported, "and then we would be very glad we had come here and located."

But Emily was not convinced that she would ever be happy to live in the town.[18] "I continue to pray for a contented mind but feel discouraged and blue yet," she wrote to Heber a few months later. "Don't forget to pray for me, dear one, for without the aid of my Father in Heaven I cannot stand this much longer and be sane."[19]

On Sunday, August 17, Wilford Woodruff and his counselors visited the small settlement. By then, the United States Supreme Court had issued its ruling on the legality of the Edmunds-Tucker Act. The court was divided on the case, but a slim majority of judges voted to uphold the law, despite the Saints' claims that it violated their religious liberty. The ruling gave government officials full rein to carry out the act's sanctions, opening possibilities for seizing more property from the Church.[20]

During a meeting with the Saints in Manassa, George Q. Cannon cautioned families to be careful. Some of the men in town were living with more than one wife, he said, and such men risked bringing trouble and persecution upon the whole community. The remark angered some men, who came to George the next day to express how hard it was on their families to live separately.[21]

Before Wilford and his counselors left, Emily hosted them and other friends for breakfast. Afterward, she and a few other women accompanied the visitors to the train station. The train was late, giving Emily a chance to visit a little longer with the First Presidency. When the train finally arrived, she clasped hands with each man in turn. "God bless you," they said to each other. "Peace be with you."

Emily longed to leave Manassa as well. "They went spinning off," she wrote Heber, "and we returned to this desolate place."[22]

THE FIRST PRESIDENCY RETURNED to Salt Lake City in late August, just in time for the one-year anniversary of Iosepa, the first settlement of Hawaiian Saints in Utah. The name *Iosepa* was the Hawaiian version of the name Joseph.[23]

When Hawaiians started joining the Church in the 1850s, the kingdom of Hawaii had restricted its people from leaving the islands, prompting Church leaders to establish Laie as a gathering place for Hawaiian Saints. But slowly the laws softened, and some Hawaiians, eager to receive the blessings of the temple, had begun gathering to Utah Territory in the 1880s.

In 1889, the First Presidency had organized a committee, which included three Hawaiian men, to find a suitable place in Utah where Hawaiian Saints could establish homes and farms. After evaluating different areas, the group proposed several locations, including a 1,900-acre ranch about sixty miles southwest of Salt Lake City. The First Presidency reviewed the committee's findings and decided to purchase the ranch for the new settlement.[24]

Throughout the following year, the Saints in Iosepa had worked hard building houses, planting crops, and caring for livestock. The first winter had been harsh, especially compared with Hawaii's tropical climate. But the settlers had persevered, hopeful that Iosepa's rich soil and ready supply of water from the nearby mountains would provide a plentiful summer harvest.[25]

The day of the celebration was warm and bright. As the members of the First Presidency, each joined by one of his wives, approached the settlement, Iosepa appeared like an oasis of green in the middle of the desert landscape. Cornstalks in the surrounding fields were tall, with large ears bursting from their husks, and the hay in the harvested fields lay in great yellow stacks.

The Hawaiian Saints gathered around their visitors, eager to greet their prophet and his counselors,

George Q. Cannon and Joseph F. Smith, who had both served missions to Hawaii as young men. The evening was full of joyful music as the Saints in Iosepa sang and played guitars, mandolins, and violins.

The celebration continued the next day with a parade followed by a lunchtime feast of meat roasted in a pit. When George gave the blessing on the food, he spoke the prayer in Hawaiian—the first time he had prayed in that language in thirty-six years.

Later that day, everyone gathered for a special meeting. Solomona, a man in his nineties whom George had baptized decades earlier, offered a fervent opening prayer. One Saint, Kaelakai Honua, spoke of the mercy of God in gathering the people of the islands of the sea to Zion. Another man, Kauleinamoku, lamented that some people had left Iosepa to return to the Pacific. He urged the Saints to be faithful and not yield to the spirit of dissatisfaction.

All around Iosepa, the people celebrated together, and Wilford, George, and Joseph delighted in their happiness. Though George had not kept up his ability to speak the Hawaiian language well, he marveled that he understood almost every word spoken at the festivities.[26]

A FEW DAYS AFTER the First Presidency returned home from Iosepa, they received news that Henry Lawrence, the new federal official appointed to seize Church property under the Edmunds-Tucker Act, was now threatening to confiscate the temples in Logan, Manti, and St. George.

A former member of the Church, Henry had been a bitter opponent of the Saints for more than two decades. He had belonged to William Godbe and Elias Harrison's New Movement and had testified against the Church at the recent trial barring immigrant Saints from citizenship.

Henry knew the Edmunds-Tucker Act protected buildings used "exclusively for purposes of the worship of God," but he intended to show that temples were used for other purposes and could therefore be seized with other properties.

On September 2, the First Presidency learned that Henry had managed to get a subpoena ordering Wilford to testify in court about Church properties. Seeking to avoid the subpoena, the presidency traveled to California to consult with several influential men who were sympathetic to the Saints' plight. But these men could offer little hope that the United States government or the American people would change their mind about the Church as long as the Saints continued to practice plural marriage.[27]

Wilford and his counselors returned to Utah a few weeks later only to learn that the Utah Commission, a group of federal officials who managed Utah's elections and monitored the Saints' compliance with antipolygamy laws, had just sent its annual report to the federal government. This year, the report falsely claimed that Church leaders were still publicly encouraging and sanctioning plural marriage. It also stated without proof that forty-one plural marriages had been performed in Utah over the last year.

In order to stamp out plural marriage once and for all, the commission recommended that Congress pass even harsher laws against the Church.[28]

The report infuriated Wilford. Although he had issued no public statement about the status of plural marriage in the Church, he had already determined that no plural marriages should be performed in Utah or anywhere else in the United States. Furthermore, he had done much over the past year to discourage new plural marriages, despite the report's claim to the opposite.[29]

On September 22, Wilford met with his counselors in the Gardo House, the official residence of the Church president in Salt Lake City, to discuss what to do about the report. George Q. Cannon proposed issuing a denial of its claims. "Perhaps no better chance has been offered to us," he said, "to officially, as leaders of the Church, make public our views concerning the doctrine and the law that has been enacted."[30]

Later, after the day's meetings, Wilford prayed for guidance. If the Church did not stop performing plural marriages, the government would keep passing laws against the Saints, a vast majority of whom did not even practice the principle. Chaos and confusion would reign in Zion. More men would go to jail, and the government would confiscate the temples. The Saints had performed hundreds of thousands of ordinances for the dead since the dedication of the new temples. If the government seized these buildings, how many of God's children, living and dead, would be barred from the sacred ordinances of the gospel?[31]

The next day, Wilford told George that he believed it was his duty as president of the Church to issue a manifesto, or public statement, to the press. He then had his secretary join him in a private room while George waited outside.

Apostle Franklin Richards, meanwhile, arrived at the Gardo House looking for the prophet. George told him that Wilford was busy and could not be disturbed. A short time later, Wilford emerged from the private room with a statement he had just dictated. His agitation over the Utah Commission's report was gone. Now his face seemed to shine, and he looked pleased and contented.

Wilford had the document read out loud. The statement denied that new plural marriages had taken place during the past year and affirmed the Church's willingness to work with the government. "Inasmuch as the nation has passed a law forbidding plural marriages," it declared, "we feel to obey that law, and leave the event in the hands of God."

"I feel it will do good," George said. He did not think the statement was ready for publication, but the ideas in it were right.[32]

The next day, the First Presidency asked three talented writers—secretary George Reynolds, newspaper editor Charles Penrose, and Presiding Bishopric counselor John Winder—to refine the language of the statement and prepare it for publication. Wilford then presented the revised document to apostles Franklin Richards, Moses Thatcher, and Marriner Merrill, and they recommended additional refinements.

Once revised, the Manifesto, as it came to be called, declared an end to future plural marriages and emphasized Wilford's resolve to obey the laws of the land and persuade the Saints to do the same.

"We are not teaching polygamy, or plural marriage, nor permitting any person to enter into its practice," it read in part. "I hereby declare my intention to submit to those laws, and to use my influence with the members of the Church over which I preside to have them do likewise."[33]

The apostles present approved the document and sent it by telegram to the press.[34]

"This whole matter has been at President Woodruff's own instance," George Q. Cannon noted that day in his journal. "He has stated that the Lord had made it plain to him that this was his duty, and he felt perfectly clear in his mind that it was the right thing."[35]

Wilford also reflected on the Manifesto in his journal. "I have arrived at a point in the history of my life as the president of The Church of Jesus Christ of Latter-day Saints," he wrote, "where I am under the necessity of acting for the temporal salvation of the Church."[36]

The government had taken a determined stand against plural marriage, he knew. So Wilford had prayed and received inspiration from the Spirit, and the Lord had revealed His will for the Saints.

CHAPTER 40

The Right Thing

B. H. Roberts, one of the seven presidents of the First Council of the Seventy, awoke on the morning of September 26, 1890, expecting to find himself nearly home.[1]

The northbound train he had been riding was due to arrive in Salt Lake City by ten o'clock that morning. But instead of making good time throughout the night, it had come to a stop somewhere amid the desert scrub of central Utah. A southbound train had derailed a few miles away, and the track was torn up all around it. B. H. and his traveling companions, four members of the Quorum of the Twelve, were stranded.

With little to do but wait, B. H. and apostle John W. Taylor decided to take a walk to the scene of the accident. Upon their arrival, they could see that only the freight cars on the derailed train had been upended. The passenger cars were still intact, so B. H. and John W. began visiting with the stranded travelers.

Inside a passenger car, John W. motioned to B. H. and held out a newspaper. B. H. took the paper and read the headlines with astonishment. President Wilford Woodruff had issued an official statement declaring that he intended to submit to the laws of the land and permit no new plural marriages.[2]

For a moment, B. H. felt a flash of light course through his body. The words "That is all right" entered his mind and spoke directly to his soul. A sense of peace and understanding lingered briefly. But then, as he reflected on the matter, his analytical mind began to spin, and questions invaded his thoughts.[3]

He thought of the time he had spent in prison for plural marriage, and the sacrifices his wives had made because of it. What about everything the Saints had suffered for honoring and defending the practice? What of the many sermons preached over the decades supporting it? B. H. believed that God would sustain the Saints through whatever hardships came their way because of the practice. Were they now taking the coward's way out?[4]

B. H. and John W. were joined by the other apostles traveling with them. Abraham Cannon, son of George Q. Cannon, did not seem surprised by the news. Francis Lyman was likewise unruffled, explaining that President Woodruff had already been discouraging new plural marriages in the United States. In his opinion, the Manifesto simply made the Church's position on the topic public. But B. H. could see that apostle John Henry Smith was agitated, just as he and John W. Taylor were.

After speaking with the southbound passengers, B. H. and the apostles walked a short distance north of the accident and caught a new train heading to Salt Lake City. As the train rumbled down the track, talk of the Manifesto dominated the conversation. B. H. felt his distress rising and finally removed himself from the apostles' company entirely.

As B. H. sat alone in his seat, his thoughts churned. For every reason his companions might give in support of the Manifesto, he felt he could come up with ten more for why the Saints should have held to the principle of plural marriage—even if it brought about the very annihilation of the Church.[5]

A FEW DAYS LATER, on September 30, Heber Grant discussed the Manifesto with other members of the Quorum of the Twelve at a meeting in the Gardo House. Issuing the statement was the right thing for the Church to do, Heber believed, though he was unsure if it would put an end to the Saints' trials.[6]

The declaration plainly stated that the Church was no longer "teaching polygamy or plural marriage, nor permitting any person to enter into its practice," but it left some matters unclear to both the Saints and the government.[7]

In conversation, Heber heard several apostles say that the Manifesto was a temporary measure, suspending plural marriage until the Saints could practice it legally. Lorenzo Snow, the president of the quorum, believed it was a necessary step to earn the goodwill of others. "The Manifesto will turn the hearts of many honest-hearted people to a feeling of friendship and respect for us," he said. "I can see the good of the Manifesto clearly and am thankful for it."[8]

"I am convinced that God was with President Woodruff when he was preparing the Manifesto for publication," Franklin Richards added. "When the Manifesto was read, I felt that it was the right thing and that it had been given at the right time."[9]

The Manifesto still unsettled John W. Taylor, who had been called to the Quorum of the Twelve shortly after Heber. After the death of his father, President John Taylor, John W. had found a purported revelation about marriage among the prophet's papers. The revelation, dated September 27, 1886, seemed to suggest to John W. that the commandment to practice plural marriage would never be revoked.[10]

Although the revelation had never been presented to the Quorum of the Twelve or accepted as scripture by the Saints, John W. believed that it was the word of God to his father. Yet he knew revelation was continuing and ongoing, addressing new situations and problems as they arose, and John W. had faith that God had spoken to Wilford as well. "I know that the Lord has given this manifesto to President Woodruff," he said, "and He can take it away when the time comes, or He can give it again."[11]

More apostles shared their feelings about the Manifesto the following day. Like John W. Taylor, John Henry Smith was still struggling to accept it. "I am willing to sustain the president in issuing the Manifesto, although I am a little at sea as to the wisdom of its having been issued," he said. "My fears are that the Manifesto will do us, as a people, more harm than good."[12]

Anthon Lund, the only monogamist in the quorum, disagreed. "I feel that the Manifesto will result in good," he said. "I give my approval to what has been done."[13]

Heber also told the quorum that he was happy with the declaration. "There is not the least reason why such a document should not be issued," he said. "President Woodruff has simply told the world what we have been doing."[14]

The next day, the apostles met with the First Presidency, and each man sustained the Manifesto as the will of God. Afterward, some apostles expressed concern that critics of the Church would be dissatisfied with the document and continue to prosecute men who did not separate from or divorce their plural wives.

"There is no telling what we might have to do in the future," Wilford said, "but at the present time, I feel that we must be true to our wives."

For Heber, the prospect of being forced to abandon his plural wives, Augusta and Emily, was unthinkable. "I confess that it would be a great trial to me," he wrote that day in his journal. "I feel that I could not endorse any such a thing."[15]

ON OCTOBER 6, GEORGE Q. CANNON arrived at the tabernacle for the third day of the Church's fall general conference. Soon after the meeting began, he stood and introduced Orson Whitney, bishop of the Salt Lake City Eighteenth Ward, who had been asked to read the Manifesto to the thousands of Saints in attendance.[16]

While George listened to the statement, he was unsure what he would say if Wilford called on him to speak. Earlier, Wilford had suggested that George might speak, but George had no desire to be the first to address the Saints on the Manifesto. In all his years of public speaking, he had never been asked to do something so difficult.[17]

The day before, George had given a sermon about the First Presidency and revelation, preparing the Saints for this meeting. "The presidency of the Church have to walk just as you walk," George had said. "They have to take steps just as you take steps. They have to depend upon the revelations of God as they come to them. They cannot see the end from the beginning, as the Lord does."

"All that we can do," he had continued, "is to seek the mind and will of God, and when that comes to us, though it may come in contact with every feeling that we have previously entertained, we have no option but to take the step that God points out and to trust to Him."[18]

When Orson finished reading the Manifesto, Lorenzo Snow presented it to the Saints for their sustaining vote. Hands went up throughout the auditorium —some decisively, some more reluctantly. Other hands did not go up at all. There did not appear to be any direct opposition, though many Saints' eyes were wet with tears.[19]

Wilford then turned to George and invited him to speak. George approached the pulpit with a prayer in his heart, but his mind was blank. As he started to speak, however, his fear left him, and words and ideas came freely. He opened the scriptures to Doctrine and Covenants 124:49, the passage Wilford had alluded to when George first heard him explain the Church's new position on plural marriage.[20]

"When I give a commandment to any of the sons of men to do a work unto my name," the Lord had declared, "and those sons of men go with all their might and with all they have to perform that work, and cease not their diligence, and their enemies come upon them and hinder them from performing that work, behold, it behooveth me to require that work no more at the hands of those sons of men, but to accept of their offerings."[21]

After reading the passage aloud, George told the congregation that the Saints had done all in their power to obey God's commandment. Now the Lord had given them new direction through His prophet. "When God makes known His mind and will," he said, "I hope that I and all Latter-day Saints will bow in submission to it."

Knowing some Saints doubted the divine origins of the Manifesto and questioned why the prophet had not issued it sooner to avoid the suffering and persecution of recent years, he counseled them to seek a testimony of the Manifesto for themselves.

"Go to your secret chambers," he urged them. "Ask God and plead with Him, in the name of Jesus, to give you a testimony as He has given it to us, and I promise you that you will not come away empty nor dissatisfied."[22]

After George finished speaking, Wilford approached the pulpit. "The Lord is preparing a people to receive His kingdom and His Church, and to build up His work," he said. "That, brethren and sisters, is our labor."

"The Lord will never permit me or any other man who stands as President of this Church to lead you astray," he continued, reassuring any Saints who questioned the divine origin of the Manifesto. "It is not in the programme. It is not in the mind of God. If I were to attempt that, the Lord would remove me out of my place."

Wilford then blessed the Saints and returned to his seat on the stand.[23]

MANY PEOPLE IN THE congregation left the tabernacle that day grateful for the Manifesto and hopeful it would reduce the persecution of the Church. They had felt spiritual strength and peace at the meeting. Other Saints, however, felt unsettled, conflicted, or even betrayed.

Despite its significant challenges, some of which were deeply painful, plural marriage had blessed the lives of many Saints. For two generations, the practice had made marriage available to virtually all who desired it. It allowed many Saints to raise large families of faithful children who became devoted parents, Church members, leaders, and missionaries. It also brought about many marriages between cultures, uniting the Church's diverse immigrant population.

Furthermore, it had bound the Saints together in a common struggle against persecution and helped them forge an identity as a peculiar, covenant people of God.[24] More than two thousand Saints had been charged for polygamy, unlawful cohabitation, or other conduct associated with plural marriage. Around 930 of them had gone to prison for their convictions. Belle Harris, a grandniece of Martin Harris who refused to testify against her husband, had been sent to prison while nursing her infant son. For many Saints, such outrages were sacrifices they had been willing to make as followers of Christ.

B. H. Roberts thought that listening to the Manifesto read from the pulpit was one of the most difficult moments of his life. Though he had no desire to oppose the declaration openly, his earlier assurance that it was right had not returned, and he could not raise his hand to support the statement.[25]

Relief Society general president Zina Young sustained the Manifesto, but it tried her heart. "We looked to God and submitted," she wrote that night in her journal.[26]

Joseph Dean, who had returned from his mission to Samoa a month earlier, was also in the tabernacle that day. He believed the Manifesto was a painful but necessary action. "Many of the Saints seemed stunned and confused and hardly knew how to vote," he wrote in his journal. "A great many of the sisters wept silently and seemed to feel worse than the brethren."[27]

The next morning dawned cold and wet. As rain pattered on rooftops, some Saints wondered how the Manifesto might affect their daily lives. The statement did not offer specific direction on how Saints already involved in plural marriages should proceed. Some plural wives worried they might be abandoned. Others were optimistic, hoping the Manifesto might pacify the government and bring an end to the fear and uncertainty of life on the underground. Many simply decided to remain in hiding until Church leaders explained in more detail how best to adapt the Manifesto to individual circumstances.[28]

When the news reached Cardston, Canada, it stunned Zina Presendia Card and her neighbors. But soon they realized that the Manifesto was precisely what the Church needed. "We feel our true position is known and appreciated now, as it could not be before the issuing of the Manifesto," she wrote in a letter to the *Woman's Exponent*. "The Saints here as a whole all feel our leaders are carrying on Christ's work to victory and are one with the Saints in the land of Zion."[29]

Later, in the *Young Woman's Journal,* Susa Gates cautioned young women not to speak lightly about the Manifesto. Plural marriage had opened covenant marriage and family opportunities for women who otherwise would not have enjoyed them, she reminded them. Now these opportunities would be unavailable.

"You, as young women of Zion, have as much interest in this matter as do your mothers and fathers. See to it that not one word of foolish, silly rejoicing passes your lips for what has been done," she counseled. "If you speak of it at all, let it be in the most solemn and sacred spirit."[30]

In Manassa, when Emily Grant first learned of the Manifesto, she *was* solemn. But her somber feelings gave way to joy when she felt a witness that the declaration was right. "I seemed to see the first ray of light I have ever seen for us through our difficulties," she wrote to her husband.[31]

AROUND THIS TIME, LORENA and Bent Larsen decided to return to Utah after months of struggling to make a living in Colorado. The farmland in Sanford had not been producing well, and Bent found it almost impossible to obtain other work. He now planned to live with his first wife, Julia, and their extended family in Monroe, Utah, while Lorena and her children would live with her brother's family in a town about a hundred miles away.[32]

After the Larsens spent days traveling alone through rocky canyons, the starkly beautiful desert town of Moab, Utah, offered a welcome place to rest.

During a previous stop, Bent and Lorena had learned that Church leaders had issued a statement about plural marriage, but they had not heard anything more about it. In Moab, however, they met people who had gone to conference in Salt Lake City. While Lorena remained at the family's tent, Bent went to learn what he could about the Manifesto.

When Bent returned, he told Lorena that the First Presidency and the Quorum of the Twelve had announced that the Church had stopped performing plural marriages and intended to submit to the laws of the nation.

Lorena could not believe what she was hearing. She had embraced plural marriage because she believed that it was God's will for her and the Saints. The sacrifices she had made to practice the principle had brought her heartache and trial. But they had also challenged her to live on a higher plane, overcome her weaknesses, and love her neighbor. Why would God now ask the Saints to turn away from the practice?

Lorena looked to Bent for comfort, but instead of offering her words of reassurance, he turned and left the tent. "Oh, yes," she thought. "It is easy for you. You can go home to your other family and be happy with her, while I must be like Hagar, sent away."[33]

Darkness flooded Lorena's mind. "If the Lord and the Church authorities have gone back on that principle," she thought, "there is nothing to any part of the gospel."[34] She had believed that plural marriage was a doctrine as fixed and immovable as God Himself. If that was not the case, why should she have faith in anything else?

Lorena then thought of her family. What did the Manifesto mean for her and her children? And what did it mean for the other women and children in the same situation? Could they still depend on their husbands and fathers for love and support? Or would they be cast adrift simply for having tried to serve the Lord and keep His commandments?

Lorena collapsed into her bedding. The darkness around her became impenetrable, and she wished the earth would open up and swallow her and her children. Then, suddenly, she felt a powerful presence in the tent. "This is no more unreasonable than the requirement the Lord made of Abraham when He commanded him to offer up his son Isaac," a voice told Lorena. "When the Lord sees that you are willing to obey in all things, the trial shall be removed."

A bright light enveloped Lorena's soul, and she felt peace and happiness. She understood that all would be well.

A short time later, Bent returned to the tent. Lorena told him about the presence that had removed her anguish. "I knew that I could not say a word to comfort you," Bent confessed, "so I went to a patch of willows and asked the Lord to send a comforter."[35]

CHAPTER 41

So Long Submerged

On the afternoon of February 25, 1891, Jane Richards, the first counselor in the Relief Society general presidency, was preparing to speak in Washington, DC, at the first conference of the National Council of Women. For the last two and a half days of the conference, she had enjoyed listening to women from across the United States speak about their efforts in education, charity work, reform, and culture. Now it was time for her address, and the auditorium was full of hundreds of people who had come to hear what the Latter-day Saints had to say.[1]

For most of its nearly fifty-year history, the Relief Society had focused on attending to the needs of the Saints. Relief Society general president Zina Young felt strongly, however, that the women's organizations in

616

the Church should work with other groups to promote causes like female suffrage. Participating in the National Council of Women was an opportunity for Relief Society and Young Ladies' Mutual Improvement Association leaders to meet and work with others who shared similar values and goals.[2]

Jane was selected to go to the conference because Emmeline Wells wanted to send women who were well educated and well informed on women's issues in Utah. She also wanted to send someone courageous, a quality she believed Jane possessed in abundance.

Joining Jane in Washington were Emmeline, Sarah Kimball, and other women's leaders in the Church. Before they left, these women were blessed and set apart by an apostle or a member of the First Presidency to represent their organizations.

In contrast with previous visits of prominent Latter-day Saint women to Washington, they were not going to lobby for the Saints. They were going as leaders of women's organizations who wanted to speak about their work, not only in Utah but also in all the other places where the Relief Society and Y.L.M.I.A. had been established.[3]

Before Jane and the other delegates from Utah could join the council, a committee had deliberated whether to admit them. Most of the women on the committee recognized the efforts of the Relief Society to promote women's suffrage, organize women on a national and international scale, and establish good relationships with prominent leaders of the national women's movement.[4] But one woman had objected to their entry, believing they had come to preach polygamy.

Other committee members had come to the Saints' defense, citing the Manifesto as proof that the Utah delegation could be trusted. In the end, the committee had voted unanimously to welcome the Relief Society and Y.L.M.I.A. into their league.[5]

When it was Jane's turn to speak, she kept her remarks brief. She told the assembly that the Relief Society believed in extending love, goodwill, peace, and joy to everyone. She also expressed gratitude for women everywhere who believed similarly.

"We may differ in opinion in some things," she said, "but our great aim is to do good to all."[6]

While in Washington, Jane spoke to many people about the Relief Society and the Saints. She admired the women she met and the work they were doing, and she wished she had five hundred copies of the Manifesto to share with people who had questions about plural marriage. Before returning home, she invited many of her new friends to visit Utah.

If they wanted to get to know the Latter-day Saints, she said, the best thing to do was spend time among them.[7]

THAT WINTER, EMILY GRANT found it more and more difficult to endure Colorado's frigid, howling winds alone.[8] Since the Church issued the Manifesto, its relationship with the United States government had begun to improve. Officials in Washington, including the president, were no longer interested in taking away the Saints' voting rights or confiscating the temples. And the U.S. Supreme Court ruled that children of polygamous marriages could once again inherit property.

Yet federal antipolygamy laws remained in force. Marshals were still arresting people for polygamy and unlawful cohabitation, although in smaller numbers.[9] If Emily left the relative safety of Manassa, her plural marriage to Heber Grant could become public, putting their family at risk.[10]

Emily's father, Daniel Wells, passed away in March 1891. She and her daughters, Dessie and Grace, returned to Salt Lake City for the funeral, and Heber agreed that she should move back to the city. He believed as long as he and Emily kept their marriage private, residing in separate houses and not being seen together in public, the family could live closer together.[11]

Family and friends wanted to throw a party to celebrate Emily's return to Salt Lake City, but she preferred to keep out of sight. "I only want a visit with my folks and friends without making myself conspicuous anywhere," she told Heber.[12] She moved in with her mother, a few blocks from Heber, and continued to communicate with him mostly through letters. Such a life was not exactly what Emily wanted, but it was far better than living hundreds of miles away.[13]

That spring, Emily and Heber's daughter Dessie turned five. Besides calling herself "Mary Harris" and Heber "Uncle Eli," Emily had called Dessie "Pattie Harris" to keep her and the family safe from the marshals. Now that their situation had changed for the better, Emily and Heber had largely dropped the pretense and begun using their real names in letters to each other.

On Dessie's birthday, Emily put her in a new dress, curled her hair, and tied it up with a new blue ribbon. "Now you are getting to be such a big girl," Emily said. "I am going to tell you a great secret." She revealed Dessie's real name and told her that Uncle Eli was actually her father.[14]

Soon after, Dessie also learned that two of her new friends, Rachel and Lutie, were her sisters, the daughters of their father and his wife Lucy. One day, ten-year-old Lutie arrived at Emily's home with her yellow pony, Flaxy, hitched up to a little cart. She wanted to take her sisters for a ride. Emily was unsure it was safe to let the girls go, but she relented. Dessie and Grace climbed into the tiny cart, and soon the sisters bounded away.[15]

Emily was grateful to finally be back at home in Salt Lake City. She disliked hiding her relationship with Heber, and she wished that her family had the freedom to go about the city as they pleased. But she could see the hand of God in her reunion with her husband, and she knew that they were happy in each other's love.

"The fact that I have stood it at all is remarkable to me," she wrote, "and I pray for strength to bear my future prospects."[16]

THAT SPRING, NINETEEN-YEAR-OLD JOHN Widtsoe celebrated his graduation from Brigham Young College in Logan. At the commencement ceremony, he received special recognition for his excellence in rhetoric, German, chemistry, algebra, and geometry.[17]

During his time at the college, John was thrilled whenever he uncovered some new piece of knowledge. The college was still new, and it did not have many books in its library or much equipment in its laboratory. Nor did its faculty have advanced academic degrees, though the teachers were excellent instructors who knew how to simplify a subject and teach it to their students.

The college principal, Joseph Tanner, was a former pupil of Karl Maeser, the famed principal of Brigham Young Academy in Provo who now served as superintendent of more than three dozen Church schools. A former missionary to Europe and the Middle East, Joseph also taught religion classes, instructing John and his fellow students in the plan of salvation and the Restoration of the gospel. Theology became one of John's favorite subjects. It shaped his character and outlook on life and made him more sensitive to the differences between right and wrong.[18]

Around the time of graduation, Joseph invited John to join him and a group of young Latter-day Saint scholars enrolling that summer at Harvard University, the oldest and most respected university in the United States. Joseph wanted the scholars to gain a first-class education, which they could then use to improve the quality of instruction in Utah's schools.[19]

Harvard was just the kind of place John's mother, Anna, had always wanted him to attend, and she supported his decision to go there, confident he would excel in his studies. To pay tuition, John took out a loan from a local bank. Five family friends—including Anthon Skanchy, the missionary who baptized Anna in Norway—also provided him with financial aid.

John left for Harvard less than a month after his graduation. A short time later, Anna negotiated a loan on her house, put it up for rent, and moved to Salt Lake City, where she and her younger son, Osborne, could find more work to support the family and pay for John's schooling.

Anna wrote frequently to John. "You will probably have many little difficulties and will probably face small disappointments at first," she told him in one letter, "but they can all be of great use to you in the future."

"God is with you, and He will bless you double what you dare imagine or pray for," she promised. "Just bow before the Lord in prayer at your appointed time, and whenever you feel like it, and with a grateful and humble heart."[20]

IN SALT LAKE CITY, Joseph F. Smith continued to live on the underground, even though the threat of arrest and prosecution had diminished. Unlike Heber Grant's plural marriages, Joseph's were publicly known, and his position in the First Presidency had long made him a target for federal marshals.

On weekdays, Joseph visited his wives and children after dark and returned to his office in the Gardo House to sleep. On weekends he risked more extended, overnight stays with his family, rotating every weekend between the homes of his five wives.[21] To live like a fugitive was discouraging. "Until the Lord relieves me in some way not now seen," he wrote his aunt Mercy Thompson, "I am doomed to remain in hiding for some time to come."[22]

In June 1891, Joseph wrote a letter to the president of the United States, Benjamin Harrison, asking for amnesty, or the removal of all criminal charges against him. With goodwill improving between the Church and the United States government, Joseph believed he could receive a pardon.[23]

By seeking amnesty, Joseph was not promising to forsake his wives, however. The Manifesto had given no direction for how Saints in existing plural marriages should act, but Wilford Woodruff had privately counseled stake presidencies and general authorities on how to interpret its message. "This manifesto only refers to future marriages and does not affect past conditions," he said. "I did not, could not, and would not promise that you would desert your wives and children. This you cannot do in honor."[24]

A few people still chose to end their plural marriages, but most people sought to comply with the Manifesto in less drastic ways. Some men continued as best they could to support their plural families, financially and emotionally, without living with them. Others continued to live with their families as if nothing had changed, even though doing so could subject them to prosecution and imprisonment.

For his part, Joseph chose to continue caring for his family as always, believing that he was complying with the Manifesto while still obeying the law forbidding cohabitation.[25]

In early September, Joseph learned of a newspaper report announcing that President Harrison had granted him amnesty. He did not want to celebrate or go out in public, however, until he had the documents in hand. "I have been so long submerged under the flood of surging events," he wrote in a letter to a friend, "if I get freedom in any form, I shall be like one raised from the dead, or born again, with new experiences to get and everything to learn anew."[26]

The amnesty letter arrived a short time later. Full of gratitude, Joseph hoped his pardon would lead to a general amnesty for all Saints who had entered plural marriage before the Manifesto. But he also knew that such a pardon might not stop the government from bringing new charges against men who continued to live with wives they had married long ago. To be safe, he chose to stay nights at the First Presidency's office while still teaching his children and supporting his large family. He and his five wives also continued to have more children.[27]

The Sunday after receiving amnesty, Joseph attended the Salt Lake City Sixteenth Ward Sunday School. He spoke to the children in class and talked afterward with several old friends and acquaintances. Later that day, he attended an afternoon meeting in the tabernacle, where he was called upon to speak.

As Joseph looked out at the Saints, his emotions nearly overwhelmed him. "It has been something over seven years since I last had the privilege of standing before a congregation of the people in this tabernacle," he said. So much had changed in his absence that he felt like a child who had been away from home for a long time.

He bore witness of the Restoration, testifying that it was the work of the Lord. "I thank God the Eternal Father that I have had this testimony put into my heart and soul," he declared, "for it gives me light, hope, joy, and consolation that no man can give or take away."

He also prayed that God would help the Saints do what was right and honorable before the Lord and before the law. "We have to live in the midst of the world as we are," he said. "We have to make the best of the circumstances in which we are placed. That is what the Lord requires at the hands of the Latter-day Saints."[28]

SHORTLY AFTER JOSEPH F. SMITH received amnesty, Wilford Woodruff declared that it was the mind and will of God that the Saints finish the temple. Workers had placed a roof on the building two years earlier, allowing carpenters and other craftsmen to work year-round. But much labor still remained on the building's exterior, including the installation of a large statue of an angel on the temple's tallest central spire. The statue would be sculpted by renowned artist Cyrus Dallin, who had grown up in Utah and received extensive artistic training in the eastern United States and Paris.

In early October, dozens of Church officers agreed to help raise $100,000 for construction, though it would likely cost more to complete the building.[29] Around this time, the First Presidency and several apostles also appealed for the return of around $400,000 worth of Church property that the government had confiscated under the Edmunds-Tucker Act.[30]

Reclaiming the Church's seized property could relieve the Saints' financial burden significantly, but it would also require some of the First Presidency and the Twelve to attend a hearing and answer questions from government lawyers about the Church's commitment to obeying antipolygamy laws.[31]

In the weeks leading up to the hearing, the Church's lawyers presented the First Presidency and members of the Twelve with questions government lawyers might ask them. Several apostles worried about how to answer questions about the future of plural marriage in the Church. Was the practice over for good, or was the Manifesto a temporary measure? And how should they answer questions about whether husbands should continue to live with and support their plural wives?

Depending on how they responded, Church leaders ran the risk of losing the good faith of the government and confusing—or even offending—the Saints.[32]

On the day of the hearing, October 19, 1891, Charles Varian, a lawyer for the United States government, questioned Wilford for several hours.[33] His questions were designed to get Wilford to clarify the Church's stance on plural marriage and the purpose of the Manifesto. Wilford, in turn, sought to answer the lawyers honestly without speaking definitively on the status of existing unions.

After the questioning began, Charles asked Wilford what the Manifesto meant for people already in plural marriages. Were they expected to cease associating with each other as husband and wife?

Wilford did not answer the question directly. "I intended the proclamation to cover the whole ground," he said, "to obey the laws of the land entirely." He knew that Saints in plural marriages had made sacred covenants with God, and he could never ask them to violate their marital vows. But each person was individually responsible for obeying the laws of the land according to his or her conscience.[34]

"Was the sole reason of this declaration because of these laws?" Charles asked, trying to gauge Church leaders' sincerity in issuing the Manifesto.

"When I was appointed president of the Church I looked this question over," Wilford replied, "and for a good while became satisfied in my own mind that plural marriage must stop in this Church."

Wilford then described how the antipolygamy laws punished not only the smaller percentage of Saints who practiced plural marriage but also the tens of thousands of Saints who did not. "It was upon that ground that I issued the Manifesto—I will say by inspiration," he explained.[35]

"Why did you not declare this Manifesto to your church as a revelation instead of by way of your personal advice and counsel?" Charles asked.

"My view is that inspiration is revelation," Wilford replied. "It is from the same source. A man is not always required to say, I think, 'Thus saith the Lord.'"

Charles then asked Wilford if the Manifesto was the direct result of the hardships brought upon the Saints by the law.

"The Lord requires, and has required many times, His people to perform a work which they could not carry out where under certain circumstances they were hindered from doing it," Wilford declared. "It is upon that ground—if I can be understood—that I view the position we are in today."[36]

THE DAY AFTER THE hearing, the *Deseret News* and other local newspapers published transcripts of Wilford's testimony to the court.[37] Some people, not grasping the prophet's guarded efforts to clarify the meaning of the Manifesto, mistakenly interpreted his words to mean that he expected husbands to abandon their plural wives.[38]

"This announcement by him as president of the Church has caused an uneasy feeling among the people," recorded one man in St. George, "and some think he has gone back on the revelation on plural marriage and its covenants and obligations." A few men in the town even used the testimony as an excuse to abandon their plural families.[39]

In private meetings, Wilford acknowledged the vagueness of his responses, but he insisted that he could not have answered the lawyer's questions in any other way. He also reiterated to the Twelve that any man who deserted or neglected his wives or children because of the Manifesto was not worthy to be a member of the Church.[40]

Wilford did not condemn men like Joseph F. Smith and George Q. Cannon who continued to have children with their plural wives. But he also believed that men could obey the law and keep their covenants by living separately from their plural families while still providing for their well-being. Within his own family, Wilford lived with his wife Emma publicly, but he continued to support and care for his other wives, Sarah and Delight, and their children.[41]

When Wilford learned that some people were wondering if he was leading the Church astray, he decided to speak further on the matter. At a stake conference in

Logan, he acknowledged that there were many Saints who were struggling to accept the change. He asked a question: Was it wiser to continue performing plural marriages, regardless of the consequences? Or to live according to the nation's laws, so that the Saints could enjoy the blessings of the temple and stay out of prison?

"If we did not stop this practice," he said, "all ordinances would be stopped throughout the land of Zion. Confusion would reign throughout Israel, and many men would be made prisoners. This trouble would have come upon the whole Church, and we should have been compelled to stop the practice."

"But I want to say this," Wilford added. "I should have let all the temples go out of our hands; I should have gone to prison myself, and let every other man go there, had not the God of heaven commanded me to do what I did do; and when the hour came that I was commanded to do that, it was all clear to me. I went before the Lord, and I wrote what the Lord told me to write."[42]

CHAPTER 42

Inspiration at
the Divine Fountain

In early January 1892, Zina Young and Emmeline Wells met in Salt Lake City with other members of the Relief Society general board to plan a "jubilee" commemoration of the Relief Society's fiftieth anniversary. The board wanted Latter-day Saint women throughout the world to join in the celebration, so they sent a letter to every Relief Society in the Church, encouraging them to hold a jubilee of their own.[1]

After extending "a heartfelt greeting" to all sisters, the letter asked the presidency of each Relief Society to invite their members and priesthood leaders to the local jubilee and to appoint an organizing committee to plan the event. Each celebration was to begin at ten o'clock in the morning on March 17, the day the Relief Society was first organized in Nauvoo, and unite two hours later in a "universal prayer of praise and thanksgiving to God."[2]

Zina relied heavily on Emmeline to help organize the jubilee in Salt Lake City to everyone's satisfaction. And by the beginning of March, Emmeline was steeped in planning. "I am trying to do what is possible toward the preparations for the jubilee," she wrote in her diary. "I am more busy than ever."[3]

The Relief Society board planned to hold the Salt Lake City jubilee in the tabernacle. For decorations, they wanted to hang large portraits of Joseph Smith, Emma Smith, Eliza R. Snow, and Zina Young behind the pulpit.[4]

Since Emma Smith, the first president of the Relief Society, had stayed in Illinois and joined the Reorganized Church of Jesus Christ of Latter Day Saints, some people believed hanging her portrait in the tabernacle was inappropriate. When debate grew intense, Zina asked President Wilford Woodruff his view on displaying the portrait. "Anyone who opposes it," he said, "must be very narrow-minded indeed."[5]

On the day of the jubilee, all four portraits hung on the tabernacle organ pipes. Beside them was a key-shaped floral arrangement symbolizing the key Joseph Smith had turned to women in 1842.[6] Zina and Emmeline sat on the stand with Bathsheba Smith, Sarah Kimball, Mary Isabella Horne, and other women who had advanced the Relief Society's mission over the last fifty years. Thousands of Relief Society members were crowded into the tabernacle. Many men were also present, including Joseph F. Smith and two members of the Twelve.[7]

Zina opened the jubilee, mindful that women across the Church were celebrating the occasion. "O that my words could be heard by all people," she said, "not only by you my brethren and sisters in this tabernacle and throughout Utah, but that they might be heard and understood by all the people of this continent, and not only this continent but the continents of Europe, Asia, Africa, and the islands of the sea."

"As sisters of this organization, we have been set apart for the purpose of comforting and consoling the sick and afflicted, the poor and distressed," she added. "If we continue to do these things in the spirit thereof, the Lord, at the time when He comes to make up His jewels, will approve of us."

"What does this woman's jubilee signify?" Emmeline asked the congregation at the close of the meeting. "Not only that fifty years ago this organization was founded by a prophet of God, but that woman is becoming emancipated from error and superstition and darkness; that light has come into the world, and the gospel has made her free; that the key of knowledge has been turned, and she has drunk inspiration at the divine fountain."[8]

AROUND THIS TIME, CHARLES Eliot, the president of Harvard University, visited Salt Lake City on a tour of the western United States. Charles was impressed with the small group of Latter-day Saints who had come to Harvard the year before, and he had accepted an invitation to speak in the tabernacle.

Seven thousand people attended the short speech. Charles championed religious liberty and praised the Saints' hard work and industry, comparing them favorably to the early English settlers who founded Harvard.[9] Later, after the *Salt Lake Tribune* and other newspapers criticized his favorable view of the Saints, Charles went on to defend them.

"I think they should now be treated, as regards their property rights and their freedom of thought and worship, precisely like Roman Catholics, Jews, Methodists, or any other religious denomination," he declared.[10]

Sitting in the audience were Anna Widtsoe, her sister Petroline, and Anna's fourteen-year-old son, Osborne. Nearly a year had passed since John, Anna's older son, had gone to Harvard, and Anna was impressed with the distinguished speaker who thought so highly of the Latter-day Saint students there.[11]

The Widtsoes were now living with Petroline in the Salt Lake City Thirteenth Ward, which had enough Scandinavian Saints to make testimony meetings a multilingual occasion. Osborne worked at the Zion's Cooperative Mercantile Institution store on Main Street while Anna and Petroline worked as dressmakers. Osborne and his mother also attended weekly lectures at the local stake academy.[12]

During the first weekend in April, snow fell in Salt Lake City as though it were the middle of winter. The morning of Wednesday, April 6, was bright and clear, however, as Anna and Osborne joined over forty thousand people on and around Temple Square to see the capstone of the Salt Lake temple fitted into place at the top of the east central spire. The dome-shaped stone was designed to support Cyrus Dallin's twelve-foot sculpture of an angel, which would be fastened to it later that day. Once the capstone and angel were in place, the exterior of the temple would be complete, leaving only the interior to finish before the dedication.[13]

The streets surrounding the temple were jammed with buggies. Some spectators stood on wagons, climbed telegraph poles, or scaled rooftops for a better view.[14] As the Widtsoes stood amid the teeming crowd, they could see President Wilford Woodruff and other Church leaders on a platform at the base of the temple.

After a band played and the Tabernacle Choir sang, Joseph F. Smith offered the opening prayer. Church architect Joseph Don Carlos Young, the son of Brigham Young and Emily Partridge, then shouted down from scaffolding at the top of the temple, "The capstone is now ready to be laid!"[15]

President Woodruff moved to the edge of the platform, looked out at the Saints, and raised his arms high. "All ye nations of the earth!" he said. "We will now lay the topstone of the temple of our God!" He pushed a button, and a current of electricity released a catch that dropped the capstone into place.[16]

Afterward, the Saints gave the Hosanna Shout and sang "The Spirit of God like a Fire Is Burning." Apostle Francis Lyman then stood before the crowd. "I propose," he said, "that this assemblage pledge themselves, collectively and individually, to furnish, as fast as it may be needed, all the money that may be required to complete the temple at the earliest time possible, so that the dedication may take place on April 6th, 1893."

The proposed date would be the fortieth anniversary of the day Brigham Young laid the temple cornerstones. George Q. Cannon called for a sustaining vote on the proposal, and the Saints raised their right hands and shouted, "Aye!"[17]

Francis pledged a large sum of his own money to complete the temple. Anna pledged five dollars for herself and ten dollars for Osborne. Knowing that John would want to pledge money as well, she contributed ten more dollars in his name.[18]

THAT SPRING, JOSEPH F. SMITH visited the home of sixty-three-year-old James Brown. As a much younger man, James had marched with the Mormon Battalion and served a mission to Tahiti and its surrounding islands with Addison and Louisa Pratt, Benjamin Grouard, and others. While laboring on the Anaa atoll in 1851, however, James had been arrested on false charges of sedition and taken to Tahiti, where he was imprisoned and eventually banished from the islands.[19] The government had forced the other missionaries to leave as well, and the mission had been closed ever since.

Now, some forty years later, Church leaders had begun expanding missionary work in the South Pacific. In July 1891, the Samoan mission had sent two young elders, Brigham Smoot and Alva Butler, to begin preaching in Tonga. Six months later, two other missionaries from the Samoan mission, Joseph Damron and William Seegmiller, renewed missionary work in French Polynesia, ministering to the long-isolated Saints in and around Tahiti.[20]

But Joseph Damron was unwell, and he and William had found that nearly all the Latter-day Saints in the area had joined the Reorganized Church of Jesus Christ of Latter Day Saints, which had sent missionaries to the South Pacific several years earlier. Both men believed the mission needed someone with more experience to lead the work in the area.[21]

At James's house in Salt Lake City, Joseph F. took out a letter he had received from the missionaries in Tahiti. "How would you like to take another mission to the Society Islands?" he asked James.

"I do not wish any man to call me to any mission," James told him.[22] He was now an old man with three wives and many children and grandchildren. His health was poor, and he had lost his leg in a firearm accident years earlier. Going to the South Pacific would be a big undertaking for someone in his condition.

Joseph F. handed the letter to James and asked him to read it. He then left with a promise that he would return the next day to find out what James thought of it.[23]

James read the letter. The young missionaries were clearly struggling. As the only one of the early missionaries still living, James had a familiarity with the people and their language that would allow him to do much good. If the First Presidency asked him to go to the Pacific, he decided, he would go. He had faith that God would not ask him to do anything without making him equal to the task.[24]

When Joseph F. Smith returned the following day, James accepted the mission call. A few weeks later, he said goodbye to his family and left the city with his son Elando, who was called to serve with him.

James, Elando, and another missionary arrived in Tahiti the following month. Elders Damron and Seegmiller escorted the new missionaries to the home of a Tahitian man named Tiniarau, who provided a bed where James and his son could sleep. After the exhausting journey, James did not leave his room for days.[25]

Before long, though, visitors began calling. One came from Anaa and said he recognized James by his voice. Others would identify him the same way, the man said, even if they did not know him by sight. Some visitors had been born after James had sailed home, but they were still glad to meet him. One older woman recognized him and began shaking his hand so persistently that he wondered if she would ever let go. She had been on Anaa, he learned, when the French officers arrested him and took him from the atoll aboard their warship.

One evening, James met yet another man from Anaa, Pohemiti, who remembered him. Pohemiti had joined the Reorganized Church, but he rejoiced to meet James again and provided food for him. If you go to Anaa, he promised the missionary, the people there will listen to you.[26]

AT HARVARD UNIVERSITY, JOHN Widtsoe received letter after letter from his mother and brother in Salt Lake City. Their words were always full of advice and encouragement. "Ma says you must be careful in your chemistry," Osborne wrote one day. "She has read of a professor losing both eyes by something exploding or something of that sort."[27]

"Everything will be right with you," Anna wrote more reassuringly. "Just dedicate yourself to doing good to everyone with all that you have and will have, so that you serve Him who is the Creator of all good things and who never tires of making everything better and more beautiful for His children."[28]

When a horse-drawn streetcar first dropped John off at Harvard one year earlier, he had been awed by the school's history and tradition. At night he would dream about acquiring all the world's knowledge without having to worry about how long it would take to master each subject.

As he began studying for his entrance exams, which he would take in the fall, he became overwhelmed by how much he had to learn. He checked out armfuls of books from the campus library and pored over their pages. But he grew discouraged as he realized how difficult it would be to master even one subject perfectly. Could he, a poor immigrant from Norway, compete with his classmates? Many of them had received a first-class education at some of the finest preparatory schools in the United States. Had his education in Utah prepared him for what lay ahead?

Homesickness only added to John's anxieties during those first months, and he had contemplated going home. But he decided to stay, and he went on to pass his entrance exams, including his English exam, even though English was his second language.

Now, with a year of schooling behind him, John was more confident in his studies. He lived in a rented house with some of the other young Latter-day Saint men studying at Harvard and neighboring schools. After much prayer, he selected chemistry as the primary focus of his study. A few other Latter-day Saint students were aspiring scientists, while others were studying for careers in engineering, law, medicine, music, architecture, and business. Like many college students, these young men often reveled in loud debates with each other on scholarly topics.[29]

In July 1892, James Talmage, a fellow chemist and respected scholar in the Church, visited Boston to research and collect laboratory instruments for a Church university in Salt Lake City.[30] James's friend and former schoolmate Susa Gates also came to Harvard to take a summer course in English.

Susa struck John as a good speaker and talented writer. She, in turn, was impressed with his refined and artistic nature, and they quickly became friends. "There is one young man here, handsome and quiet, studious and reserved," Susa wrote in a letter to her daughter Leah, who was about John's age. "He is of excellent character and is indeed the best scholar of them all. I think you would like him."

"I doubt if he can dance at all," Susa lamented, "but he has a brain as big as James Talmage's and has to my eyes a handsome face to go with it."[31]

AFTER HIDING MORE THAN two years on the underground, Lorena Larsen and her children again had a house of their own in Monroe, Utah, not far from where her husband, Bent, lived with his first wife, Julia.[32] But even though Monroe was Lorena's hometown, she did not always feel welcome there.

Throughout the Church, many plural families continued to live as they always had, confident they were doing God's will. Some Church members in Monroe, however, believed it was sinful for a man to continue having children with his plural wives. When it became clear that Lorena was expecting another baby, some of her neighbors and family members began to openly scorn her.

Bent's mother feared that Lorena would get her son thrown back in jail. Lorena's sister said that a pregnant plural wife was no better than someone who had committed adultery. And one day Lorena's own mother, who was also the ward Relief Society president, came to her home and chided her for continuing to have children with Bent.[33]

That evening, after Bent chopped some wood for her and the children, Lorena told him what her mother had said. But rather than sympathize with Lorena, Bent told her that he agreed with his mother-in-law. He had been talking the matter over with friends, and they concluded that a man with plural wives had no choice but to stay with his first wife and let the others go. He and Lorena would remain sealed, but they would have to wait until the next life to be together again.

Lorena could hardly speak. Since the Manifesto, Bent had told her again and again that he would never abandon her. Now he was going to be leaving her and her children on their own, and only weeks before she was due to give birth.

The couple talked all through the night. As Lorena cried, Bent told her that tears could not change the reality of their situation.[34]

"If I didn't believe you thought you were doing God's service," Lorena told Bent, "I could never forgive you."

After Bent was gone, Lorena prayed for strength and wisdom. Just as the sun was beginning to show over the mountains, she found Bent working in a stable behind Julia's house and told him he had to stand by her at least until their baby was born. After that, she said, he could go wherever he wanted. God was now her only friend, and she would turn to Him for help.[35]

Lorena gave birth to a daughter two weeks later. When the baby was five days old, Lorena had a dream about dying and woke up in a panic. Could she trust Bent to care for their children if she died? He had provided for her and the children throughout her pregnancy, as promised. But he rarely interacted with the children, and when he did, his quick, anxious visits often left them feeling like a stranger had dropped by for the evening.

When Lorena told Bent about her premonition, he dismissed it. "It's only a dream," he said. Still feeling uneasy, she prayed often over the next month, promising the Lord that she would endure her trials and hardships patiently and do all she could to further His work, including temple work.[36]

Five weeks after Lorena's dream, a marshal arrested her and Bent for unlawful cohabitation. The court released them on bond with the expectation that Lorena would testify in court against Bent when his trial came up later that year.

The arrest and the contempt Lorena felt from family and friends were too great for her to bear. Unsure what to do, she unburdened her soul to apostle Anthon Lund, the president of the Manti temple. Anthon wept as he listened to her story. "Walk straight ahead amid the sneers and jeers of everybody," he counseled her. "You are all right."[37]

Following the apostle's counsel, Lorena moved straight ahead with her life. Her alarming dream, and the prayers that followed, helped her become more patient, more able to endure her trials, and more thankful to the Lord for her life. Bent also saw that his neglect caused Lorena intense suffering, and he and Lorena ultimately decided to continue with their life together, though it would never be easy.

That September, Bent pleaded guilty to the charge of unlawful cohabitation, and a judge sentenced him to serve one month in jail. The punishment was not as severe as it had been years before, when Bent had served six months on a similar charge. In fact, since the Manifesto, sentences for unlawful cohabitation were often much shorter than before. But it was a reminder that if Lorena and Bent continued their relationship, the consequences could be hard to bear.[38]

Still, it was a risk the couple was now willing to take.

CHAPTER 43

A Greater Necessity
for Union

In September 1892, Francis Lyman and Anthon Lund arrived in St. George, Utah. For several weeks, the two apostles had been visiting wards and counseling Saints throughout central and southern Utah. As the Salt Lake temple neared completion, the First Presidency and the Twelve had begun encouraging the Saints to be more united. But rather than finding harmony and goodwill in their travels, Francis and Anthon had often found wards and branches rife with discord. St. George was no different.[1]

Much of the contention arose from politics. For decades, the Saints in Utah had voted for local candidates in the People's Party, a political party composed mainly of Church members. But in 1891, Church leaders disbanded the People's Party and encouraged the Saints to join either the Democrats or the Republicans, the two parties that dominated United States politics. These leaders hoped more political diversity among the Saints might increase their influence in local elections and in Washington, DC. They also believed diversity would help the Church achieve such goals as Utah statehood and general amnesty for Saints who had entered into plural marriages before the Manifesto.[2]

But now, for the first time, Saints were caught up in heated battles with one another over differing political views.[3] The conflict troubled Wilford Woodruff, and he had urged the Saints at the April 1892 general conference to stop their bickering.

"Every man has as much right—prophets, apostles, saints, and sinners—to his political convictions as he has to his religious opinions," Wilford had declared. "Don't throw filth and dirt and nonsense at one another because of any difference on political matters."

"That spirit will lead us to ruin," he warned.[4]

In St. George, as elsewhere, most Saints believed they should join the Democratic Party, since the Republican Party had typically led antipolygamy efforts against the Church. In many communities, the prevailing attitude was that a good Latter-day Saint could never be a Republican.[5]

Wilford Woodruff and other Church leaders wanted to challenge this view, especially since the United States was being governed at the time by a Republican administration.[6] As Anthon and Francis learned more about the situation in St. George, they wanted to help the Saints understand that they could differ politically without creating bitterness or division within the Church.

During an afternoon priesthood meeting, Francis reminded the men that the Church needed members in both political parties. "We don't want anyone who is a Democrat to change," he reassured them. But he said that Saints who did not feel strong ties to the Democratic Party should consider joining the Republicans. "There is much less difference between the two parties than at first thought," he noted.[7]

Francis then expressed his love for all Saints, no matter their political views. "We must not allow any bitterness in our hearts one toward another," he emphasized.[8]

Two days later, Francis and Anthon went to the St. George temple. They assisted with baptisms, endowments, and other ordinances. An uplifting spirit prevailed in the building.[9]

It was the kind of spirit the Saints needed as they prepared to dedicate another temple to the Lord.

IN SALT LAKE CITY, carpenters, electricians, and other skilled laborers were working rapidly to make sure the Salt Lake temple's interior was ready for the dedication in April 1893. On September 8, the First Presidency toured the building with architect Joseph Don Carlos Young and others. As they walked from room to room, inspecting the work in progress, the members of the presidency were pleased with what they saw.

"Everything is being done in a most finished style," George Q. Cannon noted in his journal.

George was especially impressed with the temple's modern features. "It is surprising what changes have occurred through inventions since the first plan of the temple was drawn out," he wrote. Truman Angell, the temple's original architect, had planned to warm and light the temple with stoves and candles. Now new technologies allowed the Saints to install electric lights and a steam-powered heating system throughout the building. Workers were also installing two elevators to help patrons move easily from one floor to another.[10]

Funds for construction were exhausted, however, and some people doubted the Church had the resources to finish the temple in the six months before the dedication. Beginning in 1890, the First Presidency had invested heavily in a sugar beet factory south of Salt Lake City, hoping to create a cash crop for local farmers and generate new jobs for individuals who might otherwise move away from Utah for better work opportunities. This investment, along with the loss of Church property confiscated by the federal government, left Church leaders short of valuable resources they might have used to complete the temple.[11]

Relief Societies, Mutual Improvement Associations, Primaries, and Sunday Schools tried to help ease the financial burden by collecting donations for the temple fund. But much more needed to be done.

On October 10, the First Presidency and Quorum of the Twelve met with other Church leaders, including stake presidents and bishops, in the large, partially finished assembly room on the top floor of the temple. The purpose of the meeting was to recruit local leaders to help raise funds for the temple.[12]

Shortly after George Q. Cannon opened the meeting, John Winder, a counselor in the Presiding Bishopric, reported to the assembly that it would take at least an additional $175,000 to finish the temple. Furnishing the inside would cost even more.

Wilford Woodruff spoke of his earnest desire to have the temple completed on schedule. George then urged the men in the room to use their influence to raise the needed funds. Each stake would be expected to collect a certain amount based on its size and the means of individual families.

The men in the room felt the Spirit powerfully and agreed to help. One man, John R. Murdock, recommended that all those present say how much they were personally willing to donate to the temple. One by one, the Church leaders pledged generously, promising a total contribution of more than $50,000.

Before the meeting closed, George said, "There never has been a time since the Church was organized, in my opinion, when there was a greater necessity for union in the Church than now." He testified that the First Presidency were united and constantly seeking to learn the mind and will of the Lord in how to direct the Church.

"The Lord has blessed us and acknowledged our labors," he declared. "He has made plain to us, day by day, the course that we are to take."[13]

AMONG THE CARPENTERS WORKING on the temple was Joseph Dean, the former president of the Samoan mission. Joseph had returned from the Pacific two years earlier. For a while, he had struggled to find steady work to support both of his wives, Sally and Florence, and seven children. When he was hired to work on the temple in February 1892, the job was a great blessing. But his salary and Sally's income from sewing and dressmaking were barely enough to keep the large family fed, sheltered, and clothed.[14]

In the fall of 1892, the First Presidency approved ten percent raises to temple workmen to ensure they were paid the same as other laborers in the industry. For some men, it was the highest wage they had ever been paid.[15] Joseph and his wives were grateful for the raise, but they continued to struggle to make ends meet.

They paid their tithing faithfully, however, and even donated twenty-five dollars to the temple fund.[16]

On December 1, Joseph drew his monthly paycheck of $98.17. After work, he went to a nearby store to pay a five-dollar debt. The store's owner was Joseph's bishop, and instead of simply accepting the payment, the bishop told him that their stake president had recently asked every family in the stake to donate a specific amount of money to the Church for temple construction. Joseph and his family had been asked to contribute one hundred dollars.

Joseph was stunned. Sally had recently given birth, and Joseph still needed to pay the doctor. He also owed money to five other stores and rent on Florence's home. Added together, his payment on all his debts exceeded his monthly salary, which itself was less than the stake's requested donation. How could he possibly contribute so much—especially after his family had just donated twenty-five dollars at great sacrifice?

As hard as it would be to meet his obligation, Joseph agreed to find a way to come up with the money. "I shall do my best," he wrote that night in his journal, "and trust in the Lord to see me through."[17]

THAT JANUARY, MAIHEA, AN elderly leader of the Saints on the Tuamotu Islands, called a conference on Faaite, an atoll about three hundred miles northeast of Tahiti. Rain fell heavily in the days leading up to the conference, yet determined Saints did not let the weather keep them from coming.[18]

One morning shortly before the conference, a brisk breeze brought four boats to Faaite from Takaroa, an atoll two days to the north. Among the newly arrived Saints, Maihea learned, were four white men who claimed to be missionaries of the Church, with authority to teach the restored gospel.[19]

Maihea was suspicious. Seven years earlier, a missionary of the Reorganized Church of Jesus Christ of Latter Day Saints had come to his village on the neighboring Anaa atoll. The missionary had invited the Anaa Saints to join him in worship, claiming that Brigham Young and the Saints in Utah had cut themselves off from the true church of Christ. Many Saints had accepted his invitation. But Maihea and others had refused it, recalling that Brigham Young had sent the missionaries who taught them the gospel.[20]

Unsure if these new missionaries were true representatives of the Church, Maihea and the Tuamotu Saints greeted them coldly, giving them only an unripe coconut to eat. Soon, however, Maihea learned that the oldest missionary was a one-legged man named James Brown, or Iakobo, which was the name of one of the missionaries who had taught him the gospel. Even Saints who were too young to have met James Brown personally had heard the older generation speak his name.

Since Maihea was blind and could not recognize the missionary by sight, he confronted him with questions.[21] "If you are the same that has been among us before, you have lost one leg," said Maihea, "for the Iakobo that I used to know had two legs."

Maihea then asked James if he taught the same doctrine as the man who had baptized him so many years before.

James replied that he did.

Maihea's questions continued: Have you come from Salt Lake City? Who is the president of the Church now that Brigham Young is dead? Which hand do you raise when you baptize? Is it true that you believe in plural marriage?

James answered each question, but Maihea remained unsatisfied. "What was the name of the village where the French arrested you?" he asked. Once again, James answered the question correctly.

Finally, Maihea's fear faded away, and he gladly shook James's hand. "If you had not come and satisfied us that you were the same man who was here before, it would have been useless to send these young men here," he said, referring to the missionaries with James, "for we would not have received them."

"But now," Maihea said, "we welcome you. We welcome these young men too."[22]

THAT SAME MONTH, ANTHON Lund, Francis Lyman, and B. H. Roberts visited Manassa, Colorado, at the request of the First Presidency. Four months had passed since Anthon and Francis had asked the Saints in St. George to stop fighting over politics. Since then, similar conflicts had continued to disrupt Manassa and other communities of Saints. Now, with the Salt Lake temple dedication just over two months away, Church leaders feared these communities would not be prepared for the dedication if they could not come together in fellowship and love.[23]

In Manassa, various Saints met with the three Church leaders to air their grievances. Anthon spent as many as ten hours some days listening to accusations and counteraccusations related to political, business, and personal disputes. He counted a total of sixty-five individual conflicts that Saints in Manassa wanted Church leaders to settle.[24]

After reviewing each case, he and his companions tried to resolve the most divisive complaints. Some Saints worked out their disagreements privately or agreed to apologize publicly for things they had said and done. Others, though unhappy with the recommended solutions, humbly promised to abide by them.[25]

After two weeks, Anthon, Francis, and B. H. believed that they had done all they could to help the Saints in Manassa. They knew, however, that many minor conflicts remained. "We call upon you to exert all your energies to settle whatever difficulties may still exist," they instructed the local stake presidency, "and to unite the people in the spirit of the gospel."[26]

B. H. accompanied Anthon and Francis to their train, but he did not return with them. His second wife, Celia, and their children lived in Manassa, and he wanted to spend a few more days with them.[27]

When he arrived back in Utah, B. H. turned to his journal to reflect on his efforts to overcome conflict and find peace in his own life. For over a year, he had been tormented by his struggle to sustain the Manifesto. His heart had softened, little by little, as he remembered the spiritual confirmation he had received like a flash of light when he first heard about the change.

"Perhaps I had transgressed in pushing from me the first testimony I received in relation to it and allowing my own prejudices, and my own shortsighted, human reason to stand against the inspiration of God," B. H. wrote.

"I did not understand the purposes for which the Manifesto was issued. I do not to this day," he continued. "But sure I am that it is all right. That God has a purpose in it I feel assured, and in due time it will be manifest."[28]

ON JANUARY 5, 1893, JOSEPH Dean learned that United States president Benjamin Harrison had signed a general amnesty proclamation, extending forgiveness to Saints who had practiced plural marriage but had stopped cohabiting after the Manifesto.[29]

The president had notified Church leaders a few months earlier that he would sign the proclamation. In the same dispatch, he had asked the First Presidency to pray for his wife, Caroline, who was on her deathbed. After years of conflict between the Saints and the government, the First Presidency was surprised by the request—and honored to fulfill it.[30]

For Joseph, the amnesty proclamation had little impact, since he had not abandoned his plural family after the Manifesto. But the *Deseret News* and other newspapers in Utah recognized the symbolic importance of the proclamation, and articles urged the Saints to be grateful to President Harrison for issuing it in good faith.[31]

Meanwhile, Joseph and other laborers had extended their workdays by two hours to finish the Salt Lake temple by April 6. The First Presidency visited the construction site regularly, checking on details and encouraging the craftsmen in their efforts.[32]

Joseph, for his part, was determined to do his best to build the temple and fulfill his promise to donate one hundred dollars to its completion. In February, apostle John W. Taylor canceled one hundred dollars' worth of interest on a loan he had given Joseph, and Joseph immediately saw it as a blessing. "I consider the Lord has refunded me," he wrote in his journal.[33]

By mid-March, Joseph had paid seventy-five dollars toward temple construction, and he hoped to pay the remaining twenty-five dollars in April, right before the temple's completion. He also took two of his children to see the inside of the temple. In the baptistry, he showed them a large font resting on the backs of twelve cast iron oxen—a sight that scared his five-year-old son, Jasper, who thought the animals were real.[34]

In an endowment room in the temple's basement, artists were painting beautiful murals representing the Garden of Eden, complete with waterfalls, grassy meadows, and rolling hills. A stairwell from this room led to another endowment room, where additional murals of deserts, jagged cliffs, wild animals, and dark clouds portrayed life after the Fall. Before beginning the murals, most of the artists at work had been set apart by the First Presidency and received world-class training from art instructors in Paris.[35]

Near the end of March 1893, Bishop John Winder called the workers together and exhorted them to resolve any grievances or negative feelings among the crew. The temple needed to be physically ready for dedication, but the workers needed to be spiritually ready as well.[36]

To help all the Saints reconcile themselves to God and each other, the First Presidency called for a special Churchwide fast to take place twelve days before the dedication.

"Before entering into the temple to present ourselves before the Lord in solemn assembly," they wrote in a letter to all Church members, "we shall divest ourselves of every harsh and unkind feeling against each other."[37]

On the day of the fast, a Saturday, Sally and Florence Dean gathered with other Saints to sing, speak, and pray. But Joseph could not join them. There was too much work to be done in the temple, and he and his fellow workers labored through the day, fasting all the while.[38]

In the days that followed, Joseph helped install floorboards while teams of carpet layers, curtain hangers, painters, gilders, and electricians scurried about finishing last-minute tasks. A committee of men and women then adorned the rooms with elegant furniture and other decorations. Among the items available to them were silk altar covers and other handicrafts donated by women in wards throughout the city.

More work would still need to be done after the dedication, but Joseph was sure the temple would be ready to open its doors on the appointed day. "Things are coming pretty nicely to a point after all," he wrote.[39]

ON THE DAY OF the Churchwide fast, Susa Gates received a letter from her nineteen-year-old daughter, Leah, seeking reconciliation. At the time, Susa was living in Provo while Leah was attending college in Salt Lake City. "Little did I think," Leah wrote, "that my own dear mother would be the one whose forgiveness I must beg and pardon seek for past feelings and grievances."[40]

Earlier that week, Susa had argued with Leah about Leah's father, Alma Dunford. Years before, Susa had divorced Alma when she could no longer live with his drinking and abuse. Alma had gained custody of Leah, however, so she had grown up with her father's family, away from Susa.

Alma had since remarried and had more children. Although he continued to struggle with the Word of Wisdom, Alma had become a kind husband and father who provided well for his family and raised them in the Church. Leah loved him and viewed him differently than her mother did. "You know my feelings, and I cannot help share," Leah told Susa. "I love my mother dearer than tongue can tell, but I also love my father."

Still, after the argument, Leah felt she needed to apologize. "I humbly and truly repent and beg that you will forgive and forget," she wrote.[41]

As Susa read the letter, she was sorry her daughter was burdened with remorse. Susa's father, Brigham Young, had counseled her to always place her family first, promising that every great thing she accomplished afterward would add to her glory. Since then, Susa had found success in and out of the home. At thirty-seven, she had a loving marriage, six living children and another on the way, and recognition as one of the most talented and prolific writers in the Church.[42]

But with all her success, Susa still sometimes felt that she was falling short of her lofty expectations of ideal motherhood. Her relationship with Leah had been particularly difficult. For many years after the divorce, they had not been able to interact in person. When Leah was fifteen years old, however, Susa had arranged a meeting in the Lion House, where they embraced and wept for joy. From that time forward, Susa and Leah had enjoyed a loving, affectionate relationship, and they sometimes felt more like sisters than mother and daughter.[43]

On Saturday, March 25, Susa attended the special fast meeting with her fellow Saints in Provo. Leah was never far from her mind. Susa realized that the adversary would do all he could to break the bonds of love that had so recently developed between her and her eldest daughter, and she would not allow it.

As soon as she could, she responded to Leah's letter. "My dearest, darling girl," she wrote, "know that I love you better every day." She in turn asked for Leah's forgiveness and promised to do better. "I know I am far from perfect," she admitted. "Perhaps the greatest sting of your words was, for me, in the fact that in a measure I deserved it."

"By prayer and a little effort on our part, we can learn to let these things alone," she wrote. "Give me a kiss and bury it forever."[44]

CHAPTER 44

Blessed Peace

The days leading up to the dedication of the Salt Lake temple were full of energy and commotion. Work on the temple was still in progress on the day before the doors were scheduled to open. The city streets, meanwhile, were thronged with visitors arriving hourly by train, buggy, and horseback.[1] Church leaders had decided to hold two dedication sessions a day until every Church member who wanted to participate could attend. Now tens of thousands of Saints were planning to come to Salt Lake City that spring to see the house of the Lord with their own eyes.[2]

The day before the first dedicatory session, Church leaders gave a tour of the temple to local and national reporters as well as dignitaries who were not members of the Church. Many of the guests praised the temple's craftsmanship, from its elegant spiral staircases to its delicately tiled flooring. Even the Church's staunchest critics were amazed.

"The interior was a revelation of beauty," wrote one reporter from the *Salt Lake Tribune,* "so much so that the visitors stopped and stood still involuntarily, totally engrossed in their surroundings."[3]

The next morning, April 6, 1893, dawned bright but chilly. Over two thousand Saints with recommends for the first dedicatory session began lining up outside the temple gates hours before the meeting was scheduled to begin. After the temple doors opened and the Saints started filing in, the weather grew colder and a stiff breeze began to blow. Soon, frigid rain fell and the breeze became a howling wind, blasting the Saints who huddled patiently in line.[4]

Just as the Kirtland temple could not seat everyone who wanted to attend its dedication, the Salt Lake temple's spacious assembly room was too small to accommodate everyone in the line. Even after the doors closed, crowds of Saints remained near the temple. Around ten o'clock, when the session was set to begin, the wind picked up once again, sending gravel and debris flying. To some, the devil himself seemed to be raging against the Saints and the temple they had built.[5]

Yet those who stood outside the building saw a sign that reminded them of an earlier manifestation of God's watchful care. Lifting their eyes to heaven, they glimpsed a large flock of seagulls pirouetting in the sky, circling the temple spires in the midst of the storm.[6]

INSIDE THE TEMPLE, SUSA Gates sat down at the recorder's table at the east end of the assembly room. As one of the official reporters of the dedicatory services, Susa would be taking shorthand minutes of the meeting. Even though she was just weeks away from giving birth, she planned to attend and report on every one of the dozens of scheduled sessions.[7]

Hundreds of electric lights, arranged in five hanging chandeliers, illuminated the room with dazzling brilliance. The hall had a seating capacity of twenty-two hundred and occupied the entire floor. Among the people in the room were Susa's husband, Jacob, and her mother, Lucy Young. Chairs trimmed in red velvet filled the main seating area, and rows of elevated pulpits for Church leaders stood at the eastern and western ends of the room. Every available seat was filled, and some people were standing.[8]

Soon the three hundred members of the Tabernacle Choir stood, the men dressed in dark suits and the women in white. Their voices rang out as they sang "Let All Israel Join and Sing," a hymn by Joseph Daynes, the choir's organist.[9]

President Wilford Woodruff then arose to address the Saints. "I have looked forward to this day for the last fifty years of my life," he said. As a young man, he had seen a vision of himself dedicating a magnificent temple in the mountains of the West. More recently, he had dreamed that Brigham Young had given him a set of keys for the Salt Lake temple.

"You go and unlock that temple," Brigham had said, "and let the people into it—all who want salvation."[10]

After recounting these visions to the Saints, Wilford knelt on a cushioned stool to read the dedicatory prayer. Speaking in a strong, clear voice, he pleaded with God to apply the Savior's atoning blood and forgive the Saints of their sins. "Grant that the blessings which we seek may be bestowed upon us, even a hundredfold," he prayed, "inasmuch as we seek with purity of heart and fullness of purpose to do Thy will and glorify Thy name."

For over thirty minutes, Wilford offered thanks and gave praise to God. He presented the building to the Lord, asking Him to watch over and protect it. He prayed for the priesthood quorums, the Relief Society, the missionaries, and the youth and children of the Church. He prayed for the rulers of nations and for the poor, afflicted, and oppressed. And he asked that all people might have their hearts softened and be free to accept the restored gospel.

Before closing, he asked the Lord to fortify the faith of the Saints. "Strengthen us by the memories of the glorious deliverances of the past, by the remembrance of the sacred covenants that Thou hast made with us," he prayed, "so that, when evil overshadows us, when trouble encompasses us, when we pass through the valley of humiliation, we may not falter, may not doubt, but in the strength of Thy holy name may accomplish all Thy righteous purposes."[11]

Following the prayer, Lorenzo Snow, the president of the Quorum of the Twelve, led the congregation in a jubilant Hosanna Shout. The choir and congregation then sang "The Spirit of God like a Fire Is Burning."[12]

The dedication moved Susa profoundly. Her father had broken ground on the temple a few years before she was born, so all her life faithful women and men had been consecrating their money, means, and labor to temple construction. Recently, her own mother had anonymously donated $500 to the temple fund.

All of them were sure to receive blessings, Susa believed, for offering their gifts upon the altar of sacrifice and Christlike love.[13]

Joseph F. Smith spoke later in the service, tears streaming down his face. "All the inhabitants of the earth are the people of God," he said, "and it is our duty to carry the words of life and salvation to them, and to redeem those who have died without the knowledge of the truth. This house has been erected to the name of God for that purpose."[14]

A radiant glow seemed to emanate from Joseph, and Susa thought a shaft of sunshine had come through the window to illuminate his face. "What a singular effect of sunlight," she whispered to the man next to her. "Do look at it!"

"There is no sunshine outdoors," the man whispered back, "nothing but dark clouds and gloom."

Susa glanced out the windows and saw stormy skies. She then realized that the light shining through Joseph's countenance was the Holy Spirit, descended upon him.[15]

THAT SAME DAY, RUA and Tematagi, a young couple on the Anaa atoll, attended a conference with other Saints from the Tuamotu Islands. With mission president James Brown presiding, the conference started at seven o'clock in the morning, the same time that the first dedicatory session began in Salt Lake City.[16]

For several days before the conference, missionaries and other Church members had been gathering at Putuahara, the same place on Anaa where Addison Pratt had met with more than eight hundred Saints nearly fifty years earlier. High winds had recently whipped the ocean into a fury, but the squally weather had since subsided and a warm sun was now rising over the village.[17]

Rua and Tematagi had joined the Church a few months after James Brown arrived on the islands. When he came to Anaa, James found the atoll bitterly divided over religion, but he and his son Elando had baptized a few new Saints. In accepting baptism, Rua and Tematagi were uniting their faith with Rua's younger sister, Terai, and her husband, Tefanau, who had joined the Church nine years earlier. Rua's father, Teraupua, was also a member of the Church and had recently been ordained to the Melchizedek Priesthood.[18]

After the conference began, James Brown spoke about the temple dedication and its importance. Joseph Damron, one of the elders who had reopened the Tahitian mission, spoke about building temples in the latter days. Though the Salt Lake temple was thousands of miles away, the Tuamotu Saints could celebrate the historic day and learn more about the role temples played in redeeming the living and dead.

When the meeting ended, the Saints walked down a path to the ocean to watch Elando baptize five new converts in the warm Pacific water. Among the Saints baptized was Mahue, Rua and Tematagi's nine-year-old daughter. Following the baptism, she was confirmed by her uncle Tefanau. Rua was then ordained an elder in the Melchizedek Priesthood by Terogomaihite, a local Church leader. Two other Saints from the islands were ordained elders and set apart as branch presidents.[19]

The conference concluded two days later, and the Saints agreed to meet again in three months' time. Joseph Damron and others from neighboring islands then bade farewell to their friends on Anaa. Before Joseph left, Rua presented him with a gift of a small pearl.[20]

SNOW BLANKETED THE GROUND at Temple Square on April 9 when about fifty Hawaiian Saints from the Iosepa settlement assembled at the temple gate to present their recommends.[21]

More than two years had passed since the First Presidency visited Iosepa to celebrate the founding of the settlement. The Saints had continued to work hard to cultivate their land. Although they had bought eight hundred additional acres of land and successfully raised a wide variety of crops, money was still scarce. Even so, when the First Presidency called for donations to push the temple to completion, the Iosepa Saints had donated $1,400.[22]

When they learned that a date had been scheduled for them to attend the temple dedication, the people in Iosepa were filled with new energy. They worked tirelessly to plant their spring crops before the time came to make the two-day trip to Salt Lake City. Every plow, leveler, harrow, and grain drill was put to use until the Saints were ready to depart.[23]

Although a recommend for the dedication required nothing more than membership in the Church and a desire to attend, the Iosepa Saints wanted to be sure they were spiritually prepared to enter the temple. Nearly thirty had sought rebaptism, and a special baptismal service was held at the town reservoir.[24]

After presenting their recommends at the temple gates, the Iosepa Saints entered the building and walked through its many rooms. The Saints in Laie had sent a small table inlaid with Hawaiian hardwood for the temple, and two poles decorated with the feathers of

Hawaiian birds were on display in one corner of the celestial room. Women in Hawaiian Relief Societies had crafted the poles, called kāhili, which symbolized royalty and spiritual protection.[25]

Soon the Iosepa Saints and more than two thousand others took their seats in the assembly room. Together they sang, listened to the dedicatory prayer, and gave the Hosanna Shout. After another hymn, Wilford Woodruff thanked the people for their contributions to the temple and testified of Jesus Christ.[26]

Wilford then called on George Q. Cannon to speak. "Our mission is a far greater one than that of those who have preceded us," George said. "The Saints are laying the foundation of a work, the extent of which they cannot grasp."

Before concluding, he addressed the Iosepa Saints in their own language.

"There are millions of spirits who have died but are unable to go before the presence of God because they do not possess the key," he said. He alluded to the Hawaiians on the other side of the veil who would accept the gospel, and he testified that the Church needed the Hawaiian Saints to do temple work for their kindred dead.[27]

Later, at a branch meeting in Iosepa, a man named J. Mahoe spoke of his experience at the dedication and the important lesson he learned there. "I rejoice in having been able to attend the temple and witness the happenings found therein," he said. "We need to take care of our genealogies."[28]

AT TEN O'CLOCK ON the morning of April 19, the First Presidency held a special meeting in the temple for all general authorities and stake presidencies. Once the men assembled, the presidency invited them to share their feelings about the temple dedication and the work of God in the lives of the Saints.[29]

All morning, one man after another bore powerful testimony. When they finished, Wilford stood and added his witness to theirs. "I have felt more of the Holy Ghost here at this dedication than I have ever felt before, except on one occasion," he said. He then spoke about the time when Joseph Smith gave his final charge to the apostles in Nauvoo.

"He stood upon his feet for three hours," Wilford testified. "The room seemed to be filled with consuming fire, and Joseph's face shone like amber."[30]

Wilford also spoke of seeing Brigham Young and Heber Kimball in a vision after their deaths. Both men were riding to conference in a carriage, and they invited Wilford to join them. Wilford did so and asked Brigham to speak.

"I am through with my preaching on earth," Brigham told him, "but I have come to impress upon your mind what Joseph had told me at Winter Quarters, and that is: seek always to have the Spirit of God, and it will direct you aright."[31]

Now Wilford's message to the general authorities was the same. "You want the Holy Ghost to lead and guide you," he said. "Teach the people to get the Holy

Ghost and the Spirit of the Lord, and keep it with you, and you will prosper."[32]

As a young woman, Relief Society general president Zina Young had heard angels sing in the Kirtland temple. Decades later, she had served faithfully in the Endowment House in Salt Lake City and the temples in St. George, Logan, and Manti. Now she would oversee all female ordinance workers in the Salt Lake temple.[33]

The night after the first dedicatory session, Zina bore testimony of the temple at a crowded Relief Society conference. "There has never been such a day in Israel before," she told the women. "The work of the Lord will roll on faster from this day forth."[34]

Her secretary Emmeline Wells bore a similar witness in the pages of the *Woman's Exponent*. "No event of modern times is so important," she wrote, "as the opening of this holy edifice for the administration of ordinances that pertain to the living and the dead, to the past and the present, to the endowments and covenants that unite families and kindreds in bonds inseparable."[35]

That spring, after the Saints held the final dedicatory session of the temple, Zina and Emmeline made final preparations to travel east to attend a conference of women at the World's Columbian Exposition in Chicago, a monumental fair meant to showcase the marvels of science and culture from many nations. Like the first conference of the National Council of Women two years earlier, the exposition would provide a chance for Relief Society and Young Ladies' Mutual Improvement Association leaders to represent the Church and meet with influential women from all over the world.[36]

The two friends left for Chicago on May 10. In a matter of days their train covered distances it would have taken weeks to travel nearly fifty years earlier, when the Saints first came to the Salt Lake Valley. Crossing the Mississippi River, Emmeline was overwhelmed with emotion as she thought of the past. Although the Saints had endured many trials over the last half century, they had experienced many triumphs as well.[37]

Zina also found her thoughts returning to the past. "The mantle of time is fast draping its folds around many of us," she later told Emmeline. "When we go hence to our rest after our sacrifices indescribable, may it be like Utah's most beautiful sunsets, that many in the future may have reason to praise God for the noble women of this generation."[38]

AROUND THE TIME ZINA Young and Emmeline Wells traveled to the World's Columbian Exposition, Anna Widtsoe received a letter from her son John at Harvard University. For nearly a month, John had been eagerly awaiting letters from his mother and younger brother, Osborne, about the temple dedication. But so far nothing had arrived.

"I am tired of reading the newspaper about the dedication," John wrote. "I want to hear about it more personally because there is more life in a letter than in a whole world of newspapers."[39]

The family had already written to John about the dedication, of course, but the mail service, as fast as it had become over the years, was still not fast enough for him.

Anna and Osborne had attended a dedicatory session together. Later, Osborne had attended a special session with the children and youth of the Sunday School. As he walked through the temple, he had seen a painting of three pioneer women, one of whom was Norwegian.[40] The painting was a tribute to the faith and sacrifice of the many immigrant women, including Anna, who had left their homelands to gather to Zion.

Nearly ten years had passed since the Widtsoes had made their journey to Utah. Now, in Salt Lake City, they had a small, comfortable place to live, only a few blocks from the store where Osborne worked. Anna had a dressmaking business and attended her ward Relief Society meetings. She also gathered regularly with other Scandinavian Saints at the old Social Hall.[41] She had found a home among the Saints, and she cherished her faith in the restored gospel. Before embracing it, she had been as one born blind. Now she could see.[42]

But Anna was concerned for John. He had recently written about his struggle to believe some aspects of the gospel. At Harvard, he had learned a great many things from his professors. But their lectures had also led him to question his faith. His doubts cut him to the bone. Some days he denied God's existence. Other days he affirmed it.[43]

Anna prayed daily for her son, deeply distressed by his doubts. But she knew he had to gain his own witness of the gospel. "If you have not had a testimony for yourself before, then now is the time that you should have one," she wrote John. "If you seek sincerely and live purely, then you will receive it. But everything that we have, we must work for."[44]

For Anna, the temple affirmed her faith in God's promises to His children. Even before leaving Nauvoo, the Saints had placed hope in Isaiah's prophecy of all nations gathering to the Lord's house in the top of the mountains. By the end of April 1893, more than eighty thousand men, women, and children—many of them immigrants from Europe and the islands of the sea—had entered the temple to attend a dedicatory session. A spirit of love and unity had rested over each meeting, and the Saints felt as if the word of the Lord had been fulfilled.[45]

Now, with a new century in view, the Saints could look forward to still brighter and bolder days. The four temples in Utah, representing so much sacrifice and faith, were only a beginning. "What a work there is before us if we are faithful," Brigham Young had once declared. "We shall be able to build temples, yes, thousands of them, and build temples in all countries of the world."[46]

When Anna made her way through the Salt Lake temple, she had felt the sacredness of the place. "I tried to stay in the celestial room as long as possible," she told John in a letter. "I saw it and felt as if a light was shone on me and that no place on earth had any value for me anymore."

"Everything is so glorious there," she testified, "and such a blessed peace fills the place that no language can explain it but those who have been there and received the holiness of holiness."[47]

NOTE ON SOURCES

This volume is a work of narrative nonfiction based on hundreds of historical sources. Utmost care has been taken to ensure its accuracy. Church history between 1846 and 1893 is remarkably well documented, with sources ranging from personal letters and journals to newspaper reports and institutional records like meeting minutes. Readers should not assume, however, that the narrative presented here is perfect or complete. The records of the past, and our ability to interpret them in the present, are limited.

All sources of historical knowledge contain gaps, ambiguities, and biases. They often convey only their creator's point of view. Consequently, witnesses of the same events experience, remember, and record them differently, and their diverse perspectives enable varied ways of interpreting history. The challenge of the historian is to assemble known points of view and piece together an accurate understanding of the past through careful analysis and interpretation.

Saints is a true account of the history of The Church of Jesus Christ of Latter-day Saints, based on what we know and understand at the present time from existing historical records. It is not the only possible telling of the Church's sacred history, but the scholars who researched, wrote, and edited this volume know the historical sources well, used them thoughtfully, and documented them in the endnotes and list of sources cited. Readers are invited to evaluate the sources themselves, many of which have been digitized and linked to the endnotes. It is probable that the discovery of more sources, or new readings of existing sources, will in time yield other meanings, interpretations, and possible points of view.

The narrative in *Saints* draws on primary and secondary sources. Primary sources contain information about events from those who witnessed them firsthand. Some primary sources, like letters, journals, and reports of discourses, were written at the time of the events they describe. These contemporaneous sources reflect what people thought, felt, and did in the moment, revealing how the past was interpreted when it was the present. Other primary sources, like autobiographies, were written after the fact. These reminiscent sources reveal what the past came to mean to the writer over time, often making them better than contemporary sources at recognizing the significance of past events. Since they rely on memory, however, reminiscent sources can include inaccuracies and be influenced by the author's later understandings and beliefs.

Secondary historical sources contain information from people who did not witness the events described firsthand. Such sources include later family histories and academic works. This volume is indebted to many such sources, which proved valuable for the broader contextual and interpretive work they provided.

Every source in *Saints* was evaluated for credibility, and each sentence was repeatedly checked for consistency with the sources. Lines of dialogue and other quotations come directly from historical sources. Spelling, capitalization, and punctuation in direct quotations have been silently modernized for clarity. In some instances, more significant modifications, like shifting from the past tense to present tense or standardizing grammar, have been made to quotations to improve readability. In these cases, endnotes describe the changes made. Choices about which sources to use and how to use them were made by a team of historians, writers, and editors who based decisions on both historical integrity and literary quality.

Some antagonistic sources were used to write this volume and are cited in the notes. These sources were primarily used to characterize opposition to the Church during the nineteenth century. Though largely hostile to the Church, these documents sometimes contain details that were not recorded elsewhere. Some of these details were used when other records confirmed their general accuracy. Facts from these antagonistic records were used without adopting their hostile interpretations.

As a narrative history written for a general audience, this volume presents a history of the Church in a coherent, accessible format. While drawing on the techniques of popular storytelling, it does not go beyond information found in historical sources. When the text includes even minor details, such as facial expressions or weather conditions, it is because these details are found in or reasonably deduced from the historical record.

To maintain the readability of the narrative, the volume rarely addresses challenges in or to the historical record in the text itself. Instead, such source-based discussions are found in topical essays on saints.ChurchofJesusChrist.org. Readers are encouraged to consult these essays as they study Church history.

NOTES

Some sources are referred to with a shortened citation. The "Sources Cited" section provides full citation information for all sources. Many sources are available digitally and are linked from the electronic version of the book, available at saints.ChurchofJesusChrist.org and in Gospel Library. The abbreviation CHL stands for Church History Library, The Church of Jesus Christ of Latter-day Saints, Salt Lake City.

Text in bold in the notes points to topical articles with additional information online at saints.ChurchofJesusChrist.org and in Gospel Library under "Church History Topics."

CHAPTER 1: GATHER UP A COMPANY

1. Historian's Office, General Church Minutes, Oct. 8, 1845; "Conference Minutes," *Times and Seasons,* Nov. 1, 1845, 6:1013–14. A complete report of Lucy's October 1845 conference sermon, with annotations, is available in Reeder and Holbrook, *At the Pulpit,* 21–26. **Topic: Lucy Mack Smith**
2. Lucy Mack Smith, History, 1844–45, book 5, [7]; *Saints,* volume 1, chapters 4 and 44; Black, "How Large Was the Population of Nauvoo?," 92–93. **Topic: Deaths of Joseph and Hyrum Smith**
3. Solomon Hancock and Alanson Ripley to Brigham Young, Sept. 11, 1845, Brigham Young Office Files, CHL; "Mobbing Again in Hancock!," and "Proclamation," *Nauvoo Neighbor,* Sept. 10, 1845, [2]; Gates, Journal, volume 2, Sept. 13, 1845; Glines, Reminiscences and Diary, Sept. 12, 1845; "The Crisis," and "The War," *Warsaw Signal,* Sept. 17, 1845, [2]; "The Mormon War," *American Penny Magazine,* Oct. 11, 1845, 570–71; Jacob B. Backenstos to Brigham Young, Sept. 18, 1845, Brigham Young Office Files, CHL; Orson Spencer to Thomas Ford, Oct. 23, 1845; Thomas Ford to George Miller, Oct. 30, 1845, Brigham Young History Documents, CHL; see also Leonard, *Nauvoo,* 525–42.
4. *To the Anti-Mormon Citizens of Hancock and Surrounding Counties* (Warsaw, IL: Oct. 4, 1845), Chicago Historical Society, Collection of Manuscripts about Mormons, CHL; see also Leonard, *Nauvoo,* 536–42.
5. Council of Fifty, "Record," Sept. 9, 1845, in *JSP,* CFM:471–72; "Conference Minutes," *Times and Seasons,* Nov. 1, 1845, 6:1008–11.
6. Doctrine and Covenants 29:8 (Revelation, Sept. 1830–A, at josephsmithpapers .org); Doctrine and Covenants 125:2 (Revelation, circa Early Mar. 1841, at josephsmithpapers.org); Historian's Office, General Church Minutes, Oct. 8, 1845; "Conference Minutes," *Times and Seasons,* Nov. 1, 1845, 6:1013–14.
7. Brigham Young to Wilford Woodruff, Oct. 16, 1845, Wilford Woodruff, Journals and Papers, CHL; Woodruff, Journal, Nov. 18, 1845. **Topic: Wilford Woodruff**
8. Woodruff, Journal, Nov. 18, 1845; "Address to the Saints in the British Islands," *Latter-day Saints' Millennial Star,* Dec. 1, 1845, 6:177.
9. Brigham Young to Wilford Woodruff, Oct. 16, 1845, Wilford Woodruff, Journals and Papers, CHL; "Important Notice," *Latter-day Saints' Millennial Star,* Dec. 1, 1845, 6:202; Woodruff, Journal, Nov. 20–21, 1844, and July 18, 1845. **Topic: Wilford Woodruff**
10. Brigham Young to Wilford Woodruff, Oct. 16, 1845, Wilford Woodruff, Journals and Papers, CHL.
11. Woodruff, Journal, Nov. 19–29, 1845, and July 15, 1846; "Important Notice," *Latter-day Saints' Millennial Star,* Dec. 1, 1845, 6:202; "To the Saints in Great Britain, Greeting," *Latter-day Saints' Millennial Star,* Jan. 1, 1846, 7:10.
12. Historian's Office, History of the Church, volume 14, Dec. 11, 1845, 9; Samuel Brannan to Brigham Young, Jan. 12, 1846, Brigham Young Office Files, CHL; Reports of the U.S. District Attorneys, 1845–50, Report of Suits Pending, Circuit Court of

the District of Illinois, Dec. 1845 term, Dec. 17–18, 1845, microfilm, Records of the Solicitor of the Treasury, copy at CHL; Oaks and Hill, *Carthage Conspiracy,* 202.

13. Kimball, Journal, Dec. 11, 1845; Historical Department, Journal History of the Church, Dec. 11, 1845.

14. Thomas Ford to Jacob B. Backenstos, Dec. 29, 1845, Brigham Young Office Files, CHL. Quotation edited for clarity; "Washington" in original changed to "Washington, DC."

15. Council of Fifty, "Record," Jan. 11, 1846, in *JSP,* CFM:514, 515, 518. **Topic: Council of Fifty**

16. "The Council of Fifty in Nauvoo, Illinois," in *JSP,* CFM:xxvi–xxviii; *Saints,* volume 1, chapter 11; Book of Mormon Title Page; Helaman 15:12–13; Doctrine and Covenants 3:16–20; Reeve, *Religion of a Different Color,* 75–82. **Topic: American Indians**

17. Council of Fifty, "Record," Jan. 13, 1846, in *JSP,* CFM:521–25. **Topics: Departure from Nauvoo; Pioneer Trek**

18. [Edward Kemble], "'Brooklyn Mormons' in California," *Sacramento Daily Union,* Sept. 11, 1866, 6; "To Our Brethren and Friends Scattered Abroad," *Times and Seasons,* Feb. 15, 1846, 6:1126–27; "News from America," *Latter-day Saints' Millennial Star,* Mar. 1, 1846, 7:77; "Farewell Message of Orson Pratt," *Times and Seasons,* Dec. 1, 1845, 6:1043. **Topic: Mexico**

19. "Farewell Message of Orson Pratt," *Times and Seasons,* Dec. 1, 1845, 6:1042–43; Brigham Young to Samuel Brannan, Sept. 15, 1845, Brigham Young Office Files, CHL. **Topic: Samuel Brannan**

20. "Come on Oh Israel, It Is Time to Go!," *New-York Messenger,* Extra, Dec. 13, 1845; "To Our Brethren and Friends Scattered Abroad," *Times and Seasons,* Feb. 15, 1846, 6:1127; [Edward Kemble], "'Brooklyn Mormons' in California," *Sacramento Daily Union,* Sept. 11, 1866, 6.

21. Samuel Brannan to Brigham Young, Jan. 12, 26, and 27, 1846, Brigham Young Office Files, CHL.

22. Samuel Brannan to Brigham Young, Jan. 26, 1846, Brigham Young Office Files, CHL.

23. Plewe, *Mapping Mormonism,* 72; Hansen, "Voyage of the *Brooklyn,*" 48, 54–58; "To Our Brethren and Friends Scattered Abroad," *Times and Seasons,* Feb. 15, 1846, 6:1127.

24. Historian's Office, History of the Church, volume 15, Feb. 4–8, 1846, 3–4; Plewe, *Mapping Mormonism,* 72.

25. See Nauvoo Sealing Record A, Sealings and Adoptions of the Living, 1846–57, microfilm 183,374, U.S. and Canada Record Collection, Family History Library; Bennett, "Line upon Line," 47; and McBride, *House for the Most High,* 272. **Topics: Temple Endowment; Sealing**

26. See "Plural Marriage in Kirtland and Nauvoo," Gospel Topics, topics .ChurchofJesusChrist.org. **Topic: Joseph Smith and Plural Marriage**

27. Historian's Office, History of the Church, volume 15, Feb. 3, 1846, 2–3. First sentence of quotation edited for readability; original source has "I informed the brethren that this was not wise, and that we should build more Temples, and have further opportunities to receive the blessings of the Lord."

28. Historian's Office, History of the Church, volume 15, Feb. 8, 1846, 4; Frémont, *Report of the Exploring Expedition,* 47–48; Council of Fifty, "Record," Sept. 9, 1845, in *JSP,* CFM:472–75.

29. "Conference Minutes," *Times and Seasons,* Nov. 1, 1845, 6:1008–11.

30. Historian's Office, History of the Church, volume 15, Feb. 15, 1846, 8–9.

31. "History of Brigham Young," Feb. 16, 1846, in Historian's Office, History of the Church, draft, CHL; Historian's Office, History of the Church, volume 15, Feb. 16–17, 1846, 9–11; Brigham Young to Joseph Young, Mar. 9, 1846, Brigham Young Office Files, CHL.

CHAPTER 2: GLORY ENOUGH

1. Sessions, Diary, Feb. 15, 1846; Historian's Office, History of the Church, volume 15, Feb. 17 and 28, 1846, 9–10, 36–39; Pace, Autobiography, chapter 2; Eliza R. Snow, Journal, Feb. 14 and 19, 1846; Meeks, Reminiscences, 14; Helen Mar Whitney, "Our Travels beyond the Mississippi," *Woman's Exponent,* Dec. 1, 1883, 12:102.

2. Historian's Office, History of the Church, volume 15, Feb. 16–18, 1846, 9–10, 21–22; Stout, Journal, Feb. 16–17, 1846.

3. Helen Mar Whitney, "Our Travels beyond the Mississippi," *Woman's Exponent,* Dec. 1, 1883, 12:102; Dec. 15, 1883, 12:111; Historian's Office, History of the Church, volume 15, Feb. 28, 1846, 39; Tullidge, *Women of Mormondom,* 327.

4. Historian's Office, History of the Church, volume 15, Feb. 17 and 23, 1846; Mills, "De Tal Palo Tal Astilla," 105–6.

5. *Saints,* volume 1, chapter 46; George A. Smith, in *Journal of Discourses,* June 20, 1869, 13:85.

6. Samuel Brannan to Brigham Young, Jan. 12, 26, and 27, 1846, Brigham Young Office Files, CHL; Historian's Office, History of the Church, volume 15, Feb. 17, 1846, 11.

7. Brigham Young to Jesse Little, Jan. 20, 1846, Jesse C. Little Collection, CHL; Historian's Office, History of the Church, volume 15, Feb. 17, 1846, 21.

8. Historian's Office, History of the Church, volume 15, Feb. 28, 1846, 39–40; Mar. 1, 1846, 1–2; Horace K. Whitney, Journal, Mar. 9, 1846; Brigham Young to William Huntington and Council, June 28, 1846, copy; Brigham Young to Joseph Young, Mar. 9, 1846, Brigham Young Office Files, CHL.

9. Louisa Barnes Pratt to Brigham Young, Mar. 24, 1846; Brigham Young to Addison Pratt, Aug. 28, 1845, Brigham Young Office Files, CHL; see also *Saints,* volume 1, chapter 41. **Topic: Louisa Barnes Pratt**

10. Louisa Barnes Pratt to Brigham Young, Mar. 24, 1846, Brigham Young Office Files, CHL; Louisa Barnes Pratt, Journal and Autobiography, 127.

11. Louisa Barnes Pratt, Journal and Autobiography, 127. Final sentence of quotation edited for readability; original source has "Brother Pratt will meet us in the wilderness where we locate will be sorely disappointed if his family is not with us."

12. Wells, Diary, volume 1, Mar. 1–25, 1846; Apr. 4 and 6–7, 1846; Orson Pratt, Journal, Mar. 4–5 and 24, 1846; Apr. 6, 9–10, and 30, 1846; Tullidge, *Women of Mormondom,* 312–13; Historian's Office, History of the Church, volume 15, Feb. 18, 1846, 22.

13. Historian's Office, History of the Church, volume 15, Apr. 6–7, 1846, 9–10; Sessions, Diary, Apr. 6, 1846; Clayton, Diary, Apr. 6–7, 1846.

14. Church Historian's Office, History of the Church, volume 15, Apr. 10 and 12, 1846, 12–16; Dahl, *William Clayton,* 64; Diantha F. Clayton to William Clayton, Mar. 10, 1846, CHL.

15. Clayton, Diary, Apr. 15, 1846; "Come Ye Saints," Collected Material relating to William Clayton, CHL; see also "Come, Come, Ye Saints," *Hymns,* no. 30.

16. Woodruff, Journal, Aug. 27–28, 1844, and Apr. 13, 1846; Clayton, History of the Nauvoo Temple, 57–59; "First Meeting in the Temple," *Times and Seasons,* Nov. 1, 1845, 6:1017; John Taylor, Journal, Aug. 23, 1845, 119; Scofield, *History of Hancock County,* 860.

17. Woodruff, Journal, Feb. 16–17, 1846.

18. Woodruff, Journal, Jan. 16–23, 1846; Wilford Woodruff, "To the Saints in the British Isles, Greeting," *Latter-day Saints' Millennial Star,* Feb. 1, 1846, 7:42; Wilford Woodruff to "Brother George," Dec. 18, 1845, in *Times and Seasons,* Feb. 15, 1846, 6:1129–30; see also Wilford Woodruff to Brigham Young, Apr. 1, 1845, Brigham Young Office Files, CHL.

19. Wilford Woodruff, "The Temple of the Lord," *Latter-day Saints' Millennial Star,* June 15, 1845, 6:13.

20. Doctrine and Covenants 124:31–32 (Revelation, Jan. 19, 1841, at josephsmithpapers.org).

21. Wilford Woodruff, "The Temple of the Lord," *Latter-day Saints' Millennial Star,* June 15, 1845, 6:13; Wilford Woodruff, "To the Saints in the British Isles, Greeting," *Latter-day Saints' Millennial Star,* Feb. 1, 1846, 7:42.

22. Woodruff, Journal, Mar. 6–22, 1846.
23. Woodruff, Journal, Apr. 13 and 14, 1846; "Ecclesiastical Officers and Church Appointees," in *JSP,* J3:468, available at josephsmithpapers.org; Orson Hyde to "Dear Brethren," Mar. 27, 1846, Brigham Young Office Files, CHL.
24. Woodruff, Journal, Apr. 18, 1846; Joseph Smith to James J. Strang, June 18, 1845 [1844], in *Voree Herald,* Jan. 1846, [1]; Jensen, "Gleaning the Harvest," 4; 6, note 17; John E. Page to James J. Strang, Feb. 1, 1846, in *Voree Herald,* Apr. 1846, [6]–[7]; William Smith to "Brother Strang," Mar. 11, 1846, in *Voree Herald,* Apr. 1846, [7]. **Topic: Other Latter Day Saint Movements**
25. Woodruff, Journal, Apr. 18 and 20, 1846.
26. Mendenhall, Diary, Apr. 1–4, 1846; Samuel W. Richards, Journal, Apr. 22–29, 1846; Haight, Journal, Apr. 6, 1846; Morris, Autobiography, 40–41.
27. Samuel W. Richards, Journal, Apr. 23 and 29–30, 1846; Brigham Young, in *Journal of Discourses,* Jan. 1, 1877, 18:304; Lanman, *Summer in the Wilderness,* 31–33.
28. Barney, "Ruins of the Nauvoo Temple"; *JSP,* CFM:525, note 71.
29. Historian's Office, General Church Minutes, Thomas Bullock booklet no. 8, May 1, 1846.
30. Barney, "Ruins of the Nauvoo Temple"; Historian's Office, History of the Church, volume 15, May [1], 1846, 34; Scott, Journal, May 1, 1846; Woodruff, Journal, May 1 and 3, 1846.
31. Holzapfel and Cottle, "Visit to Nauvoo," 11. **Topic: Nauvoo Temple**
32. Louisa Barnes Pratt, Journal and Autobiography, 128–29; Addison Pratt to "My Dear Family," Jan. 6, 1846, Addison Pratt Family Collection, CHL.
33. Louisa Barnes Pratt, Journal and Autobiography, 129–33; see also Doctrine and Covenants 90:30–31; 109:59; 115:6; 124:36.
34. Louisa Barnes Pratt, Journal and Autobiography, 134; Parley P. Pratt, *Autobiography,* 381. Quotation edited for clarity; word "them" added.
35. Bennett, *Mormons at the Missouri,* 45. **Topic: Pioneer Trek**
36. Historian's Office, History of the Church, volume 15, June 28, 1846, 87–89; Brigham Young to William Huntington and Council, June 28, 1846, Brigham Young Office Files, CHL.
37. Orson Pratt, Journal, Feb. 1846; Mar. 6, 1846; June 19, 1846; see also Bennett, *Mormons at the Missouri,* 32–33.
38. Brigham Young to William Huntington and Council, June 28, 1846, Brigham Young Office Files, CHL.
39. "Conference Minutes," *Times and Seasons,* Nov. 1, 1845, 6:1011; Orson Pratt, Journal, Apr. 28–29, 1846; Brigham Young to Jesse Little, Jan. 20, 1846; Jesse Little to James K. Polk, June 1, 1846, Jesse C. Little Collection, CHL.
40. Historian's Office, History of the Church, volume 15, June 29–30, 1846, 89–90; Quaife, *Diary of James K. Polk,* 444–50; Brigham Young to "the High Council of the Church," Aug. 14, 1846, Brigham Young Office Files, CHL; see also Arrington, *Great Basin Kingdom,* 21. **Topic: Mexican-American War**
41. James Allen, Circular to the Mormons, June 26, 1846, copy; S. W. Kearny to James Allen, June 19, 1846, copy, Federal and Local Government Files, 1844–76, Brigham Young Office Files, CHL; Historian's Office, History of the Church, volume 16, July 1, 1846, 3–4; July 6, 1846, 22–23; July 13, 1846, 43–47; see also Grow, *Liberty to the Downtrodden,* 58–59. Final sentence of quotation edited for readability; original source has "I proposed that the five hundred volunteers be mustered, and I would do my best to see all their families brought forward, as far as my influence extended, and feed them when I had anything to eat myself." **Topics: Thomas L. and Elizabeth Kane; Mormon Battalion**
42. Hendricks, Reminiscences, 19–20, 26; see also *Saints,* volume 1, chapters 29 and 32.
43. "Minutes of a Meeting at Head Quarters Camp of Israel," Historian's Office, General Church Minutes, July 13, 1846; Historical Department, Journal History of the Church, July 13, 1846.
44. Hendricks, Reminiscences, 26–28.

CHAPTER 3: WORD AND WILL OF THE LORD

1. Woodruff, Journal, May 8–July 11 and July 18–19, 1846; Tyler, *Concise History of the Mormon Battalion,* 118, 124–26; Stephen Kearny to James Allen, June 19, 1846, 33, Stephen Watts Kearny, Papers, Missouri Historical Society, St. Louis; Fleek, *History May Be Searched in Vain,* 136, 142. **Topic: Mormon Battalion**

2. Woodruff, Journal, July 11, 1846; Tyler, *Concise History of the Mormon Battalion,* 115–16; Kane, *The Mormons,* 27–28; Grow, *Liberty to the Downtrodden,* 8, 59–61.

3. Church Historian's Office, History of the Church, volume 16, July 18, 1846, 86–88; Tyler, *Concise History of the Mormon Battalion,* 131.

4. Historian's Office, History of the Church, volume 16, July 20, 1846, 89–90; James Allen, Authorization, Aug. 9, 1846; Big Elk, Standing Elk, and Little Chief, Authorization, Aug. 31, 1846, Thomas L. Kane Collection, CHL.

5. Wilford Woodruff to Brigham Young, Oct. 1, 1845, Brigham Young Office Files, CHL; Woodruff, Journal, July 15, 1846; see also Givens and Grow, *Parley P. Pratt,* 251–52.

6. "War in Hancock," *Sangamo Journal,* June 25, 1846, 1; Jensen, "Gleaning the Harvest," 45–52; Historian's Office, History of the Church, volume 14, Oct. 6, 1845, 165.

7. Woodruff, Journal, July 15, 1846; Historian's Office, History of the Church, volume 16, July 17, 1846, 82.

8. Brigham Young to George Miller and Captains of Fifties, Aug. 1, 1846, copy, Brigham Young Office Files, CHL; Historian's Office, History of the Church, volume 16, July 20, 1846, 89–90; see also Grow, *Liberty to the Downtrodden,* 63–64.

9. Church Historian's Office, History of the Church, volume 16, Aug. 9, 1846, 136; Woodruff, Journal, Aug. 9, 1846.

10. Crocheron, "Ship *Brooklyn,*" 83; Tullidge, *Women of Mormondom,* 446; [Edward Kemble], "'Brooklyn Mormons' in California," *Sacramento Daily Union,* Sept. 11, 1866, 6; Horner, "Voyage of the Ship 'Brooklyn,'" 795–98; Dunbar, *Romance of the Age,* 44–45.

11. [Edward Kemble], "'Brooklyn Mormons' in California," *Sacramento Daily Union,* Sept. 11, 1866, 6.

12. Crocheron, "Ship *Brooklyn,*" 83; Hansen, "Voyage of the *Brooklyn,*" 63–67; [Edward Kemble], "'Brooklyn Mormons' in California," *Sacramento Daily Union,* Sept. 11, 1866, 6; Samuel Brannan, "To the Saints in England and America," *Latter-day Saints' Millennial Star,* Oct. 15, 1847, 9:306–7.

13. Samuel Brannan to "Brother Newell"; Samuel Brannan, "To the Saints in England and America," *Latter-day Saints' Millennial Star,* Oct. 15, 1847, 9:305–7.

14. Louisa Barnes Pratt, Journal and Autobiography, Aug.–Sept. 1846, 136–39. **Topic: Word of Wisdom (D&C 89)**

15. Plewe, *Mapping Mormonism,* 76–77; Louisa Barnes Pratt, Journal and Autobiography, Aug.–Sept. 1846, 139; see also Brigham Young to Samuel Brannan, June 6, 1847, Brigham Young Office Files, CHL; and Winter Quarters Municipal High Council Records, Aug. 27–28, 1846. **Topic: Winter Quarters**

16. Louisa Barnes Pratt, Journal and Autobiography, Aug.–Sept. 1846, 140; Lund, "Pleasing to the Eyes of an Exile," 122.

17. Louisa Barnes Pratt, Journal and Autobiography, Aug.–Sept. 1846, 139–40. **Topic: Word of Wisdom (D&C 89)**

18. Louisa Barnes Pratt, Journal and Autobiography, Aug.–Sept. 1846, 140; Nauvoo Relief Society Minute Book, Apr. 28, 1842, in Derr and others, *First Fifty Years of Relief Society,* 54–55. **Topic: Healing**

19. Louisa Barnes Pratt, Journal and Autobiography, Aug.–Sept. 1846, 140–41.

20. Lund, "Pleasing to the Eyes of an Exile," 118–27; Winter Quarters Municipal High Council Records, Jan. 21, 1848; Plat of the City of Zion, circa Early June–June 25, 1833, in *JSP,* D3:121–31.

21. Woodruff, Journal, Nov. 17–21, 1846; Historian's Office, History of the Church, volume 16, Aug. 7, 1846, 9–10.

22. Bennett, *Mormons at the Missouri,* 131–34; Lorenzo Dow Young, Diary, Sept. 21–26, 1846; Kane, *The Mormons,* 48; Louisa Barnes Pratt, Journal and Autobiography, Aug.–Sept. 1846, 139–40; Lee, Journal, Mar. 6, 1847.

23. Kimball and Godfrey, "Law and Order in Winter Quarters," 172–218; Woodruff, Journal, Dec. 20, 1846.

24. Woodruff, Journal, Dec. 20, 1846, and Feb. 16, 1847; see also Mary Richards to Samuel Richards, Jan. 29, 1847, Samuel W. Richards, Papers, 1837–1929, CHL.

25. Norton, Reminiscence and Journal, 44; Stout, Journal, Dec. 15, 1846; Willard Richards, Journal, Dec. 20, 1846, and Jan. 28, 1847; Stapley, "Adoptive Sealing Ritual in Mormonism," 62–74; see also Historian's Office, History of the Church, volume 17, Feb. 23, 1847, 56–57. **Topic: Sealing**

26. Bennett, *We'll Find the Place,* 58; Plewe, *Mapping Mormonism,* 75; Bennett, *Mormons at the Missouri,* 89–90, 134, 140–41; Lund, "Pleasing to the Eyes of an Exile," 128–29.

27. Woodruff, Journal, Oct. 15, 1846; Nov. 4 and 7–12, 1846; Dec. 8–11, 18, and 31, 1846; see also Winter Quarters Municipal High Council Records, Sept. 15, 1846.

28. James Whitehead to Brigham Young, Aug. 18, 1846, Brigham Young Office Files, CHL; George Alley to Joseph Alley, Jan. 26, 1847, George Alley, Letters, CHL; Mace, Autobiography, 138–45; "Articles of Accommodation Treaty Agreement," Sept. 16, 1846, Chicago Historical Society, Collection of Manuscripts about Mormons, CHL; Bullock, Journal, Sept. 1846; Historical Department, Journal History of the Church, Sept. 18, 1846; Leonard, *Nauvoo,* 606–16.

29. Historian's Office, History of the Church, volume 16, Sept. 24 and 27, 1846, 49, 51; Brigham Young to "the High Council at Council Point," Sept. 27, 1846, Brigham Young Office Files, CHL.

30. Historian's Office, History of the Church, volume 16, Sept. 14, 1846, 34; Sept. 27, 1846, 52; Oct. 5, 1846, 7–8; Oct. 6, 1846, 11.

31. Bullock, Journal, Oct. 9, 1846; Historian's Office, History of the Church, volume 16, Oct. 5 and 9, 1846, 7–8, 14–15.

32. Society Islands Conference Report, Sept. 24, 1846, in Historian's Office, Minutes and Reports (local units), CHL; Addison Pratt, Journal, Feb. 3, 1846; Sept. 24, 1846; Nov. 1850. In his November 1850 journal report, Addison appears to misidentify the date of the conference. **Topic: French Polynesia**

33. Addison Pratt, Journal, Mar. 5, 1846; Apr. 17, 1846; Nov. 14, 1846; Woodruff, Journal, Nov. 26, 1844.

34. Grouard, Journal, 145; see also Addison Pratt, Journal, Feb. 6, 1847.

35. Addison Pratt, Journal, Nov. 7, 1846.

36. Addison Pratt, Journal, Mar. 13 and 17, 1846; Nov. 14 and 17, 1846; Jan. 9, 1847; Addison Pratt to "My Dear Family," Jan. 6, 1846, Addison Pratt Family Collection, CHL; Grouard, Journal, 165–66.

37. Grouard, Journal, 172; Addison Pratt, Journal, Nov. 1850; Addison Pratt to "My Dear Family," Jan. 6, 1846, Addison Pratt Family Collection, CHL; see also Addison Pratt, Journal, Jan. 13, 1847.

38. Addison Pratt, Journal, Nov. 14–17, 1846.

39. Historian's Office, History of the Church, volume 17, Jan. 14, 1847, 18–19; Willard Richards, Journal, Jan. 14, 1847; see also Bennett, *Mormons at the Missouri,* 148–57. **Topic: Brigham Young**

40. Doctrine and Covenants 136:1–11 (Revelation, Jan. 14, 1847, Revelations Collection, CHL); Historian's Office, History of the Church, volume 17, Jan. 15, 1847, 19.

41. Doctrine and Covenants 136:4, 8, 19, 23–27, 32 (Revelation, Jan. 14, 1847, Revelations Collection, CHL).

42. Doctrine and Covenants 136:17, 21–22, 28–31 (Revelation, Jan. 14, 1847, Revelations Collection, CHL); see also Exodus 2:23–25; 4:31; 6:6–7; 15:1.

43. Historian's Office, General Church Minutes, Jan. 17, 1847; Willard Richards, Journal, Jan. 18, 1847; Mary Richards to Samuel Richards, Jan. 29, 1847, Samuel W. Richards, Papers, 1837–1929, CHL; see also Mary Richards, Diary, May 23, 1846.

44. Willard Richards, Journal, Jan. 17, 1847; Lee, Journal, Feb. 17, 1847; Woodruff, Journal, Jan. 16 and Feb. 16, 1847; see also Irving, "Law of Adoption," 296–303. **Topic: Sealing**
45. Historian's Office, History of the Church, volume 17, Feb. 23, 1847, 56–57; Stapley, "Adoptive Sealing Ritual in Mormonism," 62–74; Jessee, "Brigham Young's Family," 475–80.
46. Woodruff, Journal, Feb. 16, 1847.
47. Woodruff, Journal, Feb. 17, 1847; Brigham Young, Vision, Feb. 17, 1847, President's Office Files, Brigham Young Office Files, CHL; Historian's Office, History of the Church, volume 17, Feb. 23, 1847, 56–58. Regarding the final quoted sentence, the version of this quotation in the Brigham Young Office Files is missing the word "Lord"; the History of the Church version supplies that word.
48. Woodruff, Journal, Sept. 4, 1847; Historian's Office, History of the Church, volume 17, Mar. 6 and 21, 1847, 65–66, 72; Lee, Journal, Feb. 15 and 27, 1847; Council of the Twelve Apostles to "the Brethren at Winter Quarters," Apr. 16, 1847, Brigham Young Office Files, CHL; see also Doctrine and Covenants 136 (Revelation, Jan. 14, 1847, Revelations Collection, CHL).
49. Council of Fifty, "Record," Sept. 9, 1845, and Jan. 11, 1846, in *JSP,* CFM:472, 513.
50. Lee, Journal, Jan. 13, 1846, 79; George A. Smith, in *Journal of Discourses,* June 20, 1869, 13:85; Council of the Twelve Apostles to "the Brethren at Winter Quarters," Apr. 16, 1846, Brigham Young Office Files, CHL; Norton, Reminiscence and Journal, July 28, 1847; Erastus Snow, in *Journal of Discourses,* Sept. 14, 1873, 16:207; see also Thomas Bullock to Henrietta Rushton Bullock, June 9, 1847, Henrietta R. Bullock Collection, CHL.
51. Clayton, Diary, Apr. 16, 1847; Whitney, *History of Utah,* 1:300–302; Horace K. Whitney, Journal, Apr. 16, 1847; Young, "Woman's Experiences with the Pioneer Band," [4]; see also Lorenzo Dow Young, Diary, Sept. 24, 1847.
52. Erastus Snow, Journal, Apr. 8 and 12–13, 1847; Historian's Office, History of the Church, volume 17, Apr. 8 and 13, 1847, 81–83; Givens and Grow, *Parley P. Pratt,* 262–63.
53. Woodruff, Journal, Apr. 14–16, 1847; Clayton, Diary, Apr. 16, 1847; Council of the Twelve Apostles to "the Brethren at Winter Quarters," Apr. 16, 1847, Brigham Young Office Files, CHL.

CHAPTER 4: AN ENSIGN TO THE NATIONS

1. "S. Brannan's Letter," *Latter-day Saints' Millennial Star,* Oct. 15, 1847, 9:305; Morgan, *Overland in 1846,* 328–29; "Emigrants in the Mountains," *California Star,* Jan. 16, 1847, [2]; "Emigration to California," *Latter-day Saints' Millennial Star,* Sept. 1, 1847, 9:269; Orson Pratt, Journal, June 30, 1847. This wagon train was known as the Donner Party or the Donner-Reed Party. **Topic: Samuel Brannan**
2. "S. Brannan's Letter," *Latter-day Saints' Millennial Star,* Oct. 15, 1847, 9:305–6.
3. Horace K. Whitney, Journal, Apr. 17–May 10, 1847; see also Egan, Journal, Apr. 16, 1847. **Topic: Pioneer Trek**
4. Clayton, Diary, May 9 and 18, 1847; Woodruff, Journal, May 8 and 18, 1847.
5. Unruh, *Plains Across,* 9–14, 64–65, 168, 254; Woodruff, Journal, May 8, 1847; Clayton, Diary, May 9, 1847; Clayton, *Latter-day Saints' Emigrants' Guide,* 7–9. In mid-May, the advance company started following the North Platte River, a tributary of the Platte River.
6. Erastus Snow, in *Journal of Discourses,* Sept. 14, 1873, 16:207.
7. Clayton, Diary, May 11, 16, and 18, 1847.
8. Kimball, Journal, May 29, 1847.
9. Kimball, Journal, May 29, 1847; Bullock, Journal, May 29, 1847.
10. Kimball, Journal, May 30, 1847; see also Bullock, Journal, May 30, 1847.

11. Bennett, *Mormons at the Missouri,* 168–73, 255; Sessions, Diary, May 9, 1847.
    Topic: Winter Quarters
12. Notice, *Gospel Herald,* Sept. 23, 1847, 115; "Pastoral Letter," *Gospel Herald,* Feb. 3, 1848, [7]; "Voree," *Voree Herald,* Sept. 1846, [4]; Lee, Journal, May 7, 1847; Stout, Journal, Apr. 27 and 30, 1847; Clark, "Mormons of the Wisconsin Territory," 58–59.
13. Historian's Office, General Church Minutes, Apr. 25 and May 2, 1847; see also "Ecclesiastical Officers and Church Appointees," in *JSP,* J3:468, at josephsmithpapers .org. Quotation edited for readability; "had called" in original changed to "has called."
14. Council of the Twelve Apostles to "the Brethren at Winter Quarters," Apr. 16, 1847, Brigham Young Office Files, CHL; Woodruff, Journal, Jan. 18–19, 1847; Sept. 4, 1847.
15. Historical Department, Office Journal, June 15, 1847; Lee, Journal, Mar. 21, 1847; Bennett, *We'll Find the Place,* 252–56.
16. Historical Department, Office Journal, June 15, 1847; Whitney, Journal, Aug. 29, 1847; Historian's Office, General Church Minutes, June 6, 1847, [9]–[10]. **Topic: Parley P. Pratt**
17. Woodruff, Journal, May 27, 1847. **Topic: Wilford Woodruff**
18. Woodruff, Journal, May 13, 1847.
19. Woodruff, Journal, May–June 1847, especially entries for May 16 and 31; see also Clayton, Diary, May 15, 1847.
20. Woodruff, Journal, June 13, 1847.
21. Whitney, Journal, June 27–28, 1847; Clayton, Diary, June 27–28, 1847; Bullock, Journal, June 27–28, 1847; Jackman, Journal, June 27–28, 1847; Historian's Office, General Church Minutes, June 28, 1847; Norton, Reminiscence and Journal, June 28, 1847.
22. Thomas Bullock to Henrietta Rushton Bullock, June 9, 1847, Henrietta R. Bullock Collection, CHL; John Pack to Julia Ives Pack, June 8, 1847, John Pack, Papers, CHL; Erastus Snow, Journal, July 9 and 19, 1847; "Interesting Items," *Latter-day Saints' Millennial Star,* Jan. 15, 1850, 12:18; see also Esplin, "A Place Prepared," 81.
23. Woodruff, Journal, June 30–July 1, 1847; Whitney, Journal, June 30, 1847; Orson Pratt, Journal, June 30, 1847; George A. Smith to John Smith, July 3, 1847, John Smith, Papers, CHL; Brigham Young to Amasa Lyman and Charles C. Rich, July 3, 1847, copy, Brigham Young Office Files, CHL.
24. Erastus Snow, Journal, July 9, 1847; Amasa Lyman, Journal, July 7–9, 1847.
25. Louisa Barnes Pratt, Journal and Autobiography, 141, 143; Addison Pratt, Journal, Sept. 28, 1848. **Topic: Louisa Barnes Pratt**
26. Louisa Barnes Pratt, Journal and Autobiography, 144–45. **Topic: Gifts of the Spirit**
27. Jackman, Journal, June 23, 1847; July 7, 14, and 16–22, 1847; Lorenzo Dow Young, Diary, July 1, 1847; Woodruff, Journal, July 1 and 9, 1847.
28. Erastus Snow, Journal, July 3, 12, and 17–19, 1847; Orson Pratt, Journal, July 12–13, 1847; Clayton, Diary, July 13, 1847.
29. Erastus Snow, Journal, July 19, 1847. Quotation edited for clarity; original source has "Halt at the first suitable spot after reaching the Lake valley and put in our seed Potatoes, Buckwheat Turnips &c regardless of our final location."
30. Willard Richards and George A. Smith to Orson Pratt, July 21, 1847, Willard Richards, Journals and Papers, CHL.
31. Kimball, Journal, July 22–23, 1847; Jackman, Journal, July 20, 1847; Orson Pratt, Journal, July 22, 1847; Erastus Snow, Journal, July 21–22, 1847.
32. Woodruff, Journal, July 24, 1847.
33. Wilford Woodruff, in *Collected Discourses,* July 24, 1888, 1:163–64; Woodruff, Journal, July 24, 1847.
34. "Pioneers' Day," *Deseret Evening News,* July 26, 1880, [2]. **Topic: Salt Lake Valley**
35. Norton, Reminiscence and Journal, July 28, 1847; Jackman, Journal, July 28, 1847.
36. Woodruff, Journal, July 24–26, 1847; Wilford Woodruff, in *Collected Discourses,* Aug. 29, 1897, 5:314–15; Snow, "Autobiography of Erastus Snow," 112.

37. Woodruff, Journal, July 26, 1847; Wilford Woodruff, in *Collected Discourses,* Aug. 29, 1897, 5:314–15; July 24, 1888, 1:163–64; Clayton, Diary, July 26, 1847; see also Berrett, *Sacred Places,* 6:465–70.

38. Brigham Young, Discourse, Apr. 6, 1853, Church History Department Pitman Shorthand Transcriptions, CHL; see also Brigham Young, Apr. 6, 1853, Historian's Office, Reports of Speeches, CHL. **Topic: Salt Lake Temple**

39. Wilford Woodruff, in *Collected Discourses,* Dec. 13, 1893, 3:421; Aug. 29, 1897, 5:315; Woodruff, Journal, Dec. 30, 1846; Wilford Woodruff, in *Journal of Discourses,* Aug. 1, 1880, 21:299–300.

40. "History of Brigham Young," July 24, 1847, in Historian's Office, History of the Church, draft, CHL; Woodruff, Journal, July 26, 1847; Clayton, Diary, July 26, 1847.

41. See Council of Fifty, "Record," Apr. 18, 1844, in *JSP,* CFM:112.

42. Woodruff, Journal, July 26, 1847; Clayton, Diary, July 26, 1847; Isaiah 2:2; 11:12.

43. Walker, "A Banner Is Unfurled," 81–82.

CHAPTER 5: BOWED DOWN TO THE GRAVE

1. James, Autobiography, [6]; "List of Names of Isaac Haight's Ten of the 2nd Fifty," First 100, Second 50, Returns, June 1847, Camp of Israel, Schedules and Reports, CHL; Historical Department, Journal History of the Church, June 15, 1847; Bennett, *We'll Find the Place,* 253–55; see also Doctrine and Covenants 136 (Revelation, Jan. 14, 1847, Revelations Collection, CHL); Historian's Office, History of the Church, volume 17, Jan. 14–15, 1847, 18–19; Daniel Spencer/Ira Eldredge Company (1847) list; and Daniel Spencer/Perrigrine Sessions Company (1847) list, Pioneer Database, history.ChurchofJesusChrist.org/overlandtravel/companies.

2. James, Autobiography, [1]–[3], [6]; *Saints,* volume 1, chapter 41; Sessions, Diary, June 10, 1846. **Topic: Jane Elizabeth Manning James**

3. James, Autobiography, [7]; Diana E. Smoot, Autobiography, 1912, [2]–[5], available at Pioneer Database, history.ChurchofJesusChrist.org/overlandtravel.

4. "Able, Elijah," Biographical Entry, Joseph Smith Papers website, josephsmithpapers .org; Daniel Spencer/Ira Eldredge Company (1847) list, Pioneer Database, history .ChurchofJesusChrist.org/overlandtravel/companies; Historian's Office, General Church Minutes, Mar. 26, 1847. **Topic: Elijah Able**

5. Amasa Lyman, Journal, Apr. 8, 1847; Clayton, Diary, Apr. 16, 1847; Brown, *Autobiography of Pioneer John Brown,* 73; Bullock, Journal, Apr. 23, 1847, 17; Brigham Young Vanguard Company (1847) list, Pioneer Database, history .ChurchofJesusChrist.org/overlandtravel/companies; *Saints,* volume 1, chapter 42. For an example of a slaveholding Latter-day Saint, see Cummings, Reminiscences and Diary, June 14, 1847.

6. Doctrine and Covenants 101:79 (Revelation, Dec. 16–17, 1833, at josephsmithpapers .org); *Saints,* volume 1, chapter 16; "Free People of Color," *The Evening and the Morning Star,* July 1833, [5]; "To His Excellency, Daniel Dunklin," *The Evening and the Morning Star,* Dec. 1833, [2]; Joseph Smith to Oliver Cowdery, circa Apr. 9, 1836, in "For the Messenger and Advocate," *Latter Day Saints' Messenger and Advocate,* Apr. 1836, 2:[1]–[3]; Historical Introduction to Letter to Oliver Cowdery, circa Apr. 9, 1836, in *JSP,* D5:231–36; Staker, *Hearken, O Ye People,* 180–88; see also "Race and the Priesthood," Gospel Topics, topics.ChurchofJesusChrist.org.

7. James, Autobiography, [1], [3]–[7].

8. "A Short Chapter on a Long Subject," *Times and Seasons,* Apr. 1, 1845, 6:857; Historian's Office, General Church Minutes, Apr. 25, 1847, [3]; see also Reeve, *Religion of a Different Color,* 22–23, 125–26, 145–46; Hudson, *Real Native Genius,* 71, 137, 187; Haynes, *Noah's Curse,* 6–8; Council of Fifty, "Record," Mar. 22, 1845, in *JSP,* CFM:360;

The Evening and the Morning Star, Extra, July 16, 1833; Appleby, Autobiography and Journal, May 19, 1847; and Parley P. Pratt, *Autobiography,* 191.

9. Council of Fifty, "Record," Mar. 22, 1845, in *JSP,* CFM:359–60; Woodruff, Journal, Dec. 25, 1869.

10. Historian's Office, General Church Minutes, Mar. 26, 1847. Brigham Young accepted the notion that black skin was a sign of God's curse but refuted the idea that black skin was evidence of a person's unrighteous actions in the premortal life. (Woodruff, Journal, Dec. 25, 1869.) **Topic: Slavery and Abolition**

11. James, Autobiography, [6]–[8]; "Race and the Priesthood," Gospel Topics, topics .ChurchofJesusChrist.org.

12. Woodruff, Journal, July 27–28 and Aug. 25–26, 1847; see also Whitney, *History of Utah,* 1:351.

13. Woodruff, Journal, July 26–30, 1847.

14. Woodruff, Journal, July 28, 1847; see also Farmer, *On Zion's Mount,* 50; Clayton, Diary, July 31 and Aug. 11, 1847; and Woodruff, Journal, July 31 and Aug. 6, 1847.

15. Woodruff, Journal, Aug. 25, 1847; Historian's Office, General Church Minutes, Aug. 22, 1847.

16. Woodruff, Journal, June 30–July 1, 1847; Wilford Woodruff, in *Collected Discourses,* Aug. 29, 1897, 5:315.

17. Brigham Young, in *Journal of Discourses,* Sept. 13, 1857, 5:231; Brown, "Evidence of Inspiration," 269; Wilford Woodruff, in *Collected Discourses,* Aug. 29, 1897, 5:315; Brigham Young to "the Saints in California," Aug. 7, 1847, draft, Brigham Young Office Files, CHL.

18. Brigham Young to "the Saints in California," Aug. 7, 1847, draft, Brigham Young Office Files, CHL.

19. Woodruff, Journal, July 24, 1847; Aug. 25, 1847; Sept. 4, 1847; Council of the Twelve Apostles to "the Brethren at Winter Quarters," Apr. 16, 1847, Brigham Young Office Files, CHL; see also Historian's Office, General Church Minutes, Sept. 4, 1847, [2].

20. Addison Pratt, Journal, Feb. 6, 1847; Mar. 26–27, 1847; Apr. 6, 1847.

21. Addison Pratt, Journal, May 1847–Aug. 1848, [1]–[11].

22. Addison Pratt, Journal, May 1847–Aug. 1848, [11].

23. Addison Pratt, Journal, May 1847–Aug. 1848, [11]–[13]; Brigham Young to Jefferson Hunt and "the Officers and Soldiers of the 'Mormon Battalion,'" Aug. 7, 1847, Brigham Young Office Files, CHL; Tyler, *Concise History of the Mormon Battalion,* 315.

24. Kimball, Journal, Aug. 26–29, 1847; Historian's Office, General Church Minutes, Sept. 4, 1847, 5.

25. Kimball, Journal, Aug. 29, 1847; Woodruff, Journal, Aug. 29 and Sept. 4, 1847; John Taylor to Brigham Young, Aug. 18, 1847, Brigham Young Office Files, CHL; Historian's Office, General Church Minutes, Sept. 3, 1847, [1], [2]; Sept. 4, 1847, [2]–[3].

26. Woodruff, Journal, Sept. 4, 1847; Historian's Office, General Church Minutes, Sept. 4, 1847. **Topic: Parley P. Pratt**

27. Historian's Office, General Church Minutes, Sept. 4, 1847, [1]–[2]; Lee, Journal, Mar. 6 and 21, 1847; Pratt, "Parley P. Pratt in Winter Quarters," 378–79, 385–88; Historical Department, Office Journal, June 15, 1847; see also Council of the Twelve Apostles to "the Brethren at Winter Quarters," Apr. 16, 1847, Brigham Young Office Files, CHL.

28. Doctrine and Covenants 136 (Revelation, Jan. 14, 1847, Revelations Collection, CHL); Historian's Office, General Church Minutes, Sept. 4, 1847, [1]–[2]; Historical Department, Office Journal, June 15, 1847.

29. Historian's Office, General Church Minutes, Sept. 4, 1847, [1]–[2]; Historical Department, Office Journal, June 15, 1847. Final sentence of quotation edited for readability; "it is not your business" in original changed to "it was not your business." **Topic: Quorum of the Twelve**

30. Historian's Office, General Church Minutes, Sept. 4, 1847, [2]–[3]. Parley Pratt quotation edited for clarity; word "take" added.

31. Historian's Office, General Church Minutes, Sept. 4, 1847, 5–6.

32. Eliza R. Snow, Journal, Sept. 8, 1847; Hendricks, Reminiscences, 28; see also "Report of the 1st Fifty 3rd Hundred and 1st Devision Our Organization at the Horne June 19th 1847," Spring 1847 Emigration Camp, Camp of Israel, Schedules and Reports, CHL.

33. Eliza R. Snow, Journal, Aug. 4 and Sept. 2, 1847; see also Hendricks, Reminiscences, 28.

34. Eliza R. Snow, Journal, Sept. 14–Oct. 2, 1847, especially entries for Oct. 1 and 2; Hendricks, Reminiscences, 28.

35. Hendricks, Reminiscences, 28; Tyler, *Concise History of the Mormon Battalion,* 300–311.

36. Hendricks, Reminiscences, 28–29.

37. Woodruff, Journal, Oct. 1–13, 1847; Historian's Office, History of the Church, volume 17, Sept. 17 and 26, 1847, 115, 116; Oct. 13, 1847, 119.

38. See Historian's Office, General Church Minutes, Nov. 16, 1847.

39. Historian's Office, General Church Minutes, Aug. 8, 1844; *Proclamation of the Twelve Apostles,* 1; Doctrine and Covenants 107:22–24; 124:126–28 (Instruction on Priesthood, between circa Mar. 1 and May 4, 1835; Revelation, Jan. 19, 1841, at josephsmithpapers.org).

40. Historian's Office, General Church Minutes, Dec. 5, 1847, 8; Apr. 6, 1848, 2; see also Bennett, *Mormons at the Missouri,* 199–209; and Arrington, *Brigham Young,* 153–56.

41. Whitney, Journal, Oct. 12, 1847; Woodruff, Journal, Oct. 12, 1847. **Topic: First Presidency**

CHAPTER 6: SEVEN THUNDERS ROLLING

1. Minute Book 2, Apr. 12, 1838; Anderson, *Investigating the Book of Mormon Witnesses,* 37–48; Gunn, *Oliver Cowdery,* 18–19, 189, 219–20; Oliver Cowdery to Phineas Young, Dec. 18, 1845, Oliver Cowdery, Letters to Phineas H. Young, CHL; Oliver Cowdery to Brigham Young and others, Dec. 25, 1843, Brigham Young Office Files, CHL; "Cowdery, Oliver," Biographical Entry, Joseph Smith Papers website, josephsmithpapers.org; see also *Saints,* volume 1, chapters 6 and 26. **Topic: Oliver Cowdery**

2. Geauga County, OH, Probate Court, Marriage Records, 1806–1920, volume C–D, 1833–51, Sept. 26, 1834, microfilm 20,256, U.S. and Canada Record Collection, Family History Library; Phineas Young to Willard Richards and Brigham Young, Dec. 14, 1842, Brigham Young Office Files, CHL; Oliver Cowdery to Phineas Young, Feb. 14, 1847, Oliver Cowdery, Letters to Phineas H. Young, CHL; see also Oliver Cowdery, Letters to Phineas H. Young, 1843–49, CHL.

3. Oliver Cowdery to Phineas Young, Dec. 18, 1845; Oliver Cowdery to Phineas Young, Feb. 14, 1847, Oliver Cowdery, Letters to Phineas H. Young, CHL.

4. Phineas Young to Willard Richards and Brigham Young, Dec. 14, 1842; Oliver Cowdery to Brigham Young and others, Dec. 25, 1843, Brigham Young Office Files, CHL; see also Oliver Cowdery to Phineas Young, Mar. 23, 1846, CHL.

5. Oliver Cowdery to Phineas Young, Mar. 23, 1846, CHL.

6. Oliver Cowdery to David Whitmer, July 28, 1847; David Whitmer to Oliver Cowdery, Sept. 8, 1847, in "Important Letters," 91–92; see also *Saints,* volume 1, chapter 7.

7. David Whitmer to Oliver Cowdery, Sept. 8, 1847, in "Important Letters," 93.

8. See Oliver Cowdery to David Whitmer, July 28, 1847, in "Important Letters," 91–93.

9. Woodruff, Journal, Oct. 17–19 and 31, 1847; Historian's Office, History of the Church, volume 17, Oct. 31, 1847, 122.

10. Woodruff, Journal, Oct. 19, 1847; Stout, Journal, Oct. 3, 5–6, and 18–19, 1847.

11. Historian's Office, History of the Church, volume 17, Oct. 31, 1847, 121–22; Woodruff, Journal, Oct. 31, 1847.

12. Woodruff, Journal, Oct. 31, 1847; Historian's Office, History of the Church, volume 17, Oct. 31, 1847, 122; Helen Mar Whitney, "Scenes and Incidents at Winter Quarters," *Woman's Exponent,* Aug. 15, 1886, 15:46.

13. Woodruff, Journal, Aug. 2, 1846; Aug. 28, 1847; Oct. 31, 1847; July 22, 1848; Woodruff, Mary Ann Jackson Woodruff Biographical Sketch, [1]–[2]; James Jackson Woodruff, "Brief Sketch of the Life of James Jackson Woodruff," in *Chronicles of Courage,* 2:127–28.

14. Historian's Office, General Church Minutes, Dec. 5, 1847, 8–10; see also Woodruff, Journal, Nov. 1–20, 1847, especially entries for Nov. 8–10 and 13–16. **Topics: Quorum of the Twelve; First Presidency**

15. Doctrine and Covenants 107:23–31 (Instruction on Priesthood, between circa Mar. 1 and circa May 4, 1835, at josephsmithpapers.org); see also Parley P. Pratt, "Proclamation," *Latter-day Saints' Millennial Star,* Mar. 1845, 5:151; and Doctrine and Covenants 124:127–28 (Revelation, Jan. 19, 1841, at josephsmithpapers.org).

16. Historian's Office, General Church Minutes, Nov. 30, 1847, [3]–4; Dec. 5, 1847, 11; Doctrine and Covenants 107:22–24, 27–28 (Instruction on Priesthood, between circa Mar. 1 and circa May 4, 1835, at josephsmithpapers.org); see also Historian's Office, General Church Minutes, Nov. 16, 1847, [6]–7.

17. Historian's Office, General Church Minutes, Nov. 30, 1847, 4. Orson Pratt quotation edited for clarity; "feelings" in original changed to "feeling," and word "member" added.

18. Historian's Office, General Church Minutes, Dec. 5, 1847, 11.

19. Tanner, Autobiography and Diary, 29–30; Horne, "Pioneer Reminiscences," 293–94; James, Autobiography, [6].

20. John Smith, Journal, 53–54; Tanner, Autobiography and Diary, 30; Horne, "Pioneer Reminiscences," 294.

21. Tanner, Autobiography and Diary, 30; Horne, "Pioneer Reminiscences," 293; Horne, "Home Life in the Pioneer Fort," 182.

22. Eliza R. Snow, Journal, Nov.–Dec. 1847, especially entries for Nov. 2–7; see also *Saints,* volume 1, chapter 37.

23. James, Autobiography, [6]–[7]; Sessions, Diary, June 10, 1846; 1850 U.S. Census, Great Salt Lake Co., Great Salt Lake, Utah Territory, 111.

24. Tanner, Autobiography and Diary, 32; Horne, "Pioneer Reminiscences," 294.

25. Eliza R. Snow, Journal, Nov. 7, 1847.

26. Historical Department, Office Journal, Nov. 23, 1847; Historian's Office, History of the Church, volume 17, Nov. 22, 1847, 125; Minutes, Discourse, and Blessings, Feb. 14–15, 1835, in *JSP,* D4:219–34; Phineas Young to Willard Richards and Brigham Young, Dec. 14, 1842; Oliver Cowdery to Brigham Young, Dec. 25, 1843; Phineas Young to Brigham Young, Nov. 26, 1844, Brigham Young Office Files, CHL.

27. Historical Department, Office Journal, Nov. 23, 1847; Brigham Young to Oliver Cowdery, Nov. 22, 1847, copy; Oliver Cowdery to Brigham Young, Feb. 27, 1848, Brigham Young Office Files, CHL.

28. Historian's Office, General Church Minutes, Dec. 5, 1847, 8–10.

29. Historian's Office, General Church Minutes, Dec. 5, 1847, 9–11; see also Woodruff, Journal, Dec. 5, 1847.

30. Historian's Office, General Church Minutes, Dec. 5, 1847, 11.

31. Historian's Office, General Church Minutes, Dec. 5, 1847, 11–13.

32. Historian's Office, General Church Minutes, Dec. 5, 1847, 13–14.

33. See Bathsheba W. Smith, Autobiography, 19; Brigham Young and Orson Hyde, in *Journal of Discourses,* Oct. 7, 1860, 8:197, 234; "Thirty-Seventh Semi-annual Conference," *Deseret News,* Oct. 9, 1867, 1; Stout, Journal, Dec. 24, 1847; and Historian's Office, General Church Minutes, Dec. 5, 1847, 13–14.

34. Historian's Office, General Church Minutes, Dec. 5, 1847, 14.

35. Historian's Office, General Church Minutes, Dec. 24, 26, and 27, 1847, 2, 8, 13, 14; see also Woodruff, Journal, Dec. 24 and 27, 1847; and Historian's Office, Journal, Dec. 27, 1847.

36. Historian's Office, General Church Minutes, Dec. 24 and 27, 1847, 2, 14–17.
37. Historian's Office, General Church Minutes, Dec. 27, 1847, 18–19. **Topics: Brigham Young; First Presidency**

CHAPTER 7: KEEP UP GOOD COURAGE

1. Horne, "Home Life in the Pioneer Fort," 182–85; Horne, "Pioneer Reminiscences," 294.
2. "Smith, John," Biographical Entry, Joseph Smith Papers website, josephsmithpapers.org.
3. John Smith to George A. Smith, Mar. 5, 1848, John Smith, Papers, CHL; John Smith, Journal, 52–53.
4. John Smith and others to D. C. Davis and Jessee D. Hunter, Nov. 16, 1847, CHL; John Smith, Charles C. Rich, and John Young to Brigham Young, Oct. 14, 1847, Brigham Young Office Files, CHL.
5. John Smith to George A. Smith, Mar. 5, 1848, John Smith, Papers, CHL; John Smith, Journal, 53.
6. John Smith, Charles C. Rich, and John Young to Brigham Young, Oct. 14, 1847; Mar. 6, 1848, Brigham Young Office Files, CHL; see also Horne, "Home Life in the Pioneer Fort," 181–82; and Horne, "Migration and Settlement of the Latter Day Saints," 24.
7. John Smith, Charles C. Rich, and John Young to Brigham Young, Oct. 14, 1847, Brigham Young Office Files, CHL; John Smith to George A. Smith, Mar. 5, 1848, John Smith, Papers, CHL; John Smith, Charles C. Rich, and John Young to Brigham Young and Council, Mar. 6, 1848, Brigham Young Office Files, CHL.
8. John Smith and others to D. C. Davis and Jessee D. Hunter, Nov. 16, 1847, CHL; John Smith, Charles C. Rich, and John Young to Brigham Young and Council, Mar. 6, 1848, Brigham Young Office Files, CHL; see also Parley P. Pratt, "To President Orson Pratt, and the Saints in Great Britain," *Latter-day Saints' Millennial Star,* Jan. 15, 1849, 11:21–22.
9. John Smith, Charles C. Rich, and John Young to Brigham Young and Council, Mar. 6, 1848, Brigham Young Office Files, CHL; John Smith and others to D. C. Davis and Jessee D. Hunter, Nov. 16, 1847, CHL.
10. Bancroft, *History of California,* 56; see also Gudde, *Bigler's Chronicle of the West,* 110–11.
11. Notice, *California Star,* Mar. 18, 1848, [2]; Notice, *California Star,* Apr. 22, 1848, [2]; Bancroft, *History of California,* 44–57; Kemble, "Confirming the Gold Discovery," 538; Bigler, Reminiscences and Diaries, volume 1, 90; Rogers, *Colusa County,* 360.
12. Bancroft, *History of California,* 56; Hittell and Bigler, "Diary of H. W. Bigler in 1847 and 1848," 244–45; Sutter, *New Helvetia Diary,* 133–38; Borrowman, Diary, May 10 and 18, 1848; see also Gudde, *Bigler's Chronicle of the West,* 110–11. **Topic: California Gold Rush**
13. Addison Pratt, Journal, May–June 1848.
14. Whitney, *History of Utah,* 1:328; Whitney, "Pioneer Women of Utah," 404–5.
15. Lorenzo Dow Young, Diary, July 24, 1847.
16. Lorenzo Dow Young, Diary, Oct. 21, 1847; Mar. 1 and 15, 1848; Apr. 3, 1848; May 19 and 27, 1848; Whitney, "Pioneer Women of Utah," 406.
17. Lorenzo Dow Young, Diary, May 19, 1848.
18. Lorenzo Dow Young, Diary, May 27, 1848; Young, *Memoirs of John R. Young,* 64–65; Smith, *Rise, Progress and Travels,* 15; see also Hartley, "Mormons, Crickets, and Gulls," 227–29.
19. Lorenzo Dow Young, Diary, May 28–29, 1848; Rich, Autobiography and Journal, 2:48; Jesse N. Smith, Autobiography and Journal, 15–16; "Discourse," *Deseret News,* Dec. 1, 1880, [2]; Hartley, "Mormons, Crickets, and Gulls," 228–30; Young, *Memoirs of John R. Young,* 65.

20. Thomas Callister to George A. Smith, Feb. 13, 1869, Historian's Office, Correspondence Files, CHL; see also John Smith, Charles C. Rich, and John Young to Brigham Young and the Twelve Apostles, June 9, 1848, copy, Brigham Young Office Files, CHL.
21. Louisa Barnes Pratt, Journal and Autobiography, 145; Samuel Brannan and Addison Pratt to Brigham Young, Oct. 17, 1847, Brigham Young Office Files, CHL. **Topic: Louisa Barnes Pratt**
22. Samuel Brannan and Addison Pratt to Brigham Young, Oct. 17, 1847, Brigham Young Office Files, CHL.
23. See Louisa Barnes Pratt, Journal and Autobiography, 152.
24. Louisa Barnes Pratt, Journal and Autobiography, 145.
25. See Jessee, "Brigham Young's Family," 475–500. For information on the 1848 Brigham Young, Heber C. Kimball, and Willard Richards companies, see the company lists on the Pioneer Database, history.ChurchofJesusChrist.org/overlandtravel/companies.
26. Louisa Barnes Pratt, Journal and Autobiography, 146.
27. Thomas Callister to George A. Smith, Feb. 13, 1869, Historian's Office, Correspondence Files, CHL; Steele, Journal, June 4, 1848.
28. Thomas Callister to George A. Smith, Feb. 13, 1869, Historian's Office, Correspondence Files, CHL; John Smith, Charles C. Rich, and John Young to Brigham Young and the Twelve Apostles, June 9, 1848, copy, Brigham Young Office Files, CHL; Steele, Journal, June 4, 1848; Stewart, *California Trail,* 135–41; Haight, Journal, June 4, 1848; Gates and Widtsoe, *Life Story of Brigham Young,* 117–18; Young, *Memoirs of John R. Young,* 64.
29. Meeks, Journal, 17; Young, *Memoirs of John R. Young,* 64–65. **Topic: Crickets and Seagulls**
30. John Smith, Charles C. Rich, and John Young to Brigham Young and the Twelve Apostles, June 9, 1848, copy, Brigham Young Office Files, CHL; see also Rich, Autobiography and Journal, 2:48. Final sentence of quotation edited for clarity; word "is" added.
31. Haight, Journal, June 4, 1848; Spencer, Diary, July 2–3, 1848; Gates and Widtsoe, *Life Story of Brigham Young,* 117–18; Young, *Memoirs of John R. Young,* 64–66.
32. John Smith, Charles C. Rich, and John Young to Brigham Young, June 21, 1848, in Historian's Office, History of the Church, volume 18, July 20, 1848, 44–45; Rich, Autobiography and Journal, 2:48; Historical Department, Journal History of the Church, May 15, 1848; A. Lathrop to Brigham Young, May 18, 1848, Brigham Young Office Files, CHL.
33. Louisa Barnes Pratt, Journal and Autobiography, 146–50; Doctrine and Covenants 59:18.

CHAPTER 8: THIS TIME OF SCARCITY

1. Louisa Barnes Pratt, Journal and Autobiography, 151–52.
2. Addison Pratt, Journal, Sept. 1848–Nov. 1849, [7]–[9]; Louisa Barnes Pratt, Journal and Autobiography, 152.
3. Louisa Barnes Pratt, Journal and Autobiography, 152.
4. Addison Pratt, Journal, Sept. 1848–Nov. 1849, [9]; Louisa Barnes Pratt, Autobiography and Journal, 152.
5. Miller, Journal, Oct. 21, 1848; Hyde and others, "Report," Apr. 5, 1849, [4], Brigham Young Office Files, CHL; Oliver Cowdery to Phineas Young, Apr. 16, 1848, in Gunn, *Oliver Cowdery,* 255–57; Historian's Office, General Church Minutes, Apr. 7, 1847; Anderson, "Reuben Miller, Recorder of Oliver Cowdery's Reaffirmations," 291; Black, "Search for Early Members of the Church," 28–31; Geauga County, Ohio, Probate Court, Marriage Records, 1806–1920, volume C–D, 1833–51, Sept. 26, 1834, microfilm 20,256, U.S. and Canada Record Collection, Family History Library; Phineas Young to Willard Richards and Brigham Young, Dec. 14, 1842, Brigham Young Office Files,

CHL; Oliver Cowdery to Phineas Young, Feb. 14, 1847, Oliver Cowdery, Letters to Phineas H. Young, CHL; see also Oliver Cowdery, Letters to Phineas H. Young, 1843–49, CHL.

6. Miller, Journal, Oct. 21, 1848; Joseph Smith, Journal, June 27, 1839, in *JSP,* J1:343; see also Minutes, Discourse, and Blessings, Feb. 14–15, 1835, in *JSP,* D4:230.

7. Miller, Journal, Oct. 21, 1848; see also Hyde and others, "Report," Apr. 5, 1849, [4], Brigham Young Office Files, CHL; and Pottawattamie High Council, Minutes, Nov. 5, 1848.

8. Hyde and others, "Report," Apr. 5, 1849, [4]–[5], Brigham Young Office Files, CHL; Pottawattamie High Council, Minutes, Nov. 5, 1848; Pottawattamie High Priests Quorum, Minutes, Nov. 5, 1848; Miller, Journal, Nov. [5], 1848; Orson Hyde to Wilford Woodruff, Nov. 11, 1848, Wilford Woodruff, Journals and Papers, CHL; Reuben Miller to Henry Sabey, Nov. 16, 1848, CHL. **Topic: Oliver Cowdery**

9. Historian's Office, History of the Church, volume 19, July 6, 1849, 97; Rohrbough, *Days of Gold,* 16–20.

10. Historian's Office, History of the Church, volume 18, Oct. 1, 1848, 67. This entry in the Manuscript History of the Church is based on the General Church Minutes. Regarding the first quoted sentence, the General Church Minutes read "If we were to go to San Francisco and dig up chunks of gold it would ruin this people if it were to be found here in this valley." (Historian's Office, General Church Minutes, Oct. 1, 1848.) **Topic: California Gold Rush**

11. Historian's Office, General Church Minutes, Oct. 8, 1848; see also Historical Department, Journal History of the Church, Oct. 8, 1848.

12. "The Council of Fifty in Nauvoo, Illinois," in *JSP,* CFM:xliv; Lee, Journal, Dec. 9, 1848, in Cleland and Brooks, *Mormon Chronicle,* 1:80. **Topic: Council of Fifty**

13. "The Council of Fifty in Nauvoo, Illinois," in *JSP,* CFM:xliv; Lee, Journal, Dec. 9, 1848, in Cleland and Brooks, *Mormon Chronicle,* 1:80; Memorial for a Territorial Government, Dec. 16, 1848, Brigham Young Office Files, CHL; Ether 2:3; see also Crawley, "Constitution of the State of Deseret," 9.

14. See Crawley, "Constitution of the State of Deseret," 9; and Historical Department, Journal History of the Church, Jan. 1849.

15. First General Epistle, Apr. 1849, in Neilson and Waite, *Settling the Valley,* 66–67, 74–75; Joseph Fielding, Journal, 145; see also Haight, Journal, Dec. 9, 1848.

16. Brown, *Life of a Pioneer,* 121–23; Historian's Office, History of the Church, volume 19, Feb. 25, 1849, 23; Historian's Office, General Church Minutes, Feb. 25, 1849.

17. Lee, Journal, [Aug. 17, 1849], in Cleland and Brooks, *Mormon Chronicle,* 1:114; Heber C. Kimball, in *Journal of Discourses,* July 19, 1863, 10:247.

18. Eliza Partridge Lyman, Journal, Oct. 18, 1848.

19. Whitney, *History of Utah,* 1:384, 386; Arrington, *Great Basin Kingdom,* 66; see also Caroline Barnes Crosby, Journal, Nov. 28, 1849. **Topic: Salt Lake Valley**

20. Eliza Partridge Lyman, Journal, Oct. 18, 1848, and Apr. 8, 1849.

21. Haight, Journal, Dec. 9, 1848; Historian's Office, History of the Church, volume 19, Apr. 17, 1849, 67; Farmer, *On Zion's Mount,* chapters 1 and 2. **Topic: American Indians**

22. First General Epistle, Apr. 1849, in Neilson and Waite, *Settling the Valley,* 66, 76; Historian's Office, General Church Minutes, Nov. 26, 1848; Brigham Young to Isaac Higbee, Oct. 18, 1849, Brigham Young Office Files, CHL; see also Arrington, *Brigham Young,* 211–13.

23. Oliver Huntington, Diary, 50–75; Stout, Journal, Feb. 28, 1849; Mar. 1 and 5, 1849.

24. Eliza Partridge Lyman, Journal, Apr. 8, 1849; Historian's Office, History of the Church, volume 19, Mar. 26, 1849, 41–42; Brigham Young to Samuel Brannan, Apr. 5, 1849, copy, Brigham Young Office Files, CHL.

25. Eliza Partridge Lyman, Journal, Apr. 13 and 19, 1849; see also Whitney, *History of Utah,* 1:384, 386; and "Early Life in the Valley!," 9.

26. Eliza Partridge Lyman, Journal, Apr. 21 and 25, 1849; see also *Saints,* volume 1, chapters 40 and 41.

27. Eliza Partridge Lyman, Journal, Apr. 18 and 25, 1849; May 18–23 and 30, 1849.
28. Louisa Barnes Pratt, Journal and Autobiography, 153–54; see also *Saints,* volume 1, chapters 36, 37, 40, 42, and 46.
29. Louisa Barnes Pratt, Journal and Autobiography, 153–54; Addison Pratt, Journal, Sept. 1848–Nov. 1849, [19]–[21], [25].
30. Addison Pratt, Journal, Sept. 1848–Nov. 1849, [17]; Louisa Barnes Pratt, Journal and Autobiography, 153, 155.
31. Addison Pratt, Journal, Sept. 1848–Nov. 1849, [21]; Louisa Barnes Pratt, Journal and Autobiography, 155; Historical Department, Journal History of the Church, Oct. 2, 1849; Historian's Office, General Church Minutes, Oct. 6, 1849, 3; Historian's Office, History of the Church, volume 19, July 21, 1849, 107. **Topic: French Polynesia**
32. Historian's Office, History of the Church, volume 19, Oct. 8, 1849, 140; First General Epistle, Apr. 1849, in Neilson and Waite, *Settling the Valley,* 83, 88; "Character of the California Emigrants," *New York Herald,* Jan. 17, 1849, [2]; Hittell, *History of California,* 690–92; Madsen, *Gold Rush Sojourners,* 33–35; Bakken and Kindell, *Encyclopedia of Immigration and Migration in the American West,* 436–39. **Topic: California Gold Rush**
33. Historian's Office, General Church Minutes, Apr. 8, 1849; Harker, Reminiscences and Journal, 1849, 44; Johnson, "Life Review," 123; Morris, Autobiography, 61; Heber C. Kimball, in *Journal of Discourses,* July 19, 1863, 10:247.
34. Louisa Barnes Pratt, Journal and Autobiography, 155; Hovey, Autobiography, 193–94; Johnson, "Life Review," 123, 125; Sessions, Diary, Aug. 20, 1849; Morris, Autobiography, 62–64; Hancock, Autobiography, 44; Thissell, *Crossing the Plains in '49,* 104; see also Madsen, *Gold Rush Sojourners,* 53–62.
35. Addison Pratt, Journal, Sept. 1848–Nov. 1849, [21]–[23]; Louisa Barnes Pratt, Journal and Autobiography, 155.
36. Louisa Barnes Pratt, Journal and Autobiography, 155–59.
37. Addison Pratt, Journal, Sept. 1848–Nov. 1849, [21]–[23]; Louisa Barnes Pratt, Journal and Autobiography, 158–59; "Hunt, Jefferson," Biographical Entry, Joseph Smith Papers website, josephsmithpapers.org.
38. Louisa Barnes Pratt, Journal and Autobiography, 158–61.
39. Addison Pratt, Journal, Sept. 1848–Nov. 1849, [27]–[29]; Louisa Barnes Pratt, Journal and Autobiography, 160–62. **Topic: Louisa Barnes Pratt**

Chapter 9: As the Spirit Dictates

1. Historian's Office, General Church Minutes, Oct. 6, 1849, draft copy, 1. **Topic: Growth of Missionary Work**
2. Second General Epistle, Oct. 1849, in Neilson and Waite, *Settling the Valley,* 85–87; Plewe, *Mapping Mormonism,* 84–85, 88–89; Historian's Office, General Church Minutes, Feb. 14–16, 1849; Historian's Office, History of the Church, volume 19, Feb. 16 and 22, 1849, 20, 22; [Cannon], "Twenty Years Ago," 6–7; Whitney, *History of Utah,* 1:372, 376, 386, 399. **Topic: Pioneer Settlements**
3. Historian's Office, General Church Minutes, Oct. 6, 1849, [1]–[2]; Second General Epistle, Oct. 1849, in Neilson and Waite, *Settling the Valley,* 83–84; see also Hansen, Diary, Oct. 6, [1849]. The reorganization of the First Presidency in 1847 and the excommunication of apostle Lyman Wight in 1848 made room for additional men to be called into the apostleship.
4. Historian's Office, General Church Minutes, Oct. 6, 1849, [1]; "An Epistle of the Twelve," *Latter-day Saints' Millennial Star,* Aug. 15, 1849, 11:246. **Topic: Pioneer Trek**
5. Second General Epistle, Oct. 1849, in Neilson and Waite, *Settling the Valley,* 85, 87–88; [Cannon], "Twenty Years Ago," 13; Brigham Young, Heber C. Kimball, and

Willard Richards to Orson Hyde, Oct. 16, 1849, Brigham Young Office Files, CHL. **Topic: Emigration**

6. Historian's Office, General Church Minutes, Oct. 6, 1849; Second General Epistle, Oct. 1849, in Neilson and Waite, *Settling the Valley,* 85, 87–88.

7. See Brigham Young to Parley P. Pratt and others, July 17, 1848, Brigham Young Office Files, CHL; Historian's Office, History of the Church, volume 19, July 8, 1849, 100–102; and Bancroft, *History of Utah,* 303–4.

8. [Cannon], "Twenty Years Ago," 6–7, 13; "Cannon, George Quayle," Biographical Entry, First Fifty Years of Relief Society website, churchhistorianspress.org; Cannon, "George Q. Cannon," 209–10; Evans and Cannon, *Cannon Family Historical Treasury,* 89; "Hoagland, Elizabeth," Biographical Entry, Journal of George Q. Cannon website, churchhistorianspress.org. **Topic: George Q. Cannon**

9. Cannon, "George Q. Cannon," 208–10; Edward Hunter–Joseph Horne Company (1847) list; Allen Taylor Company (1849) list, Pioneer Database, history .ChurchofJesusChrist.org/overlandtravel/companies; "Lambert, Mary Alice Cannon," Biographical Entry, Journal of George Q. Cannon website, churchhistorianspress.org; Obituary for Angus M. Cannon, *Salt Lake Telegram,* June 7, 1915, 2.

10. George Q. Cannon, Journal, Oct. 6–7, 1849; [Cannon], "Twenty Years Ago," 13.

11. Evans and Cannon, *Cannon Family Historical Treasury,* 119.

12. George Q. Cannon, Journal, Jan. 3, 1851; Cannon, *My First Mission,* 1.

13. Historian's Office, General Church Minutes, Oct. 6, 1849; George Q. Cannon, Journal, Oct. 6, 1849.

14. George Q. Cannon, Journal, Oct. 7–9, 1849.

15. George Q. Cannon, Journal, Oct. 11–12, 1849; [Cannon], "Twenty Years Ago," 13, 22; Harker, Reminiscences and Journal, 44.

16. Louisa Barnes Pratt, Journal and Autobiography, 165; Louisa Pratt to Willard Richards, May 5, 1850, Willard Richards, Journals and Papers, CHL.

17. Louisa Barnes Pratt, Journal and Autobiography, 165–66.

18. Historian's Office, General Church Minutes, Apr. 7, 1850, [5]; Louisa Barnes Pratt, Journal and Autobiography, 166. Quotations edited for clarity; original source has "Here are a few appointments to the nations" and "Bro Thos Thompkins go to the Islands and take Bro Pratts family."

19. Louisa Barnes Pratt, Journal and Autobiography, 166, 168–69; Historian's Office, General Church Minutes, Apr. 8, 1850.

20. Hansen, Diary, Oct. 20, [1849]; Ashby, *Autobiography of Peter Olsen Hansen,* 73–75; Constitutional Act of Denmark, section 4. **Topic: Denmark**

21. "Genealogy and Biography," [4]–[16], in Hansen, Diary, circa 1850–72, folder 1; "Hansen, Peter Olsen," in Jenson, *Latter-day Saint Biographical Encyclopedia,* 2:766; Ashby, *Autobiography of Peter Olsen Hansen,* 26; Constitutional Act of Denmark, sections 67 and 70.

22. Ashby, *Autobiography of Peter Olsen Hansen,* 75–77; see also "Genealogy and Biography," [4], in Hansen, Diary, circa 1850–72, folder 1.

23. George Q. Cannon, Journal, Sept. 24, 1850; Rohrbough, *Days of Gold,* 14–15, 139–41; Morris, Journal, May 11, 1850.

24. George Q. Cannon, Journal, Sept. 29–Oct. 2, 1850; Bigler, Reminiscences and Diaries, Sept. 23 and 25, 1850; Morris, Journal, May 11, 1850; Stanley, "First Utah Coins," 244–46.

25. George Q. Cannon, Journal, Sept. 24 and Sept. 28–Oct. 2, 1850; Bigler, Reminiscences and Diaries, Sept. 23 and 25, 1850.

26. Bigler, Reminiscences and Diaries, Sept. 25, 1850; see also George Q. Cannon, Journal, Sept. 24, 1850.

27. George Q. Cannon, Journal, Sept. 24, 1850; Bigler, Reminiscences and Diaries, Sept. 25, 1850; Rohrbough, *Days of Gold,* 87, 218, 224–26; Cannon, "George Q. Cannon," 368.

28. Bigler, Reminiscences and Diaries, Sept. 25, 1850. Quotation edited for readability; original source has "He told us that when we arrived at the islands to act as the spirit dictated in regard to our duties."

29. George Q. Cannon, Journal, Sept. 25–Oct. 16, 1850; Bigler, Reminiscences and Diaries, Sept. 25–Oct. 16, 1850.
30. George Q. Cannon, Journal, Oct. 18 and Nov. 10, 1850; Cannon, *My First Mission,* 2. Quotation edited for readability; original source has "I was in the harness and it would not do for me to baulk so I stepped forward. I spoke upon truth how professedly anxious the world were to get hold of truth. . . . Said how thankful we ought to be that we were in possession of it and of the principle whereby we might progress from one truth to another."
31. Louisa Barnes Pratt, Journal and Autobiography, 183–86; Oct. 19, 1850; Caroline Barnes Crosby, Journal, Sept. 15–Oct. 19, 1850.
32. Caroline Barnes Crosby, Journal, Oct. 19–21, 1850; Louisa Barnes Pratt, Journal and Autobiography, 185–87.
33. Louisa Barnes Pratt, Journal and Autobiography, 187–88; see also Ellsworth, *History of Louisa Barnes Pratt,* 126; and *Saints,* volume 1, chapter 46.
34. Louisa Barnes Pratt, Journal and Autobiography, 187–89; Caroline Barnes Crosby, Journal, Oct. 21, 1850; Ellsworth, *History of Louisa Barnes Pratt,* 126.
35. George Q. Cannon, Journal, Dec. 13–14 and 16, 1850; Cannon, *My First Mission,* 10–11. **Topic: Hawaii**
36. Cannon, *My First Mission,* 12; Perkins, *Na Motu,* 93–94.
37. Cannon, *My First Mission,* 14; see also Bigler, Reminiscences and Diaries, Sept. 25, 1850.
38. George Q. Cannon and others to Brigham Young, Apr. 19, 1857, Brigham Young Office Files, CHL.
39. Cannon, *My First Mission,* 15; George Q. Cannon, Journal, Dec. 20–27, 1850, and January 6–22, 1851; Keeler, Journal, Dec. 10 and 24–27, 1850; Jan. 1–4 and 20–29, 1851. **Topic: Gift of Tongues**

CHAPTER 10: TRUTH AND RIGHTEOUSNESS

1. George Q. Cannon, Journal, Mar. 2–8, 1851; Cannon, *My First Mission,* 23, 26; A Häolé, *Sandwich Island Notes,* 310.
2. George Q. Cannon, Journal, Mar. 8, 1851; Cannon, *My First Mission,* 26–27.
3. George Q. Cannon, Journal, Mar. 8, 1851; Cannon, *My First Mission,* 26–27; "Napela, Jonathan (Ionatana) Hawaii," Biographical Entry, Journal of George Q. Cannon website, churchhistorianspress.org; see also A Häolé, *Sandwich Island Notes,* 303–6. In contemporary sources, Jonathan Napela is usually referred to by his last name. **Topic: Jonathan Napela**
4. George Q. Cannon, Journal, Mar. 9, 1851. Quotation edited for readability; original source has "I told him [that] I told Mr. Conde [a Protestant missionary] that we did not take the Book of M. for the Bible, but proved one by the other."
5. George Q. Cannon, Journal, Mar. 9–10, 1851; Cannon, *My First Mission,* 28–29; see also 1 Thessalonians 5:21.
6. Brigham Young to John Bernhisel and Almon Babbitt, Sept. 10, 1850, Brigham Young Office Files, CHL; Grow, *Liberty to the Downtrodden,* 54, 81.
7. *Constitution of the State of Deseret* (Salt Lake City: Publisher unidentified, 1850); Crawley, "Constitution of the State of Deseret," 11–17; Walker, "Thomas L. Kane and Utah's Quest for Self-Government," 111–14.
8. Oliver Cowdery to Phineas H. Young, Sept. 1849, Oliver Cowdery, Letters to Phineas H. Young, CHL; Phineas H. Young to Brigham Young, Apr. 25, 1850, Brigham Young Office Files, CHL; see also Faulring, "Return of Oliver Cowdery," 152–53.
9. An Act to Establish a Territorial Government for Utah [Sept. 9, 1850], *Acts, Resolutions, and Memorials . . . of the Territory of Utah,* 27–36; John Bernhisel to Brigham Young, Aug. 9, 1850; Sept. 12, 1850; Oct. 2, 1850; Nov. 9, 1850, Brigham Young Office Files, CHL; Whitney, *History of Utah,* 1:442–51; see also "An Act," *Deseret News,* Nov. 30,

1850, [1]–[4]; and John Bernhisel to the First Presidency, Mar. 21, 1850, Brigham Young Office Files, CHL. **Topics: Utah; American Legal and Political Institutions**

10. *Three Letters to the New York Herald, from J. M. Grant,* 3–9; Harris, *Unwritten Chapter of Salt Lake,* 13–15, 30–31.

11. *Saints,* volume 1, chapters 25 and 36; Doctrine and Covenants 132:30–31, 55, 63 (Revelation, July 12, 1843, at josephsmithpapers.org); "Plural Marriage in Kirtland and Nauvoo," Gospel Topics, topics.ChurchofJesusChrist.org. **Topic: Joseph Smith and Plural Marriage**

12. See *Utah Message from the President of the United States,* 5; Harris, *Unwritten Chapter of Salt Lake,* 34–40; and Walker, "Affair of the 'Runaways,'" 15–18.

13. "Celebration of the Twenty-Fourth of July, 1851," *Deseret News,* Aug. 19, 1851, 305–6; "Report of Messrs. Brandebury, Brocchus, and Harris," Message from the President of the United States, H.R. Ex. Doc. 25, 32nd Cong., 1st Sess., 10–11 (1852).

14. "Report of Messrs. Brandebury, Brocchus, and Harris," Message from the President of the United States, H.R. Ex. Doc. 25, 32nd Cong., 1st Sess., 10–11 (1852); Brigham Young, "Beating against the Air," Report to Millard Fillmore, June 11, 1852, 25–26, Brigham Young Office Files, CHL; *Three Letters to the New York Herald, from J. M. Grant,* 8; Minutes, Sept. 14, 1851, Communications with Perry E. Brocchus, 1851–52, Brigham Young Office Files, CHL; Historian's Office, Journal, Aug. 17, 1851.

15. Judge Perry Brocchus and Brigham Young, Remarks, Sept. 8, 1851, Church History Department Pitman Shorthand Transcriptions, CHL; Woodruff, Journal, Sept. 8, 1851; Jedediah M. Grant, "Defence of the Mormons," *Deseret News,* May 15, 1852, [4].

16. Jedediah M. Grant, "Defence of the Mormons," *Deseret News,* May 15, 1852, [4].

17. Woodruff, Journal, Sept. 8, 1851; Jedediah M. Grant, "Defence of the Mormons," *Deseret News,* May 15, 1852, [4]; Judge Perry Brocchus and Brigham Young, Remarks, Sept. 8, 1851, Church History Department Pitman Shorthand Transcriptions, CHL. First sentence of quotation edited for readability; "have not injured you" in original changed to "has not injured you."

18. Jedediah M. Grant, "Defence of the Mormons," *Deseret News,* May 15, 1852, [4]; "Report of Messrs. Brandebury, Brocchus, and Harris," Message from the President of the United States, H.R. Ex. Doc. 25, 32nd Cong., 1st Sess., 15 (1852).

19. Jedediah M. Grant, "Defence of the Mormons," *Deseret News,* May 15, 1852, [4]; Judge Perry Brocchus and Brigham Young, Remarks, Sept. 8, 1851, Church History Department Pitman Shorthand Transcriptions, CHL; see also Woodruff, Journal, Sept. 8, 1851.

20. Addison Pratt, Journal, Sept. 10 and Nov. 11, 1850. **Topic: French Polynesia**

21. Addison Pratt, Journal, Nov. 11, 1850, and Jan. 28–Feb. 3, 1851; Louisa Barnes Pratt, Journal and Autobiography, [Dec. 1850] and Jan. 1851, 194–95. Louisa Pratt quotation edited for readability; original source has "my wife told me that she had been brought down to the verge of the grave by seasickness on the passage from California, but was now in good health & spirits."

22. Louisa Barnes Pratt, Journal and Autobiography, 222; [Dec. 1850]; Mar. 1, 1851; Caroline Barnes Crosby, Journal, July 20, 1851.

23. Louisa Barnes Pratt, Journal and Autobiography, [Dec. 1850] and Sept. 6, 1851; Caroline Barnes Crosby, Journal, [Oct. 1850]; Doctrine and Covenants 27:2.

24. Louisa Barnes Pratt, Journal and Autobiography, 261; Caroline Barnes Crosby, Journal, May 1851; Addison Pratt, Journal, May 4 and June 21, 1851.

25. Louisa Barnes Pratt, Journal and Autobiography, Sept. 8 and 15, 1851; Addison Pratt, Journal, May 4, 1851.

26. John Bernhisel to Brigham Young, Dec. 5, 1851, Brigham Young Office Files, CHL; "Latter Day Saints and the Government—Practical Nullification," *New York Herald,* Nov. 8, 1851, [4]; "Mormon Difficulties," *New York Herald,* Nov. 14, 1851, [2]; "Outrages at the Salt Lake," *Burlington Hawk-Eye,* Nov. 27, 1851, [3]; "Report of Messrs. Brandebury, Brocchus, and Harris," Message from the President of the United States, H.R. Ex. Doc. 25, 32nd Cong., 1st Sess., 5 (1852); see also Walker and Grow,

"National Reaction to Utah's 'Runaway' Officers," 1–52; and Walker, "Affair of the 'Runaways,'" 35–43.

27. Harris, *Unwritten Chapter of Salt Lake,* 55–56; Brigham Young to Perry Brocchus, Sept. 19, 1851, draft; Perry Brocchus to Brigham Young, Sept. 19, 1851, Brigham Young Office Files, CHL; "Extract of a Letter," Message from the President of the United States, H.R. Ex. Doc. 25, 32nd Cong., 1st Sess., 5–6 (1852); see also Brigham Young to Perry Brocchus, Sept. 20, 1851, draft, Brigham Young Office Files, CHL.

28. News item, *Deseret News,* Feb. 7, 1852, [3]; Historical Department, Office Journal, Sept. 13, 1851, 309; First Presidency to Thomas Kane, Sept. 15, 1851, Brigham Young Office Files, CHL; Willard Richards to Thomas Kane, Sept. 30, 1851, Thomas L. Kane Personal Papers, Kane Family Papers, Brigham Young University; see also Walker, "Affair of the 'Runaways,'" 37. **Topic: Thomas L. and Elizabeth Kane**

29. Historical Department, Office Journal, Sept. 28, 1851, 324; "From the Territory of Utah," *Daily Union,* Nov. 16, 1851, [3]; "Latter Day Saints and the Government— Practical Nullification," *New York Herald,* Nov. 8, 1851, [4]; John Bernhisel to Brigham Young, Mar. 10, 1852, Brigham Young Office Files, CHL; see also "Movements at Washington," *Vermont Watchman and State Journal,* Dec. 4, 1851, 1; and Walker and Grow, "National Reaction to Utah's 'Runaway' Officers," 2–5.

30. John Bernhisel to Millard Fillmore, Dec. 1, 1851; John Bernhisel to Brigham Young, Dec. 8, 1851, Brigham Young Office Files, CHL; Walker and Grow, "National Reaction to Utah's 'Runaway' Officers," 15–18.

31. Jedediah Grant to Susan Noble Grant, Mar. 7, 1852, Susan N. Grant Correspondence, CHL; John Bernhisel to Brigham Young, Mar. 10, 1852; John Bernhisel to Brigham Young, Apr. 9, 1852; John Bernhisel to Brigham Young, Jan. 10, 1852, Brigham Young Office Files, CHL; "Report of Messrs. Brandebury, Brocchus, and Harris," Message from the President of the United States, H.R. Ex. Doc. 25, 32nd Cong., 1st Sess., 8–9 (1852).

32. Jedediah Grant to Brigham Young, Dec. 30, 1851, Brigham Young Office Files, CHL; see also Jedediah Grant to Thomas Kane, Dec. 29, 1851, Thomas L. Kane Personal Papers, Kane Family Papers, Brigham Young University; see also Walker and Grow, "National Reaction to Utah's 'Runaway' Officers," 22–23.

33. Thomas Kane, Journal, Dec. 27–28, 1851; Thomas Kane to John Bernhisel, Dec. 29, 1851, draft, Thomas L. Kane Personal Papers, Kane Family Papers, Brigham Young University; see also Thomas Kane to Brigham Young, July 11, 1850, Brigham Young Office Files, CHL; "An Interesting Statement—the Mormons," *Frontier Guardian,* Sept. 5, 1851, [1]; and Walker and Grow, "National Reaction to Utah's 'Runaway' Officers," 23–24.

34. Walker and Grow, "National Reaction to Utah's 'Runaway' Officers," 22–25; Kane, Journal, Dec. 29, 1851; Thomas Kane to Brigham Young, Oct. 17, 1852; Jedediah Grant to Brigham Young, Dec. 30, 1851, Brigham Young Office Files, CHL.

35. Thomas Kane to Brigham Young, Oct. 17, 1852, Brigham Young Office Files, CHL; Thomas Kane to John Bernhisel, Dec. 29, 1851, draft, Thomas L. Kane Personal Papers, Kane Family Papers, Brigham Young University.

36. Thomas Kane to John Bernhisel, Dec. 29, 1851, draft, Thomas L. Kane Personal Papers, Kane Family Papers, Brigham Young University. **Topic: Plural Marriage in Utah**

37. Louisa Barnes Pratt, Journal and Autobiography, 212–14, 218, 220; Caroline Barnes Crosby, Journal, Oct. 21 and 30, 1851; Jan. 1, 1852.

38. Louisa Barnes Pratt, Journal and Autobiography, 223–37; Caroline Barnes Crosby, Journal, Nov. 30 and Dec. 10, 1851; Brown, *Life of a Pioneer,* 225–39; Addison Pratt, Journal, Dec. 19, 1851, and Jan. 9, 1852.

39. Louisa Barnes Pratt, Journal and Autobiography, 261–63, 266–67.

40. Louisa Barnes Pratt, Journal and Autobiography, 266; Caroline Barnes Crosby, Journal, Mar. 9–Apr. 1, 1852.

41. Louisa Barnes Pratt, Journal and Autobiography, 267–68; Caroline Barnes Crosby, Journal, Apr. 6, 1852; Addison Pratt, Journal, Apr. 1852. Louisa Pratt quotation edited for readability; original source has "I told them to be comforted, I would pray that

some future time they might come to the church of Christ in America. Even to Zion in the valley of the Rocky Mountains!"

42. Historical Department, Office Journal, Aug. 8 and 15, 1852; Grow, *Liberty to the Downtrodden,* 89–91; see also Minutes, *Deseret News,* Extra, Sept. 14, 1852, 25; and "A Brief History of the Federal Courts and Judges," *Deseret News,* May 27, 1863, [4].

43. Minutes, *Deseret News,* Extra, Sept. 14, 1852, 2, 10; see also Aaron F. Farr to George A. Smith, June 2, 1865, Missionary Reports, CHL; Robert Harrison to John Bernhisel, Feb. 3, 1853, Utah Delegate Files, Brigham Young Office Files, CHL. **Topic: Early Missionaries**

44. Minutes, *Deseret News,* Extra, Sept. 14, 1852, 2.

45. Minutes, *Deseret News,* Extra, Sept. 14, 1852, 14–22, 25; Whittaker, "Bone in the Throat," 303–4. **Topic: Plural Marriage in Utah**

46. Orson Pratt, Discourse, Aug. 29, 1852, [1], Church History Department Pitman Shorthand Transcriptions, CHL; Minutes, *Deseret News,* Extra, Sept. 14, 1852, 14–15.

47. Orson Pratt, Discourse, Aug. 29, 1852, [1]–[34], especially [19]–[28], Church History Department Pitman Shorthand Transcriptions, CHL; see also Minutes, *Deseret News,* Extra, Sept. 14, 1852, 14–22; Jacob 2:30; Genesis 16:1–3; and "Plural Marriage in The Church of Jesus Christ of Latter-day Saints," and "Plural Marriage in Kirtland and Nauvoo," Gospel Topics, topics.ChurchofJesusChrist.org.

48. Orson Pratt, Discourse, Aug. 29, 1852, [1], [16]–[27], Church History Department Pitman Shorthand Transcriptions, CHL; see also Minutes, *Deseret News,* Extra, Sept. 14, 1852, 14, 18–21.

49. Orson Pratt, Discourse, Aug. 29, 1852, [27]–[33], Church History Department Pitman Shorthand Transcriptions, CHL; Doctrine and Covenants 132:7, 45–48 (Revelation, July 12, 1843, at josephsmithpapers.org); see also Minutes, *Deseret News,* Extra, Sept. 14, 1852, 20–22.

50. Orson Pratt, Discourse, Aug. 29, 1852, [33]–[34], Church History Department Pitman Shorthand Transcriptions, CHL; Minutes, *Deseret News,* Extra, Sept. 14, 1852, 22.

51. Brigham Young, Discourse, Aug. 29, 1852, Church History Department Pitman Shorthand Transcriptions, CHL; Minutes, *Deseret News,* Extra, Sept. 14, 1852, 22–25; see also *Saints,* volume 1, chapter 14; and Doctrine and Covenants 76 (Vision, Feb. 16, 1832, at josephsmithpapers.org). **Topic: The Vision (D&C 76)**

52. Brigham Young, Discourse, Aug. 29, 1852, Church History Department Pitman Shorthand Transcriptions, CHL; Minutes, *Deseret News,* Extra, Sept. 14, 1852, 22–25.

53. Minutes, *Deseret News,* Extra, Sept. 14, 1852, 25.

54. Minutes, *Deseret News,* Extra, Sept. 14, 1852, 25–28; Doctrine and Covenants 132 (Revelation, July 12, 1843, at josephsmithpapers.org); Stout, Journal, Aug. 29, 1852; Woolley, Diary, Aug. 29, 1852.

55. Stout, Journal, Aug. 29, 1852; Historian's Office, General Church Minutes, Aug. 29, 1852, 9. **Topic: Growth of Missionary Work**

Chapter 11: A Glorious Privilege

1. Ann Eliza Logan Secrist to Jacob F. Secrist, Sept. 29, 1852; Jacob F. Secrist, "For the Satisfaction of My Wife and Children," Dec. 3, 1853, [1], Jacob F. Secrist Collection, CHL.

2. Jacob F. Secrist, "For the Satisfaction of My Wife and Children," Dec. 3, 1853, [1], Jacob F. Secrist Collection, CHL; Minutes, *Deseret News,* Extra, Sept. 14, 1852, 10.

3. Ann Eliza Logan Secrist to Jacob F. Secrist, Sept. 29, 1852, Jacob F. Secrist Collection, CHL; "Anne Eliza Secrist," in Soule, "Exerps from a History," [1]; Effie Secrist Miller, "History of Jacob Foutz Secrist," [1], Jacob F. Secrist Family Papers, CHL; see also letters between Jacob F. Secrist and Ann Eliza Logan Secrist, 1841–42, in the

Jacob F. Secrist Collection, CHL; and Ann Eliza Logan Secrist to Jacob F. Secrist, May 30 and Nov. 21, 1853, Jacob F. Secrist Collection, CHL.

4. Ann Eliza Logan Secrist to Jacob F. Secrist, Sept. 29, 1852; Jacob F. Secrist to Ann Eliza Logan Secrist, July 26, 1853, Jacob F. Secrist Collection, CHL. First sentence of quotation edited for clarity; "half" in original changed to "a half."

5. McBride, "Utah Mail Service before the Coming of the Railroad," 15–31; Jacob F. Secrist, "For the Satisfaction of My Wife and Children," Dec. 3, 1853, [8]–[9], Jacob F. Secrist Collection, CHL; see also Ann Eliza Logan Secrist to Jacob F. Secrist, Oct. 30, 1852; May 30, 1853, Jacob F. Secrist Collection, CHL.

6. Dorius, Autobiography and Journal, [1]; Jensen, "Diary of J. F. Ferdinand Dorius," [1], 34. Johan appears to have started going by the name John (the anglicized version of Johan) at some point after immigrating to the United States. **Topic: Denmark**

7. Jensen, "Diary of J. F. Ferdinand Dorius," 2, 4–8, 15; see also Stevens, Autobiography, 1.

8. Van Orden, *Building Zion,* 56; Crawley, *Descriptive Bibliography,* 2:213–16, 251–54.

9. Stevens, Autobiography, 1–2; Jensen, "Diary of J. F. Ferdinand Dorius," 4–8, 19; Dorius, "Sketch of the Life," 6.

10. Jensen, "Diary of J. F. Ferdinand Dorius," 34.

11. Mulder, *Homeward to Zion,* 41–44.

12. Jensen, "Diary of J. F. Ferdinand Dorius," 34–36; Dorius, "Sketch of the Life," 18.

13. Jensen, "Diary of J. F. Ferdinand Dorius," 36; Dorius, *Dorius Heritage,* 35–36; Dorius, "Sketch of the Life," 18–19; "Thure, Soren Christensen," Andrew Jenson Collection, CHL; Woodruff, Journal, Sept. 24, 1868. Quotation of mobbers edited for readability; original source has "They said they would show this Mormon Priest how to baptize."

14. Jensen, "Diary of J. F. Ferdinand Dorius," 36; Dorius, "Sketch of the Life," 18–19; Dorius, *Dorius Heritage,* 35–37. Quotation edited for readability; "This was" in original changed to "This is," and "were intended" in original changed to "are intended."

15. Stevens, Autobiography, 1, 4–5; Butler, "Short History," 67–68; Eli B. Kelsey Company (1852) list, Pioneer Database, history.ChurchofJesusChrist.org/overlandtravel /companies; see also Burton, *City of the Saints,* 169–70.

16. Stevens, Autobiography, 1–2, 4–5; Jenson, "Scandinavian Mission," 813; see also Eli B. Kelsey Company (1852) list, Pioneer Database, history.ChurchofJesusChrist.org /overlandtravel/companies.

17. Stevens, Autobiography, 1–2, 4–5; Jensen, "Diary of J. F. Ferdinand Dorius," 19.

18. Butler, "Short History," 70–71; Clayton, *Latter-day Saints' Emigrants' Guide,* 17–20.

19. Stevens, Autobiography, 4–5. **Topic: Pioneer Trek**

20. George Q. Cannon, Journal, Nov. 8, 1852; Cannon, *My First Mission,* 59. First sentence of quotation edited for readability; "writing" in original changed to "in writing." **Topics: George Q. Cannon; Hawaii**

21. George Q. Cannon, Journal, Jan. 5, 1852; see also entry for Mar. 8, 1851. **Topic: Jonathan Napela**

22. George Q. Cannon, Journal, May 11 and 22, 1851; Aug. 13–18, 1851; Dec. 12, 1851; Cannon, *My First Mission,* 31, 42–43.

23. Cannon, *My First Mission,* 58–61; Woods, "Jonathan Hawaii Napela," 136–37.

24. George Q. Cannon, Journal, Nov. 11–13, 1852. **Topic: Plural Marriage in Utah**

25. George Q. Cannon, Journal, Nov. 11 and 23, 1852.

26. George Q. Cannon, Journal, Nov. 29, 1852.

27. See Biography of Anne K. Smoot, 1, 5–7; and Ulvund, "Perceptions of Mormonism in Norway," 208–11, 214–16. **Topic: Norway**

28. Biography of Anne K. Smoot, 6–9; Jensen, "Diary of J. F. Ferdinand Dorius," 38, 46–47.

29. Dorius, *Dorius Heritage,* 43; Jensen, "Diary of J. F. Ferdinand Dorius," 48–49. Johan Dorius quotation edited for readability; original source has "It was in Frederikstad."

30. Dorius, *Dorius Heritage,* 43; Haslam, *Clash of Cultures,* 38–41.

31. Christian Larsen, Journal, Oct. 14–Nov. 12, 1852.

32. Christian Larsen, Journal, Nov. 12, 1852; Dorius, *Dorius Heritage,* 43–45. Second question from Norwegian officials edited for clarity; original source has "Would return to Denmark, if you was liberated from prison?"

33. Dorius, *Dorius Heritage,* 44; Jenson, *History of the Scandinavian Mission,* 65–66; "Jensen, Johan Andreas," Andrew Jenson Collection, CHL; Jensen, "Diary of J. F. Ferdinand Dorius," 50.

34. Jensen, "Diary of J. F. Ferdinand Dorius," 50.

Chapter 12: Their Faces Are Zionward

1. Brigham Young, Cornerstone Laying, Apr. 6, 1853, Church History Department Pitman Shorthand Transcriptions, CHL; Brigham Young, Apr. 6, 1853, Historian's Office, Reports of Speeches, CHL; "Minutes of the General Conference," *Deseret News,* Apr. 16, 1853, [2]; Historian's Office, History of the Church, volume 23, Apr. 6, 1853, 43; see also *Saints,* volume 1, chapter 8. **Topic: Salt Lake Temple**

2. Brigham Young, Cornerstone Laying, Apr. 6, 1853, Church History Department Pitman Shorthand Transcriptions, CHL; "Minutes of the General Conference," *Deseret News,* Apr. 16, 1853, [2]; Woodruff, Journal, Feb. 14, 1853; "The Temple," *Deseret News,* Feb. 19, 1853, [2]; Anderson, "Salt Lake Temple," 250–52, 259, 263.

3. Historian's Office, History of the Church, volume 23, Apr. 6, 1853, 43; Anderson, "Salt Lake Temple," 253.

4. Romney, Journal, Apr. [2], 1853, 29.

5. *Temple Souvenir Album,* 5, 7.

6. "Minutes of the General Conference," *Deseret News,* Apr. 16, 1853, [2]; Brigham Young, Cornerstone Laying, Apr. 6, 1853, Church History Department Pitman Shorthand Transcriptions, CHL; Brigham Young, Apr. 6, 1853, Historian's Office, Reports of Speeches, CHL; Bennett, "Line upon Line," 48–49; Anderson, "Salt Lake Temple," 254; Historian's Office, History of the Church, volume 23, Apr. 6, 1853, 43.

7. "Minutes of the General Conference," *Deseret News,* Apr. 16, 1853, [2]. **Topic: Temple Endowment**

8. Lee, Journal, Mar. 21, 1847; Woodruff, Journal, Aug. 15, 1847; Brigham Young, Discourse, Apr. 6, 1853, Church History Department Pitman Shorthand Transcriptions, CHL. **Topic: Temple Building**

9. "Minutes of the General Conference," *Deseret News,* Apr. 16, 1853, [2].

10. Ann Eliza Logan Secrist to Jacob F. Secrist, May 30, 1853; Jacob F. Secrist, "For the Satisfaction of My Wife and Children," Dec. 3, 1853, [22], Jacob F. Secrist Collection, CHL.

11. Ann Eliza Logan Secrist to Jacob F. Secrist, May 30, 1853, Jacob F. Secrist Collection, CHL; "German Mission," *Deseret News,* May 28, 1853, [2]; see also "Foreign Correspondence," *Deseret News,* Nov. 27, 1852, 4; "Liverpool Correspondence," and "Italian Correspondence," *Deseret News,* Feb. 5, 1853, [2]; and "Foreign Correspondence," *Deseret News,* May 14, 1853. **Topic: Growth of Missionary Work**

12. Ann Eliza Logan Secrist to Jacob F. Secrist, Sept. 29, 1852; Oct. 30, 1852; May 30, 1853; June 30, 1853, Jacob F. Secrist Collection, CHL.

13. Ann Eliza Logan Secrist to Jacob F. Secrist, June 30, 1853, Jacob F. Secrist Collection, CHL. Regarding the first sentence of the quotation, the original source is damaged at this point, so a word has been supplied for clarity. The original source has "I want know your mind on the subject."

14. See George Q. Cannon, Journal, Apr. 2, 1853, footnote, Journal of George Q. Cannon website, churchhistorianspress.org; Allred, Journal, Apr. 2, 1853; and Minutes, *Deseret News,* Extra, Sept. 14, 1852, 14–22. **Topic: Hawaii**

15. George Q. Cannon, Journal, Apr. 7, 1853; Woodbury, Diary, volume 2, Apr. 7 and May 22, 1853; Green, Diary, Apr. 7, 1853.

16. Reddick Allred, Journal, Mar. 24, 1853; George Q. Cannon, Journal, July 4, 1851; May 20, 1852; Oct. 6, 1852; Cannon, *My First Mission,* 42, 59–61; see also Alma 32:28. **Topic: Jonathan Napela**

17. George Q. Cannon, Journal, Jan. 27–July 22, 1853; Jonathan Napela to Brigham Young, Apr. 8, 1852, Brigham Young Office Files, CHL; Jonathan Napela to Brigham Young, Apr. 8, 1852, in "Foreign Correspondence," *Deseret News,* Nov. 27, 1852, [4].

18. George Q. Cannon, Journal, Apr. 8, 1853; Reddick Allred, Journal, Mar. 24–25 and Apr. 27, 1853; Green, Diary, Apr. 16, 18, and 20, 1853. Quotation edited for clarity; "I ever dun" in original changed to "I have ever done."

19. Green, Diary, Apr. 18 and May 17, 1853.

20. Reddick Allred, Journal, May 29–June 3, 1853; Philip B. Lewis to the First Presidency, Mar. 16, 1853, Brigham Young Office Files, CHL; George Q. Cannon, Journal, May 28 and July 22, 1853; see also "Napela, Jonathan (Ionatana) Hawaii," Biographical Entry, Journal of George Q. Cannon website, churchhistorianspress.org.

21. Walker, Journal, Apr. 18, 1853; Haven, Journal, Apr. 18, 1853. **Topic: South Africa**

22. Jesse Haven to Willard Richards, Aug. 20, 1853, Willard Richards, Journals and Papers, CHL; Haven, Journal, Apr. 18, 1853.

23. Minutes, *Deseret News,* Extra, Sept. 14, 1852, 10; *Life Incidents and Travels,* 16–17; Eighth General Epistle, Oct. 1852, in Neilson and Waite, *Settling the Valley,* 172–73.

24. *Life Incidents and Travels,* 5, 13, 16–17.

25. Walker, Journal, Apr. 18, 1853; see also Haven, Journal, Apr. 18–19, 1853.

26. Jesse Haven to Willard Richards, Aug. 20, 1853, Willard Richards, Journals and Papers, CHL; Cape of Good Hope, *Census,* iii, viii.

27. Walker, Journal, Apr. 25–26, 1853; Haven, Journal, Apr. 25–26, 1853.

28. Walker, Journal, Apr. 26 and 29, 1853; May 2, 1853.

29. Rich, "True Policy for Utah," 64–67.

30. See Brigham Young, Feb. 5, 1852, Historian's Office, Reports of Speeches, CHL; "To the Saints," *Deseret News,* Apr. 3, 1852, 2; Elder's Certificate for Elijah Able, Mar. 31, 1836, in Kirtland Elders' Certificates, 61; Nuttall, Diary, May 31, 1879; *Saints,* volume 1, chapter 27; Cannon, "Jesse Haven," 447–48; and "Race and the Priesthood," Gospel Topics, topics.ChurchofJesusChrist.org.

31. Orson Pratt, Discourse, Jan. 27, 1852, George D. Watt, Papers, CHL. Quotation edited for clarity; word "so" added at end of quotation.

32. Orson Spencer, Discourse, Jan. 27, 1852, George D. Watt, Papers, CHL; see also "Spencer, Orson," Biographical Entry, Joseph Smith Papers website, josephsmithpapers.org.

33. *Acts, Resolutions, and Memorials . . . of the Territory of Utah,* 80–82; Rich, "True Policy for Utah," 64–72. **Topic: Indian Slavery and Indentured Servitude**

34. Orson Spencer, Discourse, Jan. 27, 1852, George D. Watt, Papers, CHL; Jesse Haven to Willard Richards, Aug. 20, 1853, Willard Richards, Journals and Papers, CHL.

35. Walker, Journal, May 19, 1853; *Life Incidents and Travels,* 26; see also Stott, *Faith and Dissent,* 49, 57–58.

36. Walker, Journal, May 25, 1853; *Life Incidents and Travels,* 26–27.

37. Walker, Journal, June 24–25, 1853; *Life Incidents and Travels,* 28.

38. Haven, Journal, June 12 and 15, 1853; Aug. 16, 1853; Jesse Haven to Samuel Richards, Jan. 20, 1854, *Latter-day Saints' Millennial Star,* Mar. 18, 1854, 16:173–74; Jesse Haven, *Some of the Principal Doctrines or Belief of the Church of Jesus Christ of Latter Day Saints* (Cape Town: W. Foelscher, [1852]); Jesse Haven, William H. Walker, and Leonard I. Smith, *A Warning to All* ([Cape of Good Hope]: Publisher unidentified, [1853]); Jesse Haven, *Celestical Marriage, and the Plurality of Wives!* (Cape Town: W. Foelscher, [1854]); see also Cannon, "Jesse Haven," 448–49; and Whittaker, "Early Mormon Imprints in South Africa," 404–16.

39. *Life Incidents and Travels,* 28; Walker, Journal, Aug. 16 and Sept. 7, 1853; Haven, Journal, Aug. 16 and Sept. 7, 1853.

40. Haven, Journal, Aug. 2, 1853; South Africa (Country), Part 1, 1853–1951, 44–47, Record of Members Collection, CHL; Cannon, "Jesse Haven," 450, 452–53.
41. Walker, Journal, Sept. 13, 1853; Haven, Journal, Sept. 13, 1853.
42. Jesse Haven to Willard Richards, Aug. 20, 1853, Willard Richards, Journals and Papers, CHL. First sentence of quotation edited for readability; "a plenty of work" in original changed to "plenty of work."
43. Cannon, *My First Mission,* 61.
44. George Q. Cannon, Journal, Oct. 5, 1853; "Cannon, George Quayle," in Jenson, *Latter-day Saint Biographical Encyclopedia,* 1:44; see also George Q. Cannon, Journal, Aug. 18, 1853. Quotation edited for readability; original source has "I said that for my own part I did not consider that my mission was fully filled until I saw the Book of Mormon in press."
45. George Q. Cannon, Journal, Oct. 5–6, 1853; Brigham Young to George Q. Cannon, June 15, 1853; Sept. 30, 1853, Brigham Young Office Files, CHL; Hawaii Honolulu Mission, Manuscript History and Historical Reports, volume 1, Oct. 6, 1853.
 Topic: Hawaii
46. Hawaii Honolulu Mission, Manuscript History and Historical Reports, volume 1, Oct. 6, 1853; George Q. Cannon, Journal, Oct. 6, 1853; Hammond, Journal, Sept. 24–28, 1853.
47. George Q. Cannon, Journal, Oct. 20, 1853; Karren, Journal, Oct. 19–20, 1853; see also Sixtus Johnson, Journal, book C, Oct. 20, 1853.

Chapter 13: By Every Possible Means

1. Sixth General Epistle, Sept. 1851, in Neilson and Waite, *Settling the Valley,* 138–39; Whitney, *History of Utah,* 1:493, 495, 498, 500, 505–6; Esplin, "Buildings on the Temple Block Preceding the Tabernacle," 107–36; see also "'The Deseret Stores' and General Tithing Store-House, Salt Lake City," 1853; and "The Old Council House," in Hall, Scenes in Utah, Engraving Collection, CHL. **Topic: Salt Lake Valley**
2. Stevens, Autobiography, 5.
3. Dorius, *Dorius Heritage,* 16–17, 26, 49–51, 57–58; Dorius, "Autobiography of Carl Christian Nicoli Dorius," 8–9, 11–12; Jensen, "Diary of J. F. Ferdinand Dorius," 55–56.
4. Stevens, Autobiography, 5; John E. Forsgren Company (1853) list, Pioneer Database, history.ChurchofJesusChrist.org/overlandtravel/companies.
5. Shirts and Shirts, *Trial Furnace,* 3–4, 16–20. **Topic: Pioneer Settlements**
6. Stevens, Autobiography, 5; Historian's Office, History of the Church, volume 23, Oct. 7, 1853, 126.
7. Historian's Office, General Church Minutes, June 13, 1849; Historical Department, Journal History of the Church, June 13, 1849; Second General Epistle, Oct. 12, 1849, in Neilson and Waite, *Settling the Valley,* 86; Isaac Morley to Brigham Young and Council, Mar. 15, 1850; Apr. 17, 1850, Brigham Young Office Files, CHL.
8. Historian's Office, History of the Church, volume 20, Jan.–Feb. 1850, 17–23; Historian's Office, General Church Minutes, Jan. 31, 1850; "Special Order No. 2" to George D. Grant, Jan. 31, 1850, Department of Administrative Services, Territorial Militia Records, series 2210, Utah State Archives and Records Service, Salt Lake City; Christy, "Open Hand and Mailed Fist," 220–27; see also Farmer, *On Zion's Mount,* 67–70; and Gottfredson, *History of Indian Depredations in Utah,* 28–35.
 Topic: American Indians
9. Nelson Higgins to James Ferguson, Mar. 16, 1854, Department of Administrative Services, Territorial Militia Records, series 2210, Utah State Archives and Records; Stevens, Autobiography, 6; Christy, "Open Hand and Mailed Fist," 227, 230–33; see also Peterson, *Utah's Black Hawk War,* 63–64.

10. An Act for the Protection of the Rights of Indians, June 23, 1852; A Preamble and an Act for the Relief of Indians, Feb. 28, 1852, First Session, Utah Territory Legislative Assembly Papers, CHL; "First Judicial Court," *Deseret News,* Mar. 6, 1852, [4]; Reeve, *Religion of a Different Color,* 143–44; Jones, *Trial of Don Pedro León Luján,* 1–4, 41–52; Christy, "Walker War," 396; Cannon, "To Buy Up the Lamanite Children as Fast as They Could," 10; Van Hoak, "And Who Shall Have the Children?," 3–18; Peterson, *Utah's Black Hawk War,* 63–69; Wimmer, "Walker War Reconsidered," 52–53, 59–60. **Topic: Indian Slavery and Indentured Servitude**

11. Bean, Autobiography, 51; James McLellan to Brigham Young, July 16, 1853, Brigham Young Office Files, CHL; Love, Diary, July 16, 1853; Christy, "Walker War," 400–401; McKenzie, "Cause and Origin of the Walker War," 43–47; Wimmer, "Walker War Reconsidered," 97–100, 108–11.

12. Christy, "Walker War," 400–415; "General Orders No. 2," July 25, 1853; "Special Orders No. 21," Oct. 5, 1853, Department of Administrative Services, Territorial Militia Records, series 2210, Utah State Archives and Records Service, Salt Lake City; Brigham Young to Peter W. Conover and others, Oct. 16, 1853, Brigham Young Office Files, CHL.

13. See Stevens, Autobiography, 5–6; Whitney, *History of Utah,* 1:515–16; "Proclamation by the Governor," *Deseret News,* Oct. 1, 1853, [2]; and Wimmer, "Walker War Reconsidered," 118–24.

14. Stevens, Autobiography, 6–7; Sidwell, "Death of William Luke, Sr.," 1; "Indian Difficulties," *Deseret News,* Oct. 15, 1853, [2]; *History of Sanpete and Emery Counties,* 472. Spring Town is now known as Spring City.

15. Stevens, Autobiography, 6; Almon Babbitt, Letter to the Editor, Nov. 25, 1853, *Deseret News,* Dec. 1, 1853, [3]; George A. Smith to Daniel H. Wells, Aug. 27, 1853, Department of Administrative Services, Territorial Militia Records, series 2210, Utah State Archives and Records Service, Salt Lake City; see also Christy, "Walker War," 409; and Wimmer, "Walker War Reconsidered," 150–52.

16. Christy, "Walker War," 413–15; Historian's Office, History of the Church, volume 23, Nov. 28 and Dec. 1, 1853, 141–42; "Indian Difficulties," *Deseret News,* Nov. 24, 1853, [2].

17. Stevens, Autobiography, 6–7.

18. Great Salt Lake City Relief Society, Minutes, Jan. 24, 1854, in Derr and others, *First Fifty Years of Relief Society,* 190; "Busby, Matilda Matey Dudley Ferguson Paschall," Biographical Entry, First Fifty Years of Relief Society website, churchhistorianspress .org; see also Introduction to Great Salt Lake City Relief Society, Minutes, Jan.–June 1854, in *First Fifty Years of Relief Society,* 188.

19. Brown, Diary, 1, 3–5; Brigham Young to Peter W. Conover and others, Oct. 16, 1853, Brigham Young Office Files, CHL; Brigham Young, Discourse, Oct. 8, 1853, Church History Department Pitman Shorthand Transcriptions, CHL; Brown, *Life of a Pioneer,* 304.

20. "Minutes of the General Conference," *Deseret News,* Oct. 15, 1853, [3].

21. Helm, Reminiscences, 1; Great Salt Lake City Relief Society, Minutes, Jan. 24, 1854, in Derr and others, *First Fifty Years of Relief Society,* 190; Matilda Dudley Busby, Thirteenth Ward Relief Society Covenant, in Reeder and Holbrook, *At the Pulpit,* 29–31; see also 188. **Topic: Relief Society**

22. *Saints,* volume 1, chapter 30; Brigham Young, Discourses, Mar. 9, 1845 (Excerpts); Great Salt Lake Relief Society, Minutes, Feb. 9, 1854, in Derr and others, *First Fifty Years of Relief Society,* 168–71, 190–91. **Topics: Amanda Barnes Smith; Hawn's Mill Massacre; Female Relief Society of Nauvoo**

23. Great Salt Lake Relief Society, Minutes, Feb. 9, 1854, in Derr and others, *First Fifty Years of Relief Society,* 190–91.

24. Great Salt Lake Relief Society, Minutes, Feb. 9–June 13, 1854, in Derr and others, *First Fifty Years of Relief Society,* 191–97; Smith, Notebook, June [13], 1854; see also Ulrich, *House Full of Females,* 298–305; and Jensen, "Forgotten Relief Societies," 107–18.

25. Brown, Diary, Apr. 14, 1854; "Synopsis of the Travels and Doings," 1854, Brigham Young Office Files, CHL; Woodruff, Journal, May 3, 1854; Historical Department, Office Journal, Apr. 13–14 and May 4, 1854, 2–3, 23; George W. Bean to Brigham Young, May 1, 1854, Brigham Young Office Files, CHL; Nelson Higgins to James Ferguson, Mar. 16, 1854, Department of Administrative Services, Territorial Militia Records, series 2210, Utah State Archives and Records Service, Salt Lake City; Christy, "Walker War," 416–17; see also "Minutes," *Deseret News,* Apr. 13, 1854, [2].

26. Woodruff, Journal, May 9, 1854; Brigham Young to Grosepene, May 7, 1854; Brigham Young to Walker [Walkara], May 7, 1854, Brigham Young Office Files, CHL; Brooks, *Not by Bread Alone,* 97; see also Christy, "Walker War," 412.

27. Woodruff, Journal, May 11 and 13, 1854; "Discourse," *Deseret News,* Feb. 8, 1855, [2]; Historian's Office, General Church Minutes, May 11, 1854; Brigham Young, Discourse, May 11, 1854, Church History Department Pitman Shorthand Transcriptions, CHL; Carvalho, *Incidents of Travel and Adventure in the Far West,* 190.

28. "Discourse," *Deseret News,* Feb. 8, 1855, [2]; Carvalho, *Incidents of Travel and Adventure in the Far West,* 191–92; "Synopsis of the Travels and Doings," 1854, 5–6, Brigham Young Office Files, CHL.

29. Historian's Office, General Church Minutes, May 11, 1854; Brigham Young, Discourse, May 11, 1854, Church History Department Pitman Shorthand Transcriptions, CHL. Quotation edited for clarity; original source has "let Walker have some sleep and rest awhile and then he ma talk perhaps."

30. Woodruff, Journal, May 11, 1854; Carvalho, *Incidents of Travel and Adventure in the Far West,* 192; Historian's Office, General Church Minutes, May 11, 1854; Brigham Young, Discourse, May 11, 1854, Church History Department Pitman Shorthand Transcriptions, CHL; "Synopsis of the Travels and Doings," 1854, 6, Brigham Young Office Files, CHL.

31. Carvalho, *Incidents of Travel and Adventure in the Far West,* 192; Woodruff, Journal, May 12, 1854; "Synopsis of the Travels and Doings," 1854, 6, Brigham Young Office Files, CHL.

32. Woodruff, Journal, May 12, 1854; see also Carvalho, *Incidents of Travel and Adventure in the Far West,* 192–93. Quotation edited for readability; original source has "He said we now understand each other that they were now to have all peace so all could now go on the road in peace & not be afraid." **Topic: Word of Wisdom (D&C 89)**

33. Woodruff, Journal, May 12–18, 1854; "Synopsis of the Travels and Doings," 1854, 6–9, Brigham Young Office Files, CHL.

34. Historian's Office, General Church Minutes, May 21, 1854; see also minutes for May 14, 1854.

35. "Synopsis of the Travels and Doings," 1854, 10, Brigham Young Office Files, CHL; Woodruff, Journal, May 21, 1854; Historian's Office, General Church Minutes, June 4, 1854; see also minutes for May 21, 1854; and Ulrich, *House Full of Females,* 289, 300–305.

36. Great Salt Lake City Relief Society, Minutes, June 13, 1854, in Derr and others, *First Fifty Years of Relief Society,* 197; Smith, Notebook, June 10 and 14, 1854; Thirteenth Ward, Relief Society Record Book, June [7] and 21, 1854; Thirteenth Ward, Notes and Account Pages, 1854–57, Thirteenth Ward, Relief Society Records, CHL.

37. Brown, Diary, May 20, 1854, 51–52; "Minutes," *Deseret News,* Apr. 13, 1854, [2]; Smith, *Life of Joseph F. Smith,* 164–65; Otterstrom, "Journey to the South," 106. **Topic: Joseph F. Smith**

38. Oaks and Hill, *Carthage Conspiracy,* 184–86; Joseph F. Smith, Reminiscences, [2], [13]–[19]; Nibley, *Presidents of the Church,* 183–84; Smith, *Life of Joseph F. Smith,* 130; see also "Smith, Mary Fielding," Biographical Entry, First Fifty Years of Relief Society website, churchhistorianspress.org.

39. Joseph F. Smith, Reminiscences, [13]–[20]; see also Joseph F. Smith, "Recollections," 98–99.

40. Joseph F. Smith to Solomon Kimball, Sept. 23, 1889, letterpress copy, Joseph F. Smith, Papers, CHL; Harris, "Martha Ann Smith Harris," 14; Obituary for Mary Fielding Smith,

Deseret News, Dec. 11, 1852, [3]; "Smith, Mary Fielding," Biographical Entry, First Fifty Years of Relief Society website, churchhistorianspress.org; "Smith, Mary Fielding," in Ludlow, *Encyclopedia of Mormonism,* 3:1358–59.

41. Harris, "Martha Ann Smith Harris," 13–14; Joseph F. Smith to Samuel L. Adams, May 11, 1888, private possession; see also Joseph F. Smith correspondence with his brothers and sisters, 1853–1916, in Family Correspondence, Joseph F. Smith, Papers, CHL; Nibley, "Reminiscences of President Joseph F. Smith," 191; and Smith, *Life of Joseph F. Smith,* 163.

42. Joseph F. Smith to Samuel L. Adams, May 11, 1888, private possession; Joseph F. Smith to George A. Smith, Oct. 20, 1854, George A. Smith, Papers, CHL; Joseph F. Smith to Agnes Smith and Josephine Smith, July 5, 1857, Joseph F. Smith, Papers, CHL; Smith, *Life of Joseph F. Smith,* 164.

43. See Otterstrom, "Journey to the South," 106; and Joseph F. Smith to Agnes Smith and Josephine Smith, July 5, 1857, Joseph F. Smith, Papers, CHL.

44. Stevens, Autobiography, 7–8; *History of Sanpete and Emery Counties,* 281; "Death of Henry Stevens," *Deseret Evening News,* Aug. 21, 1899, 8.

45. Stevens, Autobiography, 7; Sanpete County, Utah Territory, Census Returns, 1856, [9]; Steele, *James and Elizabeth Allred,* 155–57; see also Cannon, "Adopted or Indentured," 341–57; and Cannon, "To Buy Up the Lamanite Children as Fast as They Could," 1–35.

46. See "Plural Marriage and Families in Early Utah," Gospel Topics, topics .ChurchofJesusChrist.org; Daynes, *More Wives Than One,* 116–18, 130; Ivins, "Notes on Mormon Polygamy," 313–14; and Jessee, "Brigham Young at Home," 23–53. **Topic: Plural Marriage in Utah**

47. Daynes, *More Wives Than One,* 101–2.

48. Sealings to Spouse, volume A1, 1851–54, entry 1734, microfilm 183,393, Sealings of Couples, Living and by Proxy, 1851–89, Special Collections, Family History Library; Stevens, Autobiography, 7–8. **Topic: Plural Marriage in Utah**

49. Silas Smith, Journal, Sept. 26, 1854.

50. Joseph F. Smith to George A. Smith, Oct. 20, 1854, George A. Smith, Papers, CHL; George Q. Cannon, Journal, July 29, 1854; Smith, *Life of Joseph F. Smith,* 168–69; Karren, Journal, Aug. 31, 1854; Green, Diary, Aug. 28–30, 1854; see also "Hammond, Francis Asbury," and "Hammond, Mary Jane Dilworth," Biographical Entries, Journal of George Q. Cannon website, churchhistorianspress.org; and Woods, "Palawai Pioneers," 11–16.

51. Joseph F. Smith to George A. Smith, Oct. 20, 1854, George A. Smith, Papers, CHL; "Hammond, Mary Jane Dilworth," Biographical Entry, Journal of George Q. Cannon website, churchhistorianspress.org; Smith, *Life of Joseph F. Smith,* 169.

52. Mary Jane Hammond, Journal, Oct. 8–10, 1854; Joseph F. Smith to George A. Smith, Oct. 20, 1854, George A. Smith, Papers, CHL; Green, Diary, Aug. 28–30, 1854.

53. Joseph F. Smith to George A. Smith, Oct. 20, 1854, George A. Smith, Papers, CHL; see also Joseph F. Smith to Samuel L. Adams, May 11, 1888, private possession.

CHAPTER 14: HARD TO BE SEPARATED

1. Jacob F. Secrist to Ann Eliza Logan Secrist, July 25, 1854; Ann Eliza Logan Secrist to Jacob F. Secrist, Mar. 30, 1855, Jacob F. Secrist Collection, CHL.

2. Ann Eliza Logan Secrist to Jacob F. Secrist, Mar. 30, 1855; Apr. 25, 1854; Jacob F. Secrist to Ann Eliza Logan Secrist, Jan. 3, 1854, Jacob F. Secrist Collection, CHL.

3. Ann Eliza Logan Secrist to Jacob F. Secrist, Oct. 30, 1853; Nov. 21, 1853; Apr. 25, 1854; Mar. 30, 1855, Jacob F. Secrist Collection, CHL.

4. Ann Eliza Logan Secrist to Jacob F. Secrist, Mar. 30, 1855; Jacob F. Secrist, "For the Satisfaction of My Wife and Children," Dec. 3, 1853, [38], [42]–[43], Jacob F. Secrist

Collection, CHL. Last sentence of quotation edited for readability; "which is simple" in original changed to "which are simple."

5. Jacob F. Secrist to "Dear Children," Jan. 23, 1854; Mar. 25, 1854, Jacob F. Secrist Collection, CHL.

6. Ann Eliza Logan Secrist to Jacob F. Secrist, Mar. 30, 1855, Jacob F. Secrist Collection, CHL.

7. George Q. Cannon, Journal, May 5, 1855; "Arrivals," *Deseret News,* Nov. 30, 1854, [3]; Historical Department, Journal History of the Church, May 5, 1855. **Topic: George Q. Cannon**

8. "Married," *Deseret News,* Dec. 21, 1854, [3]; "Hoagland, Elizabeth," Biographical Entry, Journal of George Q. Cannon website, churchhistorianspress.org; Cannon, "George Q. Cannon," 510; George Q. Cannon, Journal, Apr. 12, 1854.

9. George Q. Cannon, Journal, May 5, 1855; "Departure," *Deseret News,* May 16, 1855, [5]; Historical Department, Journal History of the Church, May 5, 1855; see also Brown, "Temple Pro Tempore," 7–8, 11–12, 55. **Topics: Endowment House; Temple Building**

10. George Q. Cannon, Journal, May 5, 1855; Historical Department, Journal History of the Church, May 5, 1855; "Hoagland, Elizabeth," Biographical Entry, Journal of George Q. Cannon website, churchhistorianspress.org; see also Obituary for Abraham Hoagland, *Deseret News,* Feb. 2, 1872, [9]; and George Q. Cannon, Journal, Apr. 12, 1854.

11. George Q. Cannon, Journal, May 10–20, 1855; William Farrer to John H. Tibbets and Hiram B. Clawson, Nov. 26, 1855, photocopy of typescript, in Farrer, Diary, CHL; Historical Department, Journal History of the Church, May 19, 1855; "Synopsis of Journey of President Young," May 19, 1855, 5, Brigham Young Office Files, CHL.

12. George Q. Cannon, Journal, May 20, 1855; Historical Department, Journal History of the Church, May 20, 1855; "Synopsis of Journey of President Young," May 20, 1855, 5, Brigham Young Office Files, CHL.

13. George Q. Cannon, Journal, May 20, 1855. Quotation edited for readability; original source has "Bro. Jedediah told me to let them know I was a Cannon & to roar."

14. Joseph F. Smith to Martha Ann Smith, Jan. 28, 1855, Joseph F. Smith Letters to Martha Ann Smith Harris, CHL. First sentence of quotation edited for readability; "grew considerable" in original changed to "grown considerably."

15. Harris, Autobiography, 1.

16. Whitney, *History of Utah,* 4:230; Gates, "Mothers in Israel," 138; Miller and Edvalson, *One Hundred Fifty Years of History of the L.D.S. Sugar House Ward,* 1–4; "Life and Labors," 19–20, Abraham O. Smoot, Papers, Brigham Young University; see also "Sugar House Ward History," [1]–[3], Sugar House Ward, Manuscript History and Historical Reports, CHL.

17. John Smith to Joseph F. Smith, Sept. 1854; James Fisher to Joseph F. Smith, July 13, 1855, Joseph F. Smith, Papers, CHL; Elias Smith, Journal, Apr. 24, 27, and 30, 1855; "The Crops and the Grasshoppers," *Deseret News,* May 23, 1855, [5].

18. Elias Smith, Journal, Apr. 24, 27, and 30, 1855; May 3, 1855; "The Grasshoppers," *Deseret News,* Apr. 25, 1855, [5]; "The Crops and the Grasshoppers," *Deseret News,* May 23, 1855, [5]; James Fisher to Joseph F. Smith, July 13, 1855, Joseph F. Smith, Papers, CHL; Love, Diary, Apr. 21, 1855. **Topic: Crickets and Seagulls**

19. Compare John Smith to Joseph F. Smith, Sept. 1854; Jan. 31, 1856, Joseph F. Smith, Papers, CHL, with Martha Ann Smith to Joseph F. Smith, Jan. 31, 1856, Joseph F. Smith, Papers, CHL.

20. Joseph F. Smith to Martha Ann Smith, June 9, 1855, Joseph F. Smith Letters to Martha Ann Smith Harris, CHL.

21. Jacob F. Secrist/Noah T. Guymon Company (1855) list, Pioneer Database, history .ChurchofJesusChrist.org/overlandtravel/companies; "Our Immigration," *Deseret News,* Aug. 8, 1855, [4]; Ashby, *Autobiography of Peter O. Hansen,* 114; Charles Smith, Reminiscences and Diary, 34; see also "Old Time 'Mormon' Camping Ground," *Deseret News,* June 22, 1887, [10]. **Topic: Pioneer Trek**

22. Jacob F. Secrist to Ann Eliza Logan Secrist, May 21, 1855, Jacob F. Secrist Collection, CHL.
23. Dorius, "Sketch of the Life," 24–25; Dorius, *Dorius Heritage,* 62.
24. Biography of Anne K. Smoot, 12–15, 19; Inger C. Johnson, Autobiography, 4–5; Mulder, *Homeward to Zion,* 65–101, 133–34. **Topic: Emigration**
25. Larsen, Autobiographical Sketch, 2; Hansen, Journal, 118–19; Neilson, Family Record, 8–9.
26. Biography of Anne K. Smoot, 18–20; Dorius, *Dorius Heritage,* 62–63; Dorius, "Sketch of the Life," 7.
27. Biography of Anne K. Smoot, 18–19; "Olsen, Annie Cathrine Christensen," *Utah Pioneer Biographies,* 22:17–18, 20; Larsen, Autobiographical Sketch, 3; Neilson, Family Record, 9; "An Old Time 'Mormon' Camping Ground," *Deseret News,* June 22, 1887, [10]. **Topic: Pioneer Trek**
28. "Minutes of a Conference," *Deseret News,* Sept. 18, 1852, [4]; Jacob F. Secrist/Noah T. Guymon Company (1855) list, Pioneer Database, history.ChurchofJesusChrist.org /overlandtravel/companies.
29. Jacob F. Secrist to Ann Eliza Logan Secrist, May 21, 1855, Jacob F. Secrist Collection, CHL; Ashby, *Autobiography of Peter O. Hansen,* 113.
30. Neilson, Family Record, 11; Larsen, Autobiographical Sketch, 3; "An Old Time 'Mormon' Camping Ground," *Deseret News,* June 22, 1887, [10]; Ashby, *Autobiography of Peter O. Hansen,* 113.
31. See Bashore, "Mortality on the Mormon Trail," 109–23.
32. Biography of Anne K. Smoot, 20–21; Jacob F. Secrist/Noah T. Guymon Company (1855) list, Pioneer Database, history.ChurchofJesusChrist.org/overlandtravel /companies; see also Charles Smith, Reminiscences and Diary, 31.
33. Charles Smith, Reminiscences and Diary, 34–36; James Faulkner to "Dear Friends," Mar. 1, 1856, CHL; Jacob F. Secrist/Noah T. Guymon Company (1855) list, Pioneer Database, history.ChurchofJesusChrist.org/overlandtravel/companies.
34. Charles Smith, Reminiscences and Diary, 36–42; Biography of Anne K. Smoot, 21; Ashby, *Autobiography of Peter O. Hansen,* 115; Inger C. Johnson, Autobiography, 12. **Topic: Salt Lake Valley**
35. "Deaths of Missionaries," *Deseret News,* Aug. 8, 1855, 173.
36. Jacob F. Secrist to Ann Eliza Logan Secrist, May 21, 1855, Jacob F. Secrist Collection, CHL.
37. Charles Smith, Reminiscences and Diary, 35, 40; Jacob F. Secrist to Ann Eliza Logan Secrist, May 21, 1855, Jacob F. Secrist Collection, CHL.
38. "Anne Eliza Secrist," in Soule, "Exerps from a History," [1]; Ann Eliza Logan Secrist to Jacob F. Secrist, June 30, 1853, Jacob F. Secrist Collection, CHL.
39. George A. Smith to "Respected Cousin," July 31, 1855, Historian's Office, Letterpress Copybook, volume 1, 229–31, CHL; Wilford Woodruff to Asa Fitch, July 31, 1856, Wilford Woodruff, Journals and Papers, CHL; George A. Smith, Letter to the Editor, July 31, 1855, *Latter-day Saints' Millennial Star,* Oct. 13, 1855, 17:651; Elias Smith, Journal, May 2 and 18, 1855; Thirteenth General Epistle, Oct. 1855, in Neilson and Waite, *Settling the Valley,* 238, 241; Carter, "Fish and the Famine of 1855–56," 96–97.
40. Thirteenth General Epistle, Oct. 1855, in Neilson and Waite, *Settling the Valley,* 242–46; "News from Elders," *Deseret News,* Oct. 31, 1855, [5]; "Elders' Correspondence," *Deseret News,* July 18, 1855, [7]; Historian's Office, General Church Minutes, Sept. 16, 1855. **Topic: Emigration**
41. Carter, "Fish and the Famine of 1855–56," 99–106; Thirteenth General Epistle, Oct. 1855, in Neilson and Waite, *Settling the Valley,* 242–44; Historian's Office, General Church Minutes, Sept. 16, 1855; Brigham Young to Amasa Lyman, Sept. 30, 1855, Brigham Young Office Files, CHL; Brigham Young to John Taylor, Sept. 30, 1855, John Taylor Collection, CHL.
42. Thirteenth General Epistle, Oct. 1855, in Neilson and Waite, *Settling the Valley,* 243–44.

43. Thirteenth General Epistle, Oct. 1855, in Neilson and Waite, *Settling the Valley,* 242–44, 248–49; Brigham Young to John Taylor, Sept. 30, 1855, John Taylor Collection, CHL. **Topic: Handcart Companies**
44. Brigham Young to Franklin D. Richards, Sept. 1855, Brigham Young Office Files, CHL.

CHAPTER 15: IN STORMS AND IN CALMS

1. "General Epistle," *Latter-day Saints' Millennial Star,* Jan. 26, 1856, 18:49–55, 58, 64; see also Thirteenth General Epistle, Oct. 1855, in Neilson and Waite, *Settling the Valley,* 237–50. **Topic: Handcart Companies**
2. See Doctrine and Covenants 29:8–11.
3. "General Epistle," *Latter-day Saints' Millennial Star,* Jan. 26, 1856, 18:56–58; Thirteenth General Epistle, Oct. 1855, in Neilson and Waite, *Settling the Valley,* 237–50; see also "Emigration by Hand-Carts," *Latter-day Saints' Millennial Star,* June 14, 1856, 18:369.
4. "Gathering of the Poor," *Latter-day Saints' Millennial Star,* Feb. 2, 1856, 18:73–74.
5. Haven, Journal, Feb. 14, 1856, and Dec. 4, 1855; "Arrivals," *Latter-day Saints' Millennial Star,* Mar. 1, 1856, 18:140; "Jesse Haven," Missionary Database, history .ChurchofJesusChrist.org/missionary; see also "Cape Conference History," [1], in South African Mission, South Africa Mission Manuscript History and Historical Reports, volume 1, part 1, 1853.
6. "The Ship 'Caravan,'" *Latter-day Saints' Millennial Star,* Mar. 1, 1856, 18:140; "Mormons at Castle Garden," *Deseret News,* June 4, 1856, [4]; see also Thurston, Reminiscence, [2]; and England, Reminiscence, 3.
7. See Haven, Journal, Nov. 3, 1855; Dec. 15, 1855; Jan. 1, 1856.
8. Jesse Haven to the First Presidency, Jan. 1856, 28–29, 32–[33], Brigham Young Office Files, CHL. Quotation edited for clarity; "two or three hundred thousand of inhabitants" in original changed to "two or three hundred thousand inhabitants." **Topic: South Africa**
9. "Departures," *Latter-day Saints' Millennial Star,* Apr. 5, 1856, 18:217; "Emigrants for Utah," *Deseret News,* July 3, 1856, [8]; Haven, Journal, Mar. 22–23 and May 25, 1856; "Departures," *Latter-day Saints' Millennial Star,* June 14, 1856, 18:377. **Topic: Emigration**
10. Haven, Journal, Mar. 5, 1856; Thirteenth General Epistle, Oct. 1855, in Neilson and Waite, *Settling the Valley,* 237–50; "Foreign Correspondence," *Latter-day Saints' Millennial Star,* Dec. 22, 1855, 17:813–14.
11. Haven, Journal, May 22 and 25, 1856; "Departures," *Latter-day Saints' Millennial Star,* June 14, 1856, 18:377; [John Jaques], "Some Reminiscences," *Salt Lake Daily Herald,* Dec. 1, 1878, 1; 1851 England and Wales Census, Macclesfield, Cheshire, England, 25; Martin, Journal, Aug. 28, 1852, and Feb. 8–21, 1853; Mormon Battalion Company C, Muster Roll, 1846, CHL; Minutes, *Deseret News,* Extra, Sept. 14, 1852, 10.
12. Haven, Journal, May 25, 1856.
13. Kingsford, Autobiographical Sketch, 1–2; [John Jaques], "Some Reminiscences," *Salt Lake Daily Herald,* Dec. 1, 1878, 1; see also Arrington, "Finest of Fabrics: Mormon Women and the Silk Industry in Early Utah," 378–80.
14. Kingsford, Autobiographical Sketch, 2, 6; Haven, Journal, June 28–July 8, 1856; [John Jaques], "Some Reminiscences," *Salt Lake Daily Herald,* Dec. 1, 1878, 1; "Correspondence from the Camp at Florence," *Mormon,* Aug. 30, 1856, [2]; Archer, Reminiscences, [124]; Smith, "Leadership, Planning, and Management," 124–61; see also William Empey Company (1854), Edward Bunker Company (1856), Edmund Ellsworth Company (1856), and Daniel D. McArthur Company (1856), Pioneer Database, history.ChurchofJesusChrist.org/overlandtravel/companies.

15. [John Jaques], "Some Reminiscences," *Salt Lake Daily Herald,* Dec. 1, 1878, 1; Kingsford, Autobiographical Sketch, 2; James G. Willie Handcart Company, Emigrating Company Journal, June 28, 1856; July 8 and 15, 1856; see also General Epistle from the Council of the Twelve Apostles, Dec. 23, 1847, Brigham Young Office Files, CHL; and Edward Martin Company (1856), William B. Hodgetts Company (1856), and John A. Hunt Company (1856), Pioneer Database, history .ChurchofJesusChrist.org/overlandtravel/companies.

16. Haven, Journal, July 22, 1856; Kingsford, Autobiographical Sketch, 2; Olsen, *Price We Paid,* 25; see also "Emigration," *Latter-day Saints' Millennial Star,* Dec. 22, 1855, 27:810; and [John Jaques], "Some Reminiscences," *Salt Lake Daily Herald,* Dec. 1, 1878, 1.

17. Haven, Journal, Aug. 19–23, 1856; Josiah Rogerson Sr., "Tells Story of Trials of the Handcart Pioneers," *Salt Lake Tribune,* Nov. 30, 1913, 11; Hamilton, Journal, Aug. 1856; [John Jaques], "Some Reminiscences," *Salt Lake Daily Herald,* Dec. 8, 1878, 1; Platt, Reminiscences, 2; Josiah Rogerson, "Martin's Handcart Company, 1856," *Salt Lake Herald,* Oct. 27, 1907, 11.

18. General Epistle from the Council of the Twelve Apostles, Dec. 23, 1847; Brigham Young to Orson Hyde and others, Oct. 9, 1848, copy, Brigham Young Office Files, CHL; Sixth General Epistle, Sept. 1851; Eighth General Epistle, Oct. 1852, in Neilson and Waite, *Settling the Valley,* 150, 171; "General Epistle," *Latter-day Saints' Millennial Star,* Mar. 15, 1848, 6:84; Erastus Snow to John Taylor, Sept. 15, 1856, in *Mormon,* Sept. 27, 1856, [2]; see also Christy, "Weather, Disaster, and Responsibility," 10–17.

19. Olsen, *Price We Paid,* 80–85, 282–94; Christy, "Weather, Disaster, and Responsibility," 19–21.

20. Josiah Rogerson, "Martin's Handcart Company, 1856," *Salt Lake Herald,* Oct. 27, 1907, 11; "Discourse," *Deseret News,* Oct. 15, 1856, [4]; see also Beecroft, Journal, Aug. 5, 1856.

21. Josiah Rogerson, "Martin's Handcart Company, 1856," *Salt Lake Herald,* Oct. 27, 1907, 11; "Discourse," *Deseret News,* Oct. 15, 1856, [4]; Haven, Journal, Aug. 22 and 24, 1856; Bond, "Handcarts West in '56," [21]; see also Beecroft, Journal, Aug. 5, 1856. Franklin Richards quotation edited for readability; original source has "When we had a meeting at Florence, we called upon the saints to express their faith to the people, and requested to know of them, even if they knew that they should be swallowed up in storms, whether they would stop or turn back."

22. "Discourse," *Deseret News,* Oct. 15, 1856, [4]; Josiah Rogerson, "Martin's Handcart Company, 1856," *Salt Lake Herald,* Oct. 27, 1907, 11.

23. Haven, Journal, Aug. 15 and 24–26, 1856; Sept. 18, 1856; Smith, "Leadership, Planning, and Management," 156–57; Kingsford, Autobiographical Sketch, 2; "Emigration to Utah," *Mormon,* Sept. 13, 1856, [2]; [John Jaques], "Some Reminiscences," *Salt Lake Daily Herald,* Dec. 1, 1878, 1; Archer, Reminiscences, 126–27, 129–30; see also Haven, Journal, Aug. 1–2, 1856.

24. Woodruff, Journal, Sept. 7 and 14, 1856; Jedediah M. Grant, in *Journal of Discourses,* Nov. 2, 1856, 4:70–75; Brigham Young, in *Journal of Discourses,* Aug. 30, 1857, 5:166–71; W. G. Mills, "God Remembers Zion!," *Deseret News,* Nov. 5, 1856, [2]; "Great Reformation," *Deseret News,* Sept. 24, 1856, [4]; Peterson, "Mormon Reformation of 1856–1857," 63–68; see also Obituary for Jedediah Morgan Grant, *Deseret News,* Dec. 10, 1856, [5]. **Topic: Reformation of 1856–57**

25. "Remarks," *Deseret News,* Oct. 1, 1856, [3]; Jedediah Grant, in *Journal of Discourses,* Sept. 21, 1856, 4:49–51; see also Sessions, *Mormon Thunder,* 210–13.

26. Martha Ann Smith to Joseph F. Smith, [circa] Apr. 1856; July 29, 1856, Joseph F. Smith, Papers, CHL; Fifth General Epistle, Apr. 1851, in Neilson and Waite, *Settling the Valley,* 128.

27. John Smith to Joseph F. Smith, July 31, 1856; Martha Ann Smith to Joseph F. Smith, July 29, 1856; Oct. 2, 1856, Joseph F. Smith, Papers, CHL; see also Edward Bunker Company (1856) list, Pioneer Database, history.ChurchofJesusChrist.org /overlandtravel/companies.

28. "Journey from Florence to G. S. L. City," *Deseret News,* Oct. 22, 1856, [2]; John Smith to Joseph F. Smith, Nov. 3, 1856, Joseph F. Smith, Papers, CHL; George D. Grant Company (1856), Pioneer Database, history.ChurchofJesusChrist.org/overlandtravel/companies.
29. John Smith to Joseph F. Smith, Nov. 3, 1856, Joseph F. Smith, Papers, CHL; see also "Journey from Florence to G. S. L. City," *Deseret News,* Oct. 22, 1856, [2].
30. Historical Department, Office Journal, Oct. 4, 1856; Historian's Office, General Church Minutes, Oct. 4, 1856; see also "Journey from Florence to G. S. L. City," *Deseret News,* Oct. 22, 1856, [2]; and Brigham Young to Orson Pratt, Oct. 30, 1856, in *Latter-day Saints' Millennial Star,* Feb. 14, 1857, 19:97, 99.
31. Brigham Young to Orson Pratt, Oct. 30, 1856, in *Latter-day Saints' Millennial Star,* Feb. 14, 1857, 19:97–99; Christy, "Weather, Disaster, and Responsibility," 23–28.
32. Historian's Office, General Church Minutes, Oct. 5, 1856; "Remarks," *Deseret News,* Oct. 15, 1856, [4], [8]. **Topic: Handcart Companies**
33. "Remarks," *Deseret News,* Oct. 15, 1856, [4], [7].
34. Lucy Meserve Smith, Account of Relief Society in 1856, as Recorded in "Historical Sketches," June 12, 1889 (Excerpt), in Derr and others, *First Fifty Years of Relief Society,* 217.
35. Historical Department, Office Journal, Oct. 4 and 7, 1856; Historian's Office, General Church Minutes, Oct. 5–6, 1856; "Offerings for the Assistance of the P. E. F. Immigrants," Oct. 1856, Perpetual Emigrating Fund Company, General Files, CHL; Cluff, Autobiography, Oct. 7, 1856, 18–19; Allred, Journal, Oct. 7, 1856; Olsen and Allphin, *Follow Me to Zion,* 222; Rescue Companies (1856) list, Pioneer Database, history.ChurchofJesusChrist.org/overlandtravel/companies.

CHAPTER 16: NOT DOUBTING NOR DESPAIRING

1. [John Jaques], "Some Reminiscences," *Salt Lake Daily Herald,* Dec. 8, 1878, 1; Haven, Journal, Oct. 8–13, 1856; Kingsford, Autobiographical Sketch, 3.
2. Jesse Haven to Brigham Young, Oct. 9, 1856, Brigham Young Office Files, CHL; Archer, Reminiscences, 145–49; Kingsford, Autobiographical Sketch, 3; see also Christy, "Weather, Disaster, and Responsibility," 23–28.
3. Kingsford, Autobiographical Sketch, 3; Haven, Journal, Oct. 12–23, 1856; [John Jaques], "Some Reminiscences," *Salt Lake Daily Herald,* Dec. 8, 1878, 1; Dec. 22, 1878, 1.
4. Kingsford, Autobiographical Sketch, 3; Josiah Rogerson, "Martin's Handcart Company, 1856 [No. 5]," *Salt Lake Herald,* Nov. 10, 1907, 5; see also Archer, Reminiscences, 158–59.
5. Kingsford, Autobiographical Sketch, 3; Carter, *Heart Throbs of the West,* 378; Archer, Reminiscences, 158–63; Binder, Reminiscences, Oct. 19, 1856; [John Jaques], "Some Reminiscences," *Salt Lake Daily Herald,* Dec. 8, 1878, 1; Josiah Rogerson, "Martin's Handcart Company, 1856 [No. 5]," *Salt Lake Herald,* Nov. 10, 1907, 3, 5.
6. Kingsford, Autobiographical Sketch, 4; Binder, Reminiscences, Oct. 20, 1856; Jones, Notes, Oct. 20, 1856; see also Josiah Rogerson, "Martin's Handcart Company, 1856 [No. 5]," *Salt Lake Herald,* Nov. 10, 1907, 5.
7. Kingsford, Autobiographical Sketch, 4; Edward Martin Company (1856) list, Pioneer Database, history.ChurchofJesusChrist.org/overlandtravel/companies; Haven, Journal, Oct. 20, 1856; Archer, Reminiscences, 163–64; Binder, Reminiscences, Oct. 20, 1856; Josiah Rogerson, "Martin's Handcart Company, 1856 [No. 6]," *Salt Lake Herald,* Nov. 17, 1907, 14. **Topic: Handcart Companies**
8. Durham, Journal, 15–16; Binder, Reminiscences, Oct. 20, 1856; Haven, Journal, Oct. 20–21, 1856.
9. Clark, "History of Louisa Mellor Clark," 3–4; George D. Grant to Brigham Young, Nov. 2, 1856, Brigham Young Office Files, CHL; Openshaw, Diary, 9; [John Jaques], "Some Reminiscences," *Salt Lake Daily Herald,* Dec. 15, 1878, 1; Bailey, Reminiscences and Journal, 6.

10. Kingsford, Autobiographical Sketch, 4–5; [John Jaques], "Some Reminiscences," *Salt Lake Daily Herald,* Dec. 15, 1878, 1; Binder, Reminiscences, Oct. 20–29, 1856.

11. Binder, Reminiscences, Oct. 20–29, 1856; Bleak, Journal, Oct. 23–28, 1856; Bailey, Reminiscences and Journal, 6; Kingsford, Autobiographical Sketch, 5; John Hunt to Brigham Young, Oct. 11, 1856, Brigham Young Office Files, CHL; Olsen, *Price We Paid,* 327–29; Josiah Rogerson, "Martin's Handcart Company, 1856 [No. 6]," *Salt Lake Herald,* Nov. 17, 1907, 14.

12. Bond, *Handcarts West in '56,* 24.

13. Kingsford, Autobiographical Sketch, 6.

14. Archer, Reminiscences, 172–73; Olsen, *Price We Paid,* 339–46; Josiah Rogerson, "Martin's Handcart Company, 1856 [No. 6]," *Salt Lake Herald,* Nov. 17, 1907, 14; Bond, *Handcarts West in '56,* 27–28; Christy, "Weather, Disaster, and Responsibility," 44. Quotation edited for readability; original source has "He then told the captain Edward Martin if he had flour enough to give us all one pound of flour each and said if there was any cattle to kill and give us one pound of beef each saying these was plenty provisions and clothing coming for us on the road but to morrow morning we must make a move from there."

15. Bleak, Journal, Oct. 28, 1856; Clark, "History of Louisa Mellor Clark," 3–4; Bond, *Handcarts West in '56,* 25, 27–29; Josiah Rogerson, "Martin's Handcart Company, 1856 [No. 6]," *Salt Lake Herald,* Nov. 17, 1907, 14; Archer, Reminiscences, 173–74; [John Jaques], "Some Reminiscences," *Salt Lake Daily Herald,* Dec. 15, 1878, 1.

16. George D. Grant to Brigham Young, Nov. 2, 1856, Brigham Young Office Files, CHL; Olsen, *Price We Paid,* 347–48.

17. Olsen, *Price We Paid,* 358–62; Orton, "Martin Handcart Company at the Sweetwater," 10–29; [John Jaques], "Some Reminiscences," *Salt Lake Daily Herald,* Dec. 15, 1878, 1.

18. Haven, Journal, Oct. 31–Nov. 10, 1856; Clayton, *Latter-day Saints' Emigrants' Guide,* 14–15; George D. Grant to Brigham Young, Nov. 2, 1856, Brigham Young Office Files, CHL; Olsen, *Price We Paid,* 369–72.

19. George D. Grant to Brigham Young, Nov. 2, 1856, Brigham Young Office Files, CHL; see also "Remarks," *Deseret News,* Nov. 19, 1856, [4].

20. Olsen, *Price We Paid,* 381–87, 391–97; Rescue Companies (1856) list, Pioneer Database, history.ChurchofJesusChrist.org/overlandtravel/companies; Historian's Office, History of the Church, volume 26, Nov. 13, 1856, 985.

21. Joseph Simmons to Horace Whitney, Nov. 24, 1856, Rachel W. Simmons Collection, CHL.

22. "Discourse," *Deseret News,* Nov. 12, 1856, [2]; Woodruff, Journal, Oct. 31, 1856; see also Historical Department, Office Journal, Oct. 31, 1856; and Archer, Reminiscences, 188.

23. "Remarks," *Deseret News,* Dec. 10, 1856, [8]; see also Historian's Office, General Church Minutes, Nov. 30, 1856, and Apr. 7, 1852.

24. "Arrival," *Deseret News,* Dec. 3, 1856, [5]; Kingsford, Autobiographical Sketch, 6; Bailey, Reminiscences and Journal, 7; Bleak, Journal, Nov. 30, 1856; Christy, "Weather, Disaster, and Responsibility," 51; Olsen, *Price We Paid,* 369–71, 383–85, 393–94; [John Jaques], "Some Reminiscences," *Salt Lake Daily Herald,* Dec. 22, 1878, 1.

25. Haven, Journal, Dec. 15, 1856.

26. Archer, Reminiscences, 185. **Topic: Handcart Companies**

Chapter 17: The Folks Are Reforming

1. Ricks, *My Candid Opinion,* ix; Joseph F. Smith, Journal, Nov. 1, 1856–Mar. 1, 1857; see also George Q. Cannon, Journal, July 27, 1851.

2. Joseph F. Smith to Martha Ann Smith, Oct. 20, 1856, Joseph F. Smith Letters to Martha Ann Smith Harris, CHL. Quotation edited for readability; "had done" in original changed to "have done."

3. John Smith to Joseph F. Smith, Jan. 6, 1857; May 31, 1856; Joseph Fisher to Joseph F. Smith, Feb. 24, 1857, Joseph F. Smith, Papers, CHL; Woodruff, Journal, Feb. 18, 1855; see also Haws, "Joseph F. Smith's Encouragement of His Brother," 134–38. Final sentence of quotation edited for readability; "went to amuse" in original changed to "gone to amuse."

4. Woodruff, Journal, Oct. 6–7, 1856; Dec. 1, 8, and 30, 1856; Historian's Office, General Church Minutes, Feb. 10, 1857; "Minutes," *Deseret News,* Oct. 1, 1856, [5].

5. King, Autobiography, volume 7, [8], [34]; Woodruff, Journal, Sept. 14, 1856; Historian's Office, General Church Minutes, Dec. 14, 1856; "Discourse," *Deseret News,* Nov. 19, 1856, [2]–[3]. **Topic: Reformation of 1856–57**

6. Mary Jane Thompson and Mercy Fielding Thompson to Joseph F. Smith, Dec. 7, 1856; Mercy Fielding Thompson to Joseph F. Smith, Jan. 6, 1857, Joseph F. Smith, Papers, CHL.

7. Mary Jane Thompson and Mercy Fielding Thompson to Joseph F. Smith, Dec. 7, 1856, Joseph F. Smith, Papers, CHL; see also Kimball, "Confession in LDS Doctrine and Practice," 49–54.

8. Joseph Fisher to Joseph F. Smith, Feb. 24, 1857, in Joseph F. Smith, Papers, CHL; "Correspondence from Great Salt Lake City," *Mormon,* Nov. 29, 1856, [3]; *Questions to Be Asked the Latter Day Saints* ([Salt Lake City]: Publisher unidentified, [1856]); Whipple, Autobiography and Journal, 116; Peterson, *Mormon Reformation,* 27–30; see also Woodruff, Journal, Oct. 27 and Nov. 4, 1856.

9. John Smith and Hellen Smith to Joseph F. Smith, Nov. 3, 1856; Hellen Smith to Joseph F. Smith, Apr. 4, 1857, Joseph F. Smith, Papers, CHL; see also Joseph Fisher to Joseph F. Smith, Feb. 24, 1857, in Joseph F. Smith, Papers, CHL; Peterson, *Mormon Reformation,* 31–32; and Whipple, Autobiography and Journal, 116.

10. William Harris and Martha Ann Smith to Joseph F. Smith, Feb. 3, 1857, Joseph F. Smith, Papers, CHL; Martha Ann Smith to Joseph F. Smith, Apr. 5, 1857, Joseph F. Smith Letters to Martha Ann Smith Harris, CHL.

11. Martha Ann Smith to Joseph F. Smith, Apr. 5, 1857, Joseph F. Smith Letters to Martha Ann Smith Harris, CHL.

12. William Harris and Martha Ann Smith to Joseph F. Smith, Feb. 3, 1857, Joseph F. Smith, Papers, CHL.

13. Wilford Woodruff to Orson Pratt, Apr. 1, 1857, in *Latter-day Saints' Millennial Star,* June 27, 1857, 19:411; Jeremy, Journal, volume 3, Apr. 5, 1857; Wilford Woodruff, Letter to the Editor, July 1, 1857, in *Latter-day Saints' Millennial Star,* Aug. 29, 1857, 19:557; see also "Discourse by President Brigham Young," and "Discourse by Prest. Joseph Young," *Deseret News,* Mar. 18, 1857, [3]–[5].

14. Ballantyne, Journal, Dec. 31, 1856; Aird, "Reasons for Disaffection in the Late 1850s," 146–47; Whipple, Autobiography and Journal, 116; Woodruff, Journal, Dec. 7 and 8, 1856; King, Autobiography, volume 7, [34]–[35]; "Discourse," *Deseret News,* Jan. 21, 1857, [5]; see also Kimball, "Confession in LDS Doctrine and Practice," 49–54; Peterson, *Mormon Reformation,* 41–42; and John Toone to Brigham Young, Dec. 20, 1856, Brigham Young Office Files, CHL.

15. "Discourse," *Deseret News,* Oct. 1, 1856, [3]; see also "Remarks," *Deseret News,* Oct. 1, 1856, [3]; Woodruff, Journal, Sept. 21, 1856; *JSP,* CFM:351, note 521; and Peterson, *Mormon Reformation,* 25.

16. Brigham Young, Sept. 14, 1856, Historian's Office, Reports of Speeches, CHL; King, Autobiography, volume 7, [34]–[35]; Stout, Journal, Apr. 16, 1857; see also Peterson, *Mormon Reformation,* 72–73.

17. Historian's Office, General Church Minutes, Mar. 17, 1848; see also Woodruff, Journal, Mar. 17, 1848; and *JSP,* CFM:351, note 521.

18. Isaac Haight to Brigham Young, Oct. 29, 1856, Brigham Young Office Files, CHL.

19. Brigham Young to Isaac Haight, Mar. 5, 1857, Letterbook, volume 3, 461–62, Brigham Young Office Files, CHL; Brigham Young to Philo Farnsworth, Apr. 4, 1857, Letterbook, volume 3, 540, Brigham Young Office Files, CHL. **Topic: Reformation of 1856–57**

20. "Memorial and Resolutions to the President of the United States, concerning Certain Officers of the Territory of Utah," Jan. 5, 1857, Governor's Office Files, 1850–67, Brigham Young Office Files, CHL.

21. "Expedition against Utah," *Deseret News,* Oct. 7, 1857, [4]–[5]; Parowan Stake, Historical Record, Aug. 9, 1857, 23–24; John Bernhisel to Brigham Young, Apr. 2, 1857, Utah Delegate Files, 1849–72, Brigham Young Office Files, CHL; "Eastern Mail," *Deseret News,* June 3, 1857, [5]; Rogers, *Unpopular Sovereignty,* 156–58.

22. John Bernhisel to Brigham Young, Apr. 2, 1857, Utah Delegate Files, 1849–72, Brigham Young Office Files, CHL; "Expedition against Utah," *Deseret News,* Oct. 7, 1857, [4]–[5]; "Mormon Rebellion," *New York Times,* May 11, 1857, 4; "Mr. Buchanan's Administration and Our Domestic Affairs," *New York Herald,* Mar. 17, 1857, 4; Rogers, *Unpopular Sovereignty,* 135–81. **Topics: Utah War; American Civil War**

23. See Woodruff, Journal, May 31, 1857; and John Bernhisel to Brigham Young, Mar. 17, 1857, Utah Delegate Files, 1849–72, Brigham Young Office Files, CHL.

24. Brigham Young to "My Dear Friend," June 29, 1857, draft, Brigham Young Office Files, CHL; Eleanor J. McComb Pratt to "Brother Snow," May 14, 1857, CHL; Eleanor J. McComb Pratt, Reminiscence, 29; Pomeroy, Statement, Apr. 11, 1898, CHL; "Tragical," *Arkansas Intelligencer,* May 15, 1857, [2]; see also Parley P. Pratt, Journal, Nov. 14, 1855; Woodruff, Journal, Jan. 3, 1858; and Givens and Grow, *Parley P. Pratt,* 366–85. **Topic: Parley P. Pratt**

25. See "Tragical," *Arkansas Intelligencer,* May 15, 1857, [2]; "Child Stealing," *Daily Missouri Republican,* May 25, 1857, [2]; Walker, Whittaker, and Allen, *Mormon History,* 202–3; and Givens and Grow, *Parley P. Pratt,* 386–88.

26. See "The Killing of Pratt—Letter from Mr. McLean," *Daily Alta California,* July 9, 1857, [2]; and Brigham Young to "Silas Smith and the Brethren on the Sandwich Islands," July 4, 1857, Letterbook, volume 3, 698–99, Brigham Young Office Files, CHL.

27. Nixon, *Abraham Owen Smoot,* 184; Harris, "Martha Ann Smith Harris," 15–16; Martha Ann Smith Harris to Joseph F. Smith, May 3, 1857; William Harris to Joseph F. Smith, July 1, 1857, Joseph F. Smith, Papers, CHL.

28. William Harris to Joseph F. Smith, July 1, 1857, Joseph F. Smith, Papers, CHL.

29. George D. Watt, "The 24th of July in the Tops of the Mountains," *Deseret News,* July 29, 1857, [5]; *Pic-nic Party at the Head Waters of Big Cottonwood* (Salt Lake City: Publisher unidentified, July 18, 1857), copy at CHL; Woodruff, Journal, July 22–24, 1857; Young, Office Journal, July 24, 1857; Tullidge, *History of Salt Lake City,* 156–59; MacKinnon, *At Sword's Point,* 563; see also Historical Department, Office Journal, July 22–24, 1857.

30. Woodruff, Journal, July 25, 1857; Daniel H. Wells and James Ferguson to "Maj. Genl. G. D. Grant," Aug. 1, 1857, Nauvoo Legion (Utah) Records, CHL; Brigham Young to "Bishop Bronson," Aug. 2, 1857, Letterbook, volume 3, 732, Brigham Young Office Files, CHL.

31. Brigham Young to George Q. Cannon, Aug. 4, 1857, Letterbook, volume 3, 735, Brigham Young Office Files, CHL; see also Brigham Young to William Crosby and William J. Cox, Aug. 4, 1857, Letterbook, volume 3, 751–54, Brigham Young Office Files, CHL; Parowan Stake, Historical Record, Aug. 23, 1857, 25; and Cannon, *Writings from the "Western Standard,"* vii.

32. Brigham Young to George Q. Cannon, Aug. 4, 1857, Letterbook, volume 3, 733–34, Brigham Young Office Files, CHL; Reavis, *Life and Military Services of Gen. William Selby Harney,* 252–56, 276–77; LeCheminant, "General Harney and the Change in Command of the Utah Expedition," 30–45; see also Clow, "General William S. Harney on the Northern Plains," 236.

33. Brigham Young to William Crosby and William J. Cox, Aug. 4, 1857, Letterbook, volume 3, 751–54, Brigham Young Office Files, CHL. **Topic: Utah War**

34. Parowan Stake, Historical Record, section B, Aug. 8, 1857, 32; George A. Smith, Journal, Dec. 7, 1850–Apr. 7, 1851; Nov. 5, 1851.

35. Elias Morris, Statement, Feb. 2, 1892, Collected Material concerning the Mountain Meadows Massacre, CHL; Seegmiller, *History of Iron County,* 64–67; see also Shirts and Shirts, *Trial Furnace,* 373–81.

36. Parowan Stake, Historical Record, section B, Aug. 8, 1857, 32; see also Parowan Stake, Historical Record, Aug. 9 and 23, 1857, 22, 25.

37. Parowan Stake, Historical Record, Aug. 9, 1857, 22–23; see also Parowan Stake, Historical Record, Aug. 23, 1857, 24; and Historical Department, Office Journal, Aug. 8–9, 1857.

Chapter 18: Too Late, Too Late

1. Liljenquist, Autobiography, [9]; Dorius, "Sketch of the Life," 47; Christian Christiansen Company (1857) list, Pioneer Database, history.ChurchofJesusChrist.org /overlandtravel/companies.

2. Dorius, "Sketch of the Life," 6–7, 11–12, 46, 49; see also Ole Nielsen Liljenquist, "Biografiske Skizzer," *Morgenstjernen,* Mar. 1833, 40.

3. Matthias Cowley to Orson Pratt, June 1, 1857, *Latter-day Saints' Millennial Star,* July 11, 1857, 19:446; Liljenquist, Autobiography, [9]; Frantzen, Reminiscence and Journal, 33.

4. Dorius, "Autobiography of Carl Christian Nicoli Dorius," 19–21. **Topic: Handcart Companies**

5. Christensen, "Reminiscence," in Jensen, "By Handcart to Utah," 337, 343–44; Liljenquist, Autobiography, [9]; Benson, "Recollections," 3–4; Frantzen, Reminiscence and Journal, 37–39; Tanner, *Biographical Sketch of James Jensen,* 23–40; Carl Dorius, Biographical Sketch, 2.

6. Dorius, "Sketch of the Life," 46, 49–50, 52; Carl Dorius, Biographical Sketch, 2–3; Dorius, "Autobiography of Carl Christian Nicoli Dorius," 19–21. Some records give Kaia as an alternate name for Karen.

7. Brigham Young to Jacob Hamblin, Aug. 4, 1857, Letterbook, volume 3, 737–38, Brigham Young Office Files, CHL; Hamblin, Journal, 37–38; Jacob Hamblin, Deposition, Nov. 28, 1871, President's Office Files, 1843–77, Brigham Young Office Files, CHL; Historical Department, Office Journal, Aug. 25, 1857; Huntington, Journal, Sept. 1, 1857.

8. See Little, *Jacob Hamblin,* 31; and Carleton, *Report on the Subject of the Massacre at the Mountain Meadows,* 10.

9. George A. Smith to Md. St. Clair, Nov. 25, 1869, Historian's Office, Letterpress Copybook, volume 2, 941–43; George A. Smith, Statement, [Nov. 1896], George A. Smith, Papers, CHL; see also Eleanor J. Pratt to "Brother Snow," May 14, 1857, CHL.

10. Walker, Turley, and Leonard, *Massacre at Mountain Meadows,* 76–83, 104–5, 244–49, 251–54; Carleton, *Report on the Subject of the Massacre at the Mountain Meadows,* 4, 6; see also Hamblin, Journal, 38–40; and Little, *Jacob Hamblin,* 45.

11. Walker, Turley, and Leonard, *Massacre at Mountain Meadows,* 80, 105–13; see also Provo Utah Central Stake, General Minutes, Aug. 16, 1857, volume 10, 907–8; "Late Horrible Massacre," *Los Angeles Star,* Oct. 17, 1857, [2]; and Arrington, *Great Basin Kingdom,* 148–51.

12. George A. Smith to Md. St. Clair, Nov. 25, 1869, Historian's Office, Letterpress Copybook, volume 2, 941–43; George A. Smith, Incidents Connected with the Mountain Meadows Massacre, [Nov. 1869], George A. Smith, Papers, CHL; Carleton, *Report on the Subject of the Massacre at the Mountain Meadows,* 6; see also Parker, *Recollections of the Mountain Meadows Massacre,* 11.

13. Carleton, *Report on the Subject of the Massacre at the Mountain Meadows,* 6; Silas Smith, Testimony, in Boreman, Transcript of John D. Lee's First Trial, 5:229; Jacob Hamblin, Testimony, in Boreman, Transcript of John D. Lee's Second Trial, 1:92.

14. Walker, Turley, and Leonard, *Massacre at Mountain Meadows,* 129–32; "Lee's Confession," *Sacramento Daily Record-Union,* Mar. 24, 1877, 3; Philip Klingensmith, Testimony, in Rogerson, Shorthand of John D. Lee's First Trial, 2:19; Boreman, Transcript of John D. Lee's First Trial, 3:2, 58–59; "History of Mormonism," *Corinne Reporter,* July 22, 1871, [2]; see also Shirts and Shirts, *Trial Furnace,* 372–87.

15. "History of Mormonism," *Corinne Reporter,* July 22, 1871, [2]; Philip Klingensmith, Testimony, in Rogerson, Shorthand of John D. Lee's First Trial, 2:19; Boreman, Transcript of John D. Lee's First Trial, 3:58–59; Bowering, Journal, fall 1857, 230; Walker, Turley, and Leonard, *Massacre at Mountain Meadows,* 132; Krenkel, *Life and Times of Joseph Fish,* 57.

16. "Christopher J. Arthur, Field Notes"; "Christopher J. Arthur, Prepared Report," Jan. 26, 1892, in Turley and Walker, *Mountain Meadows Massacre,* 80, 82; Parowan Stake, Historical Record, Aug. 9, 1857, 22–23; see also Turley and Walker, *Mountain Meadows Massacre,* 231; Plat of Cedar City, Oct. 1852, Historian's Office, Collected Historical Documents, CHL; and Shirts and Shirts, *Trial Furnace,* 289–96.

17. Krenkel, *Life and Times of Joseph Fish,* 57–58; Bowering, Journal, fall 1857, 230; "Christopher J. Arthur, Field Notes"; "Christopher J. Arthur, Prepared Report," Jan. 26, 1892, in Turley and Walker, *Mountain Meadows Massacre,* 80, 82; Charles Willden, Affidavit, Feb. 18, 1882; Elias Morris, Statement, Feb. 2, 1892, Collected Material concerning the Mountain Meadows Massacre, CHL; Walker, Turley, and Leonard, *Massacre at Mountain Meadows,* 93–94, 132–33.

18. "Nephi Johnson, Affidavit, July 22, 1908," in Turley and Walker, *Mountain Meadows Massacre,* 328.

19. Annie Hoge, Testimony, in Boreman, Transcript of John D. Lee's First Trial, 4:26–27.

20. "Lee's Confession," *Sacramento Daily Record-Union,* Mar. 24, 1877, 3; "Christopher J. Arthur, Prepared Report," Jan. 26, 1892, in Turley and Walker, *Mountain Meadows Massacre,* 82–83; see also An Act in relation to Profanity and Drunkenness, *Acts, Resolutions, and Memorials . . . of the Territory of Utah,* 89.

21. James H. Martineau to Susan, May 3, 1876, James H. Martineau Collection, CHL; John Chatterly to Andrew Jenson, Sept. 18, 1919, in Turley and Walker, *Mountain Meadows Massacre,* 278; Martineau, "Mountain Meadow Catastrophy," [2]; see also Walker, Turley, and Leonard, *Massacre at Mountain Meadows,* 55–56, 134–36, 256.

22. "Lee's Confession," *Sacramento Daily Record-Union,* Mar. 24, 1877, 3; John D. Lee to Brigham Young, May 23, 1856, Brigham Young Office Files, CHL; see also Walker, Turley, and Leonard, *Massacre at Mountain Meadows,* 59–67, 136, 139–40.

23. Lee, *Mormonism Unveiled,* 219–20; "Ellott Willden, Prepared Report," in Turley and Walker, *Mountain Meadows Massacre,* 213–14; Walker, Turley, and Leonard, *Massacre at Mountain Meadows,* 64–65; see also Knack, *Boundaries Between,* 2; and Walker, Turley, and Leonard, *Massacre at Mountain Meadows,* 137–45.

24. "Lee's Confession," *Sacramento Daily Record-Union,* Mar. 24, 1877, 3; Lee, *Mormonism Unveiled,* 218–20; see also "Daniel S. Macfarlane, Prepared Report," in Turley and Walker, *Mountain Meadows Massacre,* 109.

25. Lee, *Mormonism Unveiled,* 218, 219; see also "Elias Morris, Prepared Report—Andrew Jenson Copy," Feb. 2, 1892, in Turley and Walker, *Mountain Meadows Massacre,* 253. Quotation edited for readability; original source has "Haight said that unless something was done to prevent it, the emigrants would carry out their threats and rob every one of the out-lying settlements in the South."

26. Lee, *Mormonism Unveiled,* 219–20. Quotation edited for readability; "killed" in original changed to "kill."

27. Laban Morrill, Testimony, in Boreman, Transcript of John D. Lee's Second Trial, 1:3–4, 6, 9; Sudweeks, "Life of Laban Morrill," 1, 8–9; "Elias Morris, Prepared Report—Andrew Jenson Copy," Feb. 2, 1892, in Turley and Walker, *Mountain Meadows Massacre,* 254.

28. Laban Morrill, Testimony, in Boreman, Transcript of John D. Lee's Second Trial, 1:4, 6, 9, 10–11; Laban Morrill, Testimony, in Patterson, Shorthand Notes of John D. Lee's Second Trial, 2:[20]–[21]; Sudweeks, "Life of Laban Morrill," 8; "Elias Morris, Prepared

Report—Andrew Jenson Copy," Feb. 2, 1892, in Turley and Walker, *Mountain Meadows Massacre,* 254; Philip Klingensmith, Testimony, in Boreman, Transcript of John D. Lee's First Trial, 3:4–5.

29. Philip Klingensmith, Testimony, in Boreman, Transcript of John D. Lee's First Trial, 3:4–5; Sudweeks, "Life of Laban Morrill," 8–9; Laban Morrill, Testimony, in Boreman, Transcript of John D. Lee's Second Trial, 1:6–8; "Elias Morris, Prepared Report—Andrew Jenson Copy," Feb. 2, 1892, in Turley and Walker, *Mountain Meadows Massacre,* 254.

30. Laban Morrill, Testimony, in Boreman, Transcript of John D. Lee's Second Trial, 1:6, 8–10; Walker, Turley, and Leonard, *Massacre at Mountain Meadows,* 145–48, 157–62.

31. "Ellott Willden, Prepared Report"; "Ellott Willden, 'Additional' Prepared Report," in Turley and Walker, *Mountain Meadows Massacre,* 213–15, 222; Carleton, *Report on the Subject of the Massacre at the Mountain Meadows,* 8; Lee, *Mormonism Unveiled,* 226–27; "Lee's Confession," *Sacramento Daily Record-Union,* Mar. 24, 1877, 3; see also Joseph Clewes, "Mountain Meadows Massacre," *Salt Lake Daily Herald,* Apr. 5, 1877, [4]; and Walker, Turley, and Leonard, *Massacre at Mountain Meadows,* 158–62.

32. Jacob Hamblin to Brigham Young, Nov. 13, 1871; Jacob Hamblin, Deposition, Nov. 28, 1871, President's Office Files, 1843–77, Brigham Young Office Files, CHL; James Haslam, Testimony, in Boreman, Transcript of John D. Lee's Second Trial, 1:12; Walker, Turley, and Leonard, *Massacre at Mountain Meadows,* 162–64.

33. James Holt Haslam, Testimony, Dec. 4, 1884, [2], in "John D. Lee: Miscellaneous Papers pertaining to His Trials, Guilt, and Death," 1911, box 1, folder 18, Collected Material concerning the Mountain Meadows Massacre, CHL; James Haslam, Testimony, in Boreman, Transcript of John D. Lee's Second Trial, 1:12; Muster Roll of Company D, 2nd Battalion, in Iron Military District, Muster Rolls, 1856–57, Utah Division of Archives and Records Service, Territorial Militia Records, 1849–77, Utah State Archives and Records Service, Salt Lake City.

34. Joseph Clewes, "Mountain Meadows Massacre," *Salt Lake Daily Herald,* Apr. 5, 1877, [4].

35. "Ellott Willden, Prepared Report," in Turley and Walker, *Mountain Meadows Massacre,* 213, 216–18; see also Walker, Turley, and Leonard, *Massacre at Mountain Meadows,* 159–60, 164.

36. "Bull Valley Snort," Statement, Feb. 1894, John M. Higbee Information, Collected Material concerning the Mountain Meadows Massacre, CHL; "Ellott Willden, Prepared Report," in Turley and Walker, *Mountain Meadows Massacre,* 211; Walker, Turley, and Leonard, *Massacre at Mountain Meadows,* 173–74.

37. "Nephi Johnson Affidavit, July 22, 1908," in Turley and Walker, *Mountain Meadows Massacre,* 328; Walker, Turley, and Leonard, *Massacre at Mountain Meadows,* 169–70; see also "Lee's Confession," *Sacramento Daily Record-Union,* Mar. 24, 1877, 3.

38. Martineau, "Mountain Meadow Catastrophy," [2]; Whitney, *History of Utah,* 1:700–701; Lee, *Mormonism Unveiled,* 240; see also "Late Horrible Massacre," *Los Angeles Star,* Oct. 17, 1857, [2]; "Lee's Confession," *Sacramento Daily Record-Union,* Mar. 24, 1877, 3; and Walker, Turley, and Leonard, *Massacre at Mountain Meadows,* 174, 178–79.

39. "Lee's Confession," *Sacramento Daily Record-Union,* Mar. 24, 1877, 3; J. H. Beadle, "Interview with Jno. D. Lee of Mountain Meadows Notoriety," *Salt Lake Daily Tribune,* July 29, 1872, [2]; Philip Klingensmith, Testimony, in Boreman, Transcript of John D. Lee's First Trial, 3:82; "Nephi Johnson Affidavit, Nov. 30, 1909," in Turley and Walker, *Mountain Meadows Massacre,* 329; see also Walker, Turley, and Leonard, *Massacre at Mountain Meadows,* 172–74.

40. "Elias Morris, Prepared Report—Andrew Jenson Copy," Feb. 2, 1892; "William Barton, Prepared Report," in Turley and Walker, *Mountain Meadows Massacre,* 67–69, 254–55.

41. [Josiah Rogerson], "Review of John D. Lee's Life and Confessions," 21–22, in "John D. Lee: Miscellaneous Papers pertaining to His Trials, Guilt, and Death," 1911, box 1, folder 19, Collected Material concerning the Mountain Meadows Massacre, CHL; "Lee's Confession," *Sacramento Daily Record-Union,* Mar. 24, 1877, 3; "Daniel S. Macfarlane, Prepared Report," in Turley and Walker, *Mountain Meadows Massacre,* 110–11; Walker, Turley, and Leonard, *Massacre at Mountain Meadows,* 177–79.

Sources indicate that Elias Morris was present at the meeting of Isaac Haight and William Dame.

42. Jacob Hamblin to Brigham Young, Nov. 13, 1871, President's Office Files, 1843–77, Brigham Young Office Files, CHL; "Daniel S. Macfarlane, Prepared Report," in Turley and Walker, *Mountain Meadows Massacre,* 110–11; Walker, Turley, and Leonard, *Massacre at Mountain Meadows,* 178–79.

43. Jacob Hamblin, Deposition, Nov. 28, 1871, President's Office Files, 1843–77, Brigham Young Office Files, CHL; see also Jacob Hamblin to Brigham Young, Nov. 13, 1871, President's Office Files, 1843–77, Brigham Young Office Files, CHL.

44. Brigham Young to Isaac Haight, Sept. 10, 1857; Brigham Young to Orson Pratt Sr., Sept. 12, 1857, Letterbook, volume 3, 827, 844–48, Brigham Young Office Files, CHL; see also Young, Office Journal, Sept. 8–10, 1857.

45. Jacob Hamblin, Deposition, Nov. 28, 1871, President's Office Files, 1843–77, Brigham Young Office Files, CHL.

46. James Holt Haslam, Testimony, Dec. 4, 1884, [2]–[5], in "John D. Lee: Miscellaneous Papers pertaining to His Trials, Guilt, and Death," 1911, box 1, folder 18, Collected Material concerning the Mountain Meadows Massacre, CHL; see also Walker, Turley, and Leonard, *Massacre at Mountain Meadows,* 181–83.

47. James Holt Haslam, Testimony, Dec. 4, 1884, [5], in "John D. Lee: Miscellaneous Papers pertaining to His Trials, Guilt, and Death," 1911, box 1, folder 18, Collected Material concerning the Mountain Meadows Massacre, CHL; James Haslam, Testimony, in Boreman, Transcript of John D. Lee's Second Trial, 1:12.

48. Brigham Young to Isaac Haight, Sept. 10, 1857, Letterbook, volume 3, 827–28, Brigham Young Office Files, CHL.

49. Historical Department, Office Journal, Sept. 10, 1857; Hamilton G. Park, Affidavit, Oct. 1907, Collected Material concerning the Mountain Meadows Massacre, CHL; see also James Haslam, Testimony, in Boreman, Transcript of John D. Lee's Second Trial, 1:12.

50. Cedar City Ward, Relief Society Minute Book, Sept. 10, 1857, in Derr and others, *First Fifty Years of Relief Society,* 229–30.

51. See "Elias Morris, Prepared Report—Andrew Jenson Copy," Feb. 2, 1892, in Turley and Walker, *Mountain Meadows Massacre,* 253; Cedar City Ward, Relief Society Minute Book, Sept. 10, 1857, in Derr and others, *First Fifty Years of Relief Society,* 229–30; and Walker, Turley, and Leonard, *Massacre at Mountain Meadows,* 134–35.

52. Cedar City Ward, Relief Society Minute Book, Sept. 10, 1857, in Derr and others, *First Fifty Years of Relief Society,* 23–31; *Songs of Zion* (Publication place and publisher unidentified, [1853]), in John Freeman, Songbook, circa 1849, CHL.

53. Philip Klingensmith, Testimony; Samuel Pollock, Testimony, in Boreman, Transcript of John D. Lee's First Trial, 3:7–8, 4:68, 5:182; "Daniel S. Macfarlane, Prepared Report"; "Nephi Johnson Affidavit, July 22, 1908," in Turley and Walker, *Mountain Meadows Massacre,* 112, 329; Walker, Turley, and Leonard, *Massacre at Mountain Meadows,* 158–59, 179, 190; appendix C, 255–64.

54. See Walker, Turley, and Leonard, *Massacre at Mountain Meadows,* appendix C, 255–64.

55. "Nephi Johnson Affidavit, July 22, 1908," in Turley and Walker, *Mountain Meadows Massacre,* 330; see also "Daniel S. Macfarlane, Prepared Report," in Turley and Walker, *Mountain Meadows Massacre,* 111; and Walker, Turley, and Leonard, *Massacre at Mountain Meadows,* 179.

56. Walker, Turley, and Leonard, *Massacre at Mountain Meadows,* 187–89.

57. "Nephi Johnson Affidavit, July 22, 1908"; "Nephi Johnson Affidavit, Nov. 30, 1909," in Turley and Walker, *Mountain Meadows Massacre,* 328–30, 332; Nephi Johnson, Testimony, in Boreman, Transcript of John D. Lee's Second Trial, 1:76–77; Nephi Johnson to A. H. Lund, Mar. 1910, Collected Material concerning the Mountain Meadows Massacre, CHL.

58. "Nephi Johnson Affidavit, July 22, 1908," in Turley and Walker, *Mountain Meadows Massacre,* 329–30; Lee, *Mormonism Unveiled,* 238–40; "Lee's Confession," *Sacramento*

Daily Record-Union, Mar. 24, 1877, 3; James Lynch, Affidavit, [May 1859], in Turley, Johnson, and Carruth, *Mountain Meadows Massacre,* 1:247.

59. "Nephi Johnson Affidavit, July 22, 1908"; "Nephi Johnson Affidavit, Nov. 30, 1909," in Turley and Walker, *Mountain Meadows Massacre,* 329–30, 333; Lee, *Mormonism Unveiled,* 240; "Lee's Confession," *Sacramento Daily Record-Union,* Mar. 24, 1877, 3; Samuel McMurdy, Testimony, in Boreman, Transcript of John D. Lee's Second Trial, 1:35–36; Joel White, Testimony, in Boreman, Transcript of John D. Lee's First Trial, 3:126; "Mountain Meadows Massacre," *Daily Arkansas Gazette,* Sept. 1, 1875, [3]; Walker, Turley, and Leonard, *Massacre at Mountain Meadows,* 196–97, 202–5.

60. Nephi Johnson, Testimony, in Boreman, Transcript of John D. Lee's Second Trial, 1:76–77; Lee, *Mormonism Unveiled,* 238, 240; "Nephi Johnson Affidavit, Nov. 30, 1909," in Turley and Walker, *Mountain Meadows Massacre,* 333; "Lee's Confession," *Sacramento Daily Record-Union,* Mar. 24, 1877, 3; see also "Nephi Johnson Affidavit, July 22, 1908," in Turley and Walker, *Mountain Meadows Massacre,* 329–30.

61. "Ellott Willden, Bancroft Corrections—Prepared Report," in Turley and Walker, *Mountain Meadows Massacre,* 156–58; see also Whitney, *History of Utah,* 1:706.

62. Philip Klingensmith, Testimony; Joel White, Testimony, in Boreman, Transcript of John D. Lee's First Trial, 3:81–82, 126–27; Walker, Turley, and Leonard, *Massacre at Mountain Meadows,* 199.

63. "Ellott Willden, Bancroft Corrections—Prepared Report"; "Nephi Johnson Affidavit, Nov. 30, 1909," in Turley and Walker, *Mountain Meadows Massacre,* 158, 333; Jacob Hamblin, Testimony, in Carleton, *Report on the Subject of the Massacre at the Mountain Meadows,* 9; Samuel Pollock, Testimony, in Boreman, Transcript of John D. Lee's First Trial, 5:196; see also "Lee's Confession," *Sacramento Daily Record-Union,* Mar. 24, 1877, 3; and Walker, Turley, and Leonard, *Massacre at Mountain Meadows,* 200.

64. "Ellott Willden, Bancroft Corrections—Prepared Report," in Turley and Walker, *Mountain Meadows Massacre,* 158–59; Albert Hamblin, Testimony, in Carleton, *Report on the Subject of the Massacre at the Mountain Meadows,* 14; William Young, Testimony, in Boreman, Transcript of John D. Lee's First Trial, 4:53, 5:210–11.

65. "Ellott Willden, Bancroft Corrections—Prepared Report," in Turley and Walker, *Mountain Meadows Massacre,* 158–59; Philip Klingensmith, Testimony, in Boreman, Transcript of John D. Lee's First Trial, 3:15, 17–18; Philip Klingensmith, Testimony, in Rogerson, Shorthand of John D. Lee's First Trial, 2:27; Philip Klingensmith, Testimony, U.S. v. John D. Lee (1875), in Patterson, Shorthand Notes of John D. Lee's First Trial, 3:[2]–[3]; "Ellott Willden, Field Notes," in Turley and Walker, *Mountain Meadows Massacre,* 202.

66. Lee, *Mormonism Unveiled,* 241–42; "Nephi Johnson Affidavit, July 22, 1908," in Turley and Walker, *Mountain Meadows Massacre,* 330.

67. "Nephi Johnson Affidavit, July 22, 1908," in Turley and Walker, *Mountain Meadows Massacre,* 330; Philip Klingensmith, Testimony, in Boreman, Transcript of John D. Lee's First Trial, 3:85; Rachel Hamblin, Testimony; Albert Hamblin, Testimony, in Carleton, *Report on the Subject of the Massacre at the Mountain Meadows,* 11–12, 14; see also Jacob Hamblin, Testimony, in Carleton, *Report on the Subject of the Massacre at the Mountain Meadows,* 7–8; and Walker, Turley, and Leonard, *Massacre at Mountain Meadows,* 200, 208–9, 214–15, 246.

68. Rachel Hamblin, Testimony, in Carleton, *Report on the Subject of the Massacre at the Mountain Meadows,* 11–12.

69. Lee, *Mormonism Unveiled,* 245; "Lee's Confession," *Sacramento Daily Record-Union,* Mar. 24, 1877, 4.

70. Lee, *Mormonism Unveiled,* 245; "Ellott Willden, Bancroft Corrections—Field Notes," in Turley and Walker, *Mountain Meadows Massacre,* 144; see also "John H. Henderson, Field Notes," in Turley and Walker, *Mountain Meadows Massacre,* 76.

71. Lee, *Mormonism Unveiled,* 246; "Lee's Confession," *Sacramento Daily Record-Union,* Mar. 24, 1877, 4.

72. Lee, *Mormonism Unveiled,* 245–47; Carleton, *Report on the Subject of the Massacre at the Mountain Meadows,* 29.
73. "Lee's Confession," *Sacramento Daily Record-Union,* Mar. 24, 1877, 4; Lee, *Mormonism Unveiled,* 246. Quotation edited for readability; "was" in original changed to "were."
74. Lee, *Mormonism Unveiled,* 246–47.
75. Lee, *Mormonism Unveiled,* 247–48; Nephi Johnson, Testimony, in Boreman, Transcript of John D. Lee's Second Trial, 1:77–79; see also Walker, Turley, and Leonard, *Massacre at Mountain Meadows,* 215–16.
76. "Nephi Johnson Affidavit, July 22, 1908," in Turley and Walker, *Mountain Meadows Massacre,* 330; Brigham Young to Isaac Haight, Sept. 10, 1857, Letterbook, volume 3, 827–28, Brigham Young Office Files, CHL.
77. James Haslam, Interview by Scipio A. Kenner, Dec. 4, 1884, in Turley, Johnson, and Carruth, *Mountain Meadows Massacre,* 2:894. **Topic: Mountain Meadows Massacre**

CHAPTER 19: THE CHAMBERS OF THE LORD

1. Christian Christiansen Company (1857), Pioneer Database, history .ChurchofJesusChrist.org/overlandtravel/companies; Benson, "Recollections," 1–4; Christensen, "Reminiscence," in Jensen, "By Handcart to Utah," 337, 343–44; Dorius, "Autobiography of Carl Christian Nicoli Dorius," 20; Tanner, *Biographical Sketch of James Jensen,* 34–35, 39–40; Dorius, *Dorius Heritage,* 87–88.
2. Christensen, "Reminiscence," in Jensen, "By Handcart to Utah," 344; Dorius, "Sketch of the Life," 52; Dorius, "Autobiography of Carl Christian Nicoli Dorius," 21; see also Dorius, *Dorius Heritage,* 89–90.
3. Dorius, "Autobiography of Carl Christian Nicoli Dorius," 21; Dorius, *Dorius Heritage,* 89–90, 156–57; Endowment House Sealing Record, Book C, 210, microfilm 1,149,514, Special Collections, Family History Library; Jacob F. Secrist/Noah T. Guymon Company (1855) list, Pioneer Database, history.ChurchofJesusChrist.org /overlandtravel/companies.
4. Woodruff, Journal, Sept. 12–13, 1857; Brigham Young, *Proclamation by the Governor* (Salt Lake City: Publisher unidentified, Sept. 15, 1857); William Harney to Brigham Young, July 28, 1857, Federal and Local Government Files, 1844–76; Stewart Van Vliet to Brigham Young, Sept. 10, 1857, Brigham Young Office Files, CHL; see also "General Orders, No. 12," June 30, 1857, Federal and Local Government Files, 1844–76, Brigham Young Office Files, CHL; Historical Department, Office Journal, Sept. 18, 1857; see also Hawley, Autobiography, 12.
5. "Remarks," *Deseret News,* Sept. 23, 1857, [4]–[5]; see also Woodruff, Journal, Sept. 12–13, 1857; and Brigham Young, Aug. 16, 1857, Historian's Office, Reports of Speeches, CHL. **Topic: Utah War**
6. "Remarks," *Deseret News,* Oct. 14, 1857, [4].
7. "Minutes of the Semi-annual Conference," *Deseret News,* Oct. 14, 1857, [7]; Dorius, "Sketch of the Life," 23; Dorius, *Dorius Heritage,* 91.
8. Dorius, "Sketch of the Life," 54–55; Dorius, "Autobiography of Carl Christian Nicoli Dorius," 21; Dorius, *Dorius Heritage,* 91.
9. Woodruff, Journal, Sept. 29, 1857; see also Lee, *Mormonism Unveiled,* 251–52. **Topic: Mountain Meadows Massacre**
10. Woodruff, Journal, Sept. 29, 1857; see also Lee, *Mormonism Unveiled,* 170, 216, 251–52; Walker, Turley, and Leonard, *Massacre at Mountain Meadows,* 61–62; Woodruff, Journal, Jan. 18, 1847; and Brigham Young, Journal, Jan. 25, 1846. Brigham Young quotation edited for readability; "was" in original changed to "is."
11. John D. Lee to Brigham Young, Nov. 20, 1857; Brigham Young to James W. Denver, Jan. 6, 1858, Governor's Office Files, 1850–67, Brigham Young Office Files, CHL; Turley, Johnson, and Carruth, *Mountain Meadows Massacre,* 1:24–28.

12. "Rumored Massacre on the Plains," *Los Angeles Star,* Oct. 3, 1857, [2]; "Horrible Massacre of Emigrants!!," *Los Angeles Star,* Oct. 10, 1857, [2]; "Late Horrible Massacre," *Los Angeles Star,* Oct. 17, 1857, [2].

13. See, for example, J. Warl Christman, "Massacre by Indians of an Entire Immigrant Train," *Daily Evening Bulletin,* Oct. 12, 1857, [3]; "Horrible Massacre of Emigrants—Over 100 Persons Killed," *Daily Cleveland Herald,* Nov. 9, 1857, [2]; and "Horrible Massacre of Emigrants," *New York Herald,* Nov. 17, 1857, 2.

14. "Immigrant Massacre," *Daily Alta California,* Oct. 17, 1857, 1. Quotation edited for clarity; question mark added.

15. "Massacre of Emigrants—Reckless and Malignant Slanders," *Western Standard,* Oct. 23, 1857, [2]; "Killing of Immigrants—Mormons Falsely Accused—Further Endurance No Longer a Virtue," *Western Standard,* Nov. 6, 1857, [2].

16. Joseph F. Smith, "Report of My Mission," circa Feb. 1858, [3], in Missionary Reports, CHL; Partridge, Journal, Oct. 22, 1857; Sixtus Johnson, Journal, Oct. 22, 1857; Smith, *Life of Joseph F. Smith,* 186–88.

17. George Q. Cannon, Journal, Jan. 28–31, 1856, and Dec. 1–3, 1857.

18. See Smith, *Life of Joseph F. Smith,* 188; George Q. Cannon, Journal, Dec. 3, 1857; and Louisa Barnes Pratt, Journal and Autobiography, 371.

19. Smith, *Life of Joseph F. Smith,* 188–89; see also Nibley, "Reminiscences of President Joseph F. Smith," 192. **Topic: Joseph F. Smith**

20. Joseph F. Smith to Martha Ann Smith, June 9, 1855, Joseph F. Smith Letters to Martha Ann Smith Harris, CHL; see also Joseph F. Smith to Martha Ann Smith, Feb. 18, 1856, Joseph F. Smith Letters to Martha Ann Smith Harris, CHL.

21. Smith, *Life of Joseph F. Smith,* 189; Nibley, "Reminiscences of President Joseph F. Smith," 192.

22. See "San Bernardino," *Western Standard,* Dec. 27, 1856, [3]; William Cox to Brigham Young, Nov. 7, 1857, Brigham Young Office Files, CHL; Louisa Barnes Pratt, Journal and Autobiography, 371–72; and Plewe, *Mapping Mormonism,* 96–97.

23. Louisa Barnes Pratt, Journal and Autobiography, 295–97, 298, 301–2, 316, 371–72; "Grouard, Benjamin Franklin," Biographical Entry, Joseph Smith Papers website, josephsmithpapers.org.

24. Ellsworth, *Dear Ellen,* 41; Louisa Barnes Pratt, Journal and Autobiography, 371–73.

25. Louisa Barnes Pratt, Journal and Autobiography, 371; see also Ettling, "California, Utah, Lr. California and New Mexico," copy at CHL; and Historian's Office, History of the Church, volume 21, Mar. 20, 1851, 13. Quotation edited for clarity; exclamation point in original changed to question mark.

26. Louisa Barnes Pratt, Journal and Autobiography, 371–73, 374–75. **Topic: Louisa Barnes Pratt**

27. Woodruff, Journal, Mar. 29, 1858; Whitney, *History of Utah,* 1:631–38; Daniel Wells, John Taylor, and George A. Smith to Brigham Young, Oct. 5, 1857, Federal and Local Government Files, 1844–76, Brigham Young Office Files, CHL; Thomas L. Kane to Brigham Young, Mar. 16, 1858, draft, Thomas L. Kane Personal Papers, Kane Family Papers, Brigham Young University; "Major General Thomas L. Kane," *Latter-day Saints' Millennial Star,* Mar. 3, 1910, 72:129–33; Grow, *Liberty to the Downtrodden,* 159, 175–80; see also Pitchforth, Diary, Mar. 25, 1858. **Topic: Thomas L. and Elizabeth Kane**

28. *Series of Instructions and Remarks,* 4, 5–6, 7; see also Brigham Young to Thomas Kane, Mar. 22, 1858, Federal and Local Government Files, 1844–76, Brigham Young Office Files, CHL; and *Compilation of the Messages and Papers of the Presidents,* 7:2985–87.

29. *Series of Instructions and Remarks,* 8, 11; Historian's Office, General Church Minutes, Mar. 21, 1858; Brigham Young to Lewis Brunson, Feb. 23, 1858, copy, Brigham Young Office Files, CHL; Pitchforth, Diary, Mar. 25, 1858.

30. *Series of Instructions and Remarks,* 13–14; see also Poll, "Move South," 70–71. **Topic: Brigham Young**

31. *Series of Instructions and Remarks,* 8, 11, 13–14; Historian's Office, General Church Minutes, Mar. 21, 1858; Brigham Young to Lewis Brunson, Feb. 23, 1858, copy, Brigham Young Office Files, CHL; Pitchforth, Diary, Mar. 25, 1858.
32. Woodruff, Journal, Mar. 24, 1858; see also Historian's Office, History of the Church, volume 28, Mar. 25 and 30, 1858; Apr. 1, 1858, 281, 291–93.
33. Woodruff, Journal, Apr. 12, 1858; Alfred Cumming to Lewis Cass, May 2, 1858, Alfred Cumming, Papers, David M. Rubenstein Rare Book and Manuscript Library, Duke University, Durham, North Carolina; Daniel Wells, John Taylor, and George A. Smith to Brigham Young, Oct. 5, 1857, Brigham Young Office Files, CHL; Thomas Kane to James Buchanan, circa Mar. 15, 1858; Apr. 4, 1858, copy, Thomas L. Kane Personal Papers, Kane Family Papers, Brigham Young University; see also Stout, Journal, Mar. 8 and 14, 1858; and Grow, *Liberty to the Downtrodden,* 182.
34. Woodruff, Journal, Apr. 12, 1858; Historical Department, Office Journal, Apr. 12, 1858; Canning and Beeton, *Genteel Gentile,* xii–xiii; "Slander of Gov. Cumming," *Valley Tan,* Mar. 1, 1859, 1; Alfred Cumming, Proclamation, Nov. 21, 1857, Brigham Young Office Files, CHL.
35. Kane, Diary, Apr. 12–16, 1858; Alfred Cumming to Albert Johnston, Apr. 15, 1858, Alfred Cumming, Papers, David M. Rubenstein Rare Book and Manuscript Library, Duke University, Durham, North Carolina; Historical Department, Office Journal, Apr. 13, 1858; see also "Remarks by Governor Alfred Cumming," Apr. 25, 1858, Thomas L. Kane Personal Papers, Kane Family Papers, Brigham Young University.
36. "Remarks by Governor Alfred Cumming," Apr. 25, 1858, Thomas L. Kane Personal Papers, Kane Family Papers, Brigham Young University; see also Woodruff, Journal, Apr. 25, 1858; and Historian's Office, General Church Minutes, Apr. 25, 1858.
37. "Remarks by Governor Alfred Cumming," Apr. 25, 1858, Thomas L. Kane Personal Papers, Kane Family Papers, Brigham Young University; Historian's Office, General Church Minutes, Apr. 25, 1858; "Remarks by President Brigham Young," Apr. 25, 1858, Brigham Young Office Files, CHL; see also Alfred Cumming to Albert Johnston, Apr. 15, 1858, Alfred Cumming, Papers, David M. Rubenstein Rare Book and Manuscript Library, Duke University, Durham, North Carolina.
38. Sessions, Diary, May 25, 1858; Woodruff, Journal, May 10 and 19, 1858; Butler, "Short History," 94–95.
39. Tullidge, *Tullidge's Histories,* 30–31; Brigham Young to Elias H. Blackburn, Mar. 24, 1858, Letterbook, volume 4, 107, Brigham Young Office Files, CHL; "Highly Important from Utah," *New York Times,* July 30, 1858, 1; "Our Kansas Correspondence," *New York Herald,* June 24, 1858, 8; "A Visit to the Mormons at Provo," *American Traveller,* Aug. 7, 1858, [4]; "Reception of Governor Cumming by the Mormons," *Daily Cleveland Herald,* June 12, 1858, [2]. **Topic: Pioneer Settlements**
40. Harris, Autobiography, 1; L. Douglas Smoot, "Diana Tanner Eldredge Smoot's Later Life," in Nixon and Smoot, *Abraham Owen Smoot,* 191.
41. Booth, "History of the Fourth Provo Ward," 71; Abraham O. Smoot and others to Wilford Woodruff, June 4, 1858, Historian's Office, Correspondence Files, CHL; "Sugar House Ward," 1858, in Sugar House Ward, Manuscript History and Historical Reports, CHL.
42. Harris, "Martha Ann Smith Harris," 16.
43. Sessions, Diary, May 29 and June 1858; Poll, "Move South," 79–80; Butler, "Short History," 95–96; Tullidge, *Tullidge's Histories,* 31; Staines, Diary, May 20, 1858.
44. Tullidge, *Tullidge's Histories,* 31; "The Refugees in Provo," *New York Times,* July 30, 1858, 1; "A Visit to the Mormons at Provo," *American Traveller,* Aug. 7, 1858, [4]; Sessions, Diary, May 26 and 30, 1858; June 17, 1858.
45. Sessions, Diary, May 29, 1858; June 3–4, 12, and 14, 1858; Poll, "Move South," 79–80; Butler, "Short History," 95–96; Tullidge, *Tullidge's Histories,* 31; Staines, Diary, May 20, 1858; see also "Discourse by Elder O. Hyde," *Deseret News,* Dec. 30, 1857, [7]; and Local News Item, *Deseret News,* Oct. 13, 1858, [2].

46. Joseph F. Smith to Martha Ann Smith Harris, May 20, 1858, Joseph F. Smith Letters to Martha Ann Smith Harris, CHL; Dorius, "Sketch of the Life," 55; Dorius, *Dorius Heritage,* 91–93.
47. William Jasper Harris to Martha Ann Smith Harris, Nov. 25, 1857, in Harris, *Martha Ann,* 99–100; see also Harris, Autobiography, 1.
48. Mitchell, "Gentile Impressions of Salt Lake City," 337; Hamilton, *Reminiscences of a Veteran,* 104–5; Hammond, *Campaigns in the West,* 69–70; Poll, "Move South," 77–79.
49. Synopsis of Speeches, June 11–12, 1858, Federal and Local Government Files, 1844–76, Brigham Young Office Files, CHL; *By James Buchanan, President of the United States of America: A Proclamation* (Washington, DC: Publisher unidentified, 1858), copy at CHL; Whitney, *History of Utah,* 1:682–83; see also Poll, "Move South," 70.
50. "Additional News from Utah," *New York Times,* June 14, 1858, 1; "Cruel Panegyrics of the Administration Press," *New York Times,* June 23, 1858, 4.
51. Hamilton, *Reminiscences of a Veteran,* 104–5; Foote, Autobiography and Journal, 151–52; Historical Department, Office Journal, Mar. 25 and June 26, 1858.
52. Tullidge, *Tullidge's Histories,* 30–32; Historian's Office, History of the Church, volume 28, June 30, 1858, 759; Foote, Autobiography and Journal, 152; Sessions, Diary, July 6, 1858; Hamilton, *Reminiscences of a Veteran,* 108–9; Hammond, *Campaigns in the West,* 71–72.
53. Hamilton, *Reminiscences of a Veteran,* 108; Sessions, Diary, July 6, 1858; Hammond, *Campaigns in the West,* 71–72.
54. Tullidge, *Tullidge's Histories,* 32; Historian's Office, History of the Church, volume 28, July 2, 1858, 760–61; Poll, "Move South," 84.
55. L. Douglas Smoot, "Diana Tanner Eldredge Smoot's Later Life," in Nixon and Smoot, *Abraham Owen Smoot,* 191; Harris, Autobiography, 1; William Jasper Harris to George A. Smith, Dec. 28, 1858, in Missionary Reports, CHL.

Chapter 20: Handwriting on the Wall

1. Richards, *Called to Teach,* 172–76; Maeser, *Karl G. Maeser,* 11, 34.
2. See Maeser, *Karl G. Maeser,* 15, 29–31; and Stampp, *America in 1857,* 225–26.
3. Richards, *Called to Teach,* 174–76; Maeser, *Karl G. Maeser,* 27–28, 34.
4. Franklin D. Richards to Brigham Young, Nov. 3, 1855, Brigham Young Office Files, CHL; Maeser, "How I Became a 'Mormon,'" 24–26; Maeser, *Karl G. Maeser,* 24; Richards, "Moritz Busch's *Die Mormonen* and the Conversion of Karl G. Maeser," 53–58, 60. **Topic: Germany**
5. Maeser, "How I Became a 'Mormon,'" 25–26; see also Maeser, *Karl G. Maeser,* 24–25; and Schoenfeld, "Character Sketch of Dr. Karl G. Maeser," 181. **Topic: Gift of Tongues**
6. "Appointments," *Mormon,* Sept. 5, 1857, [3]; Maeser, *Karl G. Maeser,* 29–31, 34; Richards, *Called to Teach,* 176.
7. See Brigham Young to Samuel W. Richards and George Snider, Aug. 5, 1857, Letterbook, volume 3, 781–85, Brigham Young Office Files, CHL; "Emigration to the States Stopped for the Present," *Latter-day Saints' Millennial Star,* Oct. 17, 1857, 19:668; and Richards, *Called to Teach,* 168–72. **Topic: Emigration**
8. John F. Snedaker to Jedediah M. Grant, Oct. 18, 1856, Susan N. Grant Correspondence, CHL; William I. Appleby to Brigham Young, Aug. 25, 1857, Brigham Young Office Files, CHL.
9. George Q. Cannon to Brigham Young, Jan. 26, 1859, Brigham Young Office Files, CHL; Karl G. Maeser to Edward Collard, Feb. 19, 1859, Karl G. Maeser Letter, Brigham Young University; "Mormon Conference at Philadelphia," *New York Herald,* Aug. 29, 1858, 3; Richards, *Called to Teach,* 176–79.
10. See *Deseret News,* May 5–Sept. 1, 1858; and George Q. Cannon, Journal, Sept. 9, 1858. **Topic: Church Periodicals**

11. George Q. Cannon, Journal, Sept. 9 and 14, 1858; Cannon, *George Cannon the Immigrant,* 149–50. George Cannon quotation edited for readability; original source has "After breakfast I went to see Bro. Brigham. His first remark after the salutations was 'Are you ready?' I told him I was."

12. Brigham Young to George Q. Cannon, Sept. 7, 1858, Brigham Young Office Files, CHL; Cannon, *George Cannon the Immigrant,* 149. **Topic: Utah**

13. George Q. Cannon, Journal, Sept. 9 and 14–15, 1858. **Topic: George Q. Cannon**

14. Dorius, "Autobiography of Carl Christian Nicoli Dorius," 16–17, 22; Dorius, "Sketch of the Life," 55.

15. Stevens, Autobiography, 7–8.

16. Ephraim North Ward, Relief Society Minutes and Records, volume 1, [1].

17. Dorius, "Sketch of the Life," 10, 45, 51; Dorius, "Autobiography of Carl Christian Nicoli Dorius," 22–23; Stevens, Autobiography, 7–8; *History of Sanpete and Emery Counties,* 282–83.

18. William Black to Brigham Young, July 4, 1859; Brigham Young to William Black, July 12, 1859, Brigham Young Office Files, CHL; "History," [4], in Spring City Ward, Manuscript History and Historical Reports, CHL; Stevens, Autobiography, 6, 8. **Topic: Pioneer Settlements**

19. Stevens, Autobiography, 8–9.

20. Dorius, "Sketch of the Life," 56–57; Dorius, "Autobiography of Carl Christian Nicoli Dorius," 23.

21. Dorius, "Sketch of the Life," 57; George Q. Cannon, Journal, July–Aug. 1860; "Latest from the Plains," *Deseret News,* Aug. 8, 1860, [4].

22. George Q. Cannon to Brigham Young, Apr. 14, 1859; Oct. 14, 1859; Nov. 19, 1859, Brigham Young Office Files, CHL; George Q. Cannon, Journal, Oct. 22, 24, and 30, 1859; see also Richards, *Called to Teach,* 179–80.

23. Poll, "Antipolygamy Campaign," 108–10; *Proceedings of the First Three Republican National Conventions,* 43; Gordon, *Mormon Question,* 55–83.

24. George Q. Cannon to Brigham Young, Jan. 18, 1860, Brigham Young Office Files, CHL.

25. Historian's Office, History of the Church, volume 29, Oct. 23, 1859, 707–15; Brigham Young to George Q. Cannon, Nov. 3, 1859, photocopy, CHL.

26. "Annual Conference," *Deseret News,* Apr. 11, 1860, [5]; George Q. Cannon to Brigham Young, Dec. 13, 1859, Brigham Young Office Files, CHL.

27. George Q. Cannon to Brigham Young, June 28 and July 7, 1860, Brigham Young Office Files, CHL; see also George Q. Cannon, Journal, July 1860.

28. George Q. Cannon to Brigham Young, July 7, 1860, Brigham Young Office Files, CHL.

29. "Departure of Philadelphia Mormons for Salt Lake," *New York Herald,* May 11, 1860, 10; John Smith Company (1860) list, Pioneer Database, history .ChurchofJesusChrist.org/overlandtravel/companies; John Smith to Joseph F. Smith, Dec. 1, 1859; Apr. 18, 1860, Joseph F. Smith, Papers, CHL; see also Bean, "Reminiscences of the Granddaughter of Hyrum Smith," 10.

30. Oaks and Bentley, "Joseph Smith and the Legal Process," 193–97; 197, note 146; Leonard, *Nauvoo,* 625; *JSP,* J3:59, note 262. **Topic: Settlement of Joseph Smith's Estate**

31. John Smith to Joseph F. Smith, Apr. 18, 1860, Joseph F. Smith, Papers, CHL; "Middleton, Julia M. Smith," Biographical Entry, Joseph Smith Papers website, josephsmithpapers.org; see also biographical entries for Joseph Smith III, Frederick Granger Williams Smith, Alexander Hale Smith, and David Hyrum Smith on the Joseph Smith Papers website, josephsmithpapers.org.

32. Joseph Smith III to John Smith, Mar. 21, 1848, John Smith, Papers, Brigham Young University; Mary Audentia Smith Anderson, "Memoirs of President Joseph Smith," *Saints' Herald,* Apr. 28, 1936, 530; see also *Saints,* volume 1, chapters 36, 40, and 41; and Haws, "Joseph F. Smith's Encouragement of His Brother," 142–43. **Topic: Joseph and Emma Hale Smith Family**

33. John Smith to Joseph F. Smith, Apr. 18, 1860, Joseph F. Smith, Papers, CHL; George Q. Cannon to Brigham Young, July 7, 1860, Brigham Young Office Files,

CHL; "Schism among the Saints," *New York Times,* Apr. 11, 1860, 3; see also "Smith, Joseph, III," Biographical Entry, Joseph Smith Papers website, josephsmithpapers.org. **Topic: Other Latter Day Saint Movements**

34. Maeser, *Karl G. Maeser,* 34–35; John Smith Company (1860) list, Pioneer Database, history.ChurchofJesusChrist.org/overlandtravel/companies; see also Bean, "Reminiscences of the Granddaughter of Hyrum Smith," 10; and White, "Life Story of Thomas Gunn and Ann Houghton Gunn," 5–6.

35. "Arrival of Companies," *Deseret News,* Sept. 5, 1860, [4]; Bean, "Reminiscences of the Granddaughter of Hyrum Smith," 10; Judd, "History," 1; "Late from the Immigration," *Latter-day Saints' Millennial Star,* Oct. 20, 1860, 22:669; John Smith Company (1860) list, Pioneer Database, history.ChurchofJesusChrist.org/overlandtravel/companies; Historical Department, Office Journal, Aug. 26, 1860.

36. Woodruff, Journal, Jan. 11 and 16, 1860; Nov. 4, 1860; Gibson, *Prison of Weltevreden,* v–495.

37. Walter M. Gibson to Brigham Young, May 30, 1859, Brigham Young Office Files, CHL; Historian's Office, History of the Church, volume 29, Oct. 29, 1859, 722–23; Woodruff, Journal, Jan. 11 and 16, 1860.

38. See Woodruff, Journal, Jan. 16 and 22, 1860; Feb. 21–23 and 28, 1860; Mar. 2–3, 7, 9, and 15, 1860; Apr. 25, 1860.

39. Historian's Office, History of the Church, volume 29, Oct. 29, 1859, 722–23; Brigham Young, Discourse, Nov. 18, 1860, Church History Department Pitman Shorthand Transcriptions, CHL.

40. Woodruff, Journal, Apr. 25, 1860; see also Adler and Kamins, *Fantastic Life of Walter Murray Gibson,* 47–48.

41. Walter M. Gibson to Brigham Young, July 1, 1860, Brigham Young Office Files, CHL; Woodruff, Journal, Nov. 4, 1860; Walter M. Gibson, Discourse, Nov. 18, 1860, Church History Department Pitman Shorthand Transcriptions, CHL. Second sentence of quotation edited for clarity; "children human family" in original changed to "children of the human family."

42. Woodruff, Journal, Nov. 4, 1860.

43. Brigham Young, Discourse, Nov. 18, 1860, Church History Department Pitman Shorthand Transcriptions, CHL.

44. Walter M. Gibson, Setting Apart Blessing, Nov. 19, 1860, Church History Department Pitman Shorthand Transcriptions, CHL; Brigham Young Office, Journal, Nov. 19, 1860, Brigham Young Office Files, CHL. Quotation edited for clarity; "of children of man" in original changed to "of the children of man."

45. Woodruff, Journal, Nov. 21, 1860.

46. Doctrine and Covenants 87:1–3 (Revelation, Dec. 25, 1832, at josephsmithpapers .org); Woodworth, "Peace and War," 158–64; Woodruff, Journal, Dec. 31, 1860; see also *Saints,* volume 1, chapter 15. **Topic: Prophecies of Joseph Smith**

47. Doctrine and Covenants 87:6 (Revelation, Dec. 25, 1832, at josephsmithpapers.org).

48. Woodruff, Journal, Jan. 1, 1861. Final sentence of quotation edited for clarity; "Nations" in original changed to "nation." **Topic: American Civil War**

Chapter 21: The Same Great Work

1. Orson Pratt and Erastus Snow to Brigham Young, Apr. 29–30, 1861, Brigham Young Office Files, CHL. Quotation edited for readability; "Armies enlisting" in original changed to "Armies are enlisting."

2. McPherson, *Battle Cry of Freedom,* 234–37, 264–84; Cooper, *We Have the War upon Us,* 113–17, 129–30; Orson Pratt and Erastus Snow to Brigham Young, Jan. 3, 1861; Apr. 29–30, 1861, Brigham Young Office Files, CHL. **Topic: American Civil War**

3. "Discourse by Elder Orson Pratt," *Deseret News,* Sept. 20, 1876, [2]; see also Orson Pratt, in *Journal of Discourses,* Aug. 26, 1876, 18:224–25; Snow, Autobiography, [17]; and "Pratt, Orson," Biographical Entry, Joseph Smith Papers website, josephsmithpapers.org.

4. "Mormon Prophecy," *New York Times,* June 2, 1861, 3; see also George Q. Cannon, in *Journal of Discourses,* Nov. 2, 1879, 21:265–66; and Esplin, "Have We Not Had a Prophet among Us?," 44, 47.

5. "Mormon Prophecy," *Philadelphia Sunday Mercury,* May 5, 1861, [2]; see also "Mormon Prophecy," *Daily Argus and Democrat,* Jan. 19, 1861, [2]; and "Revelation and Prophecy by the Prophet, Seer, and Revelator, Jos. Smith," *Dawson's Daily Times and Union,* Feb. 9, 1863, [7].

6. See "News from the United States," *Latter-day Saints' Millennial Star,* Apr. 6, 1861, 23:219; Erastus Snow to George A. Smith, June 26, 1861, George A. Smith, Papers, CHL; Hartley, "Latter-day Saint Emigration during the Civil War," 240–41; and Hartley, "Great Florence Fitout of 1861," 353.

7. Orson Pratt to Brigham Young, June 14, 1861, Brigham Young Office Files, CHL; Erastus Snow to George A. Smith, June 26, 1861, George A. Smith, Papers, CHL; see also Hartley, "Latter-day Saint Emigration during the Civil War," 240–41.

8. Brigham Young to Amasa Lyman and Charles C. Rich, Sept 13, 1860, Amasa M. Lyman Collection, CHL; Rich, Diary, volume 11, Apr. 6, 1860, 1; Cannon, "Topics of the Times," 378; see also "British Mission," Missionary Database, history .ChurchofJesusChrist.org/missionary; and Hartley, "Latter-day Saint Emigration during the Civil War," 238–39.

9. Erastus Snow to George A. Smith, June 26, 1861, George A. Smith, Papers, CHL; George Q. Cannon to Brigham Young, July 7, 1860; First Presidency to "Bishop Edward Hunter and His Counselors and the Bishops throughout Utah," June 1860, Letterbook, volume 5, 552–54; First Presidency to "Bishop Edward Hunter and His Counselors and the Bishops throughout Utah," June 1860, copy; Brigham Young to John Van Cott, Aug. 9, 1860, copy; First Presidency to "Bishop Edward Hunter and the Bishops throughout the Territory," Feb. 1861, copy, Brigham Young Office Files, CHL; Hartley, "Great Florence Fitout of 1861," 345–52; Hartley, "Latter-day Saint Emigration during the Civil War," 243–44; see also Arrington, *Great Basin Kingdom,* 206–7. **Topic: Pioneer Trek**

10. Whitney, *History of Utah,* 2:25; "By Telegraph," *New York Daily Reformer,* Aug. 30, 1861, [3]; "Celebration," *Deseret News,* July 10, 1861, [4]–[5], [8]; Brigham Young, Jan. 6, 1862, Historian's Office, Reports of Speeches, CHL; Woodruff, Journal, Apr. 21, 1861; Manscill, "Rumors of Secession in the Utah Territory," 90; Dowdle, "What Means This Carnage?," 111.

11. Woodruff, Journal, Apr. 28, 1861; "Telegraph to Utah," *New York Daily Reformer,* Oct. 21, 1861, [2]. **Topic: Utah**

12. See Woodruff, Journal, May 11, 1861; Aug. 7 and 21, 1861; "Latest from the East," *Deseret News,* Oct. 2, 1861, [8]; and "Summary of War News," *Deseret News,* Dec. 25, 1861, [4].

13. "Remarks," *Deseret News,* Sept. 18, 1861, 1; see also Heber C. Kimball, in *Journal of Discourses,* Apr. 14, 1861, 9:55; and "Progress of Events," *Deseret News,* May 22, 1861, [4].

14. Brigham Young to Andrew Moffitt, June 28, 1861, Letterbook, volume 5, 815–16, Brigham Young Office Files, CHL; Ellsworth and Alford, "Mormon Motivation for Enlisting in the Civil War," 183–201; see also Jensen and Hoffman, "From Mormon Battalion Member to Civil War Soldier," 85–111.

15. Margetts, "Early Theatricals in Utah," 292–93; "Remarks," Mar. 6, 1862, *Deseret News,* May 14, 1862, 1–[2]; Spencer and Harmer, *Brigham Young at Home,* 147–48; Spencer and Harmer, *One Who Was Valiant,* 140–41; see also "Mrs. McLean," *New York Daily Tribune,* June 10, 1857, 4; and Leavitt, *Fifty Years in Theatrical Management,* 404–8.

16. Tullidge, *History of Salt Lake City,* 738–39; Lindsay, *Mormons and the Theatre,* 20–23; Jorgensen, "Mechanics' Dramatic Association," 177–79; Whitney, *Through Memory's Halls,* 23, 29; "Mrs. Marion Bowring," *Standard,* Feb. 25, 1891, 1; President's Office Journal, Mar. 8, 1861, 226, Brigham Young Office Files, CHL; see also Edward Martin Company (1856) list, Pioneer Database, history.ChurchofJesusChrist.org /overlandtravel/companies. Henry Bowring also went by the name Harry.

17. Historical Department, Office Journal, May 6, 1861; Whitney, *Drama in Utah,* 3, 6; Lindsay, *Mormons and the Theatre,* 23; Margetts, "Early Theatricals in Utah," 293; Spencer and Harmer, *One Who Was Valiant,* 140–41; Tullidge, *History of Salt Lake City,* 739; Gates and Widtsoe, *Life Story of Brigham Young,* 251.

18. Lindsay, *Mormons and the Theatre,* 23; "Fifth General Epistle," *Deseret News,* Apr. 8, 1851, [2]; Fifth General Epistle, Apr. 7, 1851, in Neilson and Waite, *Settling the Valley,* 124; see also "Seventies' Hall," *Deseret News,* May 17, 1851, [4].

19. Tullidge, *History of Salt Lake City,* 248; Spencer and Harmer, *Brigham Young at Home,* 148–49; Spencer and Harmer, *One Who Was Valiant,* 141; Arrington, *Great Basin Kingdom,* 198–99.

20. President's Office Journal, Aug. 5, 1861, 282, Brigham Young Office Files, CHL. Quotations edited for readability; original source has "HC Kimball remarked the rock looked of a very enduring character. President Young remarked he always liked to see some kind of a building going on."

21. "Theatre," *Deseret News,* Oct. 23, 1861, [5]; Dec. 25, 1861, [4]; Whitney, *Drama in Utah,* 6–7.

22. Parry, Reminiscences and Diary, 72; Tullidge, *History of Salt Lake City,* 739–40; Historical Department, Office Journal, Dec. 2, 1861; Brigham Young to J. D. T. McAllister, Nov. 9, 1861; Brigham Young to John M. Bernhisel, Dec. 21, 1861, Letterbook, volume 6, 17, 68, Brigham Young Office Files, CHL; see also Lindsay, *Mormons and the Theatre,* 20–23. **Topic: Salt Lake Temple**

23. Woodruff, Journal, Dec. 7, 1859, and Aug. 23, 1862; "Remarks," Oct. 9, 1863, *Deseret News,* Oct. 14, 1864, [5]; Brigham Young, in *Journal of Discourses,* Oct. 6, 1863, 10:254.

24. Parry, Reminiscences and Diary, 72; Brigham Young, in *Journal of Discourses,* Oct. 6, 1863, 10:254; see also Woodruff, Journal, Jan. 1, 1862. **Topic: Temple Building**

25. "New Theatre," *Deseret News,* Mar. 12, 1862, [2]–[3]; Clawson, Reminiscences, "777," [7a]–[7b]; Lindsay, *Mormons and the Theatre,* 23–27; Whitney, *Drama in Utah,* 7–8; "Remarks," Mar. 6, 1862, *Deseret News,* May 14, 1862, 1–[2].

26. George Q. Cannon, Journal, May 5, 1862; see also entries for June 13–July 3, 1855; Sept. 9 and 14, 1858; and George Q. Cannon to Brigham Young, Dec. 13, 1859, Brigham Young Office Files, CHL.

27. George Q. Cannon, Journal, Mar. 6, 1862; An Act to Establish a Territorial Government for Utah [Sept. 9, 1850], section 13, in *Acts, Resolutions, and Memorials . . . of the Territory of Utah,* 36; "Proclamation by the Governor Elect," *Deseret News,* Mar. 19, 1862, [4].

28. George Q. Cannon, Journal, May 5–6 and 31, 1862. **Topic: George Q. Cannon**

29. *Journal of the House of Representatives* [1862], 520; *Speech of Hon. Justin S. Morrill,* 3, 10–14; Rogers, *Unpopular Sovereignty,* 280–85; see also "Sermon," *Deseret News,* Sept. 17, 1856, [4]; Brigham Young, in *Journal of Discourses,* Aug. 31, 1856, 4:39; and George Q. Cannon to Brigham Young, Mar. 26, 1860, Brigham Young Office Files, CHL.

30. Poll, "Antipolygamy Campaign," 110–11; An Act to Punish and Prevent the Practice of Polygamy in the Territories of the United States and Other Places, and Disapproving and Annulling Certain Acts of the Legislative Assembly of the Territory of Utah [July 1, 1862], *Statutes at Large* [1863], 37th Cong., 2nd Sess., chapter 126, 501–2. **Topic: Antipolygamy Legislation**

31. George Q. Cannon, Journal, May 5–13, 29, and 31, 1862; June 18–24, 1862; "Departure for Washington," *Deseret News,* Apr. 30, 1862, [5]; "From Washington," *Deseret News,* July 2, 1862, [4]; An Act to Punish and Prevent the Practice of Polygamy in the Territories of the United States and Other Places, and Disapproving and Annulling

Certain Acts of the Legislative Assembly of the Territory of Utah [July 1, 1862], *Statutes at Large* [1863], 37th Cong., 2nd Sess., chapter 126, 501–2.

32. George Q. Cannon, Journal, June 13, 1862.

33. William H. Hooper and George Q. Cannon to Brigham Young, June 24 and 29, 1862, Utah Delegate Files, 1849–72, Brigham Young Office Files, CHL; George Q. Cannon, Journal, June 17–28 and July 1–2, 1862; Rives, *Congressional Globe,* 2506–7.

34. See John M. Bernhisel to Brigham Young, July 11, 1862, Utah Delegate Files, 1849–72, Brigham Young Office Files, CHL.

35. Turley, Johnson, and Carruth, *Mountain Meadows Massacre,* 1:3–6, 63–65, 201–6.

36. William H. Hooper and George Q. Cannon to Brigham Young, June 29 and July 7, 1862, Utah Delegate Files, 1849–72, Brigham Young Office Files, CHL; see also George Q. Cannon, Journal, July 1, 1862.

37. Dorius, "Autobiography of Carl Christian Nicoli Dorius," 25–26; Dorius, "Sketch of the Life," 57–58; Jenson, *History of the Scandinavian Mission,* 153; see also Dorius, *Dorius Heritage,* 97–103.

38. Dorius, "Sketch of the Life," 57; Dorius, "Autobiography of Carl Christian Nicoli Dorius," 24, 29; "Othilie Julie Birch," Apr. 14, 1867, Haderup, Ringkøbing, Denmark, volume 5, 279, "Danmark, Kirkebøger, 1484–1941," Rigsarkivet, København, Copenhagen, available at familysearch.org.

39. Dorius, "Autobiography of Carl Christian Nicoli Dorius," 24–25; Jesse N. Smith to Brigham Young, May 24, 1862, Brigham Young Office Files, CHL. **Topic: Norway**

40. Dorius, "Autobiography of Carl Christian Nicoli Dorius," 28–29.

41. Elizabeth Cannon, Journal, July 20–22, 1862.

42. See "Cannon, Elizabeth Hoagland," Biographical Entry, First Fifty Years of Relief Society website, churchhistorianspress.org.

43. Elizabeth Cannon, Journal, July 23 and 25, 1862; George Q. Cannon, Journal, July 26, 1862.

44. An Act to Punish and Prevent the Practice of Polygamy in the Territories of the United States and Other Places, and Disapproving and Annulling Certain Acts of the Legislative Assembly of the Territory of Utah [July 1, 1862], *Statutes at Large* [1863], 37th Cong., 2nd Sess., chapter 126, 501–2; Rogers, *Unpopular Sovereignty,* 285–86; William H. Hooper and George Q. Cannon to Brigham Young, June 24, 1862; John M. Bernhisel to Brigham Young, July 31, 1862; William H. Hooper and George Q. Cannon to Brigham Young, July 13, 1862, Utah Delegate Files, 1849–72, Brigham Young Office Files, CHL.

45. George Q. Cannon to Brigham Young, Sept. 18, 1862, Brigham Young Office Files, CHL; Elizabeth Cannon, Journal, Sept. 2–7, 1862; George Q. Cannon, Journal, Sept. 1–7, 1862. **Topic: Patriarchal Blessings**

46. George Q. Cannon, Journal, Sept. 7, 1862.

47. Elizabeth Cannon, Journal, Sept. 7, 1862.

CHAPTER 22: LIKE COALS OF LIVING FIRE

1. T. B. H. Stenhouse to Brigham Young, June 7, 1863, Brigham Young Office Files, CHL; "In Memory of T. B. H. Stenhouse," 91–92; Tullidge, *Tullidge's Histories,* 2:167; Brigham Young to T. B. H. Stenhouse, May 8, 1858, Brigham Young Office Files, CHL; Walker, "Stenhouses and the Making of the Mormon Image," 55.

2. See T. B. H. Stenhouse to Brigham Young, June 7, 1863, Brigham Young Office Files, CHL; Bancroft, *History of Utah,* 609; and Woodger, "Abraham Lincoln and the Mormons," 61–62, 73–74. **Topic: Antipolygamy Legislation**

3. "Departure of the Governor," *Deseret News,* May 22, 1861, [8]; Historical Department, Office Journal, Dec. 22, 1861; "Mass Meeting," and "Voice of the People," *Deseret News,* Jan. 8, 1862, [4].

4. Bancroft, *History of Utah,* 604–5; "Harding, Stephen Selwyn," in *Biographical History of Eminent and Self-Made Men of the State of Indiana,* fourth district, 78–79; "Mass Meeting in the Tabernacle," *Deseret News,* Mar. 4, 1863, [4]; John M. Bernhisel to Brigham Young, Feb. 6, 1863, Utah Delegate Files, 1849–72, Brigham Young Office Files, CHL; Citizens of Utah Territory to Abraham Lincoln, Mar. 3, 1863, copy, Federal and Local Government Files, 1844–76, Brigham Young Office Files, CHL.

5. T. B. H. Stenhouse to Brigham Young, June 7, 1863, Brigham Young Office Files, CHL; McPherson, *Battle Cry of Freedom,* 557–67, 638–46. **Topic: American Civil War**

6. Nibley, *Brigham Young,* 369; see also "Remarks," *Deseret News,* June 22, 1864, [3]; and Woodger, "Abraham Lincoln and the Mormons," 61.

7. Nibley, *Brigham Young,* 369; see also T. B. H. Stenhouse to Brigham Young, June 7, 1863; Brigham Young to George Q. Cannon, June 25, 1863, Letterbook, volume 3, 626, Brigham Young Office Files, CHL; and "Remarks," *Deseret News,* June 22, 1864, [3].

8. Bancroft, *History of Utah,* 622; News Department, "Journal of Indian Treaty Days," 75; see also Historical Department, Office Journal, June 11, 1863; Historical Department, Journal History of the Church, June 11, 1863; and Woodger, "Abraham Lincoln and the Mormons," 76.

9. Solomona and others to Alma L. Smith, July 23, 1863, verbatim copy; Solomona and others to Alma L. Smith, July 23, 1863, translated copy, Brigham Young Office Files, CHL; Hawaii Honolulu Mission, General Minutes, Apr. 25, 1858; see also Brigham Young to Henry W. Bigler and John S. Woodbury, Feb. 4, 1858, Brigham Young Office Files, CHL; and Henry W. Bigler to George A. Smith, Dec. 3, 1858, Missionary Reports, CHL.

10. Solomona and others to Alma L. Smith, July 23, 1863, translated copy, Brigham Young Office Files, CHL.

11. Brigham Young, Discourse, Nov. 18, 1860; Walter M. Gibson, Setting Apart Blessing, Nov. 19, 1860, Church History Department Pitman Shorthand Transcriptions, CHL; Brigham Young Office, Journal, Nov. 19, 1860, Brigham Young Office Files, CHL; Walter M. Gibson to Brigham Young, June 8 and 14, 1861; Sept. 19, 1861; Jan. 16, 1862, Brigham Young Office Files, CHL; "Tabernacle," *Deseret News,* Nov. 21, 1860, 1.

12. "Capt. Gibson on the Sandwich Islands," *Deseret News,* Dec. 10, 1862, [8]; see also, for example, Walter M. Gibson to Brigham Young, July 10, 1861; Sept. 2, 1861; Sept. 19, 1861; Jan. 16, 1862; July 17, 1862; Aug. 11, 1862, Brigham Young Office Files, CHL.

13. Solomona and others to Alma L. Smith, July 23, 1863, translated copy, Brigham Young Office Files, CHL; see also Walter M. Gibson to "J. W. Napela," Certificate, Oct. 9, 1862, CHL.

14. Solomona and others to Alma L. Smith, July 23, 1863, translated copy, Brigham Young Office Files, CHL.

15. Woodruff, Journal, Jan. 17, 1864; see also Jenson, "Walter Murray Gibson," 88. Quotation edited for readability; original source has "After reading the letter he said that he wanted two of the Twelve to take several of the young brethren who had been over there before & go to the islands & set the churches in order & do what is necessary."

16. Pack, "Sandwich Islands Country and Mission," 610; Cluff, "Drowning of President Snow," 392.

17. Woodruff, Journal, Jan. 17, 1864. **Topic: Hawaii**

18. Cluff, "Drowning of President Snow," 392–94; Joseph F. Smith to Levira Smith, Apr. 7, 1864, Joseph F. Smith, Papers, CHL; Pack, "Sandwich Islands Country and Mission," 611; see also George Q. Cannon, Journal, July 5, 1864.

19. Cluff, "Drowning of President Snow," 394; Pack, "Sandwich Islands Country and Mission," 611; see also *Saints,* volume 1, chapters 30 and 32.

20. Cluff, "Drowning of President Snow," 395; Pack, "Sandwich Islands Country and Mission," 611–12. **Topic: Lorenzo Snow**

21. Joseph F. Smith to Levira Smith, Apr. 7, 1864, Joseph F. Smith, Papers, CHL; Pack, "Sandwich Islands Country and Mission," 612; see also Cluff, "Drowning of President Snow," 395.

22. Joseph F. Smith to Levira Smith, Apr. 7, 1864, Joseph F. Smith, Papers, CHL; Cluff, "Fall of Walter M. Gibson," 470; Pack, "Sandwich Islands Country and Mission," 612; see also "Death of Mrs. Talula Hayselden," *Pacific Commercial Advertiser,* May 17, 1903, 10; and 1900 U.S. Census, Lahaina, Maui, Hawaiian Islands, 52[A].

23. Joseph F. Smith to Levira Smith, Apr. 7, 1864, Joseph F. Smith, Papers, CHL; see also Cluff, "Fall of Walter M. Gibson," 472.

24. Joseph F. Smith to Levira Smith, Apr. 7, 1864, Joseph F. Smith, Papers, CHL; Cluff, "My Last Mission to the Sandwich Islands," 69–70; see also Historian's Office, History of the Church, volume 34, May 4, 1864, 354.

25. Gibson, *Prison of Weltevreden,* v–495; Walter M. Gibson to Brigham Young, May 30, 1859, Brigham Young Office Files, CHL; Woodruff, Journal, Jan. 16, 1860.

26. Cluff, "Acts of Special Providence," 363; Historian's Office, History of the Church, volume 34, May 4 and 21, 1864, 355, 409; "Sandwich Island Missions," *Deseret News,* Aug. 31, 1864, [5].

27. Pack, "Sandwich Islands Country and Mission," 610, 613; Walter M. Gibson to George A. Smith, Mar. 13, 1864, George A. Smith, Papers, CHL; Cluff, "Fall of Walter M. Gibson," 470–72; Jenson, "Walter Murray Gibson," 89; Cluff, "My Last Mission to the Sandwich Islands," 69–70; Joseph F. Smith to Levira Smith, Apr. 7, 1864, Joseph F. Smith, Papers, CHL.

28. Cluff, "Fall of Walter M. Gibson," 472; see also Joseph F. Smith to Levira Smith, Apr. 7, 1864, Joseph F. Smith, Papers, CHL.

29. Joseph F. Smith to Levira Smith, Apr. 7, 1864, Joseph F. Smith, Papers, CHL.

30. Joseph F. Smith to Levira Smith, Apr. 7, 1864, Joseph F. Smith, Papers, CHL; Jenson, "Walter Murray Gibson," 94.

31. Joseph F. Smith to Levira Smith, Apr. 7, 1864; Alma Smith to Joseph F. Smith, June 22, 1864, Joseph F. Smith, Papers, CHL; Joseph F. Smith to Brigham Young, July 5, 1864, in "Sandwich Islands Mission," *Deseret News,* Aug. 31, 1864, [5]; Cluff, "Acts of Special Providence," 363–64; Pack, "Sandwich Islands Country and Mission," 692.

32. Joseph F. Smith to Levira Smith, Apr. 7, 1864; Alma Smith to Joseph F. Smith and William Cluff, May 3, 1864, Joseph F. Smith, Papers, CHL; "Sandwich Islands Mission," *Deseret News,* Nov. 11, 1864, [5]; Walter M. Gibson to "J. W. Napela," Certificate, Oct. 9, 1862, CHL; see also Walter M. Gibson to Brigham Young, Jan. 16, 1862, Brigham Young Office Files, CHL. **Topic: Jonathan Napela**

33. Joseph F. Smith to Levira Smith, Apr. 7, 1864; Joseph F. Smith to Levira Smith, Apr. 20, 1864; Alma Smith to Joseph F. Smith and William Cluff, May 3, 1864, Joseph F. Smith, Papers, CHL; Alma Smith to Brigham Young, Apr. 29, 1864, Brigham Young Office Files, CHL; Joseph F. Smith to Brigham Young, July 5, 1864, in "Sandwich Islands Mission," *Deseret News,* Aug. 31, 1864, [5].

34. Alma Smith to Joseph F. Smith, June 22, 1864, Joseph F. Smith, Papers, CHL; Joseph F. Smith to Brigham Young, July 5, 1864, in "Sandwich Islands Mission," *Deseret News,* Aug. 31, 1864, [5].

35. Brigham Young to Joseph F. Smith and others, July 28, 1864, Joseph F. Smith, Papers, CHL.

36. Joseph F. Smith to Brigham Young, Aug. 30, 1864, Brigham Young Office Files, CHL; "Sandwich Islands Mission," *Deseret News,* Nov. 30, 1864, [5].

37. "Sandwich Islands Mission," *Deseret News,* Nov. 30, 1864, [5]; Brigham Young to Joseph F. Smith, Oct. 17, 1864, Joseph F. Smith, Papers, CHL.

38. Joseph F. Smith to Brigham Young, July 5, 1864, in "Sandwich Islands Mission," *Deseret News,* Aug. 31, 1864, [5]; John R. Young to Joseph F. Smith, July 14, 1864; Joseph F. Smith to Brigham Young, Aug. 30, 1864, Joseph F. Smith, Papers, CHL.

39. Brigham Young to Joseph F. Smith, Oct. 17, 1864, Joseph F. Smith, Papers, CHL.

40. Cluff, "Acts of Special Providence," 364–65; Pack, "Sandwich Islands Country and Mission," 693–95; Hammond, Journal, Jan. 20 and 26, 1865.

CHAPTER 23: ONE HARMONIOUS WHOLE

1. Gates, "My Father as His Forty Six Children Knew Him," [3]; Gates, "Mother used to say," in Gates, "My Recollections," box 1, folder 2, item 11, 1–2. **Topic: Susa Young Gates**
2. Gates, "Lion House," 1–2; Gates, "Life in the Lion House," 20; see also Plewe, *Mapping Mormonism,* 114.
3. Gates, "Lion House," 2; Gates, "My Father as His Forty Six Children Knew Him," [6]–[7]; Gates, "Lucy Bigelow Young," 69–70; Grant, *Gospel Standards,* 223–24; 1870 U.S. Census, Salt Lake City Ward 18, Salt Lake County, Utah Territory, 701. **Topic: Heber J. Grant**
4. Gates, "My Father as His Forty Six Children Knew Him," [4]; Gates, "Mother used to say," in Gates, "My Recollections," box 1, folder 2, item 11, 2; Gates, "Life in the Lion House," 19, 32; Gates, "Family Life among the Mormons," 339, 341.
5. Gates, "Brigham Young and His Nineteen Wives," 1; Jessee, "Brigham Young at Home," 30; "Plural Marriage and Families in Early Utah," Gospel Topics, topics .ChurchofJesusChrist.org. **Topic: Brigham Young's Family**
6. Gates, "Aunt Clara Decker," in Gates, "My Recollections," box 11, folder 2, item [16] ("unfinished fragment"), 1–2; Gates, "Mother used to say," in Gates, "My Recollections," box 1, folder 2, item 11, 1–2; Gates, "Brigham Young and His Nineteen Wives," 7, 10–11; Gates, "Life in the Lion House," 26; Gates, "Alonso was a fine representative," in Gates, "My Recollections," box 11, folder 2, item [48], 4; Gates, "As the families of my Aunts increased in size," box 1, folder 5, item [14], 2.
7. Gates, "Alonso was a fine representative," in Gates, "My Recollections," box 11, folder 2, item [48], [7]; Gates, "Life in the Lion House," 39–40. **Topic: Eliza R. Snow**
8. Brigham Young, Discourse, July 13, 1865, Church History Department Pitman Shorthand Transcriptions, CHL.
9. Brigham Young, Discourse, June 18, 1865, Church History Department Pitman Shorthand Transcriptions, CHL.
10. Brigham Young, School of the Prophets, Jan. 3, 1868, Church History Department Pitman Shorthand Transcriptions, CHL.
11. Gates, "My Father as His Forty Six Children Knew Him," [4]; Dougall, "Reminiscences," 594; Gates, "And while father is ever deliberate," box 1, folder 5, item [18], 64; Heber J. Grant, in *Eighty-Ninth Annual Conference,* 7; see also Gates, "Family Life among the Mormons," 341–42.
12. Whitney, *History of Utah,* 2:223–26; see also "The Completion of the Pacific Railroad," *Deseret News,* May 19, 1869, [6].
13. Arrington, *Great Basin Kingdom,* 236–37; Union Pacific Railroad Accounts, Cash Book, 1868–72; Brigham Young to John W. Young, Feb. 5, 1867, Letterbook, volume 9, 340–43, Brigham Young Office Files, CHL; "Remarks," *Deseret News,* Sept. 16, 1868, [3]; "Governor's Message," *Deseret News,* Jan. 23, 1867, 1; Roberts, "Life Story of B. H. Roberts," 30; see also "Remarks," *Deseret News,* Aug. 7, 1867, [2]–[3]; Brigham Young, in *Journal of Discourses,* June 16, 1867, 12:63; and Cowan, "Steel Rails and the Utah Saints," 183–84, 188.
14. Brigham Young to Karl G. Maeser, May 20, 1865, Letterbook, volume 7, 629, Brigham Young Office Files, CHL; Gates, "I saw just one step cut," box 1, folder 5, item [17], [2]–[3]; Young, Autobiographical Notes, [2]–[3]; Young, "Some Unpublished Letters of President Brigham Young," 10–11; see also Gates, "Life in the Lion House," 19; and Maeser, *Karl G. Maeser,* 48.
15. Gates, "I saw just one step cut," box 1, folder 5, item [17], [2]–[3]. Quotation edited for readability; original source has "my dear teacher comforted me by telling me before the class that only those who had the courage to make mistakes ever learned worth while lessons and truths."
16. Dorius, "Sketch of the Life," 62–64; Dorius, "Autobiography of Carl Christian Nicoli Dorius," 29–30; Dorius, *Dorius Heritage,* 105, 109–10.
17. Dorius, "Autobiography of Carl Christian Nicoli Dorius," 33; Peterson, *Utah's Black Hawk War,* 102–3, 112–13.

18. Brigham Young to Orson Hyde, June 18, 1864, Letterbook, volume 7, 224, Brigham Young Office Files, CHL; see also Brigham Young to George Catlin, June 27, 1870, Letterbook, volume 12, 212, Brigham Young Office Files, CHL; and Peterson, *Utah's Black Hawk War,* 103.
19. Brigham Young to George Catlin, June 27, 1870, Letterbook, volume 12, 214, Brigham Young Office Files, CHL; Peterson, *Utah's Black Hawk War,* 3, 99–100, 104–5, 108, 110, 112–13; Coates, "George Catlin, Brigham Young, and the Plains Indians," 114–15; "Indian Hostilities," *Deseret News,* Sept. 9, 1865, [6].
20. Peterson, *Utah's Black Hawk War,* 139–44; Brigham Young to "Orson Hyde and the Bishops," Apr. 17, 1865, Letterbook, volume 7, 567–68, Brigham Young Office Files, CHL; "Indian Massacre," *Deseret News,* June 7, 1865, [6]; Gottfredson, *History of Indian Depredations in Utah,* 140–44.
21. Proceedings of a Council Held by O. H. Irish with Utah Indians at Spanish Fork, June 7, 1865, Utah American Indian Digital Archive, Main Collection, J. Willard Marriott Library, University of Utah, Salt Lake City; Indian Treaty, June 8, 1865, Federal and Local Government Files, 1844–76, Brigham Young Office Files, CHL; "Indian Treaty," *Deseret News,* June 14, 1865, [6]; Gottfredson, *History of Indian Depredations in Utah,* 153–59; Peterson, *Utah's Black Hawk War,* 148–55, 161–78.
22. Dorius, "Sketch of the Life," 63–64; Dorius, "Autobiography of Carl Christian Nicoli Dorius," 33; Kuhre, Journal, 58; Gottfredson, *History of Indian Depredations in Utah,* 169–76; Peterson, *Utah's Black Hawk War,* 178–81. **Topic: American Indians**
23. George A. Smith to Orson Hyde, Oct. 22, 1865, Historian's Office Letterpress Copybook, volume 2, 506–9; Orson Hyde to George A. Smith, Oct. 29, 1865, George A. Smith, Papers, CHL; "Conclusion of President Young's Trip to Sanpete," *Deseret News,* July 26, 1865, [2]; see also Peterson, *Utah's Black Hawk War,* 180–82.
24. Gottfredson, *History of Indian Depredations in Utah,* 176–79; Larsen, "Biographical Sketch of the Life of Oluf Christian Larsen," 45, 47; William J. Allred to George A. Smith, May 5, 1866, George A. Smith, Papers, CHL; Peterson, *Utah's Black Hawk War,* 189–90, 245–48; Winkler, "Circleville Massacre," 4–21.
25. Brigham Young, Discourse, Sept. 9, 1866, Church History Department Pitman Shorthand Transcriptions, CHL. Quotation edited for readability; original source has "I consider when a man steps out with his rifle and shoots down an innocent Indian he is guilty of murder."
26. Brigham Young, Discourse, July 28, 1866, Church History Department Pitman Shorthand Transcriptions, CHL; see also Brigham Young, in *Journal of Discourses,* July 28, 1866, 11:263; "President Young's Trip to Utah County," *Deseret News,* Aug. 2, 1866, [4]–[5]; Woodruff, Journal, July 26–29, 1866; and Brigham Young to Orson Hyde and others, Letterbook, volume 7, 746–48, Brigham Young Office Files, CHL. Second part of quotation edited for readability; "should ever had" in original changed to "should have ever had."
27. Larsen, "Biographical Sketch of the Life of Oluf Christian Larsen," 45–46; Brigham Young to Orson Hyde, July 23, 1867, Letterbook, volume 10, 317–19, Brigham Young Office Files, CHL; Jesse N. Smith to George A. Smith, Aug. 13, 1867, George A. Smith, Papers, CHL; "Black Hawk," *Deseret News,* Aug. 28, 1867, [5]; Reddick N. Allred to Robert T. Burton and William B. Pace, Aug. 13, 1867, William B. Pace Collection, CHL; Peterson, *Utah's Black Hawk War,* 340–42, 348–49.
28. Walker, "Salt Lake Tabernacle," 198–240; Grow, "One Masterpiece," 170–97.
29. See "Governor's Message," *Deseret News,* Jan. 23, 1867, 1; "Lee's Surrender," *National Intelligencer,* Apr. 16, 1865, [3]; Arrington, *Great Basin Kingdom,* 270; and "To the Leaders of the Mormon Church," and "Reply," *Deseret News,* Jan. 2, 1867, [7].
30. Doctrine and Covenants 38:27–30; 78:1–16.
31. Brigham Young, in *Journal of Discourses,* Oct. 8, 1868, 12:298; "The Deseret Alphabet," *Deseret News,* Aug. 19, 1868, [2]. **Topic: Deseret Alphabet**
32. See Arrington, *Brigham Young,* 294–95, 344–46. **Topic: Cooperative Movement**

33. "Remarks," *Deseret News,* Aug. 7, 1867, [2]–[3]; Arrington, *Great Basin Kingdom,* 235, 240–41, 247–49; Cowan, "Steel Rails and the Utah Saints," 183–84. **Topic: Railroad**

34. *Jubilee History of Latter-day Saints Sunday Schools,* 9–17; George Q. Cannon, Journal, Oct. 9 and Dec. 17, 1899; "Salutatory," 3; see also Bitton, *George Q. Cannon,* 146–47. **Topics: Sunday School; Church Periodicals**

35. Brigham Young, School of the Prophets, Dec. 2, 1867, Church History Department Pitman Shorthand Transcriptions, CHL; Doctrine and Covenants 88:127, 137 (Revelation, Jan. 3, 1833, at josephsmithpapers.org); see also *Saints,* volume 1, chapter 15; and "Remarks," *Deseret News,* Dec. 11, 1867, [7].

36. Brigham Young, School of the Prophets, Dec. 2 and 23, 1867, Church History Department Pitman Shorthand Transcriptions, CHL; see also "School of the Prophets," *Deseret News,* Dec. 4, 1867, 1; "Remarks," *Deseret News,* Dec. 11, 1867, [7]; "Names of Members of the School of the Prophets Organized Decr 9th 1867," in Roster of Members, Undated Minutes, and Attendance Roll, 1867–68, School of the Prophets Salt Lake City Records, CHL; and Arrington, *Great Basin Kingdom,* 245–49.

37. Brigham Young, Discourse, Dec. 8, 1867 (Excerpt); "Part 3: 1867–1879," in Derr and others, *First Fifty Years of Relief Society,* 248–52, 236–39; see also Cowan, "Steel Rails and the Utah Saints," 183–84. **Topic: Relief Society**

38. Eliza R. Snow, "Female Relief Society," Apr. 18 and 20, 1868; Eliza R. Snow, Account of 1868 Commission, as Recorded in "Sketch of My Life," Apr. 13, 1885 (Excerpt), in Derr and others, *First Fifty Years of Relief Society,* 270–72, 266–69; see also Nauvoo Relief Society Minute Book; Brigham Young, Discourse, Dec. 8, 1867 (Excerpt); and Brigham Young, Discourse, Apr. 8, 1868 (Excerpt), in Derr and others, *First Fifty Years of Relief Society,* 23–131, 248–52, 262.

39. Eliza R. Snow, Account of 1868 Commission, as Recorded in "Sketch of My Life," Apr. 13, 1885 (Excerpt), in Derr and others, *First Fifty Years of Relief Society,* 266–69.

40. Eliza R. Snow, "Female Relief Society," Apr. 18 and 20, 1868, in Derr and others, *First Fifty Years of Relief Society,* 271–73.

41. Thirteenth Ward, Ensign Stake, Relief Society Minutes and Records, Apr. 30, 1868; Nauvoo Relief Society Minute Book, Mar. 17 and 24, 1842; Apr. 28, 1842; Salt Lake City Thirteenth Ward Relief Society, Minutes, Apr. 18, 1868, in Derr and others, *First Fifty Years of Relief Society,* 30, 38, 53, 276–79.

42. Walker, "Rachel R. Grant," 21–28; Walker, *Qualities That Count,* 27–29; see also Grant, "How I Became a Mormon," [2].

43. Thirteenth Ward, Ensign Stake, Relief Society Minutes and Records, Apr. 30, 1868.

44. Sarah M. Kimball and Eliza R. Snow, "Duty of Officers of F R Society," circa May 1868, in Derr and others, *First Fifty Years of Relief Society,* 285–89; see also Nauvoo Relief Society Minute Book, Mar. 17, 1842, in Derr and others, *First Fifty Years of Relief Society,* 30.

45. Eliza R. Snow, Letter to Augusta B. Smith, circa May 7, 1868, in Derr and others, *First Fifty Years of Relief Society,* 280–84; Derr, Cannon, and Beecher, *Women of Covenant,* 88–92; Third Ward, Liberty Stake, Relief Society Minutes and Records, Sept. 30, 1868; see also "Female Relief Society," *Deseret News,* Apr. 22, 1868, 1.

46. See "Editorial Correspondence," *Deseret News,* Oct. 7, 1868, [2]; and Brigham Young, School of the Prophets, Dec. 2, 1867, Church History Department Pitman Shorthand Transcriptions, CHL.

47. School of the Prophets Provo Records, Apr. 15, 1868; Woodruff, Journal, Jan. 31 and Feb. 10, 1868; Smith, *Life of Joseph F. Smith,* 230.

48. Whitney, *Life of Heber C. Kimball,* 465, 482–83, 485–88, 506; "Demise of President Heber C. Kimball," *Deseret Evening News,* June 22, 1868, [2].

49. Cannon, "Change Engulfs a Frontier Settlement," 16–17; Skinner, "Civil War's Aftermath," 307; White, *Railroaded,* 31, 296; Union Pacific Railroad to Brigham Young, Contract, May 20, 1868, Union Pacific Railroad Contract Files, 1868–72, Brigham Young Office Files, CHL; "Contract for Grading Railroad," *Deseret News,* May 27, 1868, [4]; "Advantages of Two Through Lines," *Deseret News,* Mar. 10, 1869, [7]; Brigham Young to Horace S. Eldredge, Apr. 11, 1871, in *Latter-day Saints'*

Millennial Star, May 9, 1871, 33:300; see also Arrington, *Great Basin Kingdom,* 258–65.

50. Dougall, "Reminiscences," 594; see also "Discourse," *Deseret News,* Dec. 9, 1868, [2].
51. Brigham Young to the "Editor of the Religio Philosophical Journal," Jan. 7, 1869, Letterbook, volume 11, 283–86, Brigham Young Office Files, CHL.
52. Joseph Hall, "Railway Celebration at Ogden," *Deseret News,* Mar. 17, 1869, 1.
53. Historical Department, Office Journal, July 22, 1868; Woodruff, Journal, Aug. 22, 1868; Sept. 20 and 23, 1868; May 5 and 9, 1869; Derr, Cannon, and Beecher, *Women of Covenant,* 88–89; "A Great Movement Fairly Inaugurated," *Deseret News,* Mar. 17, 1869, [6]; Arrington, *Great Basin Kingdom,* 298–301; Whitney, *History of Utah,* 2:282–87. **Topic: Cooperative Movement**
54. Woodruff, Journal, May 9, 1869.
55. Whitney, *History of Utah,* 2:255–56; "Proceedings at Promontory Summit," and "Completion of the Pacific Railroad," *Deseret News,* May 19, 1869, 1, [6].
56. Brigham Young to Heber Young, May 15, 1869, Letterbook, volume 11, 527–28, Brigham Young Office Files, CHL. **Topic: Railroad**

Chapter 24: An Immense Labor

1. [George Q. Cannon], "Woman and Her Mission," *Deseret Evening News,* May 19, 1869, [2].
2. Fifteenth Ward, Relief Society Minutes and Records, volume 1, May 20, 1869; Arrington, Fox, and May, *Building the City of God,* 79–110; Wallis, "Women's Cooperative Movement in Utah," 315–31; Historical Department, Office Journal, Oct. 29, 1868; "Discourse," *Deseret News,* Oct. 21, 1868, [2]; "Remarks," *Deseret News,* May 26, 1869, [7]. **Topics: United Orders; Cooperative Movement**
3. "Co-operation," *Deseret Evening News,* Apr. 29, 1869, [3]; Reeder, "Mormon Women and the Creation of a Usable Past," 155; Sarah M. Kimball, Annual Message, circa 1868; Eliza R. Snow, Report to Philadelphia Centennial Exposition, Mar. 1876, in Derr and others, *First Fifty Years of Relief Society,* 290, 394; Wallis, "Women's Cooperative Movement in Utah," 315–31; see also *Saints,* volume 1, chapter 37.
4. Fifteenth Ward, Relief Society Minutes and Records, volume 1, Nov. 12, 1868, and July 22, 1869; Sarah M. Kimball, Annual Message, circa 1868, in Derr and others, *First Fifty Years of Relief Society,* 290; "To Pres. Young, Sister Snow, and to all," loose sheet in Fifteenth Ward, Relief Society Minutes and Records, volume 5; Derr, Cannon, and Beecher, *Women of Covenant,* 99. **Topic: Relief Society**
5. Fifteenth Ward, Relief Society Minutes and Records, volume 1, July 16, 1868; "To Pres. Young, Sister Snow, and to all," loose sheet in Fifteenth Ward, Relief Society Minutes and Records, volume 5.
6. Fifteenth Ward, Relief Society Minutes and Records, volume 1, Nov. 12, 1868; Sarah M. Kimball, "Auto-biography," *Woman's Exponent,* Sept. 1, 1883, 12:51.
7. Fifteenth Ward, Relief Society Minutes and Records, volume 1, Feb. 25 and May 13, 1869; Higbee, "President Mrs. Kimball," 87. Quotation edited for readability; original source has "Pres Kimball said she thought it was because we had acted in unison and had kept in motion that which we received."
8. Fifteenth Ward, Relief Society Minutes and Records, volume 1, May 20, 1869; "Woman and Her Mission," *Deseret Evening News,* May 19, 1869, [2]. Sarah Kimball quotation edited for readability; "woman, her abilities and duties" in original changed to "woman, and her abilities and duties."
9. Crofutt, *Crofutt's Trans-continental Tourist's Guide,* [9]–223; Francaviglia, *Over the Range,* 143–45, 151, 163; "Inauguration of the Work on the Utah Central Railroad," *Salt Lake Daily Telegraph,* May 18, 1869, [2]; "The Railroad and Its Benefits," *Deseret News,* July 7, 1869, [9]; Brigham Young, in *Journal of Discourses,* May 26, 1867, 12:54. **Topic: Railroad**

10. Historical Department, Journal History of the Church, July 1, 1866; Smith, *Life of Joseph F. Smith,* 226–28. **Topic: Joseph F. Smith**

11. Joseph F. Smith to Martha Ann Smith Harris, June 21, 1869, Carole C. King Collection, CHL; "Smith, Alexander Hale," and "Smith, David Hyrum," Biographical Entries, Joseph Smith Papers website, josephsmithpapers.org; "True Latter Day Saints' Herald," *True Latter Day Saints' Herald,* Jan. 1, 1869, 19–20; "Pleasant Chat," *True Latter Day Saints' Herald,* Mar. 15, 1869, 176–77. **Topic: Joseph and Emma Hale Smith Family**

12. Joseph F. Smith to Joseph Smith III, Mar. 18, 1868, Joseph F. Smith, Papers, CHL; "Pleasant Chat," *True Latter Day Saints' Herald,* Dec. 15, 1866, 177; Smith, "Biography of Alexander H. Smith," 399–402; see also, for example, "On Marriage," *Times and Seasons,* Oct. 1, 1842, 3:939–40; "Notice," *Times and Seasons,* Feb. 1, 1844, 5:423; and Hyrum Smith, "To the Brethren of the Church," *Times and Seasons,* Mar. 15, 1844, 5:474.

13. Doctrine and Covenants 132:18–20, 30–32, 55, 63 (Revelation, July 12, 1843, at josephsmithpapers.org).

14. Joseph F. Smith to Orson Pratt, July 19, 1875, Letterpress Copybooks, "Book C. No. 3," 1–4, Joseph F. Smith, Papers, CHL; Doctrine and Covenants 132 (Revelation, July 12, 1843, at josephsmithpapers.org).

15. Smith, "Biography of Alexander H. Smith," 402.

16. Joseph F. Smith to Martha Ann Smith Harris, June 21, 1869, Carole C. King Collection, CHL; Historical Department, Office Journal, Apr. 22 and July 26, 1869; Affidavits about Celestial Marriage, 1869–1915, CHL.

17. Kenney, "Trials of the Young Joseph F. Smith," 33–35; Joseph F. Smith to Martha Ann Smith Harris, Dec. 1, 1869, Carole C. King Collection, CHL; Beesley, Diary, Apr. 11, 1886; Divorce Certificate, June 10, 1867, Joseph F. Smith, Papers, CHL; Tait, "Wives of Joseph F. Smith," 77, 81; Joseph F. Smith to Brigham Young, Aug. 25, 1867, Brigham Young Office Files, CHL.

18. Joseph F. Smith to Joseph Smith III, Mar. 18, 1868, Joseph F. Smith, Papers, CHL; Joseph F. Smith to Orson Pratt, July 19, 1875, Letterpress Copybooks, "Book C. No. 3," 1–4, Joseph F. Smith, Papers, CHL; Notice, *Times and Seasons,* Sept. 1, 1842, 3:909; Hyrum Smith, "To the Brethren of the Church," *Times and Seasons,* Mar. 15, 1844, 5:474; Letter to the Editor, *Times and Seasons,* Nov. 15, 1844, 5:715.

19. "40 Affidavits on Celestial Marriage," Book no. 1 (second series), 1869, Affidavits about Celestial Marriage, CHL; Historical Department, Office Journal, Apr. 22 and July 26, 1869; see also *Saints,* volume 1, chapter 40; and Hales, *Joseph Smith's Polygamy,* 1:356–60; appendix C, 2:343–57. **Topic: Joseph Smith and Plural Marriage**

20. Fifteenth Ward, Relief Society Minutes and Records, volume 1, July 22, 1869. Quotation edited for readability; "had" in original changed to "has." **Topic: Relief Society**

21. Fifteenth Ward, Relief Society Minutes and Records, volume 1, July 22 and Aug. 5, 1869; Eliza R. Snow, "Dedication Hymn," in Derr and Davidson, *Eliza R. Snow,* 795–96; "Dedication," *Deseret News,* Aug. 11, 1869, [5].

22. Fifteenth Ward, Relief Society Minutes and Records, Aug. 5, 1869; "Remarks," *Deseret News,* Aug. 11, 1869, [7].

23. Fifteenth Ward, Relief Society Minutes and Records, Aug. 26, 1869.

24. Smith, "Biography of Alexander Hale Smith," 502–4; "Extracts from Elder David H. Smith's Journal," *True Latter Day Saints' Herald,* Aug. 15, 1869, 102; Sept. 1, 1869, 130; Smith, "Biography of Alexander H. Smith," 260.

25. Historical Department, Office Journal, July 19–Sept. 2, 1869; Clayton, Journal, May 1, 1843.

26. Historical Department, Office Journal, July 21–22, 26, and 28–29, 1869; Aug. 2–5 and 11, 1869; Historian's Office, History of the Church, volume 39, July 25, 1869, 689; "Sabbath Meetings," *Deseret News,* July 28, 1869, [8]; Woodruff, Journal, July 25, 1869.

27. Historical Department, Office Journal, Aug. 1, 8, 15, 21, and 22, 1869; "Extracts from Elder David H. Smith's Journal," *True Latter Day Saints' Herald,* Sept. 1, 1869, 130–31; Smith, "David H. Smith in Utah," 508–9; Smith, "Biography of Alexander Hale Smith," 504–5.

28. Smith, "David H. Smith in Utah," 509; Historical Department, Office Journal, Aug. 8, 1869; Joseph F. Smith to Martha Ann Smith Harris, Aug. 17, 1869, Carole C. King Collection, CHL; see also Avery, *From Mission to Madness*, 103.

29. [Harrison], "Josephite Platform," 280–83.

30. Walker, *Wayward Saints*, 93, 105, 149–51; Godbe, "The Situation in Utah," 406. **Topic: Godbeites**

31. "William S. Godbe," 64–65; Walker, "Commencement of the Godbeite Protest," 223–24; Beeton, "Charlotte Ives Cobb Godbe Kirby," 23–24.

32. "Godbeite Movement," 16; Godbe, "The Situation in Utah," 406; Walker, *Wayward Saints*, 100–101, 105–6; Harrison and Godbe, "Manifesto," 470. **Topic: Cooperative Movement**

33. "Mormonism," *New York Herald*, Jan. 2, 1870, 8; Albanese, *Republic of Mind and Spirit*, 178–79, 220–24; Nartonis, "Rise of 19th-Century American Spiritualism," 371; Walker, *Wayward Saints*, 112–26; Godbe, "The Situation in Utah," 406; Walker, "Commencement of the Godbeite Protest," 237–40; see also Jedediah Grant, in *Journal of Discourses*, Feb. 19, 1854, 2:10–11; and Brigham Young, in *Journal of Discourses*, May 6, 1855, 3:156–58; Sept. 1, 1859, 7:237–44.

34. "Steadying the Ark," 295; "Justifiable Obedience," 379; "True Development of the Territory," 376–78; "Our Workmen's Wages," 262–64; Walker, "Commencement of the Godbeite Protest," 237–38.

35. "True Development of the Territory," 376–78; Walker, "Commencement of the Godbeite Protest," 239; Arrington, *Brigham Young*, 299, 348–49; Arrington, *Great Basin Kingdom*, 241–44.

36. Woodruff, Journal, Oct. 17, 18, 23, and 25, 1869; [Tullidge], "Reformation in Utah," 605–6; Joseph F. Smith, Journal, Oct. 23, 1869; see also Walker, "Commencement of the Godbeite Protest," 240–41.

37. Salt Lake Stake, High Council Minute Book of Courts, volume 3, Oct. 25, 1869, 51, 58–69, 80–94; Woodruff, Journal, Oct. 25, 1869; see also Walker, *Wayward Saints*, 166; and "To Whom It May Concern," *Deseret Evening News*, Oct. 26, 1869, [3].

CHAPTER 25: THE DIGNITY OF OUR CALLING

1. Harrison, "Appeal to the People," 406–8; see also Harrison and Godbe, "Manifesto," 470–73. Quotation edited for clarity; "from out our" in original changed to "from out of our." **Topic: Godbeites**

2. "To the Latter-day Saints," *Deseret Evening News*, Oct. 26, 1869, [2].

3. "Programme of President B. Young's Trip to the Settlements South to Gunnison," 1869, Journals, Minutes, and Itineraries, 1844–77, Brigham Young Office Files, CHL; Reports for Utah County and Sanpete County, in Utah Territory Legislative Assembly, House Historical Committee Files, CHL.

4. "Remarks," *Deseret News*, Nov. 24, 1869, [8]; Gates, *History of the Young Ladies' Mutual Improvement Association*, 8–9, 30–31; see also Ladies' Cooperative Retrenchment Meeting, Minutes, Feb. 19, 1870, in Derr and others, *First Fifty Years of Relief Society*, 344–45.

5. Brigham Young, Discourse, Mar. 27, 1868 (second sermon); Brigham Young, Discourse, Apr. 6, 1868, Church History Department Pitman Shorthand Transcriptions, CHL; see also, for example, "Remarks," *Deseret News*, Apr. 29, 1868, [3]; "Remarks," *Deseret News*, May 13, 1868, [6]–[7]; "Discourse," *Deseret News*, Oct. 21, 1868, [2]–[3]; "Remarks," *Deseret News*, Oct. 13, 1869, [14]; and "Remarks," May 6, 1870, *Deseret News*, June 1, 1870, [7]. Quotation edited for clarity; original source has "The idle habits the waste extravagance of men is ridiculous in our community."

6. "Remarks," *Deseret News*, Nov. 24, 1869, [8]; Gates, *History of the Young Ladies' Mutual Improvement Association*, 30–31, 41–44; Mary Isabella Horne Address, in

Report of Relief Society Jubilee, Mar. 17, 1892, in Derr and others, *First Fifty Years of Relief Society,* 613–15.

7. Gates, *History of the Young Ladies' Mutual Improvement Association,* 31; Webster and Wheeler, *Dictionary of the English Language,* 364; Mary Isabella Horne Address, in Report of Relief Society Jubilee, Mar. 17, 1892, in Derr and others, *First Fifty Years of Relief Society,* 616; "Table Retrenchment," *Deseret News,* Feb. 23, 1870, [12].

8. Gates, *History of the Young Ladies' Mutual Improvement Association,* 30–31; "Remarks," *Deseret News,* Nov. 24, 1869, [8]; Mary Isabella Horne Address, in Report of Relief Society Jubilee, Mar. 17, 1892, in Derr and others, *First Fifty Years of Relief Society,* 616. Final sentence of quotation edited for clarity; original source has "I told her I wished to get up a society whose members would agree to have a light, nice breakfast in the morning, for themselves and children, without cooking something less than forty different kinds of food." **Topic: Retrenchment**

9. Homer, "Passing of Martin Harris," 468–69; Martin Harris Jr. to Brigham Young, Jan. 11, 1870, Brigham Young Office Files, CHL; Black and Porter, *Martin Harris,* 278–80, 284–85, 287–89, 320–41, 377–79, 385–88, 408–9; see also *Saints,* volume 1, chapters 7 and 25.

10. Homer, "Passing of Martin Harris," 469–71; "Kirtland, Ohio," *Deseret News,* Aug. 24, 1870, [5]. **Topics: Witnesses of the Book of Mormon; Kirtland Temple**

11. Derr and others, *First Fifty Years of Relief Society,* 243, 305, 312; A Bill to Provide for the Execution of the Law against the Crime of Polygamy in the Territory of Utah, and for Other Purposes, S. 286, 41st Cong., 2nd Sess. (1869); A Bill in Aid of the Execution of the Laws in the Territory of Utah, and for Other Purposes, H.R. 696, 41st Cong., 2nd Sess. (1869); see also "A Bill," *Deseret Evening News,* Jan. 4, 1870, [2]. **Topic: Antipolygamy Legislation**

12. Historical Department, Office Journal, Jan. 3, 1870; Minutes of "Ladies Mass Meeting," Jan. 6, 1870, in Derr and others, *First Fifty Years of Relief Society,* 305–10; see also Sarah M. Kimball, "Address Delivered at the Laying of the Cornerstone of the Storehouse," in Fifteenth Ward, Relief Society Minutes and Records, volume 1, Nov. 12, 1868.

13. Minutes of "Ladies Mass Meeting," Jan. 6, 1870, in Derr and others, *First Fifty Years of Relief Society,* 307–10; Givens, *Viper on the Hearth,* chapters 6 and 7; Bunker and Bitton, *Mormon Graphic Image,* 16–26.

14. Minutes of "Great Indignation Meeting," Jan. 13, 1870, in Derr and others, *First Fifty Years of Relief Society,* 311, 313, 332; Maughan, Autobiography, volume 2, Jan. 13 and Feb. 1, 1870; Campbell, *Man Cannot Speak for Her,* 4–5, 9–12; Ulrich, *House Full of Females,* xi–xii; see also "Polygamy," *New York Herald,* Jan. 23, 1870, 4.

15. Minutes of "Great Indignation Meeting," Jan. 13, 1870, in Derr and others, *First Fifty Years of Relief Society,* 313, 318–19.

16. Minutes of "Great Indignation Meeting," Jan. 13, 1870, in Derr and others, *First Fifty Years of Relief Society,* 313–32; see also *Saints,* volume 1, chapter 30. **Topics: Amanda Barnes Smith; Eliza R. Snow**

17. See Ulrich, *House Full of Females,* xii.

18. "Indignation Meetings in the Settlements," *Deseret News,* Feb. 2, 1870, 1; "Indignation Meetings," *Deseret News,* Feb. 9, 1870, 12; "Ladies' Mass Meetings," *Deseret News,* Mar. 9, 1870, 1; Maughan, Autobiography, volume 2, Jan. 13 and 30, 1870; see also Phipps, "Marriage and Redemption," 451–64.

19. Minutes of "Ladies Mass Meeting," Jan. 6, 1870, in Derr and others, *First Fifty Years of Relief Society,* 308; House Record of Attendance, 1870; House Minutes, 19th Sess., Jan. 27–Feb. 10, 1870, Utah Territory Legislative Assembly Papers, CHL; Joseph F. Smith, Journal, Jan. 27 and Feb. 9, 1870; see also Women Suffrage Act, 1870, Utah Territory Legislative Assembly Papers, CHL.

20. Resolution Proposing an Amendment to the Constitution of the United States [Feb. 27, 1869], *Statutes at Large* [1869], 40th Cong., 3rd Sess., Res. 14, 346; Gordon, "Liberty of Self-Degradation," 285; Nelson, *Fourteenth Amendment,* 55–58, 87, 98–99, 136–38.

21. "New Plan," and "Female Suffrage in Utah," *Deseret News,* Mar. 24, 1869, [6]; Bill to Discourage Polygamy in Utah, H.R. 64, 41st Cong., 1st Sess. (1869); Tullidge, *History of Salt Lake City,* 435; see also Alexander, "Experiment in Progressive Legislation," 21, 24–27.

22. School of the Prophets Salt Lake City Records, Jan. 29, 1870; Joseph F. Smith, Journal, Jan. 29 and Feb. 10, 1870; "Nineteenth Annual Session of the Legislature," *Deseret News,* Jan. 12, 1870, [8]; Introduction to "Female Suffrage in Utah," Feb. 8, 1870; Eliza R. Snow and others to Stephen A. Mann, Feb. 19, 1870, in Derr and others, *First Fifty Years of Relief Society,* 333–34, 350–52. **Topic: Women's Suffrage**

23. See Historical Department, Office Journal, Jan. 3, 1870; and Tullidge, *History of Salt Lake City,* 467.

24. "Extracts from Elder David H. Smith's Journal," *True Latter Day Saints' Herald,* Jan. 1, 1870, 9–11; Smith, "Biography of Alexander Hale Smith," 505; Avery, *From Mission to Madness,* 111–13. **Topic: Godbeites**

25. Tullidge, "Oracles Speak," 523; "New Movement," 531; Harrison and Godbe, "Manifesto," 471–72; Walker, "Commencement of the Godbeite Protest," 233–34, 243–44.

26. Godbe and Harrison, "Prospectus," 474–75; Baskin, *Reminiscences of Early Utah,* 23–27; Walker, *Wayward Saints,* 221–29.

27. Joseph F. Smith, Journal, Jan. 1 and 15, 1870; School of the Prophets Salt Lake City Records, Jan. 21–22 and Apr. 23, 1870.

28. Joseph F. Smith, Journal, Jan. 16 and 29, 1870; School of the Prophets Salt Lake City Records, Jan. 22 and 29, 1870; Mar. 26, 1870.

29. *Congressional Globe,* 41st Cong., 2nd Sess., Mar. 23, 1870, 2180–81; "Action by the House on the Cullom Bill," *Deseret Evening News,* Mar. 24, 1870, [2]; School of the Prophets Salt Lake City Records, Mar. 26, 1870. Daniel Wells quotation edited for clarity; "councils" in original changed to "counsels," and word "with" added.

30. Joseph F. Smith to Martha Ann Smith Harris, Mar. 29, 1870, Carole C. King Collection, CHL.

31. Gates, *History of the Young Ladies' Mutual Improvement Association,* 31; Ladies' Cooperative Retrenchment Meeting, Minutes, Feb. 10, 1870; Mary Isabella Horne Address, in Report of Relief Society Jubilee, Mar. 17, 1892, in Derr and others, *First Fifty Years of Relief Society,* 338–42, 616. **Topic: Retrenchment**

32. See Gates, *History of the Young Ladies' Mutual Improvement Association,* 9–11.

33. Historical Department, Office Journal, May 25, 1870, 71; Dougall, "Reminiscences," 594; Gates, "Historical Sketch of the Y. L. M. I. A," 231–32.

34. Dougall, "Reminiscences," 594–95; see also Gates, *History of the Young Ladies' Mutual Improvement Association,* 10–11.

35. Ladies Cooperative Retrenchment Association Minutes, May 28, 1870, Zina D. Young Papers, Zina Card Brown Family Collection, CHL; see also Young Ladies' Department of the Ladies' Cooperative Retrenchment Association, Resolutions, May 27, 1870, in Derr and others, *First Fifty Years of Relief Society,* 353–57.

36. Young Ladies' Department of the Ladies' Cooperative Retrenchment Association, Resolutions, May 27, 1870, in Derr and others, *First Fifty Years of Relief Society,* 353–57; Ladies Cooperative Retrenchment Association Minutes, May 28, 1870, Zina D. Young Papers, Zina Card Brown Family Collection, CHL.

37. Young Ladies' Department of the Ladies' Cooperative Retrenchment Association, Resolutions, May 27, 1870, in Derr and others, *First Fifty Years of Relief Society,* 355. **Topic: Young Women Organizations**

CHAPTER 26: FOR THE BEST GOOD OF ZION

1. "Local and Other Matters," *Deseret News,* July 27, 1870, [12]; Santaquin Ward, Relief Society Minutes and Records, volume 1, May 28 and July 9, 1870.

2. School of the Prophets Salt Lake City Records, May 14 and 21, 1870. Quotation edited for clarity; original source has "They may determine to send armies here to destroy us, and scatter us, and lay waste our habitations, but it would not prove our religion to be false—There are many who expect to fatten on our overthrow and pick the bones of the Mormons."

3. See "Organization of the Church of Zion," *Mormon Tribune,* Jan. 29, 1870, 36; Walker, *Wayward Saints,* 198–205; and Joseph F. Smith, Journal, Mar. 10, 1870. **Topic: Godbeites**

4. Amasa Lyman, Journal, volume 34, May 8–12, 1870; Francis Marion Lyman, Journal, May 8, 1870; Hefner, "From Apostle to Apostate," 90–104; Lyman, *Amasa Mason Lyman,* 427–34.

5. School of the Prophets Salt Lake City Records, Apr. 23, 1870; July 16 and 23, 1870. First quotation edited for readability; "He intended to use his influence" in original changed to "I intend to use my influence."

6. Homer, "Passing of Martin Harris," 471; Black and Porter, *Martin Harris,* 418, 429; "Personal," *Salt Lake Daily Herald,* Aug. 31, 1870, [2]; Martin Harris Jr. to Brigham Young, Jan. 11, 1870, Brigham Young Office Files, CHL.

7. "Martin Harris—One of the Witnesses of the Book of Mormon," *Deseret News,* Sept. 7, 1870, [6]; "Martin Harris," *Salt Lake Daily Herald,* Sept. 3, 1870, [3]; "Harris, Martin," Biographical Entry, Joseph Smith Papers website, josephsmithpapers.org; Thomas B. Marsh, "Remarks," *Deseret News,* Sept. 16, 1857, [4]; "Further Remarks by President Brigham Young," *Deseret News,* Sept. 16, 1857, [5]; "Marsh, Thomas Baldwin," Biographical Entry, Joseph Smith Papers website, josephsmithpapers.org.

8. Homer, "Passing of Martin Harris," 471–72; Joseph F. Smith, Journal, Sept. 4, 1870; Woodruff, Journal, Sept. 4, 1870; "Testimony of Martin Harris," Sept. 4, 1870, Edward Stevenson Collection, CHL.

9. "Testimony of Martin Harris," Sept. 4, 1870, Edward Stevenson Collection, CHL.

10. Joseph F. Smith, Journal, Sept. 17, 1870; Woodruff, Journal, Sept. 17, 1870; Black and Porter, *Martin Harris,* 407, 437–39, 471–72.

11. "Fortieth Semi-annual Conference," *Deseret Evening News,* Oct. 10, 1870, [2]. **Topic: Witnesses of the Book of Mormon**

12. Gates, "Lucy Bigelow Young," 71–73; Susa Young Gates, Journal, Nov. 25, 1870. **Topic: Susa Young Gates**

13. Gates, "Lucy Bigelow Young," 69–73; Susa Young Gates, Journal, Nov. 25, 1870; Snow, *Biography and Family Record of Lorenzo Snow,* 385–89.

14. Susa Young Gates, Journal, Nov. 25, 1870; Gates, "Lucy Bigelow Young," 72–73.

15. George A. Smith, Journal, Nov. 25–Dec. 8, 1870; see also Gates, "Lucy Bigelow Young," 72–75; and Susa Young Gates, Journal, Nov. 30, 1870.

16. Bleak, Annals of the Southern Utah Mission, 1850–69, 75–76; 1871, 55–56; St. George Utah Stake Manuscript History, May 27, 1861, 36; [Brigham Young] to Orson Hyde, Oct. 13, 1861, in Historian's Office, Letterpress Copybook, volume 1, 985–86; John Taylor, in *Journal of Discourses,* Nov. 9, 1881, 23:11, 13–14; Charles L. Walker, Journal, June 21, 1863, and Feb. 14, 1865; Bradshaw, *Under Dixie Sun,* 293–95, 332–33; Arrington, *Great Basin Kingdom,* 216–22.

17. Bleak, Annals of the Southern Utah Mission, 1850–69, 75–76, 362, 450; 1871, 2–3; Bradshaw, *Under Dixie Sun,* 295–97, 325–31, 332–33; see also "Mac" to George Reynolds, Nov. 12, 1871, in "Correspondence," *Latter-Day Saints' Millennial Star,* Dec. 19, 1871, 33:812; and Kane, *Twelve Mormon Homes,* 138. **Topic: Pioneer Settlements**

18. Gates, "Lucy Bigelow Young," 75–77; John Taylor, in *Journal of Discourses,* Nov. 9, 1881, 23:14; "Discourse," *Deseret News,* Sept. 24, 1873, [4]; Bennett, "Line upon Line," 50–53. **Topic: Endowment House**

19. "Council in Prest. Erastus Snow's House," Jan. 31, 1871, Journals, Minutes, and Itineraries, 1844–77, Brigham Young Office Files, CHL; see also Bleak, Annals of the Southern Utah Mission, 1871, 8–10.

20. Historical Department, Office Journal, Feb. 10, 1871; Brigham Young to Erastus Snow, Apr. 5, 1871, Letterbook, volume 12, 627–29, Brigham Young Office Files, CHL; Charles L. Walker, Journal, Nov. 1–6, 1871; Bleak, Annals of the Southern Utah Mission, Feb. 15, 1873, 33.

21. See Amasa Lyman, Journal, volumes 23, 34, May 11, 1870–May 28, 1871; and Isaac Morley to Brigham Young and "Council," Mar. 15, 1850, Brigham Young Office Files, CHL. For specific details on séances, see entries in volume 34 of Amasa Lyman's journal for Jan. 31, 1871; Feb. 13, 1871; Mar. 6 and 9–10, 1871; and Apr. 4, 1871; and in volume 25 of his journal for Mar. 17–21 and 27, 1871.

22. Walker, *Wayward Saints,* 202, 207–9, 215, 232–34, 274–76, 291; Walker, "Stenhouses," 51–62.

23. Brigham Young to Albert Carrington, Apr. 23, 1870, Letterbook, volume 12, 101, Brigham Young Office Files, CHL; Walker, *Wayward Saints,* 204; Whitney, *History of Utah,* 2:487–88, 542–43, 554–55, 628; "Death of Judge McKean," *Salt Lake Daily Tribune,* Jan. 7, 1879, [2]; Phipps, "Marriage and Redemption," 461–64; Alexander, "Federal Authority versus Polygamic Theocracy," 86; see also Tullidge, *Life of Brigham Young,* 420–21. **Topic: Antipolygamy Legislation**

24. "Important Legal Decision," *Salt Lake Tribune,* Oct. 15, 1870, 2; "Judicial Decision," *Deseret News,* Oct. 19, 1870, [12]; "That Ruling," *Deseret News,* Oct. 19, 1870, [4]; "The Ruling of Chief Justice McKean," *Deseret News,* Oct. 19, 1870, [12]; Alexander, "Federal Authority versus Polygamic Theocracy," 88.

25. Brigham Young to Erastus Snow, Apr. 5, 1871, Letterbook, volume 12, 628, Brigham Young Office Files, CHL; "Utah Conspiracy," *Deseret News,* Oct. 11, 1871, [8]; Historical Department, Office Journal, Sept. 26–27, 1871; Alexander, "Federal Authority versus Polygamic Theocracy," 89, 93; Baskin, *Reminiscences of Early Utah,* 28, 38, 54.

26. Historical Department, Office Journal, Sept. 27, 1871; *Saints,* volume 1, chapter 44; Grow and Walker, *Prophet and the Reformer,* 427–31. Quotation edited for readability; "Things were" in original changed to "Things are."

27. Editorial, *Deseret Evening News,* Oct. 3, 1871, [2]; "Great Excitement," *Deseret Evening News,* Oct. 3, 1871, [3]; "Senseless Rumors," *Salt Lake Daily Herald,* Oct. 3, 1871, [2]; "Press on Utah Matters," *Salt Lake Daily Herald,* Oct. 10, 1871, [2].

28. Thomas Fitch to Brigham Young, Sept. 23, 1871, Brigham Young Office Files, CHL; Historical Department, Office Journal, Sept. 27, 1871; D. McKenzie to James Cumming, Oct. 3, 1871, Letterbook, volume 12, 865, Brigham Young Office Files, CHL.

29. Woodruff, Journal, Oct. 9–10, 1871; Whitney, *History of Utah,* 2:598.

30. "Plea in Abatement in the Case of the People vs. Brigham Young," *Deseret Evening News,* Oct. 11, 1871, [2]; "Local and Other Matters," *Deseret Evening News,* Oct. 10, 1871, [3]; "Courts versus Religion," *Salt Lake Daily Herald,* Oct. 10, 1871, [3]; "Courts versus Religion," *Salt Lake Daily Herald,* Oct. 11, 1871, [2]; "Third District Court," *Salt Lake Daily Herald,* Oct. 12, 1871, [3]; "Opinion of Judge McKean," *Salt Lake Daily Herald,* Oct. 13, 1871, [1]; see also "A Day in Court," *Deseret Evening News,* Sept. 19, 1871, [2].

31. "Opinion of Chief Justice McKean," *Deseret Evening News,* Oct. 12, 1871, [2]; "Opinion of Judge McKean," *Salt Lake Daily Herald,* Oct. 13, 1871, [1].

32. "Local and Other Matters," *Deseret Evening News,* Oct. 16, 1871, [3]; Whitney, *History of Utah,* 2:603, 629–30, 642; George A. Smith, Journal, Oct. 24, 1871; "St. Brigham's Counsel," *New York Herald,* Nov. 16, 1871, 5; see also Daniel Wells to Brigham Young, Oct. 25, 1871; Oct. 29, 1871, Brigham Young Office Files, CHL.

33. Charles L. Walker, Journal, Nov. 5–9, 1871; Gates, "Lucy Bigelow Young," 80–81.

34. George A. Smith, Journal, Nov. 1–9, 1871; Brigham Young and George A. Smith to Daniel H. Wells, Oct. 28, 1871, President's Office Files, Brigham Young Office Files, CHL; Daniel H. Wells to Brigham Young and George A. Smith, [Nov. 9, 1871], Brigham Young Office Files, CHL.

35. Gates, "Lucy Bigelow Young," 81; "Mrs. Susa Young Gates," [1], in Susa Young Gates Personal Papers, Susa Young Gates, Papers, CHL.

36. George A. Smith, Journal, Nov. 9, 1871; Charles L. Walker, Journal, Nov. 9, 1871; Gates, "Lucy Bigelow Young," 80–81; Bush, "Brigham Young in Life and Death," 79, 89; Heath, "Sacred Shout," 115–23. **Topic: Temple Building**

37. George A. Smith, Journal, Nov. 30, 1871; Dec. 4 and 15, 1871; Grow and Walker, *Prophet and the Reformer,* 427–32; Brigham Young to Daniel Wells, Dec. 12, 1871, Telegram; Brigham Young and George A. Smith to Daniel Wells, Dec. 15, 1871, President's Office Files, Brigham Young Office Files, CHL.

38. George A. Smith, Journal, Dec. 15, 1871; Grow and Walker, *Prophet and the Reformer,* 440–46; Brigham Young and George A. Smith to Daniel Wells, Oct. 26, 1871; Brigham Young to Daniel Wells, Oct. 28, 1871, Telegram, President's Office Files, Brigham Young Office Files, CHL.

39. Brigham Young and George A. Smith to Daniel H. Wells, Dec. 15, 1871, President's Office Files, Brigham Young Office Files, CHL; George A. Smith, Journal, Dec. 15–16, 1871; Roberts, *Comprehensive History,* 5:402–3.

40. "Journal of Pres. Young and Party," Dec. 19, 1871, in Historical Department, Office Journal, Dec. 23–28, 1871. Quotation edited for readability; "would overrule" in original changed to "will overrule."

CHAPTER 27: FIRE IN THE DRY GRASS

1. "President Young Again in Court," *Salt Lake Daily Herald,* Jan. 3, 1872, [2]; "Give Him Time," *Salt Lake Daily Tribune and Utah Mining Gazette,* Nov. 29, 1871, [2]; "Oh Dear!," *Salt Lake Daily Tribune and Utah Mining Gazette,* Dec. 23, 1871, [2]; "Home or Not at Home," *Salt Lake Daily Tribune and Utah Mining Gazette,* Dec. 27, 1871, [2].

2. Brigham Young and George A. Smith to Daniel H. Wells, Dec. 15, 1871, President's Office Files, Brigham Young Office Files, CHL; Daniel H. Wells to Brigham Young, Dec. 22, 1871, Brigham Young Office Files, CHL.

3. "Journal of Pres. Young and Party," Dec. 26, 1871, in Historical Department, Office Journal, Dec. 23–28, 1871; Historical Department, Office Journal, Jan. 2, 1872; "Application for the Admission of President Young to Bail," *Salt Lake Daily Herald,* Jan. 3, 1872, [3]; "Brigham Young on Trial," *Salt Lake Daily Tribune and Utah Mining Gazette,* Jan. 3, 1872, [2].

4. "Brigham Young on Trial," *Salt Lake Daily Tribune and Utah Mining Gazette,* Jan. 3, 1872, [2]; Tullidge, *History of Salt Lake City,* 553–57; Whitney, *History of Utah,* 2:661–63; Historical Department, Office Journal, Jan. 22 and 29, 1872; "Minutes of a Surprise Meeting," *Deseret Evening News,* Jan. 24, 1872, [2].

5. George Q. Cannon to Brigham Young, Mar. 16, 1872; Mar. 25, 1872, Brigham Young Office Files, CHL; "St. Brigham's Counsel," *New York Herald,* Nov. 16, 1871, 5.

6. George Q. Cannon to Brigham Young, Apr. 15, 1872, Brigham Young Office Files, CHL.

7. "The Clinton-Engelbrecht Decision," *Deseret News,* May 8, 1872, [10]–[11]. Quotation edited for readability; "of opinion" in original changed to "of the opinion."

8. George Q. Cannon to Brigham Young, Apr. 15, 1872, Brigham Young Office Files, CHL; "By Telegraph," *Deseret Evening News,* Apr. 16, 1872, [1]; "Local and Other Matters," *Deseret Evening News,* Apr. 16, 1872, [3]; Historical Department, Office Journal, Apr. 25, 1872; "President Brigham Young," *Salt Lake Daily Herald,* Apr. 26, 1872, [2].

9. George Q. Cannon to Brigham Young, Apr. 15, 1872, Brigham Young Office Files, CHL.

10. Cluff, Autobiography, 132; H. H. Cluff, Letter to the Editor, Apr. 7, 1872, in "Correspondence," *Deseret News,* May 8, 1872, [13]; George Nebeker to Joseph F. Smith, Apr. 29, 1872, and H. H. Cluff, Letter to the Editor, Apr. 1872, in "From the Sandwich Islands," *Deseret News,* May 29, 1872, [9]; "Elder George Nebeker," *Deseret News,* Nov. 15, 1871, [7]; H. H. Cluff, "Sandwich Islands," *Deseret News,* Oct. 4, 1871, [9]; "Napela, Jonathan (Ionatana) Hawaii," Biographical Entry, Journal of

George Q. Cannon website, churchhistorianspress.org; see also Moffat, Woods, and Walker, *Gathering to La'ie,* 29–47. **Topic: Hawaii**

11. William King to George Nebeker, Dec. 4, 1871, in "Correspondence," *Deseret News,* Jan. 24, 1872, [3].

12. H. H. Cluff, Letter to the Editor, Apr. 1872, in "From the Sandwich Islands," *Deseret News,* May 29, 1872, [9].

13. Cluff, Autobiography, 134–35; George Nebeker, Letter to the Editor, Aug. 19, 1872, in "Correspondence," *Deseret News,* Sept. 25, 1872, [10]; H. H. Cluff, Letter to the Editor, Oct. 12, 1872, in "Correspondence," *Deseret News,* Nov. 20, 1872, [10]; Woods, "Jonathan Napela," 32–33; Zambŭcka, *High Chiefess,* 25; "Kaleohano, H. K.," Biographical Entry, Journal of George Q. Cannon website, churchhistorianspress.org. In contemporary sources, H. K. Kaleohano is usually referred to by his last name.

14. See "Mrs. Stenhouse's Book," *Salt Lake Daily Tribune and Utah Mining Gazette,* Feb. 26, 1872, [2]; "Mrs. Stenhouse on Polygamy," *Salt Lake Daily Tribune and Utah Mining Gazette,* Mar. 1, 1872, [2]; "Polygamy," *Chicago Tribune,* Mar. 17, 1872, [6]; "Reviews of New Books," *New York Herald,* Mar. 25, 1872, 10; "Mormonism," *Alexandria Gazette,* Mar. 28, 1872, [1]; "Giving Her Husband to a Second Wife," *New North-West,* Apr. 13, 1872, [4]; Walker, "Stenhouses and the Making of a Mormon Image," 59, 62; and Stenhouse, *Exposé of Polygamy,* 13, 85–88, 96.

15. "Woman's Exponent," *Woman's Exponent,* June 1, 1872, 1:[8]; "'Enslaved' Women of Utah," *Woman's Exponent,* July 1, 1872, 1:[20]; "Richards, Louisa Lula Greene," Biographical Entry, First Fifty Years of Relief Society website, churchhistorianspress.org.

16. Lula Greene Richards to Zina S. Whitney, Jan. 20, 1893, Louisa Lula Greene Richards, Papers, CHL; Richards, "How 'The Exponent' Was Started," 605–7; Smithfield Branch, Young Women's Mutual Improvement Association Minutes and Records, May 25, 1871, CHL; Campbell, *Man Cannot Speak for Her,* 4–5, 9–12; "Prospectus of Woman's Exponent, a Utah Ladies' Journal."

17. See "Woman's Exponent," *Woman's Exponent,* June 1, 1872, 1:[8]. **Topic: Church Periodicals**

18. "Woman's Voice," *Woman's Exponent,* July 15, 1872, 1:30.

19. Christensen, *Sagwitch,* 2, 23–26, 81. **Topic: American Indians**

20. Christensen, *Sagwitch,* 18–23, 26–40. **Topic: Sagwitch**

21. Christensen, *Sagwitch,* 41–58; 216–17, note 26; Martineau, Journal, Feb. 1, 1863, in Godfrey and Martineau-McCarty, *Uncommon Pioneer,* 132.

22. Peter Maughan to Brigham Young, Feb. 4, 1863, Brigham Young Office Files, CHL; Christensen, *Sagwitch,* 57–81; Madsen, *Shoshoni Frontier,* 194–95.

23. Christensen, *Sagwitch,* 30, 71, 81; Parry, Interview, 8, 17.

24. Hill, "Indian Vision," 12:11; Hill, "My First Day's Work," 10:309; Christensen, *Sagwitch,* 84–87; Parry, Interview, 14.

25. Hill, "George Washington Hill"; Hill, "My First Day's Work," 10:309; see also Christensen, *Sagwitch,* 59, 85, 88; and Parry, Interview, 8–10, 14.

26. Hill, "George Washington Hill"; see also Christensen, *Sagwitch,* 88–89.

27. Hill, "My First Day's Work," 10:309; Hill, "George Washington Hill"; George Washington Hill to Brigham Young, May 6, 1873, Brigham Young Office Files, CHL; Hill, "Brief Acct," 1.

28. George Washington Hill to Brigham Young, May 6, 1873, Brigham Young Office Files, CHL. Quotation edited for clarity; "nor never spent" in original changed to "nor ever spent," and word "I" added.

29. George Washington Hill to Dimick Huntington, May 7, 1873, Brigham Young Office Files, CHL.

30. B. Morris Young to Brigham Young, July 6, 1873, Brigham Young Office Files, CHL; Woods, "Jonathan Napela," 34–35; Woods, *Kalaupapa,* 18–22, 28–34, 37–40; Korn, *News from Molokai,* 7; 16, note 8; Kekuaokalani [Peter Kaeo] to Emma [Kaleleonalani], July 9, 1873, in Korn, *News from Molokai,* 18; Jonathan Napela to E. O. Hall, Apr. 29, 1873; May 1, 1873; July 24, 1873; Jonathan Napela to S. G.

Wilder, May 10, 1873; May 19, 1873, Board of Health Incoming Letters, Hawaii State Archives. **Topic: Jonathan Napela**

31. Kekuaokalani [Peter Kaeo] to Emma [Kaleleonalani], July 4, 1873; July 7, 1873; July 9, 1873; July 10, 1873, in Korn, *News from Molokai*, 11, 12–13, 17–18, 19–20; Korn, *News from Molokai*, 7. Quotation edited for readability; "was" in original changed to "is."

32. Kekuaokalani [Peter Kaeo] to Emma [Kaleleonalani], Aug. 31, 1873; Oct. 23, 1873, in Korn, *News from Molokai*, 80–81, 139; Korn, *News from Molokai*, 140, note 1; Woods, *Kalaupapa*, 37.

33. Jonathan Napela to E. O. Hall, Oct. 23, 1873, Board of Health Incoming Letters, Hawaii State Archives; Kekuaokalani [Peter Kaeo] to Emma [Kaleleonalani], Oct. 23, 1873, in Korn, *News from Molokai*, 139; Woods, *Kalaupapa*, 39.

34. *Congressional Record* [1874], volume 2, 7–8; Bitton, *George Q. Cannon*, 93–103, 117–25, 171–72, 184. **Topic: George Q. Cannon**

35. George Q. Cannon, Journal, Dec. 1, 1873.

36. George Q. Cannon to George Reynolds, Apr. 24, 1872, George Reynolds, Papers, Brigham Young University; *Congressional Record* [1874], volume 2, 3599–600; George Q. Cannon, Journal, Feb. 5 and 6, 1873; May 5, 1874; Bitton, *George Q. Cannon*, 187–88.

37. Fanny Stenhouse, *Tell It All* (Hartford, CT: A. D. Worthington, 1874); T. B. H. Stenhouse, *Rocky Mountain Saints* (New York: D. Appleton, 1873); George Q. Cannon, Journal, Feb. 21, 1873; "Home Again," *Salt Lake Daily Tribune*, May 8, 1873, [2]; "Anti-polygamy Lecture," *Salt Lake Daily Herald*, July 3, 1874, [3]; "Lecture by Mrs. Stenhouse," *Salt Lake Daily Herald*, Nov. 19, 1874, [3].

38. "Mrs. Young," *Boston Post*, May 2, 1874, [4]; "Ann Eliza's Life," *Daily Rocky Mountain News*, Dec. 10, 1873, [4]; "The Divorce Suit," *Salt Lake Daily Tribune*, Aug. 1, 1873, [2]; "The Ann Eliza Divorce Case," *Salt Lake Daily Tribune*, Aug. 23, 1873, [3]; Young, *Wife No. 19*, 553–58; see also "Mormonism," *National Republican*, Apr. 14, 1874, 8.

39. Kane, *Twelve Mormon Homes*; Grow, *Liberty to the Downtrodden*, 262–70; George Q. Cannon to Brigham Young, George A. Smith, and Daniel H. Wells, June 15, 1874, Brigham Young Office Files, CHL; George Q. Cannon, Journal, May 5–June 21, 1874, especially entry for June 19, 1874; An Act in relation to Courts and Judicial Officers in the Territory of Utah, June 23, 1874, in *Statutes at Large* [1875], 18:253–56. **Topic: Thomas L. and Elizabeth Kane**

40. "Got Home," *Salt Lake Daily Herald*, July 2, 1874, [3]; "Third District Court," *Salt Lake Daily Herald*, Oct. 22, 1874, [3]; Reynolds, Journal, Oct. 21–26, 1874; "Genuine Polygamy Indictment," *Deseret Evening News*, Oct. 26, 1874, [3]; Wells, "Living Martyr," 154; Whitney, *History of Utah*, 3:45–47; Van Orden, *Prisoner for Conscience' Sake*, 37; 65, note 11. **Topic: Antipolygamy Legislation**

CHAPTER 28: UNTIL THE COMING OF THE SON OF MAN

1. Historical Department, Office Journal, June 19, 1875.

2. Reynolds, Journal, Oct. 21–23, 1874; Van Orden, *Prisoner for Conscience' Sake*, 60–63, 68–74.

3. "Young vs. Young," *Salt Lake Daily Tribune*, Mar. 12, 1875, [4]; "The order granting alimony," President's Office Files, Legal Files, Brigham Young Office Files, CHL; Historical Department, Office Journal, Feb. 26, 1875; Mar. 11, 1875; and May 10, 1875; Arrington, *Brigham Young*, 334–35, 373; Firmage and Mangrum, *Zion in the Courts*, 249–51; Whitney, *History of Utah*, 2:603–7; see also Van Orden, *Prisoner for Conscience' Sake*, 67.

4. Moroni Ward, North Sanpete Stake, Relief Society Minutes, June 21, 1875, 97–98; Sanpete Stake, Minutes, June 23, 1875, [15]–[16]; Brackenridge, "Evolution of an Anti-Mormon Story," 82–85.

5. See Moses 7:18.

6. Arrington, Fox, and May, *Building the City of God,* 136–45; Arrington, *Great Basin Kingdom,* 141, 323–30, 389. **Topic: United Orders**

7. Sanpete Stake, Minutes, June 23, 1875, [13]–[14], [40]. Brigham Young quotation edited for readability; "United Order" in original changed to "The United Order."

8. Sanpete Stake, Minutes, June 25, 1875, [44]–[45], [49]–[52], [67]; June 26, 1875, [34]; George Q. Cannon, Journal, June 25, 1875.

9. Jones, *Forty Years among the Indians,* 220–21; Duke, "Meliton Gonzalez Trejo," 714–15.

10. See Jones, *Forty Years among the Indians,* 220; "Book of Mormon in Spanish," *Deseret News,* Apr. 16, 1884, [8]; and "Parley P. Pratt, October 31, 1852: Report of His Mission to Chile."

11. See "Meliton Gonzalez Trejo," Missionary Database, history.ChurchofJesusChrist.org /missionary.

12. *Trozos selectos del Libro de Mormon* (Salt Lake City: Impreso para Daniel W. Jones en la imprenta del Deseret News, 1875).

13. Jones, *Forty Years among the Indians,* 219–33; see also Geilman, "Taking the Gospel to Mexico: Meliton Gonzalez Trejo," note 12.

14. Daniel Webster Jones, "Report of the Mexican Mission," Oct. 5, 1876, 1; James Z. Stewart, Mission Report, Aug. 6, 1876, [1], Missionary Reports, CHL. **Topic: Mexico**

15. "Visit of President Grant," *Deseret News,* Oct. 6, 1875, [8]; "Visit of President Grant," *Deseret News,* Oct. 6, 1875, [12].

16. Simon, *Personal Memoirs of Julia Dent Grant,* 184–85; Tullidge, *History of Salt Lake City,* 620–23; "Visit of President Grant," *Deseret News,* Oct. 6, 1875, [12].

17. "Minute Book of the Deacon's Quorum Salt Lake City," Nov. 11, 1873, 23; May 12, 1874, 55; Dec. 14, 1875, 163; "Worthy Couple Married 66 Years," *Deseret News,* May 10, 1924, section 3, vii; Hartley, "Samuel D. Chambers," 47–50.

18. Hartley, "Samuel D. Chambers," 47–50; "Leggroan, Edward 'Ned,'" Biographical Entry, Century of Black Mormons website, exhibits.lib.utah.edu/s /century-of-black-mormons; 1870 U.S. Census, 1st Ward, Salt Lake City, Salt Lake County, Utah Territory, 553[A]; 1880 U.S. Census, 1st and 10th Wards, Salt Lake City, Salt Lake County, Utah Territory, 10C; "8th Ward Liberty Stake Record of Members Early–1905," [12], Record of Members Collection, CHL; "Worthy Couple Married 66 Years," *Deseret News,* May 10, 1924, section 3, vii.

19. "Minute Book of the Deacon's Quorum Salt Lake City," 1873–76; Salt Lake City Eighth Ward, Liberty Stake, Relief Society Minute Book B, 2; "Worthy Couple Married 66 Years," *Deseret News,* May 10, 1924, section 3, vii; "Minutes of Meetings Held in the 8th. Ward G. S. L. City," Teachers Meeting, Oct. 14, 1874; Reiter, "Black Saviors on Mount Zion," 100–104, 120–21; "Leggroan, Edward 'Ned,'" Biographical Entry, Century of Black Mormons website, exhibits.lib.utah.edu/s /century-of-black-mormons. **Topic: Priesthood and Temple Restriction**

20. "Minute Book of the Deacon's Quorum Salt Lake City," Jan. 12, 1876, 167.

21. "Death and Destruction," *Salt Lake Daily Herald,* Apr. 6, 1876, [3]; "Terrible Disaster," *Deseret Evening News,* Apr. 6, 1876, [3]; "The Explosion," *Salt Lake Daily Herald,* Apr. 7, 1876, [3]; Richards, *Called to Teach,* 358–59; Maeser, *Karl G. Maeser,* 76.

22. Maeser, *Karl G. Maeser,* 76–77; Richards, *Called to Teach,* 358–59.

23. Maeser, *Karl G. Maeser,* 77; see also Richards, *Called to Teach,* 251–86, 328–29, 348.

24. Moroni Ward, North Sanpete Stake, Relief Society Minutes, June 21, 1875, 97–98.

25. Richards, *Called to Teach,* 223, note 38; 330–32; 360–61; Jessee, *Letters of Brigham Young to His Sons,* 161, 199, 217, 264; Brackenridge, "Evolution of an Anti-Mormon Story," 86. **Topic: Church Academies**

26. Maeser, *Karl G. Maeser,* 77, 79; Richards, *Called to Teach,* 363–65; Maeser, *School and Fireside,* 189; see also "Going to Provo," *Deseret News,* Apr. 12, 1876, [13].

27. Anderson, "Past of Mutual Improvement," 2–3. **Topics: Heber J. Grant; Young Men Organizations**

28. Heber J. Grant, "When I was a small boy," box 176, folder 13, item 2, 12–13, in Heber J. Grant Collection, CHL; Shumway, "Dancing the Buckles off Their Shoes in Pioneer Utah," 40–41.

29. Heber J. Grant, "When I was a small boy," box 176, folder 13, item 2, 12–16, in Heber J. Grant Collection, CHL; Grant and Taylor, "When Brigham Young Watched a Waltz," 654, 678.

30. Historical Department, Office Journal, Nov. 1, 1876; see also Woodruff, Journal, Jan. 1, 1877.

31. "Discourse by President Brigham Young," *Deseret News,* Sept. 24, 1873, 532; see also Mackley, *Wilford Woodruff's Witness,* 170.

32. Woodruff, Journal, Nov. 9–10, 1876; Booth, St. George Temple, CHL.

33. Charles L. Walker, Journal, Jan. 1, 1877.

34. Woodruff, Journal, Jan. 1, 1877; *Interviews with Living Pioneers,* 40–41; see also "Dedication Services at the Temple at St. George," *Deseret News,* Jan. 17, 1877, [8].

35. Alma Bailey Dunford and Susa Amelia Young, Dec. 1, 1872, 379, Sealings of Couples, Living and By Proxy, 1851–89, volume H, microfilm 183,398, U.S. and Canada Record Collection, Family History Library; Alma Dunford to Isaac Dunford and Leah Bailey Dunford, Dec. 21, 1872, Isaac Dunford Family Correspondence, CHL; Charles L. Walker, Journal, Jan. 9, 1877; Woodruff, Journal, Jan. 9 and 11, 1877; Feb. 1, 1877; Bennett, "Which Is the Wisest Course?," 5–43.

36. Woodruff, Journal, Jan. 14, 1877; Mackley, *Wilford Woodruff's Witness,* 168; Bennett, "Line upon Line," 61–62; see also Bennett, *Temples Rising,* 78–79, 210–12.

37. Nuttall, Diary, Feb. 7, 1877.

38. Yorgason, Schmutz, and Alder, *All That Was Promised,* 282–84; Woodruff, "History of the St George Temple," [2]. Quotation edited for clarity; "ensample" in original changed to "example." **Topic: Temple Endowment**

CHAPTER 29: TO DIE IN THE HARNESS

1. Woodruff, Journal, Apr. 16, 1877; "Discourse by Prest. Brigham Young," *Deseret News,* May 23, 1877, [7].

2. "Brigham Young," *New York Herald,* May 6, 1877, 8; see also "Interview with Brigham Young," *Deseret Evening News,* May 12, 1877, [2].

3. Turley, Johnson, and Carruth, *Mountain Meadows Massacre,* 2:601–4; Briggs, "Mountain Meadows Massacre," 314–17.

4. Lee, Journal, July 20, 1871, and Sept. 24, 1875, in Cleland and Brooks, *Mormon Chronicle,* 2:164–65, 369; Turley, Johnson, and Carruth, *Mountain Meadows Massacre,* 1:9, 407–11, 465–67, 525–40; "John D. Lee," *Salt Lake Daily Tribune,* Feb. 21, 1877, [3].

5. Turley, Johnson, and Carruth, *Mountain Meadows Massacre,* 2:853–57, 885; Brigham Young to Isaac Haight, Sept. 10, 1857, Letterbook, volume 3, 827–28, Brigham Young Office Files, CHL; *Saints,* volume 2, chapter 18.

6. Reeves, "Divert the Minds of the People," 291–315; Brigham Young to W. E. Pack, Aug. 6, 1877, Letterbook, volume 15, 118–19, Brigham Young Office Files, CHL; "Brigham Young," *New York Herald,* May 6, 1877, 8. **Topic: Mountain Meadows Massacre**

7. "Brigham Young," *New York Herald,* May 6, 1877, 8.

8. Salt Lake Stake, General Minutes, volume 2, Aug. 11, 1877, 45–46; Woodruff, Journal, Apr. 25, 1877. **Topic: Adjustments to Priesthood Organization**

9. Woodruff, Journal, Apr. 10, 1875; Historical Department, Journal History of the Church, Apr. 10, 1875; Mecham, "Changes in Seniority to the Quorum of the Twelve," 29–44; Bishop, "Precept upon Precept," 255, 257. **Topic: Succession of Church Leadership**

10. Hartley, "Priesthood Reorganization of 1877," 6–8, 11, 32.

11. Circular of the First Presidency, 1–4; Hartley, "Priesthood Reorganization of 1877," 3–36; Salt Lake Stake, General Minutes, volume 2, Aug. 11, 1877, 45–46; Brigham Young to William C. Staines, May 11, 1877, Letterbook, volume 14, 810, Brigham Young Office Files, CHL; Young Ladies' Department of the Ladies' Cooperative Retrenchment Association, Resolutions, May 27, 1870, in Derr and others, *First Fifty Years of Relief Society,* 354–55; Hartley, "From Men to Boys," 80–136.

12. Brigham Young to Wilford Woodruff, June 12, 1877, Letterbook, volume 14, 916, Brigham Young Office Files, CHL; Brigham Young Jr., Journal, June 20, 1877.

13. Francis Marion Lyman, Journal, June 20, 1877.

14. Lyman, *Francis Marion Lyman,* 51–64, 68–69, 84–85; Francis Marion Lyman, Journal, Jan. 12, 1877.

15. Francis Marion Lyman, Journal, Jan. 2, 20, and 26, 1877; Feb. 6, 1877; Lyman, *Francis Marion Lyman,* 81–82.

16. Francis Marion Lyman, Journal, Mar. 31, 1877; Apr. 8, 1877; June 20, 1877.

17. Francis Marion Lyman, Journal, June 24, 1877; Tooele Utah Stake, General Minutes, June 24, 1877, 4–5, 7.

18. Hartley, *My Fellow Servants,* 239.

19. Francis Marion Lyman, Journal, June 24 and 26, 1877; July 21, 30, and 31, 1877; Aug. 1 and 2, 1877.

20. Tooele Utah Stake, General Minutes, Dec. 18, 1877, and Mar. 2, 1878.

21. Weber Stake Relief Society, Minutes, July 19, 1877, in Derr and others, *First Fifty Years of Relief Society,* 405–7; "Richards, Jane Snyder," Biographical Entry, First Fifty Years of Relief Society website, churchhistorianspress.org.

22. Salt Lake Stake, Relief Society Record Book, June 22, 1878, 9; Nauvoo Relief Society Minute Book, Mar. 9, 1844, in Derr and others, *First Fifty Years of Relief Society,* 129.

23. Jane Snyder Richards, Autobiographical Sketch, [5]–[8]; Weber Stake Relief Society, Minutes, Oct. 30, 1877, in Derr and others, *First Fifty Years of Relief Society,* 416; Richards, History of the Relief Society in Weber County, 3. **Topic: Healing**

24. Weber Stake Relief Society, Minutes, July 19, 1877, in Derr and others, *First Fifty Years of Relief Society,* 405–9. **Topic: Relief Society**

25. Salt Lake Stake, Relief Society Record Book, June 22, 1878, 9; Weber Stake Relief Society, Minutes, July 19, 1877; John Taylor, Discourse, Oct. 21, 1877 (Excerpt); Weber Stake Relief Society, Minutes, Oct. 30, 1877, in Derr and others, *First Fifty Years of Relief Society,* 405–9, 412, 417; "Home Affairs," *Woman's Exponent,* Aug. 1, 1877, 6:37; "R. S. Reports," *Woman's Exponent,* Jan. 1, 1878, 6:114; Middleton, Journal, May 28, 1877; "Our Country Contemporaries," *Deseret News,* June 6, 1877, 1.

26. Weber Stake, Relief Society Minutes and Records, volume 5, Aug. 3 and 9, 1877, 260–62.

27. Susa Young to Zina Young Williams, May 18, 1878, 1–[3], Early Papers and Memorabilia, Susa Young Gates, Papers, CHL; Brigham Young, Discourse, Aug. 17, 1867, Church History Department Pitman Shorthand Transcriptions, CHL; Peterson and Walker, "Brigham Young's Word of Wisdom Legacy," 29–64; *Saints,* volume 1, chapter 15. **Topic: Word of Wisdom (D&C 89)**

28. Gates, "As the families of my Aunts increased in size," box 1, folder 5, item [14], 6; *Isaac and Leah Bailey Dunford Family Story,* 10–11, 295; Brigham Young to Susy Dunford [Susa Young], Aug. 13, 1877, Susa Young Gates, Papers, CHL.

29. Gates, "As the families of my Aunts increased in size," box 1, folder 5, item [14], 6; Edward W. Tullidge, *The Women of Mormondom* (New York: Tullidge and Crandall, 1877); see also Gates, *History of the Young Ladies' Mutual Improvement Association,* 124.

30. Gates, "As the families of my Aunts increased in size," box 1, folder 5, item [14], 6, 9–10. Susie Young Dunford quotation edited for readability; "I wished I knew" in original changed to "I wish I knew."

31. Gates, "As the families of my Aunts increased in size," box 1, folder 5, item [14], 9–10; see also "Young, Brigham," Biographical Entry, Joseph Smith Papers website, josephsmithpapers.org. Susie Young Dunford quotation edited for readability; original

source has "I am glad I told him then how proud and grateful I was that I had been permitted to come upon the earth as his daughter." **Topic: Susa Young Gates**

32. Gates and Widtsoe, *Life Story of Brigham Young,* 360–62; Brigham Young Jr., Journal, Aug. 18–19 and 23–24, 1877; Presiding Bishopric, Bishops Meeting Minutes, Aug. 23, 1877; Richard W. Young, Diary, Aug. 29, 1877; Obituary for Brigham Young, *Deseret Evening News,* Aug. 30, 1877, [2]; see also Historical Department, Office Journal, Aug. 18–19 and 24–25, 1877; and George Q. Cannon, Journal, Aug. 23–29, 1877. Brigham's brother Joseph was one of many family members in the room at the time of Brigham's death. Brigham's family members believed Brigham was calling out to the prophet Joseph Smith rather than to his brother Joseph. (Arrington, *Brigham Young,* 399; Gates and Widtsoe, *Life Story of Brigham Young,* 361–62.) **Topic: Brigham Young**

CHAPTER 30: A STEADY, ONWARD MOVEMENT

1. "Lying in State—Preparations for the Funeral," *Deseret Evening News,* Sept. 1, 1877, [2]; Account of the Funeral Proceedings, [1]–[2]; Woodruff, Journal, Aug. 29–Sept. 1, 1877; "Monday's Celebration," *Deseret News,* Jan. 12, 1870, [7]; Hannah Tapfield King, "Mormonism," *Woman's Exponent,* Nov. 15, 1877, 91; Isaiah 35:1; Howard B. Grose, "Across Continent Sketches," *Watchman,* Aug. 12, 1897, 78:14; Arrington, Fox, and May, *Building the City of God,* 54–57; Arrington, *Brigham Young,* 402–3; Plewe, *Mapping Mormonism,* 88–89. **Topic: Brigham Young**
2. "Funeral of President Brigham Young," *Deseret Evening News,* Sept. 3, 1877, [2]; Walker, "Salt Lake Tabernacle," 217; Eliza R. Snow, "Funeral of President Brigham Young," in Derr and Davidson, *Eliza R. Snow,* 900; Gates, "As the families of my Aunts increased in size," box 1, folder 5, item [14], 8.
3. **Topic: John Taylor**
4. "Funeral of President Brigham Young," *Deseret Evening News,* Sept. 3, 1877, [2].
5. "Death of Brigham Young," *New-York Times,* Aug. 30, 1877, 1–2; "Brigham Young as a Ruler," *Salt Lake Daily Tribune,* Aug. 30, 1877, [2].
6. Reynolds, Journal, Dec. 21, 1875, and [Oct. 1876]; Van Orden, *Prisoner for Conscience' Sake,* 74–79, 84–90.
7. "Funeral of President Brigham Young," *Deseret Evening News,* Sept. 3, 1877, [2].
8. Susa Young to Zina Young Williams, May 18, 1878, [1]–[4], Early Papers and Memorabilia, Susa Young Gates, Papers, CHL. **Topic: Susa Young Gates**
9. Susa Young to Zina Young Williams, May 18, 1878, [2], [4]–[5], Early Papers and Memorabilia, Susa Young Gates, Papers, CHL; Gates, "As the families of my Aunts increased in size," box 1, folder 5, item [14], 6.
10. Susa Young to Zina Young Williams, May 18, 1878, [11], Early Papers and Memorabilia, Susa Young Gates, Papers, CHL; Embry, *Mormon Polygamous Families,* 253; "Plural Marriage and Families in Early Utah," Gospel Topics, topics .ChurchofJesusChrist.org. **Topic: Plural Marriage in Utah**
11. Madsen, "Utah Law and the Case of Plural Wives," 431–34; Campbell and Campbell, "Divorce among Mormon Polygamists," 4–23; Arrington, *Brigham Young,* 318–20.
12. Grossberg, *Governing the Hearth,* 238, 240, 250–53; Susan Y. Dunford v. Alma B. Dunford, Divorce Decree, May 6, 1878, Washington Co., Probate Court Civil and Criminal Record Books, series 3168, 68–69, Utah Division of Archives and Records Service, Utah State Archives, Salt Lake City; Susa Young to Zina Young Williams, May 18, 1878, [5]–[8], [18]–[19], Early Papers and Memorabilia, Susa Young Gates, Papers, CHL; *Isaac and Leah Bailey Dunford Family Story,* 10–11, 17, 65–66.
13. Susa Young to Zina Young Williams, May 18, 1878, [19]–[20], [25]–[26], Early Papers and Memorabilia, Susa Young Gates, Papers, CHL.
14. "The Old B. Y. Academy," 337. **Topic: Church Academies**

15. Henry P. Richards, Diary, Jan. 26, 1878; Woods, "Jonathan Napela," 34–36. **Topic: Jonathan Napela**

16. Henry P. Richards, Diary, Jan. 19–20 and 26, 1878; Henry P. Richards, "A Visit to the Lepers," *Deseret News,* Apr. 3, 1878, [10]; "Kalawaia, K.," and "Nihipali, Nehemia Kahuelaau," Andrew Jenson Collection, CHL; "Richards, Henry Phinehas," in Jenson, *Latter-day Saint Biographical Encyclopedia,* 1:813.

17. Henry P. Richards, Diary, Jan. 26–27, 1878; Korn, *News from Molokai,* 192. For information on Father Damien, see Woods, *Kalaupapa,* 28–34; Daws, *Holy Man,* 97–99; and Stewart, *Leper Priest of Moloka'i,* 157–58.

18. Henry P. Richards, Diary, Jan. 27–28, 1878; Woods, *Kalaupapa,* 19–25.

19. "Home Affairs," *Woman's Exponent,* July 15, 1878, 7:29; Wells, Diary, volume 4, July 10, 1878; Madsen, *Emmeline B. Wells,* 164, 167, 176; Rogers, *Life Sketches,* 181.

20. Aurelia Spencer Rogers, Reminiscences of Aug. 1878, as Published in "History of Primary Work," 1898, in Derr and others, *First Fifty Years of Relief Society,* 431–34; Wells, Diary, volume 4, July 10, 1878; Snow, "Sketch of My Life," 38; Farmington Ward, Primary Association Minutes and Records, volume 1, Aug. 11, 1878; Rogers, *Life Sketches,* 35, 41, 47–48. **Topic: Primary**

21. Farmington Ward, Primary Association Minutes and Records, volume 1, Aug. 11, 1878.

22. Farmington Ward, Primary Association Minutes and Records, volume 1, Aug. 11 and 25, 1878; Sept. 7 and 14, 1878; Aurelia Spencer Rogers, Reminiscences of Aug. 1878, as Published in "History of Primary Work," 1898, in Derr and others, *First Fifty Years of Relief Society,* 430.

23. Orson Pratt and Joseph F. Smith to John Taylor and the Council of the Twelve, Sept. 17, 1878, Joseph F. Smith, Papers, CHL; Joseph F. Smith, Journal, Sept. 2 and 7, 1878; Neilson and Schaefer, "Excavating Early Mormon History," 359–61; Orson Pratt to Marian Pratt, Sept. 18, 1878, CHL; *Saints,* volume 1, chapter 19; Whitmer, *Address to All Believers in Christ;* "Whitmer, John," Biographical Entry, Joseph Smith Papers website, josephsmithpapers.org.

24. Orson Pratt and Joseph F. Smith to John Taylor and the Council of the Twelve, Sept. 17, 1878, Joseph F. Smith, Papers, CHL; Joseph F. Smith, Journal, Sept. 7, 1878; see also Orson Pratt to Marian Pratt, Sept. 18, 1878, CHL; and *Saints,* volume 1, chapter 7.

25. Orson Pratt and Joseph F. Smith to John Taylor and the Council of the Twelve, Sept. 17, 1878, Joseph F. Smith, Papers, CHL; Joseph F. Smith, Journal, Sept. 8, 1878. **Topic: Witnesses of the Book of Mormon**

26. Carl Dorius, Diary, Nov. 5, 1878. It appears Ane Sophie often went by her maiden name, Christoffersen, in Utah.

27. Dorius, "Sketch of the Life," 66–67; Carl Dorius, Diary, 1874 and Nov. 5, 1878.

28. Dorius, *Dorius Heritage,* 6–7, 155–56; Stevens, Autobiography, 1, 8–10.

29. Dorius, "Sketch of the Life," 3; Dorius, *Dorius Heritage,* 155–56.

30. Carl Dorius, Diary, Nov. 5, 1878; St. George Temple, Baptisms for the Dead, Book H, 411–12, microfilm 170,847; St. George Temple, Endowments for the Dead, Book D, 13–16, microfilm 170,543, U.S. and Canada Record Collection, Family History Library; St. George Temple, Sealings for the Dead, Couples, Book B, 378–81, microfilm 170,596; St. George Temple, Sealings of Children to Parents, Book A, 107, microfilm 170,583, U.S. and Canada Record Collection, Family History Library. **Topic: Denmark**

31. Wells, Diary, volume 5, Jan. 1, 1879; Madsen, *Emmeline B. Wells,* 183. **Topic: Women's Suffrage**

32. "Part 3: 1867–1879," in Derr and others, *First Fifty Years of Relief Society,* 242–46; Stanton, *Eighty Years and More,* 283–87.

33. Madsen, *Advocate for Women,* 160–68.

34. Henderson, *Crickets and Grasshoppers in Utah,* 20; "Grain Meeting," *Woman's Exponent,* Dec. 1, 1877, 6:102; Wells, "The Mission of Saving Grain," 47; see also Committees on the Grain Movement, Minutes, Nov. 17, 1876, in Derr and others, *First Fifty Years of Relief Society,* 399–401.

35. Emmeline B. Wells [Blanche Beechwood, pseud.], "Why, Ah! Why," *Woman's Exponent,* Sept. 30, 1874, 3:67; Madsen, *Advocate for Women,* 50–55.
36. Wells, Diary, volume 4, Jan. 4, 1878. **Topic: Emmeline B. Wells**
37. Wells, Diary, volume 5, Jan. 9, 1879; "Washington," *Salt Lake Daily Tribune,* Jan. 7, 1879, [1]; Reynolds v. United States, 98 U.S. 145 (1879); George Q. Cannon, Journal, Jan. 11, 1879. **Topic: Antipolygamy Legislation**
38. "The Utah Ladies in Washington," *Deseret Evening News,* Jan. 18, 1879, [2].
39. "Miss Grundy," "Mormon Ladies Calling at the White House," *Woman's Exponent,* Mar. 15, 1879, 7:212; Wells, Diary, volume 5, Jan. 13, 1879; George Q. Cannon, Journal, Jan. 13, 1879. Quotation edited for readability; second instance of word "made" added.
40. Wells, Diary, volume 5, Jan. 14–30, 1879; *Memorial of Emeline B. Wells and Zina Young Williams.*
41. Madsen, *Advocate for Women,* 163–68; George Q. Cannon, Journal, Jan. 18, 1879.
42. Van Orden, *Prisoner for Conscience' Sake,* 90; Wells, Diary, volume 5, Jan. 14 and 18, 1879; [Emmeline B. Wells], "Visit to Washington," *Woman's Exponent,* Feb. 15, 1879, 7:194; Madsen, *Advocate for Women,* 167.

Chapter 31: The Shattered Threads of Life

1. "The Supreme Court Decision," *Deseret Evening News,* Jan. 25, 1879, [1]; Historical Department, Office Journal, Jan. 13, 1879; Doctrine and Covenants 58:21; see also *Supreme Court Decision,* 3, 6, 11–12. Ovando Hollister quotation edited for clarity; question mark added. **Topic: Antipolygamy Legislation**
2. Wilkinson, *Brigham Young University,* 1:46, 99, 111, 125; "Dr. Karl G. Maeser," 482–83; Susa Young to Jacob Gates, Feb. 3, 1879, Susa Young Gates, Papers, CHL; Wilkinson, *Brigham Young University,* 1:191, 194.
3. "The Old B. Y. Academy," 339–40; "Dr. Karl G. Maeser," 483; "Talmage, James Edward," in Jenson, *Latter-day Saint Biographical Encyclopedia,* 3:788.
4. Nixon and Smoot, *Abraham Owen Smoot,* 22–23, 227; Wilkinson, *Brigham Young University,* 1:66; "The Old B. Y. Academy," 341; Merrill, *Reed Smoot,* 4–5.
5. "The Old B. Y. Academy," 339; "Dr. Karl G. Maeser," 484; Harrington, *Early Procedure, Scenes and Personnel of the Brigham Young University,* 1–2; Buchanan, "Brigham Young and the Schools of Utah," 435–59; Wilkinson, *Brigham Young University,* 1:65–66, 523–27. **Topic: Church Academies**
6. "The Old B. Y. Academy," 338–39; Gates, "I saw just one step cut," box 1, folder 5, item [17], [2]–[3]; Maeser, *Karl G. Maeser,* 48; Susa Young to Jacob Gates, Feb. 3, 1879, Susa Young Gates, Papers, CHL; see, for example, Karl G. Maeser Religious Lecture Minutes, Dec. 2 and 5, 1878; Jan. 6, 9, 13, 16, 20, 21, and 28, 1879. First Karl Maeser quotation edited for clarity; "Miss Susa" in original changed to "Miss Susie."
7. Susa Young to Jacob Gates, Feb. 3, 1879; Jacob Gates to Susa Young, Mar. 18, 1879, Susa Young Gates, Papers, CHL; "Home Affairs," *Woman's Exponent,* July 15, 1879, 8:28; Zina D. Young, "Correspondence," *Woman's Exponent,* Aug. 30, 1879, 8:53; see also Susa Young Gates to Zina Huntington Young, May 5, 1888, Young Woman's Journal Files, Susa Young Gates, Papers, CHL. For additional correspondence between Susa Young and Jacob Gates during this period, see Family Correspondence, Susa Young Gates, Papers, CHL. **Topic: Susa Young Gates**
8. Reynolds, Journal, June 16, 1879; George Reynolds to "My dear Family," June 22, 1879, Correspondence and Clippings, George Reynolds, Journals, CHL; George Reynolds to "Elder J. Nicholson," July 19, 1879, in *Latter-day Saints' Millennial Star,* Aug. 18, 1879, 41:518; see also Van Orden, *Prisoner for Conscience' Sake,* 96–97; and Reynolds, Journal, Dec. 17, 1879, and Feb. 9, 1880.

9. George Reynolds to "Elder J. Nicholson," July 19, 1879, in *Latter-day Saints' Millennial Star,* Aug. 18, 1879, 41:518–19; George Q. Cannon, Journal, June 5, 13, 16, 20, 22, 23, and 28, 1879; see also Van Orden, *Prisoner for Conscience' Sake,* 93, 98.

10. Reynolds, Journal, [July] 1879; George Reynolds to "Elder J. Nicholson," July 19, 1879, in *Latter-day Saints' Millennial Star,* Aug. 18, 1879, 41:518–19; George Reynolds to "My dear Family," June 22, 1879, Correspondence and Clippings, George Reynolds, Journals, CHL.

11. Clawson, Autobiography, [32], [38]–[39], [48], [50]; Driggs, "There Is No Law in Georgia for Mormons," 750; Hoopes and Hoopes, *Making of a Mormon Apostle,* 3, 15–16.

12. Hoopes and Hoopes, *Making of a Mormon Apostle,* 15, 18–20, 22, 24; Clawson, Autobiography, [50], [57]; "Last Letter from Elder Joseph Standing," *Deseret News,* Aug. 13, 1879, [11]; Driggs, "Joseph Standing Murder Case of 1879," 746–53, 762–63; Nicholson, *Martyrdom of Joseph Standing,* 15–16, 38–39.

13. Clawson, Autobiography, [53]–[60]; Nicholson, *Martyrdom of Joseph Standing,* 17–21, 26–31; "The Murder of Joseph Standing," *Deseret Evening News,* Aug. 1, 1879, [3]; "The Assassination," *Salt Lake Daily Herald,* Aug. 1, 1879, [3]; Driggs, "Joseph Standing Murder Case of 1879," 759, 762–65; "That Mormon Murder in Whitfield," *Georgia Weekly Telegraph,* July 29, 1879, [6]; see also Mason, *Mormon Menace,* 5–8, 24, 47–48, 61–62. Quotation edited for clarity; question mark added at end of "Isn't this terrible that he should have shot himself."

14. "The Funeral Services of Elder Joseph Standing," *Deseret News,* Aug. 6, 1879, [13].

15. Clawson, Autobiography, [61]–[70]; Nicholson, *Martyrdom of Joseph Standing,* 53; "The Murder of Joseph Standing," *Deseret Evening News,* Aug. 1, 1879, [3].

16. "The Funeral Services of Elder Joseph Standing," *Deseret News,* Aug. 6, 1879, [13]; "Remarks by Prest. John Taylor," *Deseret News,* Aug. 13, 1879, [11].

17. Arrington, *History of Idaho,* 1:165–80; Peterson, *Take Up Your Mission,* 38–42; Arrington, *Brigham Young,* 173–74, 381–84, 402; Allen and Leonard, *Story of the Latter-day Saints,* 369–71, 392–99; "Latter-day Saint Settlements in San Luis Valley," 2; Andrew Jenson, "San Luis Stake," [1]–[2], in San Luis Colorado Stake, Manuscript History and Historical Reports, CHL; Miller, *Hole-in-the-Rock,* 4–9; McPherson, *A History of San Juan County,* 97. **Topic: Pioneer Settlements**

18. "Remarks by Prest. John Taylor," *Deseret News,* Aug. 13, 1879, [11].

19. Zina D. Young, "Correspondence," *Woman's Exponent,* Aug. 30, 1879, 8:53. **Topic: Hawaii**

20. Hawaii Honolulu Mission, Manuscript History and Historical Reports, volume 4, Apr. 6, 1879; "Population of Hawaii by Islands and Districts," *Census Bulletin,* Nov. 16, 1900, no. 13, 2.

21. Zina D. Young, "Correspondence," *Woman's Exponent,* Aug. 30, 1879, 8:53; Zina D. H. Young, Diary, July 19, 1879; Spurrier, *Sandwich Islands Saints,* 163–68; Woods, "Jonathan Napela," 34–36; see also "Home Affairs," *Woman's Exponent,* Oct. 1, 1879, 8:68–69.

22. Zina D. Young, "Correspondence," *Woman's Exponent,* Aug. 30, 1879, 8:53; Zina D. H. Young, Diary, July 25, 1879; see also entries for Aug. 1879.

23. Zina D. Young, "My Last Week at Laie," *Woman's Exponent,* Nov. 1, 1879, 8:85; "O My Father," *Hymns,* no. 292; Eliza R. Snow, "My Father in Heaven," Oct. 1845, in Derr and others, *First Fifty Years of Relief Society,* 173–75; *Saints,* volume 1, chapter 34.

24. Zina D. H. Young, Diary, Aug. 27, 1879; Susa Young to Jacob Gates, Aug. 13, 1879, Susa Young Gates, Papers, CHL.

25. Zina D. Young, "My Last Week at Laie," *Woman's Exponent,* Nov. 1, 1879, 8:85; Zina D. H. Young, Diary, Aug. 30–Sept. 1, 1879; Susa Young to Jacob Gates, no date, "Thursday Morning, Stateroom 8 o'clock," Susa Young Gates, Papers, CHL.

26. Tullis, *Mormons in Mexico,* 33–36; Smith and Tamez, "Plotino C. Rhodakanaty," 58–59; Stewart, Diary, Nov. 1–15, 1879. **Topics: Mexico; Growth of Missionary Work**

27. Stewart, Diary, Nov. 14–16, 1879; Plotino Rhodakanaty to John Taylor and the Quorum of the Twelve Apostles, Dec. 15, 1878, First Presidency (John Taylor)

Correspondence, CHL; Tullis, *Mormons in Mexico,* 35; Smith and Tamez, "Plotino C. Rhodakanaty," 55, 58–60.

28. *La voz del desierto,* Mexico City, 1879, copy at Brigham Young University; Smith and Tamez, "Plotino C. Rhodakanaty," 61–62.

29. Thatcher, Journal, Nov. 20, 1879.

30. Thatcher, Journal, Nov. 20–30, 1879; Dec. 2 and 31, 1879; Jan. 8, 1880; Tullis, *Mormons in Mexico,* 36; Moses Thatcher to John Taylor, Jan. 13, 1880, First Presidency (John Taylor) Correspondence, CHL. **Topic: Mexico**

CHAPTER 32: STAND UP AND TAKE THE PELTING

1. George Q. Cannon, Journal, Nov. 25, 1879; George Q. Cannon to John Taylor, Dec. 4, 1879, First Presidency (John Taylor) Correspondence, CHL; Bitton, *George Q. Cannon,* 235. **Topic: George Q. Cannon**

2. George Q. Cannon, Journal, Jan. 27 and Mar. 19, 1880; "The Mormon Problem," *Deseret Evening News,* Jan. 30, 1880, [2].

3. *Compilation of the Messages and Papers of the Presidents,* 10:4511–12.

4. George Q. Cannon, Journal, Dec. 10 and 12, 1879; *Journal of the House of Representatives,* Dec. 10, 1879, 76; George Q. Cannon to John Taylor, Jan. 13, 1880, First Presidency (John Taylor) Correspondence, CHL; see also George Q. Cannon, Journal, June 16, 1880. Final sentence of quotation edited for clarity; "draw of" in original changed to "draw off." **Topic: Antipolygamy Legislation**

5. Taylor, Mission Papers, volume 2, July 10, 1903; Mexican Mission, Manuscript History and Historical Reports, Feb. and Apr. 1880, 8–9; July 7, 1903; "List of Baptisms in Mexico," in Thatcher, Journal, volume 6.

6. Taylor, Mission Papers, volume 2, July 10, 1903; Cummings, Mission Journal, Oct. 24, 1886; Melitón Trejo to John Taylor, July 7, 1880, First Presidency (John Taylor) Correspondence, CHL; Christensen, "Solitary Saint in Mexico," 463–64. **Topic: Mexico**

7. Christensen, "Solitary Saint in Mexico," 463; Melitón Trejo to John Taylor, July 7, 1880, First Presidency (John Taylor) Correspondence, CHL; Decideria Quintanar, 1893, no. 173, in Registros civiles del municipio de Nopala, 1876–1958, México, Hidalgo, Registro Civil, 1861–1967, microfilm 674,770, International Film Collection, FHL.

8. Taylor, Mission Papers, volume 2, July 10, 1903; Christensen, "Solitary Saint in Mexico," 463.

9. Taylor, Mission Papers, volume 2, July 10, 1903; Stewart, Diary, Feb. 9 and 17, 1880; Christensen, "Solitary Saint in Mexico," 463–66; Mexican Mission, Manuscript History and Historical Reports, July 7, 1903; see also Parley P. Pratt, *A Voice of Warning and Instruction to All People* . . . (New York: W. Sandford, 1837).

10. Stewart, Diary, Apr. 17 and 26, 1880; Christensen, "Solitary Saint in Mexico," 467–68; Mexican Mission, Manuscript History and Historical Reports, July 7, 1903; "List of Baptisms in Mexico," in Thatcher, Journal, volume 6; Melitón Trejo to John Taylor, July 7, 1880, First Presidency (John Taylor) Correspondence, CHL.

11. Udall, Autobiography and Diaries, volume 1, 1, 3–5; Louisa Barnes Pratt, Journal and Autobiography, 370–75, 390, 429, 436, 535; "Pratt, Addison," Biographical Entry, Joseph Smith Papers website, josephsmithpapers.org. **Topic: Ida Hunt Udall**

12. Udall, Autobiography and Diaries, volume 1, 4–5, 10, 17–20; Louisa Barnes Pratt, Journal and Autobiography, 537–38, 540, 542, 544–45; Crosby, Journal, Oct. 3, 1879; Ellsworth, *Mormon Odyssey,* 36–39.

13. Jesse N. Smith, Autobiography and Journal, Apr. 6, 1880; Eastern Arizona Stake, Manuscript History and Historical Reports, Sept. 28, 1878; Ellsworth, *Mormon Odyssey,* 39–41.

14. "Plural Marriage in The Church of Jesus Christ of Latter-day Saints"; "Plural Marriage and Families in Early Utah," Gospel Topics, topics.ChurchofJesusChrist.org; Daynes, *More Wives Than One,* 101–2, 173–74.

15. Woodruff, Journal, Feb. 12, 1870; see also George Q. Cannon, in *Journal of Discourses,* Oct. 8, 1882, 23:278.

16. Ellsworth, *Mormon Odyssey,* 40–41; Udall, Autobiography and Diaries, volume 1, 20–21.

17. Leviticus 25:10; *Year of Jubilee,* 6; "Circular from the Twelve Apostles," *Deseret Evening News,* Apr. 17, 1880, [2]; Quorum of the Twelve Apostles, Circular Letter, Apr. 16, 1880 (Excerpt), in Derr and others, *First Fifty Years of Relief Society,* 451–53; see also Roberts, *Life of John Taylor,* 332–33. **Topic: John Taylor**

18. Nauvoo Relief Society Minute Book, Mar. 17, 1842; Salt Lake Stake Relief Society, Report, June 18 and 19, 1880, in Derr and others, *First Fifty Years of Relief Society,* 32, 36, 467–72; *Saints,* volume 1, chapter 37; see also Biographical Entries on First Fifty Years of Relief Society website, churchhistorianspress.org. **Topics: Relief Society; Eliza R. Snow; Young Women Organizations**

19. General Relief Society Meeting, Report, July 17, 1880; Belinda Marden Pratt, Diary Entry, Sept. 5, 1880, in Derr and others, *First Fifty Years of Relief Society,* 478, 480–82.

20. George Q. Cannon, Journal, Oct. 6 and 9, 1880; Woodruff, Journal, Oct. 9, 1880; "Fiftieth Semi-annual Conference," *Deseret News,* Oct. 13, 1880, [12]; Bishop, "Precept upon Precept," 259–62. **Topics: First Presidency; Succession of Church Leadership**

21. "Fiftieth Semi-annual Conference," *Salt Lake Daily Herald,* Oct. 12, 1880, 3; see also "Fiftieth Semi-annual Conference," *Deseret News,* Oct. 13, 1880, [12].

22. Widtsoe, *In the Gospel Net,* 58, 60, 62–68; Ulvund, "Perceptions of Mormonism in Norway," 208–30. **Topic: Norway**

23. "The Reynolds Case in the Cabinet," *Salt Lake Daily Herald,* June 15, 1879, 1; "Garfield's Inaugural Address," *Deseret News,* Mar. 9, 1881, [8]–[9]; "The Great Tragedy," *National Republican,* July 4, 1881, 1; "Talmage on Mormonism," *Daily Gazette,* Oct. 5, 1881, 1; "Talmage on Guiteau," *Evening Critic,* Oct. 4, 1881, [4].

24. John Taylor, in *Journal of Discourses,* July 3, 1881, 22:140.

25. "Dead!," *National Republican,* Sept. 20, 1881, 1; *Papers relating to the Foreign Relations of the United States,* xxiii–xxiv.

26. George Q. Cannon, Journal, Jan. 20, 23, and 27, 1882; Feb. 11 and 16, 1882; *Congressional Record* [1882], 67–68; An Act to Amend Section Fifty-Three Hundred and Fifty-Two of the Revised Statutes of the United States, in Reference to Bigamy, and for Other Purposes [Mar. 22, 1882], *Statutes at Large* [1883], 47th Cong., 1st Sess., chapter 47, 30–32; see also Bitton, *George Q. Cannon,* 251–53. **Topic: Antipolygamy Legislation**

27. George Q. Cannon, Journal, Jan. 24 and 26, 1882; see also entries for Mar. 1, 1880; Nov. 30, 1880; Jan. 18–19, 1882; and Bitton, *George Q. Cannon,* 250–51.

28. An Act to Amend Section Fifty-Three Hundred and Fifty-Two of the Revised Statutes of the United States, in Reference to Bigamy, and for Other Purposes [Mar. 22, 1882], *Statutes at Large* [1883], 47th Cong., 1st Sess., chapter 47, 30–32; "Forty-Seventh Congress," and "The Edmunds Bill," *Salt Lake Daily Herald,* Mar. 15, 1882, 1, [5]; *Speech of Hon. George Q. Cannon,* 3–4, 10; George Q. Cannon, Journal, Apr. 19, 1882; George Q. Cannon to John Taylor, Apr. 19, 1882, 2–5, First Presidency (John Taylor) Correspondence, CHL; see also Bitton, *George Q. Cannon,* 256–58.

29. Ida Hunt to Eliza Luella Udall, Jan. 29, 1882, Udall Family Correspondence Collection, CHL; Udall, *Arizona Pioneer Mormon,* 97–99; Udall, Autobiography and Diaries, volume 1, 20.

30. Ellsworth, *Mormon Odyssey,* 43–46; Udall, *Arizona Pioneer Mormon,* 97–99; Ida Hunt to Eliza Luella Udall, Jan. 29, 1882; Eliza Luella Udall to Ida Hunt, Mar. 12, 1882, Udall Family Correspondence Collection, CHL.

31. Ida Hunt to Eliza Luella Udall, Jan. 29, 1882, Udall Family Correspondence Collection, CHL.
32. Eliza Luella Udall to Ida Hunt, Mar. 12, 1882, Udall Family Correspondence Collection, CHL.
33. Udall, Autobiography and Diaries, volume 1, 22–28; Udall, *Arizona Pioneer Mormon,* 101; Ellsworth, *Mormon Odyssey,* 47, 54.

CHAPTER 33: UNTIL THE STORM BLOWS PAST

1. McDonnel, Reminiscence, part 1, [68]–[70]; part 2, [17]–[22]; Bromley, Journal, Dec. 24–25, 1882; New Zealand Auckland Mission, Manuscript History, volume 2, part 1, Dec. 25, 1882; William Burnett, Letter to the Editor, *Deseret News,* Mar. 7, 1883, [15]; Britsch, *Unto the Islands of the Sea,* 265.
2. Britsch, *Unto the Islands of the Sea,* 260–61; Barber, "Matakite, Mormon Conversions, and Māori-Israelite Identity," 169–73; Britsch, "Maori Traditions and the Mormon Church," 38–40.
3. Greenwood, Journal, Apr. 5, 1883; Meha, "A Prophetic Utterance of Paora Potangaroa," 298; Cowley, "Maori Chief Predicts," 696–97; Underwood, "Mormonism and the Shaping of Maori Religious Identity," 117–19; Ballara and Cairns, "Te Potangaroa, Paora."
4. McDonnel, Reminiscence, part 1, [69]–[70].
5. McDonnel, Reminiscence, part 1, [70]–[73].
6. McDonnel, Reminiscence, part 1, [74]; part 2, [44], [64]–[70]; McDonnel, "Start of the Mission," 8–9.
7. Newton, *Mormon and Maori,* xxiii, 1; Newton, *Tiki and Temple,* 5–30; Britsch, *Unto the Islands of the Sea,* 195–97; Bromley, Journal, Dec. 11, 1880, and Jan. 14, 1881; Bromley, "Introduction of the Gospel to the Maories," 6.
8. McDonnel, Reminiscence, part 1, [1]–[8], [34]–[45]; Bromley, Journal, Apr. 5, 1881; June 13, 1881; Oct. 20, 1881; New Zealand Auckland Mission, Manuscript History, volume 2, part 1, Oct. 18, 1881. **Topic: New Zealand**
9. McDonnel, Reminiscence, part 1, [74]–[85]; part 2, [1]–[7]; Bromley, Journal, Dec. 24, 1882; McDonnel, "Start of the Mission," 4–5; New Zealand Auckland Mission, Manuscript History, volume 2, part 1, Dec. 25, 1882. **Topic: Healing**
10. Bromley, Journal, Dec. 25–26, 1882, and Feb. 26, 1883; McDonnel, Reminiscence, part 2, [11]–[14], [30]–[31]; "Cox, Thomas Lewis," Andrew Jenson Collection, CHL.
11. Andrew and Blank, "Four Mormon Temples," 51–56; Anton Skanchy to Anna Gaarden Widtsoe, May 27, 1882; Aug. 27, 1882, Anna K. Gaarden Widtsoe Papers, Widtsoe Family Papers, CHL; see also letters from Anton Skanchy to Anna Gaarden Widtsoe, 1881–83, Anna K. Gaarden Widtsoe Papers, Widtsoe Family Papers, CHL.
12. Widtsoe, *In the Gospel Net,* 67–68, 72–75; "Widtsoe, Anna Karine Gaarden," in Jenson, *Latter-day Saint Biographical Encyclopedia,* 3:735; Hunsaker, "History of the Norwegian Mission," 65–66, 68–69. **Topic: Norway**
13. Anna Gaarden Widtsoe to Petroline Gaarden, Sept. 14, 1883, Anna K. Gaarden Widtsoe Papers, Widtsoe Family Papers, CHL.
14. Widtsoe, *In the Gospel Net,* 70–73; Haslam, *Clash of Cultures,* 33–34, 45, 70–72, 82–85; Anna Gaarden Widtsoe to Petroline Gaarden, Sept. 14, 1883, Anna K. Gaarden Widtsoe Papers, Widtsoe Family Papers, CHL.
15. "Scandinavian Mission Emigration List 'G,'" 1881–1886," 82[a]–82[b]; Trondheim Branch, Relief Society Minutes and Records, Aug. 16, 1883, 41–42; Widtsoe, *In the Gospel Net,* 74, 76; Anna Gaarden Widtsoe to Petroline Gaarden, Sept. 14, 1883, Anna K. Gaarden Widtsoe Papers, Widtsoe Family Papers, CHL. **Topic: Emigration**
16. Snowflake Arizona Stake, Young Women's Mutual Improvement Association Minutes and Records, Dec. 7, 1883; Mar. 7, 1884; Sept. 12, 1884; Snowflake Arizona Stake, Relief Society Minutes and Records, Mar. 7, 1884.

17. *Apache Chief,* May 30, 1884, quoted in Fish, *Life and Times of Joseph Fish,* 253; Udall, Autobiography and Diaries, volume 1, 47–50; Ellsworth, *Mormon Odyssey,* 43–47; David K. Udall and others to John Taylor, Mar. 27, 1884, First Presidency (John Taylor) Correspondence, CHL; Bair and Jensen, "Prosecution of the Mormons," 28–30.

18. Udall, Autobiography and Diaries, volume 1, 36–38, 48–50, 56–57; James, "Between Two Fires," 51.

19. Udall, Autobiography and Diaries, volume 1, 47–50, 56–57; Bair and Jensen, "Prosecution of the Mormons," 25–26, 29; An Act to Amend Section Fifty-Three Hundred and Fifty-Two of the Revised Statutes of the United States, in Reference to Bigamy, and for Other Purposes [Mar. 22, 1882], *Statutes at Large* [1883], 47th Cong., 1st Sess., chapter 47, 30–31, secs. 1, 3; Firmage and Mangrum, *Zion in the Courts,* 161. Quotation edited for readability; original source has "They thought the next call would be for me, and it might come any moment."

20. Udall, Autobiography and Diaries, volume 1, 56–58.

21. Snowflake Ward, Young Women's Mutual Improvement Association Minutes and Records, July 21, 1884. **Topic: Ida Hunt Udall**

22. Whitney, *History of Utah,* 3:275–78; Clawson, Autobiography, [93]; "A Comedy of Errors," *Salt Lake Daily Herald,* Oct. 18, 1884, 8; "Evidence Ended," *Salt Lake Daily Herald,* Oct. 19, 1884, 12. **Topic: Antipolygamy Legislation**

23. "A Comedy of Errors," *Salt Lake Daily Herald,* Oct. 18, 1884, 5, 8; Whitney, *History of Utah,* 3:295–307.

24. "A Brilliant Defense," *Salt Lake Daily Herald,* Oct. 21, 1884, 8, 5; "Unable to Agree," *Salt Lake Daily Herald,* Oct. 22, 1884, 8; "The Long Agony," *Salt Lake Daily Herald,* Oct. 23, 1884, 8; "The Climax," *Salt Lake Daily Herald,* Oct. 25, 1884, 8.

25. "The Climax," *Salt Lake Daily Herald,* Oct. 25, 1884, 8; "Lydia Spencer's Reasons," *Salt Lake Daily Herald,* Oct. 26, 1884, 12; Hoopes and Hoopes, *Making of a Mormon Apostle,* 88.

26. "Found Guilty," *Salt Lake Daily Herald,* Oct. 26, 1884, 12; "Lydia Spencer's Reasons," *Salt Lake Daily Herald,* Oct. 26, 1884, 12; "Lydia Spencer," *Deseret News,* Oct. 29, 1884, [12]; Gordon, *Mormon Question,* 157.

27. "No Bail," *Salt Lake Daily Herald,* Nov. 4, 1884, 7; see also Whitney, *History of Utah,* 3:317–19; and Clawson, Autobiography, [95]–[97].

28. Panek, "Search and Seizure in Utah," 319–31; James, "Between Two Fires," 51, 52–53; John Taylor, in *Journal of Discourses,* Oct. 19, 1884, 25:344–51; see also "Discourse by President John Taylor," *Deseret Evening News,* Feb. 14, 1885, [1].

29. John Taylor and George Q. Cannon to Jesse N. Smith and others, Dec. 8, 1884, First Presidency (John Taylor) Correspondence, CHL; see also Romney, *Mormon Colonies in Mexico,* 51–53.

30. "Discourse by President John Taylor," *Deseret Evening News,* Feb. 14, 1885, [1]; Jesse N. Smith, Autobiography and Journal, Jan. 3 and 18, 1885; Joseph F. Smith to Sarah Richards Smith, Jan. 14, 1885, Sarah Ellen R. Smith Collection, CHL; Erastus Snow to E. W. Snow, Jan. 15, 1885, Erastus Snow Correspondence, CHL; McIntyre and Barton, *Christopher Layton,* 151.

31. Erastus Snow to E. W. Snow, Jan. 15, 1885, Erastus Snow Correspondence, CHL; Joseph F. Smith to Sarah Richards Smith, Jan. 17, 1885, Sarah Ellen R. Smith Collection, CHL; Joseph F. Smith, Journal, Jan. 1 and 15–18, 1885; Francis Marion Lyman, Journal, Jan. 14–15, 1885.

32. Thatcher, Diary, Jan. 17, 18, and 23, 1885; Francis Marion Lyman, Journal, Jan. 17, 18, and 23, 1885; Jesse N. Smith, Autobiography and Journal, Jan. 18, 1885; McIntyre and Barton, *Christopher Layton,* 151; Joseph F. Smith, Journal, Jan. 23, 1885. **Topic: Colonies in Mexico**

33. Joseph F. Smith, Journal, Jan. 20 and 24–25, 1885; Francis Marion Lyman, Journal, Jan. 18, 23–25, and 27, 1885; Thatcher, Diary, Jan. 23, 1885; Franklin D. Richards, Journal, Jan. 27, 1885; Abraham H. Cannon, Diary, Jan. 27, 1885; George Q. Cannon,

Journal, Jan. 23 and 27, 1885; "Discourse by President John Taylor," *Deseret Evening News,* Feb. 14, 1885, [1].

34. "Discourse by President John Taylor," *Deseret Evening News,* Feb. 14, 1885, [1].

35. George Q. Cannon, Journal, Feb. 1, 1885.

CHAPTER 34: NOTHING TO FEAR FROM THE WICKED

1. Udall, Autobiography and Diaries, volume 1, 96, 100.

2. David Udall to Ida Udall, Nov. 30, 1884; Mar. 8, 1885, copied in Udall, Autobiography and Diaries, volume 1, 82, 101; "The Arizona Anti-'Mormon' Outrages," *Deseret News,* Mar. 18, 1885, [7]; Bair and Jensen, "Prosecution of the Mormons," 32.

3. "The Arizona Anti-'Mormon' Outrages," *Deseret News,* Mar. 18, 1885, [7]; David Udall to Ida Udall, Dec. 6, 1884, copied in Udall, Autobiography and Diaries, volume 1, 84–85.

4. Udall, Autobiography and Diaries, volume 1, 62, 65, 75, 86–100; volume 2, Mar. 8, 1885.

5. Udall, Autobiography and Diaries, volume 1, 67, 95, 100, 103.

6. Udall, Autobiography and Diaries, volume 1, 102–3, 113.

7. Logan Temple, Baptisms for the Dead, 1884–1943, volume B, 329–31, microfilm 177,838; Logan Temple, Endowments for the Dead, 1884–1970, volume A, 387, 391–92, microfilm 177,955, U.S. and Canada Record Collection, Family History Library; Washakie Ward, Record of Members, 2–3, 22–37, 44–45, 64–79.

8. Box Elder Stake, General Minutes, 59; Logan Temple, Ward Account Book, 123, 152, 290, 300, 336, 421, 466; Charles Ora Card to Isaac Zundel, Apr. 21, 1882, Logan Temple Letterpress Copybook, 143–44; "Mortar Mixers," *Logan Herald-Journal,* article nos. [123], [125–26], 151, in Everton, Scrapbooks, CHL.

9. "Zundell, Isaac E. D.," in Jenson, *Latter-day Saint Biographical Encyclopedia,* 1:561; Dibble, "Mormon Mission to the Shoshoni Indians, Part III," 284–93.

10. Endowment House, Sealings of Couples, Living and By Proxy, 1851–89, volume J, 1874–75, entry 2483, microfilm 183,400, Special Collections, U.S. and Canada Record Collection, Family History Library; Woodruff, Journal, Feb. 22, 1875.

11. *Year of Jubilee,* 103; Isaac Zundel to John Taylor, Nov. 30, 1886, First Presidency (John Taylor) Correspondence, CHL. **Topic: Sagwitch**

12. Hill, "Brief Acct," 3, 11–14; "The Indian Ejectment," *Deseret News,* Sept. 1, 1875, [5]; George W. Hill to Brigham Young, Aug. 15, 1876, Brigham Young Office Files, CHL. **Topic: American Indians**

13. Isaac E. D. Zundel, Alexander Hunsaker, and Moroni Ward to John Taylor, May 23, 1880; Isaac E. D. Zundel to John Taylor, Dec. 8, 1880; Isaac E. D. Zundel to John Hess, Dec. 8, 1880, First Presidency (John Taylor) Correspondence, CHL; *History of Box Elder County,* 153.

14. Christensen, *Sagwitch,* 165.

15. Charles Ora Card to Isaac Zundel, Apr. 21, 1882, Logan Temple Letterpress Copybook, 143–44; "Mortar Mixers," *Logan Herald-Journal,* article nos. [123], [125–26], 151, in Everton, Scrapbooks, CHL; Box Elder Stake, General Minutes, 59; Logan Temple, Ward Account Book, 123, 152, 290, 300, 336, 421, 466.

16. "Mortar Mixers," *Logan Herald-Journal,* article nos. [124], [125], 151, in Everton, Scrapbooks, CHL; J. H. M., Letter to the Editor, Mar. 22, 1863, *Deseret News,* Apr. 1, 1863, [3].

17. Logan Temple, Baptisms for the Dead, 1884–1943, volume B, 329–31, microfilm 177,838; Logan Temple, Endowments for the Dead, 1884–1970, volume A, 387, 391–92, microfilm 177,955, U.S. and Canada Record Collection, Family History Library; Washakie Ward, Record of Members, 2–3, 22–37, 44–45, 64–79.

18. "Joseph Smith," *Salt Lake Daily Tribune,* June 23, 1885, [4]; Launius, "Methods and Motives," 113. **Topics: Other Latter Day Saint Movements; Joseph and Emma Hale Smith Family**

19. Helen Mar Kimball Whitney, Diary, June 21, 1885 [CHL]; Nov. 19, 1885 [Utah State University]; Whitney, *Plural Marriage;* Whitney, Autobiography, [2]. **Topic: Helen Mar Kimball Whitney**

20. Whitney, Autobiography, [1]–[3]; Helen Mar Kimball Whitney, "Scenes and Incidents in Nauvoo," *Woman's Exponent,* Nov. 15, 1882, 11:90; Fluhman, "Subject That Can Bear Investigation," 105–12; Hales, *Joseph Smith's Polygamy,* 2:294–98. **Topic: Joseph Smith and Plural Marriage**

21. Whitney, Autobiography, [3]; Helen Mar Kimball Whitney, "The Last Chapter of Scenes in Nauvoo," *Woman's Exponent,* Nov. 1, 1883, 12:[81]; Bennett, *Journey West,* xxiii–xxvi. **Topic: Sealing**

22. Whitney, Autobiography, [3]; Whitney, *Through Memory's Halls,* 22; Hatch and Compton, *Widow's Tale,* 3–6.

23. Helen Mar Kimball Whitney, Diary, Nov. 21–[22], 1884 [CHL].

24. Whitney, *Why We Practice Plural Marriage,* 9, 23–24, 65–66; Whitney, *Plural Marriage,* 37. **Topic: Plural Marriage in Utah**

25. Whitney, *Why We Practice Plural Marriage,* 3–[72]; Helen Mar Kimball Whitney, Diary, Dec. 17, 18, and 31, 1884; Jan. 1, 2, and 3, 1885; Feb. 3, 1885 [CHL]; Mar. 5 and 6, 1886 [Utah State University].

26. Helen Mar Kimball Whitney, "Hypocrisy of the Crusaders, and Encouragement for the Faithful," *Deseret Evening News,* Aug. 15, 1885, [5]; Helen Mar Kimball Whitney, "History Repeating Itself," *Deseret News,* May 13, 1885, [6].

27. Whitney, *Plural Marriage,* 3–9.

28. Helen Mar Kimball Whitney, Diary, Nov. 19, 1885 [Utah State University]. Quotation edited for readability; "I'd been more bold" in original changed to "I would have been more bold."

29. Whitney, Autobiography, [3]; Helen Mar Kimball Whitney, "The Last Chapter of Scenes in Nauvoo," *Woman's Exponent,* Nov. 1, 1883, 12:[81]; see Isaiah 48:10.

30. Udall, Autobiography and Diaries, volume 1, 113, 115–16, 132–33, 156–57.

31. Udall, Autobiography and Diaries, volume 1, 126–27; Udall, *Arizona Pioneer Mormon,* 116–18; Hiram B. Clawson to John Taylor and George Q. Cannon, Aug. 21, 1885, First Presidency (John Taylor) Correspondence, CHL.

32. David Udall to Ida Udall, July 16, 1885, copied in Udall, Autobiography and Diaries, volume 1, 121; Udall, Autobiography and Diaries, volume 1, 109–11.

33. Udall, Autobiography and Diaries, volume 1, 126; David Udall to Ida Udall, Aug. 4, 1885, copied in Udall, Autobiography and Diaries, volume 1, 126–27.

34. Udall, Autobiography and Diaries, volume 1, 128–33, 139, 151, 153, 155, 170.

35. Udall, Autobiography and Diaries, volume 1, 155, 157, 158, 159–65; Eliza Luella Udall to Ida Udall, Aug. 31, 1885; David K. Udall to Family, Sept. 20, 1885; David K. Udall to Family, Oct. 5, 1885; David K. Udall to Family, Oct. 18, 1885, Udall Family Correspondence Collection, CHL; David Udall to "Lois Pratt" [Ida Udall], Nov. 29, 1885, copied in Udall, Autobiography and Diaries, volume 1, 168–69.

36. Perkins and Woodger, "Administration from the Underground," appendix B, 365; Susa Young Gates to Lucy Bigelow Young, Oct. 12, 1885, Susa Young Gates, Papers, CHL; Jacob F. Gates to John Taylor, Oct. 12, 1885, First Presidency Missionary Calls and Recommendations, CHL. First sentence of quotation edited for readability; "he dont think" in original changed to "he doesn't think." **Topic: Susa Young Gates**

37. Jacob F. Gates to John Taylor, Oct. 12, 1885, First Presidency Missionary Calls and Recommendations, CHL.

38. Jacob F. Gates to George Reynolds, Oct. 21, 1885, First Presidency Missionary Calls and Recommendations, CHL; Susa Young Gates to Lucy Bigelow Young, Oct. 19, 1885, Susa Young Gates, Papers, CHL.

39. "Mother and Father," *Salt Lake Daily Herald,* Oct. 29, 1885, 8.

40. Jacob F. Gates to Jacob Gates, Nov. 12, 1885, Susa Young Gates, Papers, CHL; Beesley, Diary, Oct. 28 and Nov. 9–10, 1885, 3, 4–6.

41. Susa Young Gates [Homespun, pseud.], "A Tropical Picture," *Woman's Exponent,* Jan. 1, 1886, 14:118; Jacob F. Gates to Jacob Gates, Nov. 12, 1885; Jacob F. Gates to Emma F. Gates, July 13, 1886, Susa Young Gates, Papers, CHL; Moffat, Woods, and Walker, *Gathering to La'ie,* 29–51. **Topic: Hawaii**

42. Jacob F. Gates to Jacob Gates, Nov. 12, 1885, Susa Young Gates, Papers, CHL.

43. Bailey Dunford to Susa Young Gates, Dec. 6, 1885, Susa Young Gates, Papers, CHL. Quotation edited for readability; "I wish you was" in original changed to "I wish you were."

44. George Reynolds to Joseph F. Smith, Mar. 26, 1885, Joseph F. Smith, Papers, CHL; George Q. Cannon, Journal, Jan. 27, 1885; Feb. 1, 6, 14, and 16, 1885; Apr. 3, 5, 12, 19, and 23, 1885; May 14 and 27, 1885; June 19, 1885; July 14–17, 1885; Oct. 3, 1885; Jan. 1–2, 1886; John Taylor to Joseph F. Smith, Mar. 12, 1885, Joseph F. Smith, Papers, CHL.

45. See George Q. Cannon, Journal, Feb.–June 1885; and George Reynolds to Joseph F. Smith, Feb. 12, 1885, Joseph F. Smith, Papers, CHL.

46. George Q. Cannon, Journal, Nov. 20, 1885; "Apostle Lorenzo Snow," *Deseret News,* Nov. 25, 1885, [12].

47. "Mr. Snow Speaks," *Salt Lake Daily Herald,* Jan. 17, 1886, 12; Lorenzo Snow, in *Journal of Discourses,* Jan. 10, 1886, 26:365; "In the Snow Case," *Salt Lake Daily Herald,* Feb. 7, 1886, 10. **Topic: Lorenzo Snow**

48. Hedges and Holzapfel, *Within These Prison Walls,* xxxiv; "Raid on the Cannon Farm," *Deseret Evening News,* Feb. 8, 1886, [3]; "Another Raid," *Deseret Evening News,* Feb. 10, 1886, [3].

49. George Q. Cannon, Journal, Feb. 27, 1886; Abraham H. Cannon, Diary, Feb. 10–11, 1886.

50. George Q. Cannon, Journal, Feb. 27, 1886; "The Great Prisoner," *Deseret Evening News,* Feb. 17, 1886, [3].

CHAPTER 35: A DAY OF TRIAL

1. George Q. Cannon, Journal, Feb. 17 and 27, 1886; Abraham H. Cannon, Diary, Feb. 17, 1886; "Captured Artillery," *Salt Lake Daily Tribune,* Feb. 18, 1886, [4]. **Topic: George Q. Cannon**

2. George Q. Cannon, Journal, Feb. 27, 1886.

3. George Q. Cannon, Journal, Feb. 17 and 27–28, 1886; Mar. 2 and 17, 1886; "Letter from the Secretary of the Treasury," *Executive Documents of the Senate of the United States,* 52nd Cong., 2nd Sess., Ex. Doc. No. 43, 3; see also Walker, "Grant's Watershed," 206–8.

4. George Q. Cannon, Journal, Feb. 28–Mar. 2 and Mar. 5, 1886.

5. Wells, Diary, volume 2, Jan. 28, 1886; Madsen, *Emmeline B. Wells,* 217–18; "Items from Washington," *Woman's Exponent,* Feb. 15, 1886, 14:140. **Topics: Emmeline B. Wells; Antipolygamy Legislation**

6. "The Latest from Edmunds," *Woman's Exponent,* Feb. 1, 1886, 14:134–36; see also An Act to Amend an Act Entitled "An Act to Amend Section Fifty-Three Hundred and Fifty Two . . ." [Mar. 3, 1887], *Statutes at Large* [1887], 49th Cong., 2nd Sess., chapter 397, 635–41.

7. "Items from Washington," *Woman's Exponent,* Feb. 15, 1886, 14:140; "Notes from Washington," *Woman's Exponent,* May 1, 1886, 14:180–81; see also Madsen, *Emmeline B. Wells,* 218–20; and Wells, Diary, volume 2, Jan. 28, 1886.

8. Emmeline Wells to Orson F. Whitney, Mar. 2, 1886, Orson F. Whitney Collection, CHL; *"Mormon" Women's Protest,* 1886 (Excerpt), in Derr and others, *First Fifty Years of Relief Society,* 517, 520; Madsen, *Emmeline B. Wells,* 225.

9. "Letter to the Sisters at Home," *Woman's Exponent,* Apr. 1, 1886, 14:164; Madsen, *Emmeline B. Wells,* 225; *"Mormon" Women's Protest,* 1886 (Excerpt), in Derr and others, *First Fifty Years of Relief Society,* 522–25; "Ferguson, Ellen Brooke," Biographical Entry, First Fifty Years of Relief Society website, churchhistorianspress.org.

10. "Notes from Washington," *Woman's Exponent,* May 1, 1886, 14:180; "Items from Washington," *Woman's Exponent,* Feb. 15, 1886, 14:140; "Report," *Deseret News,* June 3, 1885, [13]; see also "'The Rotunda'—Kirtland—The 'Memorial,'" *Woman's Exponent,* Apr. 15, 1886, 14:169.

11. "Notes from Washington," *Woman's Exponent,* May 1, 1886, 14:180.

12. See Daynes, *More Wives Than One,* 175; and Antrei and Scow, *Other Forty-Niners,* 152.

13. Ephraim South Ward, Primary Association Minutes, Jan. 23, 1886, 50; see also Stevens, Autobiography, 15.

14. Bradley, "Hide and Seek," 147–48.

15. See Dorius, "Autobiography of Carl Christian Nicoli Dorius," 39.

16. Dorius, *Dorius Heritage,* 212–14; see also Dorius, "Autobiography of Carl Christian Nicoli Dorius," 26; and Jensen, "Diary of J. F. Ferdinand Dorius," 5.

17. Dorius, *Dorius Heritage,* 149–54; Stevens, Autobiography, 8–10, 12; 1880 U.S. Census, West Point, Ephraim Precinct, Sanpete County, Utah Territory, 444D; "David Eugene Stevens," Utah Department of Heritage and Arts, Utah Division of State History, Cemeteries and Burials database, http://history.utah.gov/cemeteries/.

18. Death Certificate for Charles Henry Stevens, Mar. 6, 1935; Death Certificate for Alma Stevens, Mar. 6, 1932, Utah Department of Health, Office of Vital Records and Statistics, Utah State Archives and Records Service, Salt Lake City; "Elizabeth Sophia Stevens Nielson"; "Margret Augusta Taylor"; "William Henry Taylor," Utah Department of Heritage and Arts, Utah Division of State History, Cemeteries and Burials database, http://history.utah.gov/cemeteries/. Full biographical research for Augusta Dorius Stevens and Henry Stevens in possession of editors.

19. Eliza R. Snow, Discourse, Aug. 14, 1873, in Derr and others, *First Fifty Years of Relief Society,* 387–88; "Minutes of a Special Meeting of the F. R. Societies of Provo," *Woman's Exponent,* Sept. 15, 1872, 1:58; Stevens, Autobiography, 13; "Biographical Sketch of R. B. Pratt," 534; "The Women of Utah," *Woman's Exponent,* Sept. 1, 1888, 17:49–50; Report of Deseret Hospital Dedication, July 17, 1882, in Derr and others, *First Fifty Years of Relief Society,* 497–506; Derr, Cannon, and Beecher, *Women of Covenant,* 106–7. **Topic: Pioneer Women and Medicine**

20. See Firmage and Mangrum, *Zion in the Courts,* 174, 188–90; Bradley, "Hide and Seek," 146–47; and Stevens, Autobiography, 13.

21. Ephraim South Ward, Primary Association Minutes, Oct. 11, 1884, 36; Jan. 10, 1885, 39; Apr. 20, 1885, 43; Dec. 26, 1885, 49; June 21, 1886, 52.

22. Ephraim South Ward, Primary Association Minutes, Oct. 11, 1884, 36; Apr. 6, 1885, 42; *Circular of the First Presidency,* 5; see also Sanpete Stake, General Minutes, July 10, 1887, 49.

23. Ephraim South Ward, Primary Association Minutes, Mar. 15, 1886, 51; see also Jan. 2, 1886, 49. Quotation edited for readability; "it was a day of trial" in original changed to "it is a day of trial."

24. Udall, Autobiography and Diaries, volume 1, 170–72, 175.

25. See, for example, Udall, Autobiography and Diaries, volume 1, 180–81, 205.

26. Udall, Autobiography and Diaries, volume 1, 206–7, 209.

27. Udall, Autobiography and Diaries, volume 1, 211, 217.

28. Udall, Autobiography and Diaries, volume 2, [15]; see also Ellsworth, *Mormon Odyssey,* 185; and Bair and Jensen, "Prosecution of the Mormons," 44.

29. Ellsworth, *Mormon Odyssey,* 186. **Topic: Ida Hunt Udall**

30. Hawaii Honolulu Mission, Manuscript History and Historical Reports, volume 5, Feb. 1, 1887.

31. Susa Young Gates to Lucy Bigelow Young and "Sister," Dec. 30, 1886, Susa Young Gates, Papers, CHL.

32. Susa Young Gates to Lucy Bigelow Young, Mar. 6, 1887, Jacob F. Gates Papers, Susa Young Gates, Papers, CHL; Susa Young Gates, Journal, Feb. 22 and Apr. 22, 1888; Joseph F. Smith, Journal, Feb. 22–23, 1887.

33. Susa Young Gates, Journal, Feb. 24, 1888; Susa Young Gates to Lucy Bigelow Young, Mar. 6, 1887, Jacob F. Gates Papers, Susa Young Gates, Papers, CHL; Hawaii Honolulu Mission, Manuscript History and Historical Reports, volume 5, Mar. 2, 1887.

34. Joseph F. Smith, Journal, Feb. 23 and Mar. 2, 1887.

35. Susa Young Gates to Lucy Bigelow Young, Mar. 6, 1887, Jacob F. Gates Papers, Susa Young Gates, Papers, CHL; Joseph F. Smith, Journal, June 6 and July 7, 1870.

36. An Act to Amend an Act Entitled "An Act to Amend Section Fifty-Three Hundred and Fifty Two . . ." [Mar. 3, 1887], *Statutes at Large* [1887], 49th Cong., 2nd Sess., chapter 397, 635–41; Firmage and Mangrum, *Zion in the Courts,* 197–99, 231–36; Daynes, *More Wives Than One,* 176; see also "At the Capital," *Salt Lake Daily Herald,* Mar. 13, 1887, 8.

37. Cox, "Mormon Colonies in Mexico," 23–29.

38. Godfrey, "Canada's Brigham Young," 226–34.

39. George Q. Cannon to Joseph F. Smith, May 21, 1887, Joseph F. Smith, Papers, CHL; George Q. Cannon, Journal, Nov. 22, 1886; Mar. 4, 1887; Apr. 17, 19, 20, and 21, 1887; May 7, 11, 20, and 24, 1887; June 24, 1887; July 2, 1887; Nuttall, Diary, June 26, 1887.

40. George Q. Cannon, Journal, May 24, 1887.

41. George Q. Cannon to Joseph F. Smith, Oct. 23, 1886; May 21, 1887; May 26, 1887, Joseph F. Smith, Papers, CHL.

42. George Q. Cannon, Journal, June 23, 1887; July 1, 2, 10, 11, 13, and 18, 1887; Nuttall, Diary, July 1–31, 1887. **Topic: John Taylor**

43. George Q. Cannon, Journal, July 18, 1887; Joseph F. Smith, Journal, July 18, 1887.

44. George Q. Cannon, Journal, July 25 and 26, 1887; Joseph F. Smith, Journal, July 25, 1887. **Topics: Wilford Woodruff; Succession of Church Leadership**

CHAPTER 36: THE WEAK THING OF THIS WORLD

1. Woodruff, Journal, July 28–29, 1887; Joseph F. Smith, Journal, July 29, 1887; George Q. Cannon, Journal, July 29, 1887; "Laid to Rest," *Salt Lake Daily Herald,* July 30, 1887, 8; [Emmeline B. Wells], "In Memoriam," *Woman's Exponent,* Aug. 1, 1887, 16:37. **Topics: John Taylor; Wilford Woodruff**

2. George Q. Cannon, Journal, July 29, 1887; Woodruff, Journal, Nov. 9–12, 1885, and July 25, 1887.

3. Woodruff, Journal, Aug. 3, 1887; "From President Woodruff," *Salt Lake Daily Herald,* Aug. 6, 1887, 5. **Topic: Succession of Church Leadership**

4. Truman O. Angell Sr. and Truman O. Angell Jr. to John Taylor, Apr. 28, 1885, First Presidency (John Taylor) Correspondence, CHL; George Q. Cannon, Journal, July 14, 1885; May 3, 13, and 19, 1886; Aug. 15 and 18, 1887; Sept. 10, 1887; West Towers Transverse Section, Sept. 1884; Tower Sections, Nov. 1887, Stone Mason Sections, Architect's Office, Salt Lake Temple Architectural Drawings, CHL.

5. Francis Marion Lyman, Journal, Aug. 13, 1887; Franklin D. Richards, Journal, Aug. 4, 1887; George Q. Cannon, Journal, Aug. 15 and 18, 1887; Oct. 7–8, 1887; Woodruff, Journal, Oct. 9, 1887.

6. Grant, Journal, loose copy, Aug. 3, 1887; Francis Marion Lyman, Journal, Aug. 3, 1887; Franklin D. Richards, Journal, Oct. 5, 1887; Woodruff, Journal, Aug. 3, 1887; George Q. Cannon, Journal, Aug. 5 and Oct. 8, 1887; Walker, "Grant's Watershed," 195–96, 198–99, 202–8, 211–16. **Topic: George Q. Cannon**

7. George Q. Cannon, Journal, Sept. 13, 1887.

8. Franklin D. Richards, Journal, Oct. 5, 1887; Grant, Journal, Oct. 5, 1887; Woodruff, Journal, Oct. 5–6, 1887; Francis Marion Lyman, Journal, Oct. 5, 1887; see also Walker, "Grant's Watershed," 214–17.

9. Gray, *Amerika Samoa*, 11–13; "A Brief Account of the History of the Samoan Mission," Manuscript History of the Samoan Mission, 1–[2]; Hart, Hart, and Harris, *Expanded Samoan Mission History*, 8. **Topics: Samoa; American Samoa**

10. McBride, "Mormon Beginnings in Samoa," 57–62; Harris, *Building the Kingdom in Samoa*, 3–6; Britsch, "Founding of the Samoan Mission," 13–15; "The Great Crusade," *Deseret News*, Nov. 15, 1871, [7]. **Topic: Hawaii**

11. Britsch, "Founding of the Samoan Mission," 15; Harris, *Building the Kingdom in Samoa*, 6; Hart, Hart, and Harris, *Expanded Samoan Mission History*, 8–9; "Correspondence," *Deseret News*, Sept. 25, 1872, [10].

12. Britsch, "Founding of the Samoan Mission," 6; Harris, *Building the Kingdom in Samoa*, 6; Joseph H. Dean to Wilford Woodruff and George Q. Cannon, Feb. 13, 1888, First Presidency, Mission Administration Correspondence, CHL.

13. Wood, "My Samoan Experience," 210; McBride, "Mormon Beginnings in Samoa," 66–67.

14. "A Brief Account of the History of the Samoan Mission," Manuscript History of the Samoan Mission, [2].

15. Britsch, "Founding of the Samoan Mission," 14–15; McBride, "Mormon Beginnings in Samoa," 62–63, 65–67; Joseph H. Dean to Wilford Woodruff and George Q. Cannon, July 7, 1888, First Presidency, Mission Administration Correspondence, CHL.

16. "A Brief Account of the History of the Samoan Mission," Manuscript History of the Samoan Mission, [2].

17. Anna Gaarden Widtsoe to Petroline Gaarden, Aug. 28, 1887; Nov. 9, 1887, Anna K. Gaarden Widtsoe Papers, Widtsoe Family Papers, CHL; Widtsoe, *In the Gospel Net*, 78, 84.

18. Widtsoe, *In the Gospel Net*, 78–80, 92–94; Widtsoe, *In a Sunlit Land*, 8–9, 19–20.

19. Garr, "History of Brigham Young College," 4–9; Godfrey, *Logan, Utah*, 38–40; Widtsoe, *In the Gospel Net*, 92–94; Widtsoe, *In a Sunlit Land*, 19–21. **Topic: Church Academies**

20. Widtsoe, *In a Sunlit Land*, 10–11, 13; Widtsoe, *In the Gospel Net*, 81–82, 86–88; Logan First Ward, Relief Society Minutes and Records, volume 1, July 3, 1884. **Topic: Young Men Organizations**

21. Widtsoe, *In the Gospel Net*, 81–82, 86–87. **Topic: Word of Wisdom (D&C 89)**

22. Logan Temple, Baptisms for the Dead, volume F, Apr. 12 and 19, 1887, 342, 347, microfilm 177,845, U.S. and Canada Record Collection, Family History Library; Widtsoe, *In the Gospel Net*, 88.

23. "Death of Sister E. R. Snow Smith," *Deseret News*, Dec. 7, 1887, [8]; "Eliza Roxie Snow Smith," *Woman's Exponent*, Dec. 15, 1887, 16:108–10. **Topic: Eliza R. Snow**

24. [Emmeline B. Wells], "Pen Sketch of an Illustrious Woman," *Woman's Exponent*, Feb. 1, 1881, 9:131; Provo Second Ward, Relief Society Minutes and Records, volume 1, Sept. 1869, 14–19; Eliza R. Snow, Discourse, Aug. 14, 1873, in Derr and others, *First Fifty Years of Relief Society*, 384.

25. "Eliza Roxie Snow Smith," *Woman's Exponent*, Dec. 15, 1887, 16:109.

26. "Young, Zina Diantha Huntington Jacobs," Biographical Entry, First Fifty Years of Relief Society website, churchhistorianspress.org; "General Conference," *Deseret News*, Apr. 11, 1888, [13]; Derr, Cannon, and Beecher, *Women of Covenant*, 127.

27. "Young, Zina Diantha Huntington Jacobs," Biographical Entry, First Fifty Years of Relief Society website, churchhistorianspress.org; "General Conference," *Deseret News*, Apr. 11, 1888, [13]; Derr, Cannon, and Beecher, *Women of Covenant*, 127; Salt Lake Stake Relief Society, Report, June 18 and 19, 1880; General Relief Society Meeting, Report, July 17, 1880, in Derr and others, *First Fifty Years of Relief Society*, 467–77; Bradley and Woodward, *4 Zinas*, 316–18.

28. Derr, Cannon, and Beecher, *Women of Covenant*, 127–30; Wells, "Zina D. H. Young," 43–48. **Topics: Zina D. H. Jacobs Young; Pioneer Women and Medicine**

29. Derr, Cannon, and Beecher, *Women of Covenant,* 130; George Q. Cannon, Journal, Aug. 19, 1886; Godfrey, "Canada's Brigham Young," 226.

30. Zina Young Card to Zina Huntington Young, Oct. 6, 1887, Zina Card Brown Family Collection, CHL.

31. Zina Huntington Young to Susa Young Gates, June 19, 1888, Susa Young Gates, Papers, CHL; "On the Canadian Frontier," Church History website, history .ChurchofJesusChrist.org; Brown, "Biographical Sketch of the Life of Zina Young Williams Card," 14. **Topic: Canada**

32. Zina Huntington Young to Susa Young Gates, June 19, 1888, Susa Young Gates, Papers, CHL; Bradley and Woodward, *4 Zinas,* 249–67.

33. Brown, "Biographical Sketch of the Life of Zina Young Williams Card," 1, 14–15; Bradley and Woodward, *4 Zinas,* 283–84.

34. Cardston Ward, Relief Society Minutes and Records, volume 1, June 11, 1888; see also entries for May 24–Aug. 30, 1888.

35. Zina Huntington Young to Susa Young Gates, June 19, 1888, Susa Young Gates, Papers, CHL; Bradley and Woodward, *4 Zinas,* 288–89, 322–23.

36. Joseph H. Dean, Journal, May 23, 1887; Franklin D. Richards, Journal, May 23, 1887; Britsch, "Founding of the Samoan Mission," 16. **Topic: Growth of Missionary Work**

37. Britsch, "Founding of the Samoan Mission," 16–17; "Joseph Henry Dean," and "Sarah Allen Arnold Dean," Missionary Database, history.ChurchofJesusChrist.org/missionary; Joseph H. Dean, Journal, Mar. 28 and May 16–25, 1887; "The Jos. Dean Trial," *Salt Lake Democrat,* May 14, 1887, [6]; "Not Guilty," *Salt Lake Daily Herald,* May 15, 1887, 3; "The Case of Joseph Dean," *Salt Lake Daily Tribune,* May 15, 1887, [2].

38. Joseph H. Dean to Wilford Woodruff and George Q. Cannon, Feb. 13, 1888, First Presidency, Mission Administration Correspondence, CHL; Hart, Hart, and Harris, *Expanded Samoan Mission History,* 8–9.

39. Joseph H. Dean, Journal, Feb. 9, 1888; May 11, 1888; June 1 and 10–11, 1888; Hart, Hart, and Harris, *Expanded Samoan Mission History,* 9.

40. Joseph H. Dean to Wilford Woodruff and George Q. Cannon, July 7, 1888, First Presidency, Mission Administration Correspondence, CHL; Joseph H. Dean, Journal, June 18, 20–21, and 24–25, 1888; Britsch, "Founding of the Samoan Mission," 18–19.

CHAPTER 37: TO THE THRONE OF GRACE

1. Woodruff, Journal, May 13–14, 1888; George Q. Cannon, Journal, May 13–14, 1888.

2. Woodruff, Journal, May 16–17 and 21, 1888; George Q. Cannon, Journal, May 13 and 17, 1888; "Dedication of the Temple at Manti," *Deseret News,* May 16, 1888, [8]; see also Rasmussen and Nielson, *Manti Temple,* 46.

3. "The Manti Temple," *Deseret Evening News,* Oct. 5, 1877, [3]; Stubbs, "History of the Manti Temple," 26–28, 33–35, 46, 56–59; Rasmussen and Nielson, *Manti Temple,* 33, 104. **Topic: Temple Building**

4. George Q. Cannon, Journal, Mar. 19–26, 1888; Woodruff, Journal, Mar. 20–26, 1888; Walker, "Grant's Watershed," 216–18.

5. An Act to Amend an Act Entitled "An Act to Amend Section Fifty-Three Hundred and Fifty-Two . . ." [Mar. 3, 1887], *Statutes at Large* [1887], 49th Cong., 2nd Sess., chapter 397, 637; Woodruff, Journal, Nov. 5 and 16, 1887; "The Receiver Takes the Tithing Office," *Deseret News,* Nov. 16, 1887, [8]; "As a Matter of History," *Salt Lake Daily Herald,* Nov. 26, 1887, 8; George Q. Cannon, Journal, Nov. 15, 1887; see also An Act to Punish and Prevent the Practice of Polygamy in the Territories of the United States and Other Places, and Disapproving and Annulling Certain Acts of the Legislative Assembly of the Territory of Utah [July 1, 1862], *Statutes at Large* [1863], 37th Cong., 2nd Sess., chapter 126, 501–2. **Topic: Antipolygamy Legislation**

6. Monnett, "Emergence of the Academies," 60–64, 74–79, 101–9; George Q. Cannon, Journal, Jan. 26–27 and Apr. 7, 1888; "General Conference," *Deseret News,* Apr. 11, 1888, [13]. **Topic: Church Academies**

7. Woodruff, Journal, May 17, 1888; George Q. Cannon, Journal, May 17, 1888; "Another Temple," and "Demand the Tabernacle," *Deseret News,* May 23, 1888, [9], [11]; see also Rasmussen and Nielson, *Manti Temple,* 46–47. **Topic: Temple Dedications and Dedicatory Prayers**

8. "The House of the Lord," *Deseret News,* May 30, 1888, [9]; Rasmussen and Nielson, *Manti Temple,* 47–57; Bennett, *Temples Rising,* 264.

9. Susa Young Gates to Zina Huntington Young, May 5, 1888; Susa Young Gates to Wilford Woodruff, Aug. 23, 1888, Young Woman's Journal Files, General Information, Susa Young Gates, Papers, CHL; "The New Year, 1881," *Woman's Exponent,* Jan. 1, 1884, 12:116; Tait, "Susa Young Gates and the Cultural Work of Home Literature," 54–56. **Topic: Susa Young Gates**

10. Susa Young Gates, Journal, Apr. 8, 1888; May 18 and 25, 1888.

11. Susa Young Gates, Journal, Feb. 19, 1888; Apr. 22 and 24, 1888; May 24, 1888; Susa Young Gates to Jacob F. Gates, Mar. 18, 1887, Susa Young Gates, Papers, CHL.

12. Susa Young Gates to Zina Huntington Young, May 5, 1888, Young Woman's Journal Files, General Information, Susa Young Gates, Papers, CHL.

13. Susa Young Gates to Emmeline B. Wells, May 5, 1888; Romania Bunnell Penrose to Susa Young Gates, June 26, 1888, Young Woman's Journal Files, Alphabetical Correspondence Files, Susa Young Gates, Papers, CHL; Derr and others, *First Fifty Years of Relief Society,* 387, note 416. **Topics: Church Periodicals; Emmeline B. Wells**

14. Susa Young Gates, Journal, July 12 and Aug. 24, 1888; Joseph F. Smith to Susa Young Gates, Aug. 10, 1888, Young Woman's Journal Files, General Information, Susa Young Gates, Papers, CHL. Quotation edited for clarity; "different to" in original changed to "different from."

15. Susa Young Gates to Elmina Shepherd Taylor, Maria Young Dougall, and Mattie Horne Tingey, Aug. 23, 1888; Wilford Woodruff to Susa Young Gates, Oct. 2, 1888, Young Woman's Journal Files, General Information, Susa Young Gates, Papers, CHL; "Letter of the Presidency," 19; Susa Young Gates, Journal, Oct. 19, 1888.

16. Alexander, "Odyssey of a Latter-day Prophet" [2010], 284–85; George Q. Cannon, Journal, Feb. 28, 1886, and Sept. 13, 1888; see also entries for Aug. 16 and Sept. 15, 1887. **Topic: George Q. Cannon**

17. Alexander, *Things in Heaven and Earth,* 248–49; Sigman, "Everything Lawyers Know about Polygamy Is Wrong," 117–19, 129–31; Poll, "Legislative Antipolygamy Campaign," 117–19; see also An Act to Amend an Act Entitled "An Act to Amend Section Fifty-Three Hundred and Fifty-Two . . ." [Mar. 3, 1887], *Statutes at Large* [1887], 49th Cong., 2nd Sess., chapter 397, 635–41. **Topic: Utah**

18. Abraham H. Cannon, Diary, Sept. 8, 1888; George Q. Cannon, Journal, Aug. 2 and Sept. 12–17, 1888; Franklin D. Richards, Journal, Sept. 14, 1888.

19. Whitney, *History of Utah,* 3:633–35; Lyman, *Political Deliverance,* 99–100; Abraham H. Cannon, Diary, Sept. 17, 1888; Woodruff, Journal, Sept. 17, 1888; "Apostle George Q. Cannon," *Deseret Evening News,* Sept. 17, 1888, [3]; see also Utah Commission, *Edmunds Act,* 3.

20. George Q. Cannon, Journal, Sept. 14–17, 1888; "Governor's Message," *Deseret News,* Dec. 14, 1859, [5]; Bashore, "Life behind Bars," 24; Hill, "History of Utah State Prison," 49.

21. George Q. Cannon, Journal, Sept. 17, 1888.

22. George Q. Cannon, Journal, Sept. 27–30, 1888.

23. Bitton, *George Q. Cannon,* 293–96; Walker, "Grant's Watershed," 218–19; George Q. Cannon, Journal, Sept. 17–30 and Nov. 6–21, 1888; see also entry for Feb. 18–20, 1889.

24. See Woodruff, Journal, Feb. 2, 1888; and Whitchurch and Perry, "Friends and Enemies in Washington," 229, note 95. **Topic: Joseph F. Smith**

25. See Joseph F. Smith, Journal, Sept. 3 and 22, 1888.

26. Joseph F. Smith, Journal, Jan. 5–12, 1889.
27. *Admission of Utah,* 7–8.
28. Joseph F. Smith, Journal, Jan. 12–14, 16, 20, and 22, 1889; Feb. 1, 5–6, 11, 15, and 19–20, 1889.
29. Joseph F. Smith, Journal, Sept. 12 and 14, 1888; see also George Q. Cannon, Journal, Sept. 12–13, 1888.
30. Joseph F. Smith, Journal, Feb. 1, 1889.
31. Alexander, "Odyssey of a Latter-day Prophet" [1991], 181; George Q. Cannon, Journal, Dec. 12, 1888, and Feb. 17, 1889; "He Gives Himself Up," *Salt Lake Daily Herald,* Dec. 13, 1888, 8; Woodruff, Journal, Sept. 17, 1888; Walker, "Grant's Watershed," 215–16.
32. Woodruff, Journal, Nov. 1888–Jan. 1889, especially entries for Nov. 24, Dec. 22, and Jan. 19.
33. George Q. Cannon, Journal, Feb. 21–22, 1889; Abraham H. Cannon, Diary, Feb. 20–22, 1889; Woodruff, Journal, Aug. 3, 1887, and Feb. 22, 1889; "Serenaded," *Deseret Evening News,* Feb. 23, 1889, [3]; see also Walker, "Grant's Watershed," 222–25.
34. Derr, Cannon, and Beecher, *Women of Covenant,* 128, 131; Franklin D. Richards, Journal, Oct. 11, 1888; "Relief Society Central Board," *Woman's Exponent,* Oct. 15, 1888, 17:76; Zina Young Card to Zina Huntington Young, May 25 and 30, 1889, Zina Card Brown Family Collection, CHL. **Topics: Relief Society; Zina D. H. Jacobs Young**
35. Derr, Cannon, and Beecher, *Women of Covenant,* 128; Madsen, *Emmeline B. Wells,* 264–65; Wells, Diary, volume 12, Jan. 19 and Mar. 24, 1889.
36. Wells, Diary, volume 11, June 12, 1888. **Topic: Emmeline B. Wells**
37. An Act to Amend an Act Entitled "An Act to Amend Section Fifty-Three Hundred and Fifty-Two . . ." [Mar. 3, 1887], *Statutes at Large* [1887], 49th Cong., 2nd Sess., chapter 397, 639; Wells, Diary, volume 12, Jan. 3, 1889; Derr, Cannon, and Beecher, *Women of Covenant,* 138–39; Nuttall, Diary, Jan. 2 and 4, 1889. **Topic: Women's Suffrage**
38. Derr, Cannon, and Beecher, *Women of Covenant,* 138; "Woman Suffrage Meeting," *Woman's Exponent,* May 1, 1889, 17:182; see also Bohman, "Fresh Perspective," 207–9; and Madsen, "Schism in the Sisterhood," 247.
39. Franklin D. Richards to Wilford Woodruff, Oct. 31, 1888, First Presidency General Authorities Correspondence, CHL; "Mutual Improvement Conference," *Deseret News,* Oct. 13, 1880, [13].
40. Zina D. H. Young, Discourse, Apr. 6, 1889, in Derr and others, *First Fifty Years of Relief Society,* 564–69; "First General Conference of the Relief Society," *Woman's Exponent,* Apr. 15, 1889, 17:172–73; Sonne, *Saints on the Seas,* xi; Madsen, *I Walked to Zion,* vii; Plewe, *Mapping Mormonism,* 104. First sentence of quotation edited for clarity; "chords" in original changed to "cords." **Topic: Emigration**
41. Nuttall, Diary, Feb. 19–20 and Apr. 5, 1889; Doctrine and Covenants 121:41–42; see also Walker, "Grant's Watershed," 219. **Topic: Wilford Woodruff**
42. Nuttall, Diary, Apr. 5, 1889; Grant, Journal, Apr. 5, 1889. Final Wilford Woodruff quotation edited for clarity; word "more" added.
43. "The General Conference," *Deseret Evening News,* Apr. 9, 1889, [2]; Woodruff, Journal, Apr. 5, 1889. **Topic: Succession of Church Leadership**
44. "Discourse," *Deseret Weekly,* Apr. 20, 1889, 513–14. Final sentence of quotation edited for clarity; two instances of "ensample" in original changed to "example."

CHAPTER 38: MINE OWN DUE TIME AND WAY

1. Joseph H. Dean to Wilford Woodruff, George Q. Cannon, and Joseph F. Smith, Feb. 10, 1889; Joseph H. Dean to Wilford Woodruff and George Q. Cannon, Aug. 7, 1888; Joseph H. Dean to Wilford Woodruff, Oct. 30, 1888, First Presidency,

Mission Administration Correspondence, CHL; see also Gilson, *Samoa,* 393–94. **Topics: Samoa; American Samoa**

2. Joseph H. Dean to Wilford Woodruff and George Q. Cannon, Aug. 7, 1888; Joseph H. Dean to Wilford Woodruff, Oct. 30, 1888; Joseph H. Dean to Wilford Woodruff, George Q. Cannon, and Joseph F. Smith, Feb. 10, 1889, First Presidency, Mission Administration Correspondence, CHL; see also, for example, Florence Dean, Journal, Nov. 9 and 30, 1888; Dec. 7 and 14, 1888.

3. Joseph H. Dean to Wilford Woodruff, George Q. Cannon, and Joseph F. Smith, Feb. 10, 1889, First Presidency, Mission Administration Correspondence, CHL; see also Joseph H. Dean, Journal, Feb. 19 and Mar. 13–14, 1889.

4. Joseph H. Dean, Journal, Mar. 12 and 14, 1889; Beesley, Journal, Mar. 12, 1889; "Elders from Zion Who Have Labored in the Samoan Mission," in Samoa Mission Manuscript History and Historical Reports, CHL; Wood, "Notable Incidents of Missionary Life," 633.

5. Joseph H. Dean, Journal, Mar. 11–12, 1889; Wood, Journal, Mar. 11–12, 1889; Beesley, Journal, Mar. 11–12, 1889; see also Joseph H. Dean, Journal, Mar. 14 and 21, 1889.

6. "Life Sketch of Lorena Eugenia Washburn Larsen," 1, 108, 128, 139, 149, 146 [second numbering], 149 [second numbering]; "Liberated," *Deseret Evening News,* Sept. 18, 1888, [3]; "Local Briefs," *Salt Lake Daily Herald,* Sept. 19, 1888, 8.

7. "Life Sketch of Lorena Eugenia Washburn Larsen," 151 [second numbering]–156.

8. "Life Sketch of Lorena Eugenia Washburn Larsen," 158, 166.

9. "Life Sketch of Lorena Eugenia Washburn Larsen," 139, 151, 161–62, 168.

10. "Life Sketch of Lorena Eugenia Washburn Larsen," 164–65.

11. Joseph H. Dean, Journal, Mar. 14, 1889; see also "Dissatisfaction in Apia," *Deseret Evening News,* Aug. 4, 1890, [3]. Quotation edited for readability; "was" in original changed to "is."

12. Joseph H. Dean, Journal, Mar. 15, 1889; Wood, Journal, Mar. 13, 1889; see also Britsch, "Founding of the Samoan Mission," 21.

13. Joseph H. Dean, Journal, Mar. 12, 14, and 21, 1889; Beesley, Journal, Mar. 12, 1889.

14. Joseph H. Dean, Journal, Mar. 14–17, 1889; Wood, Journal, Mar. 15–17, 1889; Beesley, Journal, Mar. 15–16, 1889.

15. "President Edward James Wood," *Cardston News,* Oct. 27, 1936, [5]; Joseph H. Dean, Journal, Mar. 16, 1889; Beesley, Journal, Mar. 17, 1889; Wood, Journal, Mar. 18, 1889.

16. Wood, Journal, Mar. 16–17, 1889; Joseph H. Dean, Journal, Mar. 17, 1889; Beesley, Journal, Mar. 17, 1889; Wood, "Notable Incidents of Missionary Life," 633.

17. Wood, "Notable Incidents of Missionary Life," 633; Joseph H. Dean, Journal, Mar. 21, 1889, and Jan. 3, 1890; Beesley, Journal, Mar. 21, 1889; Wood, Journal, Mar. 21, 1889.

18. Joseph H. Dean, Journal, Mar. 22–25, 1889; Wood, Journal, Mar. 23 and 25, 1889; Beesley, Journal, Mar. 23, 1889.

19. "Life Sketch of Lorena Eugenia Washburn Larsen," 167; see also Flower, "Mormon Colonization of the San Luis Valley," 90–94.

20. "Life Sketch of Lorena Eugenia Washburn Larsen," 167–201.

21. Firmage and Mangrum, *Zion in the Courts,* 231–33, 243–44, 257; Groberg, "Mormon Disfranchisements of 1882 to 1892," 400–404; "The Church Suit," *Deseret Weekly,* Jan. 26, 1889, 154–60; Wells, "Idaho Anti-Mormon Test Oath," 235.

22. See "Life Sketch of Lorena Eugenia Washburn Larsen," 213–15.

23. Wilford Woodruff, George Q. Cannon, and Joseph F. Smith to Charles W. Penrose, Nov. 27, 1887, First Presidency, Political Letterpress Copybook, CHL; George Q. Cannon, Journal, Nov. 2 and 22, 1887; Apr. 9, 1888; Woodruff, Journal, Mar. 13, 1889; Franklin D. Richards, Journal, Mar. 13, 1889; Clark, *Messages of the First Presidency,* 169; Alexander, *Things in Heaven and Earth,* 248, 254. **Topic: Antipolygamy Legislation**

24. See "Plural Marriages and Families in Early Utah," and "The Manifesto and the End of Plural Marriage," Gospel Topics, topics.ChurchofJesusChrist.org.

25. George Q. Cannon, Journal, Sept. 9, 1889.

26. *Young Woman's Journal* 1, no. 1 (Oct. 1889); "Y.L.M.I.A. Conference," *Deseret Weekly,* June 29, 1889, 22; "Local and Other Briefs," *Salt Lake Herald,* Aug. 16, 1889, 8; "Prospectus of the Young Woman's Journal," *Salt Lake Herald,* Aug. 18, 1889, 5; "Prospectus of the 'Young Woman's Journal,'" *Utah Enquirer,* Aug. 30, 1889, [2]; "The Young Woman's Journal," *Woman's Exponent,* Sept. 1, 1889, 18:55. **Topic: Susa Young Gates**

27. Zina E. Crocheron to Susa Young Gates, July 10, 1889; Josephine Spencer to Susa Young Gates, Aug. 19, 1889; M. A. Y. Greenhalgh to Susa Young Gates, Aug. 22, 1889, Young Woman's Journal Files, Susa Young Gates, Papers, CHL; Emily H. Woodmansee to Susa Young Gates, July 16, 1889; Sarah E. Russell to Susa Young Gates, Aug. 16, 1889, General Correspondence, Susa Young Gates, Papers, CHL; "Woman's Exponent," *Woman's Exponent,* June 1, 1872, 1:[8]; "Salutatory," 3; Wells, "Salutation," 12. **Topic: Church Periodicals**

28. Arrington, *Great Basin Kingdom,* 112–30, 254; "Home Literature," 299–301. Final sentence of quotation edited for readability; "that shall" in original changed to "which shall."

29. *Young Woman's Journal,* Oct. 1889, 1:1, 9–12, 19, 22, 29–31.

30. [Gates], "Editor's Department," 32.

31. "Naturalization of 'Mormons,'" *Deseret Evening News,* Nov. 30, 1889, [2]; "More Endowment Scare," *Semi-weekly Standard,* Nov. 20, 1889, [3]; Flake, *Politics of American Religious Identity,* 82.

32. George Q. Cannon, Journal, Nov. 21, 1889.

33. Woodruff, Journal, Nov. 24, 1889; Nuttall, Diary, Nov. 23–24, 1889.

34. Woodruff, Journal, Nov. 24, 1889.

35. George Q. Cannon, Journal, Nov. 25, 1889; Woodruff, Journal, Nov. 24, 1889.

CHAPTER 39: IN THE HANDS OF GOD

1. Nuttall, Diary, Dec. 14, 1889; George Q. Cannon, Journal, Dec. 5, 6, and 12, 1889; see also George Q. Cannon, Journal, Oct. 7, 1889; *History of Sanpete and Emery Counties,* 326; "Official Declaration," *Deseret Weekly,* Dec. 21, 1889, 809–10; and "Judge Anderson's Decision," and "Naturalization of 'Mormons,'" *Deseret Evening News,* Nov. 30, 1889, [2].

2. Sjodahl, "Anthon H. Lund," 707, 709–11; Lund, "Ministry of Anthon H. Lund," 84, 87.

3. Nuttall, Diary, Dec. 14, 1889; Lund, "Ministry of Anthon H. Lund," 84, 85–87, 96; George Q. Cannon, Journal, Oct. 6, 1889; F. W. Otterstrom, "Report of Funeral Services for President Anthon H. Lund," *Deseret News,* Mar. 12, 1921, section 4, vi; Sjodahl, "Anthon H. Lund," 706, 708, 711.

4. George Q. Cannon, Journal, Oct. 7, 1889.

5. "Official Declaration," *Deseret Weekly,* Dec. 21, 1889, 809–10; Joseph F. Smith, Journal, Dec. 14, 1889; see also Nuttall, Diary, Dec. 14, 1889.

6. Jane Manning James to Joseph F. Smith, Feb. 7, 1890, Joseph F. Smith, Papers, CHL; Jane Manning James to John Taylor, Dec. 27, 1884, First Presidency (John Taylor) Correspondence, CHL. **Topic: Jane Elizabeth Manning James**

7. Newell, *Your Sister in the Gospel,* 70, 72–73, 94–97, 107, 109; see also Jane Manning James to Joseph F. Smith, Feb. 7, 1890, Joseph F. Smith, Papers, CHL.

8. Jane Manning James to John Taylor, Dec. 27, 1884, First Presidency (John Taylor) Correspondence, CHL; Jane Manning James to Joseph F. Smith, Feb. 7, 1890, Joseph F. Smith, Papers, CHL; see also James, Autobiography, [3]–[4]; and Newell, *Your Sister in the Gospel,* 48–50, 113–14. **Topic: Sealing**

9. Newell, *Your Sister in the Gospel,* 105–6; "Race and the Priesthood," Gospel Topics, topics.ChurchofJesusChrist.org; "Able, Elijah," Biographical Entry, Century

of Black Mormons website, exhibits.lib.utah.edu/s/century-of-black-mormons.
Topics: Priesthood and Temple Restriction; Elijah Able

10. Jane Manning James to John Taylor, Dec. 27, 1884, First Presidency (John Taylor) Correspondence, CHL.

11. Angus M. Cannon to Jane Manning James, June 16, 1888, Angus M. Cannon Collection, CHL; Newell, *Your Sister in the Gospel,* 106–7.

12. Jane Manning James to Joseph F. Smith, Feb. 7, 1890, Joseph F. Smith, Papers, CHL.

13. Jane Manning James to Joseph F. Smith, Apr. 12, 1890, Joseph F. Smith, Papers, CHL; Eighth Ward, Relief Society Minutes and Records, volume 5, Nov. 5, 1885, 17; Aug. 7, 1890, 99; Nov. 6, 1890, 103; Newell, *Your Sister in the Gospel,* 141. Jane James quotation edited for readability; original source has "Sister Jane James, knew that this was the work of God, felt to rejoice that she was a member with us, had never seen a time when she felt like backing out."

14. Emily Wells Grant to Heber J. Grant, Apr. 27, 1890, Heber J. Grant Collection, CHL; Grant, Journal, Apr. 25–26, 1890; John Henry Smith, Diary, Apr. 24–27, 1890; see also Boyle, "Appreciation," 672.

15. Grant, Journal, Apr. 24–26, 1890; Emily Wells Grant to Heber J. Grant, Jan. 10, 1886; Apr. 27, 1890; Aug. 11, 1890, Heber J. Grant Collection, CHL; Heber J. Grant to Melvin Wells, Apr. 22, 1936, in Grant, Journal, Apr. 22, 1936; Heber J. Grant, Memo, Nov. 15, 1881; Heber J. Grant to Grace Grant Evans, Nov. 5, 1941, Heber J. Grant, Letterpress Copybook, volume 80, 464–65, Heber J. Grant Collection, CHL; Joseph F. Smith, Journal, May 26–27, 1884; Walker, "Mormon 'Widow' in Colorado," 176–78.

16. Walker, "Mormon 'Widow' in Colorado," 178–79; George Q. Cannon, Journal, Aug. 19 and 24, 1890; Grant, Journal, Dec. 4, 1889; Emily Wells Grant to Heber J. Grant, Dec. 7, 1889; Dec. 11, 1889; Dec. 16, 1889; Mar. 9, 1890; June 24, 1890; Oct. 13, 1890, Heber J. Grant Collection, CHL.

17. Emily Wells Grant to Heber J. Grant, Dec. 27, 1889, Heber J. Grant Collection, CHL.

18. Emily Wells Grant to Heber J. Grant, May 9, 1890, Heber J. Grant Collection, CHL.

19. Emily Wells Grant to Heber J. Grant, July 11, 1890, Heber J. Grant Collection, CHL.

20. George Q. Cannon, Journal, May 19, 1890; "The Church Suits," *Salt Lake Herald,* May 20, 1890, 1; see also Alexander, "Odyssey of a Latter-day Prophet" [2010], 299–302. **Topic: Antipolygamy Legislation**

21. Emily Wells Grant to Heber J. Grant, July 27, 1890, Heber J. Grant Collection, CHL; George Q. Cannon, Journal, Aug. 17, 18, and 24, 1890.

22. Emily Wells Grant to Heber J. Grant, Aug. 19 and 31, 1890, Heber J. Grant Collection, CHL; see also George Q. Cannon, Journal, Aug. 20, 1890. Last sentence of quotation edited for clarity; word "place" added.

23. Joseph F. Smith, Journal, Aug. 20–28, 1890; Andrew Jenson, "Utah Hawaiian Colony," *Deseret Evening News,* May 19, 1893, 6. **Topic: Hawaii**

24. Andrew Jenson, "Utah Hawaiian Colony," *Deseret Evening News,* May 19, 1893, 6; Kester, *Remembering Iosepa,* 76–78, 82, 84, 97–98, 105–7; Joseph F. Smith, Journal, May 24, 1889; June 21, 1889; July 21, 1889.

25. See Andrew Jenson, "Utah Hawaiian Colony," *Deseret Evening News,* May 19, 1893, 6; Kester, *Remembering Iosepa,* 1079; Albert F. Philips, "Know Utah," *Salt Lake Telegram,* Dec. 20, 1928, 6; Jackson and Jackson, "Iosepa," 323; and George Q. Cannon, Journal, Aug. 27, 1890.

26. Joseph F. Smith, Journal, Aug. 27–28, 1890; George Q. Cannon, Journal, Aug. 26–28, 1890. An alternative spelling for Kauleinamoku is Kaulainamoku.

27. Alexander, "Odyssey of a Latter-day Prophet" [1991], 201–3; McCormick and Sillito, "Henry W. Lawrence," 220–29; "The End Is Not Yet," *Salt Lake Herald,* Nov. 22, 1889, 5; An Act to Amend an Act Entitled "An Act to Amend Section Fifty-Three Hundred and Fifty-Two . . ." [Mar. 3, 1887], *Statutes at Large* [1887], 49th Cong., 2nd Sess., chapter 397, 637; Abraham H. Cannon, Diary, Sept. 1, 1890; George Q. Cannon, Journal, Sept. 1–21, 1890; Woodruff, Journal, Sept. 2–21, 1890; "Locked Horns Again," *Salt Lake Herald,* Sept. 3, 1890, 5.

28. George Q. Cannon, Journal, Sept. 22, 1890; *Report of the Utah Commission,* 20–27; see also An Act to Amend Section Fifty-Three Hundred and Fifty-Two of the Revised Statutes of the United States, in Reference to Bigamy, and for Other Purposes [Mar. 22, 1882], *Statutes at Large* [1883], 47th Cong., 1st Sess., chapter 47, 30, section 9.

29. George Q. Cannon, Journal, June 30, 1890; Abraham H. Cannon, Diary, July 10, 1890; Joseph F. Smith to Charles W. Nibley, July 18, 1890, Letterpress Copybooks, Joseph F. Smith, Papers, CHL.

30. George Q. Cannon, Journal, Sept. 22, 1890; see also entry for Sept. 23, 1890; and Joseph F. Smith, Journal, Sept. 23, 1890. Quotation edited for readability; original source has "I remarked that perhaps no better chance had been offered to us to officially, as leaders of the Church, make public our views concerning the doctrine and the law that had been enacted."

31. "Remarks Made by President Wilford Woodruff," *Deseret Evening News,* Nov. 7, 1891, 4; Bennett, *Temples Rising,* 202–17; see also Woodruff, Journal, Sept. 24 and 25, 1890.

32. George Q. Cannon, Journal, Sept. 23–24, 1890; Joseph F. Smith, Journal, Sept. 23, 1890; Grant, Journal, Sept. 30, 1890. Last sentence of quotation edited for readability; original source has "I told him I felt it would do good." **Topics: Manifesto; Wilford Woodruff**

33. George Q. Cannon, Journal, Sept. 24, 1890; Joseph F. Smith, Journal, Sept. 24, 1890; see also Doctrine and Covenants, Official Declaration 1.

34. Joseph F. Smith, Journal, Sept. 24, 1890.

35. George Q. Cannon, Journal, Sept. 24, 1890.

36. Woodruff, Journal, Sept. 25, 1890.

CHAPTER 40: THE RIGHT THING

1. "General Conference," *Deseret Evening News,* Apr. 7, 1890, [2]; Madsen, *Defender of the Faith,* 346–56; Roberts, Diary, 38; Francis Marion Lyman, Journal, Sept. 26, 1890.

2. Roberts, Diary, 38–39; see also "Official Declaration," *Deseret Evening News,* Sept. 25, 1890, [2]. **Topic: Manifesto**

3. Roberts, Diary, 39; see also George Q. Cannon, Journal, Dec. 6, 1891.

4. Roberts, Diary, 39–41.

5. Roberts, Diary, 39–42; Abraham H. Cannon, Diary, Sept. 26, 1890; Francis Marion Lyman, Journal, Sept. 26, 1890.

6. Grant, Journal, Sept. 30, 1890; Abraham H. Cannon, Diary, Oct. 1, 1890. **Topic: Heber J. Grant**

7. "Official Declaration," *Deseret Evening News,* Nov. 25, 1890, [2]; see also Doctrine and Covenants, Official Declaration 1.

8. Grant, Journal, Sept. 30 and Oct. 1, 1890; Abraham H. Cannon, Diary, Sept. 30, 1890; Franklin D. Richards, Journal, Sept. 30, 1890. First sentence of quotation edited for readability; "would turn" in original changed to "will turn."

9. Grant, Journal, Sept. 30, 1890. First sentence of quotation edited for readability; "he was convinced" in original changed to "I am convinced."

10. Abraham H. Cannon, Diary, Sept. 30, 1890; George Q. Cannon, Journal, Oct. 16, 1882, and Apr. 4, 1884; Grant, Journal, Sept. 30, 1890; Francis Marion Lyman, Journal, Feb. 22, 1911.

11. Grant, Journal, Sept. 30, 1890; see also Francis Marion Lyman, Journal, Feb. 22, 1911.

12. Grant, Journal, Oct. 1, 1890; see also Abraham H. Cannon, Diary, Oct. 1, 1890. First sentence of quotation edited for readability; two instances of "he was" in original changed to "I am."

13. Abraham H. Cannon, Diary, Oct. 1, 1890. Final sentence of quotation edited for readability; "I gave" in original changed to "I give," and "had been done" in original changed to "has been done."

14. Grant, Journal, Oct. 1, 1890; see also Abraham H. Cannon, Diary, Oct. 1, 1890. Quotation edited for readability; original source has "There was not the least reason why such a document should not be issued. . . . President Woodruff had simply told the world what we had been doing."
15. Grant, Journal, Oct. 2, 1890. Wilford Woodruff quotation edited for readability; "There was no telling" in original changed to "There is no telling," and "he felt" in original changed to "I feel."
16. George Q. Cannon, Journal, Oct. 6, 1890; "General Conference," *Deseret Weekly,* Oct. 11, 1890, 525; see also "The Address Is Endorsed," *Salt Lake Tribune,* Oct. 7, 1890, 5.
17. George Q. Cannon, Journal, Oct. 6, 1890. **Topic: George Q. Cannon**
18. "Discourse," *Deseret Weekly,* Nov. 8, 1890, 649–50.
19. George Q. Cannon, Journal, Oct. 6, 1890; "General Conference," *Deseret Weekly,* Oct. 11, 1890, 526; Joseph H. Dean, Journal, Oct. 6, 1890; Roberts, Diary, 42; Merrill, Journal, Oct. 6, 1890; Grant, Journal, Oct. 6, 1890; Byron Allred, Journal, 131.
20. George Q. Cannon, Journal, Sept. 9, 1889, and Oct. 6, 1890; "Remarks," *Deseret Weekly,* Oct. 18, 1890, 550; see also *President Woodruff's Manifesto,* 3.
21. "Remarks," *Deseret Weekly,* Oct. 18, 1890, 550; Doctrine and Covenants 124:49.
22. "Remarks," *Deseret Weekly,* Oct. 18, 1890, 550–51.
23. "Remarks," *Deseret Evening News,* Oct. 11, 1890, [2], in "Excerpts from Three Addresses by President Wilford Woodruff regarding the Manifesto," in Doctrine and Covenants, Official Declaration 1.
24. "Plural Marriage and Families in Early Utah," Gospel Topics, topics .ChurchofJesusChrist.org. **Topic: Plural Marriage in Utah**
25. Gordon, *Mormon Question,* 275, note 16; "Just Compare the Two Cases," *Deseret Evening News,* May 18, 1883, [2]; "Contempt Case," *Salt Lake Daily Herald,* May 18, 1883, 8; "The Belle Harris Case," *Sacramento Daily Record-Union,* May 22, 1883, [2]; Joseph H. Dean, Journal, Oct. 6, 1890; Condie, Autobiography and Journal, Oct. 6, 1890; Jensen, *Little Gold Pieces,* 130; Franklin D. Richards, Journal, Oct. 6, 1890; Roberts, Diary, 42.
26. "Young, Zina Diantha Huntington Jacobs," Biographical Entry, First Fifty Years of Relief Society website, churchhistorianspress.org; Zina D. H. Young, Diary, Oct. 6, 1890. Quotation edited for clarity; original source has "To day the harts of all were tried but looked to God & Submitted."
27. Joseph H. Dean, Journal, Sept. 4 and Oct. 6, 1890.
28. Helen Mar Kimball Whitney, Diary, Oct. 7, 1890 [Utah State University]; Joseph H. Dean, Journal, Oct. 8, 1890; Hansen, Autobiography, 48–49; "Life Sketch of Lorena Eugenia Washburn Larsen," 240; Emily Wells Grant to Heber J. Grant, Oct. 13, 1890, Heber J. Grant Collection, CHL; Shipps, "Principle Revoked," 113, 117–18; Tanner, *Mormon Mother,* 114–15.
29. Zina Y. Card, Letter to the *Exponent,* Nov. 20, 1890, in Derr and others, *First Fifty Years of Relief Society,* 578.
30. [Gates], "Editor's Department," 191, 284–85.
31. Emily Wells Grant to Heber J. Grant, Oct. 13, 1890, Heber J. Grant Collection, CHL.
32. "Life Sketch of Lorena Eugenia Washburn Larsen," 212 [second numbering], 231, 233, 245, 247; *Autobiography of Lorena Eugenia Washburn Larsen,* 78.
33. "Life Sketch of Lorena Eugenia Washburn Larsen," 188, 231–40; see also Genesis 21:9–21.
34. "Life Sketch of Lorena Eugenia Washburn Larsen," 240. Quotation edited for readability; "had gone" in original changed to "have gone," and "there was nothing" in original changed to "there is nothing."
35. "Life Sketch of Lorena Eugenia Washburn Larsen," 240–41.

CHAPTER 41: SO LONG SUBMERGED

1. "R.S. Reports," *Woman's Exponent,* May 15, 1891, 19:174; Emmeline B. Wells, "A Glimpse of Washington," Mar. 1, 1891, in Derr and others, *First Fifty Years of Relief Society,* 579–88; Wells, Diary, volume 14, Jan. 23–25, 1891; see also Avery, *Transactions of the National Council of Women of the United States,* 5–8, 258.

2. "Woman Suffrage Meeting," *Woman's Exponent,* May 1, 1889, 17:182; Ryan, "Latter-day Saints in the National Council of Women," 132–35. **Topic: Relief Society**

3. Wells, Diary, volume 14, Jan. 19–23, 1891; Ryan, "Latter-day Saints in the National Council of Women," 134–35; Avery, *Transactions of the National Council of Women of the United States,* 256–60.

4. Emmeline B. Wells, "A Glimpse of Washington," Mar. 1, 1891, in Derr and others, *First Fifty Years of Relief Society,* 579–81; Robbins, *History and Minutes of the National Council of Women of the United States,* 25–26; Ryan, "Latter-day Saints in the National Council of Women," 131–32. **Topic: Women's Suffrage**

5. Thomas, "Report of the Y. L. M. I. Delegate to the Woman's National Council at Washington, D. C.," 381–82; Emmeline B. Wells, "A Glimpse of Washington," Mar. 1, 1891, in Derr and others, *First Fifty Years of Relief Society,* 579–88; Wells, Diary, volume 14, Feb. 21, 1891.

6. Avery, *Transactions of the National Council of Women of the United States,* 258.

7. "R.S. Reports," *Woman's Exponent,* May 15, 1891, 19:174.

8. Emily Wells Grant to Heber J. Grant, Feb. 11, 1891; Mar. 18, 1891, Heber J. Grant Collection, CHL.

9. George Q. Cannon, Journal, Dec. 2, 1890, and Feb. 13, 1891; Abraham H. Cannon, Diary, Mar. 8–9 and 11, 1892; Joseph F. Smith, Journal, Dec. 5, 1890; "First District Court," *Deseret Evening News,* Jan. 7, 1891, [3]; "Will Obey the Law," *Salt Lake Herald,* Feb. 18, 1891, 8; "U. S. Supreme Court," *Deseret Evening News,* Jan. 20, 1891, 1; Evans, "Judicial Prosecution of Prisoners for LDS Plural Marriage," 73, 117–32; "The Manifesto and the End of Plural Marriage," Gospel Topics, topics .ChurchofJesusChrist.org.

10. Emily Wells Grant to Heber J. Grant, Oct. 27, 1890; Mar. 18, 1891, Heber J. Grant Collection, CHL.

11. Emily Wells Grant to Heber J. Grant, Mar. 18, 1891; Mar. 20, 1891; Apr. 5, 1891, Heber J. Grant Collection, CHL.

12. Boyle, "Appreciation," 672; Emily Wells Grant to Heber J. Grant, Mar. 20, 1891, Heber J. Grant Collection, CHL; see also Walker, "Mormon 'Widow' in Colorado," 189–90.

13. Emily Wells Grant to Heber J. Grant, Apr. 5, 1891; May 7, 1891; May 27, 1891; June 6, [1892], Heber J. Grant Collection, CHL; Grant, Journal, June 18, 1889, and May 29–31, 1891.

14. Emily Wells Grant to Heber J. Grant, undated fragment [circa 1887]; Mar. 20, 1891, Heber J. Grant Collection, CHL; Boyle, "Appreciation," 672; "The Manifesto and the End of Plural Marriage," Gospel Topics, topics.ChurchofJesusChrist.org. Dessie may have known before her birthday that Uncle Eli was her father. (Emily Wells Grant to Heber J. Grant, Jan. 23, 1891, Heber J. Grant Collection, CHL.)

15. Cannon, Autobiography, 10–11; Emily Wells Grant to Heber J. Grant, Mar. 18, 1891, Heber J. Grant Collection, CHL.

16. Emily Wells Grant to Heber J. Grant, May 5, 1891; Nov. 1, 1891; June 6, 1892, Heber J. Grant Collection, CHL. Quotation edited for clarity; "and pray" in original changed to "and I pray."

17. Widtsoe, *In the Gospel Net,* 94; Widtsoe, *In a Sunlit Land,* 26; "Commencement Day," *Logan Journal,* May 20, 1891, 8.

18. Widtsoe, *In a Sunlit Land,* 21–22, 24–25; "Church Schools," *Daily Enquirer,* Jan. 17, 1891, [4]; Ward, *A Life Divided,* 22–29; Tanner, "Grammar Department. Historical

Work," 339–40; Richards, "Educational Legacy of Karl G. Maeser," 27. **Topic: Church Academies**

19. Widtsoe, *In a Sunlit Land,* 26–27; Widtsoe, *In the Gospel Net,* 94–95; Simpson, *American Universities and the Birth of Modern Mormonism,* 41–42.

20. Widtsoe, *In a Sunlit Land,* 26–27; Widtsoe, *In the Gospel Net,* 94–95; "Widtsoe, Anna Karine Gaarden," in Jenson, *Latter-day Saint Biographical Encyclopedia,* 3:735; Anna Gaarden Widtsoe to John A. Widtsoe, June 24, 1891, Anna K. Gaarden Widtsoe Papers, Widtsoe Family Papers, CHL.

21. Joseph F. Smith, Journal, Nov. 7, 9, 14, 18, 23, and 30, 1890; Dec. 6, 14, 21, 28, and 31, 1890; Abraham H. Cannon, Diary, June 4, 1891; Stephen L. Richards, in *Eighty-Ninth Annual Conference,* 56; see also Joseph F. Smith to Mercy Fielding Thompson, July 21, 1891, Letterpress Copybooks, 65–70, Joseph F. Smith, Papers, CHL; and "The Manifesto and the End of Plural Marriage," Gospel Topics, topics.ChurchofJesusChrist.org. **Topic: Joseph F. Smith**

22. Joseph F. Smith to Mercy Fielding Thompson, Nov. 18, 1890, Letterpress Copybooks, 313–14, Joseph F. Smith, Papers, CHL.

23. Joseph F. Smith to Benjamin Harrison, June 22, 1891, Joseph F. Smith, Papers, CHL; Joseph F. Smith, Journal, Dec. 5, 1890.

24. Abraham H. Cannon, Diary, Oct. 7, 1890; George Q. Cannon, Journal, Oct. 7, 1890.

25. Wilford Woodruff and Joseph F. Smith to H. S. Palmer, May 10, 1890; Joseph F. Smith to J. E. D. Zundell, Dec. 21, 1891, Letterpress Copybooks, 86–87, 210–11, Joseph F. Smith, Papers, CHL; Grant, Journal, Oct. 7, 1891; Merrill, Journal, Oct. 25, 1891; Shipps, "Principle Revoked," 113–24; "The Manifesto and the End of Plural Marriage," Gospel Topics, topics.ChurchofJesusChrist.org.

26. Joseph F. Smith, Journal, Sept. 7, 1891; Joseph F. Smith to Charles W. Nibley, Sept. 14, 1891, Letterpress Copybooks, 132–33, Joseph F. Smith, Papers, CHL; George Q. Cannon, Journal, Sept. 2, 1891.

27. Joseph F. Smith, Journal, Sept. 21 and 29, 1891; Oct. 8, 1891; Benjamin Harrison to Joseph F. Smith, Sept. 10, 1891, Joseph F. Smith, Papers, CHL; Joseph F. Smith to George F. Richards, Sept. 22, 1891; Joseph F. Smith to Harvey Cluff, Sept. 22, 1891, Letterpress Copybooks, 143–46, Joseph F. Smith, Papers, CHL; Holzapfel and Shupe, *Joseph F. Smith,* 36–40, 44, 47–56, 64–67; see also Joseph F. Smith, Journal, Sept. 18–Oct. 13, 1891; and Wilford Woodruff and Joseph F. Smith to H. S. Palmer, May 10, 1890, Letterpress Copybooks, 86–87, Joseph F. Smith, Papers, CHL.

28. "Sunday Services," *Deseret Evening News,* Sept. 28, 1891, 5. First two sentences of quotation edited for readability; original source has "It had been something over seven years since he last had the privilege of standing before a congregation of the people in that Tabernacle. . . . He thanked God the Eternal Father that he had had this testimony put into his heart and soul, for it gave him light, hope, joy and consolation that no man could give or take away."

29. Abraham H. Cannon, Diary, Oct. 7, 1891; Grant, Journal, Oct. 7, 1891; Merrill, Journal, Oct. 7, 1891; George Q. Cannon, Journal, July 21 and Oct. 7, 1891; "The Temple," *Salt Lake Herald,* Oct. 4, 1891, 23; "The Last Tile," *Deseret Evening News,* Aug. 15, 1889, [3]; Cyrus E. Dallin to Gaylen S. Young, July 30, 1938, CHL; Horne, "Cyrus Edwin Dallin," 491–97. **Topic: Salt Lake Temple**

30. Francis Marion Lyman, Journal, Aug. 20, 1891; "The Church Personal Property," *Deseret Evening News,* Oct. 19, 1891, 4. **Topic: Antipolygamy Legislation**

31. George Q. Cannon, Journal, Aug. 6, 1891; Abraham H. Cannon, Diary, Aug. 20, 1891; Francis Marion Lyman, Journal, Aug. 20, 1891; "The Church Personal Property," *Deseret Evening News,* Oct. 19, 1891, 4; see also Alexander, *Things in Heaven and Earth,* 271.

32. Woodruff, Journal, Oct. 12, 1891; George Q. Cannon, Journal, July 13, 1891; Oct. 2, 7, 12, and 17, 1891; Abraham H. Cannon, Diary, Oct. 7 and 12, 1891; Francis Marion Lyman, Journal, Aug. 23 and Oct. 12, 1891; see also Alexander, *Things in Heaven and Earth,* 271–72.

33. Woodruff, Journal, Oct. 19, 1891; "The Church Cases," *Deseret Evening News,* Oct. 19, 1891, 4; George Q. Cannon, Journal, Oct. 19, 1891; see also Lyman, "Political Background of the Woodruff Manifesto," 31.

34. "Taking of Testimony," *Deseret Evening News,* Oct. 20, 1891, 4–5; see also "The Escheated Property," *Salt Lake Tribune,* Oct. 20, 1891, 6; George Q. Cannon, Journal, Nov. 12, 1891; and Abraham H. Cannon, Diary, Apr. 1, 1892.

35. "The Escheated Property," *Salt Lake Tribune,* Oct. 20, 1891, 6; see also "Taking of Testimony," *Deseret Evening News,* Oct. 20, 1891, 5. **Topic: Manifesto**

36. "Taking of Testimony," *Deseret Evening News,* Oct. 20, 1891, 5; "The Escheated Property," *Salt Lake Tribune,* Oct. 20, 1891, 6. First sentence of quotation edited for clarity; "declare this to your church" in original changed to "declare this Manifesto to your church."

37. "Taking of Testimony," *Deseret Evening News,* Oct. 20, 1891, 4–5; "The Escheated Property," *Salt Lake Tribune,* Oct. 20, 1891, 5–6; "Whose Is It?," *Salt Lake Herald,* Oct. 20, 1891, 6.

38. George Q. Cannon, Journal, Oct. 21, 1891; Woodruff, Journal, Oct. 25, 1891; "Remarks," *Deseret Evening News,* Nov. 7, 1891, 4.

39. Charles L. Walker, Journal, Oct. 20, 1891.

40. George Q. Cannon, Journal, Oct. 21, 1891; "Remarks," *Deseret Evening News,* Nov. 7, 1891, 4; Abraham H. Cannon, Diary, Nov. 12, 1891.

41. Merrill, Journal, Nov. 1, 1891; Alexander, "Odyssey of a Latter-day Prophet" [2011], 63–64, 73–74; see also "General Conference," *Deseret Weekly,* Apr. 11, 1891, [27].

42. George Q. Cannon, Journal, Oct. 21, 1891; "Remarks," *Deseret Weekly,* Nov. 14, 1891, 659–60, in "Excerpts from Three Addresses by President Wilford Woodruff regarding the Manifesto," in Doctrine and Covenants, Official Declaration 1; see also "Quarterly Conference," *Logan Journal,* Nov. 4, 1891, 1. First sentence of quotation edited for clarity; "If we had not stopped it" in original changed to "If we did not stop this practice."

Chapter 42: Inspiration at the Divine Fountain

1. Wells, Diary, volume 15, Jan. 5 and 8, 1892. **Topic: Relief Society**

2. Zina D. H. Young, Jane S. Richards, and Bathsheba W. Smith, "Letter of Greeting," Jan. 21, 1892, Relief Society Historical Files, CHL; see also Derr and others, *First Fifty Years of Relief Society,* 590.

3. Wells, Diary, volume 15, Mar. 2–4, 1892.

4. Report of Relief Society Jubilee, Mar. 17, 1892, in Derr and others, *First Fifty Years of Relief Society,* 591; Wells, Diary, volume 15, Mar. 7, 1892.

5. Wells, Diary, volume 15, Mar. 15, 1892. Quotation edited for readability; "opposed" in original changed to "opposes." **Topic: Emma Hale Smith**

6. Wells, Diary, volume 15, Mar. 14 and 17, 1892; Report of Relief Society Jubilee, Mar. 17, 1892; Nauvoo Relief Society Minute Book, Apr. 28, 1842, in Derr and others, *First Fifty Years of Relief Society,* 591, 59; *Saints,* volume 1, chapter 37.

7. Wells, Diary, volume 15, Mar. 17, 1892; Abraham H. Cannon, Diary, Mar. 17, 1892; Report of Relief Society Jubilee, Mar. 17, 1892, in Derr and others, *First Fifty Years of Relief Society,* 591.

8. Report of Relief Society Jubilee, Mar. 17, 1892, in Derr and others, *First Fifty Years of Relief Society,* 592–93, 610; Wells, Diary, volume 15, Mar. 17, 1892. Last sentence of quotation edited for readability; "has drank" in original changed to "has drunk." Emmeline Wells's address was read by apostle Abraham H. Cannon.

9. "Mormons at Harvard," *Provo Daily Enquirer,* Mar. 14, 1892, [2]; "President Eliot's Address," *Deseret Evening News,* Mar. 17, 1892, 5; "President Eliot's Visit," *Salt Lake Tribune,* Mar. 17, 1892, 5.

10. "President Eliot Replies," *Deseret Evening News,* Mar. 26, 1892, 8; "Soft Word to Mormons," *New York Sun,* Mar. 25, 1892, [1]; "President Eliot's Visit," *Deseret Evening News,* Mar. 29, 1892, 5; see also "Eliot's Status," *Salt Lake Tribune,* Mar. 18, 1892, 4.

11. Anna Widtsoe to John A. Widtsoe, Mar. 24, 1892; Osborne Widtsoe to John A. Widtsoe, Apr. 10, 1892, Widtsoe Family Papers, CHL; see also Widtsoe, *In a Sunlit Land,* 34.

12. Osborne Widtsoe to John A. Widtsoe, Nov. 1, 1891; Jan. 17, 1892; Apr. 24, 1892; May 8, 1892; June 7, 1892, Widtsoe Family Papers, CHL. **Topic: Church Academies**

13. Joseph H. Dean, Journal, Apr. 3, 1892; Woodruff, Journal, Apr. 6 and 11, 1892; George Q. Cannon, Journal, Apr. 6, 1892; "Temple Capstone," *Salt Lake Herald,* Apr. 7, 1892, 6; "The Temple," *Sunday Herald* (Salt Lake City), Apr. 3, 1892, 3; John Nicholson, "At the Tabernacle," *Deseret Evening News,* Apr. 6, 1892, 4, 8; Francis Marion Lyman, Journal, Apr. 6, 1892; Talmage, Journal, Apr. 6, 1892; Osborne Widtsoe to John A. Widtsoe, Apr. 10, 1892, Widtsoe Family Papers, CHL. **Topics: Angel Moroni; Salt Lake Temple**

14. "Temple Capstone," *Salt Lake Herald,* Apr. 7, 1892, 6; John Nicholson, "At the Tabernacle," *Deseret Evening News,* Apr. 6, 1892, 4, 8.

15. John Nicholson, "At the Tabernacle," *Deseret Evening News,* Apr. 6, 1892, 8; Osborne Widtsoe to John A. Widtsoe, Apr. 10, 1892, Widtsoe Family Papers, CHL.

16. John Nicholson, "At the Tabernacle," *Deseret Evening News,* Apr. 6, 1892, 8; Talmage, Journal, Apr. 6, 1892; Joseph H. Dean, Journal, Apr. 6, 1892; "Temple Capstone," *Salt Lake Herald,* Apr. 7, 1892, 6.

17. John Nicholson, "At the Tabernacle," *Deseret Evening News,* Apr. 6, 1892, 8; Francis Marion Lyman, Journal, Apr. 6, 1892; Joseph H. Dean, Journal, Apr. 6, 1892; George Q. Cannon, Journal, Apr. 6, 1892; "Temple Capstone," *Salt Lake Herald,* Apr. 7, 1892, 6; see also Osborne Widtsoe to John A. Widtsoe, Apr. 10, 1892, Widtsoe Family Papers, CHL.

18. Francis Marion Lyman, Journal, Apr. 6, 1892; Osborne Widtsoe to John A. Widtsoe, Apr. 10, 1892; May 8, 1892, Widtsoe Family Papers, CHL.

19. Brown, *Life of a Pioneer,* 129, 168, 204–13, 223–37, 267–70, 480. **Topic: French Polynesia**

20. Britsch, *Unto the Islands of the Sea,* 16–23, 431; Damron, Diary, Nov. 29, 1891, 6; Jan. 28, 1892, 60; Seegmiller, Journal, Nov. 29, 1891, and Jan. 27, 1892.

21. Abraham H. Cannon, Diary, Mar. 31, 1892; Damron, Diary, Feb. 8 and 11, 1892, 74, 77; Joseph W. Damron and William A. Seegmiller to the First Presidency, May 12, 1892, First Presidency, Mission Administration Correspondence, CHL; Britsch, *Unto the Islands of the Sea,* 21–22.

22. Brown, Reminiscences and Journal, Mar. 30, 1892; Brown, *Life of a Pioneer,* 478. Quotations edited for readability; "asked me how I would" in original changed to "how would you," and "did not wish" in original changed to "do not wish." The question mark has also been added for clarity.

23. Brown, *Life of a Pioneer,* 438–39, 445–46, 478; Brown, Reminiscences and Journal, Mar. 30, 1892.

24. Brown, Reminiscences and Journal, Mar. 30, 1892; George Q. Cannon, Journal, Apr. 11, 1892; Brown, *Life of a Pioneer,* 478–79.

25. Brown, *Life of a Pioneer,* 478–83; Brown, Reminiscences and Journal, June 1, 1892; Damron, Diary, May 24–June 1, 1892; Seegmiller, Journal, June 1, 1892; James Brown to First Presidency, June 10, 1892, First Presidency, Mission Administration Correspondence, CHL.

26. Brown, *Life of a Pioneer,* 483–85; James Brown to First Presidency, June 10, 1892, First Presidency, Mission Administration Correspondence, CHL; Damron, Diary, June 10, 1892; Seegmiller, Journal, June 10, 1892.

27. Osborne Widtsoe to John A. Widtsoe, Apr. 24, 1892, Widtsoe Family Papers, CHL.

28. Anna Gaarden Widtsoe to John A. Widtsoe, Aug. 9, 1892, Widtsoe Family Papers, CHL.

29. Widtsoe, *In a Sunlit Land,* 28–32; John A. Widtsoe to John H. Squires, Sept. 22, 1892, John A. Widtsoe, Papers, CHL; see also Morison, *Three Centuries of Harvard,* 421–22; and McLachlan, *American Boarding Schools,* 205–6.

30. Talmage, Journal, June 29–30 and July 12–13, 1892; John A. Widtsoe to Anna Gaarden Widtsoe, July 12, 1892, Anna K. Gaarden Widtsoe Papers, Widtsoe Family Papers, CHL.

31. John A. Widtsoe to Anna Gaarden Widtsoe, July 4, 1892; Aug. 17, 1892, Anna K. Gaarden Widtsoe Papers, Widtsoe Family Papers, CHL; Susa Young Gates to Leah Dunford, July 10, 1892; Aug. 7, 1892, Widtsoe Family Papers, CHL; Widtsoe, *In a Sunlit Land,* 38.

32. *Autobiography of Lorena Eugenia Washburn Larsen,* 57, 109, 111–12.

33. *Autobiography of Lorena Eugenia Washburn Larsen,* 109–11.

34. *Autobiography of Lorena Eugenia Washburn Larsen,* 110–12.

35. *Autobiography of Lorena Eugenia Washburn Larsen,* 112. Quotation edited for readability; original source has "I told him that if I didn't believe that he thought he was doing God's service, I could never forgive him."

36. *Autobiography of Lorena Eugenia Washburn Larsen,* 112–13, 124–25; "Life Sketch of Lorena Eugenia Washburn Larsen," 254, 257; Larsen, "Memories of My Father."

37. "Bent Larson and His Plural," *Salt Lake Times,* Mar. 28, 1892, 5; United States of America v. Bent Larsen, Case No. 1381, 1892, Territorial Case Files of the U.S. District Courts of Utah, National Archives, Washington, DC; *Autobiography of Lorena Eugenia Washburn Larsen,* 110.

38. Larsen, "Story of Bent Rolfsen Larsen," 6; Larsen, "Memories of My Father"; "Provo," *Salt Lake Herald,* Sept. 23, 1892, 3; "District Court," *Provo Daily Enquirer,* Nov. 7, 1892, [4]. **Topic: Manifesto**

Chapter 43: A Greater Necessity for Union

1. Francis Marion Lyman, Journal, Aug. 20–Sept. 12, 1892; Lund, Journal, Aug. 20–Sept. 23, 1892; "Stake Conferences," *Deseret Weekly,* Sept. 24, 1892, 419; "General Conference," *Deseret Evening News,* Apr. 4, 1892, 4–5; Apr. 5, 1892, 4; Abraham H. Cannon, Diary, Jan. 12 and 24–25, 1892; Feb. 8 and 14, 1892; Mar. 21, 1892; Apr. 1, 1892; Grant, Journal, July 12, 1892; Card, Journal, Jan. 12, 1892; Charles L. Walker, Journal, Oct. 1, 1892.

2. Walker, *Wayward Saints,* 217–18; George Q. Cannon, Journal, Feb. 19, 1891; May 11, 25, 27, and 28, 1891; June 3, 11, and 29, 1891; July 1, 1891. **Topic: Political Neutrality**

3. "Quarterly Conference," *Logan Journal,* Nov. 4, 1891, 1.

4. "General Conference," *Deseret Evening News,* Apr. 5, 1892, 4. Quotation edited for readability; original source has "Every man had as much right—Prophets, Apostles, Saints and sinners—to his political convictions as he had to his religious opinions. . . . That spirit would lead them to ruin. . . . 'Don't throw filth and dirt and nonsense at one another, because of any difference on political matters.'"

5. George Q. Cannon, Journal, Jan. 10, 1877; "General Conference," *Deseret Evening News,* Apr. 5, 1892, 4; see also Lund, Journal, Sept. 11, 1892.

6. Francis Marion Lyman, Journal, Sept. 11, 1892; Lund, Journal, Sept. 11, 1892; George Q. Cannon, Journal, Feb. 25, 1891.

7. Lund, Journal, Sept. 11, 1892; Francis Marion Lyman, Journal, Sept. 11, 1892.

8. Francis Marion Lyman, Journal, Sept. 11, 1892. Quotation edited for readability; original source has "they must not allow any bitterness in their hearts one toward another."

9. Lund, Journal, Sept. 13, 1892.

10. George Q. Cannon, Journal, Sept. 7–8, 1892; see also Eugene Young, "Inside the New Mormon Temple," *Harper's Weekly,* May 27, 1893, 510; and "Angell, Truman Osborn," in Jenson, *Latter-day Saint Biographical Encyclopedia,* 4:693. **Topic: Salt Lake Temple**

11. George Q. Cannon, Journal, May 1, 1890; Sept. 8, 1892; Oct. 10, 1892; June–July 1898; Joseph F. Smith, Journal, Oct. 13, 1890; Dec. 3, 1890; Jan. 29, 1891; Sept. 2,

1891; Godfrey, *Religion, Politics, and Sugar,* 26–36; Arrington, *Beet Sugar in the West,* 11–13; see also Arrington, *Great Basin Kingdom,* 400–401.

12. George Q. Cannon, Journal, Oct. 10, 1892; see, for example, "Relief Society Report," *Woman's Exponent,* Oct. 15, 1890, 19:68; "Fast Day May First," *Woman's Exponent,* May 15, 1892, 20:164; "R. S., Y. L. M. I. A., and P. A. Reports," *Woman's Exponent,* June 1, 1892, 20:174; "Ladies Semi-monthly Meetings," *Woman's Exponent,* Aug. 1, 1892, 21:22; Cedar Fort Ward, Young Women's Mutual Improvement Association Minutes and Records, volume 1, 65; and Seventeenth Ward, General Minutes, volume 12, 45–52.

13. George Q. Cannon, Journal, Oct. 10, 1892; see also "General Conference," *Deseret News,* Apr. 13, 1887, [4]; Woodruff, Journal, Oct. 10, 1892; Abraham H. Cannon, Diary, Oct. 10, 1892; and Middleton, Notes, Oct. 10, 1892, CHL. Quotation edited for readability; original source has "There never had been a time since the Church was organized, in my opinion, when there was a greater necessity for union in the Church than now. . . . The Lord had blessed us and acknowledged our labors. . . . He had made plain to us day by day the course that we were to take." **Topic: Temple Building**

14. Joseph H. Dean, Journal, Sept. 1890–Dec. 1892, especially entries for Sept. 4, 1890; Feb. 2 and 5, 1892; Mar. 8, 1892; Nov. 5, 1892; and Dec. 31, 1892; "Joseph Henry Dean," Missionary Database, history.ChurchofJesusChrist.org/missionary.

15. Joseph H. Dean, Journal, Sept. 8, 1892; George Q. Cannon, Journal, Sept. 7, 1892; Kirkham, Journal, Sept. 9, 1892.

16. Joseph H. Dean, Journal, Aug. 1 and 4, 1892; Sept. 1 and 6, 1892; Oct. 1, 4, and 30, 1892; Nov. 5, 1892; Dec. 31, 1892.

17. Joseph H. Dean, Journal, Sept. 17, 1892; Nov. 4, 1892; Dec. 1, 3, and 31, 1892.

18. Damron, Mission Report, Dec. 4, 29, and 31, 1892; Damron, Diary, Dec. 30–31, 1892, and Jan. 2, 1893. **Topic: French Polynesia**

19. Damron, Diary, Dec. 29–31, 1892; Jan. 2 and 6, 1893; Cannon, "Tahiti and the Society Island Mission," 317; "Society Islands Mission," Tahiti Papeete Mission, Manuscript History and Historical Reports, volume 2, part 2, Dec. 31, 1892.

20. Butterworth, *Roots of the Reorganization,* 132–37, 143–47; Cannon, "Tahiti and the Society Island Mission," 285–86; "Letter from Elder T. W. Smith," *Saints' Herald,* July 23, 1887, 484; Brown, *Life of a Pioneer,* 209, 499.

21. Damron, Diary, Dec. 31, 1892–Jan. 2, 1893; Brown, *Life of a Pioneer,* 498–99; "Society Islands Mission," Tahiti Papeete Mission, Manuscript History and Historical Reports, volume 2, part 2, Dec. 31, 1892; Cannon, "Tahiti and the Society Island Mission," 285–86, 317; Damron, Mission Report, Dec. 31, 1892; see also James Brown to the First Presidency, Jan. 23, 1893, First Presidency, Mission Administration Correspondence, CHL.

22. "Society Islands Mission," Tahiti Papeete Mission, Manuscript History and Historical Reports, volume 2, part 2, Dec. 31, 1892. First sentence of quotation edited for readability; original source has "he remarked that if I was the same that had been among them before I had lost one leg, for the Iakabo that he used to know had two legs."

23. Francis Marion Lyman, Journal, Jan. 25–27, 1893; "Remarks," *Deseret Weekly,* Dec. 3, 1892, 737–38; Woodruff, Journal, Nov. 1, 1892; Christen Jensen to George Q. Cannon, Jan. 5, 1893, First Presidency, Court Case Files, CHL; "The Recent General Conference," *Deseret Evening News,* Apr. 7, 1892, 4; Albert R. Smith to Wilford Woodruff, Mar. 3, 1893, Wilford Woodruff, Stake Correspondence Files, CHL; "Discourse," *Deseret Weekly,* Mar. 25, 1893, 418; see also "Preparations for the Dedication," 235–36.

24. Lund, Journal, Jan. 26–Feb. 8, 1893, especially entries for Jan. 28, Jan. 30, and Feb. 6; Francis Marion Lyman, Journal, Jan. 26–Feb. 8, 1893, especially entry for Jan. 28; Roberts, Diary, 106–21.

25. Lund, Journal, Jan. 26–Feb. 8, 1893, especially entries for Jan. 30, Feb. 1, Feb. 3, Feb. 5, and Feb. 8; Francis Marion Lyman, Journal, Jan. 26–Feb. 8, 1893, especially entries for Jan. 30, Feb. 5, and Feb. 8; Roberts, Diary, 106–21.

26. Lund, Journal, Feb. 8, 1893; Francis Marion Lyman, Journal, Feb. 8, 1893. Quotation edited for clarity; original source has "we call upon you to exert all your energies to settle whatever difficulties may still exist and unite in urging the bishops to promptly allay all ill feeling and to unite the people in the spirit of the Gospel."
27. Lund, Journal, Feb. 8, 1893; Roberts, Diary, 119–21.
28. Roberts, Diary, 29, 36–37, 42–43.
29. Joseph H. Dean, Journal, Jan. 5, 1893; "Amnesty," *Deseret Evening News,* Jan. 5, 1893, 1.
30. George Q. Cannon, Journal, Oct. 13, 1892; Woodruff, Journal, Oct. 13, 1892; Franklin D. Richards, Journal, Oct. 13, 1892; see also "Rest at Last," *Deseret Evening News,* Oct. 25, 1892, 1.
31. Joseph H. Dean, Journal, Jan. 5, 1893; "The Proclamation's Import," *Deseret Evening News,* Jan. 6, 1893, 4; "Harrison's Amnesty Proclamation," *Salt Lake Herald,* Jan. 5, 1893, 4; "That 'Inconsequential Paper,'" *Daily Enquirer,* Jan. 6, 1893, [2].
32. Joseph H. Dean, Journal, Dec. 31, 1892, and Jan. 25, 1893; George Q. Cannon, Journal, Jan. 3 and Mar. 18, 1893.
33. Joseph H. Dean, Journal, Feb. 2 and 6, 1893; Mar. 1, 1893; Apr. 1, 1893.
34. Joseph H. Dean, Journal, Jan. [Feb.] 9 and Mar. 18, 1893; see also "Dedicated to the Lord," *Salt Lake Herald,* Apr. 7, 1893, 6.
35. Talmage, *House of the Lord,* 186–88, 267, 275; Eugene Young, "Inside the New Mormon Temple," *Harper's Weekly,* May 27, 1893, 510; George Q. Cannon, Journal, June 20, 1890, and Jan 12, 1893; Hafen, "Art Student in Paris," 485; "Local and Other Briefs," *Salt Lake Herald,* June 22, 1890, 8. **Topic: Salt Lake Temple**
36. Joseph H. Dean, Journal, Mar. 1 and 23, 1893; Apr. 1, 1893.
37. "An Address," *Deseret Evening News,* Mar. 18, 1893, 4.
38. Joseph H. Dean, Journal, Mar. 25, 1893.
39. Joseph H. Dean, Journal, Apr. 3, 1893; "Donated to the Salt Lake Temple," Mar. 31, 1893, Ancient Documents, Santa Monica Correspondence Files, Joseph F. Smith, Papers, CHL; see also George Q. Cannon, Journal, Jan. 4, 1893.
40. Leah Dunford to Susa Young Gates, Mar. 24, 1893, Susa Young Gates, Papers, CHL; see also *Isaac and Leah Bailey Dunford Family Story,* 64.
41. Leah Dunford to Susa Young Gates, Mar. 24, 1893, Susa Young Gates, Papers, CHL; Widtsoe, "Alma Bailey Dunford," 4; Susa Young to Zina Young Card, May 18, 1878, Susa Young Gates, Papers, CHL; *Isaac and Leah Bailey Dunford Family Story,* 66, 68–69, 70, 76; Dunford, Interview, 17; see also Alma B. Dunford to Leah Dunford, July 11, 1893; July 28, 1893; Sept. 11, 1893, Widtsoe Family Papers, CHL.
42. Susa Young Gates to Leah Dunford, Mar. 27, 1893, Widtsoe Family Papers, CHL; [Gates], "Editor's Department," 449; *Isaac and Leah Bailey Dunford Family Story,* 74; "Gates, Susa Young," in Jenson, *Latter-day Saint Biographical Encyclopedia,* 2:626–27; "One Family Group Genealogy," Susa Young Gates, Papers, CHL.
43. Susa Young Gates to Leah Dunford, Mar. 27, 1893, Widtsoe Family Papers, CHL; Widtsoe, Interview, 11. **Topic: Susa Young Gates**
44. Susa Young Gates to Leah Dunford, Mar. 27, 1893, Widtsoe Family Papers, CHL.

CHAPTER 44: BLESSED PEACE

1. "A Multitude Is Coming," *Salt Lake Herald,* Apr. 2, 1893, 8; Joseph H. Dean, Journal, Apr. 5, 1893; "Crowds of Visitors," *Salt Lake Herald,* Mar. 9, 1893, 8; see also "An Address," *Deseret Evening News,* Mar. 18, 1893, 4.
2. George Q. Cannon, Journal, Aug. 4, 1892; Woodruff, Journal, Mar. 14, 1893; "A Multitude Is Coming," *Salt Lake Herald,* Apr. 2, 1893, 8; "The Meetings and Attendance," *Deseret Weekly,* May 6, 1893, 614; see also Hammond, Journal, Apr. 4, 1893.

3. Joseph H. Dean, Journal, Apr. 5, 1893; George Q. Cannon, Journal, Apr. 6, 1893; Whitaker, Autobiography and Journals, 46; "Viewing the Temple," and "A Voice from the South," *Deseret Evening News,* Apr. 6, 1893, 1, 5; "The Temple Dedication," *Salt Lake Tribune,* Apr. 6, 1893, 5. **Topic: Salt Lake Temple**

4. Griggs, Journal, Apr. 6, 1893; Joseph H. Dean, Journal, Apr. 6, 1893; Anderson, "Salt Lake Temple," 286; "Angry Elements," *Deseret Evening News,* Apr. 6, 1893, 1.

5. Griggs, Journal, Apr. 6, 1893; Anderson, "Salt Lake Temple," 286, 292; Flake, Autobiography and Journal, [47]; "Angry Elements," *Deseret Evening News,* Apr. 6, 1893, 1; Joseph H. Dean, Journal, Apr. 6, 1893.

6. "A Singular Circumstance," *Deseret Evening News,* Apr. 6, 1893, 8. **Topic: Crickets and Seagulls**

7. Gates, "More than a Halo," 683; Gates, "Mrs. Susa Young Gates in Genealogy and Temple Work," 3–5; Gates, "Lucy Bigelow Young," 149f–150. **Topic: Susa Young Gates**

8. Talmage, *House of the Lord,* 198; "The Interior," *Deseret Evening News,* Apr. 5, 1893, 1; Anderson, "Salt Lake Temple," 286; Gates, "Mrs. Susa Young Gates in Genealogy and Temple Work," 3–4; Gates, "Lucy Bigelow Young," 150–51; Hammond, Journal, Apr. 6, 1893; George Q. Cannon, Journal, Apr. 6, 1893.

9. [Emmeline B. Wells], "Temple Dedication," *Woman's Exponent,* Apr. 15 and May 1, 1893, 21:156; McAllister, Journal, Apr. 6, 1893.

10. Salt Lake Temple Dedication Services, Apr. 6, 1893, 1; Woodruff, Journal, Mar. 12, 1887, and Dec. 31, 1893.

11. "Annual Conference," *Deseret Evening News,* Apr. 6, 1893, 5; see also Salt Lake Temple Dedication Services, Apr. 6, 1893, 1; Joseph H. Dean, Journal, Apr. 6, 1893; Francis Marion Lyman, Journal, Apr. 6, 1893; Hammond, Journal, Apr. 6, 1893; and Woodruff, Journal, Mar. 17–18, 1893. **Topic: Temple Dedications and Dedicatory Prayers**

12. George Q. Cannon, Journal, Apr. 6, 1893; "Annual Conference," *Deseret Evening News,* Apr. 6, 1893, 5; Salt Lake Temple Dedication Services, Apr. 6, 1893, 18.

13. [Gates], "Precious Promise," 376; "The Temple," *Deseret News,* Feb. 19, 1853, [2]; Caldwell, "Susa Young Gates," 1; Gates, "Lucy Bigelow Young," 150.

14. Salt Lake Temple Dedication Services, Apr. 6, 1893, 20.

15. Gates, "More than a Halo," 683; see also Gates, "Mrs. Susa Young Gates in Genealogy and Temple Work," 4–5.

16. See Damron, Diary, Apr. 5 and 6, 1893; Society Islands Mission, Membership Records, 256, 258; "Society Islands Mission," Tahiti Papeete Mission, Manuscript History and Historical Reports, volume 2, part 2, Apr. 6, 1893; and Brown, *Life of a Pioneer,* 503. **Topic: French Polynesia**

17. Damron, Diary, Mar. 31, 1893; Apr. 1 and 6, 1893; Society Islands Conference Report, Sept. 24, 1846, in Historian's Office, Minutes and Reports (local units), CHL; "Society Islands Mission," Tahiti Papeete Mission, Manuscript History and Historical Reports, volume 2, part 2, Apr. 6, 1893; James Brown to the First Presidency, May 9, 1893, First Presidency, Mission Administration Correspondence, CHL.

18. Society Islands Mission, Membership Records, 256–58; James Brown to the First Presidency, May 9, 1893, First Presidency, Mission Administration Correspondence, CHL.

19. Damron, Diary, Apr. 6, 1893; Brown, *Life of a Pioneer,* 503; Society Islands Mission, Membership Records, 256–58.

20. Damron, Diary, Apr. 5 and 8, 1893.

21. Cluff, Journal, Mar. 21, 24, 26, and 28, 1893; Apr. 1, 2, and 9, 1893; see also "Temple Dedication," *Deseret Evening News,* Apr. 6, 1893, 10. **Topic: Hawaii**

22. Atkin, "History of Iosepa," 24, 37, 47; "From the Hawaiian Colony," *Deseret Evening News,* July 13, 1892, 8; Panek, "Life at Iosepa," 70; Cluff, Journal, May 1, 1892.

23. Cluff, Journal, Mar. 24 and 28, 1893; see also Panek, "Life at Iosepa," 71.

24. Cluff, Journal, Mar. 20, 1893; Apr. 1 and 2, 1893; see also Woodruff, Journal, Mar. 14, 1893.

25. Cluff, Journal, Apr. 6 and 9, 1893; "Beautiful Table," *Daily Bulletin,* Mar. 3, 1893, [3]; Osborne J. Widtsoe to John Widtsoe, Apr. 23, 1893, Widtsoe Family Papers, CHL; Rose, Conant, and Kjellgren, "Hawaiian Standing *Kāhili,*" 274, 279; Matthew Noall to the First Presidency, Oct. 10, 1892; Feb. 28, 1893, First Presidency, Mission Administration Correspondence, CHL.
26. "Temple Dedication," *Deseret Evening News,* Apr. 6, 1893, 10; Salt Lake Temple Dedication Services, Apr. 9, 1893, 35.
27. George Q. Cannon, Journal, Apr. 9, 1893; Salt Lake Temple Dedication Services, Apr. 9, 1893, 35–36; Iosepa Branch, Historical Records, Apr. 23, 1893. Last sentence of quotation edited for readability; "they did not" in original changed to "they do not."
28. Iosepa Branch, Historical Records, Apr. 23, 1893. Quotation edited for clarity; word "witness" added.
29. George Q. Cannon, Journal, Apr. 19, 1893; Cowley, Journal, Apr. 19, 1893.
30. George Q. Cannon, Journal, Apr. 19, 1893; Lund, Journal, Apr. 19, 1893; Nuttall, Diary, Apr. 19, 1893; see also *Saints,* volume 1, chapter 42.
31. Lund, Journal, Apr. 19, 1893. Quotation edited for clarity; word "with" added.
32. Nuttall, Diary, Apr. 19, 1893.
33. [Gates], "Sketch of Sister Zina D. Young," 293–94; Bradley and Woodward, *4 Zinas,* 364–65.
34. Relief Society General Board, Minutes, Apr. 6–7, 1893. Quotation edited for readability; "had" in original changed to "has," and "would" in original changed to "will."
35. [Emmeline B. Wells], "Temple Dedication," *Woman's Exponent,* Apr. 15 and May 1, 1893, 21:156.
36. "The Meetings and Attendance," *Deseret Evening News,* Apr. 25, 1893, 4; Handy, *Official Directory of the World's Columbian Exposition,* 42, 191–92; [Emmeline B. Wells], "Women and the World's Fair," *Woman's Exponent,* Dec. 1, 1892, 21:84; Neilson, *Exhibiting Mormonism,* 84–94; Gates, *History of the Young Ladies' Mutual Improvement Association,* 93, 202; see also Wells, Diary, volume 16, May 5, 1893.
    Topics: Zina D. H. Jacobs Young; Emmeline B. Wells
37. Wells, Diary, volume 16, May 10 and 12, 1893; "World's Fair Exodus," *Salt Lake Herald,* May 11, 1893, 2.
38. Zina D. H. Young to Emmeline B. Wells, Aug. 14, 1893, Zina Card Brown Family Collection, CHL.
39. John A. Widtsoe to Anna Gaarden Widtsoe, Apr. 30, 1893, Widtsoe Family Papers, CHL; see also Anna Gaarden Widtsoe to John A. Widtsoe, May 11, 1893, Widtsoe Family Papers, CHL.
40. Osborne Widtsoe to John A. Widtsoe, Apr. 2, 1893; Apr. 23, 1893; Anna Gaarden Widtsoe to John A. Widtsoe, Apr. 25, 1893, Widtsoe Family Papers, CHL.
41. Widtsoe, *In the Gospel Net,* 89–90, 94–95; "Widtsoe, Anna Karine Gaarden," in Jenson, *Latter-day Saint Biographical Encyclopedia,* 3:734–35; see also, for example, "The Scandinavian Hotel," *Sunday Herald* (Salt Lake City), Feb. 26, 1893, 8; and "The Clubs Will Meet," *Sunday Herald,* Apr. 23, 1893, 8.
42. Anna Gaarden Widtsoe to John A. Widtsoe, May 11, 1893, Widtsoe Family Papers, CHL.
43. Anna Gaarden Widtsoe to John A. Widtsoe, May 11, 1893, Widtsoe Family Papers, CHL; Widtsoe, *In a Sunlit Land,* 31, 36–38; John A. Widtsoe, "For 50th Anniversary Volume of Class of '94 Harvard," 3, John A. Widtsoe, Papers, CHL; John Widtsoe to Carl L. Anderson, Mar. 23, 1914, John A. Widtsoe, Papers, CHL; see also Reuben, *Making of the Modern University,* 133–35; and Marsden, *Soul of the American University,* 50.
44. Anna Gaarden Widtsoe to John A. Widtsoe, May 11, 1893, Widtsoe Family Papers, CHL.
45. Anna Gaarden Widtsoe to John A. Widtsoe, May 11, 1893, Widtsoe Family Papers, CHL; Isaiah 2:2; Lee, Journal, Jan. 13, 1846, 79; Joseph H. Dean, Journal, Apr. 24, 1893; "Temple Dedication," *Deseret Evening News,* Apr. 6, 1893, 10; "Meetings and Attendance," *Deseret Evening News,* Apr. 25, 1893, 4; Hammond, Journal, Apr. 4 and 7, 1893; Lund, Journal, Apr. 18, 1893; see also *Saints,* volume 1, chapter 46.

46. Brigham Young, School of the Prophets, Jan. 25, 1868, Church History Department Pitman Shorthand Transcriptions, CHL; see also "Remarks," *Deseret News,* Oct. 14, 1863, [4]–[5]; Talmage, *House of the Lord,* 23; and Holzapfel, *Every Stone a Sermon,* 91–95. Quotation edited for clarity; expansion from original shorthand has "we shall be able to build temples yes thousands of them and build temples all countries."
47. Anna Gaarden Widtsoe to John A. Widtsoe, Apr. 25, 1893, Widtsoe Family Papers, CHL.

SOURCES CITED

This list serves as a comprehensive guide to all sources cited in the second volume of *Saints: The Story of the Church of Jesus Christ in the Latter Days*. In entries for manuscript sources, dates identify when the manuscript was created, which is not necessarily the time period the manuscript covers. Volumes of *The Joseph Smith Papers* are listed under "JSP." Many sources are available digitally, and links are found in the electronic version of the book, available at saints.ChurchofJesusChrist.org and in Gospel Library.

Citation of a source does not imply that it is endorsed by the Church. For more information about the types of sources used in *Saints*, see "Note on Sources."

The poems of Eliza R. Snow that appear in epigraphs for each of the four parts come from Jill Mulvay Derr and Karen Lynn Davidson, eds., *Eliza R. Snow: The Complete Poetry* (Provo, UT: Brigham Young University Press; Salt Lake City: University of Utah Press, 2009).

The following abbreviations are used in this list of sources cited:

BYU: L. Tom Perry Special Collections, Harold B. Lee Library, Brigham Young University, Provo, Utah
CHL: Church History Library, The Church of Jesus Christ of Latter-day Saints, Salt Lake City
FHL: Family History Library, The Church of Jesus Christ of Latter-day Saints, Salt Lake City

Account of the Funeral Proceedings for President Brigham Young, Sept. 1, 1877. CHL.
Acts, Resolutions, and Memorials, Passed by the First Annual, and Special Sessions, of the Legislative Assembly, of the Territory of Utah, Begun and Held at Great Salt Lake City, on the 22nd Day of September, A. D., 1851. Also the Constitution of the United States, and the Act Organizing the Territory of Utah. Salt Lake City: Legislative Assembly, 1852.
Addison Pratt Family Collection, 1831–1924. CHL.
Adler, Jacob, and Robert M. Kamins. *The Fantastic Life of Walter Murray Gibson: Hawaii's Minister of Everything*. Honolulu: University of Hawaii Press, 1986.
The Admission of Utah. Arguments in Favor of the Admission of Utah as a State, Made before the House Committee on Territories, Second Session, Fiftieth Congress, January 12–22, 1889. Washington, DC: Government Printing Office, 1889.
Affidavits about Celestial Marriage, 1869–1915. CHL.
A Häolé [George Washington Bates]. *Sandwich Island Notes*. New York: Harper and Brothers, 1854.
Aird, Polly. "'You Nasty Apostates, Clear Out': Reasons for Disaffection in the Late 1850s." *Journal of Mormon History* 30, no. 2 (Fall 2004): 129–207.
Albanese, Catherine L. *A Republic of Mind and Spirit: A Cultural History of American Metaphysical Religion*. New Haven, CT: Yale University Press, 2007.
Alexander, Thomas G. "An Experiment in Progressive Legislation: The Granting of Woman Suffrage in Utah in 1870." *Utah Historical Quarterly* 38, no. 1 (Winter 1970): 20–30.
———. "Federal Authority versus Polygamic Theocracy: James B. McKean and the Mormons, 1870–1875." *Dialogue: A Journal of Mormon Thought* 1, no. 3 (Autumn 1966): 85–100.
———. "The Odyssey of a Latter-day Prophet: Wilford Woodruff and the Manifesto of 1890." *Journal of Mormon History* 17 (1991): 169–206.
———. "The Odyssey of a Latter-day Prophet: Wilford Woodruff and the Manifesto of 1890." In *Banner of the Gospel: Wilford Woodruff*, edited by Alexander L. Baugh and Susan Easton Black, 277–325. Provo, UT: Religious Studies Center, Brigham Young University; Salt Lake City: Deseret Book, 2010.
———. "The Odyssey of a Latter-day Prophet: Wilford Woodruff and the Manifesto of 1890." In *In the Whirlpool: The Pre-Manifesto Letters of President Wilford Woodruff to the William Atkin Family, 1885–1890*, edited by Reid L. Neilson, with contributions by Thomas G. Alexander and Jan Shipps, 57–96. Norman, OK: Arthur H. Clark, 2011.

————. *Things in Heaven and Earth: The Life and Times of Wilford Woodruff, a Mormon Prophet*. Salt Lake City: Signature Books, 1993.

Alexandria Gazette. Alexandria, VA. 1834–1974.

Allen, James B., and Glen M. Leonard. *The Story of the Latter-day Saints*. Salt Lake City: Deseret Book, 1976.

Alley, George. Letters, 1844–59. CHL.

Allred, Byron H. Journals, circa 1894 and 1898–1912. CHL.

Allred, Reddick. Journals, 1852–63. Daughters of Utah Pioneers Collection, 1828–1963. CHL.

American Penny Magazine, and Family Newspaper. New York City. 1845–46.

American Traveller. Boston. 1845–85.

Anderson, Edward H. "The Past of Mutual Improvement." *Improvement Era* 1, no. 1 (Nov. 1897): 1–10.

Anderson, James A. "Salt Lake Temple." *Contributor* 14, no. 6 (Apr. 1893): 243–303.

Anderson, Richard Lloyd. *Investigating the Book of Mormon Witnesses*. Salt Lake City: Deseret Book, 1981.

————. "Reuben Miller, Recorder of Oliver Cowdery's Reaffirmations." *BYU Studies* 8, no. 3 (Spring 1968): 277–93.

Andrew, David S., and Laurel B. Blank. "The Four Mormon Temples in Utah." *Journal of the Society of Architectural Historians* 30, no. 1 (Mar. 1971): 51–56.

Antrei, Albert C. T., and Ruth D. Scow, eds. *The Other Forty-Niners: A Topical History of Sanpete County, Utah, 1849–1983*. Salt Lake City: Western Epics, 1982.

Appleby, William I. Autobiography and Journal, 1848–56. CHL.

Archer, Patience L. Rozsa. Reminiscences, circa 1890. CHL.

Architect's Office. Salt Lake Temple Architectural Drawings, 1853–93. CHL.

Arkansas Intelligencer. Van Buren. 1842–59.

Arrington, Chris Rigby. "The Finest of Fabrics: Mormon Women and the Silk Industry in Early Utah." *Utah Historical Quarterly* 46, no. 4 (Fall 1978): 376–96.

Arrington, Leonard J. *Brigham Young: American Moses*. Urbana: University of Illinois Press, 1986.

————. *Great Basin Kingdom: An Economic History of the Latter-day Saints, 1830–1900*. Cambridge, MA: Harvard University Press, 1958.

————. *History of Idaho*. 2 vols. Moscow: University of Idaho Press; Boise: Idaho State Historical Society, 1994.

Arrington, Leonard J., Feramorz Y. Fox, and Dean L. May. *Building the City of God: Community and Cooperation among the Mormons*. Salt Lake City: Deseret Book, 1976.

Ashby, Leland Hansen, comp. *An Autobiography of Peter Olsen Hansen, 1818–1895*. Salt Lake City: By the compiler, 1988.

Atkin, Dennis H. "A History of Iosepa, the Utah Polynesian Colony." Master's thesis, Brigham Young University, 1958.

Avery, Rachel Foster, ed. *Transactions of the National Council of Women of the United States, Assembled in Washington, D.C., February 22 to 25, 1891*. Philadelphia: Executive Board of the National Council of Women, 1891.

Avery, Valeen Tippetts. *From Mission to Madness: Last Son of the Mormon Prophet*. Urbana: University of Illinois Press, 1998.

Bailey, Langley A. Reminiscences and Journal, circa 1920–29. CHL.

Bair, JoAnn W., and Richard L. Jensen. "Prosecution of the Mormons in Arizona Territory in the 1880s." *Arizona and the West* 19, no. 1 (Spring 1977): 25–46.

Bakken, Gordon Morris, and Alexandra Kindell, eds. *Encyclopedia of Immigration and Migration in the American West*. Vol. 1, *A–L*. Thousand Oaks, CA: Sage, 2006.

Ballantyne, Richard. Journals, 1852–96. Richard Ballantyne, Papers, 1852–96. CHL.

Ballara, Angela, and Keith Cairns. "Te Potangaroa, Paora." *Dictionary of New Zealand Biography*, 1990. Available at Te Ara: The Encyclopedia of New Zealand, accessed Feb. 7, 2019, https://teara.govt.nz/en/biographies/1t57/te-potangaroa-paora.

Bancroft, Hubert H. *History of California*. Vol. 6, *1848–1859*. The Works of Hubert Howe Bancroft, vol. 23. San Francisco: History Company, 1888.

————. *History of Utah, 1540–1886*. The Works of Hubert Howe Bancroft, vol. 26. San Francisco: History Company, 1889.

Barber, Ian G. "Matakite, Mormon Conversions, and Māori-Israelite Identity Work in Colonial New Zealand." *Journal of Mormon History* 41, no. 3 (July 2015): 167–220.

Barney, Elvira Stevens. "Ruins of the Nauvoo Temple as Stood in 1857," 1906. CHL.

Bashore, Melvin L. "Life behind Bars: Mormon Cohabs of the 1880s." *Utah Historical Quarterly* 47, no. 1 (Winter 1979): 22–41.

Bashore, Melvin L., H. Dennis Tolley, and BYU Pioneer Mortality Team. "Mortality on the Mormon Trail, 1847–1868." *BYU Studies Quarterly* 53, no. 4 (2014): 109–23.

Baskin, Robert Newton. *Reminiscences of Early Utah*. [Salt Lake City]: By the author, 1914.

Bean, George W. Autobiography, 1897. George W. Bean, Papers, 1852–56, 1891–97. CHL.

Bean, Nellie Stary. "Reminiscences of the Granddaughter of Hyrum Smith." *Relief Society Magazine* 9, no. 1 (Jan. 1922): 8–10.

Beecroft, Joseph. Journals, 1844–82. 11 vols. Beecroft Family Papers, 1842–1907. CHL.

Beesley, Adelbert. Missionary Journals, 1888–91. CHL.

Beesley, Fredrick. Diary, 1885–86. CHL.

Beeton, Beverly. "A Feminist among the Mormons: Charlotte Ives Cobb Godbe Kirby." *Utah Historical Quarterly* 59, no. 1 (Winter 1991): 22–31.

Bennett, Richard E. *The Journey West: The Mormon Pioneer Journals of Horace K. Whitney with Insights by Helen Mar Kimball Whitney*. Provo, UT: Religious Studies Center, Brigham Young University; Salt Lake City: Deseret Book, 2018.

————. "'Line upon Line, Precept upon Precept': Reflections on the 1877 Commencement of the Performance of Endowments and Sealings for the Dead." *BYU Studies* 44, no. 3 (2005): 38–77.

————. *Mormons at the Missouri, 1846–1852: "And Should We Die . . ."*. Norman: University of Oklahoma Press, 1987.

————. *Temples Rising: A Heritage of Sacrifice*. Salt Lake City: Deseret Book, 2019.

————. *We'll Find the Place: The Mormon Exodus, 1846–1848*. Salt Lake City: Deseret Book, 1997.

————. "'Which Is the Wisest Course?': The Transformation in Mormon Temple Consciousness, 1870–1898." *BYU Studies Quarterly* 52, no. 2 (2013): 5–43.

Benson, Kersten Ericksen. "Recollections of Kersten Erickson Benson Coming to Zion in 1857," circa 1905. Kersten E. Benson Biographical File, no date. CHL.

Berrett, LaMar C., ed. *Sacred Places: A Comprehensive Guide to Early LDS Historical Sites*. 6 vols. Salt Lake City: Deseret Book, 1999–2007.

Bigler, Henry W. Reminiscences and Diaries, 1846–50. 3 vols. Typescript. CHL.

A Bill in Aid of the Execution of the Laws in the Territory of Utah, and for Other Purposes. H.R. 696, 41st Cong., 2nd Sess. (1869). Copy at CHL.

A Bill to Discourage Polygamy in Utah by Granting the Right of Suffrage to the Women of That Territory. H.R. 64, 41st Cong., 1st Sess. (1869). Copy at CHL.

A Bill to Provide for the Execution of the Law against the Crime of Polygamy in the Territory of Utah, and for Other Purposes. S. 286, 41st Cong., 2nd Sess. (1869). Copy at CHL.

Binder, William Lawrence Spicer. Reminiscences, no date. CHL.

A Biographical History of Eminent and Self-Made Men of the State of Indiana. Vol. 1. Cincinnati: Western Biographical, 1880.

"A Biographical Sketch of R. B. Pratt." *Young Woman's Journal* 2, no. 12 (Sept. 1891): 531–36.

Biography of Anne K. Smoot, 1910. BYU.

Bishop, Patrick A. "Precept upon Precept: The Succession of John Taylor." In *Champion of Liberty: John Taylor*, edited by Mary Jane Woodger, 233–72. Provo, UT: Religious Studies Center, Brigham Young University, 2009.

Bitton, Davis. *George Q. Cannon: A Biography*. Salt Lake City: Deseret Book, 1999.

Black, Susan Easton. "How Large Was the Population of Nauvoo?" *BYU Studies* 35, no. 2 (1995): 91–94.

————. "The Search for Early Members of the Church." *Ensign*, July 1989, 28–31.

Black, Susan Easton, and Larry C. Porter. *Martin Harris: Uncompromising Witness of the Book of Mormon*. Provo, UT: BYU Studies, 2018.

Bleak, James G. Annals of the Southern Utah Mission, circa 1903–6. CHL.

———. Journal, 1854–60. CHL.

Board of Health. Incoming Letters of the Board of Health, 1850–1941 (bulk 1850–1904), Series 334. Hawaii State Archives, Honolulu.

Bohman, Lisa Bryner. "A Fresh Perspective: The Woman Suffrage Associations of Beaver and Farmington, Utah." In *Battle for the Ballot: Essays on Woman Suffrage in Utah, 1870–1896*, edited by Carol Cornwall Madsen, 203–19. Logan: Utah State University Press, 1997.

Bond, John. "Handcarts West in '56." Microfilm. Utah State Archives. Salt Lake City.

———. *Handcarts West in '56*. Publication place and publisher unidentified, 1970.

The Book of Mormon: Another Testament of Jesus Christ. Salt Lake City: The Church of Jesus Christ of Latter-day Saints, 2013.

Booth, James J. St. George Temple, circa 1877. Photograph. CHL.

Booth, John E. "A History of the Fourth Provo Ward." Copied 1941. Copy at CHL.

Boreman, Jacob S. Transcript of John D. Lee's First Trial, no date. Jacob Smith Boreman, Papers, 1857–1912. Huntington Library, San Marino, CA. Transcript available at http://mountainmeadowsmassacre.com.

———. Transcript of John D. Lee's Second Trial, no date. Jacob Smith Boreman, Papers, 1857–1912. Huntington Library, San Marino, CA. Transcript available at http://mountain meadowsmassacre.com.

Borrowman, John. Diaries, 1846–60. CHL.

Boston Post. Boston. 1842–1956.

Bowering, George K. Journal, 1842–75. CHL.

Box Elder Stake. General Minutes, 1877–1927. CHL.

Boyle, Dessie Grant. "An Appreciation." *Relief Society Magazine* 23, no. 11 (Nov. 1936): 672–73.

Brackenridge, R. Douglas. "'Are You That Damned Presbyterian Devil?' The Evolution of an Anti-Mormon Story." *Journal of Mormon History* 21, no. 1 (Spring 1995): 80–105.

Bradley, Martha Sonntag. "'Hide and Seek': Children on the Underground." *Utah Historical Quarterly* 51, no. 2 (Spring 1983): 133–53.

Bradley, Martha Sonntag, and Mary Brown Firmage Woodward. *4 Zinas*. Salt Lake City: Signature Books, 2000.

Bradshaw, Hazel, ed. *Under Dixie Sun: A History of Washington County by Those Who Loved Their Forebears*. Illustrations by Nellie Jenson. [St. George, UT]: Washington County Chapter Daughters of Utah Pioneers, 1950.

Briggs, Robert H. "The Mountain Meadows Massacre: An Analytical Narrative Based on Participant Confessions." *Utah Historical Quarterly* 74, no. 4 (Fall 2006): 313–33.

Brigham Young History Documents, 1844–66. CHL.

Brigham Young Office Files, 1832–78 (bulk 1844–77). CHL.

Britsch, R. Lanier. "The Founding of the Samoan Mission." *BYU Studies* 18, no. 1 (Fall 1977): 12–26.

———. "Maori Traditions and the Mormon Church." *New Era*, June 1981, 38–46.

———. *Unto the Islands of the Sea: A History of the Latter-day Saints in the Pacific*. Salt Lake City: Deseret Book, 1986.

Bromley, William M. "Introduction of the Gospel to the Maories." *Juvenile Instructor* 22, no. 1 (Jan. 1, 1887): 6–7.

———. Journals and Notebook, 1871–1905. CHL.

Brooks, Juanita, ed. *Not by Bread Alone: The Journal of Martha Spence Heywood, 1850–56*. Salt Lake City: Utah State Historical Society, 1978.

Brown, James S. *Life of a Pioneer: Being the Autobiography of James S. Brown*. Salt Lake City: George Q. Cannon and Sons, 1900.

———. Reminiscences and Journals, 1849–1900. CHL.

Brown, John. "An Evidence of Inspiration." *Juvenile Instructor* 16, no. 23 (Dec. 1, 1881): 269.

Brown, John Zimmerman, ed. *Autobiography of Pioneer John Brown, 1820–1896*. Salt Lake City: By the author, 1941.

Brown, Lisle G. "'Temple Pro Tempore': The Salt Lake City Endowment House." *Journal of Mormon History* 34, no. 4 (Fall 2008): 1–68.

Brown, Thomas D. Diary, 1854–57. CHL.

Brown, Zina Young Card. "A Biographical Sketch of the Life of Zina Young Williams Card," circa 1930. Zina Card Brown Family Collection, 1806–1972. CHL.

Buchanan, Frederick S. "Education among the Mormons: Brigham Young and the Schools of Utah." *History of Education Quarterly* 22, no. 4 (Winter 1982): 435–59.

Bullock, Henrietta Rushton. Collection, 1836–89, 1914. CHL.

Bullock, Thomas. Journals, 1843–49. CHL.

Bunker, Gary L., and Davis Bitton. *The Mormon Graphic Image, 1834–1914: Cartoons, Caricatures, and Illustrations*. Salt Lake City: University of Utah Press, 1983.

Burlington Hawk-Eye. Burlington, IA. 1845–185?.

Burton, Richard F. *The City of the Saints, and across the Rocky Mountains to California*. New York: Harper and Brothers, 1862.

Bush, Lester E., Jr. "Brigham Young in Life and Death: A Medical Overview." *Journal of Mormon History* 5 (1978): 79–103.

Butler, John L. "A Short History or the Byography of John L Butler Partly from His Own Writing," 1863. In John L. Butler, Autobiography, circa 1859. CHL.

By James Buchanan, President of the United States of America: A Proclamation. Washington, DC: 1858. Copy at CHL.

Caldwell, Estelle Neff. "Susa Young Gates," no date. In Susa Young Gates, Papers, circa 1870–1933. CHL.

California Star. San Francisco. 1847–48.

Campbell, Eugene E., and Bruce L. Campbell. "Divorce among Mormon Polygamists: Extent and Explanations." *Utah Historical Quarterly* 46, no. 1 (Winter 1978): 4–23.

Campbell, Karlyn Kohrs. *Man Cannot Speak for Her: A Critical Study of Early Feminist Rhetoric*. Vol. 1. New York: Greenwood, 1989.

Camp of Israel. Schedules and Reports, 1845–49. CHL.

Canning, Ray R., and Beverly Beeton, eds. *The Genteel Gentile: Letters of Elizabeth Cumming, 1857–1858*. Salt Lake City: University of Utah Library, 1977.

Cannon, Abraham H. Diaries, 1879–95. CHL.

Cannon, Angus M. Collection, 1854–1920. CHL.

Cannon, Brian Q. "Adopted or Indentured, 1850–1870: Native Children in Mormon Households." In *Nearly Everything Imaginable: The Everyday Life of Utah's Mormon Pioneers*, edited by Ronald W. Walker and Doris R. Dant, 341–57. Provo, UT: Brigham Young University Press, 1999.

———. "Change Engulfs a Frontier Settlement: Ogden and Its Residents Respond to the Railroad." *Journal of Mormon History* 12 (1985): 15–28.

———. "'To Buy Up the Lamanite Children as Fast as They Could': Indentured Servitude and Its Legacy in Mormon Society." *Journal of Mormon History* 44, no. 2 (Apr. 2018): 1–35.

Cannon, Elizabeth Hoagland. Journal, July–Oct. 1862. CHL.

Cannon, George Q. Journal, Sept.–Dec. 1888. In M. Hamlin Cannon Papers, Colorado College, Colorado Springs, CO. Also available at churchhistorianspress.org.

———. Journals, 1849–1901. 50 vols. CHL. Also available at churchhistorianspress.org.

———. *My First Mission*. Faith-Promoting Series. Salt Lake City: Juvenile Instructor, 1879.

———. "Topics of the Times." *Juvenile Instructor* 18, no. 24 (Dec. 15, 1883): 377–78.

———. *Writings from the "Western Standard," Published in San Francisco, California*. Liverpool: By the author, 1864.

[Cannon, George Q.]. "Twenty Years Ago: A Sketch." *Juvenile Instructor* 4, no. 1 (Jan. 2, 1869): 6–7; 4, no. 2 (Jan. 16, 1869): 13–14; 4, no. 3 (Jan. 30, 1869): 21–22.

Cannon, Jeffrey G. "Mormonism's Jesse Haven and the Early Focus on Proselytizing the Afrikaner at the Cape of Good Hope, 1853–1855." *Dutch Reformed Theological*

Journal/Nederduitse Gereformeerde Teologiese Tydskrif 48, nos. 3 and 4 (Sept. and Dec. 2007): 446–56.

Cannon, John Q. *George Cannon the Immigrant. Isle of Man, 1794—St. Louis, U. S. A., 1844. His Ancestry, His Life, His Native Land, His Posterity.* Salt Lake City: [Deseret News], 1927.

Cannon, Joseph J. "George Q. Cannon." *Instructor* 79, no. 5 (May 1944): 206–10; 79, no. 8 (Aug. 1944): 367–71.

Cannon, Lucy Grant. Autobiography, 1952. Typescript. Cannon and Willis Families Papers, 1891–2003. BYU.

Cape of Good Hope. *Census of the Colony of the Cape of Good Hope. 1865.* Cape Town, South Africa: Saul Solomon, 1866.

Cardston News. Cardston, Alberta, Canada. 1925–58.

Cardston Ward, Alberta Stake. Relief Society Minutes and Records, 1887–1911. 7 vols. CHL.

Carleton, James Henry. *Report on the Subject of the Massacre at the Mountain Meadows, in Utah Territory, in September, 1857, of One Hundred and Twenty Men, Women and Children, Who Were from Arkansas.* Little Rock, AR: True Democrat, 1860.

Carter, D. Robert. "Fish and the Famine of 1855–56." *Journal of Mormon History* 27, no. 2 (Fall 2001): 92–124.

Carter, Kate, comp. *Heart Throbs of the West: "A Unique Volume Treating Definite Subjects of Western History."* Vol. 6. Salt Lake City: Daughters of Utah Pioneers, 1945.

Carvalho, S. N. *Incidents of Travel and Adventure in the Far West; with Col. Fremont's Last Expedition across the Rocky Mountains: Including Three Months' Residence in Utah, and a Perilous Trip across the Great American Desert, to the Pacific.* New York: Derby and Jackson, 1857.

Census Bulletin. Washington, DC. 1880–1960.

Century of Black Mormons. University of Utah, Salt Lake City. Accessed Sept. 30, 2019. https://exhibits.lib.utah.edu/s/century-of-black-mormons.

Chicago Historical Society. Collection of Manuscripts about Mormons, 1832–1954. CHL.

Chicago Tribune. Chicago. 1847–.

Christensen, Carl Christian Anton. "Reminiscence," no date. In Richard L. Jensen, "By Handcart to Utah: The Account of C. C. A. Christensen." *Nebraska History* 66, no. 4 (Winter 1985): 333–48.

Christensen, Clinton D. "Solitary Saint in Mexico: Desideria Quintanar de Yañez (1814–1893)." In *1775–1820,* edited by Richard E. Turley Jr. and Brittany A. Chapman, 461–72. Vol. 1 of *Women of Faith in the Latter Days.* Salt Lake City: Deseret Book, 2011.

Christensen, Scott R. *Sagwitch: Shoshone Chieftain, Mormon Elder, 1822–1887.* Logan: Utah State University Press, 1999.

Christy, Howard A. "Open Hand and Mailed Fist: Mormon-Indian Relations in Utah, 1847–52." *Utah Historical Quarterly* 46, no. 3 (Summer 1978): 216–35.

———. "The Walker War: Defense and Conciliation as a Strategy." *Utah Historical Quarterly* 47, no. 4 (Fall 1979): 395–420.

———. "Weather, Disaster, and Responsibility: An Essay on the Willie and Martin Handcart Story." *BYU Studies* 37, no. 1 (1997–98): 6–74.

Chronicles of Courage. 8 vols. Salt Lake City: Daughters of Utah Pioneers, 1990–97.

Church History Department Pitman Shorthand Transcriptions, 2013–17. CHL.

Circular of the First Presidency of The Church of Jesus Christ of Latter-day Saints. Salt Lake City: Publisher unidentified, 1877.

Clark, David L. "The Mormons of the Wisconsin Territory: 1835–1848." *BYU Studies* 37, no. 2 (1997–98): 57–85.

Clark, James R., ed. *Messages of the First Presidency of The Church of Jesus Christ of Latter-day Saints, 1833–1964.* Vol. 3. Salt Lake City: Bookcraft, 1966.

Clark, Louisa Mellor. "History of Louisa Mellor Clark," 1881. International Society Daughters of Utah Pioneers, History Department, Salt Lake City.

Clawson, Margaret G. Reminiscences, part 2, circa 1904–11. CHL.

Clawson, Rudger. Autobiography, circa 1926–35. CHL.

Clayton, Diantha F. Letter to William Clayton, Mar. 10, 1846. CHL.

Clayton, William. Diaries, 1846–53. CHL.

———. History of the Nauvoo Temple, circa 1845. CHL.

———. Journals, 1842–46. CHL.

———. *The Latter-day Saints' Emigrants' Guide: Being a Table of Distances, Showing All the Springs, Creeks, Rivers, Hills, Mountains, Camping Places, and All Other Notable Places, from Council Bluffs, to the Valley of the Great Salt Lake*. St. Louis: Chambers and Knapp, 1848.

Cleland, Robert Glass, and Juanita Brooks. *A Mormon Chronicle: The Diaries of John D. Lee, 1848–1876*. 2 vols. San Marino, CA: Huntington Library, 1955.

Clow, Richmond L. "General William S. Harney on the Northern Plains." *South Dakota History* 16, no. 3 (Fall 1986): 229–48.

Cluff, Harvey H. Autobiography, 1868–88. Harvey H. Cluff, Autobiography, Journals, and Scrapbook, 1868–1916. CHL.

———. Journal, 1888–1912. Harvey H. Cluff, Autobiography, Journals, and Scrapbook, 1868–1916. CHL.

Cluff, W. W. "Acts of Special Providence in Missionary Experience." *Improvement Era* 2, no. 5 (Mar. 1899): 363–65.

———. "The Drowning of President Snow." *Juvenile Instructor* 36, no. 13 (July 1, 1901): 392–95.

———. "The Fall of Walter M. Gibson." *Juvenile Instructor* 36, no. 15 (Aug. 1, 1901): 470–73.

———. "My Last Mission to the Sandwich Islands." In *Fragments of Experience, Sixth Book of the Faith-Promoting Series*. Salt Lake City: Juvenile Instructor, 1882.

Coates, Larry C. "George Catlin, Brigham Young, and the Plains Indians." *BYU Studies* 17, no. 1 (Autumn 1976): 114–18.

Collected Material concerning the Mountain Meadows Massacre, 1859–1961. CHL.

Collected Material relating to William Clayton, circa 1842–72. CHL.

A Compilation of the Messages and Papers of the Presidents Prepared under the Direction of the Joint Committee on Printing, of the House and Senate, pursuant to an Act of the Fifty-Second Congress of the United States. . . . 20 vols. James D. Richardson, 1897.

Condie, Gibson. Autobiography and Journal, 1858–1910. CHL.

The Congressional Globe: Containing the Debates and Proceedings of the Second Session Forty-First Congress; together with an Appendix, Embracing the Laws Passed at That Session. Washington, DC: Office of the Congressional Globe, 1870.

Congressional Record: Containing the Proceedings and Debates of the Forty-Third Congress, First Session. Vol. 2. Washington, DC: Government Printing Office, 1874.

Congressional Record: Containing the Proceedings and Debates of the Forty-Seventh Congress, First Session. Vol. 13. Washington, DC: Government Printing Office, 1882.

The Constitutional Act of Denmark of June 5th 1953. Translated by Birgitte Wern. Folketing Copenhagen, 2013.

Constitution of the State of Deseret. Salt Lake City: Publisher unidentified, 1850.

Cooper, William J. *We Have the War upon Us: The Onset of the Civil War, November 1860– April 1861.* New York: Knopf, 2012.

Corinne Reporter. Corinne, UT. 1869–71.

Cowan, Richard O. "Steel Rails and the Utah Saints." *Journal of Mormon History* 27, no. 2 (Fall 2001): 177–96.

Cowdery, Oliver. Letters to Phineas H. Young, 1843–49. CHL.

———. Letter to Phineas Young, Mar. 23, 1846. CHL.

Cowley, Matthew. "Maori Chief Predicts Coming of L. D. S. Missionaries." *Improvement Era* 53, no. 9 (Sept. 1950): 696–98, 754–56. Also printed in *Te Karere* [45], no. 11 (Nov. 1950): 365–68.

Cowley, Matthias F. Journals and Autobiography, 1877–1940. CHL.

Cox, Clarence William, Jr. "The Mormon Colonies in Chihuahua, Mexico." Master's thesis, University of Southern California, 1969.

Crawley, Peter. "The Constitution of the State of Deseret." *BYU Studies* 29, no. 4 (Fall 1989): 7–22.

———. *A Descriptive Bibliography of the Mormon Church.* 3 vols. Provo, UT: Religious Studies Center, Brigham Young University, 2005.

Crocheron, Augusta Joyce. "The Ship *Brooklyn.*" *Tullidge's Monthly Magazine—The Western Galaxy* 1, no. 1 (Mar. 1888): 78–84.

Crofutt, George A. *Crofutt's Trans-continental Tourist's Guide.* . . . Vol. 3. 2nd ed. New York: By the author, 1871.

Crosby, Caroline Barnes. Journals, 1848–82. Jonathan and Caroline B. Crosby, Papers, 1848–82. CHL.

Cumming, Alfred. Papers, 1792–1889. David M. Rubenstein Rare Book and Manuscript Library, Duke University, Durham, NC.

Cummings, Benjamin Franklin. Reminiscences and Diaries, 1842–79. CHL. Portions also available in the Pioneer Database at https://history.ChurchofJesusChrist.org/overlandtravel /sources/6119/cummings-benjamin-franklin-reminiscences-and-diaries-1842-1879-fd-1-8-p.

Cummings, Horace H. Mission Journal, 1885–88. CHL.

Dahl, Paul E. *William Clayton: Missionary, Pioneer, and Public Servant.* Boise, ID: J. Grant Stevenson, 1964.

Daily Alta California. San Francisco. 1849–91.

Daily Argus and Democrat. Madison, WI. 1857–61.

Daily Arkansas Gazette. Little Rock. 1866–89.

Daily Bulletin. Honolulu. 1882–95.

Daily Cleveland Herald. Cleveland. 1853–74.

Daily Enquirer. Provo, UT. 1889–1908.

Daily Evening Bulletin. San Francisco. 1855–95.

Daily Gazette. Wilmington, DE. 1874–83.

Daily Missouri Republican. St. Louis. 1822–1919.

Daily Rocky Mountain News. Denver. 1860–79.

Daily Union. Washington, DC. 1845–57.

Dallin, Cyrus E. Letter to Gaylen S. Young, July 30, 1938. CHL.

Damron, Joseph W. Diaries, 1891–1945. Microfilm. CHL.

———. Mission Report, circa 1895. CHL.

"Danmark Kirkebøger, 1484–1941." Rigsarkivet, København, Copenhagen. Available at https://www.familysearch.org/ark:/61903/1:1:QG88-FRYJ.

Daws, Gavan. *Holy Man: Father Damien of Molokai.* Honolulu: University of Hawaii Press, 1973.

Dawson's Daily Times and Union. Fort Wayne, IN. 1863–65.

Daynes, Kathryn M. *More Wives Than One.* Urbana: University of Illinois Press, 2001.

Dean, Florence R. Journal, 1887–88. CHL.

Dean, Joseph H. Journals, 1876–1944. CHL.

Department of Administrative Services, Division of Archives and Records Service. Territorial Militia Records, 1849–77; 1905–[circa 1917]. Series 2210. Utah State Archives and Records, Salt Lake City. Also available at https://www.familysearch.org/search/collection/1462415.

Derr, Jill Mulvay, Janath Russell Cannon, and Maureen Ursenbach Beecher. *Women of Covenant: The Story of Relief Society.* Salt Lake City: Deseret Book; Provo, UT: Brigham Young University Press, 1992.

Derr, Jill Mulvay, and Karen Lynn Davidson, eds. *Eliza R. Snow: The Complete Poetry.* Provo, UT: Brigham Young University Press; Salt Lake City: University of Utah Press, 2009.

Derr, Jill Mulvay, Carol Cornwall Madsen, Kate Holbrook, and Matthew J. Grow, eds. *The First Fifty Years of Relief Society: Key Documents in Latter-day Saint Women's History.* Salt Lake City: Church Historian's Press, 2016.

Deseret News. Salt Lake City. 1850–.

Dibble, Charles E. "The Mormon Mission to the Shoshoni Indians, Part III." *Utah Humanities Review* 1 (July 1947): 279–93.

The Doctrine and Covenants of The Church of Jesus Christ of Latter-day Saints: Containing Revelations Given to Joseph Smith, the Prophet, with Some Additions by His Successors in the Presidency of the Church. Salt Lake City: The Church of Jesus Christ of Latter-day Saints, 2013.

Dorius, Carl Christian Nikolai. "Autobiography of Carl Christian Nicoli Dorius." Translated by Anne Sophia Dorius Johnson. Presented by Orpha Dorius Edwards. 1954. Typescript. Pioneer Memorial Museum, International Society Daughters of Utah Pioneers, Salt Lake City.

———. Biographical Sketch, 1955. With Anna Sophia Dorius Johnson. CHL.

———. Diary, 1860–93. CHL.

Dorius, Earl N. *The Dorius Heritage.* Salt Lake City: By the author, 1979.

Dorius, John. "A Sketch of the Life of Nicoli Dorius and a Life History of John Ferdinand Fredrick Dorius and His Wife Kaia Frantzen Dorius," 1974. Typescript. CHL.

Dorius, John F. F. Autobiography and Journal, circa 1851–53. CHL.

Dougall, Maria Young. "Reminiscences." *Young Woman's Journal* 30, no. 11 (Nov. 1919): 594–95.

Dowdle, Brett D. " 'What Means This Carnage?': The Civil War in Mormon Thought." In *Civil War Saints,* edited by Kenneth L. Alford, 107–25. Provo, UT: Religious Studies Center, Brigham Young University; Salt Lake City: Deseret Book, 2012.

Driggs, Ken. " 'There Is No Law in Georgia for Mormons': The Joseph Standing Murder Case of 1879." *Georgia Historical Quarterly* 73, no. 4 (Winter 1989): 745–72.

"Dr. Karl G. Maeser." *Young Woman's Journal* 3, no. 11 (Aug. 1892): 481–86.

Duke, K. E. "Meliton Gonzalez Trejo: Translator of the Book of Mormon into Spanish." *Improvement Era* 59, no. 10 (Oct. 1956): 714–15, 753.

Dunbar, Edward E. *The Romance of the Age; or, The Discovery of Gold in California.* New York: D. Appleton, 1867.

Durham, Thomas. Journal, 1854–71. CHL.

"Early Life in the Valley!" *Juvenile Instructor* 9, no. 1 (Jan. 3, 1874): 9.

Eastern Arizona Stake. Manuscript History and Historical Reports, 1878–81. CHL.

Egan, Howard. Journals, 1847–56. Western Americana Collection. Beinecke Rare Book and Manuscript Library, Yale University, New Haven, CT. Also available in Howard R. Egan, *Pioneering the West 1846–1878: Major Howard Egan's Diary. . . .* (Richmond, UT: By the author, 1917).

1851 England and Wales Census. Available at FamilySearch. https://www.familysearch.org /search/collection/2563939. From "1851, England, Scotland and Wales census." Database with images. Findmypast. https://www.findmypast.com. Original at PRO HO 107, the National Archives of the United Kingdom, Kew, Surrey.

Eighth Ward, Liberty Stake. Relief Society Minutes and Records, 1867–1969. CHL.

Eighty-Ninth Annual Conference of The Church of Jesus Christ of Latter-day Saints. Held in the Tabernacle and Assembly Hall, Salt Lake City, Utah, June 1st, 2nd and 3rd, 1919, with a Full Report of the Discourses. Salt Lake City: Deseret News, 1919.

Ellsworth, Brant W., and Kenneth L. Alford. "Mormon Motivation for Enlisting in the Civil War." In *Civil War Saints,* edited by Kenneth L. Alford, 183–201. Provo, UT: Religious Studies Center, Brigham Young University; Salt Lake City: Deseret Book, 2012.

Ellsworth, Maria S. *Mormon Odyssey: The Story of Ida Hunt Udall, Plural Wife.* Urbana: University of Illinois Press, 1992.

Ellsworth, S. George. *Dear Ellen: Two Mormon Women and Their Letters.* Salt Lake City: Tanner Trust Fund, University of Utah Library, 1974.

———, ed. *The History of Louisa Barnes Pratt: Being the Autobiography of a Mormon Missionary Widow and Pioneer, a New England Youth, at Nauvoo and Salt Lake City, Mission to the Society Islands, Mormon Life in California, Pioneering in Beaver, Utah.* Logan: Utah State University Press, 1998.

Embry, Jessie L. *Mormon Polygamous Families: Life in the Principle.* Salt Lake City: Greg Kofford Books, 2008.

England, Eliza Seamons. Reminiscence, no date. Typescript. Collected Information on the Seamons and Related Families, circa 1980. CHL.

Ephraim North Ward, Sanpete Stake. Relief Society Minutes and Records, 1856–1973. CHL.

Ephraim South Ward, Sanpete South Stake. Primary Association Minutes and Records, 1879–1973. CHL.

Erastus Snow Correspondence, 1848–87. CHL.

Esplin, Ronald K. "'A Place Prepared': Joseph, Brigham and the Quest for Promised Refuge in the West." *Journal of Mormon History* 9 (1982): 85–111.

Esplin, Scott C. "Buildings on the Temple Block Preceding the Tabernacle." In *An Old and Wonderful Friend,* edited by Scott C. Esplin, 107–36. Provo, UT: Religious Studies Center, Brigham Young University, 2007.

———. "'Have We Not Had a Prophet among Us?': Joseph Smith's Civil War Prophecy." In *Civil War Saints,* edited by Kenneth L. Alford, 41–59. Provo, UT: Religious Studies Center, Brigham Young University; Salt Lake City: Deseret Book, 2012.

Ettling, Thomas, cartographer. *California, Utah, Lr. California and New Mexico.* Map. [London]: Day and Son Lithographers to the Queen, 1858. Copy at CHL.

Evans, Beatrice Cannon, and Janath Russell Cannon. *Cannon Family Historical Treasury.* 2nd ed. Salt Lake City: George Cannon Family Association, 1995.

Evans, Rosa Mae McClellan. "Judicial Prosecution of Prisoners for LDS Plural Marriage: Prison Sentences, 1884–1895." Master's thesis, Brigham Young University, 1986.

The Evening and the Morning Star. Independence, MO, July 1832–July 1833; Kirtland, OH, Dec. 1833–Sept. 1834.

Evening Critic. Washington, DC. 1881–85.

Everton, Marion K. Scrapbooks, no date. CHL.

The Executive Documents of the Senate of the United States for the Second Session of the Fifty-Second Congress and the Special Session of the Senate Convened March 4, 1893. 1892–'93. Washington, DC: Government Printing Office, 1893.

Farmer, Jared. *On Zion's Mount: Mormons, Indians, and the American Landscape.* Cambridge, MA: Harvard University Press, 2010.

Farmington Ward, Davis Stake. Primary Association Minutes and Records, 1878–1949. 33 vols. CHL.

Farrer, William. Diary, 1849–54. CHL.

Faulkner, James. Letter to "Dear Friends," Mar. 1, 1856. CHL.

Faulring, Scott H. "The Return of Oliver Cowdery." In *The Disciple as Witness: Essays on Latter-day Saint History and Doctrine in Honor of Richard Lloyd Anderson,* edited by Stephen D. Ricks, Donald W. Parry, and Andrew H. Hedges, 117–74. Provo, UT: Foundation for Ancient Research and Mormon Studies, 2000.

Fielding, Joseph. Journals, 1837–59. CHL.

Fifteenth Ward, Riverside Stake. Relief Society Minutes and Records, 1868–1968. CHL.

Firmage, Edwin Brown, and Richard Collin Mangrum. *Zion in the Courts: A Legal History of The Church of Jesus Christ of Latter-day Saints, 1830–1900.* Urbana: University of Illinois Press, 1988.

The First Fifty Years of Relief Society. Church History Department, The Church of Jesus Christ of Latter-day Saints. http://churchhistorianspress.org.

First Presidency. General Authorities Correspondence, 1887–1918. CHL.

———. John Taylor Underground Letterpress Copybook, 1886–87. CHL.

———. Mission Administration Correspondence, 1877–1918. CHL.

———. Missionary Calls and Recommendations, 1877–1918. CHL.

———. Political Letterpress Copybook, 1887–1902. CHL.

———. Temple Administration Files, 1877–1914. CHL.

First Presidency (John Taylor) Correspondence, 1877–87. CHL.

Fish, Joseph. *The Life and Times of Joseph Fish, Mormon Pioneer,* edited by John H. Krenkel. Danville, IL: Interstate, 1970.

Flake, Kathleen. *The Politics of American Religious Identity: The Seating of Senator Reed Smoot, Mormon Apostle.* Chapel Hill: University of North Carolina Press, 2004.

Flake, Lucy H. Autobiography and Journal, Mar.–Aug. 1894. Lucy H. Flake, Journals, 1894–99. BYU.

Fleek, Sherman L. *History May Be Searched in Vain: A Military History of the Mormon Battalion*. Spokane, WA: Arthur H. Clark, 2008.

Flower, Judson Harold, Jr. "Mormon Colonization of the San Luis Valley, Colorado, 1878–1900." Master's thesis, Brigham Young University, 1966.

Fluhman, J. Spencer. "'A Subject That Can Bear Investigation': Anguish, Faith, and Joseph Smith's Youngest Plural Wife." In *No Weapon Shall Prosper: New Light on Sensitive Issues*, edited by Robert L. Millet, 105–19. Provo, UT: Religious Studies Center, Brigham Young University, 2011.

Foote, Warren. Autobiography and Journal, 1837–79. Copy. Warren Foote, Papers, 1837–1941. CHL.

Francaviglia, Richard V. *Over the Range: A History of the Promontory Summit Route of the Pacific Railroad*. Logan: Utah State University Press, 2008.

Frantzen, John. Reminiscence and Journal, 1889–92. Typescript. CHL.

Frémont, John C. *Report of the Exploring Expedition to the Rocky Mountains in the Year 1842, and to Oregon and North California in the Years 1843–'44*. Washington, DC: Gales and Seaton, 1845.

Frontier Guardian. Kanesville [Council Bluffs], IA. 1849–52.

Garr, Arnold K. "A History of Brigham Young College, Logan, Utah." Master's thesis, Utah State University, 1973.

Gates, Jacob. Journals, 1836–61. 7 vols. CHL.

Gates, Susa Young. "And while father is ever deliberate," no date. Box 1, folder 5, item [18], Susa Young Gates, Papers, 1852–1932. Utah State Historical Society, Salt Lake City.

———. "As the families of my Aunts increased in size," no date. Box 1, folder 5, item [14], Susa Young Gates, Papers, 1852–1932. Utah State Historical Society, Salt Lake City.

———. "Brigham Young and His Nineteen Wives," no date. Box 11, folder 1, item [3], Susa Young Gates, Papers, 1852–1932. Utah State Historical Society, Salt Lake City.

———. "Family Life among the Mormons." *North American Review* 150 (Mar. 1890): 339–50.

———. "Historical Sketch of the Y. L. M. I. A." *Young Woman's Journal* 3, no. 5 (Feb. 1892): 231–33.

———. *History of the Young Ladies' Mutual Improvement Association of The Church of Jesus Christ of Latter-day Saints. From November 1869 to June 1910*. Salt Lake City: Deseret News, 1911.

———. "I saw just one step cut," no date. Box 1, folder 5, item [17], Susa Young Gates, Papers, 1852–1932. Utah State Historical Society, Salt Lake City.

———. Journals, 1870–1933. Journals, Notebooks, and Scrapbooks, Susa Young Gates, Papers, circa 1870–1933. CHL.

———. "Life in the Lion House," no date. Box 11, folder 2, item [52], Susa Young Gates, Papers, 1852–1932. Utah State Historical Society, Salt Lake City.

———. "The Lion House," no date. Box 10, folder 5, item [1], Susa Young Gates, Papers, 1852–1932. Utah State Historical Society, Salt Lake City.

———. "Lucy Bigelow Young," no date. Biographical Treatment, in Susa Young Gates, Papers, 1852–1932. Utah State Historical Society, Salt Lake City.

———. "More Than a Halo." *Juvenile Instructor* 42, no. 22 (Nov. 15, 1907): 683–84.

———. "Mothers in Israel." *Relief Society Magazine* 3, no. 3 (Mar. 1916): 123–48.

———. "Mrs. Susa Young Gates in Genealogy and Temple Work," no date. Susa Young Gates, Papers, circa 1870–1933. CHL.

———. "My Father as His Forty Six Children Knew Him," no date. Box 1, folder 5, item [7], Susa Young Gates, Papers, 1852–1932. Utah State Historical Society, Salt Lake City.

———. "My Recollections," no date. Box 1, folder 2, item 11, Susa Young Gates, Papers, 1852–1932. Utah State Historical Society, Salt Lake City.

———. "My Recollections," no date. Box 11, folder 2, item [16] ("unfinished fragment"), Susa Young Gates, Papers, 1852–1932. Utah State Historical Society, Salt Lake City.

———. "My Recollections," no date. Box 11, folder 2, item [48], Susa Young Gates, Papers, 1852–1932. Utah State Historical Society, Salt Lake City.

———. Papers, 1852–1932. Utah State Historical Society, Salt Lake City.

————. Papers, circa 1870–1933. CHL.

[Gates, Susa Young]. "The Editor's Department." *Young Woman's Journal* 1, no. 1 (Oct. 1889): 32; 2, no. 4 (Jan. 1891): 190–91; 2, no. 6 (Mar. 1891): 283–85; 5, no. 9 (June 1894): 448–52.

————. "A Precious Promise Made in the Temple." *Young Woman's Journal* 4, no. 8 (May 1893): 376–78.

————. "Sketch of Sister Zina D. Young." *Young Woman's Journal* 4, no. 7 (Apr. 1893): 292–94.

Gates, Susa Young, and Leah D. Widtsoe. *The Life Story of Brigham Young: Mormon Leader, Founder of Salt Lake City, and Builder of an Empire in the Uncharted Wastes of Western America.* London: Jarrolds, 1930.

Geilman, Matthew G. "Taking the Gospel to Mexico: Meliton Gonzalez Trejo: Translator, Missionary, Colonizer." Pioneers in Every Land, Church History Department, The Church of Jesus Christ of Latter-day Saints. Published Oct. 30, 2014. https://history .ChurchofJesusChrist.org/article/meliton-trejo-translator-missionary-colonist.

Georgia Weekly Telegraph. Macon. 1869–80.

Gibson, Walter M. Certificate to Jonathan W. Napela, Oct. 9, 1862. CHL.

————. *The Prison of Weltevreden; and a Glance at the East Indian Archipelago.* New York: J. C. Riker, 1855.

Gilson, R. P. *Samoa, 1830 to 1900: The Politics of a Multi-cultural Community.* Melbourne, Australia: Oxford University Press, 1970.

Givens, Terryl L. *The Viper on the Hearth: Mormons, Myths, and the Construction of Heresy.* Updated ed. New York: Oxford University Press, 2013.

Givens, Terryl L., and Matthew J. Grow. *Parley P. Pratt: The Apostle Paul of Mormonism.* New York: Oxford University Press, 2011.

Glines, James H. Reminiscences and Diary, 1845–99. Copy at CHL.

Godbe, William S. "The Situation in Utah." *Medium and Daybreak* 2, no. 89 (Dec. 15, 1871): 406–7.

Godbe, W. S., and E. L. T. Harrison. "Prospectus. The Mormon Tribune, the Organ of Liberty and Progress, to Be Published Every Saturday, Salt Lake City, Utah Territory, E. L. T. Harrison, Editor." *Utah Magazine* 3, no. 30 (Nov. 27, 1869): 474–75.

"Godbeite Movement." *Tullidge's Quarterly Magazine* 1, no. 1 (Oct. 1880): 14–19.

Godfrey, Donald G. "'Canada's Brigham Young': Charles Ora Card, Southern Alberta Pioneer." *American Review of Canadian Studies* 28, no. 2 (Summer 1988): 223–38.

Godfrey, Donald G., and Rebecca S. Martineau-McCarty, eds. *An Uncommon Pioneer: The Journals of James Henry Martineau, 1828–1918.* Provo, UT: Religious Studies Center, Brigham Young University, 2008.

Godfrey, Kenneth W. *Logan, Utah: A One Hundred Fifty Year History.* [Logan, UT]: Exemplar, 2010.

Gordon, Sarah Barringer. "The Liberty of Self-Degradation: Polygamy, Woman Suffrage, and Consent in Nineteenth-Century America." *Journal of American History* 83, no. 3 (Dec. 1996): 815–47.

————. *The Mormon Question: Polygamy and Constitutional Conflict in Nineteenth-Century America.* Chapel Hill: University of North Carolina Press, 2002.

Gospel Herald. Voree, WI. 1847–50.

"Gospel Topics." The Church of Jesus Christ of Latter-day Saints. http://www.topics .ChurchofJesusChrist.org.

Gottfredson, Peter, ed. and comp. *History of Indian Depredations in Utah.* Salt Lake City: Skelton, 1919.

Grant, Heber J. Collection, 1852–1945 (bulk 1880–1945). CHL.

————. *Gospel Standards: Selections from the Sermons and Writings of Heber J. Grant.* Compiled by G. Homer Durham under the direction of John A. Widtsoe and Richard L. Evans. Salt Lake City: Improvement Era, 1941.

————. Journals, 1880–1945. Heber J. Grant Collection, 1852–1945 (bulk 1880–1945). CHL.

Grant, Heber J., and Rachel Grant Taylor. "When Brigham Young Watched a Waltz." *Improvement Era* 44, no. 11 (Nov. 1941): 654, 678.

Grant, Rachel Ridgway Ivins. "How I Became a Mormon," circa 1898. CHL.

Gray, J. A. C. *Amerika Samoa: A History of American Samoa and Its United States Naval Administration.* Annapolis, MD: United States Naval Institute, 1960.

Green, Ephraim. Diary, 1852–55. Mormon Missionary Diaries. BYU.

Greenwood, Alma. Journal, vol. 1, 1883. Mormon Missionary Diaries. BYU.

Griggs, Thomas C. Journal, Jan. 1893–Nov. 1894. Thomas C. Griggs, Journals, 1861–1903. CHL.

Groberg, Joseph H. "The Mormon Disfranchisements of 1882 to 1892." *BYU Studies* 16, no. 3 (Spring 1976): 399–408.

Grossberg, Michael. *Governing the Hearth: Law and the Family in Nineteenth-Century America.* Chapel Hill: University of North Carolina Press, 1985.

Grouard, Benjamin F. Journal, 1843–46. CHL.

Grow, Matthew J. *"Liberty to the Downtrodden": Thomas L. Kane, Romantic Reformer.* New Haven: Yale University Press, 2009.

Grow, Matthew J., and Ronald W. Walker. *The Prophet and the Reformer: The Letters of Brigham Young and Thomas Kane.* New York: Oxford University Press, 2015.

Grow, Nathan D. "One Masterpiece, Four Masters: Reconsidering the Authorship of the Salt Lake Tabernacle." *Journal of Mormon History* 31, no. 3 (Fall 2005): 171–97.

Gudde, Erwin G. *Bigler's Chronicle of the West: The Conquest of California, Discovery of Gold, and Mormon Settlement as Reflected in Henry William Bigler's Diaries.* Berkeley: University of California Press, 1962.

Gunn, Stanley R. *Oliver Cowdery: Second Elder and Scribe.* Salt Lake City: Bookcraft, 1962.

Haight, Isaac C. Journal, 1842–50. CHL. Also available in the Pioneer Database at https://history.ChurchofJesusChrist.org/overlandtravel/sources/6125 /haight-isaac-chauncey-journal-1842-june-1850-apr.

Hales, Brian C. *Joseph Smith's Polygamy.* 3 vols. Salt Lake City: Greg Kofford Books, 2013.

Hall, Charles B. Engraving Collection, no date. CHL.

Hamblin, Jacob. Journal, 1854–58. CHL.

Hamilton, Henry. Journals, 1851–1900. CHL.

Hamilton, Henry S. *Reminiscences of a Veteran.* Concord, NH: Republican Press, 1897.

Hammond, Francis A. Journals, 1852–57, 1864–67, 1883–93. CHL.

Hammond, George P., ed. *Campaigns in the West, 1856–1861: The Journal and Letters of Colonel John Van Deusen Du Bois with Pencil Sketches by Joseph Heger.* Tucson: Arizona Pioneers Historical Society, 1949.

Hammond, Mary Jane Dilworth. Journal, vol. 1, 1853–55. Mormon Missionary Diaries. BYU.

Hancock, Mosiah L. Autobiography, no date. Typescript. CHL.

Handy, Moses P. *The Official Directory of the World's Columbian Exposition, May 1st to October 30th, 1893.* Chicago: World's Columbian Exposition, 1893.

Hansen, Andrew. Autobiography, 1911–32. Andrew J. and Caroline P. Hansen Papers, 1883–1932. CHL.

Hansen, Lorin K. "Voyage of the *Brooklyn.*" *Dialogue: A Journal of Mormon Thought* 21, no. 3 (Autumn 1988): 47–72.

Hansen, Peter Olsen. Diaries, circa 1850–95. CHL.

———. Journal, circa 1876. Peter Olsen Hansen, Papers, 1869–93. CHL.

Harker, Joseph. Reminiscences and Journal, 1855–95. CHL.

Harrington, Daniel. *Early Procedure, Scenes and Personnel of the Brigham Young University.* Provo, UT: Brigham Young University, 1935.

Harris, Martha Ann Smith. Autobiography, circa 1920. Typescript. CHL.

Harris, R. Carl, ed. *Building the Kingdom in Samoa, 1888–2005.* Heber, UT: Harris Video Cases, 2006.

Harris, Richard P. "Martha Ann Smith Harris." *Relief Society Magazine* 11 (Jan. 1924): 11–18.

Harris, Ruth Mae Barney, comp. *Martha Ann: Daughter of Hyrum and Mary Fielding Smith.* Orem, UT: Likes, 2002.

Sources Cited

Harris, Sarah Hollister. *An Unwritten Chapter of Salt Lake 1851–1901.* New York: By the author, 1901.

Harrison, Elias L. T. "An Appeal to the People." *Utah Magazine* 3, no. 26 (Oct. 30, 1869): 406–8.

[Harrison, Elias L. T.]. "The Josephite Platform." *Utah Magazine* 3, no. 18 (Sept. 4, 1869): 280–83.

Harrison, Elias L. T., and William S. Godbe. "Manifesto from W. S. Godbe and E. L. T. Harrison." *Utah Magazine* 3, no. 30 (Nov. 27, 1869): 470–73.

Hart, Jennie M., John W. Hart, and R. Carl Harris. *The Expanded Samoan Mission History, 1888–1900.* Publication place unidentified: By the authors; Provo, UT: Brigham Young University Media Services, 1988.

Hartley, William G. "From Men to Boys: LDS Aaronic Priesthood Offices, 1829–1996." *Journal of Mormon History* 22, no. 1 (Spring 1996): 80–136.

———. "The Great Florence Fitout of 1861." *BYU Studies* 24, no. 3 (Summer 1984): 341–71.

———. "Latter-day Saint Emigration during the Civil War." In *Civil War Saints,* edited by Kenneth L. Alford, 237–65. Provo, UT: Religious Studies Center, Brigham Young University; Salt Lake City: Deseret Book, 2012.

———. "Mormons, Crickets, and Gulls: A New Look at an Old Story." *Utah Historical Quarterly* 38, no. 3 (Summer 1970): 224–39.

———. *My Fellow Servants: Essays on the History of the Priesthood.* Provo, UT: BYU Studies, 2010.

———. "The Priesthood Reorganization of 1877: Brigham Young's Last Achievement." BYU.

———. "Samuel D. Chambers." *New Era,* June 1974, 47–50.

Haslam, Gerald Myron. *Clash of Cultures: The Norwegian Experience with Mormonism, 1842–1920.* American University Studies. Series 9, History. Vol. 7. New York: Peter Lang, 1984.

Hatch, Charles M., and Todd M. Compton, eds. *A Widow's Tale: The 1884–1896 Diary of Helen Mar Kimball Whitney.* Logan: Utah State University Press, 2003.

Haven, Jesse. *Celestial Marriage, and the Plurality of Wives!* Cape Town, South Africa: W. Foelscher, [1854].

———. Journals, 1852–92. CHL.

———. *Some of the Principal Doctrines or Belief of the Church of Jesus Christ, of Latter Day Saints.* Cape Town, South Africa: W. Foelscher, [1852].

Haven, Jesse, William H. Walker, and Leonard I. Smith. *A Warning to All.* Cape of Good Hope: Publisher unidentified, [1853].

Hawaii Honolulu Mission. General Minutes, 1851–1972. CHL.

———. Manuscript History and Historical Reports, 1850–1978. CHL.

Hawley, Asa S. Autobiography, no date. Typescript. CHL.

Haws, J. B. "Joseph F. Smith's Encouragement of His Brother, Patriarch John Smith." In *Joseph F. Smith: Reflections on the Man and His Times,* edited by Craig K. Manscill, Brian D. Reeves, Guy L. Dorius, and J. B. Haws, 133–58. Provo, UT: Religious Studies Center, Brigham Young University; Salt Lake City: Deseret Book, 2013.

Haynes, Stephen R. *Noah's Curse: The Biblical Justification of American Slavery.* New York: Oxford University Press, 2002.

Heath, Steven H. "The Sacred Shout." *Dialogue: A Journal of Mormon Thought* 19, no. 3 (Fall 1986): 115–23.

Hedges, Andrew H., and Richard Neitzel Holzapfel. *Within These Prison Walls: Lorenzo Snow's Record Book, 1886–1897.* Provo, UT: Religious Studies Center, Brigham Young University; Salt Lake City: Deseret Book, 2010.

Hefner, Loretta L. "From Apostle to Apostate: The Personal Struggle of Amasa Mason Lyman." *Dialogue: A Journal of Mormon Thought* 16, no. 1 (Spring 1983): 90–104.

Helm, Elsie. Reminiscences. Private possession. Copy in Public Member Photos and Scanned Documents, Matilda Matey Dudley, 1818–95, at ancestry.com.

Henderson, W. W. *Crickets and Grasshoppers in Utah.* Logan: Utah Agricultural Experiment Station, Utah State Agricultural College, 1931.

Hendricks, Drusilla D. Reminiscences, circa 1877. Typescript. CHL.

Higbee, Janelle M. "President Mrs. Kimball: A Rhetoric of Words and Works." Master's thesis, Brigham Young University, 1998.

Hill, George Washington. "A Brief Acct of the Labors of G W Hill While Engaged on a Mission to the House of Israel," Oct. 1, 1876. In George W. Hill, Report, Oct. 1, 1876. CHL.

———. "An Indian Vision." *Juvenile Instructor* 12, no. 1 (Jan. 1, 1877): 11.

———. "My First Day's Work." *Juvenile Instructor* 10, no. 26 (Dec. 25, 1875): 309.

Hill, James B. "History of Utah State Prison, 1850–1952." Master's thesis, Brigham Young University, 1952.

Hill, Joseph John. "George Washington Hill," circa 1936. Transcript at FamilySearch, accessed Jan. 10, 2019, https://www.familysearch.org/photos/artifacts/36789957?p=20886584.

Historian's Office. Collected Historical Documents, circa 1851–69. CHL.

———. Correspondence Files, 1856–1926. CHL.

———. General Church Minutes, 1839–77. CHL.

———. History of the Church, 1839–circa 1882. 69 vols. CHL.

———. History of the Church, draft, 1845–67. CHL.

———. Letterpress Copybooks, 1854–79, 1885–86. CHL.

———. Minutes and Reports (local units), 1840–86. CHL.

———. Reports of Speeches, 1845–85. CHL.

Historical Department. Journal History of the Church, 1896–2001. CHL.

———. Office Journal, 1844–2012. CHL.

History of Box Elder County. Compiled by Box Elder County Daughters of the Pioneers. [Salt Lake City: Paragon, 1938].

History of Sanpete and Emery Counties, Utah, with Sketches of Cities, Towns, and Villages, Chronology of Important Events, Records of Indian Wars, Portraits of Prominent Persons, and Biographies of Representative Citizens. Ogden, UT: W. H. Lever, 1898.

Hittell, John S., ed., and Henry W. Bigler. "Diary of H. W. Bigler in 1847 and 1848." *Overland Monthly* 10 (July–Dec. 1887): 233–45.

Hittell, Theodore H. *History of California*. Vol. 2. San Francisco: N. J. Stone, 1897.

The Holy Bible, Containing the Old and New Testaments Translated Out of the Original Tongues: And with the Former Translations Diligently Compared and Revised, by His Majesty's Special Command. Authorized King James Version with Explanatory Notes and Cross References to the Standard Works of The Church of Jesus Christ of Latter-day Saints. Salt Lake City: The Church of Jesus Christ of Latter-day Saints, 2013.

Holzapfel, Richard Neitzel. *Every Stone a Sermon*. Salt Lake City: Bookcraft, 1992.

Holzapfel, Richard Neitzel, and T. Jeffrey Cottle. "A Visit to Nauvoo: September 1846." *Nauvoo Journal* 7, no. 1 (Spring 1995): 3–12.

Holzapfel, Richard Neitzel, and R. Q. Shupe. *Joseph F. Smith: Portrait of a Prophet*. Salt Lake City: Deseret Book, 2000.

"Home Literature." *Contributor* 9, no. 8 (June 1888): 297–302.

Homer, William Harrison. "The Passing of Martin Harris." *Improvement Era* 29, no. 5 (Mar. 1926): 468–72.

Hoopes, David S., and Roy Hoopes. *The Making of a Mormon Apostle: The Story of Rudger Clawson*. Lanham, MD: Madison Books, 1990.

Horne, Alice Merrill. "Cyrus Edwin Dallin." *Young Woman's Journal* 21, no. 9 (Sept. 1910): 491–97.

Horne, Mary Isabella. "Home Life in the Pioneer Fort." *Juvenile Instructor* 29, no. 6 (Mar. 15, 1894): 181–85.

———. "Migration and Settlement of the Latter Day Saints," 1884. Hubert H. Bancroft, Utah and the Mormons Collection, before 1889. Microfilm. CHL.

———. "Pioneer Reminiscences." *Young Woman's Journal* 13, no. 7 (July 7, 1902): 292–95.

Horner, John M. "Voyage of the Ship 'Brooklyn.'" *Improvement Era* 9, no. 10 (Aug. 1906): 794–98.

Hovey, Joseph G. Autobiography, 1845–56. Joseph G. Hovey, Papers, 1845–56, circa 1933. CHL.

Hudson, Angela Pulley. *Real Native Genius: How an Ex-slave and a White Mormon Became Famous Indians*. Chapel Hill: University of North Carolina Press, 2015.

Hunsaker, Curtis B. "History of the Norwegian Mission from 1851 to 1960." Master's thesis, Brigham Young University, 1965.

Huntington, Dimick B. Journal, 1857–59. CHL.

Huntington, Oliver B. Diary and Reminiscences, 1843–1900. Typescript. CHL.

Hymns of The Church of Jesus Christ of Latter-day Saints. Salt Lake City: The Church of Jesus Christ of Latter-day Saints, 1985.

"Important Letters." *Ensign of Liberty of the Church of Christ* 1, no. 6. (May 1848): 91–93.

"In Memory of T. B. H. Stenhouse." *Tullidge's Quarterly Magazine* 2, no. 1 (Apr. 1882): 91–92.

International Film Collection. CHL.

Interviews with Living Pioneers. Provo, UT: Brigham Young University, 1939. Copy at CHL.

Iosepa Branch. Historical Records, 1889–1917. CHL.

Irving, Gordon. "The Law of Adoption: One Phase of the Development of the Mormon Concept of Salvation, 1830–1900." *BYU Studies* 14, no. 3 (Spring 1974): 291–314.

The Isaac and Leah Bailey Dunford Family Story. 2nd ed. Bountiful, UT: Isaac and Leah Bailey Dunford Family Association, 2006.

Isaac Dunford Family Correspondence, 1865–82. CHL.

Ivins, Stanley S. "Notes on Mormon Polygamy." *Utah Historical Quarterly* 35, no. 4 (Fall 1967): 309–21.

Jackman, Levi. Journal, Mar. 1847–Apr. 1849. Trails of Hope: Overland Diaries and Letters, 1846–69. Digital Collections, Harold B. Lee Library, Brigham Young University, Provo, UT.

Jackson, Richard H., and Mark W. Jackson. "Iosepa: The Hawaiian Experience in Settling the Mormon West." *Utah Historical Quarterly* 76, no. 4 (Fall 2008): 316–37.

Jacob F. Secrist Family Papers, 1854–2008. CHL.

James, Jane Manning. Autobiography, circa 1902. CHL.

James, Kimberly Jensen. "'Between Two Fires': Women on the 'Underground' of Mormon Polygamy." *Journal of Mormon History* 8 (1981): 49–61.

James G. Willie Handcart Company. Emigrating Company Journal, May–Nov. 1856. Typescript. CHL.

Jensen, Devan, and Paul A. Hoffman. "From Mormon Battalion Member to Civil War Soldier: The Military Service of Henry Wells Jackson." *Mormon Historical Studies* 15, no. 1 (Spring 2014): 85–111.

Jensen, Juliaetta Bateman. *Little Gold Pieces: The Story of My Mormon Mother's Life*. Salt Lake City: Stanway, 1948.

Jensen, Richard L. "Diary of J. F. Ferdinand Dorius including a Brief Sketch of His Earlier Life," 1977. Typescript. In John F. F. Dorius, Autobiography and Journal, circa 1851–53. CHL.

———. "Forgotten Relief Societies, 1844–67." *Dialogue: A Journal of Mormon Thought* 16, no. 1 (Spring 1983): 105–25.

Jensen, Robin Scott. "Gleaning the Harvest: Strangite Missionary Work, 1846–1850." Master's thesis, Brigham Young University, 2005.

Jenson, Andrew. Collection, circa 1841–1942. CHL.

———. *History of the Scandinavian Mission*. Salt Lake City: Deseret News, 1927.

———. *Latter-day Saint Biographical Encyclopedia*. 4 vols. Salt Lake City: Deseret News, 1910–36.

———. "The Scandinavian Mission." *Improvement Era* 12, no. 10 (Aug. 1909): 809–18.

———. "Walter Murray Gibson: A Sketch of His Life and Adventures, in Two Chapters." *Improvement Era* 4, no. 1 (Nov. 1900): 5–13; 4, no. 2 (Dec. 1900): 86–95.

Jeremy, Thomas E. Journals, 1852–86. 17 vols. Thomas E. Jeremy Collection, 1827–1931. CHL.

Jessee, Dean C. "Brigham Young's Family: The Wilderness Years." *BYU Studies* 19, no. 4 (Summer 1979): 474–500.

———, ed. *Letters of Brigham Young to His Sons*. With a foreword by J. H. Adamson. Salt Lake City: Deseret Book, 1974.

———. "'A Man of God and a Good Kind Father': Brigham Young at Home." *BYU Studies* 40, no. 2 (2001): 23–53.

Johnson, Benjamin Franklin. "A Life Review," after 1893. Benjamin F. Johnson, Papers, 1852–1923. CHL.

Johnson, Inger C. Autobiography. In Inger C. Johnson Autobiography and Lester F. Nielsen Journal, 1907–9. CHL.

Johnson, Sixtus. Journal. Typescript. In "Leaves from the Family Tree of Sixtus Ellis Johnson," 1955. BYU.

Jones, Albert. Notes, circa 1906. CHL.

Jones, Daniel W. *Forty Years among the Indians: A True yet Thrilling Narrative of the Author's Experiences among the Natives*. Salt Lake City: Juvenile Instructor, 1890.

Jones, Sondra. *The Trial of Don Pedro León Luján: The Attack against Indian Slavery and Mexican Traders in Utah*. Salt Lake City: University of Utah Press, 2000.

Jorgensen, Lynne Watkins. "The Mechanics' Dramatic Association: London and Salt Lake City." *Journal of Mormon History* 23, no. 2 (Fall 1997): 155–84.

The Joseph Smith Papers. Church History Department, The Church of Jesus Christ of Latter-day Saints. http://josephsmithpapers.org.

Journal of Discourses. 26 vols. Liverpool: F. D. Richards, 1855–86.

The Journal of George Q. Cannon. 1849–1901. Church History Department, The Church of Jesus Christ of Latter-day Saints. http://churchhistorianspress.org.

Journal of the House of Representatives of the United States: Being the Second Session of the Thirty-Seventh Congress; Begun and Held at the City of Washington, December 2, 1861, the Eighty-Sixth Year of the Independence of the United States. Washington, DC: Government Printing Office, 1862.

Journal of the House of Representatives of the United States, Being the Second Session of the Forty-Sixth Congress, Begun and Held at the City of Washington, December 1, 1879, in the One Hundred and Fourth Year of the Independence of the United States. Washington, DC: Government Printing Office, 1880.

JSP, CFM / Grow, Matthew J., Ronald K. Esplin, Mark Ashurst-McGee, Gerrit J. Dirkmaat, and Jeffrey D. Mahas, eds. *Council of Fifty, Minutes, March 1844–January 1846*. Administrative Records series of *The Joseph Smith Papers*, edited by Ronald K. Esplin, Matthew J. Grow, and Matthew C. Godfrey. Salt Lake City: Church Historian's Press, 2016.

JSP, D3 / Dirkmaat, Gerrit J., Brent M. Rogers, Grant Underwood, Robert J. Woodford, and William G. Hartley, eds. *Documents, Volume 3: February 1833–March 1834*. Vol. 3 of the Documents series of *The Joseph Smith Papers*, edited by Ronald K. Esplin and Matthew J. Grow. Salt Lake City: Church Historian's Press, 2014.

JSP, D4 / Godfrey, Matthew C., Brenden W. Rensink, Alex D. Smith, Max H Parkin, and Alexander L. Baugh, eds. *Documents, Volume 4: April 1834–September 1835*. Vol. 4 of the Documents series of *The Joseph Smith Papers*, edited by Ronald K. Esplin, Matthew J. Grow, and Matthew C. Godfrey. Salt Lake City: Church Historian's Press, 2016.

JSP, D5 / Rogers, Brent M., Elizabeth A. Kuehn, Christian K. Heimburger, Max H Parkin, Alexander L. Baugh, and Steven C. Harper, eds. *Documents, Volume 5: October 1835–January 1838*. Vol. 5 of the Documents series of *The Joseph Smith Papers*, edited by Ronald K. Esplin, Matthew J. Grow, and Matthew C. Godfrey. Salt Lake City: Church Historian's Press, 2017.

JSP, J1 / Jessee, Dean C., Mark Ashurst-McGee, and Richard L. Jensen, eds. *Journals, Volume 1: 1832–1839*. Vol. 1 of the Journals series of *The Joseph Smith Papers*, edited by Dean C. Jessee, Ronald K. Esplin, and Richard Lyman Bushman. Salt Lake City: Church Historian's Press, 2008.

JSP, J3 / Hedges, Andrew H., Alex D. Smith, and Brent M. Rogers, eds. *Journals, Volume 3: May 1843–June 1844*. Vol. 3 of the Journals series of *The Joseph Smith Papers*, edited by Ronald K. Esplin and Matthew J. Grow. Salt Lake City: Church Historian's Press, 2015.

Sources Cited

Jubilee History of Latter-day Saints Sunday Schools. 1849–1899. Salt Lake City: Deseret Sunday School Union, 1900.

Judd, Lois Gunn. "History," 1924. Typescript. Pioneer Memorial Museum, International Society Daughters of Utah Pioneers, Salt Lake City.

"Justifiable Obedience." *Utah Magazine* 3, no. 24 (Oct. 16, 1869): 379.

Kane, Elizabeth Wood. *Twelve Mormon Homes Visited in Succession on a Journey through Utah to Arizona.* Utah, the Mormons, and the West, edited by Everett L. Cooley, Brigham D. Madsen, S. Lyman Tyler, and Margery W. Ward, vol. 4. Salt Lake City: Tanner Trust Fund, University of Utah Library, 1974.

Kane, Thomas L. Collection, 1762–1982. Microfilm. CHL.

———. Diary, 1858. BYU.

———. Journal, Nov. 1851–Sept. 1852. Thomas L. Kane Personal Papers, 1835–86. Kane Family Papers, 1690–1982. BYU.

———. *The Mormons, a Discourse Delivered before the Historical Society of Pennsylvania: March 26, 1850.* Philadelphia: King and Baird, 1850.

———. Personal Papers, 1835–86. Kane Family Papers, 1690–1982. BYU.

Karl G. Maeser Religious Lecture Minutes. 1878–79. BYU.

Karren, Thomas. Journals, 1853–54. CHL.

Kearny, Stephen Watts. Papers, 1810–1962. Missouri Historical Society Archives, St. Louis.

Keeler, James. Journals, 1850–59, 1876–90. CHL.

Kemble, E. C. "Confirming the Gold Discovery." *Century Illustrated Monthly Magazine* 41 (Feb. 1891): 538–39.

Kenney, Scott G. "Before the Beard: Trials of the Young Joseph F. Smith." *Sunstone,* no. 120 (Nov. 2001): 20–42.

Kester, Matthew. *Remembering Iosepa: History, Place, and Religion in the American West.* New York: Oxford University Press, 2013.

Kimball, Edward L. "Confession in LDS Doctrine and Practice." *BYU Studies* 36, no. 2 (1996–97): 7–73.

Kimball, Edward L., and Kenneth W. Godfrey. "Law and Order in Winter Quarters." *Journal of Mormon History* 32, no. 1 (Spring 2006): 172–218.

Kimball, Heber C. Journal, Nov. 1845–Jan. 1846. CHL.

King, Carole C. Collection, 1854–1916. CHL.

King, Hannah Tapfield. Autobiography, circa 1864–72. 7 vols. CHL.

Kingsford, Elizabeth H. Autobiographical Sketch, no date. Typescript. CHL.

Kirtland Elders' Certificates / Kirtland Elders Quorum. "Record of Certificates of Membership and Ordinations of the First Members and Elders of the Church of Jesus Christ of Latter Day Saints Dating from March 21st 1836 to June 18th 1838 Kirtland Geauga Co. Ohio," 1836–38. CHL.

Knack, Martha C. *Boundaries Between: The Southern Paiutes, 1775–1995.* Lincoln: University of Nebraska Press, 2001.

Korn, Alfons L. *News from Molokai: Letters between Peter Kaeo and Queen Emma, 1873–1876.* Honolulu: University of Hawaii Press, 1976.

Krenkel, John H., ed. *Life and Times of Joseph Fish.* Danville, IL: Interstate, 1970.

Kuhre, Martin P. Journal, 1861–65. Typescript. CHL.

Lanman, Charles. *A Summer in the Wilderness; Embracing a Canoe Voyage up the Mississippi and around Lake Superior.* New York: D. Appleton, 1847.

Larsen, Bent Rolfsen. "Memories of My Father Bent Rolfsen Larsen," 1963. B. F. Larsen Collection, 1910–70. BYU.

Larsen, Christian J. Journals, 1851–1914. CHL.

Larsen, Hans P. Autobiographical Sketch, 1928. Typescript. CHL.

Larsen, Lorena Eugenia Washburn. *Autobiography of Lorena Eugenia Washburn Larsen.* Published by her children. [Provo, UT]: Brigham Young University Press, 1962.

———. "The Story of Bent Rolfsen Larsen." Typescript. Lorena W. Larsen, Papers, no date. CHL.

Larsen, Oluf Christian. "A Biographical Sketch of the Life of Oluf Christian Larsen Dictated by Himself and Written by His Son Oluf Larsen Dedicated to His Posterity Who Might Desire to Read It," 1916. CHL.

Latter Day Saints' Messenger and Advocate. Kirtland, OH. 1834–37.

Latter-day Saints' Millennial Star. Liverpool. 1840–1970.

Launius, Roger D. "Methods and Motives: Joseph Smith III's Opposition to Polygamy, 1860–90." *Dialogue: A Journal of Mormon Thought* 20, no. 4 (Winter 1987): 105–20.

La voz del desierto. Periodico mormonico. Organo de la Rama mexicana de "La Iglesia Cristiana de los Santos de los Ultimos Dias." Mexico City, 1879. Copy at BYU.

Leavitt, M. B. *Fifty Years in Theatrical Management.* New York: Broadway, 1912.

LeCheminant, Wilford Hill. "A Crisis Averted? General Harney and the Change in Command of the Utah Expedition." *Utah Historical Quarterly* 51, no. 1 (Winter 1983): 30–45.

Lee, John D. Journal, Nov. 1846–July 1847. John D. Lee, Papers, 1841–77. Huntington Library, San Marino, CA. Also available in Charles Kelly, ed., *Journals of John D. Lee, 1846–47 and 1859* (Salt Lake City: Western, 1938).

———. *Mormonism Unveiled; or, The Life and Confessions of the Late Mormon Bishop, John D. Lee; (Written by Himself) Embracing a History of Mormonism from Its Inception down to the Present Time, with an Exposition of the Secret History, Signs, Symbols and Crimes of the Mormon Church.* Edited by William Bishop. St. Louis: Bryan, Brand; New York: W. H. Stelle, 1877.

Leonard, Glen M. *Nauvoo: A Place of Peace, a People of Promise.* Salt Lake City: Deseret Book; Provo, UT: Brigham Young University Press, 2002.

"Letter of the Presidency." *Young Woman's Journal* 1, no. 1 (Oct. 1889): 19.

The Life Incidents and Travels of Elder William Holmes Walker and His Association with Joseph Smith, the Prophet. Publication place unidentified: Elizabeth Jane Walker Piepgrass, 1943.

"Life Sketch of Lorena Eugenia Washburn Larsen." Willard and Celia Luce Collection, 1929–2008. 19th Century Western and Mormon Manuscripts. BYU. Also available as *Autobiography of Lorena Eugenia Washburn Larsen,* published by her children (Provo, UT: Brigham Young University Press, 1962).

Liljenquist, Ola N. Autobiography, circa 1881. Typescript. CHL.

Lindsay, John S. *The Mormons and the Theatre; or, The History of Theatricals in Utah.* Salt Lake City: Publisher unidentified, 1905.

Little, James A. *Jacob Hamblin, a Narrative of His Personal Experience, as a Frontiersman, Missionary to the Indians, and Explorer, Disclosing Interpositions of Providence, Severe Privations, Perilous Situations and Remarkable Escapes.* Salt Lake City: Juvenile Instructor, 1881.

Little, Jesse C. Collection, 1844–1967. CHL.

Logan First Ward, Logan Stake. Relief Society Minutes and Records, 1881–1973. CHL.

Logan Journal. Logan, UT. 1889–91.

Logan Temple. Letterpress Copybook, 1877–1908. CHL.

———. Ward Account Book, 1881–83. CHL.

Los Angeles Star. Los Angeles. 1851–64.

Love, Andrew. Diary, 1852–75. CHL.

Ludlow, Daniel H., ed. *Encyclopedia of Mormonism.* 4 vols. New York: Macmillan, 1992.

Lund, Anthon. Journals, 1860–1921. CHL.

Lund, Jennifer L. "Out of the Swan's Nest: The Ministry of Anthon H. Lund, Scandinavian Apostle." *Journal of Mormon History* 29, no. 2 (Fall 2003): 77–105.

———. "'Pleasing to the Eyes of an Exile': The Latter-day Saint Sojourn at Winter Quarters, 1846–1848." *BYU Studies* 39, no. 2 (2000): 112–43.

Lyman, Albert R. *Biography: Francis Marion Lyman, 1840–1916, Apostle, 1880–1916.* Delta, UT: Melvin A. Lyman, 1958.

Lyman, Amasa M. Collection, 1832–77. CHL.

———. Journals, 1832–77. 44 vols. Amasa M. Lyman Collection, 1832–77. CHL.

Lyman, Edward Leo. *Amasa Mason Lyman, Mormon Apostle and Apostate: A Study in Dedication*. Salt Lake City: University of Utah Press, 2009.

———. "The Political Background of the Woodruff Manifesto." *Dialogue: A Journal of Mormon Thought* 24, no. 3 (Fall 1991): 21–39.

———. *Political Deliverance: The Mormon Quest for Utah Statehood*. With a foreword by Leonard J. Arrington. Urbana: University of Illinois Press, 1986.

Lyman, Eliza Maria Partridge. Journal, 1846–85. CHL.

Lyman, Francis Marion. Journals, 1860–1916. CHL.

Mace, Wandle. Autobiography, circa 1890. CHL.

MacKinnon, William P., ed. *At Sword's Point, Part 2: A Documentary History of the Utah War, 1858–1859*. Kingdom in the West: The Mormons and the American Frontier, edited by Will Bagley, vol. 11. Norman, OK: Arthur H. Clark, 2016.

Mackley, Jennifer Ann. *Wilford Woodruff's Witness: The Development of Temple Doctrine*. Seattle: High Desert, 2014.

Madsen, Brigham D. *Gold Rush Sojourners in Great Salt Lake City 1849 and 1850*. Salt Lake City: University of Utah Press, 1983.

———. *The Shoshoni Frontier and the Bear River Massacre*. Salt Lake City: University of Utah Press, 1985.

Madsen, Carol Cornwall. *An Advocate for Women: The Public Life of Emmeline B. Wells, 1870–1920*. Provo, UT: Brigham Young University Press; Salt Lake City: Deseret Book, 2006.

———. "'At Their Peril': Utah Law and the Case of Plural Wives, 1850–1900." *Western Historical Quarterly* 21, no. 4 (Nov. 1990): 425–44.

———. *Emmeline B. Wells: An Intimate History*. Salt Lake City: University of Utah Press, 2017.

———. "Schism in the Sisterhood: Mormon Women and Partisan Politics, 1890–1900." In *Battle for the Ballot: Essays on Woman Suffrage in Utah, 1870–1896,* edited by Carol Cornwall Madsen, 245–71. Logan: Utah State University Press, 1997.

Madsen, Susan Arrington. *I Walked to Zion: True Stories of Young Pioneers on the Mormon Trail*. Salt Lake City: Deseret Book, 1994.

Madsen, Truman G. *Defender of the Faith: The B. H. Roberts Story*. Salt Lake City: Bookcraft, 1980.

Maeser, Karl G. "How I Became a 'Mormon.'" *Improvement Era* 3, no. 1 (Nov. 1899): 23–26.

———. *School and Fireside*. [Provo, UT]: Skelton, 1897.

Maeser, Reinhard. *Karl G. Maeser: A Biography*. Provo, UT: Brigham Young University, 1928.

Manscill, Craig K. "Rumors of Secession in the Utah Territory, 1847–61." In *Civil War Saints,* edited by Kenneth L. Alford, 83–91. Provo, UT: Religious Studies Center, Brigham Young University; Salt Lake City: Deseret Book, 2012.

Manuscript History of the Samoan Mission, circa 1930. CHL.

Margetts, Phil. "Early Theatricals in Utah." *Juvenile Instructor* 38, no. 10 (May 15, 1903): 289–93.

Marsden, George M. *The Soul of the American University: From the Protestant Establishment to Established Nonbelief*. New York: Oxford University Press, 1994.

Martin, Edward. Journal, 1852–55. CHL.

Martineau, James Henry. Collection, 1822–1932. CHL.

———. "The Mountain Meadow Catastrophy," July 23, 1907. CHL.

Mason, Patrick Q. *The Mormon Menace: Violence and Anti-Mormonism in the Postbellum South*. New York: Oxford University Press, 2011.

Maughan, Mary Ann Weston. Autobiography, 1894–98. Typescript. CHL. Also available as Mary Ann Weston Maughan, Journal, in *Joel E. Ricks Collection of Transcriptions,* vol. 1 (Logan: Library of the Utah State Agricultural College, 1955).

McAllister, John D. T. Journals, 1851–1906. CHL.

McBride, Matthew. S. *A House for the Most High: The Story of the Original Nauvoo Temple*. Salt Lake City: Greg Kofford Books, 2007.

McBride, Ralph L. "Utah Mail Service before the Coming of the Railroad, 1869." Master's thesis, Brigham Young University, 1957.

McBride, Spencer. "Mormon Beginnings in Samoa: Kimo Belio, Samuela Manoa and Walter Murray Gibson." *Mormon Pacific Historical Society* 27, no. 1 (2006): 57–73.

McCormick, John S., and John R. Sillito. "Henry W. Lawrence: A Life in Dissent." In *Differing Visions: Dissenters in Mormon History,* edited by Roger D. Launius and Linda Thatcher, 220–40. Urbana: University of Illinois Press, 1994.

McDonnel, William J. Reminiscence, circa 1889. 2 parts. CHL.

———. "The Start of the Mission among the Maoris of New Zealand." Part 1. Typescript. In William J. McDonnel, Reminiscence, circa 1889. CHL.

McIntyre, Myron W., and Noel R. Barton, eds. *Christopher Layton.* [Salt Lake City]: Christopher Layton Family Organization, 1966.

McKenzie, George. "Cause and Origin of the Walker War." In *History of Indian Depredations in Utah,* compiled and edited by Peter Gottfredson, 43–47. Salt Lake City: Skelton, 1919.

McLachlan, James. *American Boarding Schools: A Historical Study.* New York: Charles Scribner's Sons, 1970.

McPherson, James M. *Battle Cry of Freedom: The Civil War Era.* Edited by C. Vann Woodward. Vol. 6 of *The Oxford History of the United States.* New York: Oxford University Press, 1988.

McPherson, Robert S. *A History of San Juan County: In the Palm of Time.* Salt Lake City: Utah State Historical Society, 1995.

Mecham, Travis Q. "Changes in Seniority to the Quorum of the Twelve Apostles of The Church of Jesus Christ of Latter-day Saints." Master's thesis, Utah State University, 2009.

Meeks, Priddy. Journal, 1879–86. Typescript. Microfilm 161,939. U.S. and Canada Record Collection. FHL.

———. Reminiscences, 1879. CHL.

Meha, Stuart. "A Prophetic Utterance of Paora Potangaroa." *Te Karere* 43, no. 10 (Oct. 1948): 298–99.

Memorial of Emeline B. Wells and Zina Young Williams, of Salt Lake City, Utah Territory, to the Senate and House of Representatives of the United States, in Congress Assembled: Asking for a Repeal of the Anti-polygamy Law of 1862, and for Legislation to Protect the Women and Children of Utah Territory. Washington, DC, 1879.

Mendenhall, William. Diaries, 1842–96. CHL.

Merrill, Marriner W. Journals, 1889–1906. CHL.

Merrill, Milton R. *Reed Smoot: Apostle in Politics.* New York: Columbia University, 1950.

Message from the President of the United States, Transmitting Information in reference to the Condition of Affairs in the Territory of Utah, Jan. 9, 1852. H.R. Ex. Doc. 25, 32nd Cong., 1st Sess. (1852).

Mexican Mission. Manuscript History and Historical Reports, 1874–1977. CHL.

Middleton, Charles F. Journals, 1855–1915. 12 vols. Charles F. Middleton Collection, 1836–1941. CHL.

Miller, Charlene, and Alice Edvalson, comps. *One Hundred Fifty Years of History of the L.D.S. Sugar House Ward, 1854 to 2004.* Publication place and publisher unidentified, 2004.

Miller, David E. *Hole-in-the-Rock: An Epic in the Colonization of the Great American West.* Salt Lake City: University of Utah Press, 1966.

Miller, Effie Secrist. "History of Jacob Foutz Secrist." Jacob F. Secrist Family Papers, 1854–2008. CHL.

Miller, Reuben. Journals, 1848–49. CHL.

———. Letter to Henry Sabey, Nov. 16, 1848. CHL.

Mills, H. W. "De Tal Palo Tal Astilla." *Annual Publication, Historical Society of Southern California* 10, no. 3 (1917): 86–174.

Minute Book 2 / "The Conference Minutes and Record Book of Christ's Church of Latter Day Saints," 1838, 1842, 1844. CHL.

"Minute Book of the Deacon's Quorum Salt Lake City. 1873." Vol. 2. Salt Lake Stake, Aaronic Priesthood Minutes and Records, 1857–64, 1873–77. CHL.

"Minutes of Meetings Held in the 8th. Ward G. S. L. City." Eighth Ward, Liberty Stake, General Minutes, 1856–1976. CHL.

Missionary Database. Church History Department, The Church of Jesus Christ of Latter-day Saints. http://history.ChurchofJesusChrist.org/missionary.

Missionary Reports, 1831–1900. CHL.

Mitchell, Martin. "Gentile Impressions of Salt Lake City, Utah, 1849–1870." *Geographical Review* 87, no. 3 (July 1997): 334–52.

Moffat, Riley M., Fred E. Woods, and Jeffrey N. Walker. *Gathering to La'ie*. Mormons in the Pacific Series. Laie, HI: Jonathan Napela Center for Hawaiian and Pacific Islands Studies, 2011.

Monnett, John D., Jr. "The Mormon Church and Its Private School System in Utah: The Emergence of the Academies, 1880–1892." PhD diss., University of Utah, 1984.

Morgan, Dale. *Overland in 1846: Diaries and Letters of the California-Oregon Trail*. Vol. 1. Lincoln: University of Nebraska Press, 1993.

Morgenstjernen. Salt Lake City. 1882–95.

Morison, Samuel Eliot. *Three Centuries of Harvard, 1636–1936*. Cambridge, MA: Belknap Press of Harvard University, 1936.

Mormon. New York City. 1855–57.

Mormon Battalion Company C. Muster Roll, 1846. CHL.

Mormon Tribune. Salt Lake City, 1870.

Moroni Ward, North Sanpete Stake. Relief Society Minutes and Records, 1871–1920. CHL.

Morris, George. Autobiography, circa 1880–90. Typescript. CHL.

Morris, Thomas. Journal, 1849–50. Typescript. CHL.

The Mountain Meadows Massacre. https://mountainmeadowsmassacre.com.

Mulder, William. *Homeward to Zion: The Mormon Migration from Scandinavia*. Minneapolis: University of Minnesota Press, 2000.

Nartonis, David K. "The Rise of 19th-Century American Spiritualism, 1854–1873." *Journal for the Scientific Study of Religion* 49, no. 2 (June 2010): 361–73.

National Intelligencer. Washington, DC. 1810–69.

National Republican. Washington, DC. 1872–88.

Nauvoo Legion. Great Salt Lake Military District. Nauvoo Legion (Utah) Records, 1852–58. CHL.

Nauvoo Neighbor. Nauvoo, IL. 1843–45.

Neilson, Peter. Family Record, no date. CHL.

Neilson, Reid L. *Exhibiting Mormonism: The Latter-day Saints and the 1893 Chicago World's Fair*. New York: Oxford University Press, 2011.

Neilson, Reid L., and Mitchell K. Schaefer. "Excavating Early Mormon History: The 1878 History Fact-Finding Mission of Apostles Joseph F. Smith and Orson Pratt." In *Joseph F. Smith: Reflections on the Man and His Times*, edited by Craig K. Manscill, Brian D. Reeves, Guy L. Dorius, and J. B. Haws, 359–78. Provo, UT: Religious Studies Center, Brigham Young University; Salt Lake City: Deseret Book, 2013.

Neilson, Reid L., and Nathan N. Waite, eds. *Settling the Valley, Proclaiming the Gospel: The General Epistles of the Mormon First Presidency*. New York: Oxford University Press, 2017.

Nelson, William E. *The Fourteenth Amendment: From Political Principle to Judicial Doctrine*. Cambridge, MA: Harvard University Press, 1988.

Newell, Quincy D. *Your Sister in the Gospel: The Life of Jane Manning James, a Nineteenth-Century Black Mormon*. New York: Oxford University Press, 2019.

"New Movement." *Utah Magazine* 3, no. 34 (Dec. 25, 1869): 531.

New North-West. Deer Lodge, MT. 1869–97.

News Department. "Journal of Indian Treaty Days." *Washington Historical Quarterly* 11, no. 1 (Jan. 1920): 75–76.

Newton, Marjorie. *Mormon and Maori*. Salt Lake City: Greg Kofford Books, 2014.

———. *Tiki and Temple: The Mormon Mission in New Zealand, 1854–1958*. Salt Lake City: Greg Kofford Books, 2012.

New York Daily Tribune. New York City. 1842–66.

New York Herald. New York City. 1835–1924.

New-York Messenger. New York City. 1845.

New York Reformer. Watertown, NY. 1850–67.

New York Sun. New York City. 1833–1916.

New York Times. New York City. 1851–.

New Zealand Auckland Mission. Manuscript History and Historical Reports, 1854–1974. CHL.

Nibley, Charles W. "Reminiscences of President Joseph F. Smith." *Improvement Era* 22, no. 3 (Jan. 1919): 191–98.

Nibley, Preston. *Brigham Young: The Man and His Work.* Salt Lake City: Deseret News, 1936.

———. *The Presidents of the Church.* Salt Lake City: Deseret Book, 1974.

Nicholson, John. *The Martyrdom of Joseph Standing; or, The Murder of a "Mormon" Missionary. A True Story.* Salt Lake City: Deseret News, 1886.

Nixon, Loretta D., and L. Douglas Smoot. *Abraham Owen Smoot: A Testament of His Life.* Provo, UT: Brigham Young University Press, 1994.

Norton, Jacob. Reminiscence and Journal, 1844–52. CHL.

Nuttall, L. John. Diaries, 1876–1904. Microfilm. L. John Nuttall, Papers, 1854–1903. CHL. Originals at BYU.

Oaks, Dallin H., and Joseph I. Bentley. "Joseph Smith and Legal Process: In the Wake of the Steamboat *Nauvoo.*" *BYU Studies* 19, no. 2 (Winter 1979): 167–99.

Oaks, Dallin H., and Marvin S. Hill. *Carthage Conspiracy: The Trial of the Accused Assassins of Joseph Smith.* Urbana: University of Illinois Press, 1975.

"The Old B. Y. Academy." *Young Woman's Journal* 3, no. 8 (May 1892): 336–43.

Olsen, Andrew D. *The Price We Paid: The Extraordinary Story of the Willie and Martin Handcart Pioneers.* Salt Lake City: Deseret Book, 2006.

Olsen, Andrew D., and Jolene S. Allphin. *Follow Me to Zion: Stories from the Willie Handcart Pioneers.* With art by Julie Rogers. Salt Lake City: Deseret Book, 2013.

"On the Canadian Frontier: Stories of Life in the Charles and Zina Card Home." Church History website, The Church of Jesus Christ of Latter-day Saints. Published May 18, 2012. https://history.ChurchofJesusChrist.org/article/life-in-card-home-cardston.

Openshaw, Samuel. Diary, 1856. CHL.

Orton, Chad M. "The Martin Handcart Company at the Sweetwater: Another Look." *BYU Studies* 45, no. 3 (2006): 5–37.

Otterstrom, F. W. "A Journey to the South: Gems from President Smith's Talks to the People on the Way." *Improvement Era* 21, no. 2 (Dec. 1917): 97–111.

"Our Workmen's Wages." *Utah Magazine* 3, no. 17 (Aug. 28, 1869): 262–64.

Pace, William B. Autobiography, 1904. Typescript. CHL.

———. Collection, circa 1857–1970. CHL.

Pacific Commercial Advertiser. Honolulu. 1856–88.

Pack, John. Papers, 1833–82. CHL.

Pack, Marvin E. "The Sandwich Islands Country and Mission." *Contributor* 17, no. 10 (Aug. 1896): 608–14; 17, no. 11 (Sept. 1896): 692–96.

Panek, Tracey E. "Life at Iosepa, Utah's Polynesian Colony." *Utah Historical Quarterly* 60, no. 1 (Winter 1992): 64–77.

———. "Search and Seizure in Utah: Recounting the Antipolygamy Raids." *Utah Historical Quarterly* 62, no. 4 (Fall 1994): 316–34.

Papers relating to the Foreign Relations of the United States, Transmitted to Congress, with the Annual Message of the President, December 5, 1881. Washington, DC: Government Printing Office, 1882.

Parker, B. G. *Recollections of the Mountain Meadows Massacre.* Plano, CA: Fred W. Reed, 1901.

"Parley P. Pratt, October 31, 1852: Report of His Mission to Chile." Transcribed by LaJean Purcell Carruth. Church History website, The Church of Jesus Christ of Latter-day Saints. Published Apr. 29, 2013. https://history.ChurchofJesusChrist.org/article /lost-sermons-parley-p-pratt-october-1852.

Parowan Stake. Historical Record, 1855–60. CHL.

Parry, John. Reminiscences and Diary, 1857–67. CHL.

Parry, Mae O. Timbimboo. Interview by Scott R. Christensen and A. J. Simmonds, Mar. 9, 1988. Photocopy of typescript. CHL.

Partridge, Edward, Jr. Journals, 1854–99. CHL.

Patterson, Adam. Shorthand Notes of John D. Lee's Second Trial, no date. Jacob S. Boreman Collection, Huntington Library, San Marino, CA. Transcript available at http://mountain meadowsmassacre.com.

The Pearl of Great Price: A Selection from the Revelations, Translations, and Narrations of Joseph Smith, First Prophet, Seer, and Revelator to The Church of Jesus Christ of Latter-day Saints. Salt Lake City: The Church of Jesus Christ of Latter-day Saints, 2013.

Perkins, Edward T. *Na Motu; or, Reef-Rovings in the South Seas. A Narrative of Adventures at the Hawaiian, Georgian and Society Islands; with Maps, Twelve Original Illustrations, and an Appendix*. New York: Pudney and Russell, 1854.

Perkins, Eric, and Mary Jane Woodger. "Administration from the Underground." In *Champion of Liberty: John Taylor*, edited by Mary Jane Woodger, 347–70. Provo, UT: Religious Studies Center, Brigham Young University, 2009.

Perpetual Emigrating Fund Company. General Files, 1850–87. CHL.

Peterson, Charles. *Take Up Your Mission: Mormon Colonizing along the Little Colorado River, 1870–1900*. Tucson: University of Arizona Press, 1973.

Peterson, John Alton. *Utah's Black Hawk War*. Salt Lake City: University of Utah Press, 1998.

Peterson, Paul H. *The Mormon Reformation*. Dissertations in Latter-day Saint History. Provo, UT: Joseph Fielding Smith Institute for Latter-day Saint History; BYU Studies, 2002.

———. "The Mormon Reformation of 1856–1857: The Rhetoric and Reality." *Journal of Mormon History* 15 (1989): 59–87.

Peterson, Paul H., and Ronald W. Walker. "Brigham Young's Word of Wisdom Legacy." *BYU Studies* 42, nos. 3 and 4 (2003): 29–64.

Philadelphia Sunday Mercury. Philadelphia. 1860–63.

Phipps, Kelly Elizabeth. "Marriage and Redemption: Mormon Polygamy in the Congressional Imagination, 1862–1887." *Virginia Law Review* 95, no. 2 (Apr. 2009): 435–87.

Pic-nic Party at the Head Waters of Big Cottonwood. Great Salt Lake City: July 18, 1857. Copy at CHL.

Pioneer Database. Church History Department, The Church of Jesus Christ of Latter-day Saints. http://history.ChurchofJesusChrist.org/overlandtravel.

Pitchforth, Samuel. Diary, 1857–61. CHL.

Platt, Benjamin. Reminiscences, 1899–1905. CHL.

Plewe, Brandon S., ed. *Mapping Mormonism: An Atlas of Latter-day Saint History*. Provo, UT: Brigham Young University Press, 2012.

Poll, Richard D. "The Legislative Antipolygamy Campaign." *BYU Studies* 26, no. 4 (Fall 1986): 107–21.

———. "The Move South." *BYU Studies* 29, no. 4 (Fall 1989): 65–88.

Pomeroy, Franklin T. Statement, Apr. 11, 1898. CHL.

Pottawattamie High Council. Minutes, 1846–52. CHL.

Pottawattamie High Priests Quorum. Minutes, 1848–51. CHL.

Pratt, Addison. Autobiography and Journals, 1843–52. CHL.

Pratt, Eleanor J. McComb. Letter to "Brother Snow," May 14, 1857. CHL.

———. Reminiscence, circa 1857. Eleanor J. McComb Pratt, Papers, circa 1857. CHL.

Pratt, Louisa Barnes. Journal and Autobiography, 1850–80. CHL.

Pratt, Orson. Journal, Feb.–July 1846; May–July 1847. Orson Pratt, Autobiography and Journals, 1833–47. CHL.

———. Letter to Marian Ross Pratt, Sept. 18, 1878. CHL.

Pratt, Parley P. *The Autobiography of Parley Parker Pratt, One of the Twelve Apostles of The Church of Jesus Christ of Latter-day Saints, Embracing His Life, Ministry and Travels, with Extracts, in Prose and Verse, from His Miscellaneous Writings*. Edited by Parley P. Pratt Jr. New York: Russell Brothers, 1874.

———. Journal, 1855–56. CHL.

———. *A Voice of Warning and Instruction to All People, Containing a Declaration of the Faith and Doctrine of the Church of the Latter Day Saints, Commonly Called Mormons*. New York: W. Sandford, 1837.

Pratt, Stephen F. "Parley P. Pratt in Winter Quarters and the Trail West." *BYU Studies* 24 (Summer 1984): 373–88.

President Woodruff's Manifesto. Proceedings at the Semi-annual General Conference of The Church of Jesus Christ of Latter-day Saints, Monday Forenoon, October 6, 1890. [Salt Lake City]: Publisher unidentified, 1890.

Presiding Bishopric. Bishops Meeting Minutes, 1851–84. CHL.

Proceedings of a Council Held by O. H. Irish with Utah Indians at Spanish Fork, June 7, 1865. Utah American Indian Digital Archive, Main Collection, J. Willard Marriott Library, University of Utah, Salt Lake City.

Proceedings of the First Three Republican National Conventions of 1856, 1860 and 1864, including Proceedings of the Antecedent National Convention Held at Pittsburg, in February, 1856, as Reported by Horace Greeley. Minneapolis: Charles W. Johnson, 1893.

Proclamation of the Twelve Apostles of the Church of Jesus Christ, of Latter-day Saints. To All the Kings of the World; to the President of the United States of America; to the Governors of the Several States; and to the Rulers and People of All Nations. New York: [Prophet Office], 1845.

"Prospectus of Woman's Exponent, a Utah Ladies' Journal." In Peter Maughan, Papers, 1848–92. Special Collections and Archives, Merrill-Cazier Library, Utah State University, Logan.

Provo Daily Enquirer. Provo, UT. 1891–97.

Provo Second Ward, Utah Stake. Relief Society Minutes and Records, 1869–1973. CHL.

Provo Utah Central Stake. General Minutes, 1849–1977. CHL.

Quaife, Milo Milton, ed. *The Diary of James K. Polk, during His Presidency, 1845 to 1849. Now First Printed from the Original Manuscript in the Collections of the Chicago Historical Society.* Vol. 1. Chicago: A. C. McClurg, 1910.

Questions to Be Asked the Latter Day Saints. [Salt Lake City: 1856]. Copy at CHL.

Rasmussen, Victor J., and Myrtle Hancock Nielson. *The Manti Temple.* Manti, UT: Manti Temple Centennial Committee, 1988.

Reavis, L. U. *The Life and Military Services of Gen. William Selby Harney.* St. Louis: Bryan, Brand, 1878.

Record of Members Collection, 1836–1970. CHL.

Records of the Solicitor of the Treasury / National Archives Reference Service Report, Sept. 23, 1964. "Record Group 206, Records of the Solicitor of the Treasury, and Record Group 46, Records of the United States Senate: Records relating to the Mormons in Illinois, 1839–1848 (Records Dated 1840–1852), including Memorials of Mormons to Congress, 1840–1844, Some of Which Relate to Outrages Committed against the Mormons in Missouri, 1831–1839." Microfilm. Washington, DC: National Archives and Records Service, General Services Administration, 1964. Copy at CHL in Records Related to Church Interaction with Federal Government, 1840–52.

Reeder, Jennifer. "'To Do Something Extraordinary': Mormon Women and the Creation of a Usable Past." PhD diss., George Mason University, 2013.

Reeder, Jennifer, and Kate Holbrook, eds. *At the Pulpit: 185 Years of Discourses by Latter-day Saint Women.* Salt Lake City: Church Historian's Press, 2017.

Reeve, W. Paul. *Religion of a Different Color: Race and the Mormon Struggle for Whiteness.* New York: Oxford University Press, 2015.

Reeves, Brian D. "'Divert the Minds of the People': Mountain Meadows Massacre Recitals and Missionary Work." In *Go Ye into All the World: The Growth and Development of Mormon Missionary Work,* edited by Reid L. Neilson and Fred E. Woods, 291–315. Provo, UT: Religious Studies Center, Brigham Young University, 2012.

Reiter, Tonya. "Black Saviors on Mount Zion: Proxy Baptisms and Latter-day Saints of African Descent." *Journal of Mormon History* 43, no. 4 (Oct. 2017): 100–123.

Relief Society General Board. Minutes, 1842–2007. CHL.

Relief Society Historical Files. 1888–1984. CHL.

Report of the Utah Commission to the Secretary of the Interior. 1890. Washington, DC: Government Printing Office, 1890.

Reuben, Julie A. *The Making of the Modern University: Intellectual Transformation and the Marginalization of Morality.* Chicago: University of Chicago Press, 1996.

Revelations Collection, 1831–circa 1844, 1847, 1861, circa 1876. CHL.

Reynolds, George. Journals, 1861–81. CHL.

———. Papers, circa 1863–1920. BYU.

Rich, Charles C. Diaries, 1833–62. 15 vols. Charles C. Rich Collection, 1832–1908. CHL.

Rich, Christopher B., Jr. "The True Policy for Utah: Servitude, Slavery, and 'An Act in relation to Service.'" *Utah Historical Quarterly* 80, no. 1 (Winter 2012): 54–74.

Rich, Sarah P. Autobiography and Journal, 1885–90. CHL.

Richards, A. LeGrand. *Called to Teach: The Legacy of Karl G. Maeser.* Provo, UT: Religious Studies Center, Brigham Young University; Salt Lake City: Deseret Book, 2014.

———. "The Educational Legacy of Karl G. Maeser." *Religious Educator: Perspectives on the Restored Gospel* 17, no. 1 (2016): 22–39.

———. "Moritz Busch's Die Mormonen and the Conversion of Karl G. Maeser." *BYU Studies* 45, no. 4 (2006): 1–22.

Richards, Franklin D. Journals, 1844–99. Richards Family Collection, 1837–1961. CHL.

Richards, Henry P. Diaries. 1854–1900. Henry P. Richards, Papers, 1854–1900. CHL.

Richards, Jane Snyder. Autobiographical Sketch, 1881. CHL.

———. History of the Relief Society in Weber County, 1887. Jane S. Richards Papers, Richards Family Collection, 1837–1961. CHL.

Richards, Louisa Lula Greene. "How 'The Exponent' Was Started." *Relief Society Magazine* 14, no. 12 (Dec. 1927): 605–8.

———. Papers, circa 1860–1940. CHL.

Richards, Mary Haskin Parker. Diaries, 1846–48. CHL. Also available in Maureen Carr Ward, ed., *Winter Quarters, the 1846–1848 Life Writings of Mary Haskin Parker Richards* (Logan: Utah State University, 1991), 63–81.

———. Diary, May–July 1846. CHL.

Richards, Samuel W. Journal, vol. 1, 1846. Samuel W. Richards, Journals and Family Record, 1846–76. CHL.

———. Papers, circa 1847–59. CHL.

Richards, Willard. Journals, 1836–52. Willard Richards, Journals and Papers, 1821–54. CHL.

———. Journals and Papers, 1821–54. CHL.

Ricks, Nathaniel R., ed. *"My Candid Opinion": The Sandwich Island Diaries of Joseph F. Smith, 1856–1857.* Salt Lake City: Smith-Pettit Foundation, 2011.

Rives, John C. *The Congressional Globe: Containing the Debates and Proceedings of the Second Session of the Thirty-Seventh Congress.* Washington, DC: Congressional Globe, 1862.

Robbins, Louise Barnum, ed. *History and Minutes of the National Council of Women of the United States, Organized in Washington, D. C., March 31, 1888.* Boston: E. B. Stillings, 1898.

Roberts, Brigham Henry. *A Comprehensive History of The Church of Jesus Christ of Latter-day Saints: Century I.* 6 vols. Salt Lake City: Deseret News, 1930.

———. Diary, 1890–93. American Westward Migration Pioneer Diaries, J. Willard Marriott Library, University of Utah, Salt Lake City.

———. *The Life of John Taylor, Third President of The Church of Jesus Christ of Latter-day Saints.* Salt Lake City: George Q. Cannon and Sons, 1892.

———. "The Life Story of B. H. Roberts," circa 1933. CHL. Also available as Gary James Bergera, ed., *The Autobiography of B. H. Roberts* (Salt Lake City: Signature Books, 1990).

Rogers, Aurelia Spencer. *Life Sketches of Orson Spencer and Others, and History of Primary Work.* [Salt Lake City]: George Q. Cannon and Sons, 1898.

Rogers, Brent M. *Unpopular Sovereignty: Mormons and the Federal Management of Early Utah Territory.* Lincoln: University of Nebraska Press, 2017.

Rogers, Justus H. *Colusa County: Its History Traced from a State of Nature through the Early Period of Settlement and Development, to the Present Day with a Description of Its Resources, Statistical Tables, Etc.* Orland, CA: Publisher unidentified, 1891.

Rogerson, Josiah. Shorthand of John D. Lee's First Trial, no date. Josiah Rogerson, Transcripts and Notes of John D. Lee Trials, 1875–85. CHL. Transcript available at http://mountain meadowsmassacre.com.

Rohrbough, Malcolm J. *Days of Gold: The California Gold Rush and the American Nation*. Berkeley and Los Angeles: University of California Press, 1997.

Romney, Miles. Journal, circa 1850–circa 1855. Typescript. CHL.

Romney, Thomas Cottam. *The Mormon Colonies in Mexico*. Salt Lake City: University of Utah Press, 2005.

Rose, Roger G., Sheila Conant, and Eric P. Kjellgren. "Hawaiian Standing *Kāhili* in the Bishop Museum: An Ethnological and Biological Analysis." *Journal of the Polynesian Society* 102, no. 3 (Sept. 1993): 273–304.

Ryan, Rebekah J. "In the World: Latter-day Saints in the National Council of Women, 1888–1987." In *Summer Fellows' Papers 2003: Latter-day Saint Women in the Twentieth Century,* edited by Claudia L. Bushman, 131–47. Provo, UT: Joseph Fielding Smith Institute for Latter-day Saint History at Brigham Young University, 2004.

Sacramento Daily Record-Union. Sacramento, CA. Feb. 1875–Jan. 1891.

Sacramento Daily Union. Sacramento, CA. 1851–99.

Saint George Utah Stake. Manuscript History and Historical Reports, 1850–1977. CHL.

Saints' Herald. Independence, MO. 1860–.

Saints: The Story of the Church of Jesus Christ in the Latter Days. Vol. 1, *The Standard of Truth, 1815–1846*. Salt Lake City: The Church of Jesus Christ of Latter-day Saints, 2018.

Salt Lake City Eighth Ward, Liberty Stake. Relief Society Minute Book B, 1872–84. Eighth Ward, Liberty Stake, Relief Society Minutes and Records, 1867–1969. CHL.

Salt Lake Daily Telegraph. Salt Lake City. 1864–70.

Salt Lake Democrat. Salt Lake City. 1885–87.

Salt Lake Herald. Salt Lake City. 1870–1909.

Salt Lake Stake. General Minutes, 1869–1977. 8 vols. CHL.

———. High Council Minute Book of Courts, vol. 3, 1869–72. Salt Lake Stake, Confidential Minutes, 1869–1977. CHL.

———. Relief Society Record Book, 1868–1903. CHL.

Salt Lake Telegram. Salt Lake City. 1902–52.

Salt Lake Temple Dedication Services, 1893. CHL.

Salt Lake Times. Salt Lake City. 1875–92.

Salt Lake Tribune. Salt Lake City. 1871–.

"Salutatory." *Juvenile Instructor* 1, no. 1 (Jan. 1, 1866): 3.

Samoa Mission Manuscript History and Historical Reports, 1863–1966. CHL.

Sangamo Journal. Springfield, IL. 1831–47.

San Luis Colorado Stake. Manuscript History and Historical Reports, 1877–1977. CHL.

Sanpete Stake. General Minutes, 1877–1906. CHL.

———. Minutes, June 23, 25–28, 1875. CHL.

Santaquin Ward, Nebo Stake. Relief Society Minutes and Records, 1868–1920. CHL.

"Scandinavian Mission Emigration List 'G' 1881–1886." European Mission Emigration Records, Scandinavian Mission, 1852–1920. CHL.

Schoenfeld, Edward. "A Character Sketch of Dr. Karl G. Maeser." *Juvenile Instructor* 36, no. 6 (Mar. 15, 1901): 179–83.

School of the Prophets Provo Records, 1868–72. CHL.

School of the Prophets Salt Lake City Records, 1867–72. CHL.

Scofield, Charles J., ed. *History of Hancock County*. Vol. 2 of *Historical Encyclopedia of Illinois and History of Hancock County*. Chicago: Munsell, 1921.

Scott, James A. Journal, Mar.–July 1846. CHL.

Secrist, Jacob F. Collection, 1841–74. CHL.

Seegmiller, Janet Burton. *A History of Iron County: Community above Self.* Utah Centennial County History Series. Salt Lake City: Utah State Historical Society; Iron County Commission, 1998.

Seegmiller, William A. Journals, 1891–95, 1909–11. CHL.

Sources Cited

Semi-weekly Standard. Ogden, UT. 1888–1908.
A Series of Instructions and Remarks by President Brigham Young, at a Special Council, Tabernacle, March 21, 1858. [Salt Lake City: 1858]. Copy at CHL.
Sessions, Gene A. *Mormon Thunder: A Documentary History of Jedediah Morgan Grant.* Urbana: University of Illinois Press, 1982.
Sessions, Patty B. Diary, Feb. 1846–Dec. 1867. 6 vols. Patty B. Sessions, Diaries and Account Book, 1846–66, 1880. CHL. Also available in Donna Toland Smart, ed., *Mormon Midwife: The 1846–1888 Diary of Patty Bartlett Sessions,* Life Writings of Frontier Women 2 (Logan: Utah State University Press, 1997).
Shipps, Jan. "The Principle Revoked: Mormon Reactions to Wilford Woodruff's 1890 Manifesto." In *In the Whirlpool: The Pre-Manifesto Letters of President Wilford Woodruff to the William Atkin Family, 1885–1890,* edited by Reid L. Neilson, with contributions by Thomas G. Alexander and Jan Shipps, 112–24. Norman, OK: Arthur H. Clark, 2011.
Shirts, Morris A., and Kathryn H. Shirts. *A Trial Furnace: Southern Utah's Iron Mission.* Provo, UT: Brigham Young University Press, 2001.
Shumway, Larry V. "Dancing the Buckles off Their Shoes in Pioneer Utah." *BYU Studies* 37, no. 3 (1997–98): 6–50.
Sidwell, A. B. "Death of William Luke, Sr.," 1889. In William Luke Correspondence, 1849. CHL.
Sigman, Shayna M. "Everything Lawyers Know about Polygamy Is Wrong." *Cornell Journal of Law and Public Policy* 16, no. 1 (Fall 2006): 101–85.
Simmons, Rachel W. Collection, 1862–1971. CHL.
Simon, John Y., ed. *The Personal Memoirs of Julia Dent Grant (Mrs. Ulysses S. Grant).* Carbondale: Southern Illinois University Press, 1975.
Simpson, Thomas W. *American Universities and the Birth of Modern Mormonism, 1867–1940.* Chapel Hill: University of North Carolina Press, 2016.
Sjodahl, Janne M. "Apostle Anthon H Lund." *Juvenile Instructor* 35, no. 21 (Nov. 1900): 707, 709–11.
Skinner, Andrew C. "Civil War's Aftermath: Reconstruction, Abolition, and Polygamy." In *Civil War Saints,* edited by Kenneth L. Alford, 295–315. Provo, UT: Religious Studies Center, Brigham Young University, 2012.
Smith, Amanda Barnes. Notebook, 1854–66. CHL.
Smith, Bathsheba W. Autobiography, circa 1875–1906. CHL.
Smith, Bill, and Jared M. Tamez. "Plotino C. Rhodakanaty: Mormonism's Greek Austrian Mexican Socialist." In *Just South of Zion: The Mormons in Mexico and Its Borderlands,* edited by Jason H. Dormady and Jared M. Tamez, 55–72. Albuquerque: University of New Mexico Press, 2015.
Smith, Charles. Reminiscences and Diary, 1842–1905. Typescript. CHL.
Smith, Don H. "Leadership, Planning, and Management of the 1856 Mormon Handcart Emigration." *Annals of Iowa* 65 (Spring/Summer 2006): 124–61.
Smith, Elbert A. "David H. Smith in Utah." *Autumn Leaves* 25, no. 11 (Nov. 1912): 507–12.
Smith, Elias. Journal, 1854–58. Elias Smith, Journals, 1836–88. CHL.
Smith, George Albert. Journals, 1839–75. George A. Smith, Papers, 1834–77. CHL.
———. Papers, 1834–77. CHL.
———. *The Rise, Progress and Travels of The Church of Jesus Christ of Latter-day Saints, Being a Series of Answers to Questions, including the Revelation on Celestial Marriage, and a Brief Account of the Settlement of Salt Lake Valley, with Interesting Statistics.* Salt Lake City: Deseret News, 1869.
Smith, Inez. "Biography of Alexander Hale Smith.—Part 6." *Autumn Leaves* 25, no. 11 (Nov. 1912): 501–6.
Smith, Jesse N. Autobiography and Journal, 1855–1906. CHL.
Smith, John. Journal, 1846–54. John Smith, Papers, 1833–54. CHL.
———. Papers, 1833–54. CHL.
Smith, John, Charles C. Rich, John Young, and the High Council. Letter to D. C. Davis and Jesse D. Hunter, Nov. 16, 1847. CHL.

Smith, Joseph F. Letters to Martha Ann Smith Harris, 1855–97. CHL. Also available in Richard Neitzel Holzapfel and David M. Whitchurch, eds., *My Dear Sister: Letters between Joseph F. Smith and His Sister Martha Ann Smith Harris* (Provo, UT: Religious Studies Center, Brigham Young University, in cooperation with Deseret Book, Salt Lake City, 2018).

———. Letter to Samuel L. Adams, May 11, 1888. Private possession. Copy at http://www .sanders-mcarthurfamily.org/.

———. Papers, 1854–1918. CHL.

———. "Recollections." *Juvenile Instructor* 6, no. 13 (June 24, 1871): 98–99.

———. Reminiscences, 1838–circa 1848. Joseph F. Smith, Papers, 1854–1918. CHL.

Smith, Joseph Fielding, comp. *Life of Joseph F. Smith, Sixth President of The Church of Jesus Christ of Latter-day Saints.* Salt Lake City: Deseret News, 1938.

Smith, Lucy Mack. History, 1844–45. 18 books. CHL. Also available at the Joseph Smith Papers website, josephsmithpapers.org/paper-summary/lucy-mack-smith-history-1845.

Smith, Sarah Ellen Richards. Collection, 1868–95. CHL.

Smith, Silas. Journal, May 1854–June 1855. Typescript. CHL.

Smith, Vida E. "Biography of Alexander H. Smith." *Journal of History* 4, no. 4 (Oct. 1911): 394–411.

Smithfield Branch, Cache Stake. Young Women's Mutual Improvement Association Minutes and Records, 1871–1900. CHL.

Smoot, Abraham O. Papers, 1837–94. BYU.

Smoot, Diana E. Autobiography, 1912. BYU. Available at Pioneer Database, https://history.ChurchofJesusChrist.org/overlandtravel/sources/6130 /smoot-diana-eldredge-autobiography-1912-2-5-mss-sc-1587.

Snow, Eliza R. *Biography and Family Record of Lorenzo Snow, One of the Twelve Apostles of The Church of Jesus Christ of Latter-day Saints.* Salt Lake City: Deseret News, 1884.

———. Journals, 1846–1951. CHL. Also available in Maureen Ursenbach Beecher, ed., *The Personal Writings of Eliza Roxcy Snow* (Logan: Utah State University Press, 2000).

———. "Sketch of My Life," Apr. 13, 1885. Utah and the Mormons Collection, no date. CHL.

Snow, Erastus. Autobiography, 1875. Typescript. CHL.

———. "Autobiography of Erastus Snow." *Utah Genealogical and Historical Magazine* 14, no. 3 (July 1923): 104–13.

———. Journals, 1835–51, 1856–57. CHL.

Snowflake Arizona Stake. Relief Society Minutes and Records, 1880–1973. CHL.

———. Young Women's Mutual Improvement Association Minutes and Records, 1882–1973. CHL.

Snowflake Ward, Snowflake Stake. Young Women's Mutual Improvement Association Minutes and Records, 1880–1973. CHL.

"Society Islands Mission." In Tahiti Papeete Mission, Manuscript History and Historical Reports, 1843–1978. CHL.

Society Islands Mission. Membership Records, circa 1892–1905. CHL.

Songs of Zion. Publication place and publisher unidentified, [1853]. In John Freeman, Songbook, circa 1849. CHL.

Sonne, Conway B. *Saints on the Seas: A Maritime History of Mormon Migration, 1830–1890.* Salt Lake City: University of Utah Press, 1983.

Soule, Orson P. "Exerps from a History by Orson P. Soule, Salt Lake City Utah." Jacob F. Secrist Family Papers, 1854–2008. CHL.

South African Mission. South Africa Mission Manuscript History and Historical Reports, 1853–1977. CHL.

Speech of Hon. George Q. Cannon, of Utah, in the House of Representatives, Wednesday, April 19, 1882. Washington, DC: Publisher unidentified, 1882.

Speech of Hon. Justin S. Morrill, of Vermont, on Utah Territory and Its Laws—Polygamy and Its License; Delivered in the House of Representatives, February 23, 1857. Washington, DC: Congressional Globe, 1857.

Spencer, Clarissa Young, and Mabel Harmer. *Brigham Young at Home*. Salt Lake City: Deseret Book, 1974.

———. *One Who Was Valiant*. Caldwell, ID: Caxton Printers, 1940.

Spencer, Daniel. Diaries, 1845–57. Vol. 2. Typescript. CHL. Also available in the Pioneer Database at https://history.ChurchofJesusChrist.org/overlandtravel/sources/6131/spencer-daniel-diaries-1845-1857-vol-2.

Spring City Ward, Sanpete North Stake. Manuscript History and Historical Reports, 1853–1983. CHL.

Spurrier, Joseph H. *Sandwich Islands Saints: Early Mormon Converts in the Hawaiian Islands*. Publication place and publisher unidentified, 1989.

Staines, William C. Camp Journal, June–Oct. 1847. In Camp of Israel, Schedules and Reports, 1845–49. CHL.

———. Diary, 1857–59. CHL.

Staker, Mark L. *Hearken, O Ye People: The Historical Setting for Joseph Smith's Ohio Revelations*. Salt Lake City: Greg Kofford Books, 2009.

Stampp, Kenneth M. *America in 1857: A Nation on the Brink*. New York: Oxford University Press, 1990.

Standard. Ogden, UT. 1888–1902.

Stanley, Reva Holdaway. "The First Utah Coins Minted from California Gold." *California Historical Society Quarterly* 15, no. 3 (Sept. 1936): 244–46.

Stanton, Elizabeth Cady. *Eighty Years and More (1815–1897): Reminiscences of Elizabeth Cady Stanton*. New York City: European Publishing, 1898.

Stapley, Jonathan A. "Adoptive Sealing Ritual in Mormonism." *Journal of Mormon History* 37, no. 3 (Summer 2011): 53–118.

The Statutes at Large, Treaties, and Proclamations, of the United States of America. From December 5, 1859, to March 3, 1863. Arranged in Chronological Order and Carefully Collated with the Originals at Washington. . . . Edited by George P. Sanger. Boston: Little, Brown, 1863.

The Statutes at Large, Treaties, and Proclamations, of the United States of America. From December 1867, to March 1869. Arranged in Chronological Order and Carefully Collated with the Originals at Washington. . . . Vol. 15. Edited by George P. Sanger. Boston: Little, Brown, 1869.

The Statutes at Large of the United States, from December, 1873, to March, 1875, and Recent Treaties, Postal Conventions, and Executive Proclamations. Vol. 18, part 3. Washington, DC: Government Printing Office, 1875.

The Statutes at Large of the United States of America, from December, 1881, to March, 1883, and Recent Treaties, Postal Conventions, and Executive Proclamations. Vol. 22. Washington, DC: Government Printing Office, 1883.

The Statutes at Large of the United States of America, from December, 1885, to March, 1887, and Recent Treaties, Postal Conventions, and Executive Proclamations. Vol. 24. Washington, DC: Government Printing Office, 1887.

"Steadying the Ark." *Utah Magazine* 3, no. 19 (Sept. 11, 1869): 295.

Steele, John. Journal, 1846–77. John Steele, Reminiscences and Journals, 1846–98. CHL.

Steele, Linda Allred. *James and Elizabeth Allred*. Vernal, UT: By the author, 1995.

Stenhouse, [Fanny]. *Exposé of Polygamy in Utah: A Lady's Life among the Mormons, a Record of Personal Experience as One of the Wives of a Mormon Elder during a Period of More Than Twenty Years*. New York: American News, 1872.

———. *"Tell It All": The Story of a Life's Experience in Mormonism*. Hartford, CT: A. D. Worthington, 1874.

Stenhouse, T. B. H. *The Rocky Mountain Saints: A Full and Complete History of the Mormons*. New York: D. Appleton, 1873.

Stevens, Augusta Dorius. Autobiography, 1922. Photocopy of typescript. CHL.

Stevenson, Edward. Collection, 1849–1922. CHL.

Stewart, George R. *The California Trail: An Epic with Many Heroes*. New York: McGraw-Hill, 1962.

Stewart, James Z. Diaries, 1873–84. James Z. Stewart, Papers, 1873–1927. CHL.

Stewart, Richard. *Leper Priest of Moloka'i: The Father Damien Story.* Honolulu: University of Hawaii Press, 2000.

Stott, Clifford L. *Faith and Dissent: The Nicholas Paul Story.* Publication place unidentified: By the author, 2007.

Stout, Hosea. Journals, 1845–69. Hosea Stout, Papers, 1829–70. Utah State Historical Society, Salt Lake City.

Stubbs, Glen R. "A History of the Manti Temple." Master's thesis, Brigham Young University, 1960.

Stuy, Brian H., comp. and ed. *Collected Discourses Delivered by President Wilford Woodruff, His Two Counselors, the Twelve Apostles, and Others.* 5 vols. Burbank, CA: B. H. S., 1987–91; Woodland Hills, UT: B. H. S., 1992.

Sudweeks, Joseph. "The Life of Laban Morrill." Harold B. Lee Library, Brigham Young University, Provo, UT.

Sugar House Ward, Sugar House Stake. Manuscript History and Historical Reports, 1849–1984. CHL.

Sunday Herald. Salt Lake City. 1889–95.

The Supreme Court Decision in the Reynolds Case. Interview between President John Taylor, and O. J. Hollister, Esq., United States Collector of Internal Revenue for Utah Territory, and Correspondent of the New York Tribune. [Salt Lake City]: Publisher unidentified, 1879.

Susan N. Grant Correspondence, circa 1849–61. CHL.

Sutter, John A. *New Helvetia Diary: A Record of Events Kept by John A. Sutter and His Clerks at New Helvetia, California, from September 9, 1845, to May 25, 1848.* San Francisco: Grabhorn, 1939.

Tahiti Papeete Mission. Manuscript History and Historical Reports, 1843–1978. CHL.

Tait, Lisa Olsen. "'A Modern Patriarchal Family': The Wives of Joseph F. Smith in the Relief Society Magazine, 1915–19." In *Joseph F. Smith: Reflections on the Man and His Times,* edited by Craig K. Manscill, Brian D. Reeves, Guy L. Dorius, and J. B. Haws, 74–95. Provo, UT: Religious Studies Center, Brigham Young University; Salt Lake City: Deseret Book, 2013.

———. "Mormon Culture Meets Popular Fiction: Susa Young Gates and the Cultural Work of Home Literature." Master's thesis, Brigham Young University, 1998.

Talmage, James E. *The House of the Lord: A Study of Holy Sanctuaries Ancient and Modern, including Forty-Six Plates Illustrative of Modern Temples.* Salt Lake City: Deseret News, 1912.

———. Journals, 1879–1933. Microfilm. CHL.

Tanner, Annie Clark. *A Mormon Mother: An Autobiography.* Salt Lake City: Deseret News, 1941.

Tanner, J. M. *A Biographical Sketch of James Jensen.* Salt Lake City: Deseret News, 1911.

Tanner, John M. "Grammar Department. Historical Work." *Young Woman's Journal* 3, no. 8 (May 1892): 339–40.

Tanner, Mary Jane Mount. Autobiography and Diary, 1872–79. Mary Jane Mount Tanner, Papers, 1837–1908. Special Collections, J. Willard Marriott Library, University of Utah, Salt Lake City.

Taylor, Alonzo L. Mission Papers, 1891, 1902–4. CHL.

Taylor, John. Collection, 1829–94. CHL.

———. Journal, 1844–45. CHL.

Temple Souvenir Album, April, 1892, Illustrated with Portraits of the Architects, Views of the Building, Plan of Electric Lights, Engine-House and Grounds, including Views of Logan, Manti, Nauvoo and Kirtland Temples, and Places of Interest in Salt Lake City. Salt Lake City: Magazine Printing Company, 1892.

Territorial Case Files of the U.S. District Courts of Utah, 1870–96. National Archives, Washington, DC.

Thatcher, Moses. Diary and Notebook, 1884–85, 1887, 1902. CHL.

———. Journal, 1866–68, 1879–81. 6 vols. CHL.

Third Ward, Liberty Stake. Relief Society Minutes and Records, 1868–1967. CHL.

Thirteenth Ward, Ensign Stake. Relief Society Minutes and Records, 1868–1906. CHL.

———. Relief Society Records, 1854–57. CHL.

Thissell, G. W. *Crossing the Plains in '49*. Oakland, CA: Publisher unidentified, 1903.

Thomas, Carrie S. "Report of the Y. L. M. I. Delegate to the Woman's National Council at Washington, D. C." *Young Woman's Journal* 2, no. 8 (May 1891): 381–82.

Three Letters to the New York Herald, from J. M. Grant, of Utah. [New York]: Publisher unidentified, [1852].

Thurston, Mary Seamons. Reminiscence, no date. Typescript. Collected Information on the Seamons and Related Families, circa 1980. CHL.

Times and Seasons. Commerce/Nauvoo, IL. Nov. 1839–Feb. 1846.

Tooele Utah Stake. General Minutes, 1877–1977. CHL.

Trondheim Branch, Scandinavian Mission. Relief Society Minutes and Records, 1882–91, 1901–42. CHL.

Trozos selectos del Libro de Mormon. Salt Lake City: Impreso para Daniel W. Jones en la imprenta del Deseret News, 1875.

"True Development of the Territory." *Utah Magazine* 3, no. 24 (Oct. 16, 1869): 376–78.

True Latter Day Saints' Herald. See *Saints' Herald*.

Tullidge, Edward W. *History of Salt Lake City*. Salt Lake City: Star, 1886.

———. *Life of Brigham Young; or, Utah and Her Founders*. New York: Publisher unidentified, 1876.

———. "The Oracles Speak." *Utah Magazine* 3, no. 33 (Dec. 18, 1869): 521–23.

———. *Tullidge's Histories*. Vol. 2, *Containing the History of all the Northern, Eastern and Western Counties of Utah; also the Counties of Southern Idaho*. Salt Lake City: Juvenile Instructor, 1889.

———. *The Women of Mormondom*. New York: Tullidge and Crandall, 1877.

[Tullidge, Edward W.]. "Reformation in Utah." *Harper's New Monthly Magazine* (Nov. 1871): 602–10.

Tullis, F. LaMond. *Mormons in Mexico: The Dynamics of Faith and Culture*. Logan: Utah State University Press, 1987.

Turley, Richard E., Jr., Janiece L. Johnson, and LaJean Purcell Carruth, eds. *Mountain Meadows Massacre: Collected Legal Papers*. 2 vols. Norman: University of Oklahoma Press, 2017.

Turley, Richard E., Jr., and Ronald W. Walker, eds. *Mountain Meadows Massacre: The Andrew Jenson and David H. Morris Collections*. Provo, UT: Brigham Young University Press, 2009.

Tyler, Daniel. *A Concise History of the Mormon Battalion in the Mexican War, 1846–1847*. Salt Lake City: Publisher unidentified, 1881.

Udall, David King. *Arizona Pioneer Mormon: David King Udall, His Story and His Family, 1851–1938*. Written in collaboration with his daughter Pearl Udall Nelson. Tucson: Arizona Silhouettes, 1959.

Udall, Ida Hunt. Autobiography and Diaries, 1873–1905. 2 vols. CHL.

Udall Family Correspondence Collection, 1859–1950. CHL.

Ulrich, Laurel Thatcher. *A House Full of Females: Plural Marriage and Women's Rights in Early Mormonism, 1835–1870*. New York: Knopf, 2017.

Ulvund, Frode. "Travelling Images and Projected Representations: Perceptions of Mormonism in Norway, c. 1840–1860." *Scandinavian Journal of History* 41, no. 2 (2016): 208–30.

Underwood, Grant. "Mormonism and the Shaping of Maori Religious Identity." In *Voyages of Faith: Explorations in Mormon Pacific History*, edited by Grant Underwood, 107–26. Provo, UT: Brigham Young University, 2000.

Unruh, John D., Jr. *The Plains Across: The Overland Emigrants and the Trans-Mississippi West, 1840–60*. Urbana: University of Illinois Press, 1979.

U.S. and Canada Record Collection. FHL.

U.S. Bureau of the Census. Population Schedules. Microfilm. FHL.

U.S. Reports: Reynolds v. United States, 98 U.S. 145 (1879).

Utah Commission. *The Edmunds Act, Reports of the Commission, Rules, Regulations, and Decisions, and Population, Registration and Election Tables, &c.* Salt Lake City: Tribune, 1883.

Utah Department of Health, Office of Vital Records and Statistics, Utah State Archives and Records Service, Salt Lake City.

Utah Department of Heritage and Arts, Utah Division of State History, Cemeteries and Burials database. Accessed Sept. 25, 2019. http://history.utah.gov/cemeteries/.

Utah Enquirer. Provo. 1888–95.

Utah Message from the President of the United States, Transmitting Information in reference to the Condition of Affairs in the Territory of Utah. Washington, DC: Publisher unidentified, 1852.

Utah Pioneer Biographies. 1935–64. 44 vols. Typescript. Available at FHL.

Utah Territory. Census Returns, Feb. 1856. CHL.

Utah Territory and Legislative Assembly Papers, 1852–72. CHL.

Utah Territory Legislative Assembly. House Historical Committee Files, 1866–68. CHL.

Valley Tan. Salt Lake City. 1858–60.

Van Hoak, Stephen P. "And Who Shall Have the Children?: The Indian Slave Trade in the Southern Great Basin, 1800–1865." *Nevada Historical Quarterly* 41, no. 1 (Spring 1998): 3–25.

Van Orden, Bruce A. *Building Zion: The Latter-day Saints in Europe.* Salt Lake City: Deseret Book, 1996.

———. *Prisoner for Conscience' Sake: The Life of George Reynolds.* Salt Lake City: Deseret Book, 1992.

Vermont Watchman and State Journal. Montpelier. 1836–83.

Voree Herald. Voree, WI. Jan.–Oct. 1846.

Walker, Charles Lowell. Journals, 1854–99. 12 vols. Charles L. Walker, Papers, 1854–99. CHL. Also available in A. Karl Larson and Katharine Miles Larson, eds., *Diary of Charles Lowell Walker,* 2 vols. (Logan: Utah State University Press, 1980).

Walker, Ronald W. "The Affair of the 'Runaways': Utah's First Encounter with the Federal Officers." *Journal of Mormon History* 39, no. 4 (Fall 2013): 1–43.

———. "'A Banner Is Unfurled': Mormonism's Ensign Peak." *Dialogue: A Journal of Mormon Thought* 26 (Winter 1993): 71–91.

———. "The Commencement of the Godbeite Protest: Another View." *Utah Historical Quarterly* 42, no. 3 (Summer 1974): 217–44.

———. "Grant's Watershed: Succession in the Presidency, 1887–1889." *BYU Studies* 43, no. 1 (2004): 195–229.

———. "A Mormon 'Widow' in Colorado: The Exile of Emily Wells Grant." *BYU Studies* 43, no. 1 (2004): 175–93.

———. *Qualities That Count: Heber J. Grant as Businessman, Missionary, and Apostle.* Provo, UT: Brigham Young University Press, 2004.

———. "Rachel R. Grant: The Continuing Legacy of the Feminine Ideal." In *Supporting Saints: Life Stories of Nineteenth-Century Mormons,* edited by Donald Q. Cannon and David J. Whittaker, 17–42. Provo, UT: Religious Studies Center, Brigham Young University, 1985.

———. "The Salt Lake Tabernacle in the Nineteenth Century: A Glimpse of Early Mormonism." *Journal of Mormon History* 32, no. 3 (Fall 2005): 198–240.

———. "The Stenhouses and the Making of a Mormon Image." *Journal of Mormon History* 1 (1974): 51–72.

———. "Thomas L. Kane and Utah's Quest for Self-Government, 1846–51." *Utah Historical Quarterly* 69, no. 2 (Spring 2001): 100–19.

———. *Wayward Saints: The Godbeites and Brigham Young.* Urbana: University of Illinois Press, 1998.

Walker, Ronald W., and Matthew J. Grow. "The People Are 'Hogaffed or Humbugged': The 1851–52 National Reaction to Utah's 'Runaway' Officers." *Journal of Mormon History* 40, no. 1 (Winter 2014): 1–52.

Walker, Ronald W., Richard E. Turley Jr., and Glen M. Leonard. *Massacre at Mountain Meadows: An American Tragedy.* Oxford: Oxford University Press, 2008.

Walker, Ronald W., David J. Whittaker, and James B. Allen. *Mormon History.* Urbana: University of Illinois Press, 2001.

Walker, William H. Journal, 1852–53. CHL.

Wallis, Eileen V. "The Women's Cooperative Movement in Utah, 1869–1915." *Utah Historical Quarterly* 71, no. 4 (Fall 2003): 315–31.

Ward, Margery W. *A Life Divided: The Biography of Joseph Marion Tanner, 1859–1927.* Salt Lake City: Publishers Press, 1980.

Warsaw Signal. Warsaw, IL. 1841–42, 1844–53.

Washakie Ward, Malad Stake. Record of Members, 1885–86, 1938. CHL.

Washington County, Utah, Probate Court. Civil and Criminal Record Books, 1856–86. Series 3168. Utah Division of Archives and Records Service, Utah State Archives, Salt Lake City.

Watchman. Boston. 1876–1913.

Watt, George D. Papers, circa 1846–65. CHL.

Weber Stake. Stake Relief Society Minutes and Records, 1867–1968. 22 vols. CHL.

Webster, William G., and William A. Wheeler. *A Dictionary of the English Language, Explanatory, Pronouncing, Etymological, and Synonymous. . . .* New York: Ivison, Blakeman, Taylor, 1874.

Wells, Emmeline B. Diaries, 1844–1920. 47 vols. BYU. Diary for 1844–46 also available in Carol Cornwall Madsen, *Journey to Zion: Voices from the Mormon Trail* (Salt Lake City: Deseret Book, 1997), 113–29.

———. "The Mission of Saving Grain." *Relief Society Magazine* 2, no. 2 (Feb. 1915): 47–49.

———. "Zina D. H. Young—a Character Sketch." *Improvement Era* 5, no. 1 (Nov. 1901): 43–48.

Wells, Junius F. "A Living Martyr." *Contributor* 2, no. 5 (Feb. 1881): 154–57.

———. "Salutation." *Contributor* 1, no. 1 (Oct. 1879): 12.

Wells, Merle W. "The Idaho Anti-Mormon Test Oath, 1884–1892." *Pacific Historical Review* 24, no. 3 (Aug. 1955): 235–52.

Western Standard. San Francisco. 1856–57.

Whipple, Nelson W. Autobiography and Journal, 1859–87. CHL.

Whitaker, John A. Autobiography and Journals, 1883–1960. CHL.

Whitchurch, David M., and Mallory Hales Perry. "Friends and Enemies in Washington: Joseph F. Smith's Letter to Susa Young Gates, March 21, 1889." *Mormon Historical Studies* 13, nos. 1 and 2 (Spring/Fall 2012): 211–29.

White, George A. "The Life Story of Thomas Gunn and Ann Houghton Gunn and Their Parents and Brothers and Sisters." In Thomas and Ann Houghton Gunn Biographical Sketch, 1941. CHL.

White, Richard. *Railroaded: The Transcontinentals and the Making of Modern America.* New York: W. W. Norton, 2011.

Whitmer, David. *An Address to All Believers in Christ.* Richmond, MO: David Whitmer, 1887.

Whitney, Helen Mar Kimball. Autobiography, Mar. 30, 1881. Helen Mar Kimball Whitney, Papers, 1881–82. CHL.

———. Diaries, 1876, 1883–85. Helen Mar Kimball Whitney Papers, Helen B. Fleming Collection, 1836–1963. CHL. Portions available in Charles M. Hatch and Todd M. Compton, eds., *A Widow's Tale: The 1884–1896 Diary of Helen Mar Kimball Whitney,* Life Writings of Frontier Women 6 (Logan: Utah State University Press, 2003).

———. Diaries, 1885–96. Helen Mar Kimball Whitney Papers, 1841–1900. Special Collections and Archives, Merrill-Cazier Library, Utah State University, Logan. Also available in Charles M. Hatch and Todd M. Compton, eds., *A Widow's Tale: The 1884–1896 Diary of Helen Mar Kimball Whitney,* Life Writings of Frontier Women 6 (Logan: Utah State University Press, 2003).

———. *Plural Marriage as Taught by the Prophet Joseph. A Reply to Joseph Smith, Editor of the Lamoni (Iowa) "Herald."* Salt Lake City: Juvenile Instructor, 1882.

———. *Why We Practice Plural Marriage.* Salt Lake City: Juvenile Instructor, 1884.

Whitney, Horace G. *The Drama in Utah: The Story of the Salt Lake Theatre.* Salt Lake City: Deseret News, 1915.

Whitney, Horace K. Journals, 1843 and 1846–47. CHL.

Whitney, Orson F. Collection, 1851–1931. CHL.

———. *History of Utah.* 4 vols. Salt Lake City: George Q. Cannon and Sons, 1892–1904.

———. "Home Literature." *Contributor* 9, no. 8 (June 1888): 297–302.

———. *Life of Heber C. Kimball. An Apostle: The Father and Founder of the British Mission.* Salt Lake City: Kimball Family, 1888.

———. "Pioneer Women of Utah." *Contributor* 11, no. 11 (Sept. 1890): 404–8.

———. *Through Memory's Halls: The Life Story of Orson F. Whitney as Told by Himself.* Independence, MO: By the author, 1930.

Whittaker, David J. "The Bone in the Throat: Orson Pratt and the Public Announcement of Plural Marriage." *Western Historical Quarterly* 18, no. 3 (July 1987): 293–314.

———. "Early Mormon Imprints in South Africa." *BYU Studies* (Summer 1980): 404–16.

Widtsoe, John A. *In a Sunlit Land: The Autobiography of John A. Widtsoe.* Salt Lake City: Milton R. Hunter and G. Homer Durham, 1953.

———. *In the Gospel Net: The Story of Anna Karine Gaarden Widtsoe.* Salt Lake City: Improvement Era, 1942.

———. Papers, no date. CHL.

Widtsoe, Leah D. Interview, Salt Lake City, 1965. CHL.

Widtsoe Family Papers, 1824–1953. CHL.

Wilkinson, Ernest L. *Brigham Young University: The First One Hundred Years.* 4 vols. Provo, UT: Brigham Young University Press, 1975.

"William S. Godbe." *Tullidge's Quarterly Magazine* 1, no. 1 (Oct. 1880): 64–66.

Wimmer, Ryan E. "The Walker War Reconsidered." Master's thesis, Brigham Young University, 2010.

Winkler, Albert. "The Circleville Massacre: A Brutal Incident in Utah's Black Hawk War." *Utah Historical Quarterly* 55, no. 1 (Winter 1987): 4–21.

Winter Quarters Municipal High Council Records, 1846–48. CHL.

Woman's Exponent. Salt Lake City. 1872–1914.

Wood, Edward J. Collection, 1884–1982. CHL.

———. Journals, circa 1884–1933. Edward J. Wood Collection, 1884–1982. CHL.

———. "My Samoan Experience." *Juvenile Instructor* 28, no. 7 (Apr. 1, 1893): 209–11.

———. "Notable Incidents of Missionary Life." *Juvenile Instructor* 28, no. 20 (Oct. 15, 1893): 632–35.

Woodbury, John Stillman. Diaries, 1851–77. 13 vols. Mormon Missionary Diaries, 1832–circa 1960. BYU.

Woodger, Mary Jane. "Abraham Lincoln and the Mormons." In *Civil War Saints,* edited by Kenneth L. Alford, 61–81. Provo, UT: Religious Studies Center, Brigham Young University, 2012.

Woodruff, James Jackson. Mary Ann Jackson Woodruff Biographical Sketch, Apr. 1917. CHL.

Woodruff, Wilford. "History of the St George Temple. It's Cost and Dedication and the Labor Thereon," Mar. 26, 1883. In David H. Cannon Collection, 1883–1924. CHL.

———. Journals, 1833–98. Wilford Woodruff, Journals and Papers, 1828–98. CHL.

———. Journals and Papers, 1828–98. CHL.

Woods, Fred E. "Jonathan Napela: A Noble Hawaiian Convert." In *Regional Studies in Latter-day Saint Church History: The Pacific Isles,* edited by Reid L. Neilson, Steven C. Harper, Craig K. Manscill, and Mary Jane Woodger, 23–36. Provo, UT: Religious Studies Center, Brigham Young University, 2008.

———. *Kalaupapa: The Mormon Experience in an Exiled Community.* Provo, UT: Religious Studies Center, Brigham Young University, 2017.

———. "A Most Influential Mormon Islander: Jonathan Hawaii Napela." *Hawaiian Journal of History* 42 (2008): 135–57.

———. "The Palawai Pioneers on the Island of Lanai: The First Hawaiian Latter-day Saint Gathering Place (1854–1864)." *Mormon Historical Studies* 5, no. 2 (Fall 2004): 3–35.

Woodworth, Jed. "Peace and War: D&C 87." In *Revelations in Context: The Stories behind the Sections of the Doctrine and Covenants,* edited by Matthew McBride and James Goldberg, 158–64. Salt Lake City: The Church of Jesus Christ of Latter-day Saints, 2016.

Woolley, Samuel A. Diary, June–Dec. 1852. Samuel A. Woolley, Papers, 1846–99. CHL.

The Year of Jubilee. A Full Report of the Proceedings of the Fiftieth Annual Conference of The Church of Jesus Christ of Latter-day Saints, Held in the Large Tabernacle, Salt Lake City, Utah, April 6th, 7th and 8th, A. D. 1880. Salt Lake City: Deseret News, 1880.

Yorgason, Blaine M., Richard A. Schmutz, and Douglas D. Alder. *All That Was Promised: The St. George Temple and the Unfolding of the Restoration.* Salt Lake City: Deseret Book, 2013.

Young, Ann Eliza. *Wife No. 19; or, The Story of a Life in Bondage, Being a Complete Exposé of Mormonism, and Revealing the Sorrows, Sacrifices and Sufferings of Women in Polygamy.* Hartford, CT: Dustin, Gilman, 1876.

Young, Brigham. Journals, 1832–77. Brigham Young Office Files, 1832–78 (bulk 1844–77). CHL.

———. Letter to George Q. Cannon, Nov. 3, 1859. Photocopy. CHL.

———. Office Journal, May–Sept. 1857. CHL.

———. *Proclamation by the Governor.* Salt Lake City: Publisher unidentified, Sept. 15, 1857. Copy at CHL.

Young, Brigham, Jr. Journals, 1862–1900. CHL.

Young, Clara Decker. "A Woman's Experiences with the Pioneer Band," 1884. In Hubert H. Bancroft, Utah and the Mormons Collection, before 1889. Microfilm. CHL. Also available as Clara Decker Young, "A Woman's Experiences with the Pioneer Band," *Utah Historical Quarterly* 14 (1946): 173–76.

Young, John R. *Memoirs of John R. Young, Utah Pioneer, 1847.* Salt Lake City: Deseret News, 1920.

Young, Joseph Don Carlos. Autobiographical Notes, 1935–36. In George C. Young Collection, 1857–1963. CHL.

Young, Lorenzo Dow. Diary, 1846–52. Lorenzo D. Young, Papers, 1846–94. CHL.

Young, Richard W. Diary, 1877–78, 1882–83. CHL.

Young, Willard. "Some Unpublished Letters of President Brigham Young." *Utah Genealogical and Historical Magazine* 17 (Jan. 1926): 10–18.

Young, Zina Diantha Huntington. Diaries and Notebooks, 1848–97. Zina Card Brown Family Collection, 1806–1972. CHL.

Zambŭcka, Kristin. *The High Chiefess Ruth Keelikolani.* Honolulu: Mana, 1977.

Zina Card Brown Family Collection, 1806–1972. CHL.

ACKNOWLEDGMENTS

Hundreds of people contributed to this new history of the Church, and we are grateful to each one of them. We are indebted to the generations of historians employed by the Church who have meticulously collected and preserved the records on which this book is based. Special thanks to James Goldberg, David Golding, Elizabeth Mott, Jennifer Reeder, and Ryan Saltzgiver for creating the supplemental materials online. The digitization of sources was led by Audrey Spainhower Dunshee and completed by staff of the Church History Department's Preservation Division and Enhanced Processing team.

All staff members, missionaries, and volunteers in the Church History Department contributed directly or indirectly to this book. In particular, we thank the following for their feedback on draft material: Matthew Godfrey, LaJean Purcell Carruth, Chad Foulger, David Grua, Kate Holbrook, Jennifer Reeder, and Brent Rogers of the Publications Division; Jenny Lund, Jacob Olmstead, Chad Orton, Benjamin Pykles, Emily Utt, and Aaron West of the Historic Sites Division; Clint Christensen, Scott Christensen, and Matthew Geilman of the Global Support and Acquisitions Division; and Christine Cox, Emily Marie Crumpton, Keith Erekson, Brandon Metcalf, and Tyson Thorpe of the Library Division. We also thank James Goldberg and Angela Hallstrom for helping shape the literary structure of the book and Catherine Reese Newton, Alex Hugie, Lorin Groesbeck, and Petra Javadi-Evans for editorial contributions. The members of the Church Historian's Press Editorial Board provided ongoing support.

Many expert readers reviewed chapters. These include Allen Andersen, Jill Andersen, Ian Barber, Laurel Barlow, Richard Bennett, M. Joseph Brough, Claudia Bushman, Richard Lyman Bushman, Néstor Curbelo, Kathryn Daynes, Jill Mulvay Derr, Devin G. Durrant, Sharon Eubank, Christian Euvrard, J. Spencer Fluhman, Jennefer Free, Fiona Givens, Terryl Givens, Melissa Wei-Tsing Inouye, Khumbulani Mdletshe, Dmitry Mikulin, Marjorie Newton, Andrew Olsen, Bonnie L. Oscarson, Darren Parry, W. Paul Reeve, Carlos F. Rivas, Cristina Sanches, Jorge L. Saldivar, Russell Stevenson, Laurel Thatcher Ulrich, Marissa A. Widdison, and Jared Yang. We also thank Dean Hughes, Jay A. Parry, and Larry E. Morris for helping research and write early drafts of this volume. Sarah Clement Reed, Michael Knudson, Emily Brignone, Savannah Woolsey Larson, Heather Olsen, Kristlynn Roth, and Annie Smith offered valuable assistance translating the letters of Anna and John Widtsoe.

Greg Newbold created the engaging artwork. John Heath, Debra Abercrombie, and Miryelle Resek contributed to the outreach effort. Deborah Gates, Kiersten Olson, Jo Lyn Curtis, Cindy Pond, and Debi Robins provided administrative assistance. Nick Olvera provided project management.

Members of several Church departments contributed, including a cross-departmental team made up of Irene Caso, Drew Conrad, Irinna Danielson, David Dickson, Norm Gardner, Paul Murphy, Alan Paulsen, and Jen Ward. Eliza Nevin of the Publishing Services Department oversaw the final publication process, and Patric Gerber, Alyssa Aramaki, Katrina Cannon, Heather Claridge, Hillary Olsen Errante, Stacie Heaps, Christopher Kugler, Lindsey Maughan, Taylor Nelson, Katie Parker, Benson Y. Parkinson,

Heather Randall, Greg Scoggin, Preston Shewell, and Kat Tilby provided production assistance. Other contributors include Nic A. Benner, Alan Blake, Christopher Blake Clark, Matt Evans, Brooke Frandsen, Jeff Hatch, Jim McKenna, Jared Moon, Casey Olson, Benjamin Peterson, Paul VanDerHoeven, Gary Walton, and Scott Welty. Translators carefully prepared the entire text in thirteen languages.

We appreciate the contributions of Steven C. Harper, who served as general editor of *Saints,* and of past Church History Department executives Elder J. Devn Cornish, Reid L. Neilson, and Richard E. Turley Jr., who helped guide the project for many years. We especially thank Elder Steven E. Snow, emeritus General Authority Seventy, who served for seven years as Church Historian and Recorder and executive director of the Church History Department, and without whom this book could not have been published.

INDEX

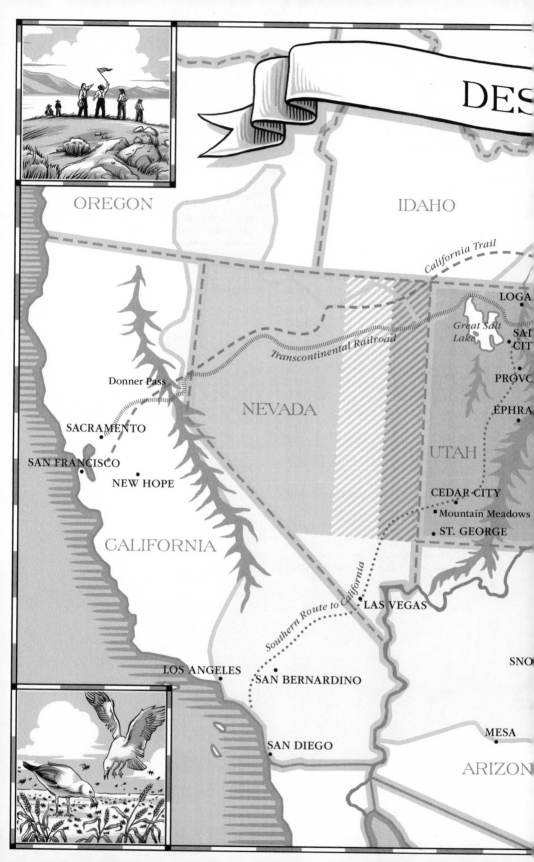

DES

OREGON

IDAHO

California Trail

LOGA

Great Salt Lake

SAI CIT

PROV

EPHRA

Donner Pass

Transcontinental Railroad

NEVADA

SACRAMENTO

SAN FRANCISCO

NEW HOPE

UTAH

CALIFORNIA

CEDAR CITY

■ Mountain Meadows

• ST. GEORGE

Southern Route to California

LAS VEGAS

LOS ANGELES

SAN BERNARDINO

SNO

MESA

SAN DIEGO

ARIZON